# Constellations
## in my Palm

*Chisako Sakuragi & Yukine Honami*

*Juné*

# Constellations In My Palm

| | |
|---|---|
| Translation | Sachiko Sato |
| Lettering | Samantha Yamanaka |
| Graphic Design | Wendy Lee/Fred Lui |
| Editing | Samantha Yamanaka |
| Editor in Chief | Fred Lui |
| Publisher | Hikaru Sasahara |

English Edition Published by
DIGITAL MANGA PUBLISHING
A division of DIGITAL MANGA, Inc.
1487 W 178th Street, Suite 300
Gardena, CA 90248

www.dmpbooks.com

First Edition: September 2007
ISBN-10: 1-56970-798-7
ISBN-13: 978-1-56970-798-2

1 3 5 7 9 10 8 6 4 2

Printed in China

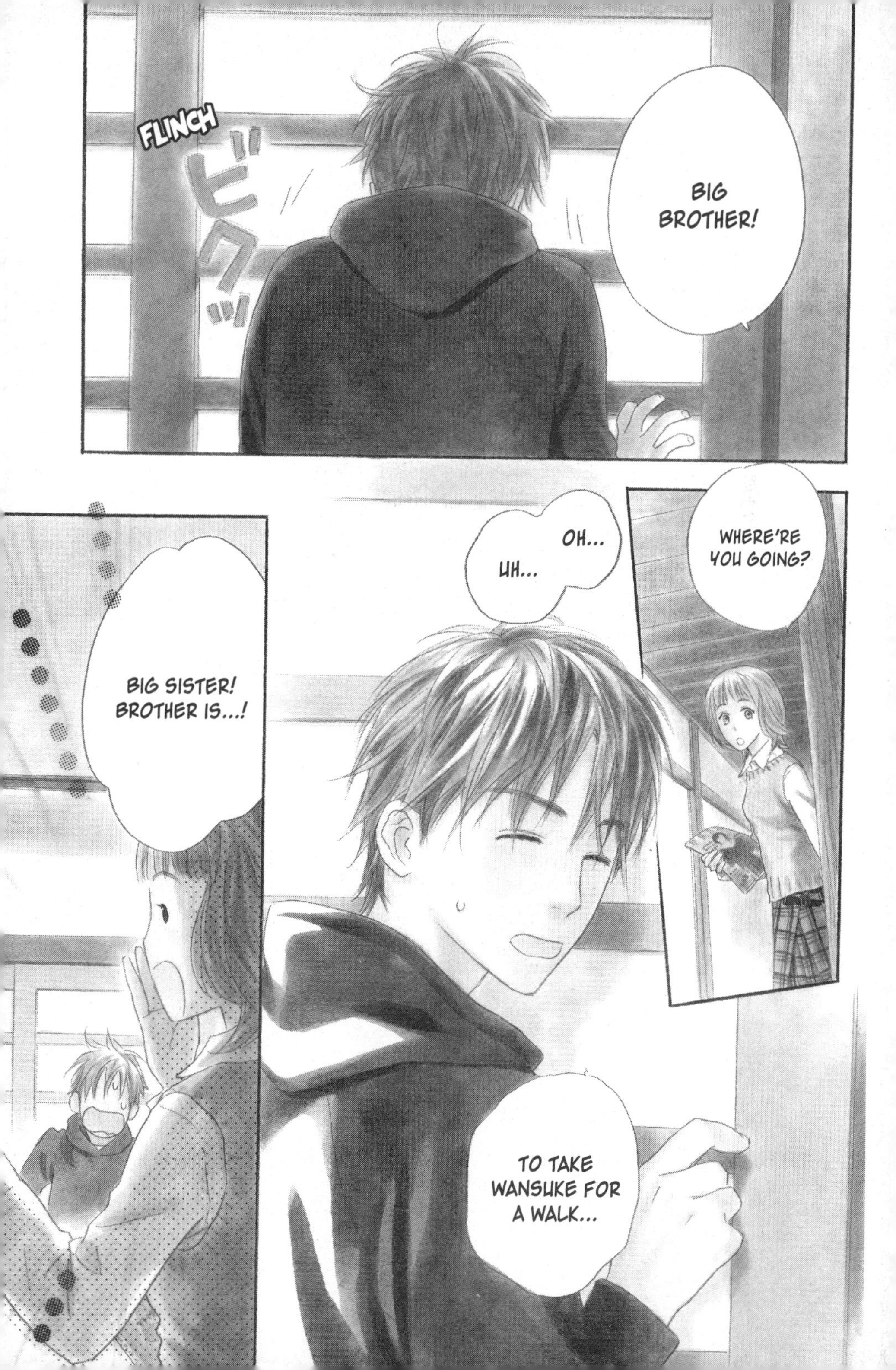
BIG BROTHER!
FLINCH
ビクッ
WHERE'RE YOU GOING?
OH... UH...
TO TAKE WANSUKE FOR A WALK...
BIG SISTER! BROTHER IS...!

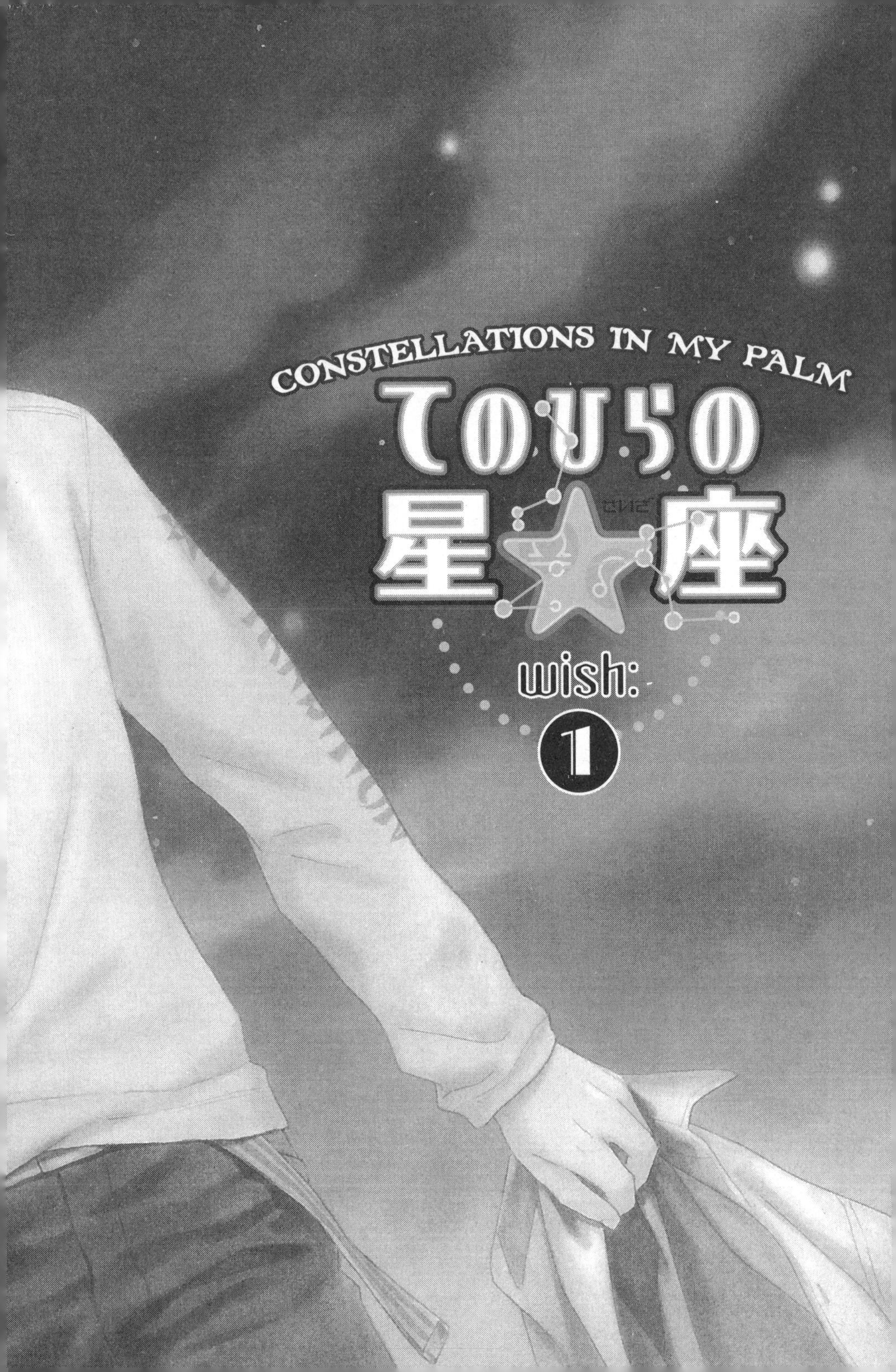
CONSTELLATIONS IN MY PALM
てのひらの星座
wish:
1

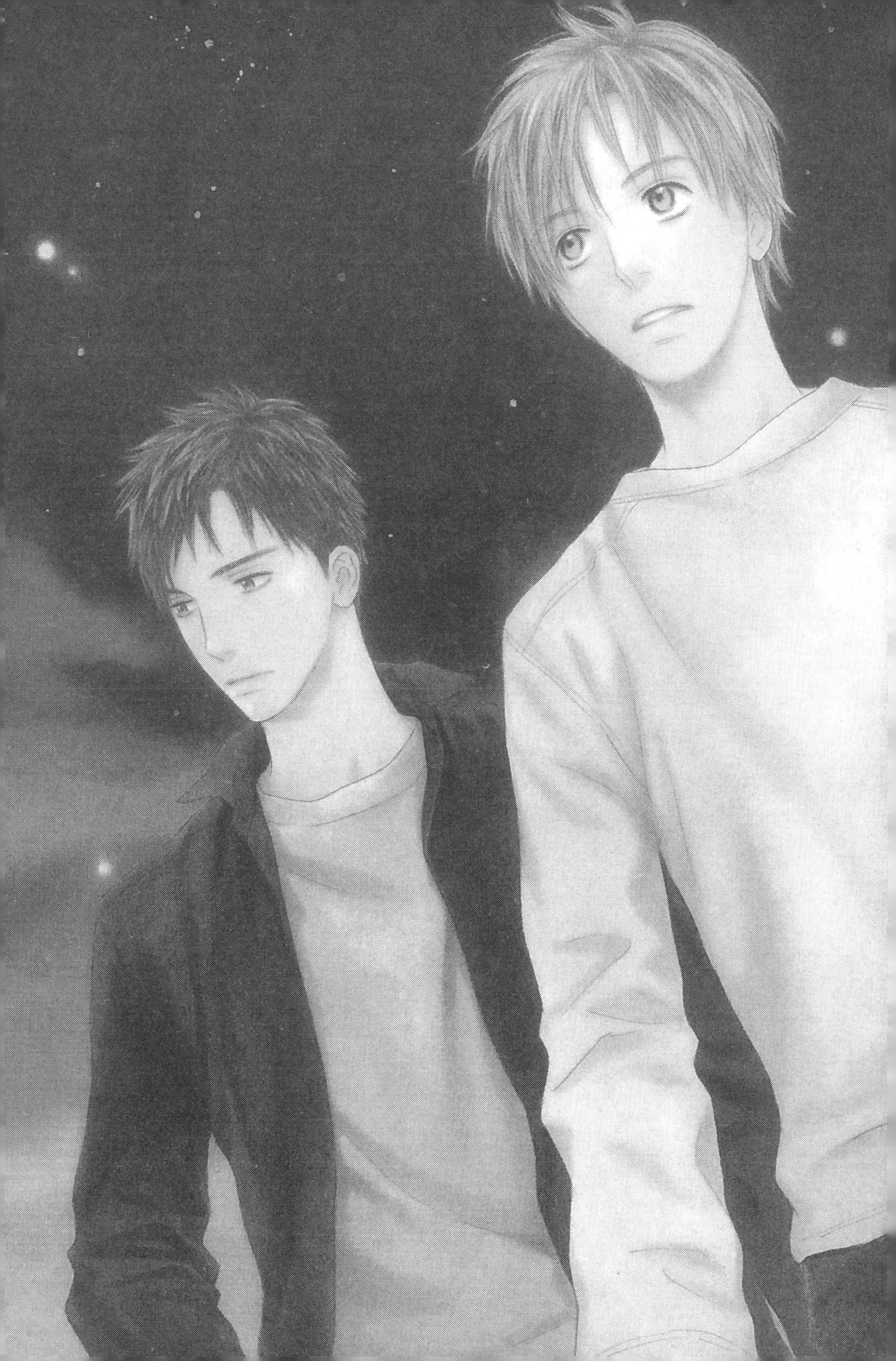

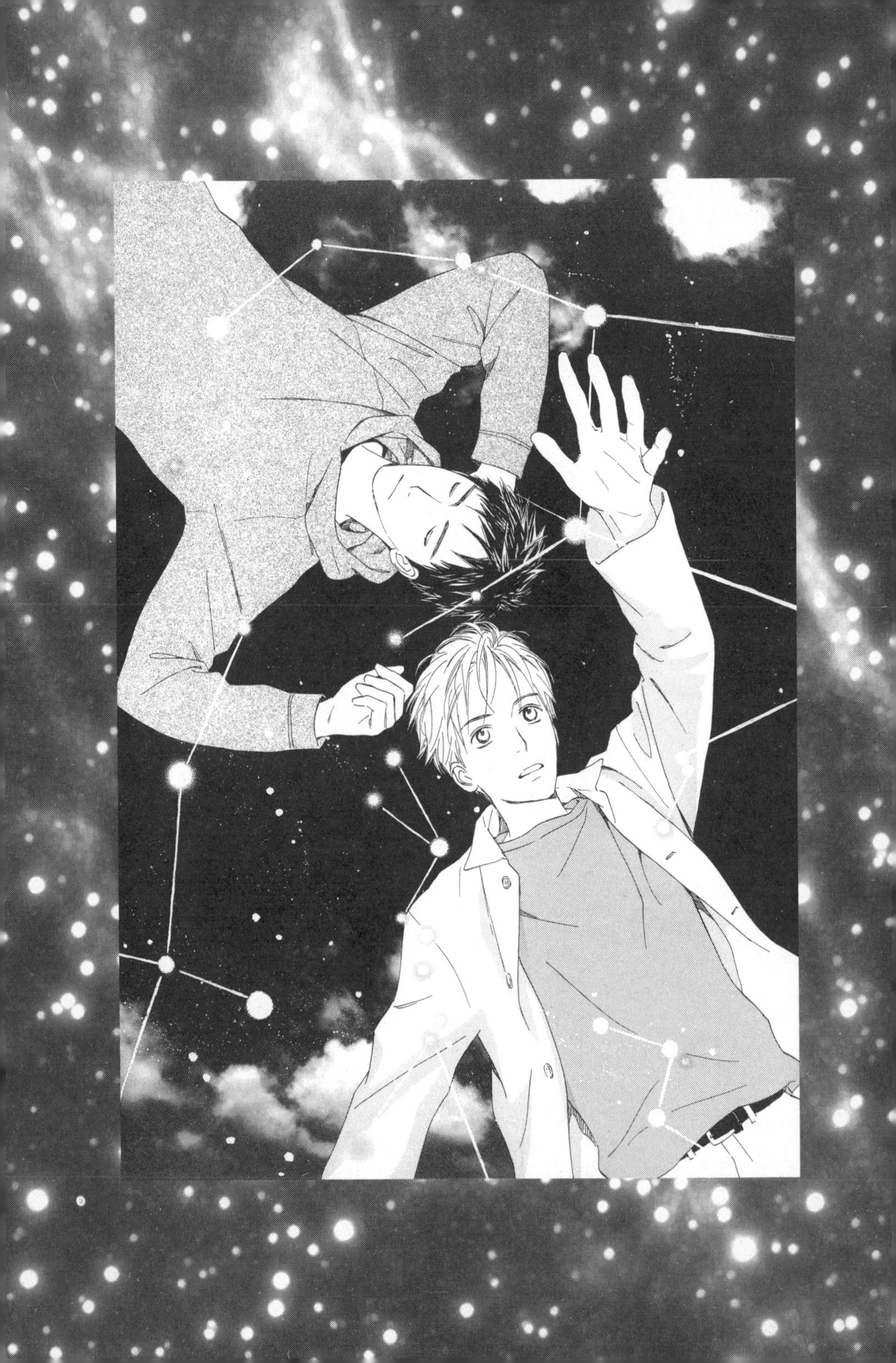

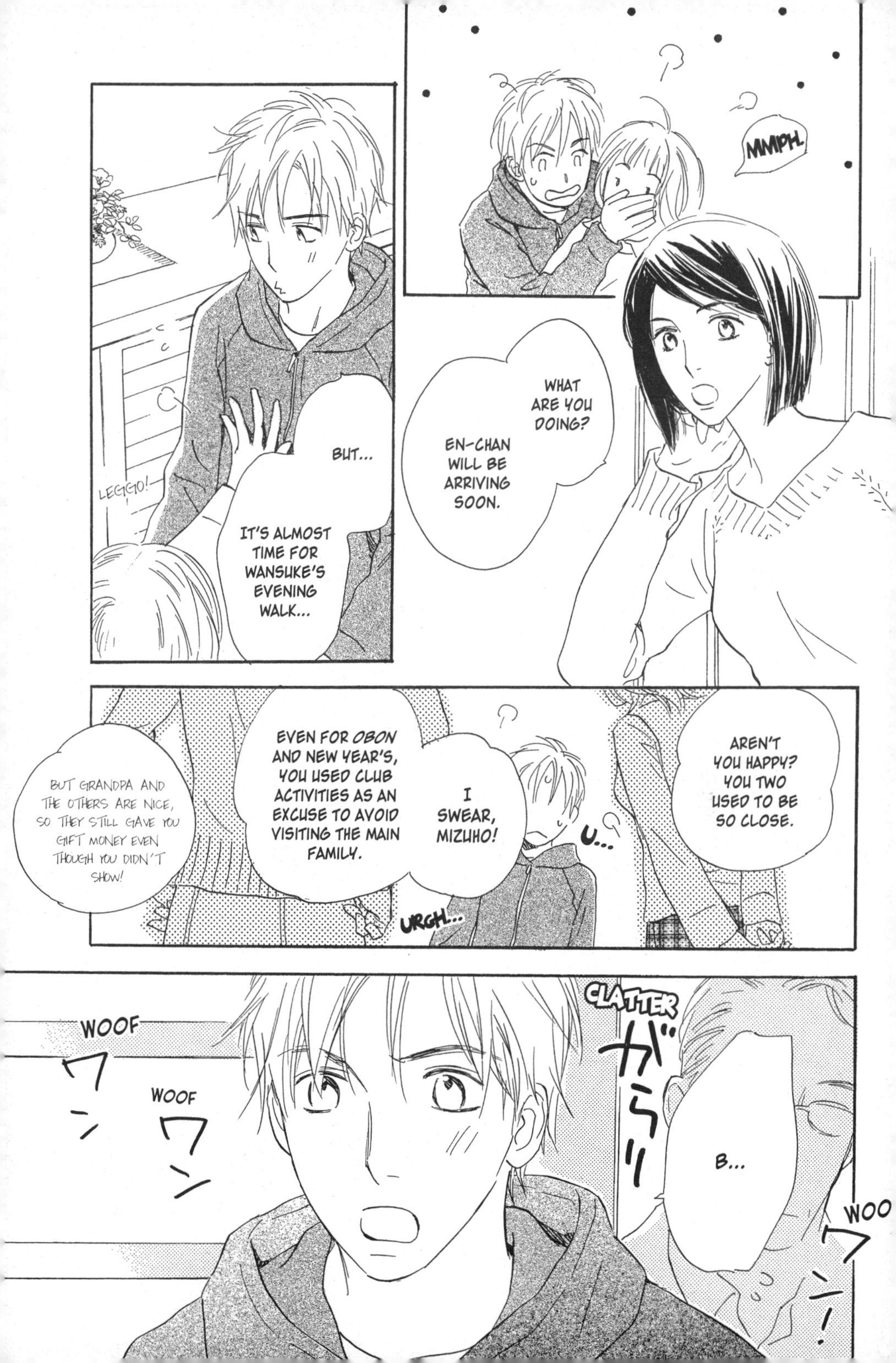
MMPH.
WHAT ARE YOU DOING?
EN-CHAN WILL BE ARRIVING SOON.
BUT...
IT'S ALMOST TIME FOR WANSUKE'S EVENING WALK...
LEGGGO!
AREN'T YOU HAPPY? YOU TWO USED TO BE SO CLOSE.
U...
I SWEAR, MIZUHO!
URGH...
EVEN FOR *OBON* AND NEW YEAR'S, YOU USED CLUB ACTIVITIES AS AN EXCUSE TO AVOID VISITING THE MAIN FAMILY.
BUT GRANDPA AND THE OTHERS ARE NICE, SO THEY STILL GAVE YOU GIFT MONEY EVEN THOUGH YOU DIDN'T SHOW!
WOO
ワン
B...
CLATTER
がらり
WOOF
ワン
WOOF
ワン

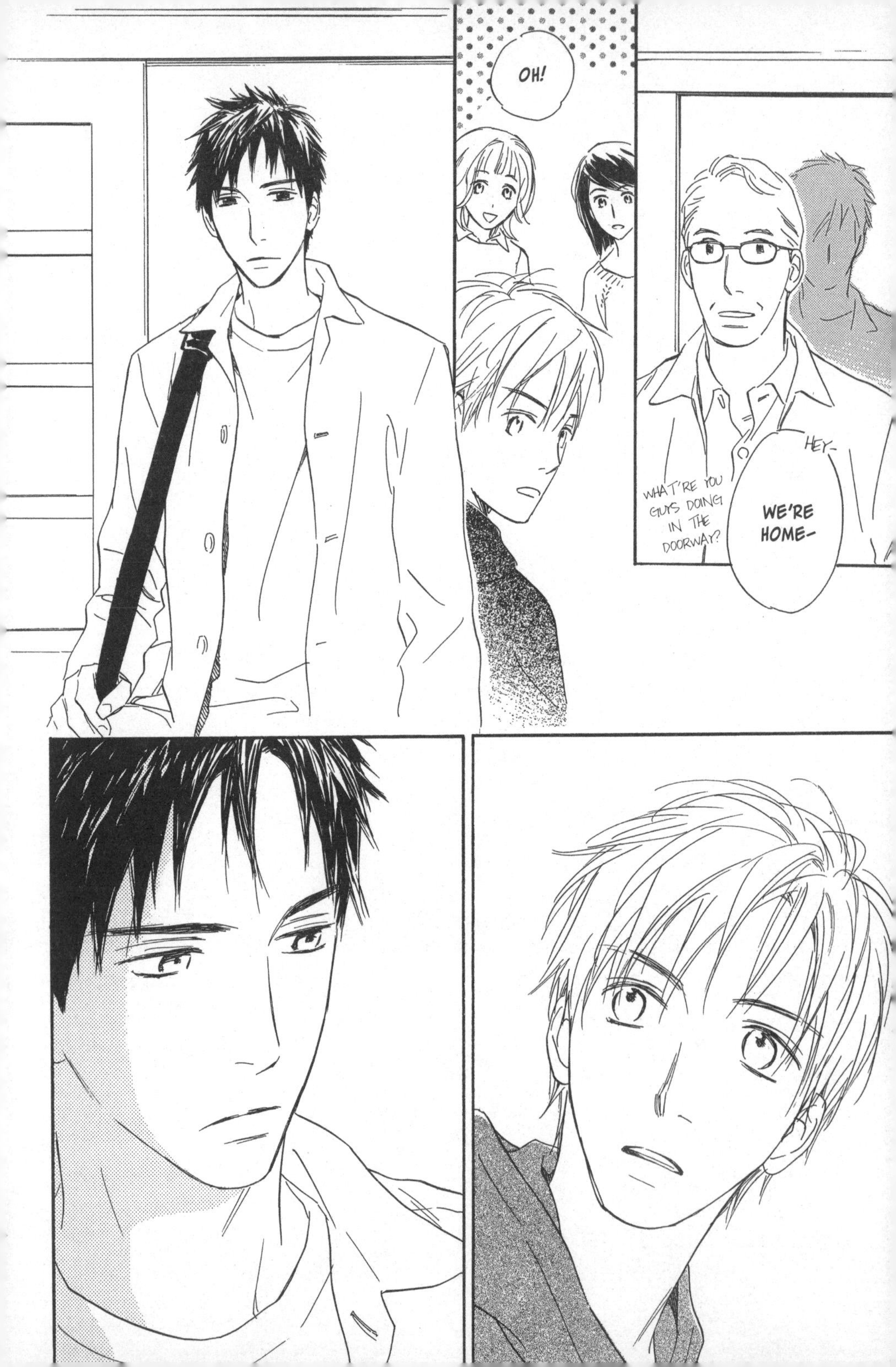
HEY-
WE'RE HOME-
WHAT'RE YOU GUYS DOING IN THE DOORWAY?
OH!

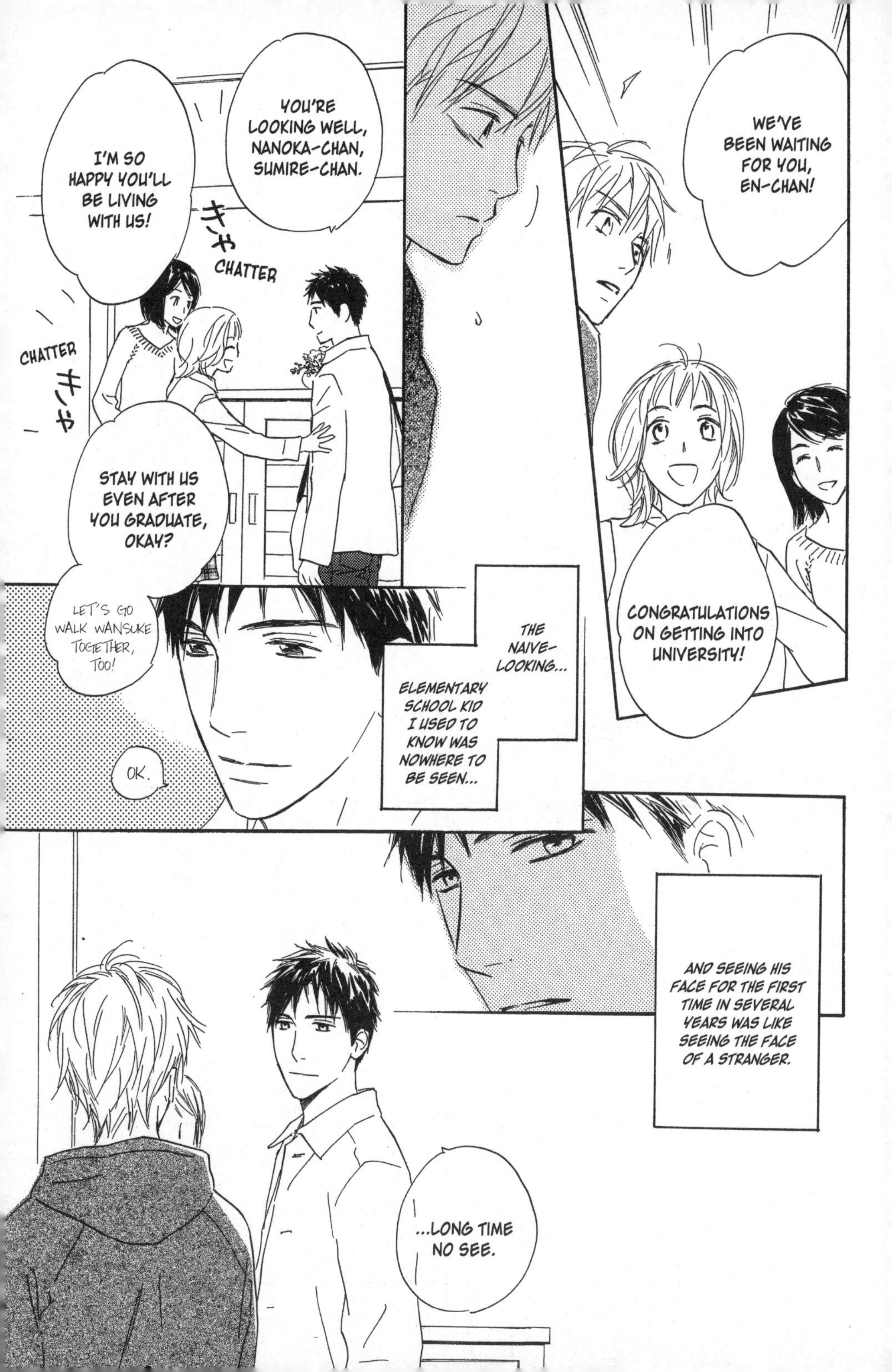
WE'VE BEEN WAITING FOR YOU, EN-CHAN!
CONGRATULATIONS ON GETTING INTO UNIVERSITY!
YOU'RE LOOKING WELL, NANOKA-CHAN, SUMIRE-CHAN.
I'M SO HAPPY YOU'LL BE LIVING WITH US!
キャ CHATTER
CHATTER キャ
STAY WITH US EVEN AFTER YOU GRADUATE, OKAY?
THE NAIVE-LOOKING...
ELEMENTARY SCHOOL KID I USED TO KNOW WAS NOWHERE TO BE SEEN...
LET'S GO WALK WANSUKE TOGETHER, TOO!
OK.
AND SEEING HIS FACE FOR THE FIRST TIME IN SEVERAL YEARS WAS LIKE SEEING THE FACE OF A STRANGER.
...LONG TIME NO SEE.

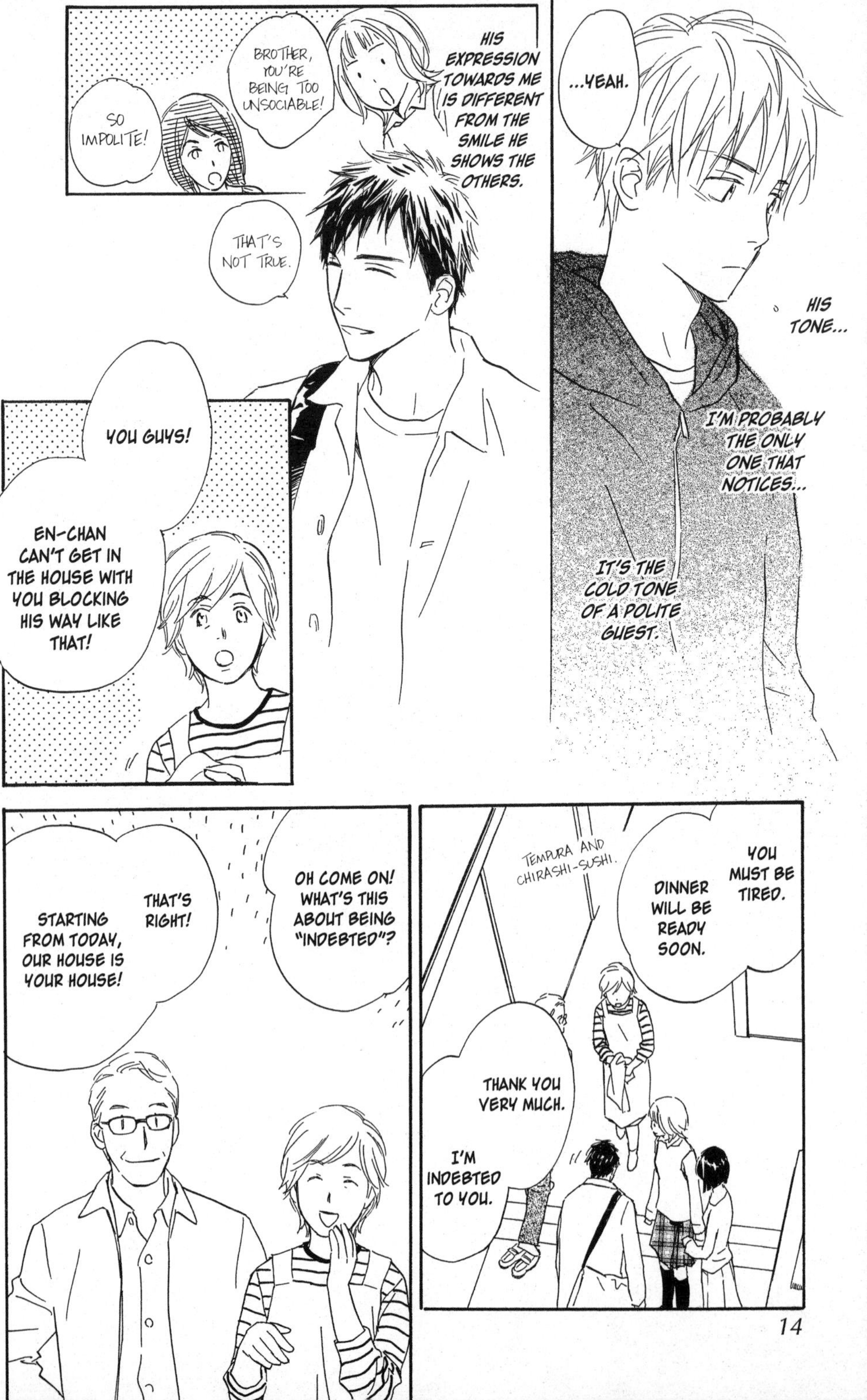
...YEAH.
HIS TONE...
I'M PROBABLY THE ONLY ONE THAT NOTICES...
IT'S THE COLD TONE OF A POLITE GUEST.
HIS EXPRESSION TOWARDS ME IS DIFFERENT FROM THE SMILE HE SHOWS THE OTHERS.
BROTHER, YOU'RE BEING TOO UNSOCIABLE!
SO IMPOLITE!
THAT'S NOT TRUE.
YOU GUYS!
EN-CHAN CAN'T GET IN THE HOUSE WITH YOU BLOCKING HIS WAY LIKE THAT!
YOU MUST BE TIRED.
DINNER WILL BE READY SOON.
TEMPURA AND CHIRASHI-SUSHI.
THANK YOU VERY MUCH.
I'M INDEBTED TO YOU.
OH COME ON! WHAT'S THIS ABOUT BEING "INDEBTED"?
THAT'S RIGHT!
STARTING FROM TODAY, OUR HOUSE IS YOUR HOUSE!

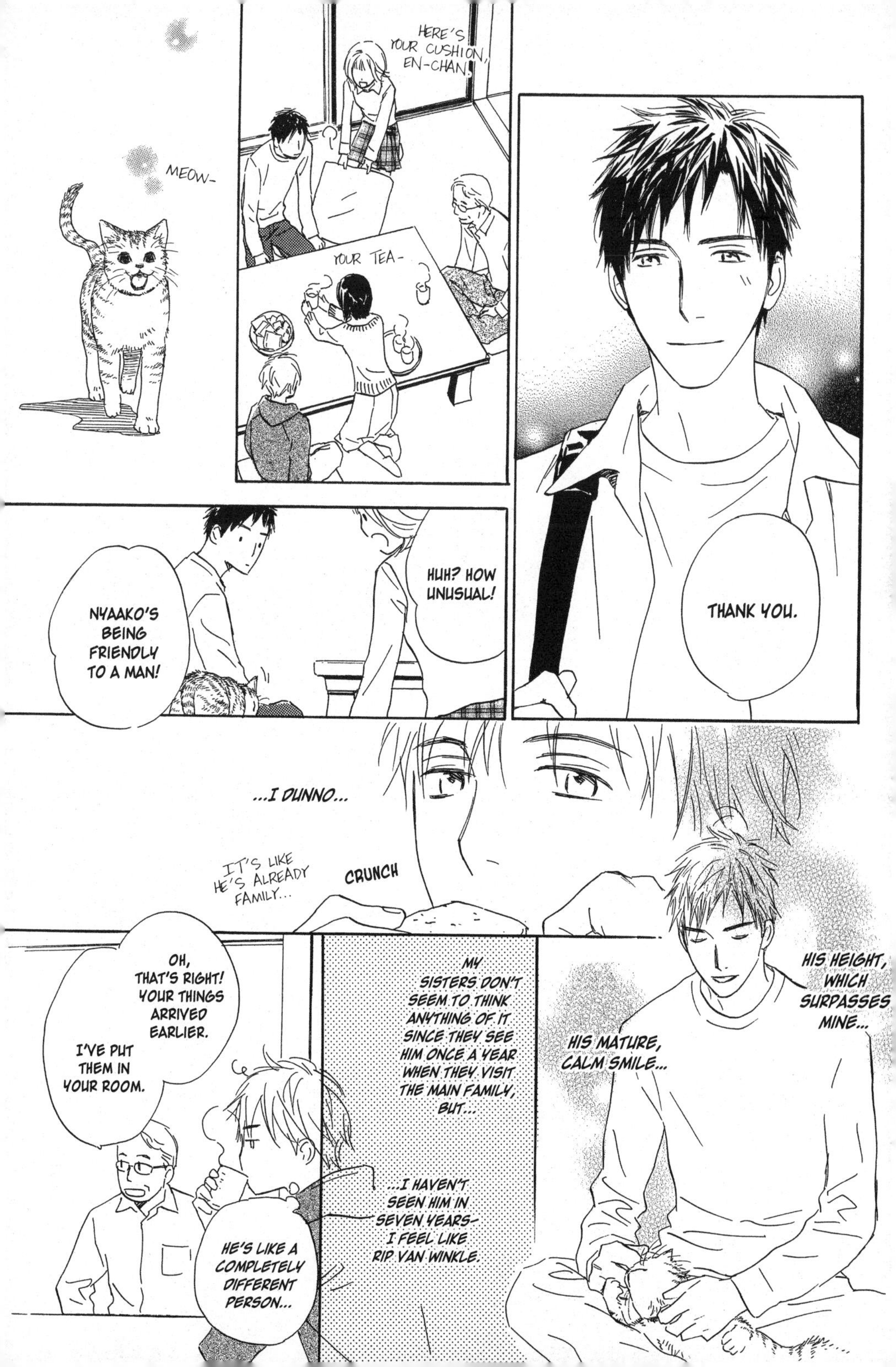
THANK YOU.
HERE'S YOUR CUSHION, EN-CHAN.
YOUR TEA-
MEOW-
HUH? HOW UNUSUAL!
NYAAKO'S BEING FRIENDLY TO A MAN!
...I DUNNO...
CRUNCH
IT'S LIKE HE'S ALREADY FAMILY...
HIS HEIGHT, WHICH SURPASSES MINE...
HIS MATURE, CALM SMILE...
MY SISTERS DON'T SEEM TO THINK ANYTHING OF IT SINCE THEY SEE HIM ONCE A YEAR WHEN THEY VISIT THE MAIN FAMILY, BUT...
...I HAVEN'T SEEN HIM IN SEVEN YEARS- I FEEL LIKE RIP VAN WINKLE.
OH, THAT'S RIGHT! YOUR THINGS ARRIVED EARLIER.
I'VE PUT THEM IN YOUR ROOM.
HE'S LIKE A COMPLETELY DIFFERENT PERSON...

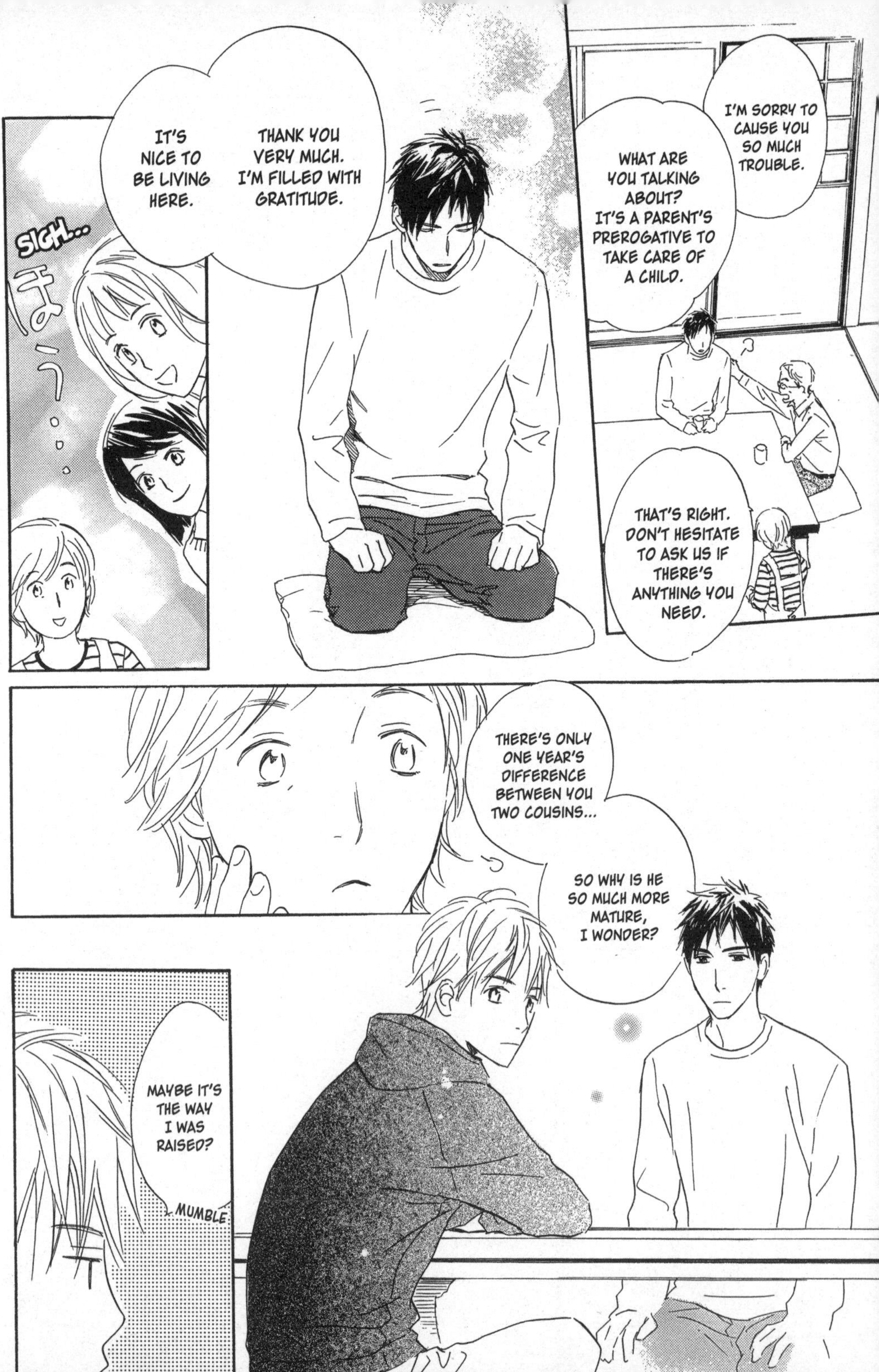

I'M SORRY TO CAUSE YOU SO MUCH TROUBLE.
WHAT ARE YOU TALKING ABOUT? IT'S A PARENT'S PREROGATIVE TO TAKE CARE OF A CHILD.
THAT'S RIGHT. DON'T HESITATE TO ASK US IF THERE'S ANYTHING YOU NEED.
THANK YOU VERY MUCH. I'M FILLED WITH GRATITUDE.
IT'S NICE TO BE LIVING HERE.
SIGH...
ほぅ...
THERE'S ONLY ONE YEAR'S DIFFERENCE BETWEEN YOU TWO COUSINS...
SO WHY IS HE SO MUCH MORE MATURE, I WONDER?
MAYBE IT'S THE WAY I WAS RAISED?
MUMBLE

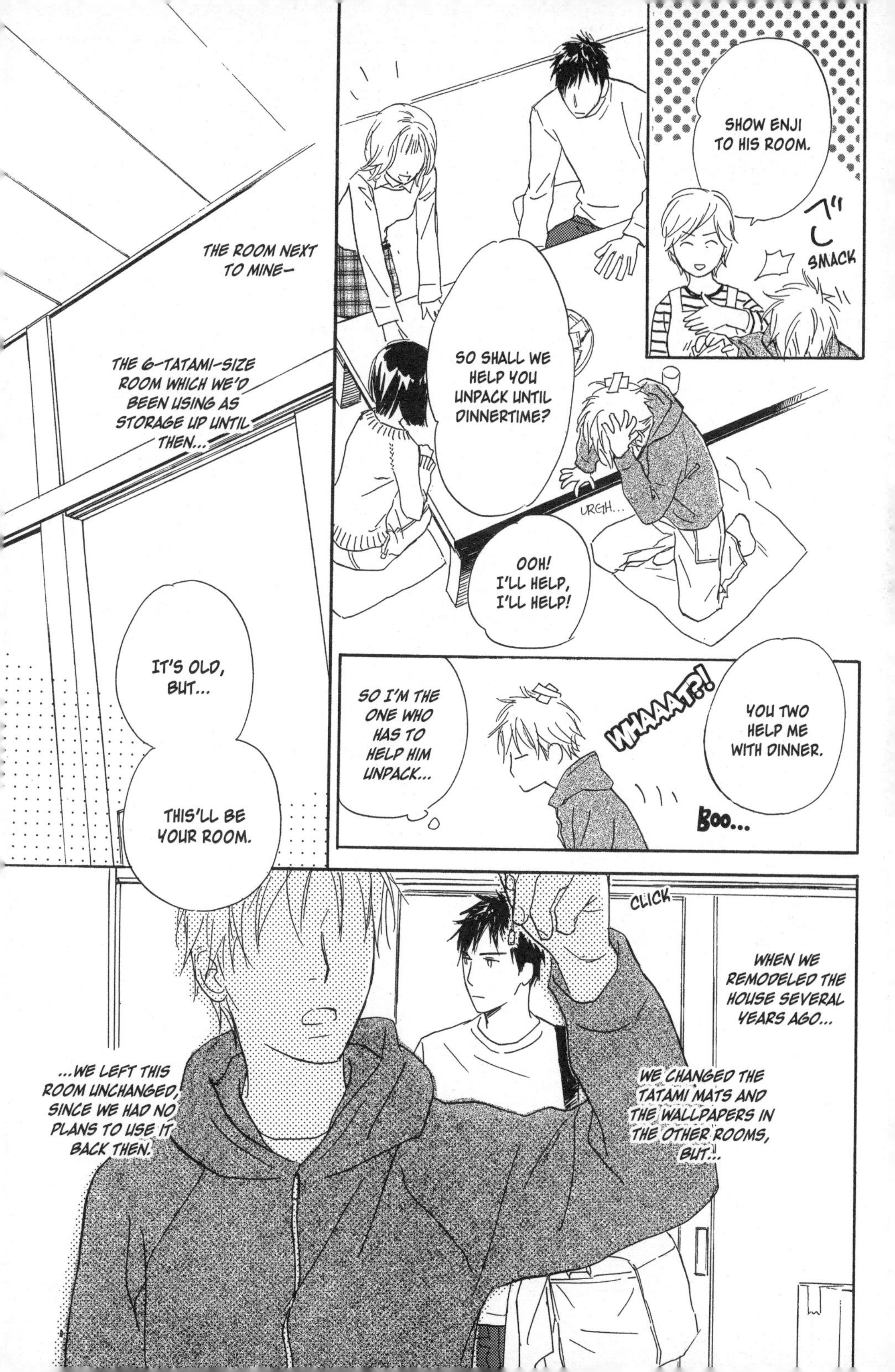

SHOW ENJI TO HIS ROOM.
べし
SMACK
SO SHALL WE HELP YOU UNPACK UNTIL DINNERTIME?
OOH! I'LL HELP, I'LL HELP!
URGH...
YOU TWO HELP ME WITH DINNER.
WHAAAT?!
BOO...
SO I'M THE ONE WHO HAS TO HELP HIM UNPACK...
THE ROOM NEXT TO MINE—
THE 6-TATAMI-SIZE ROOM WHICH WE'D BEEN USING AS STORAGE UP UNTIL THEN...
IT'S OLD, BUT...
THIS'LL BE YOUR ROOM.
CLICK
WHEN WE REMODELED THE HOUSE SEVERAL YEARS AGO...
WE CHANGED THE TATAMI MATS AND THE WALLPAPERS IN THE OTHER ROOMS, BUT...
...WE LEFT THIS ROOM UNCHANGED, SINCE WE HAD NO PLANS TO USE IT BACK THEN.

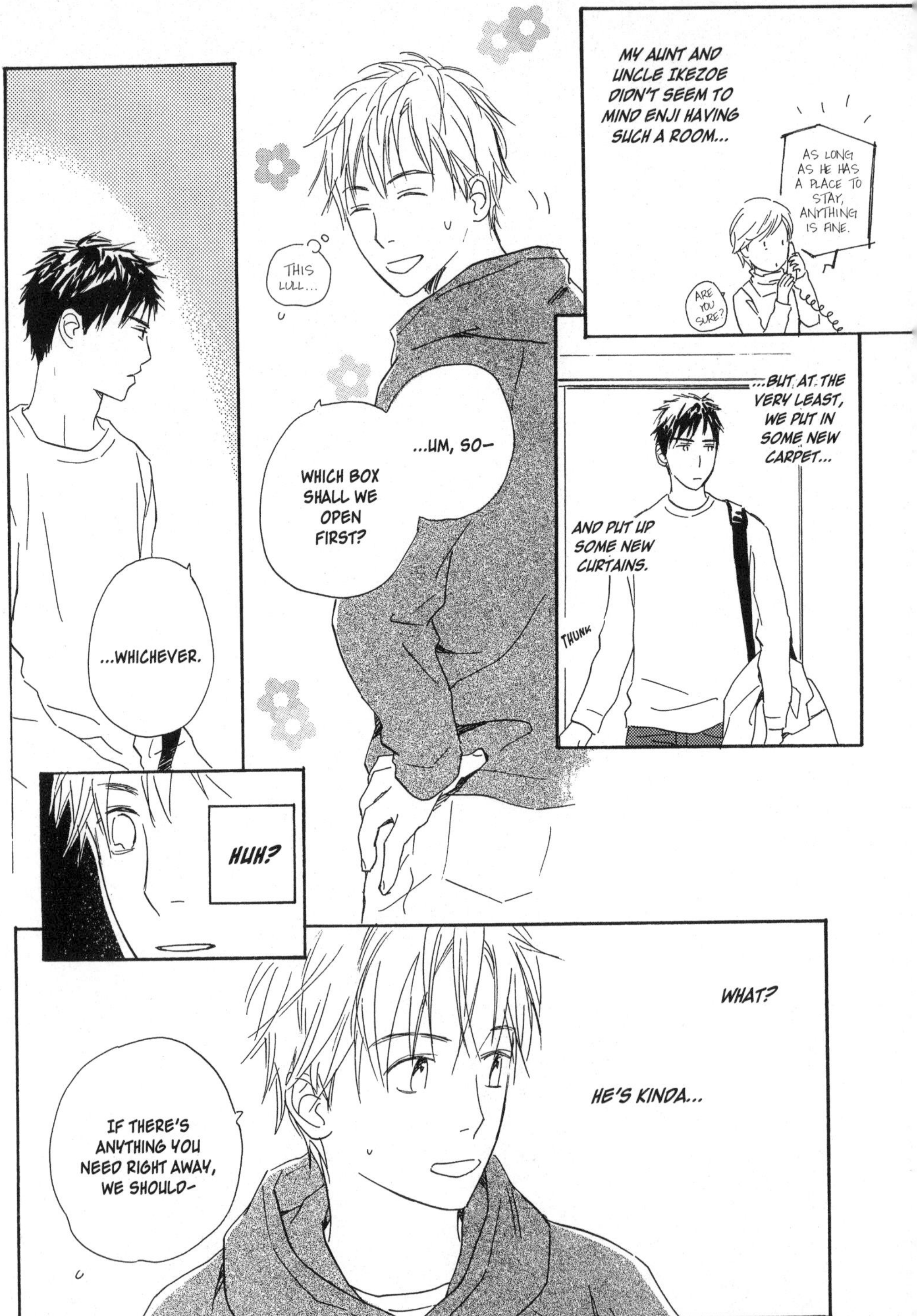
MY AUNT AND UNCLE IKEZOE DIDN'T SEEM TO MIND ENJI HAVING SUCH A ROOM...
AS LONG AS HE HAS A PLACE TO STAY, ANYTHING IS FINE.
ARE YOU SURE?
...BUT AT THE VERY LEAST, WE PUT IN SOME NEW CARPET...
AND PUT UP SOME NEW CURTAINS.
THUNK
THIS LULL...
...UM, SO-
WHICH BOX SHALL WE OPEN FIRST?
...WHICHEVER.
HUH?
WHAT?
HE'S KINDA...
IF THERE'S ANYTHING YOU NEED RIGHT AWAY, WE SHOULD-

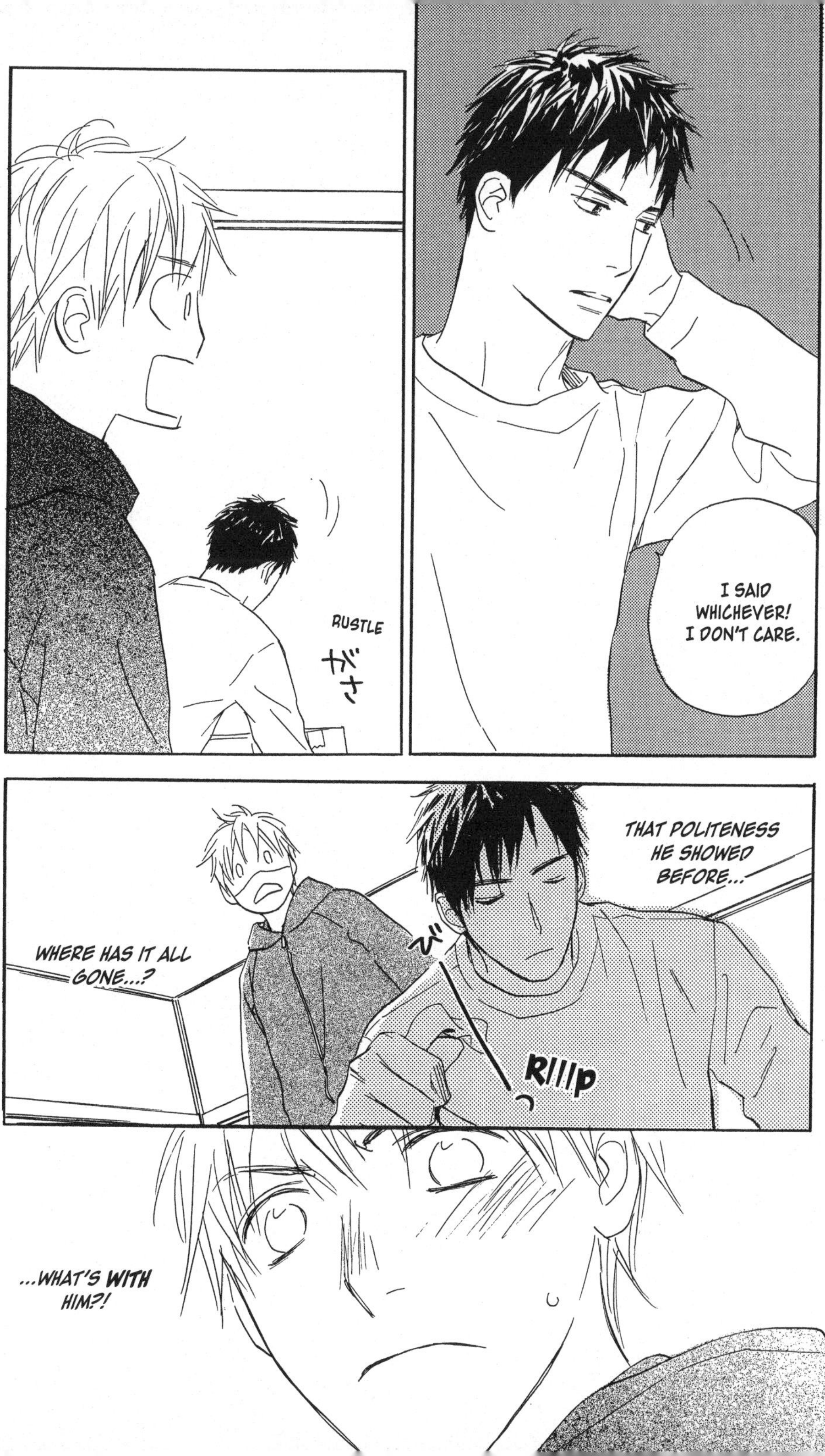
I SAID WHICHEVER! I DON'T CARE.
RUSTLE
ガさ
THAT POLITENESS HE SHOWED BEFORE...
び
RIIIP
WHERE HAS IT ALL GONE...?
...WHAT'S WITH HIM?!

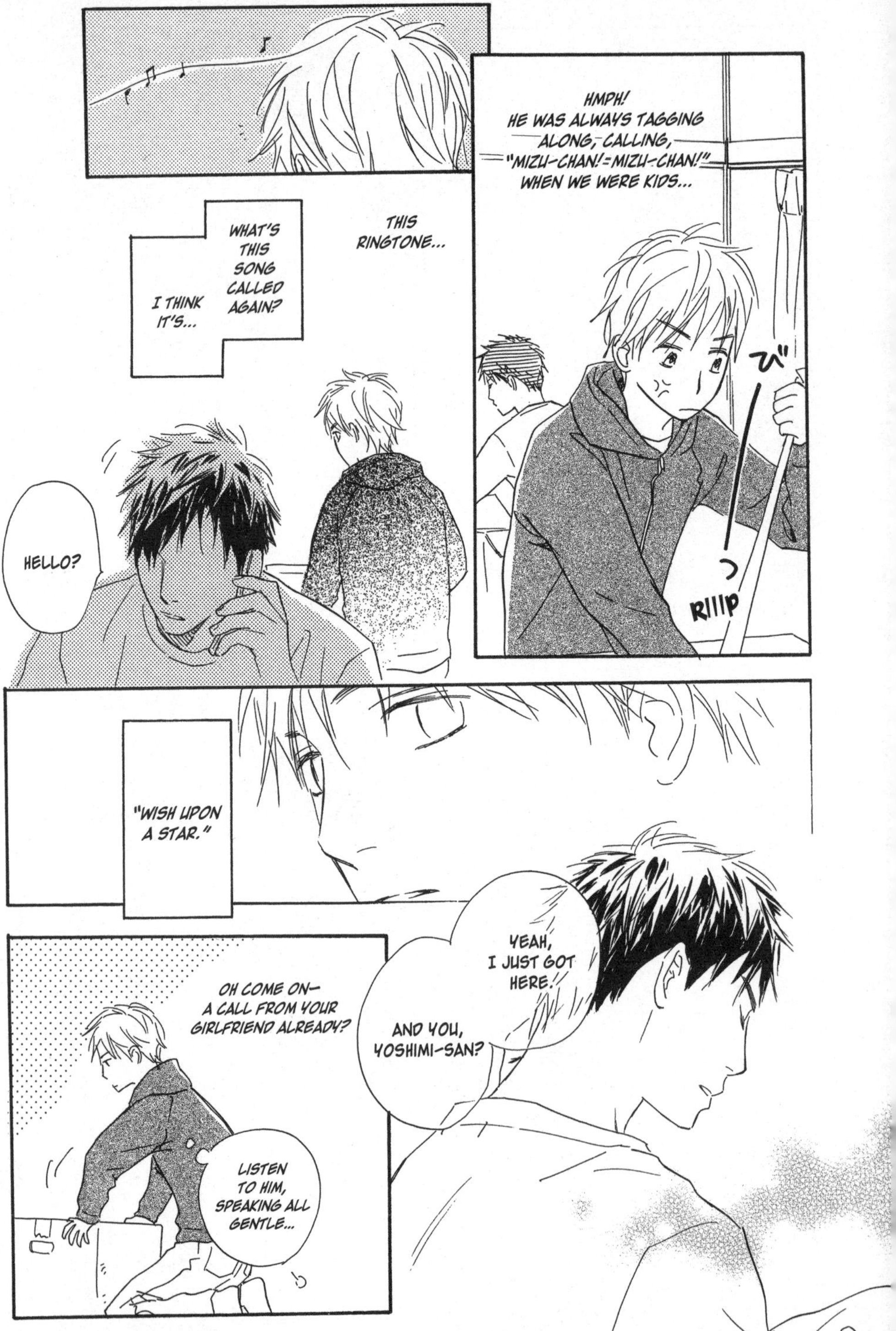
HMPH!
HE WAS ALWAYS TAGGING ALONG, CALLING, "MIZU-CHAN!" "MIZU-CHAN!" WHEN WE WERE KIDS...
び
っ
RIIIP
THIS RINGTONE...
WHAT'S THIS SONG CALLED AGAIN?
I THINK IT'S...
HELLO?
"WISH UPON A STAR."
YEAH, I JUST GOT HERE.
AND YOU, YOSHIMI-SAN?
OH COME ON— A CALL FROM YOUR GIRLFRIEND ALREADY?
LISTEN TO HIM, SPEAKING ALL GENTLE...

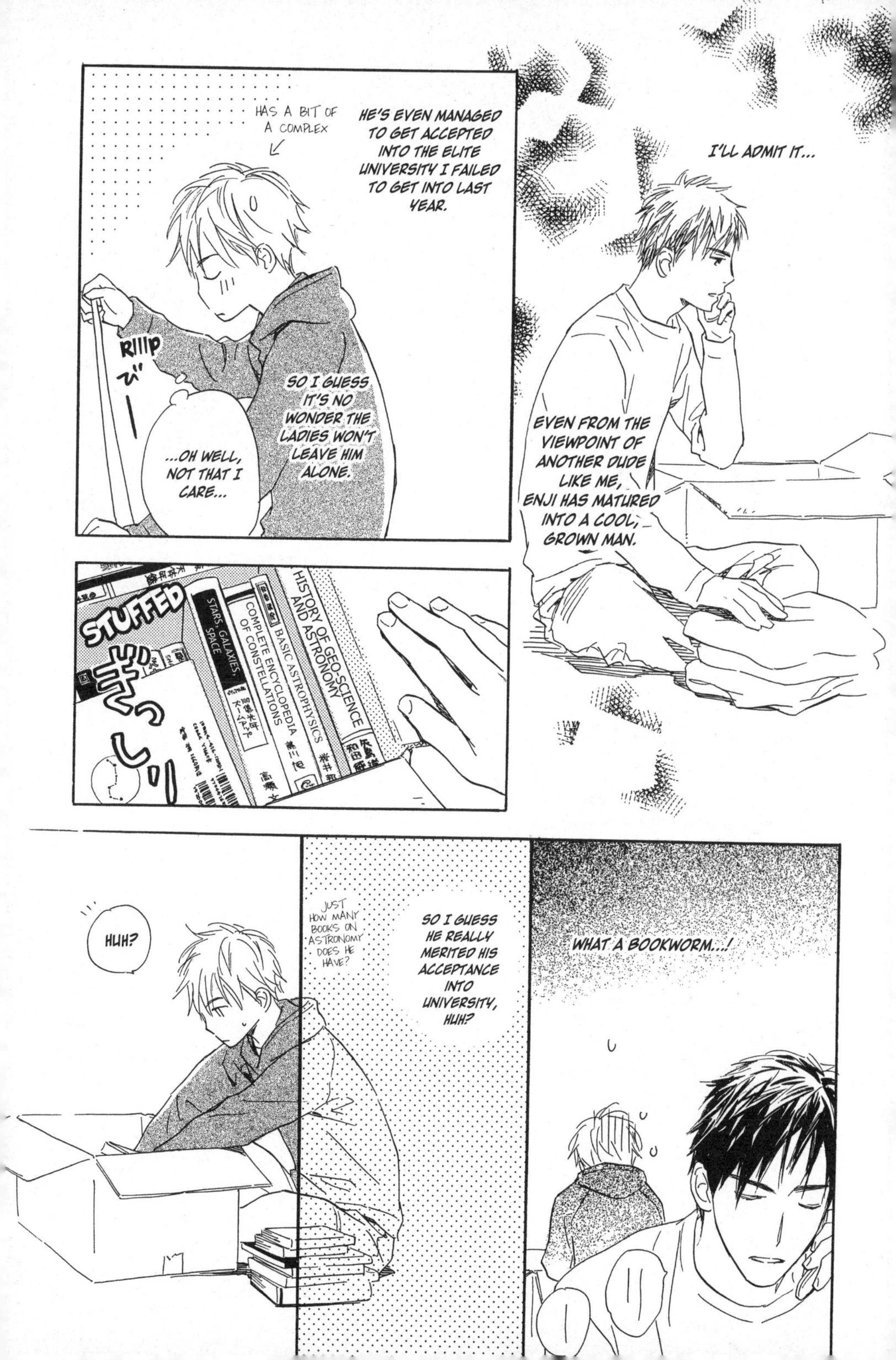
I'LL ADMIT IT...
EVEN FROM THE VIEWPOINT OF ANOTHER DUDE LIKE ME, ENJI HAS MATURED INTO A COOL, GROWN MAN.
HE'S EVEN MANAGED TO GET ACCEPTED INTO THE ELITE UNIVERSITY I FAILED TO GET INTO LAST YEAR.
HAS A BIT OF A COMPLEX
SO I GUESS IT'S NO WONDER THE LADIES WON'T LEAVE HIM ALONE.
...OH WELL, NOT THAT I CARE...
RIIIP
STUFFED
HISTORY OF GEO-SCIENCE AND ASTRONOMY
BASIC ASTROPHYSICS
COMPLETE ENCYCLOPEDIA OF CONSTELLATIONS
STARS, GALAXIES, SPACE
WHAT A BOOKWORM...!
SO I GUESS HE REALLY MERITED HIS ACCEPTANCE INTO UNIVERSITY, HUH?
JUST HOW MANY BOOKS ON ASTRONOMY DOES HE HAVE?
HUH?

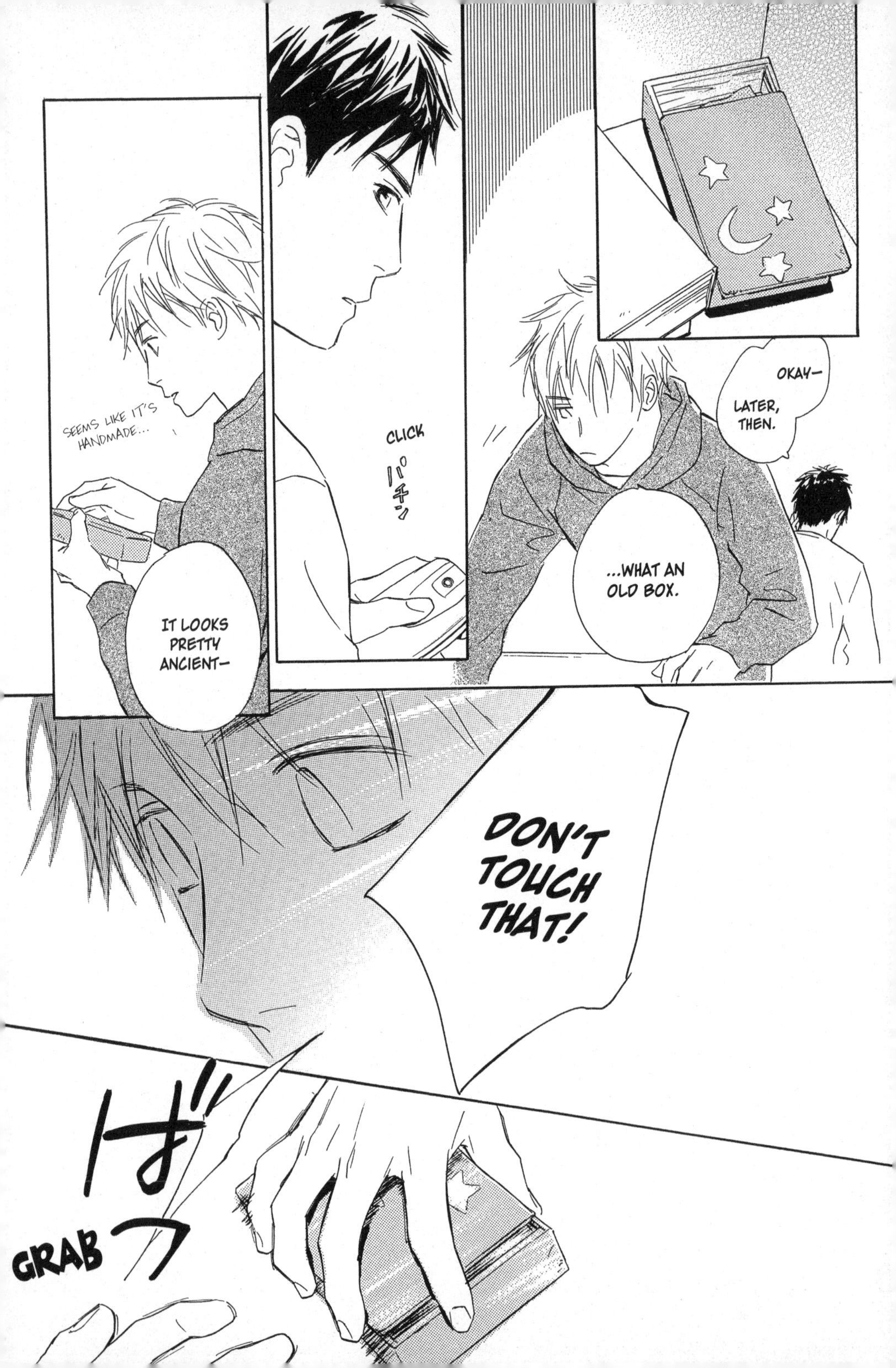
OKAY— LATER, THEN.
...WHAT AN OLD BOX.
CLICK
パチン
SEEMS LIKE IT'S HANDMADE...
IT LOOKS PRETTY ANCIENT—
DON'T TOUCH THAT!
ばっ
GRAB

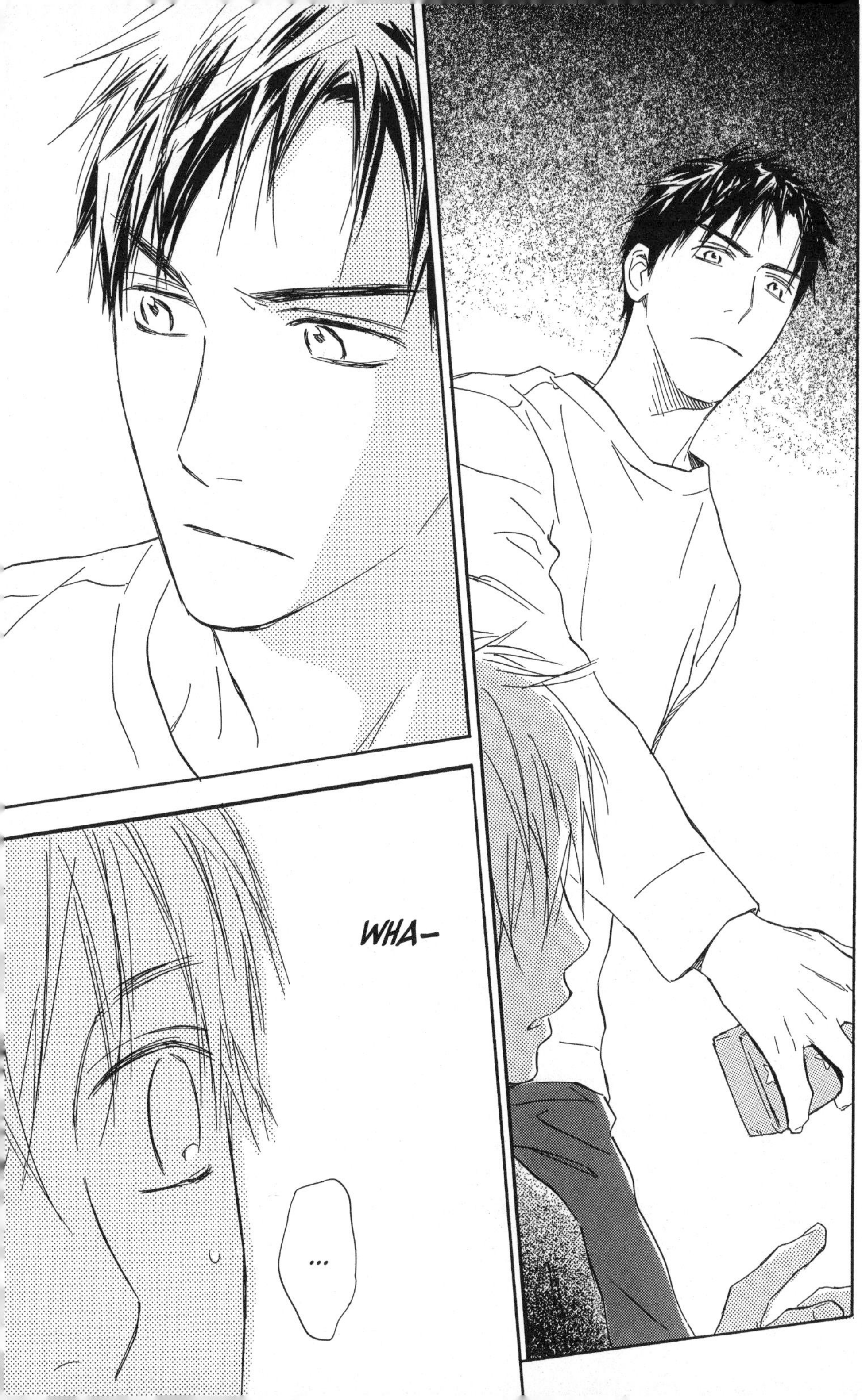
WHA-
...

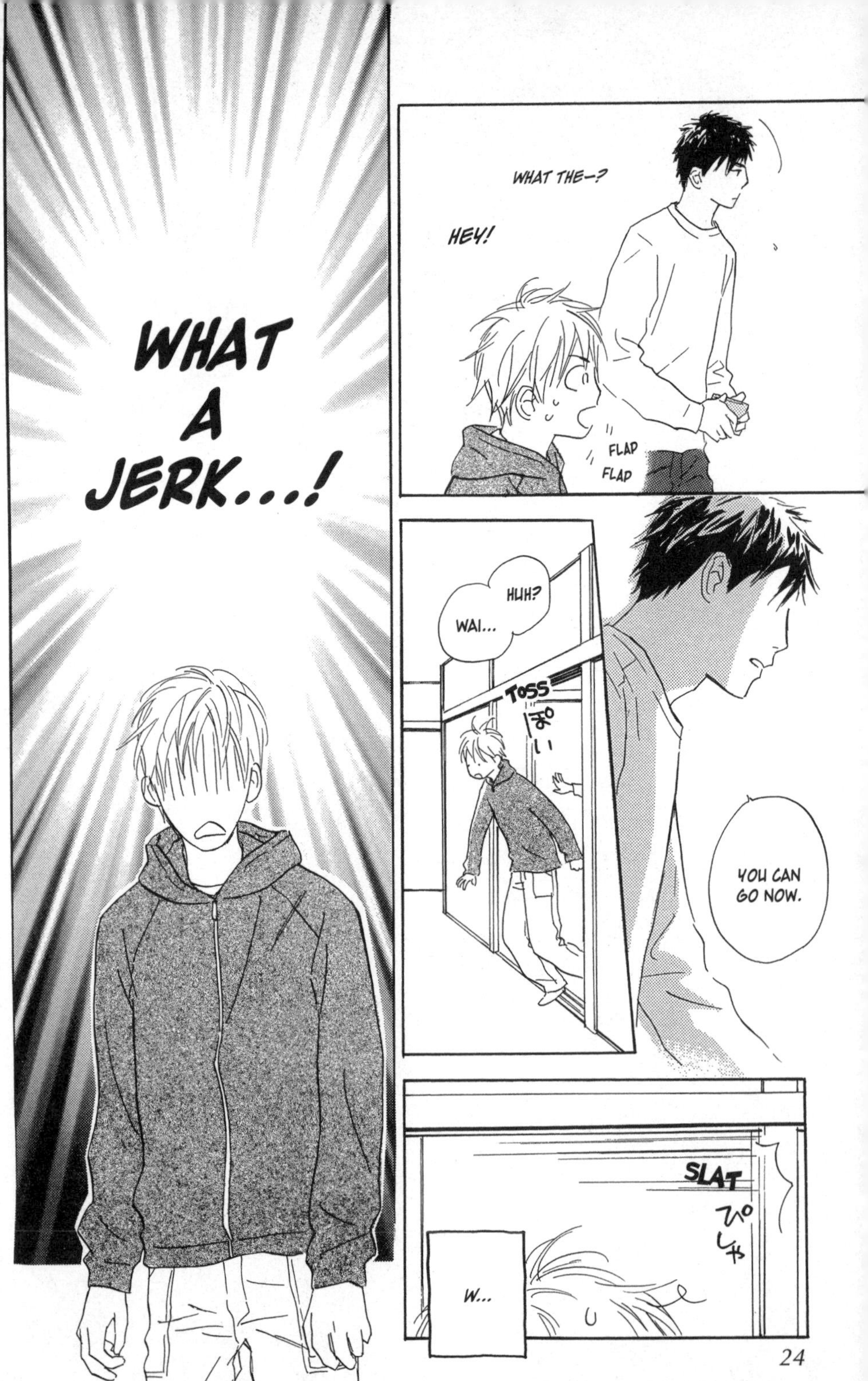
WHAT THE–?
HEY!
FLAP
FLAP
HUH?
WAI...
TOSS
ぽい
YOU CAN GO NOW.
SLAT
ぴしゃ
W...
WHAT A JERK...!

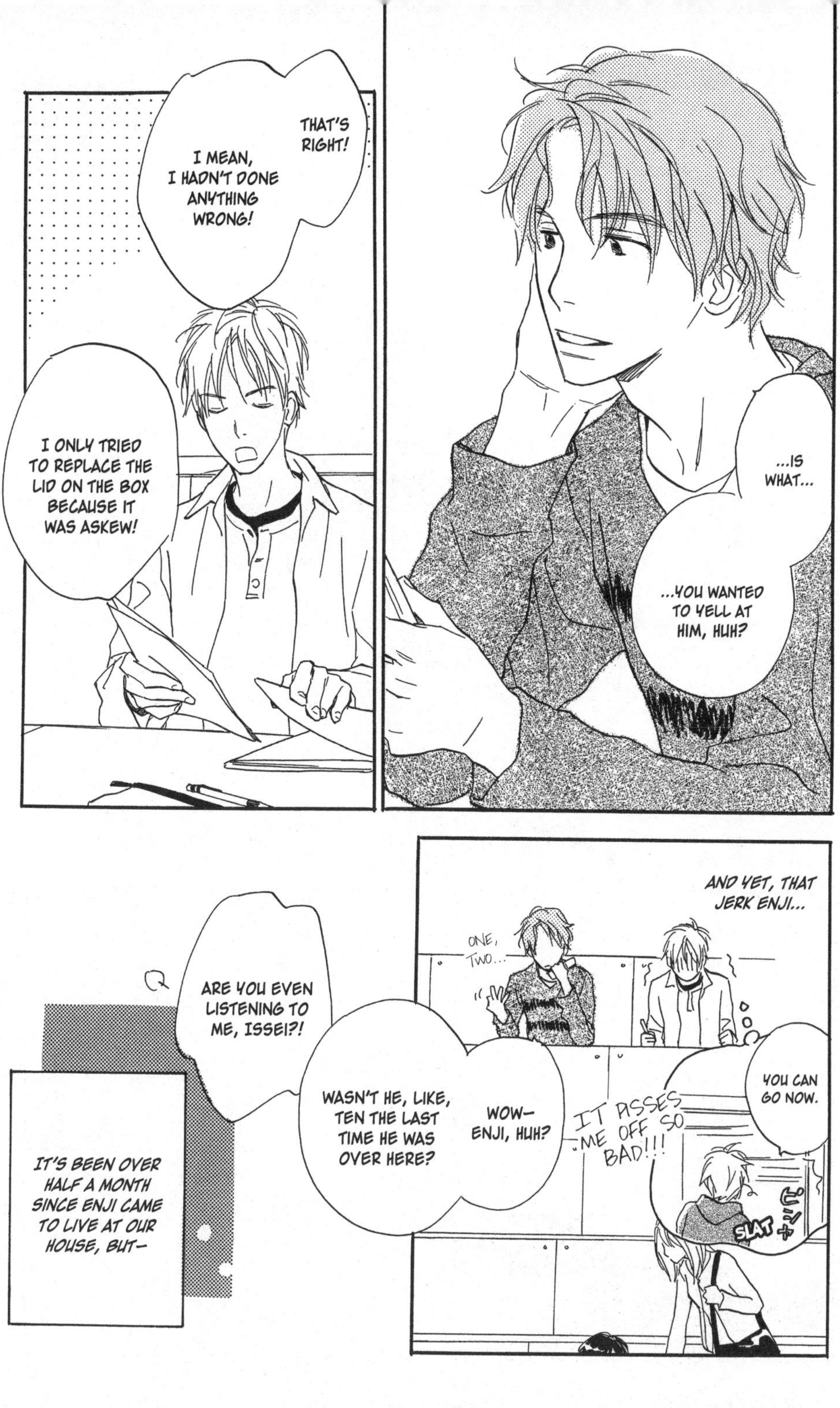
...IS WHAT...
...YOU WANTED TO YELL AT HIM, HUH?
THAT'S RIGHT!
I MEAN, I HADN'T DONE ANYTHING WRONG!
I ONLY TRIED TO REPLACE THE LID ON THE BOX BECAUSE IT WAS ASKEW!
AND YET, THAT JERK ENJI...
ONE, TWO...
YOU CAN GO NOW.
SLAT
IT PISSES ME OFF SO BAD!!!
WOW— ENJI, HUH?
WASN'T HE, LIKE, TEN THE LAST TIME HE WAS OVER HERE?
ARE YOU EVEN LISTENING TO ME, ISSEI?!
IT'S BEEN OVER HALF A MONTH SINCE ENJI CAME TO LIVE AT OUR HOUSE, BUT—

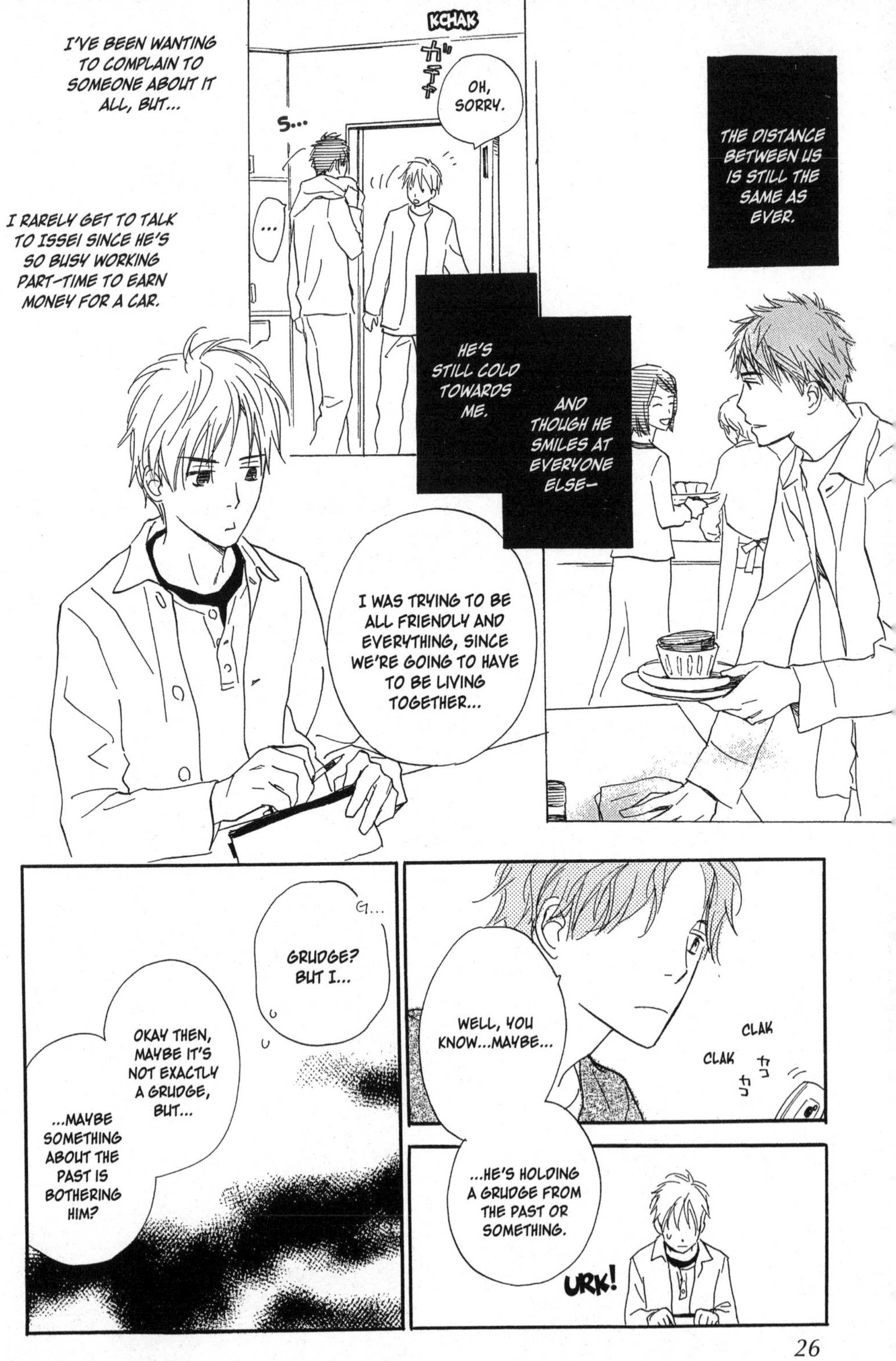
THE DISTANCE BETWEEN US IS STILL THE SAME AS EVER.
KCHAK
ガチャ
OH, SORRY.
S...
...
I'VE BEEN WANTING TO COMPLAIN TO SOMEONE ABOUT IT ALL, BUT...
I RARELY GET TO TALK TO ISSEI SINCE HE'S SO BUSY WORKING PART-TIME TO EARN MONEY FOR A CAR.
HE'S STILL COLD TOWARDS ME.
AND THOUGH HE SMILES AT EVERYONE ELSE—
I WAS TRYING TO BE ALL FRIENDLY AND EVERYTHING, SINCE WE'RE GOING TO HAVE TO BE LIVING TOGETHER...
WELL, YOU KNOW...MAYBE...
CLAK
CLAK
カコ
カコ
...HE'S HOLDING A GRUDGE FROM THE PAST OR SOMETHING.
URK!
G...
GRUDGE? BUT I...
OKAY THEN, MAYBE IT'S NOT EXACTLY A GRUDGE, BUT...
...MAYBE SOMETHING ABOUT THE PAST IS BOTHERING HIM?

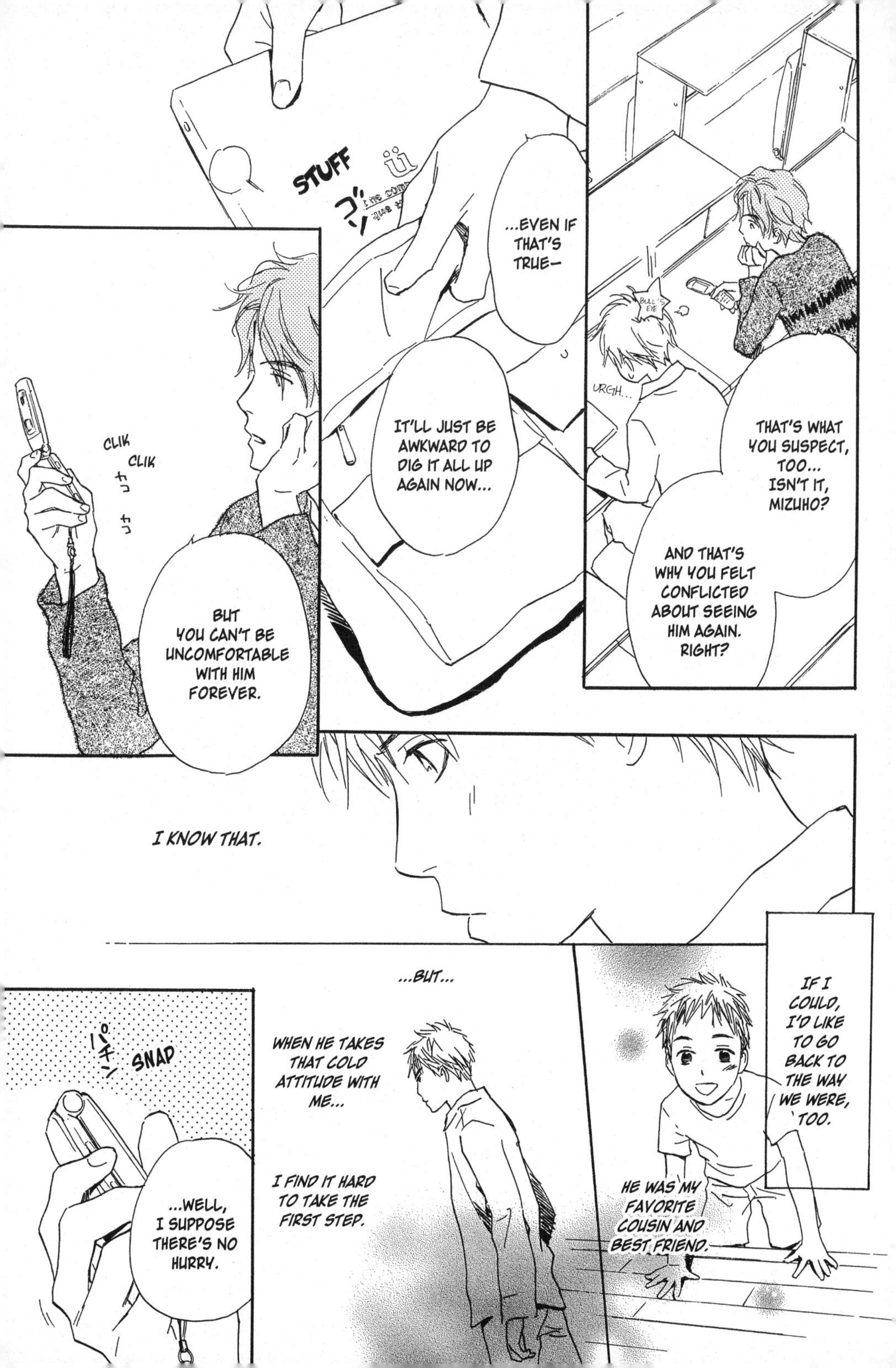
BULL'S EYE
URGH...
THAT'S WHAT YOU SUSPECT, TOO... ISN'T IT, MIZUHO?
AND THAT'S WHY YOU FELT CONFLICTED ABOUT SEEING HIM AGAIN. RIGHT?
STUFF
...EVEN IF THAT'S TRUE—
IT'LL JUST BE AWKWARD TO DIG IT ALL UP AGAIN NOW...
CLIK CLIK
BUT YOU CAN'T BE UNCOMFORTABLE WITH HIM FOREVER.
I KNOW THAT.
IF I COULD, I'D LIKE TO GO BACK TO THE WAY WE WERE, TOO.
HE WAS MY FAVORITE COUSIN AND BEST FRIEND.
...BUT...
WHEN HE TAKES THAT COLD ATTITUDE WITH ME...
I FIND IT HARD TO TAKE THE FIRST STEP.
パチン
SNAP
...WELL, I SUPPOSE THERE'S NO HURRY.

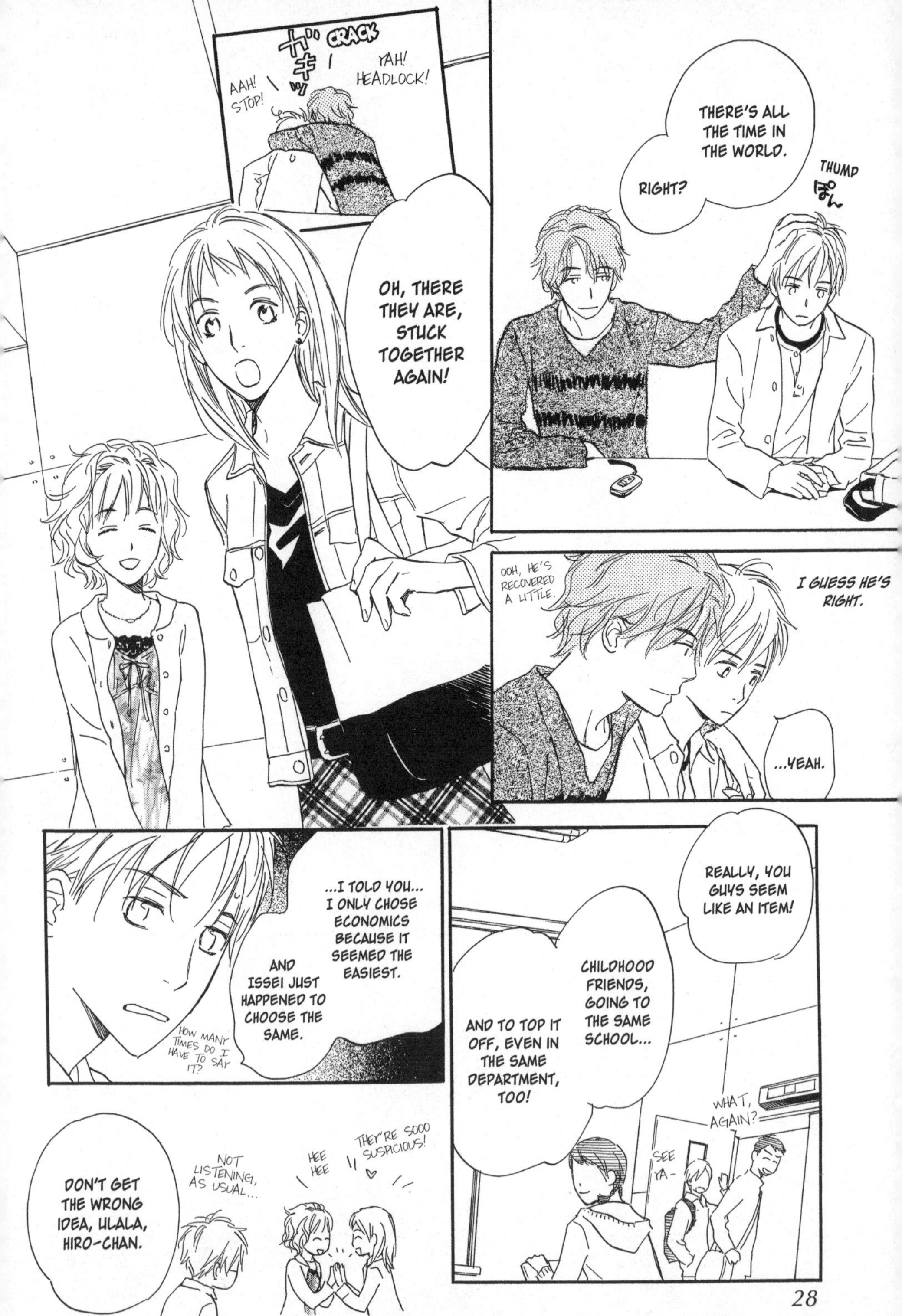
There's all the time in the world.
Right?
THUMP
ぽん
Ooh, he's recovered a little.
I guess he's right.
...Yeah.
ガギッ
CRACK
Yah! Headlock!
Aah! Stop!
Oh, there they are, stuck together again!
Really, you guys seem like an item!
Childhood friends, going to the same school...
And to top it off, even in the same department, too!
What, again?
See ya-
...I told you... I only chose economics because it seemed the easiest.
And Issei just happened to choose the same.
How many times do I have to say it?
They're sooo suspicious!
Hee hee
Not listening, as usual...
Don't get the wrong idea, Ulala, Hiro-chan.

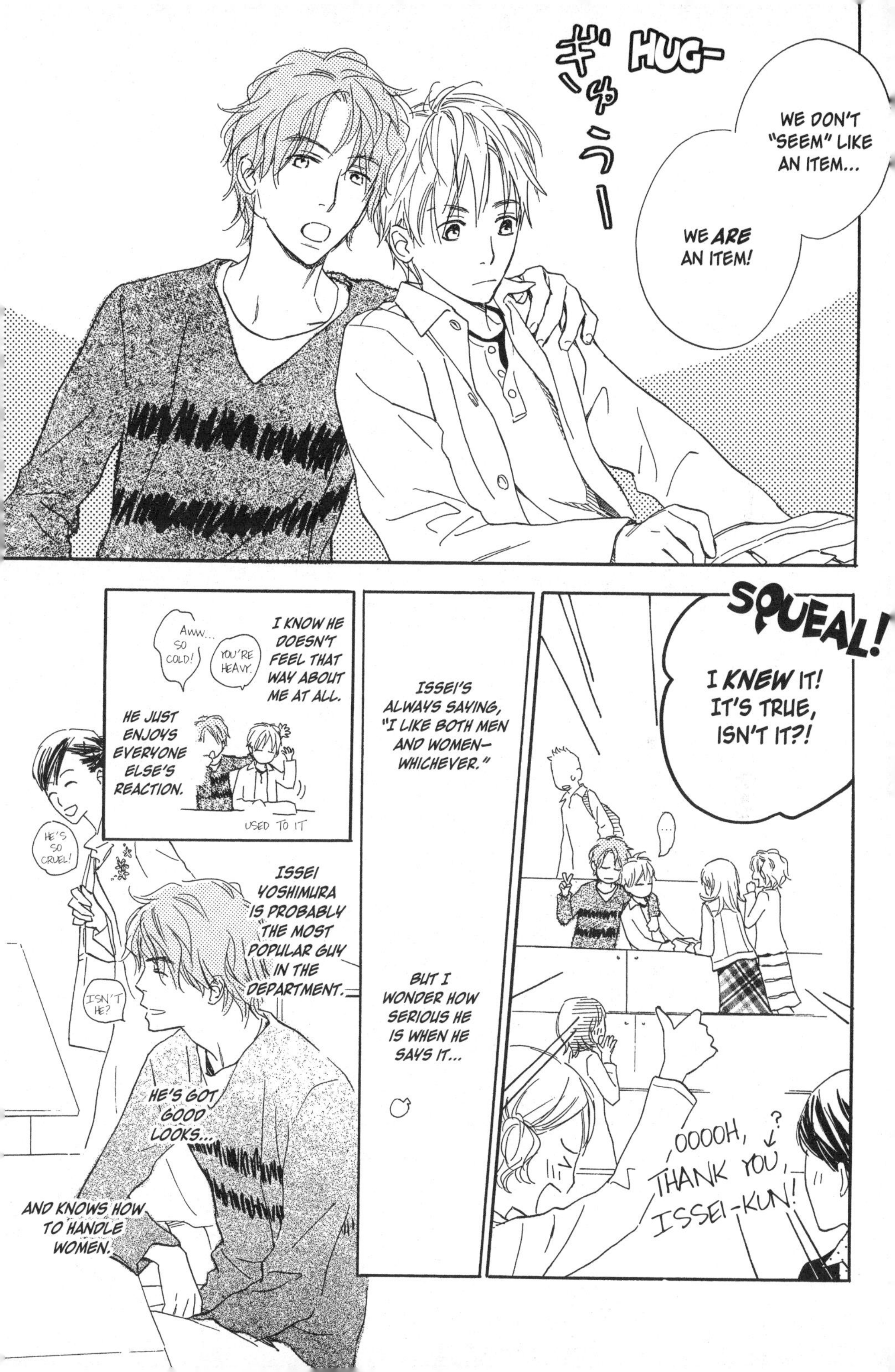

ぎゅうー
HUG-
WE DON'T "SEEM" LIKE AN ITEM...
WE ARE AN ITEM!
SQUEAL!
I KNEW IT! IT'S TRUE, ISN'T IT?!
...
OOOOH, THANK YOU, ISSEI-KUN!
?
ISSEI'S ALWAYS SAYING, "I LIKE BOTH MEN AND WOMEN-WHICHEVER."
BUT I WONDER HOW SERIOUS HE IS WHEN HE SAYS IT...
I KNOW HE DOESN'T FEEL THAT WAY ABOUT ME AT ALL.
AWW... SO COLD!
YOU'RE HEAVY.
HE JUST ENJOYS EVERYONE ELSE'S REACTION.
USED TO IT
ISSEI YOSHIMURA IS PROBABLY THE MOST POPULAR GUY IN THE DEPARTMENT.
HE'S SO CRUEL!
ISN'T HE?
HE'S GOT GOOD LOOKS...
AND KNOWS HOW TO HANDLE WOMEN.

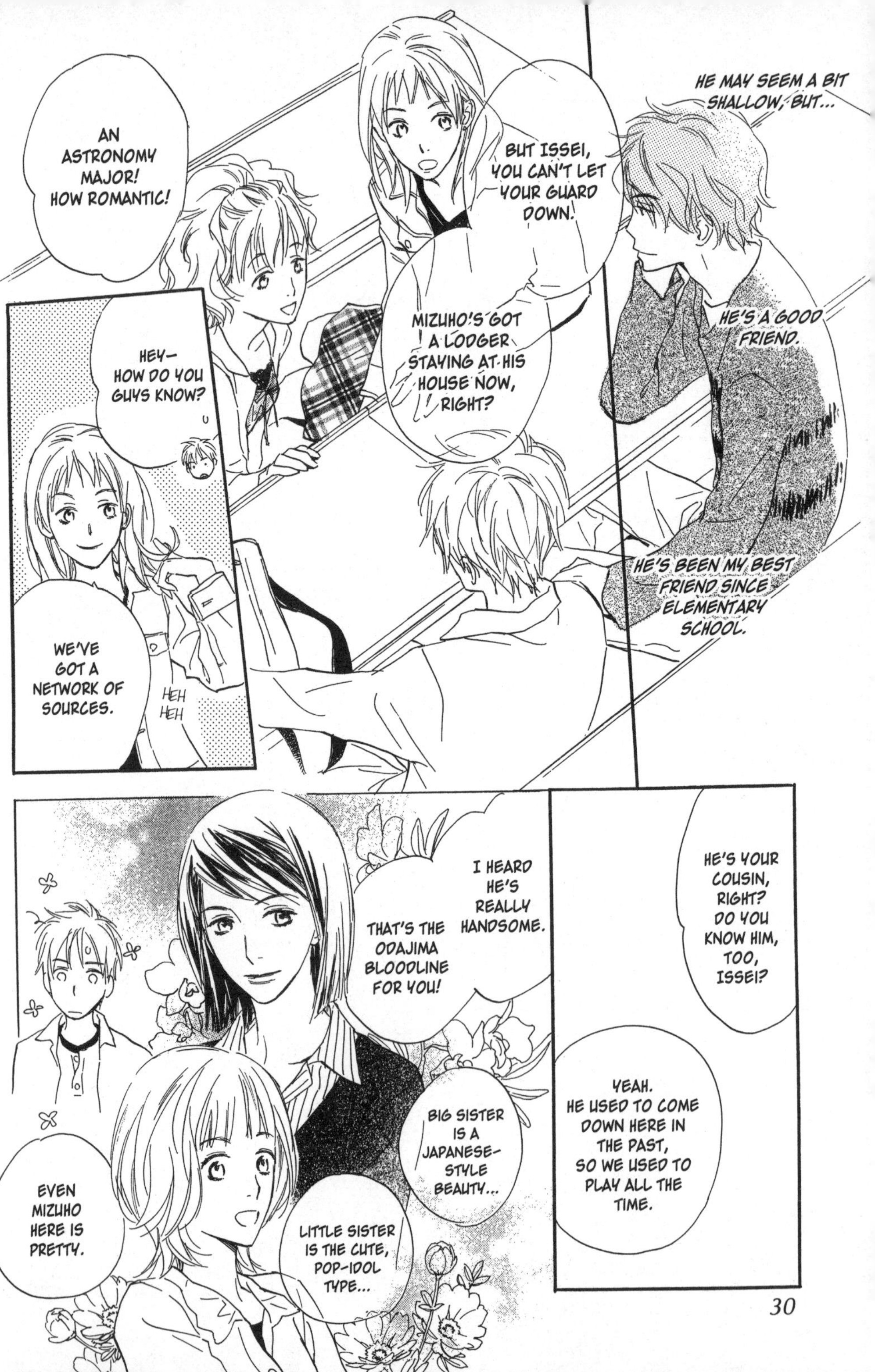
HE MAY SEEM A BIT SHALLOW, BUT...
HE'S A GOOD FRIEND.
HE'S BEEN MY BEST FRIEND SINCE ELEMENTARY SCHOOL.
BUT ISSEI, YOU CAN'T LET YOUR GUARD DOWN.
MIZUHO'S GOT A LODGER STAYING AT HIS HOUSE NOW, RIGHT?
AN ASTRONOMY MAJOR! HOW ROMANTIC!
HEY— HOW DO YOU GUYS KNOW?
WE'VE GOT A NETWORK OF SOURCES.
HEH HEH
HE'S YOUR COUSIN, RIGHT? DO YOU KNOW HIM, TOO, ISSEI?
YEAH. HE USED TO COME DOWN HERE IN THE PAST, SO WE USED TO PLAY ALL THE TIME.
I HEARD HE'S REALLY HANDSOME.
THAT'S THE ODAJIMA BLOODLINE FOR YOU!
BIG SISTER IS A JAPANESE-STYLE BEAUTY...
LITTLE SISTER IS THE CUTE, POP-IDOL TYPE...
EVEN MIZUHO HERE IS PRETTY.

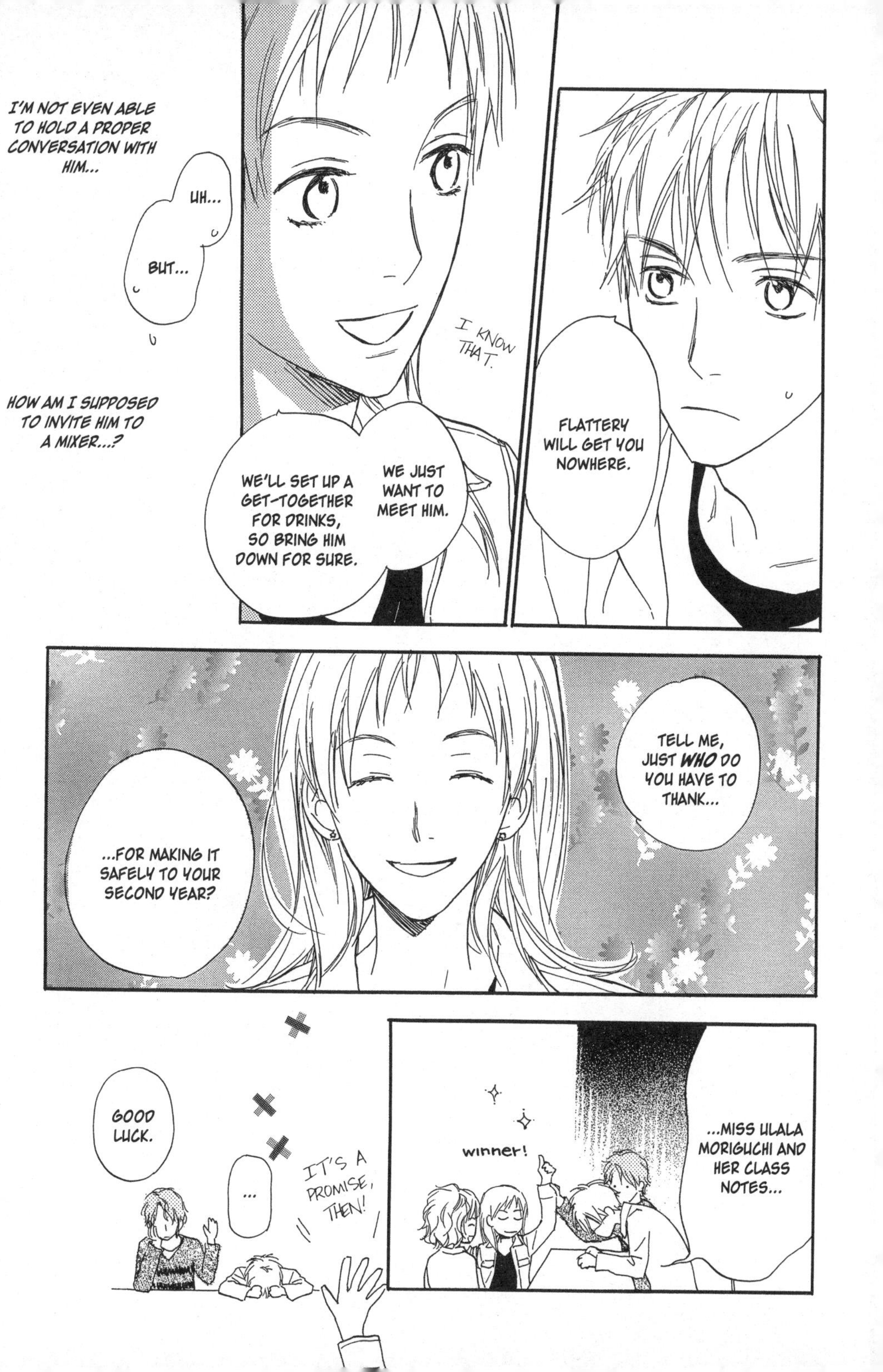
FLATTERY WILL GET YOU NOWHERE.
I KNOW THAT.
WE JUST WANT TO MEET HIM.
WE'LL SET UP A GET-TOGETHER FOR DRINKS, SO BRING HIM DOWN FOR SURE.
I'M NOT EVEN ABLE TO HOLD A PROPER CONVERSATION WITH HIM...
UH...
BUT...
HOW AM I SUPPOSED TO INVITE HIM TO A MIXER...?
TELL ME, JUST **WHO** DO YOU HAVE TO THANK...
...FOR MAKING IT SAFELY TO YOUR SECOND YEAR?
...MISS ULALA MORIGUCHI AND HER CLASS NOTES...
winner!
IT'S A PROMISE, THEN!
...
GOOD LUCK.

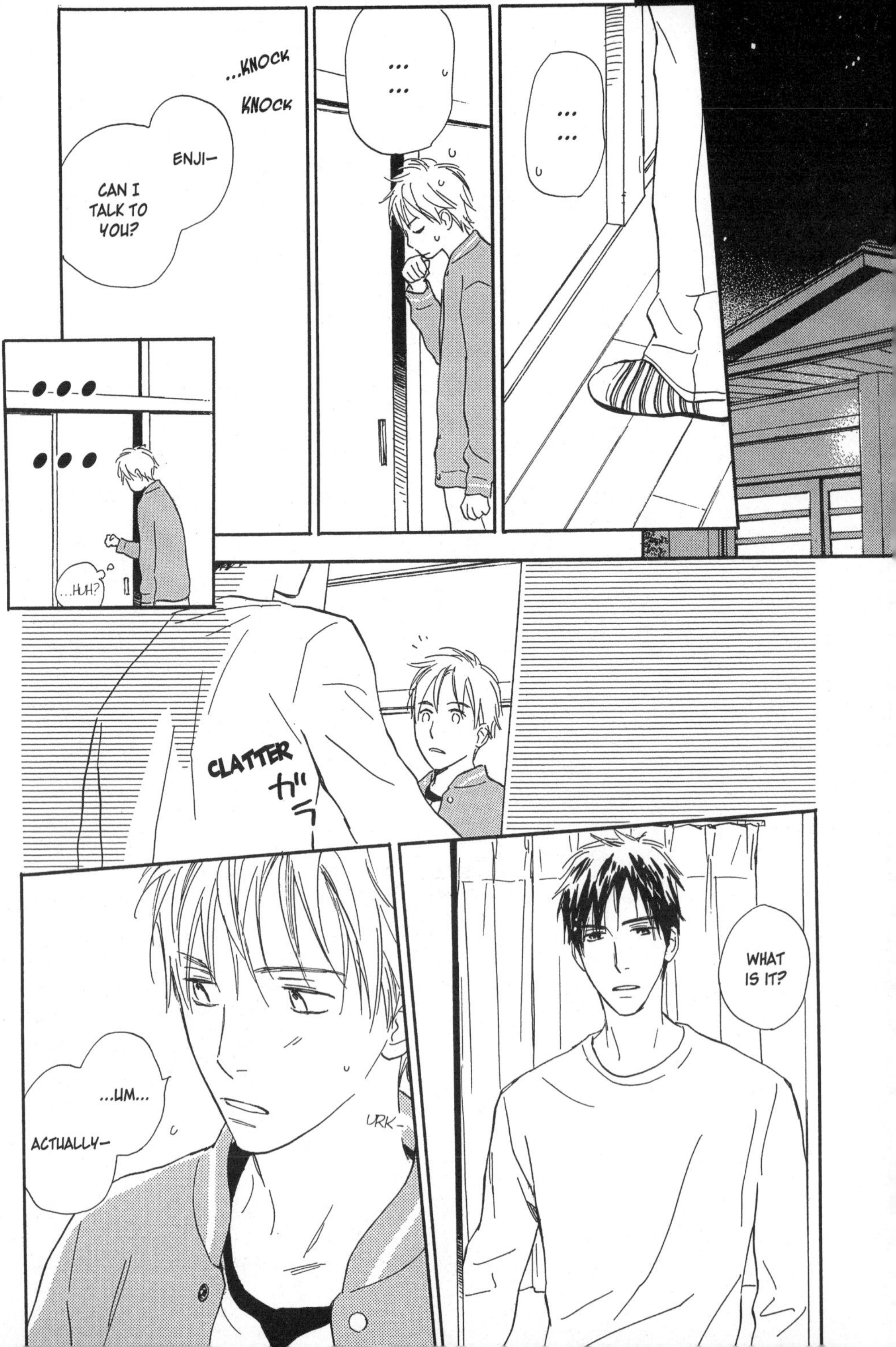
... ...
... ...
...KNOCK KNOCK
ENJI— CAN I TALK TO YOU?
• • •
• • •
...HUH?
CLATTER
ガラ
WHAT IS IT?
URK—
...UM...
ACTUALLY—

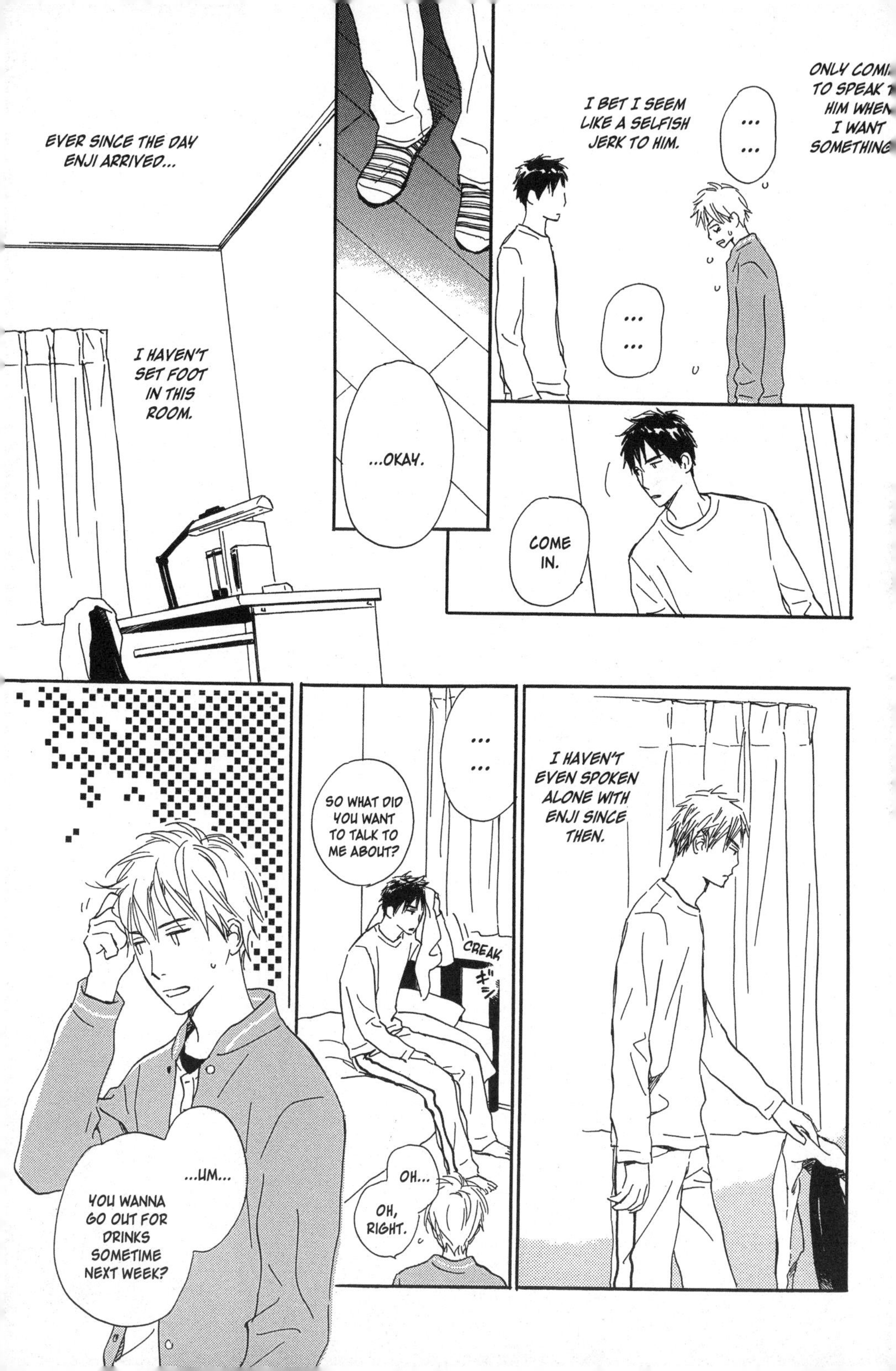
ONLY COMI TO SPEAK T HIM WHEN I WANT SOMETHING
... ...
I BET I SEEM LIKE A SELFISH JERK TO HIM.
... ...
COME IN.
...OKAY.
EVER SINCE THE DAY ENJI ARRIVED...
I HAVEN'T SET FOOT IN THIS ROOM.
I HAVEN'T EVEN SPOKEN ALONE WITH ENJI SINCE THEN.
... ...
SO WHAT DID YOU WANT TO TALK TO ME ABOUT?
CREAK
OH...
OH, RIGHT.
...UM...
YOU WANNA GO OUT FOR DRINKS SOMETIME NEXT WEEK?

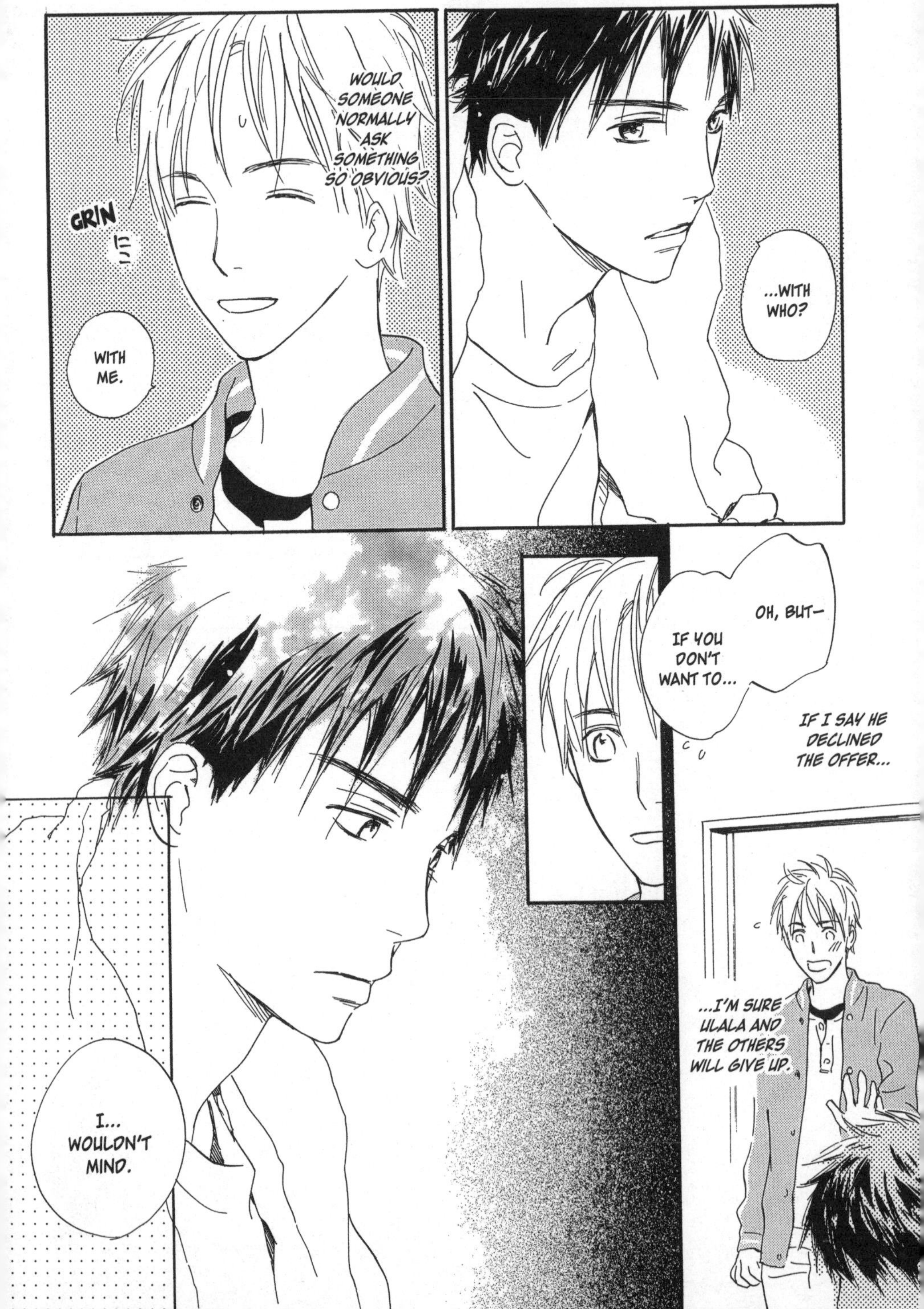
...WITH WHO?
WOULD SOMEONE NORMALLY ASK SOMETHING SO OBVIOUS?
GRIN
WITH ME.
OH, BUT—
IF YOU DON'T WANT TO...
IF I SAY HE DECLINED THE OFFER...
...I'M SURE ULALA AND THE OTHERS WILL GIVE UP.
I... WOULDN'T MIND.

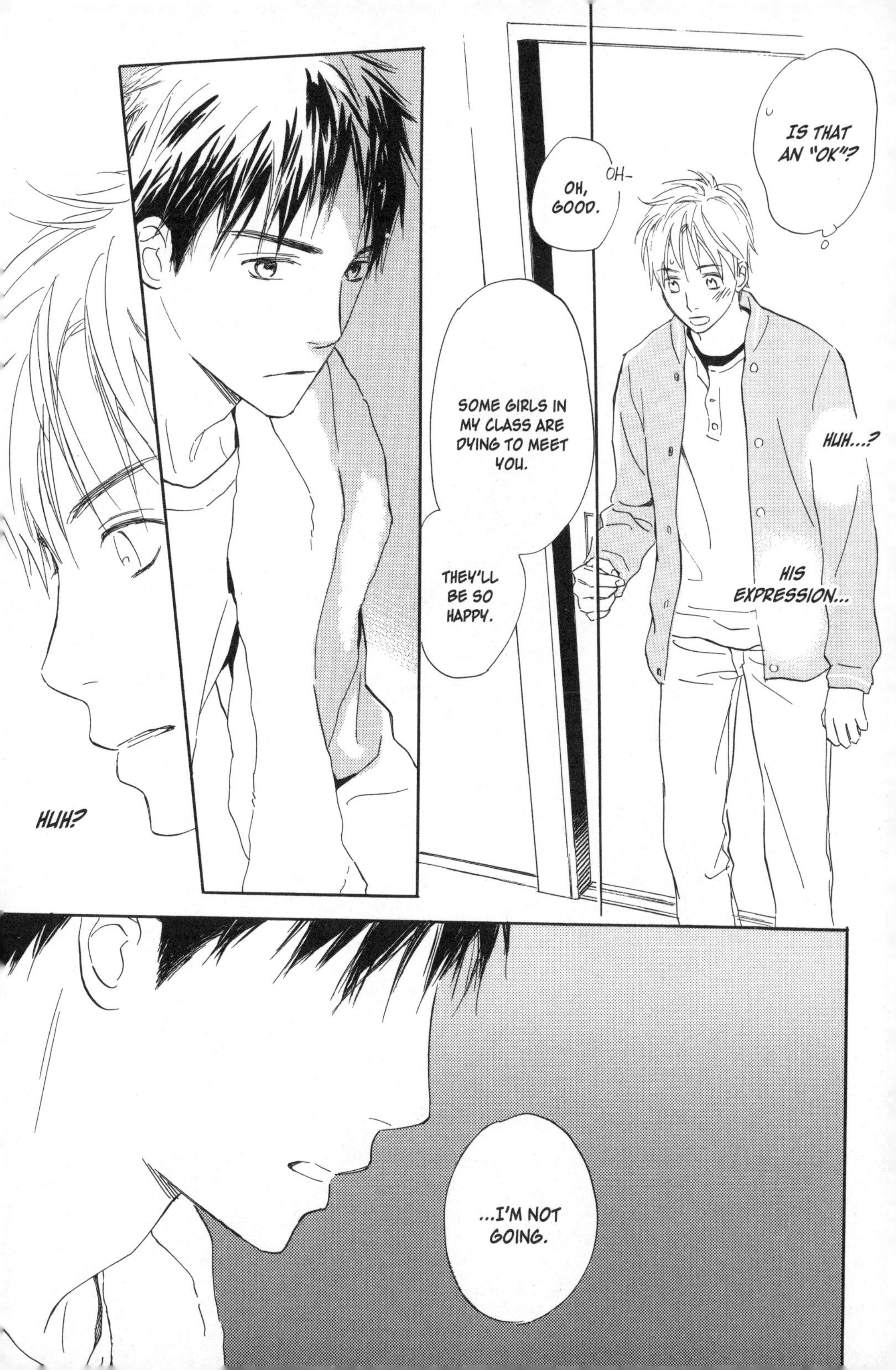
IS THAT AN "OK"?
OH-
OH, GOOD.
SOME GIRLS IN MY CLASS ARE DYING TO MEET YOU.
THEY'LL BE SO HAPPY.
HUH...?
HIS EXPRESSION...
HUH?
...I'M NOT GOING.

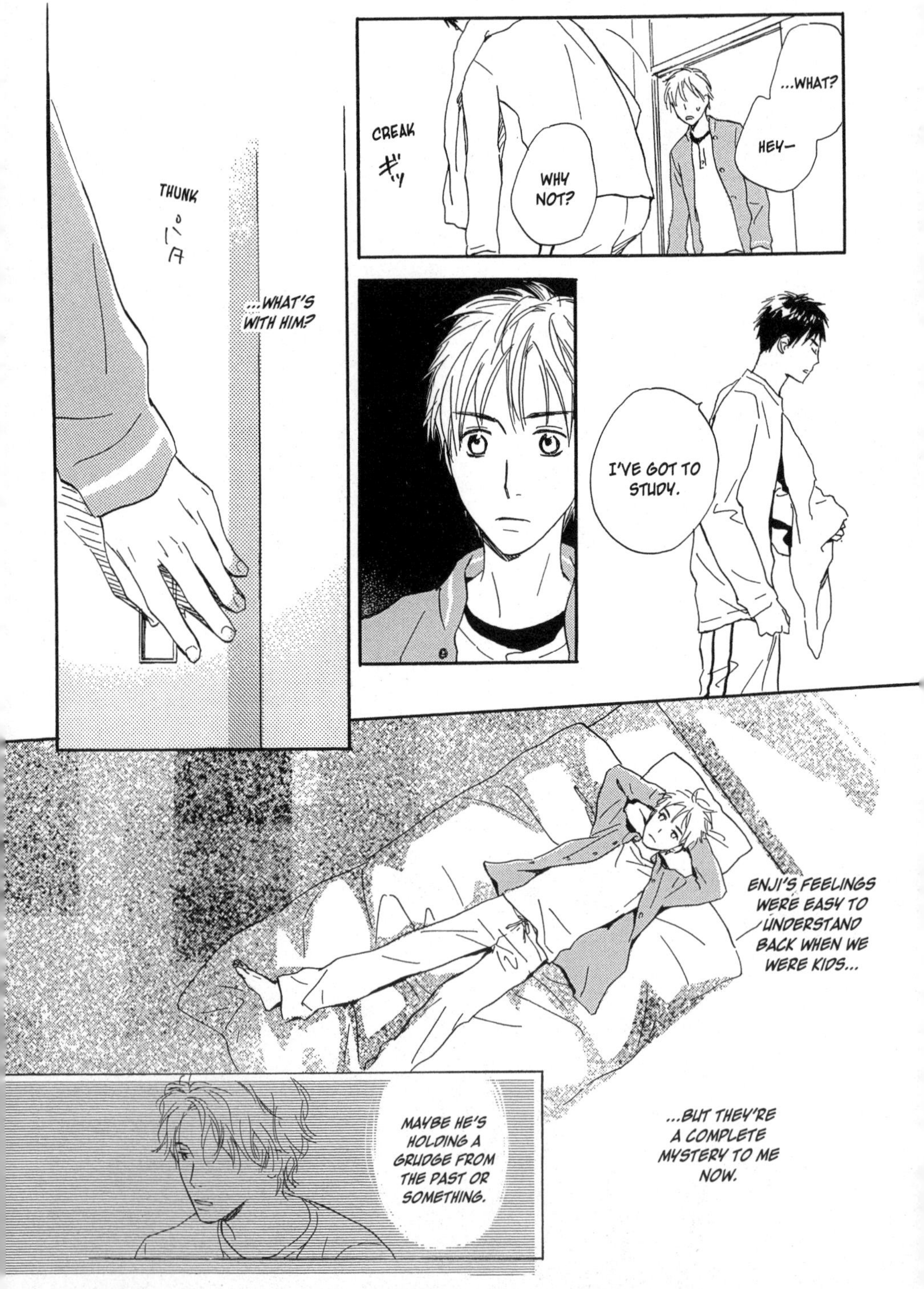
...WHAT?
HEY—
WHY NOT?
CREAK
ギッ
I'VE GOT TO STUDY.
THUNK
パタ
...WHAT'S WITH HIM?
ENJI'S FEELINGS WERE EASY TO UNDERSTAND BACK WHEN WE WERE KIDS...
...BUT THEY'RE A COMPLETE MYSTERY TO ME NOW.
MAYBE HE'S HOLDING A GRUDGE FROM THE PAST OR SOMETHING.

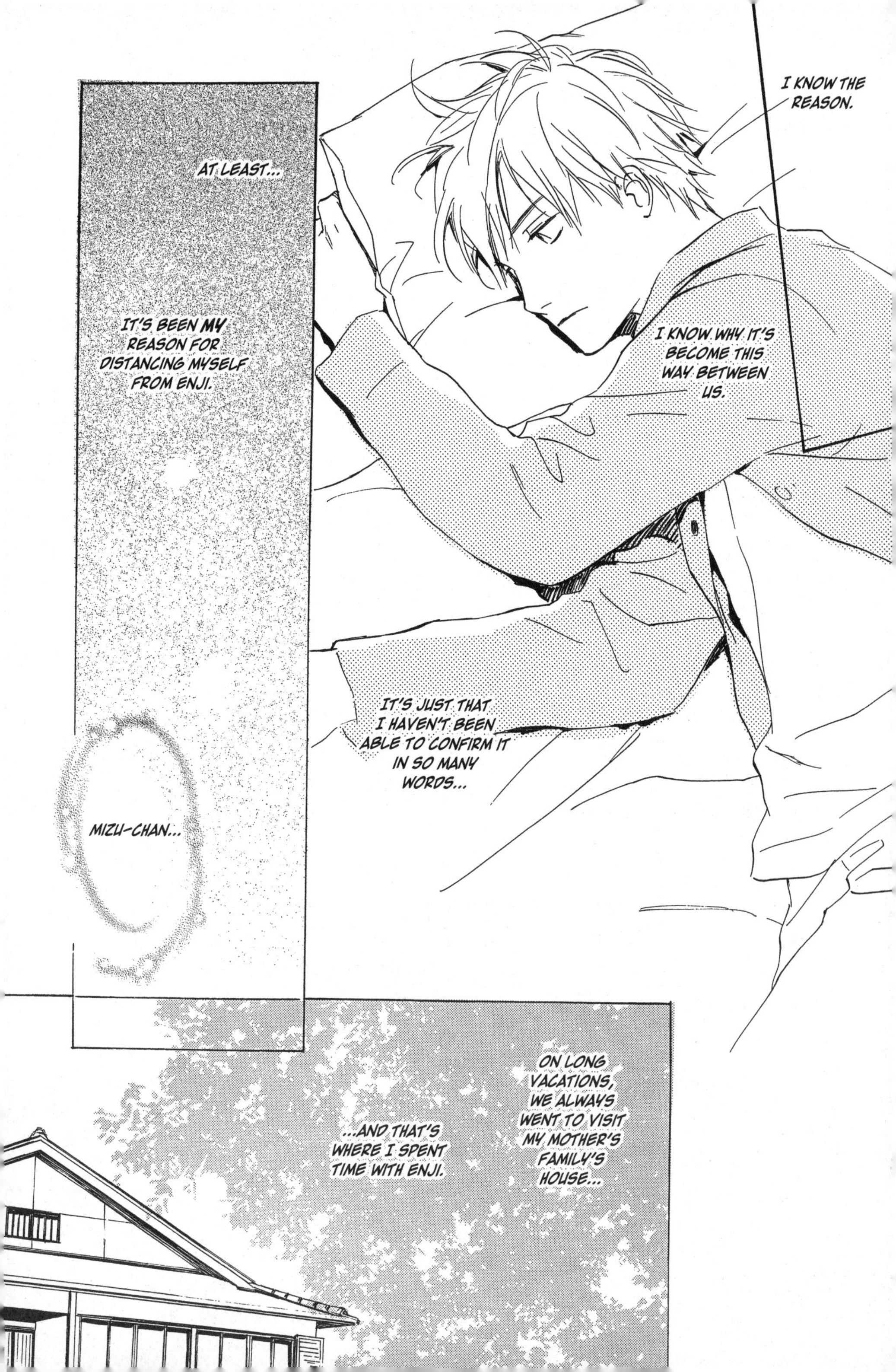
I KNOW THE REASON.
I KNOW WHY IT'S BECOME THIS WAY BETWEEN US.
IT'S JUST THAT I HAVEN'T BEEN ABLE TO CONFIRM IT IN SO MANY WORDS...
AT LEAST...
IT'S BEEN MY REASON FOR DISTANCING MYSELF FROM ENJI.
MIZU-CHAN...
ON LONG VACATIONS, WE ALWAYS WENT TO VISIT MY MOTHER'S FAMILY'S HOUSE...
...AND THAT'S WHERE I SPENT TIME WITH ENJI.

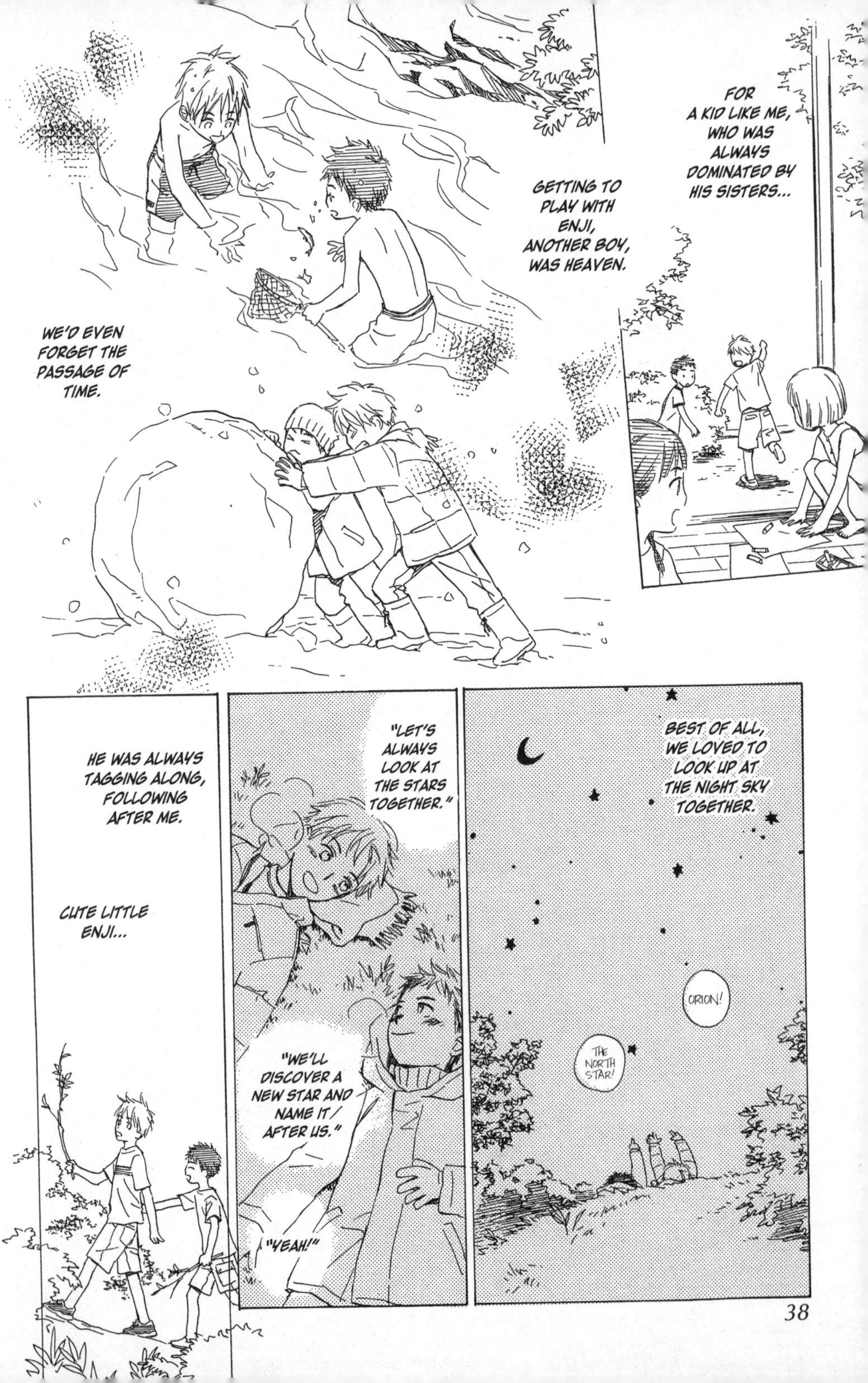
FOR A KID LIKE ME, WHO WAS ALWAYS DOMINATED BY HIS SISTERS...
GETTING TO PLAY WITH ENJI, ANOTHER BOY, WAS HEAVEN.
WE'D EVEN FORGET THE PASSAGE OF TIME.
BEST OF ALL, WE LOVED TO LOOK UP AT THE NIGHT SKY TOGETHER.
ORION!
THE NORTH STAR!
"LET'S ALWAYS LOOK AT THE STARS TOGETHER."
"WE'LL DISCOVER A NEW STAR AND NAME IT AFTER US."
"YEAH!"
HE WAS ALWAYS TAGGING ALONG, FOLLOWING AFTER ME.
CUTE LITTLE ENJI...

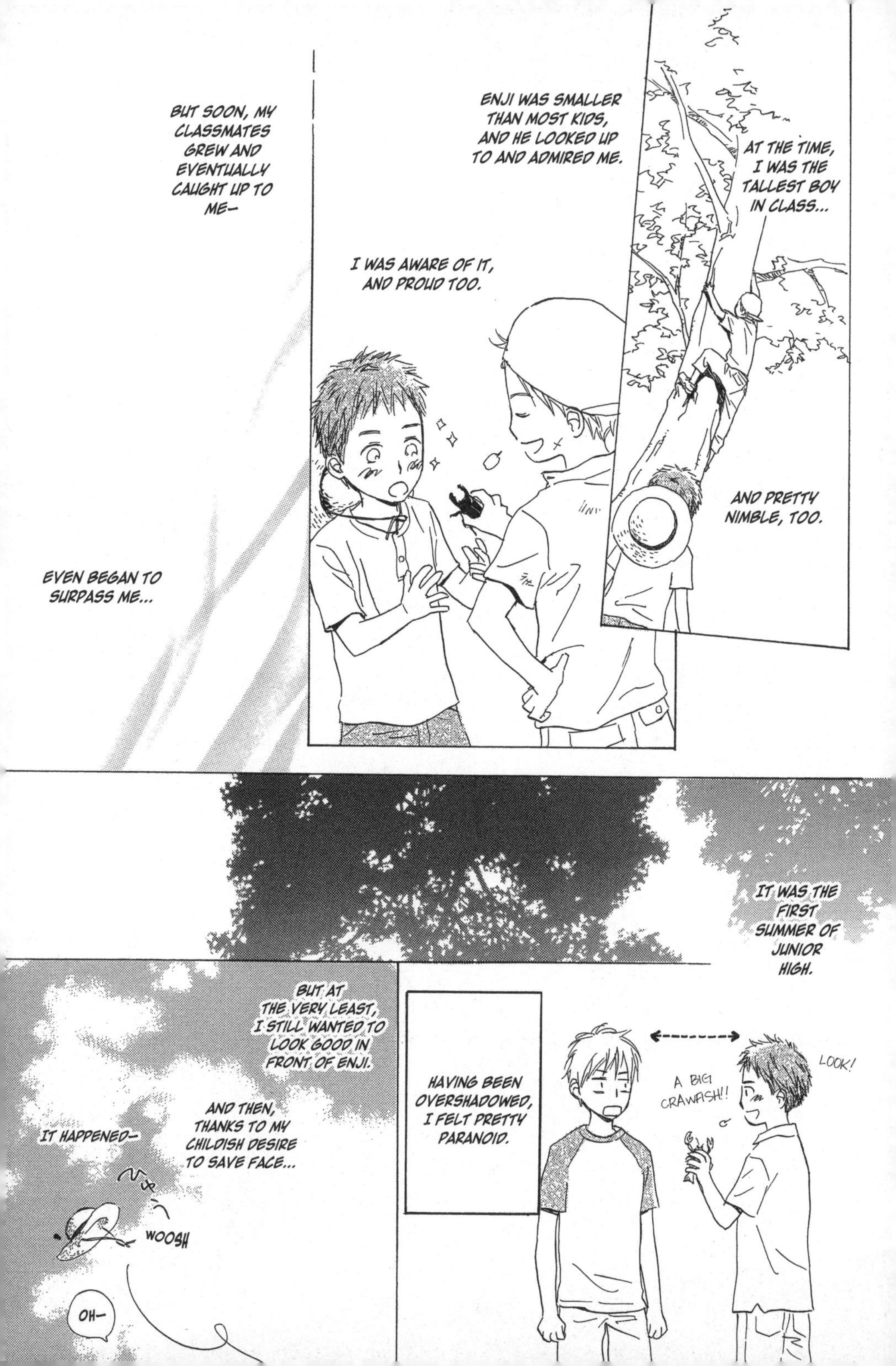
AT THE TIME, I WAS THE TALLEST BOY IN CLASS...
AND PRETTY NIMBLE, TOO.
ENJI WAS SMALLER THAN MOST KIDS, AND HE LOOKED UP TO AND ADMIRED ME.
I WAS AWARE OF IT, AND PROUD TOO.
BUT SOON, MY CLASSMATES GREW AND EVENTUALLY CAUGHT UP TO ME—
EVEN BEGAN TO SURPASS ME...
IT WAS THE FIRST SUMMER OF JUNIOR HIGH.
LOOK!
A BIG CRAWFISH!!
HAVING BEEN OVERSHADOWED, I FELT PRETTY PARANOID.
BUT AT THE VERY LEAST, I STILL WANTED TO LOOK GOOD IN FRONT OF ENJI.
AND THEN, THANKS TO MY CHILDISH DESIRE TO SAVE FACE...
IT HAPPENED—
WOOSH
OH—

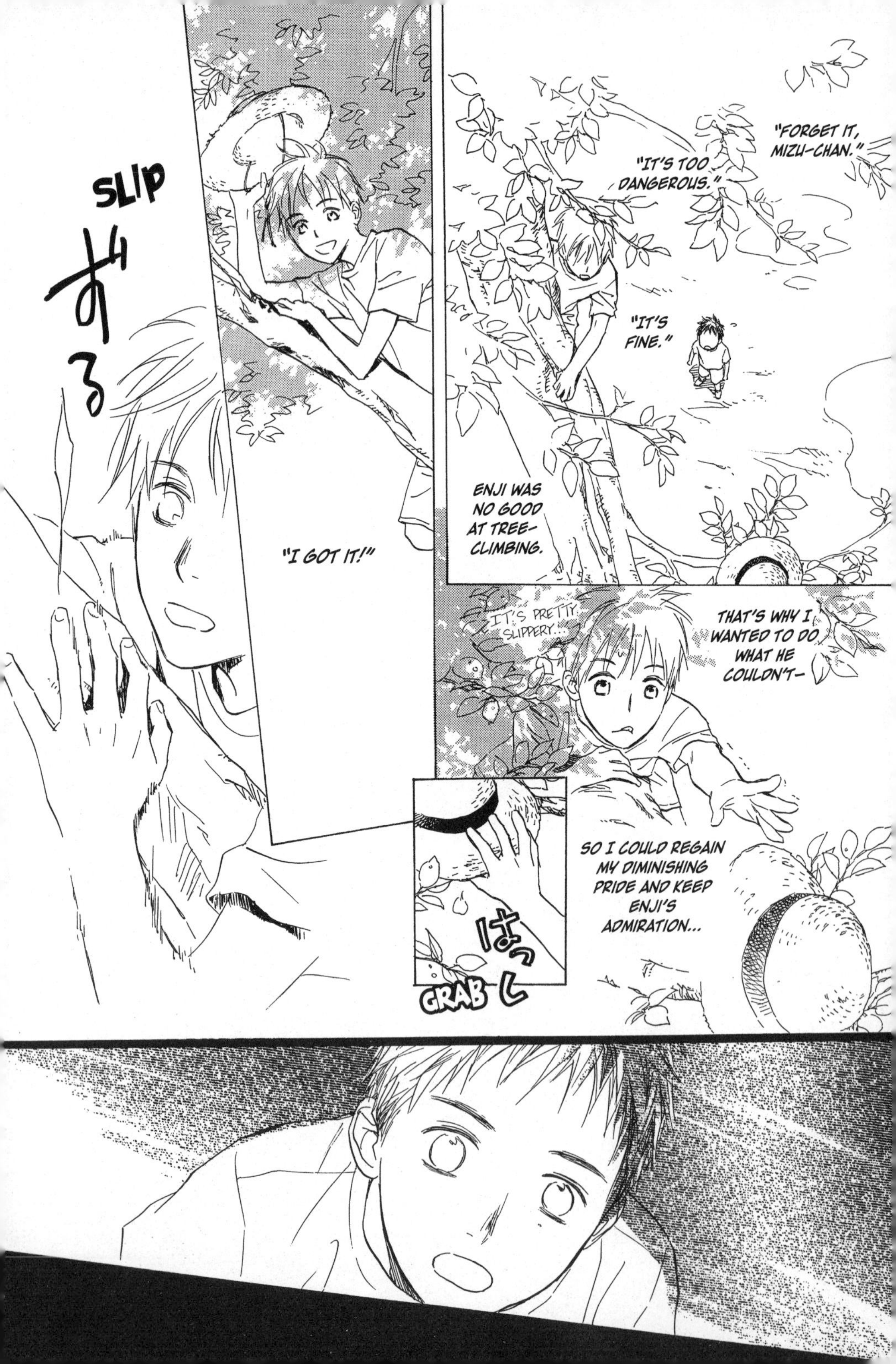
"FORGET IT, MIZU-CHAN."
"IT'S TOO DANGEROUS."
"IT'S FINE."
ENJI WAS NO GOOD AT TREE-CLIMBING.
IT'S PRETTY SLIPPERY...
THAT'S WHY I WANTED TO DO WHAT HE COULDN'T—
SO I COULD REGAIN MY DIMINISHING PRIDE AND KEEP ENJI'S ADMIRATION...
はっし
GRAB
"I GOT IT!"
ずる
SLIP

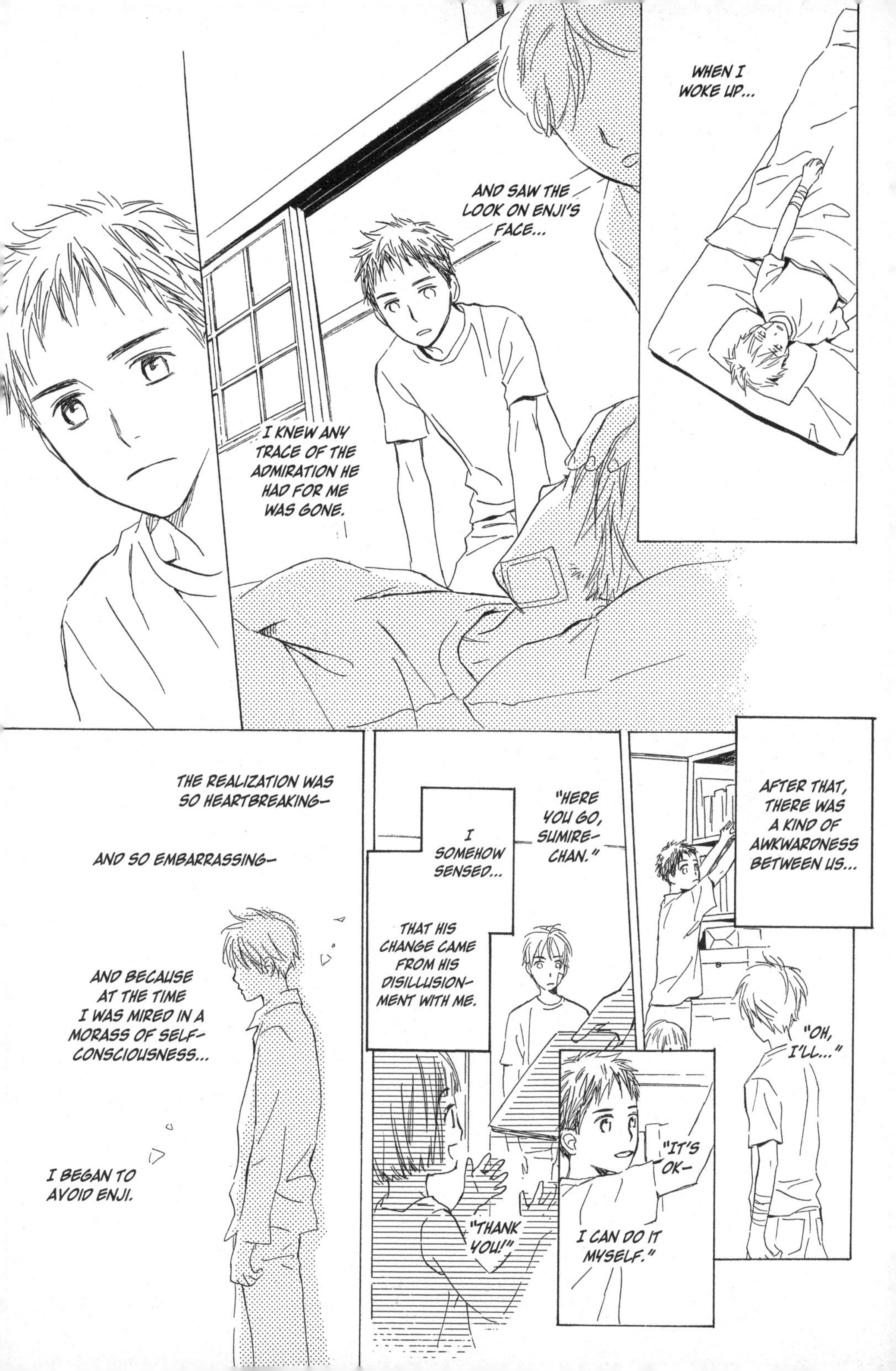
WHEN I WOKE UP...
AND SAW THE LOOK ON ENJI'S FACE...
I KNEW ANY TRACE OF THE ADMIRATION HE HAD FOR ME WAS GONE.
AFTER THAT, THERE WAS A KIND OF AWKWARDNESS BETWEEN US...
"OH, I'LL..."
"IT'S OK—
I CAN DO IT MYSELF."
"HERE YOU GO, SUMIRE-CHAN."
I SOMEHOW SENSED...
THAT HIS CHANGE CAME FROM HIS DISILLUSIONMENT WITH ME.
"THANK YOU!"
THE REALIZATION WAS SO HEARTBREAKING—
AND SO EMBARRASSING—
AND BECAUSE AT THE TIME I WAS MIRED IN A MORASS OF SELF-CONSCIOUSNESS...
I BEGAN TO AVOID ENJI.

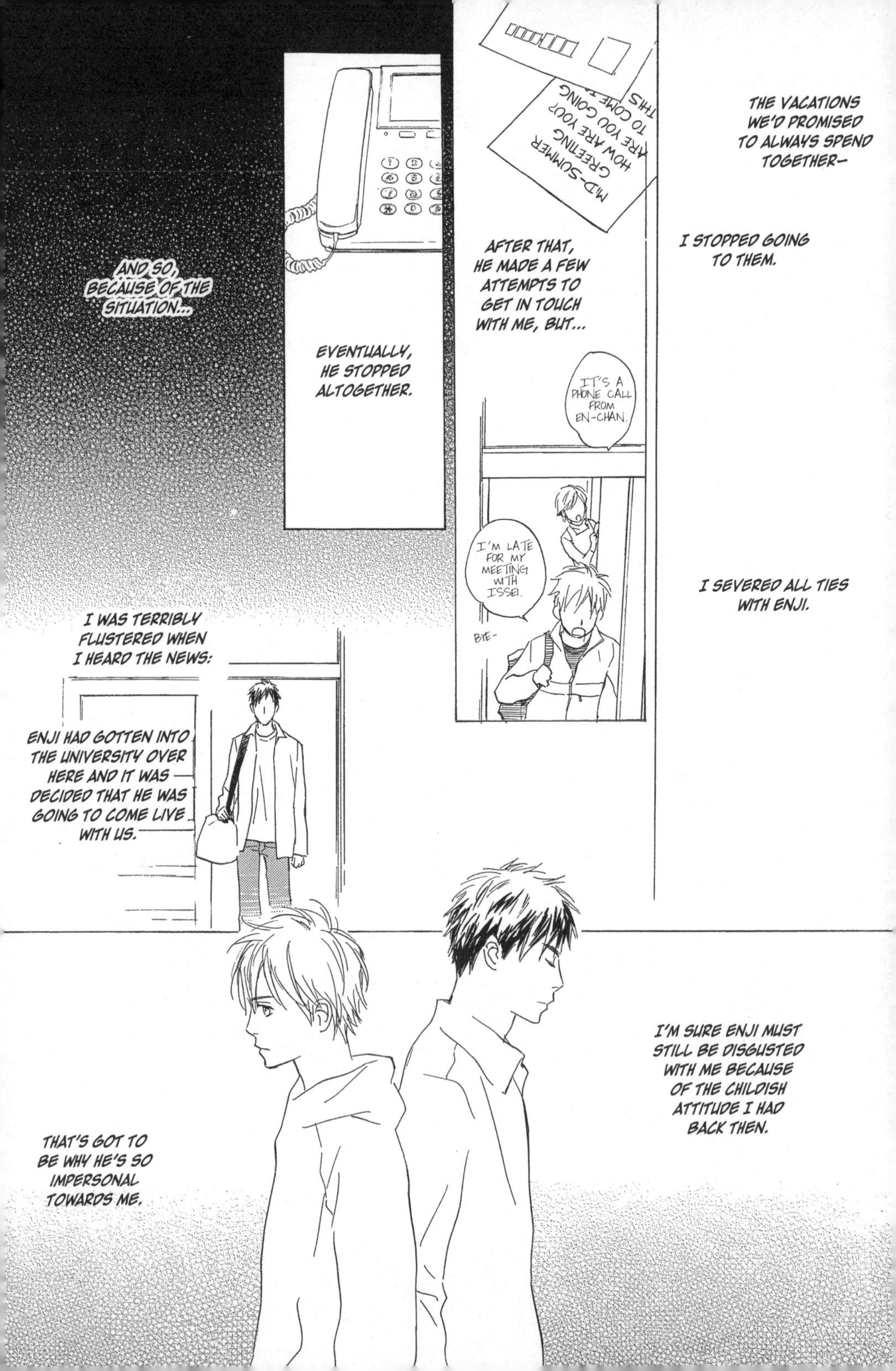
THE VACATIONS WE'D PROMISED TO ALWAYS SPEND TOGETHER—
I STOPPED GOING TO THEM.
I SEVERED ALL TIES WITH ENJI.
MID-SUMMER GREETING
HOW ARE YOU?
ARE YOU GOING TO COME THIS
AFTER THAT, HE MADE A FEW ATTEMPTS TO GET IN TOUCH WITH ME, BUT...
IT'S A PHONE CALL FROM EN-CHAN.
I'M LATE FOR MY MEETING WITH ISSEI.
BYE-
EVENTUALLY, HE STOPPED ALTOGETHER.
AND SO, BECAUSE OF THE SITUATION...
I WAS TERRIBLY FLUSTERED WHEN I HEARD THE NEWS:
ENJI HAD GOTTEN INTO THE UNIVERSITY OVER HERE AND IT WAS DECIDED THAT HE WAS GOING TO COME LIVE WITH US.
I'M SURE ENJI MUST STILL BE DISGUSTED WITH ME BECAUSE OF THE CHILDISH ATTITUDE I HAD BACK THEN.
THAT'S GOT TO BE WHY HE'S SO IMPERSONAL TOWARDS ME.

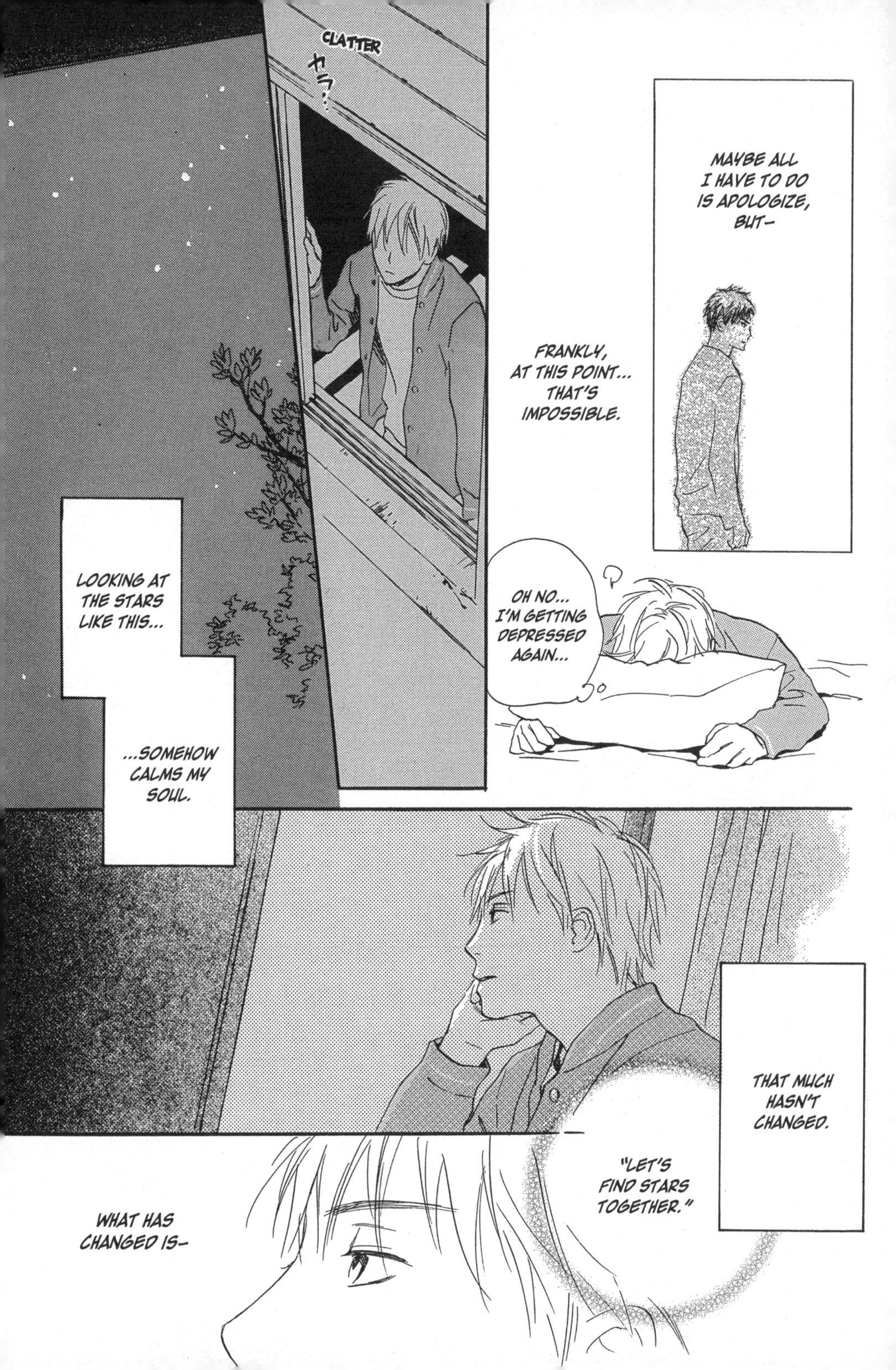
MAYBE ALL I HAVE TO DO IS APOLOGIZE, BUT–
FRANKLY, AT THIS POINT... THAT'S IMPOSSIBLE.
OH NO... I'M GETTING DEPRESSED AGAIN...
CLATTER
カラ…
LOOKING AT THE STARS LIKE THIS...
...SOMEHOW CALMS MY SOUL.
THAT MUCH HASN'T CHANGED.
"LET'S FIND STARS TOGETHER."
WHAT HAS CHANGED IS–

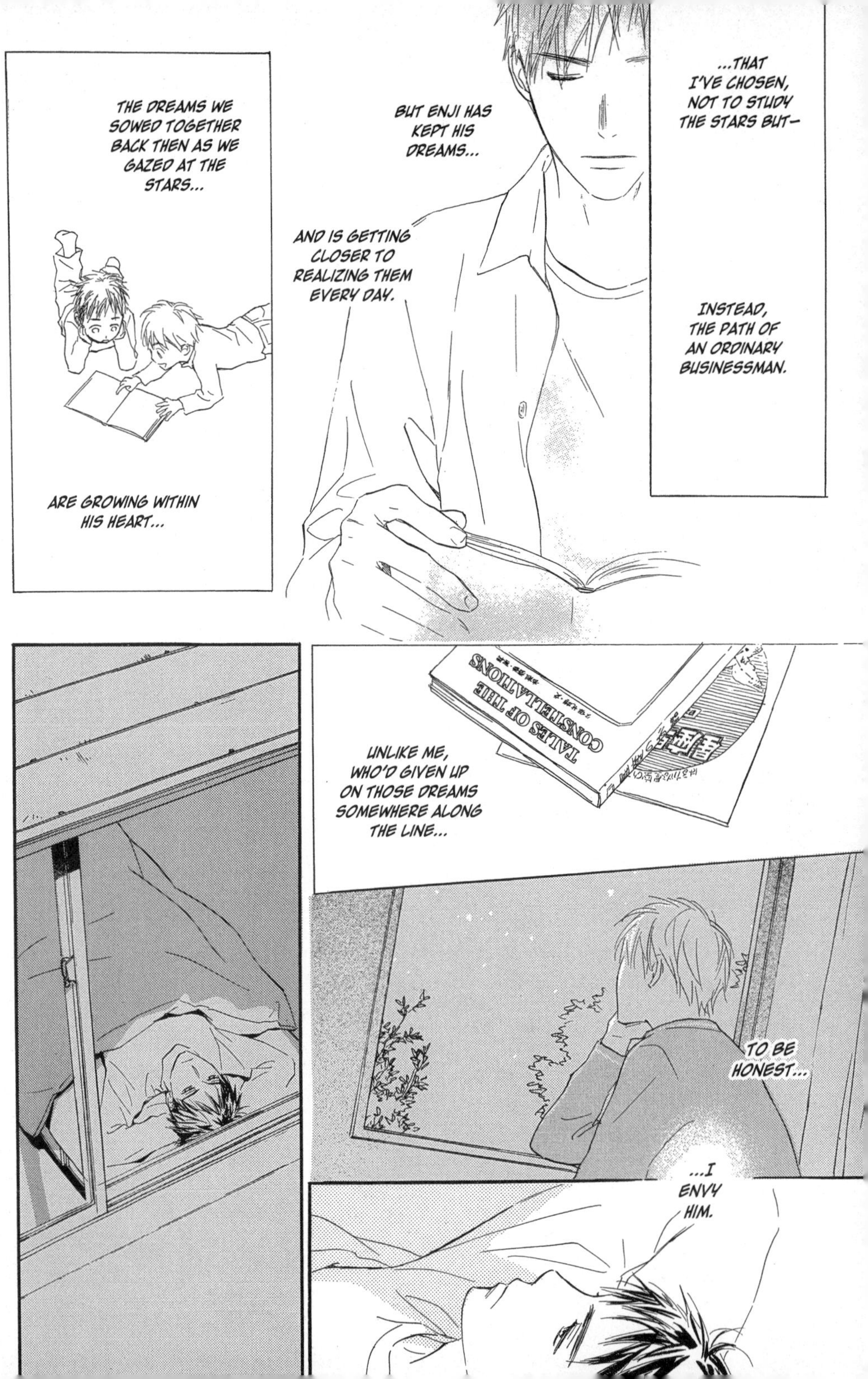
...THAT I'VE CHOSEN, NOT TO STUDY THE STARS BUT—
INSTEAD, THE PATH OF AN ORDINARY BUSINESSMAN.
BUT ENJI HAS KEPT HIS DREAMS...
AND IS GETTING CLOSER TO REALIZING THEM EVERY DAY.
THE DREAMS WE SOWED TOGETHER BACK THEN AS WE GAZED AT THE STARS...
ARE GROWING WITHIN HIS HEART...
TALES OF THE CONSTELLATIONS
UNLIKE ME, WHO'D GIVEN UP ON THOSE DREAMS SOMEWHERE ALONG THE LINE...
TO BE HONEST...
...I ENVY HIM.

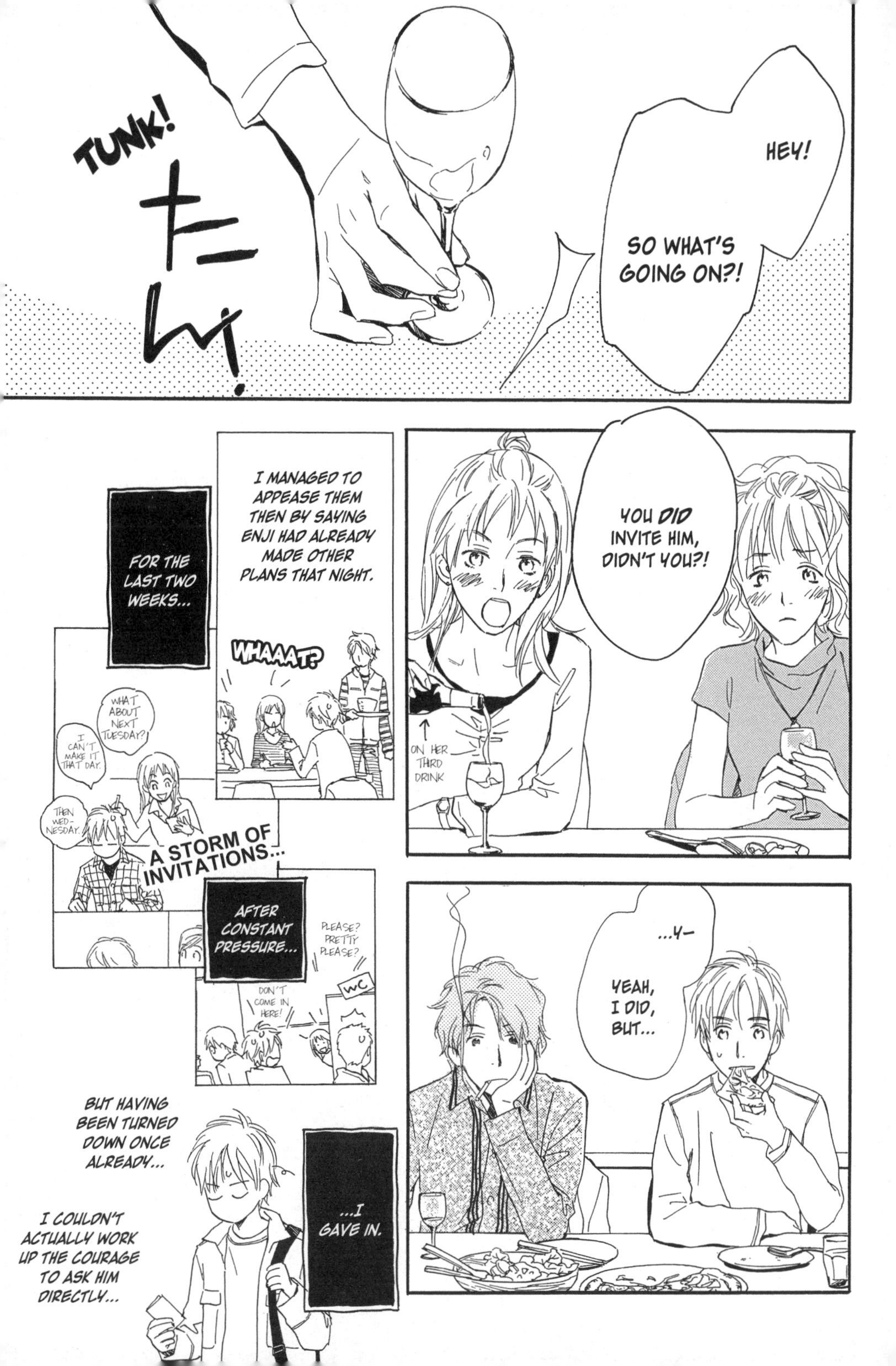

HEY!
SO WHAT'S GOING ON?!
TUNK!
たーん!
YOU DID INVITE HIM, DIDN'T YOU?!
ON HER THIRD DRINK
...Y—
YEAH, I DID, BUT...
I MANAGED TO APPEASE THEM THEN BY SAYING ENJI HAD ALREADY MADE OTHER PLANS THAT NIGHT.
WHAAAT?
FOR THE LAST TWO WEEKS...
WHAT ABOUT NEXT TUESDAY?
I CAN'T MAKE IT THAT DAY.
THEN WEDNESDAY.
A STORM OF INVITATIONS...
AFTER CONSTANT PRESSURE...
PLEASE? PRETTY PLEASE?
WC
DON'T COME IN HERE!
...I GAVE IN.
BUT HAVING BEEN TURNED DOWN ONCE ALREADY...
I COULDN'T ACTUALLY WORK UP THE COURAGE TO ASK HIM DIRECTLY...

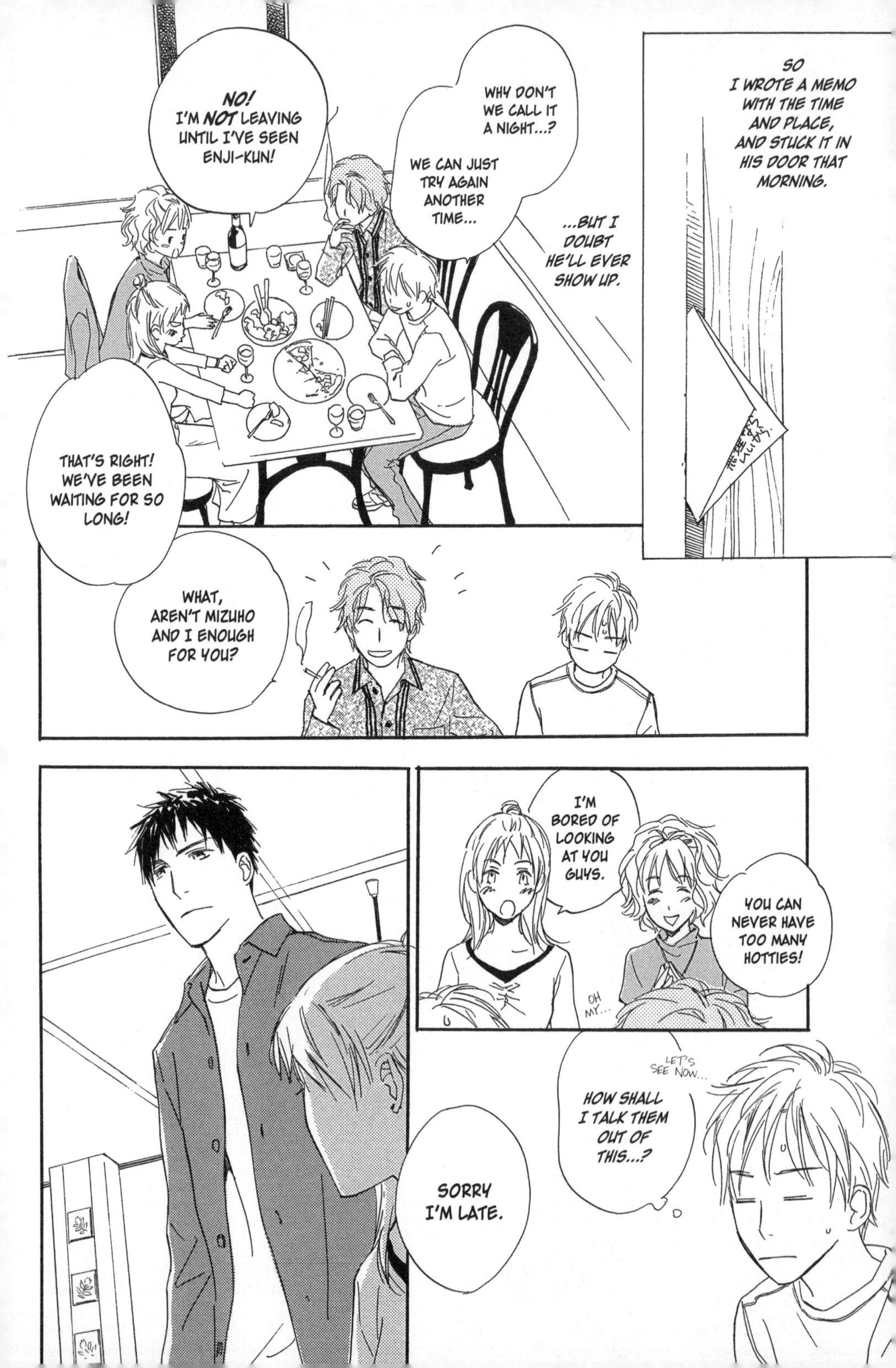
SO I WROTE A MEMO WITH THE TIME AND PLACE, AND STUCK IT IN HIS DOOR THAT MORNING.
...BUT I DOUBT HE'LL EVER SHOW UP.
WHY DON'T WE CALL IT A NIGHT...?
WE CAN JUST TRY AGAIN ANOTHER TIME...
NO! I'M NOT LEAVING UNTIL I'VE SEEN ENJI-KUN!
THAT'S RIGHT! WE'VE BEEN WAITING FOR SO LONG!
WHAT, AREN'T MIZUHO AND I ENOUGH FOR YOU?
I'M BORED OF LOOKING AT YOU GUYS.
YOU CAN NEVER HAVE TOO MANY HOTTIES!
OH MY...
LET'S SEE NOW...
HOW SHALL I TALK THEM OUT OF THIS...?
SORRY I'M LATE.

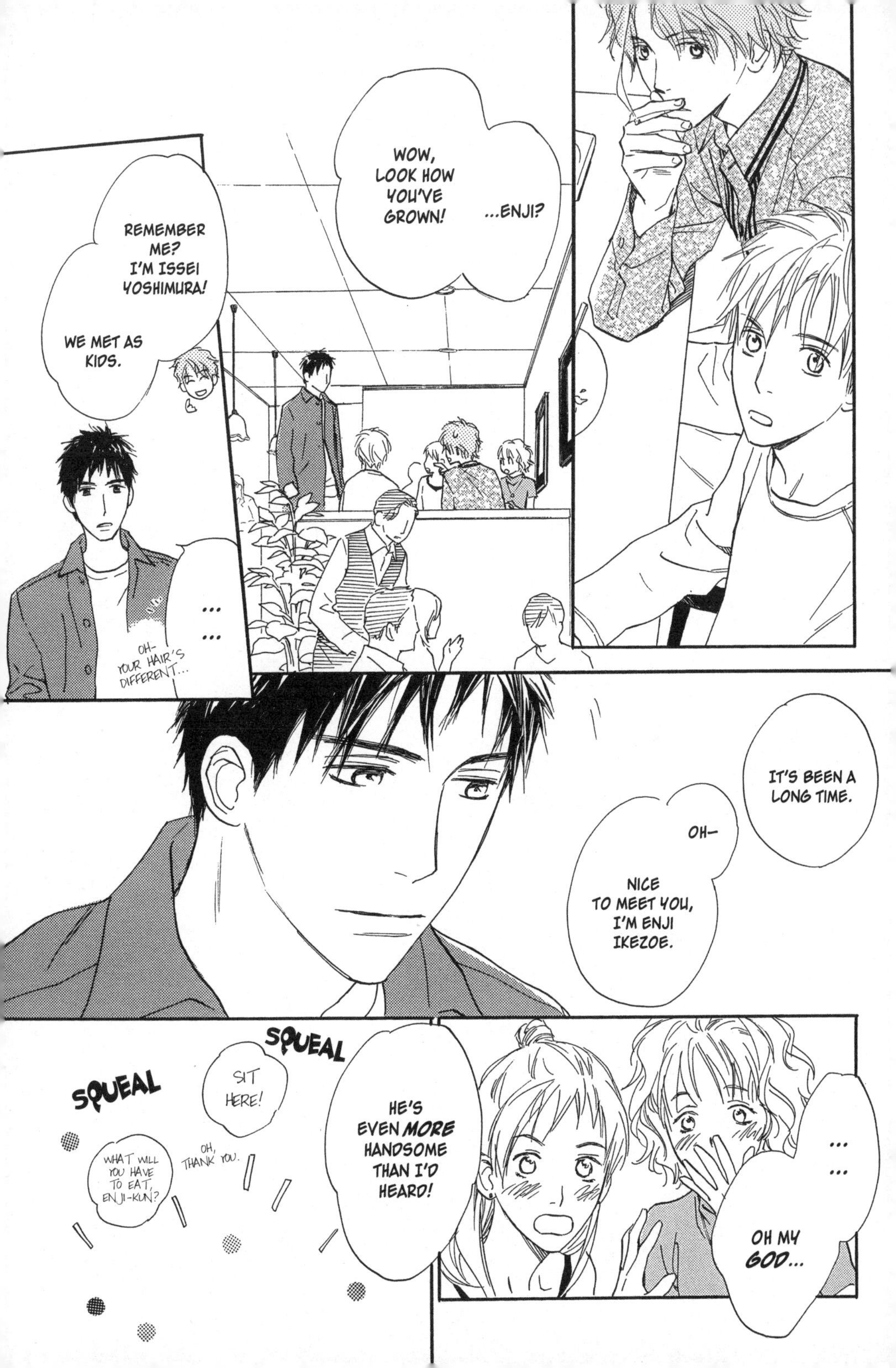
...ENJI?
WOW, LOOK HOW YOU'VE GROWN!
REMEMBER ME? I'M ISSEI YOSHIMURA!
WE MET AS KIDS.
...
...
OH- YOUR HAIR'S DIFFERENT...
IT'S BEEN A LONG TIME.
OH—
NICE TO MEET YOU, I'M ENJI IKEZOE.
...
...
OH MY GOD...
HE'S EVEN MORE HANDSOME THAN I'D HEARD!
SQUEAL
SIT HERE!
SQUEAL
OH, THANK YOU.
WHAT WILL YOU HAVE TO EAT, ENJI-KUN?

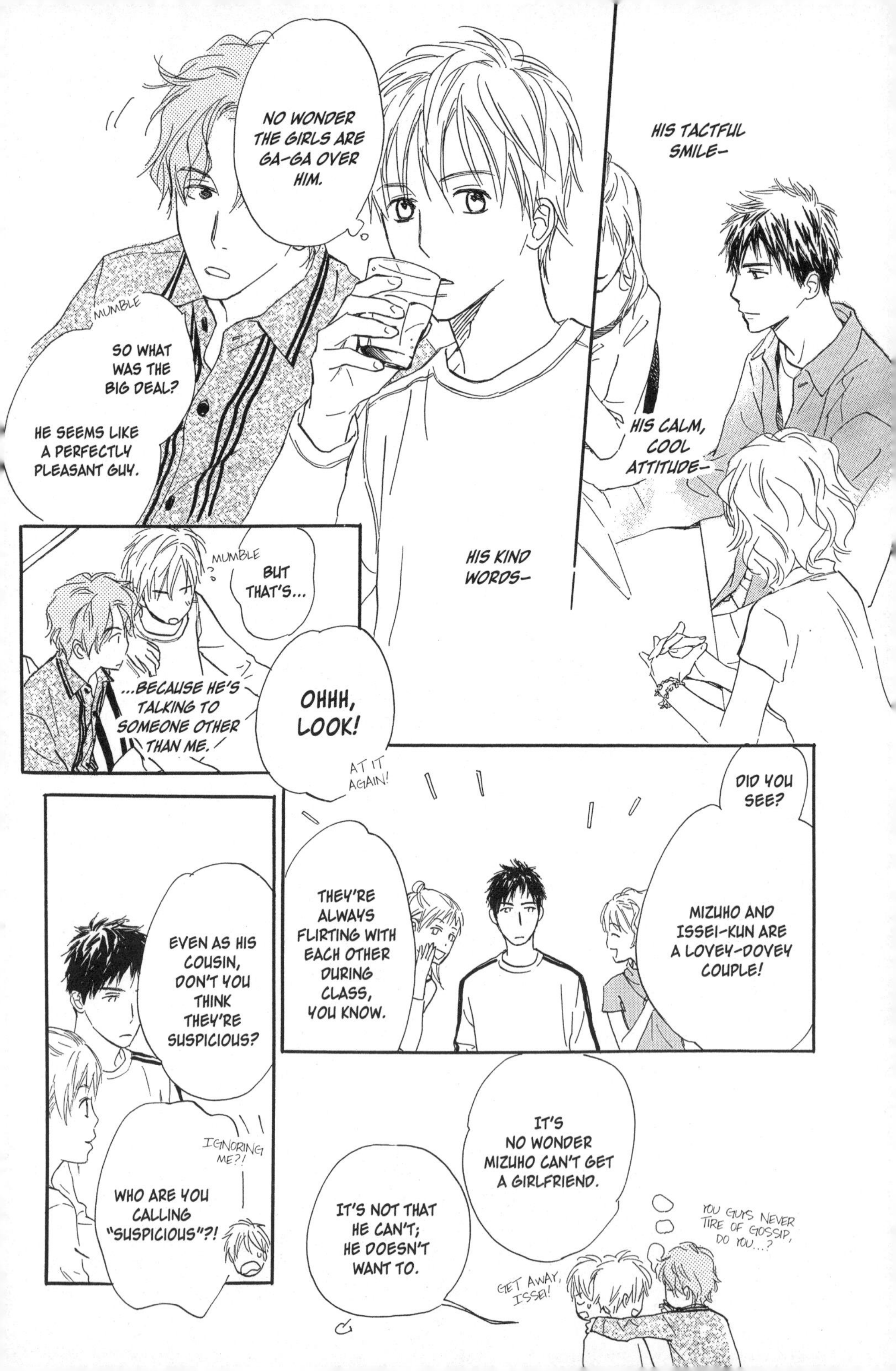
HIS TACTFUL SMILE–
HIS CALM, COOL ATTITUDE–
HIS KIND WORDS–
NO WONDER THE GIRLS ARE GA-GA OVER HIM.
MUMBLE
SO WHAT WAS THE BIG DEAL?
HE SEEMS LIKE A PERFECTLY PLEASANT GUY.
MUMBLE
BUT THAT'S...
...BECAUSE HE'S TALKING TO SOMEONE OTHER THAN ME.
OHHH, LOOK!
AT IT AGAIN!
DID YOU SEE?
MIZUHO AND ISSEI-KUN ARE A LOVEY-DOVEY COUPLE!
THEY'RE ALWAYS FLIRTING WITH EACH OTHER DURING CLASS, YOU KNOW.
EVEN AS HIS COUSIN, DON'T YOU THINK THEY'RE SUSPICIOUS?
IGNORING ME?!
WHO ARE YOU CALLING "SUSPICIOUS"?!
IT'S NO WONDER MIZUHO CAN'T GET A GIRLFRIEND.
IT'S NOT THAT HE CAN'T; HE DOESN'T WANT TO.
YOU GUYS NEVER TIRE OF GOSSIP, DO YOU...?
GET AWAY, ISSEI!

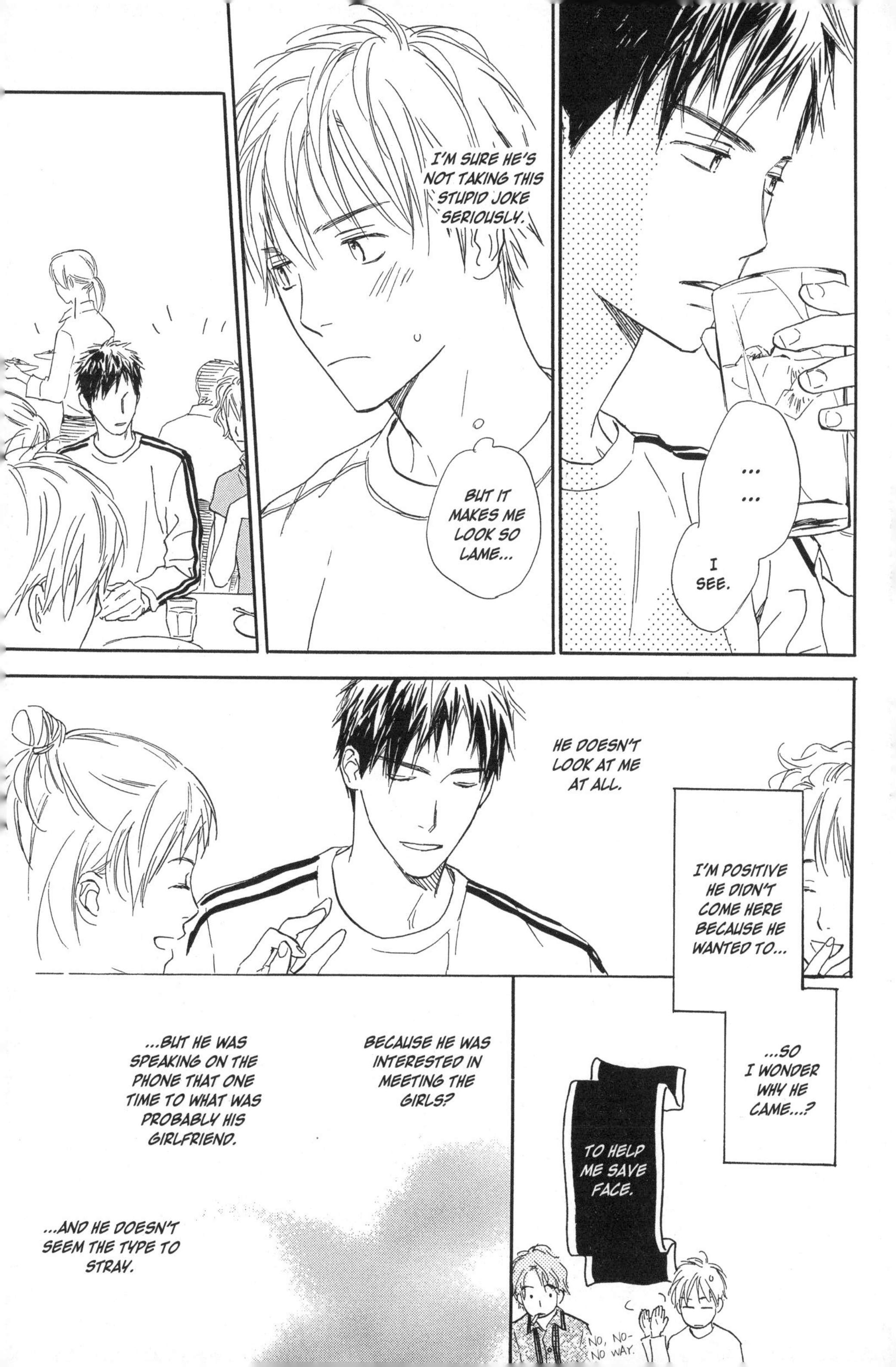

... ... I SEE.
I'M SURE HE'S NOT TAKING THIS STUPID JOKE SERIOUSLY.
BUT IT MAKES ME LOOK SO LAME...
HE DOESN'T LOOK AT ME AT ALL.
I'M POSITIVE HE DIDN'T COME HERE BECAUSE HE WANTED TO...
...SO I WONDER WHY HE CAME...?
TO HELP ME SAVE FACE.
NO, NO-NO WAY.
BECAUSE HE WAS INTERESTED IN MEETING THE GIRLS?
...BUT HE WAS SPEAKING ON THE PHONE THAT ONE TIME TO WHAT WAS PROBABLY HIS GIRLFRIEND.
...AND HE DOESN'T SEEM THE TYPE TO STRAY.

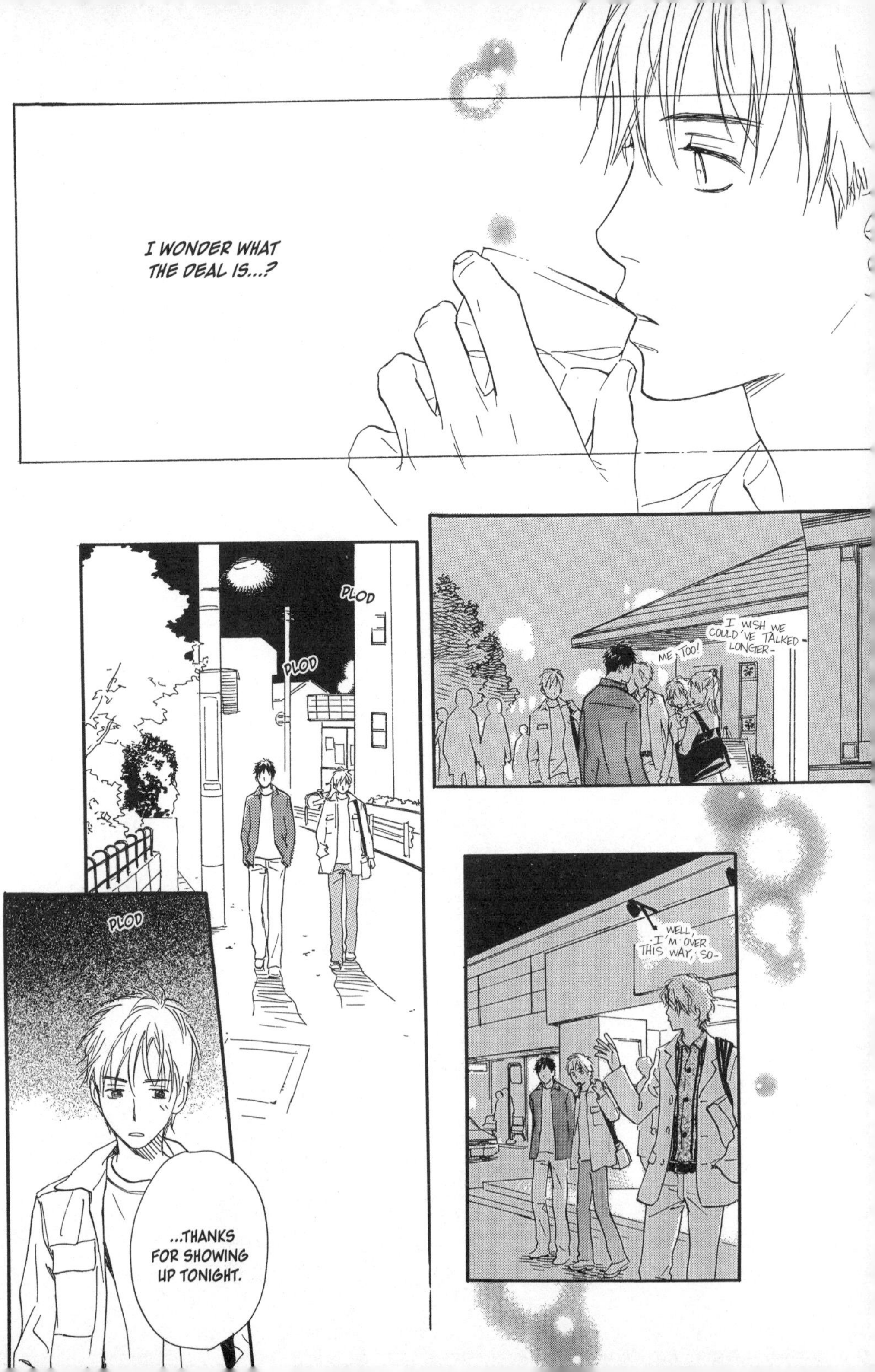
I WONDER WHAT THE DEAL IS...?
I WISH WE COULD'VE TALKED LONGER-
ME TOO!
WELL, I'M OVER THIS WAY, SO-
PLOD
PLOD
PLOD
...THANKS FOR SHOWING UP TONIGHT.

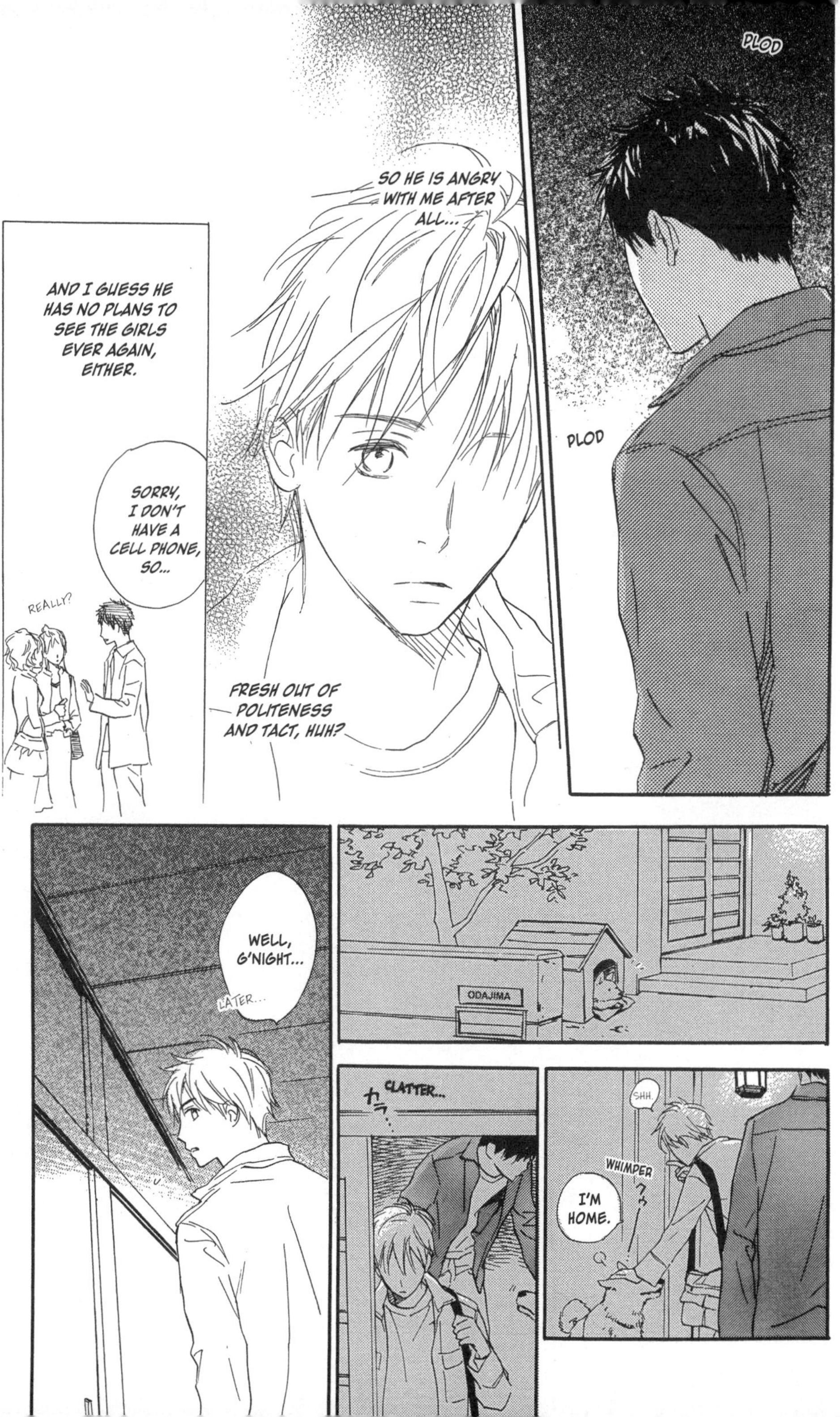
PLOD
PLOD
SO HE IS ANGRY WITH ME AFTER ALL...
FRESH OUT OF POLITENESS AND TACT, HUH?
AND I GUESS HE HAS NO PLANS TO SEE THE GIRLS EVER AGAIN, EITHER.
SORRY, I DON'T HAVE A CELL PHONE, SO...
REALLY?
ODAJIMA
SHH.
WHIMPER
I'M HOME.
CLATTER...
WELL, G'NIGHT...
LATER...

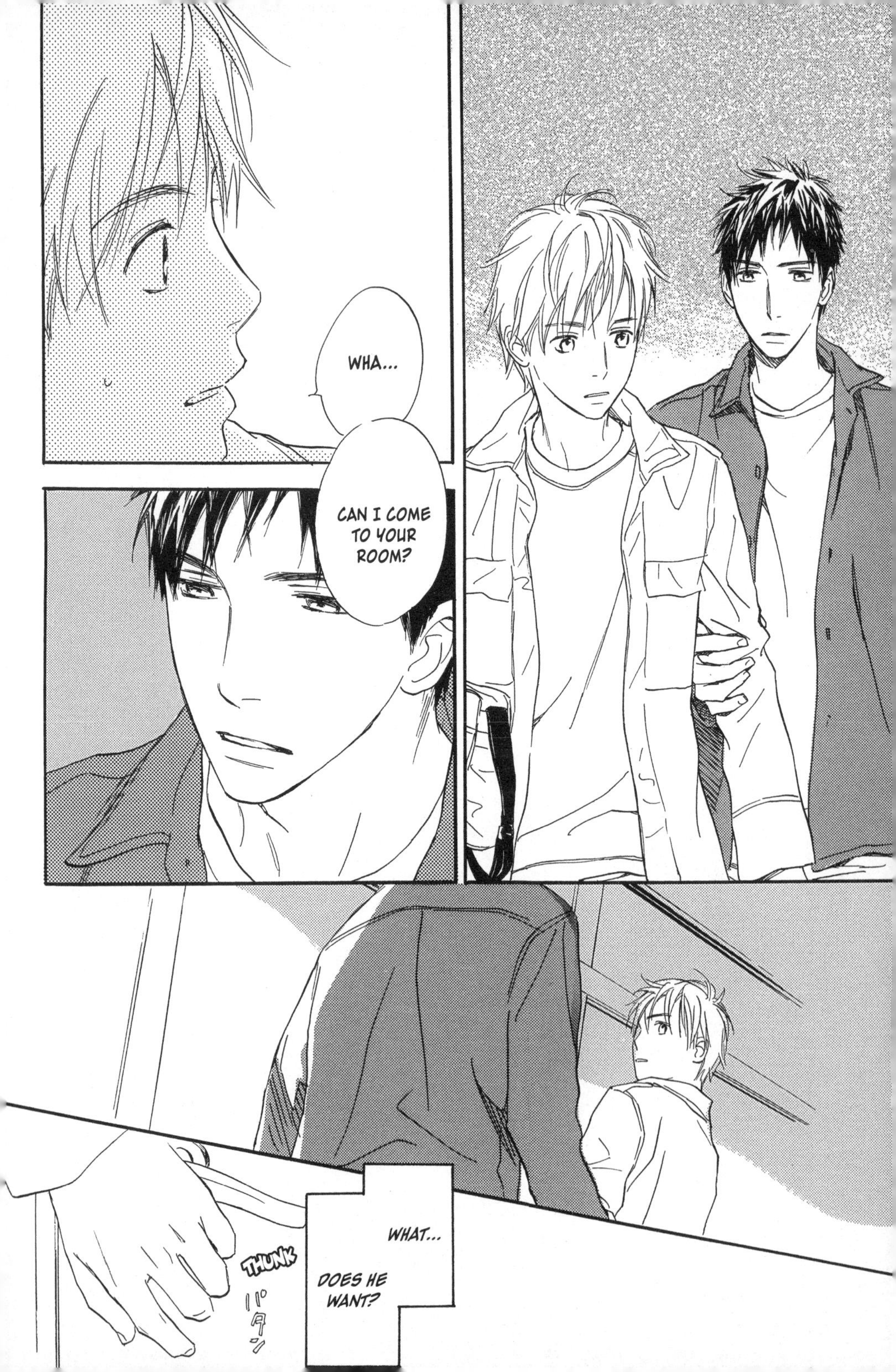
WHA...
CAN I COME TO YOUR ROOM?
THUNK
パタン
WHAT...
DOES HE WANT?

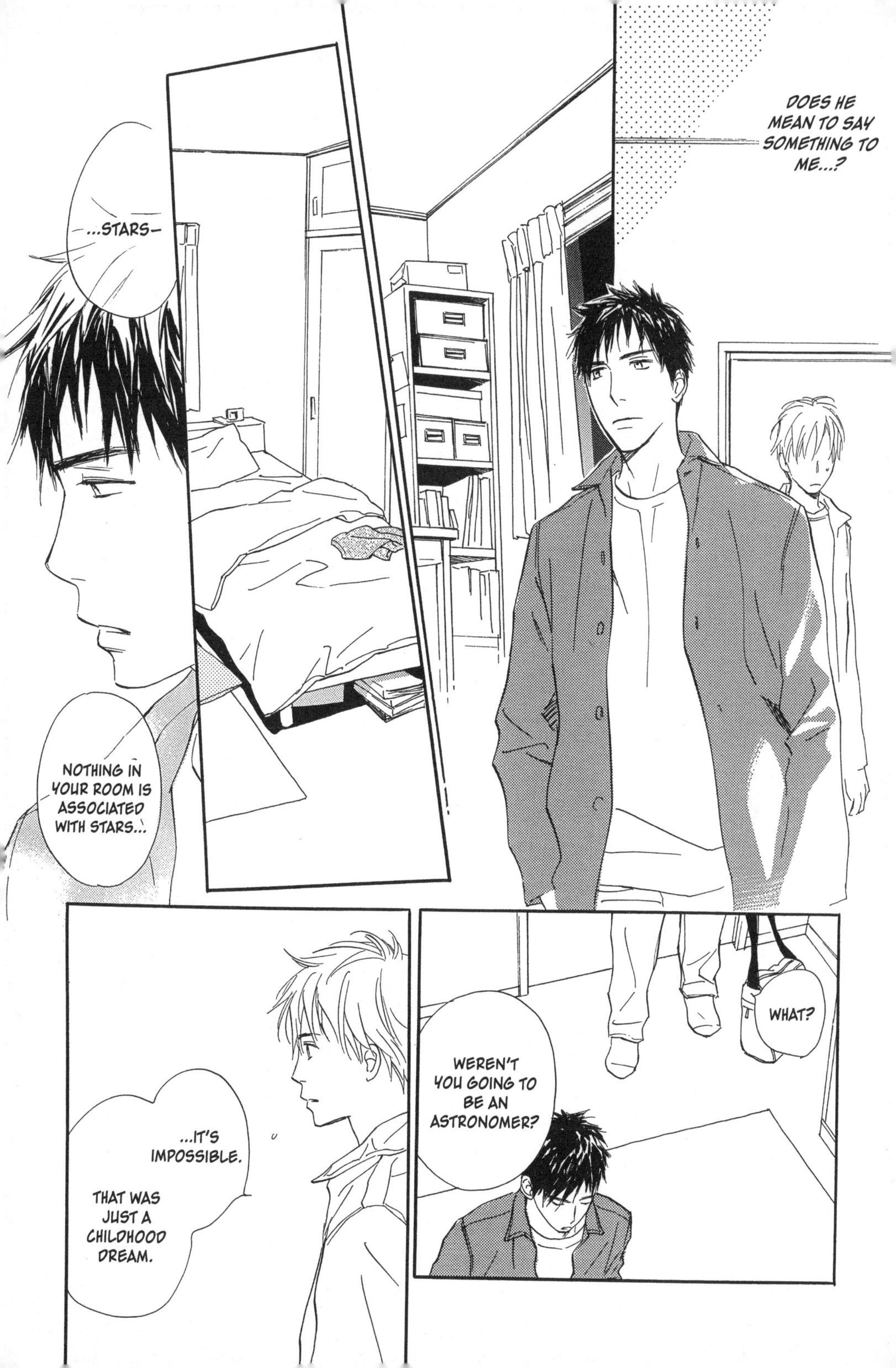
DOES HE MEAN TO SAY SOMETHING TO ME...?
...STARS—
NOTHING IN YOUR ROOM IS ASSOCIATED WITH STARS...
WHAT?
WEREN'T YOU GOING TO BE AN ASTRONOMER?
...IT'S IMPOSSIBLE.
THAT WAS JUST A CHILDHOOD DREAM.

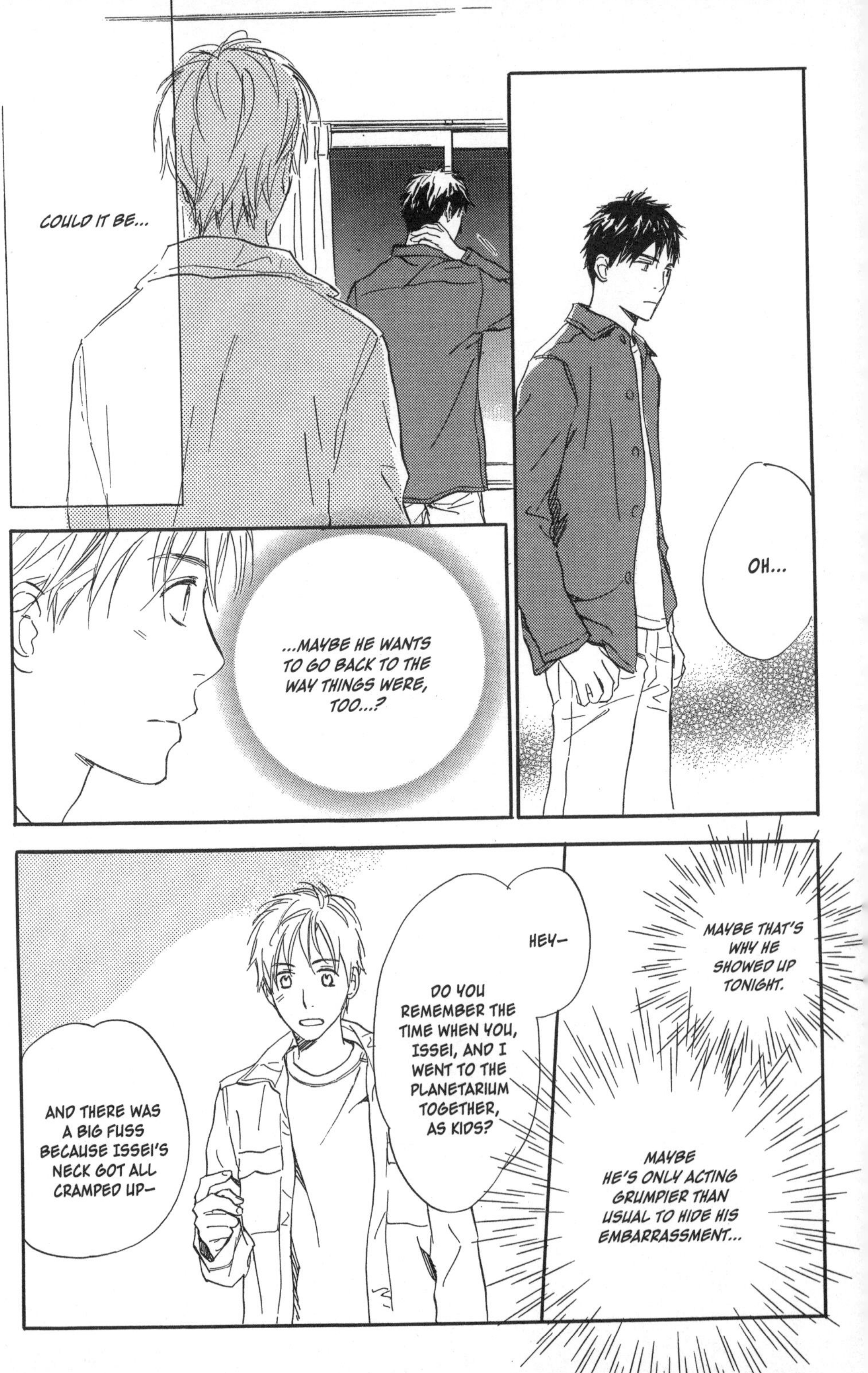
OH...
COULD IT BE...
...MAYBE HE WANTS TO GO BACK TO THE WAY THINGS WERE, TOO...?
MAYBE THAT'S WHY HE SHOWED UP TONIGHT.
MAYBE HE'S ONLY ACTING GRUMPIER THAN USUAL TO HIDE HIS EMBARRASSMENT...
HEY—
DO YOU REMEMBER THE TIME WHEN YOU, ISSEI, AND I WENT TO THE PLANETARIUM TOGETHER, AS KIDS?
AND THERE WAS A BIG FUSS BECAUSE ISSEI'S NECK GOT ALL CRAMPED UP—

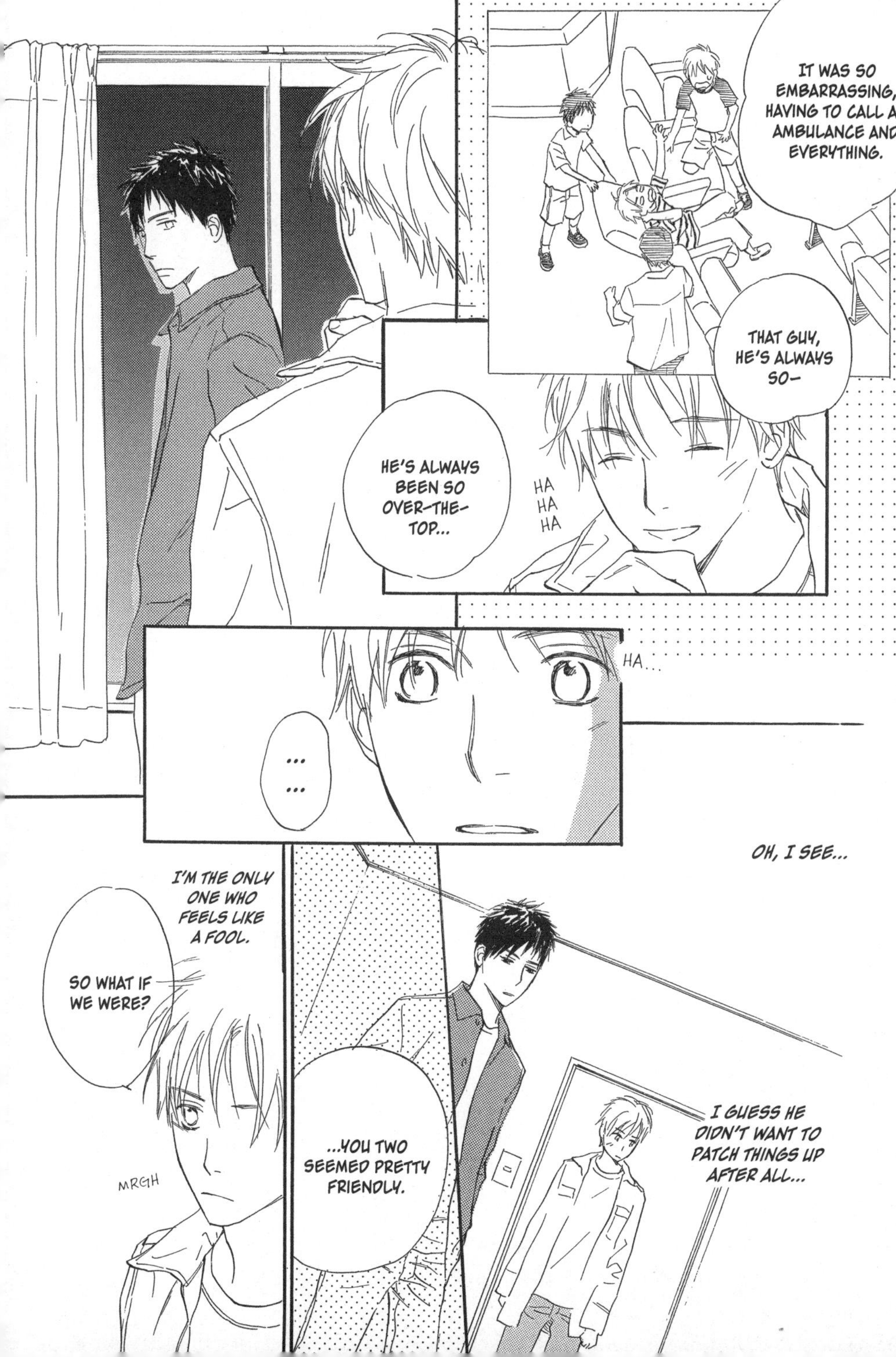
IT WAS SO EMBARRASSING, HAVING TO CALL AN AMBULANCE AND EVERYTHING.
THAT GUY, HE'S ALWAYS SO—
HE'S ALWAYS BEEN SO OVER-THE-TOP...
HA HA HA
HA...
......
OH, I SEE...
I GUESS HE DIDN'T WANT TO PATCH THINGS UP AFTER ALL...
...YOU TWO SEEMED PRETTY FRIENDLY.
I'M THE ONLY ONE WHO FEELS LIKE A FOOL.
SO WHAT IF WE WERE?
MRGH

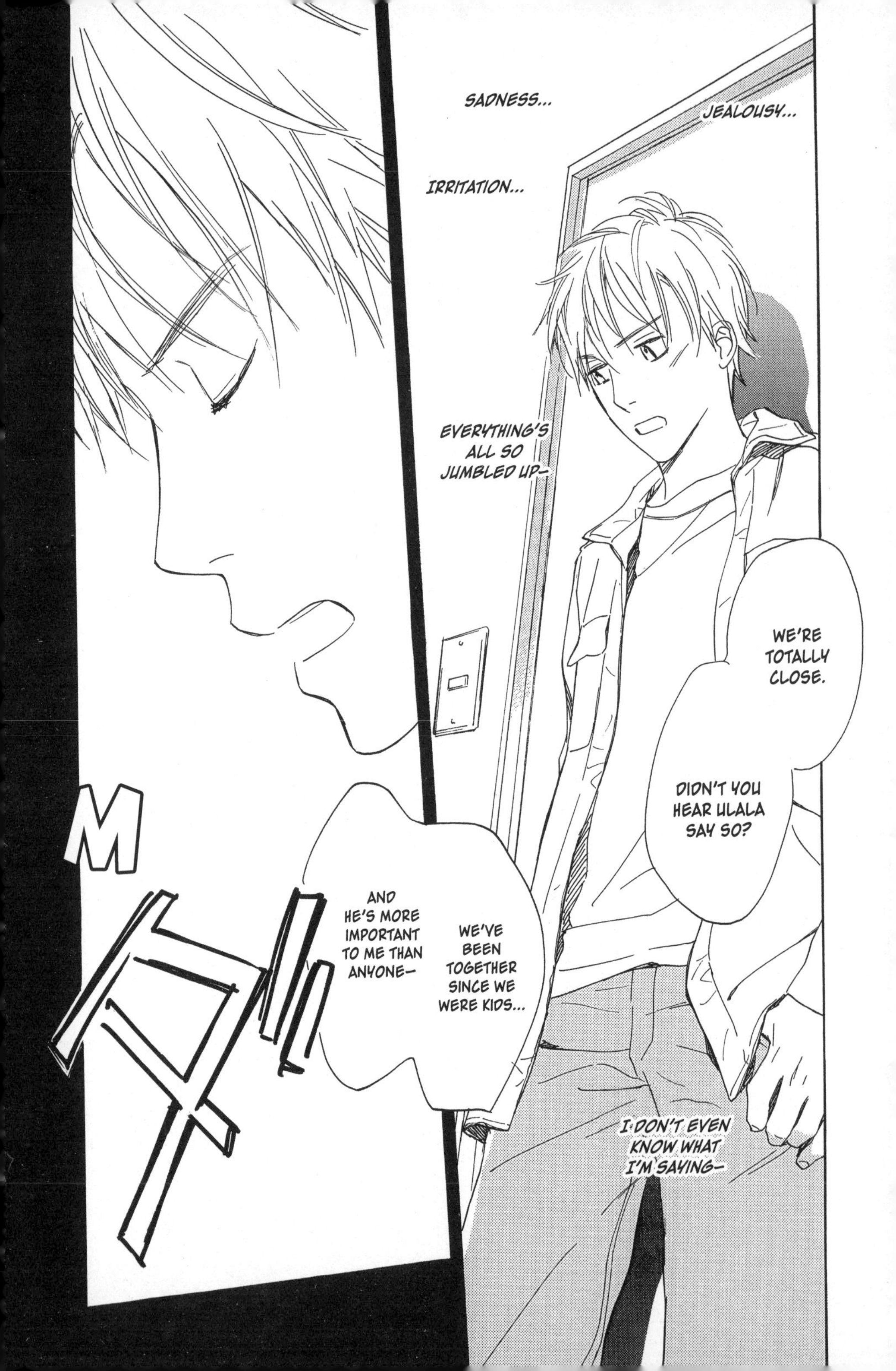
SADNESS...
JEALOUSY...
IRRITATION...
EVERYTHING'S ALL SO JUMBLED UP–
WE'RE TOTALLY CLOSE.
DIDN'T YOU HEAR ULALA SAY SO?
WE'VE BEEN TOGETHER SINCE WE WERE KIDS...
AND HE'S MORE IMPORTANT TO ME THAN ANYONE–
I DON'T EVEN KNOW WHAT I'M SAYING–
M

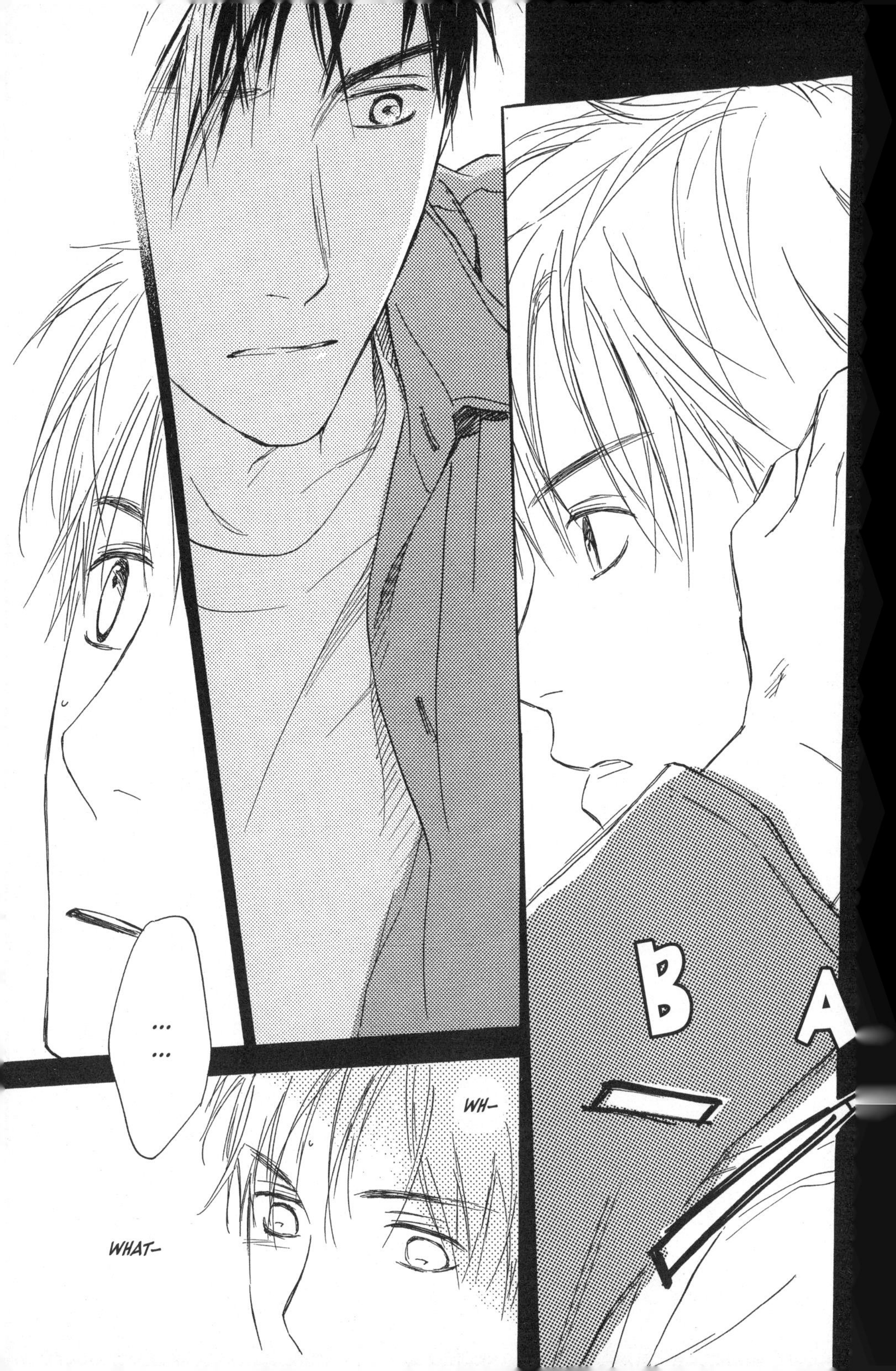
BA
...
...
WH-
WHAT-

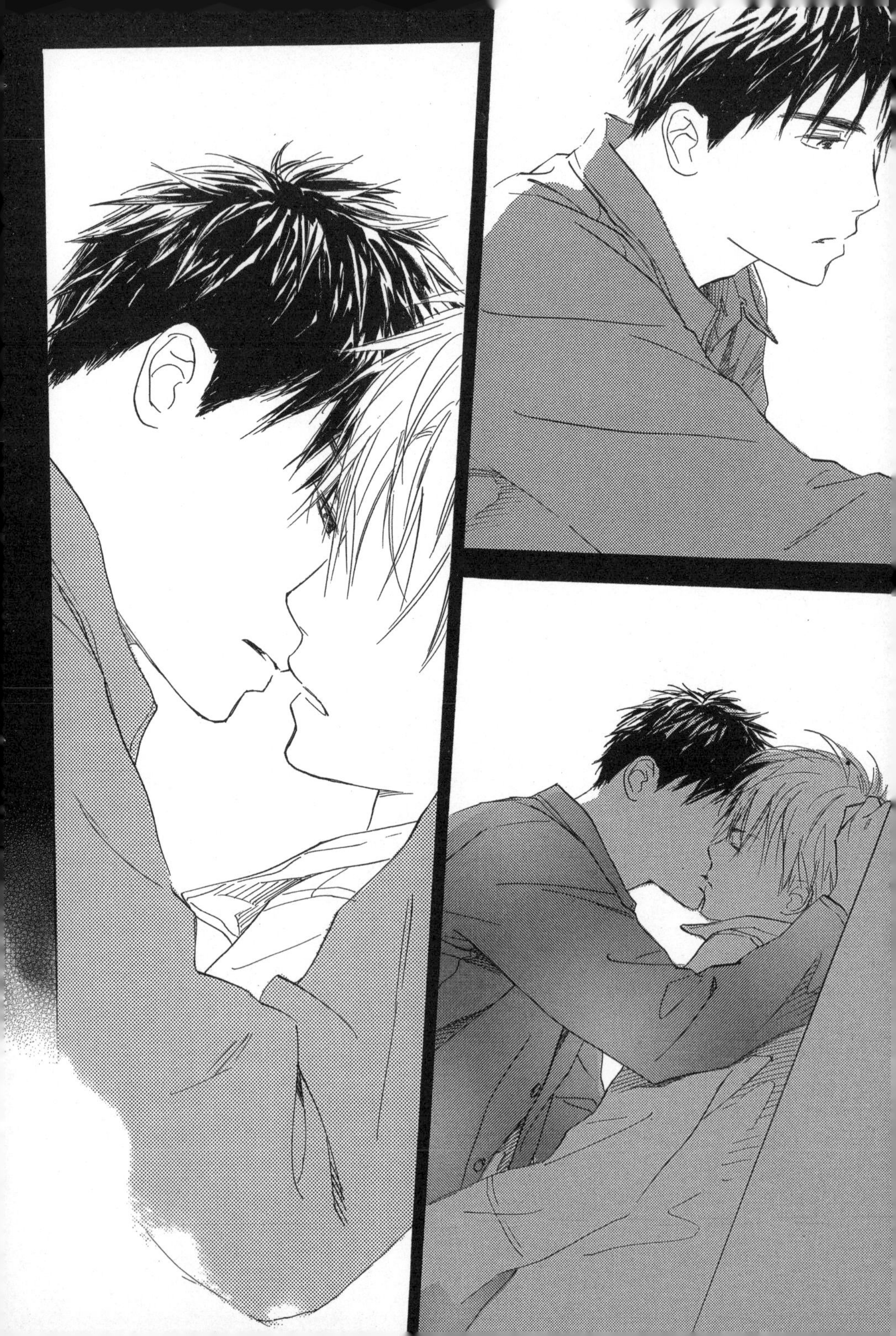

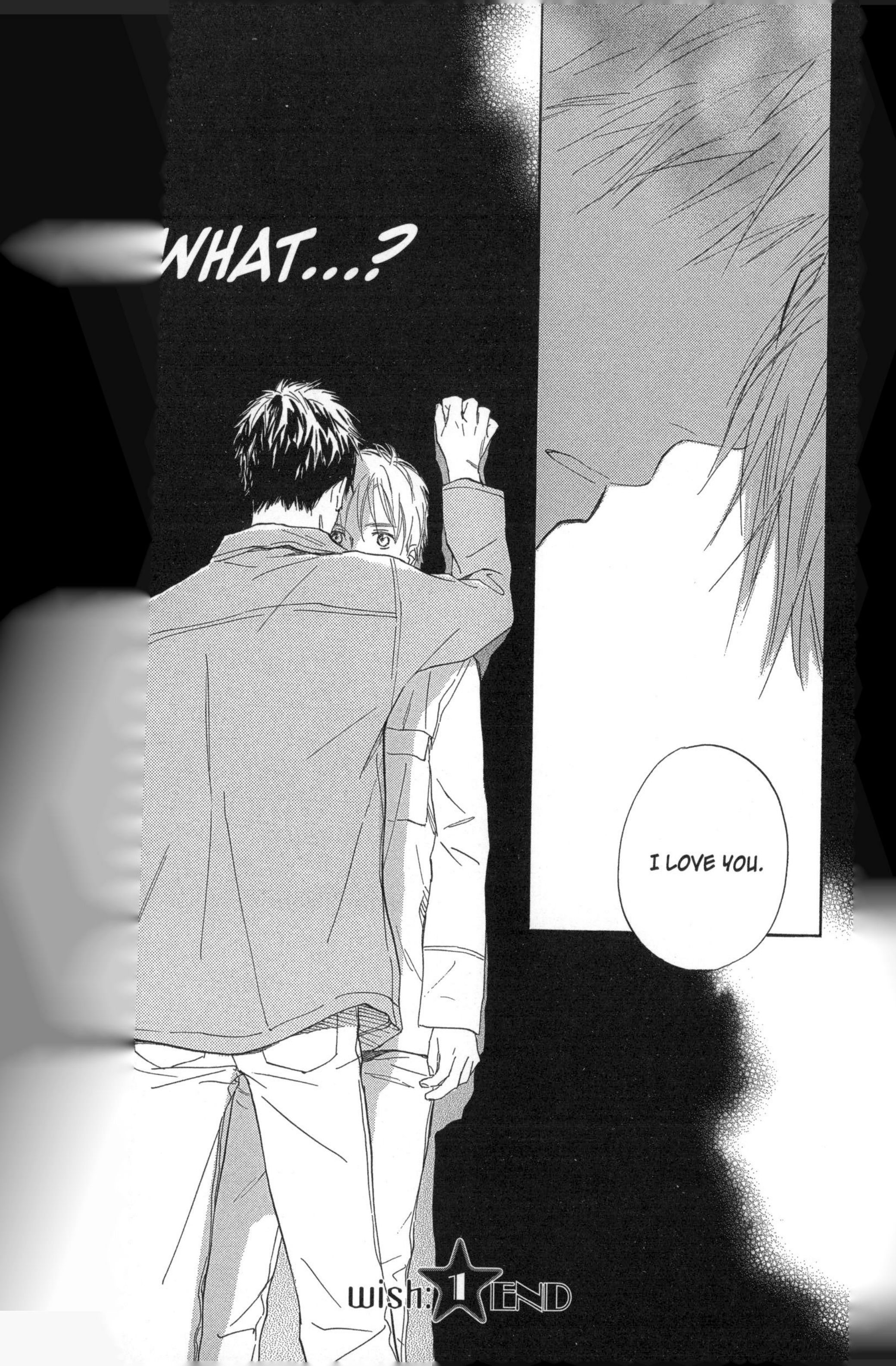
I LOVE YOU.
WHAT...?
wish: 1 END

✿ THANK YOU VERY MUCH FOR TAKING THIS BOOK IN HAND. I AM HONAMI. DURING MY WORK ON THIS PROJECT, I STARTED TO SPEND A LOT MORE TIME LOOKING UP AT THE STARS. THE CLEAR NIGHTS WHEN THE STARS ARE CLEARLY VISIBLE ARE BEAUTIFUL, OF COURSE, BUT THE SLIGHTLY OVERCAST NIGHTS ARE NICE, TOO, WHEN THE MOON CAN BE SEEN AS A DIM BLUR BEHIND A VEIL OF CLOUDS. OBVIOUSLY, THE CONSTELLATIONS NOTED IN BOOKS CAN BE FOUND UP IN THE SKY; BUT ACTUALLY SEEING THEM WITH MY OWN EYES IS SOMEHOW AWE-INSPIRING. I'M SURE MIZUHO AND ENJI MUST KNOW A LOT ABOUT THEM, AND I BET THEY'RE ABLE TO POINT THEM ALL OUT IN THE SKY.

✿ WHEN YOU THINK ABOUT IT, THE PEOPLE WHO NAMED THE CONSTELLATIONS SURE HAD SOME GREAT IMAGINATIONS, BEING ABLE TO SEE ALL KINDS OF ANIMALS AND THINGS UP THERE IN THE INFINITE MASS OF STARS. SOMETIMES I WONDER, "HOW DID THEY EVER SEE THAT ANIMAL IN THIS COMBINATION OF STARS?!" FOR SOME OF THE CONSTELLATIONS I HAVE TO ASK, "DO YOU REALLY THINK SO...?" AND WITH OTHERS, I HAVE TO OUTRIGHT LAUGH- LIKE "THE SCULPTOR'S WORKSHOP" AND "THE TRIANGLE" (IT'S EXACTLY WHAT IT IS!). THE NIGHT SKY BECOMES FUN WHEN YOU'RE ABLE TO SPOT THE CONSTELLATIONS.

✿ SAKURAGI SENSEI, THANK YOU VERY MUCH. I'M SORRY I WAS INADEQUATE IN SO MANY WAYS...! THIS STORY FEATURED QUITE A FEW GIRLS AND IT ADDED A "FLOWERINESS" (I THINK?) THAT MADE IT FUN. APOLOGIES ARE ALSO DUE TO MY EDITOR M-SAMA...I AM DEEPLY THANKFUL TO YOU. AND LAST BUT NOT LEAST, IF YOU READERS ENJOY THIS BOOK EVEN A LITTLE, IT WOULD MAKE ME VERY HAPPY.

YUKINE HONAMI

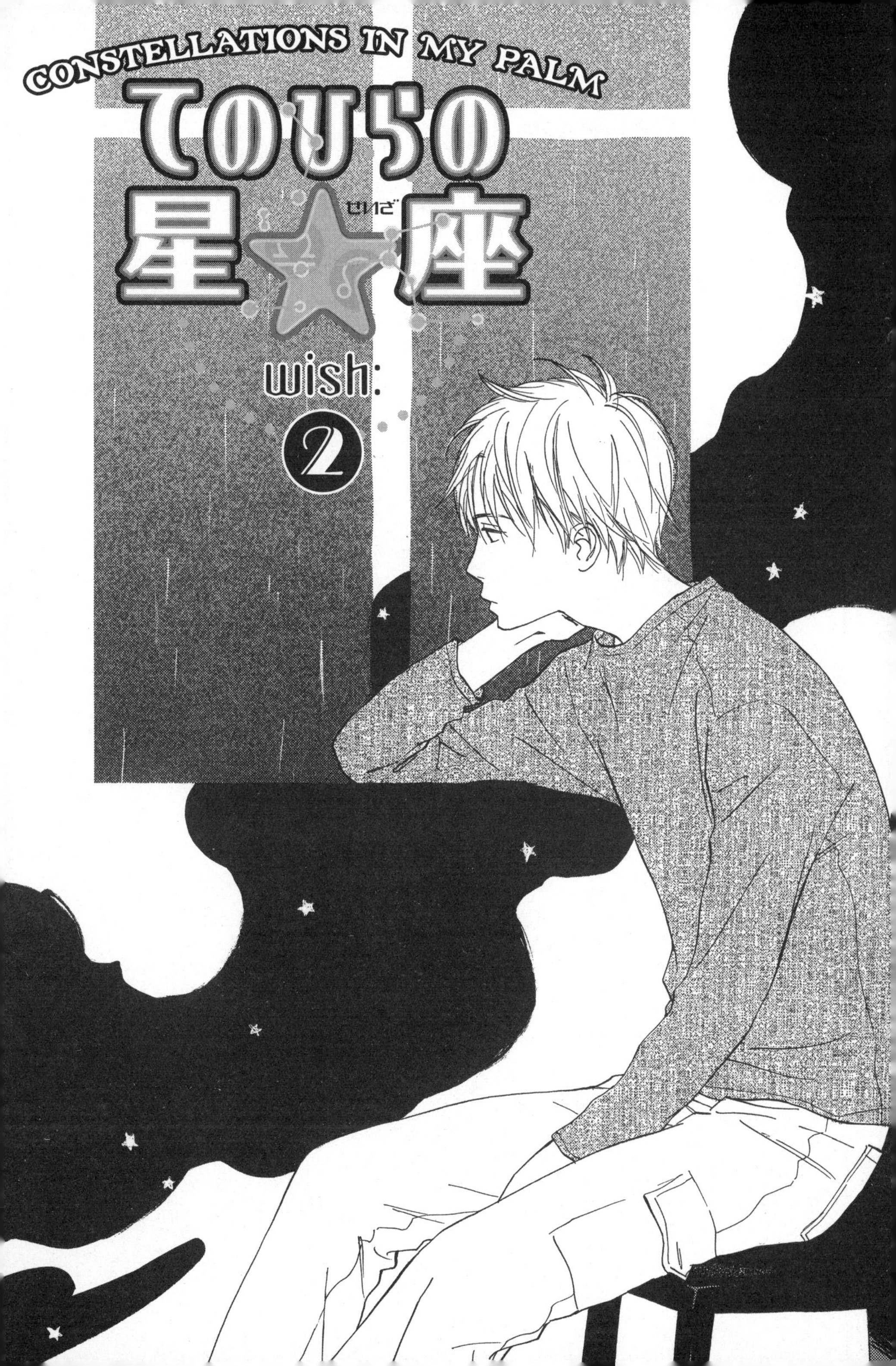
CONSTELLATIONS IN MY PALM
てのひらの星座
せいざ
wish:
2

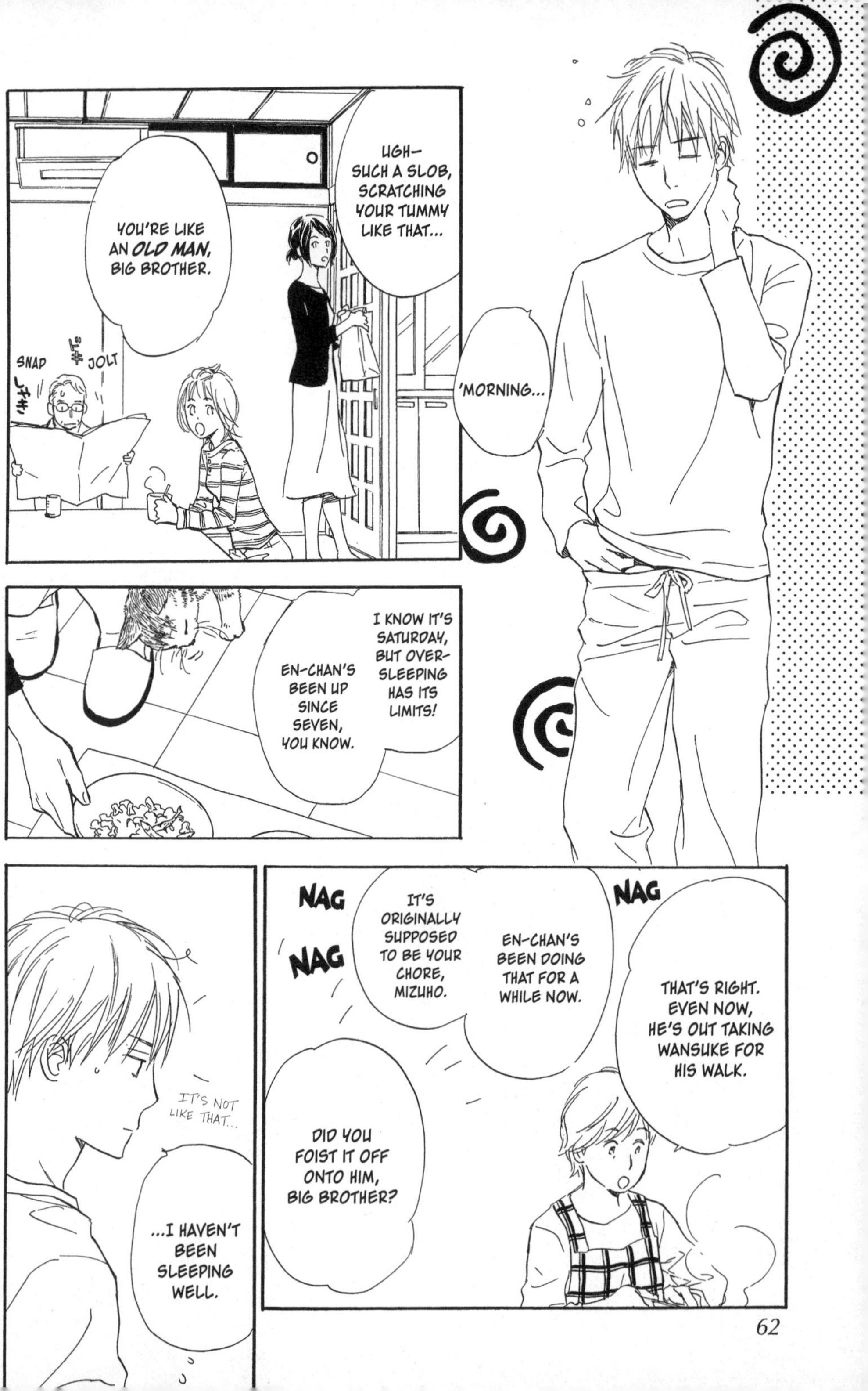
'MORNING...
UGH— SUCH A SLOB, SCRATCHING YOUR TUMMY LIKE THAT...
YOU'RE LIKE AN ***OLD MAN***, BIG BROTHER.
JOLT
SNAP
I KNOW IT'S SATURDAY, BUT OVER-SLEEPING HAS ITS LIMITS!
EN-CHAN'S BEEN UP SINCE SEVEN, YOU KNOW.
NAG
THAT'S RIGHT. EVEN NOW, HE'S OUT TAKING WANSUKE FOR HIS WALK.
NAG
EN-CHAN'S BEEN DOING THAT FOR A WHILE NOW.
IT'S ORIGINALLY SUPPOSED TO BE YOUR CHORE, MIZUHO.
NAG
DID YOU FOIST IT OFF ONTO HIM, BIG BROTHER?
IT'S NOT LIKE THAT...
...I HAVEN'T BEEN SLEEPING WELL.

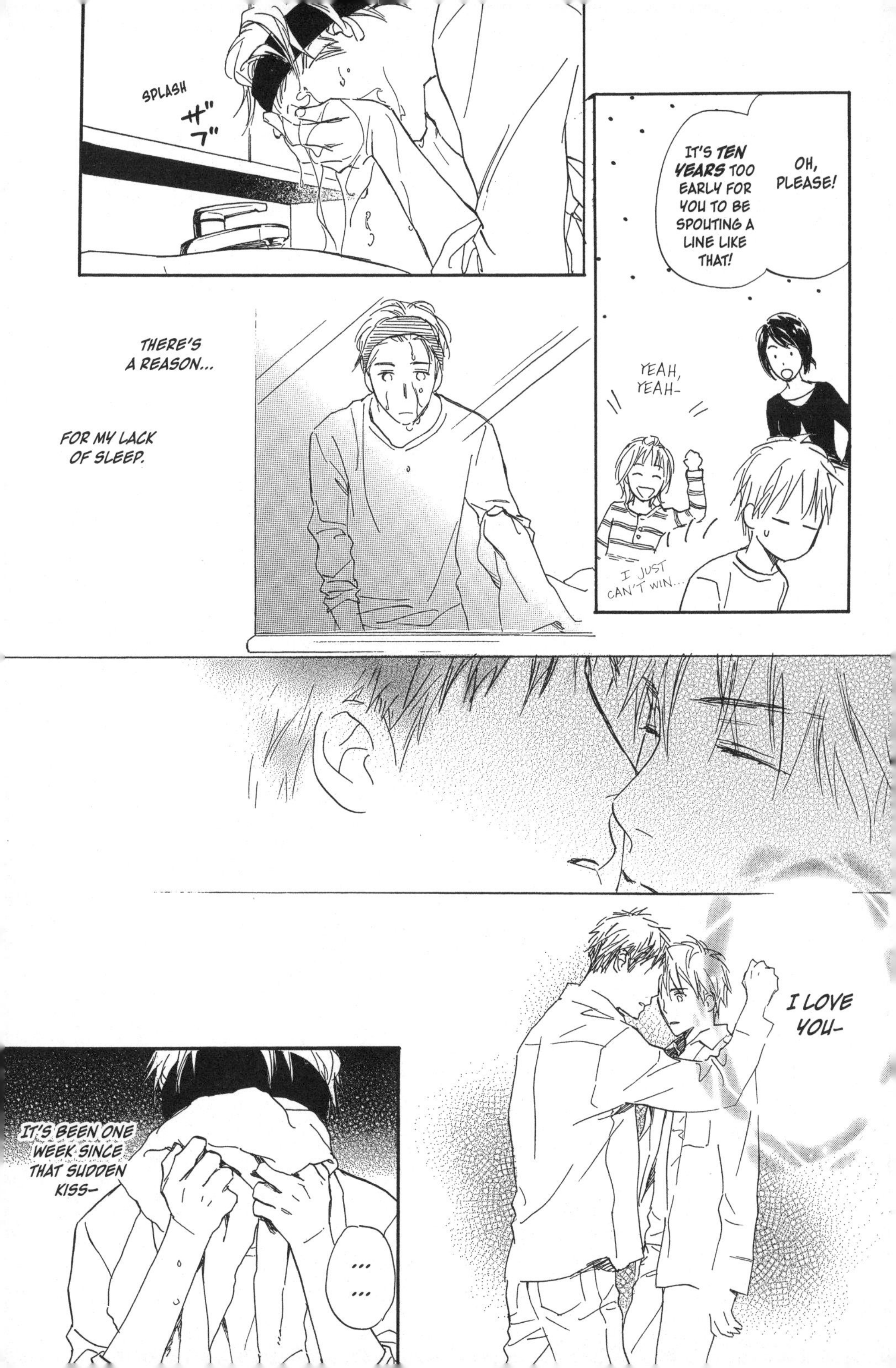
OH, PLEASE!
IT'S TEN YEARS TOO EARLY FOR YOU TO BE SPOUTING A LINE LIKE THAT!
YEAH, YEAH-
I JUST CAN'T WIN...
SPLASH
ザブ
THERE'S A REASON...
FOR MY LACK OF SLEEP.
I LOVE YOU-
IT'S BEEN ONE WEEK SINCE THAT SUDDEN KISS-
......

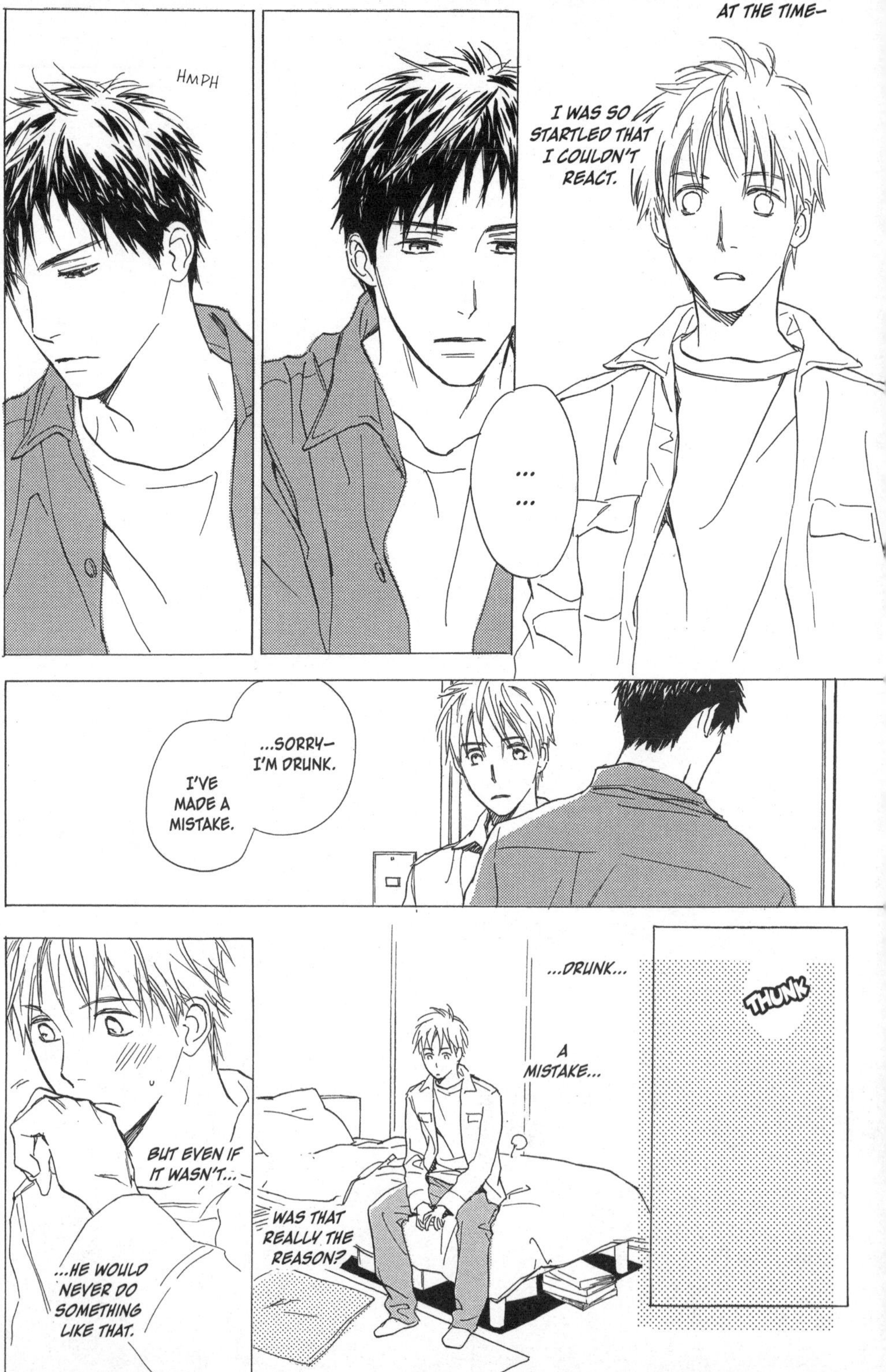
AT THE TIME—
I WAS SO STARTLED THAT I COULDN'T REACT.
... ...
HMPH
...SORRY— I'M DRUNK.
I'VE MADE A MISTAKE.
THUNK
...DRUNK...
A MISTAKE...
WAS THAT REALLY THE REASON?
BUT EVEN IF IT WASN'T...
...HE WOULD NEVER DO SOMETHING LIKE THAT.

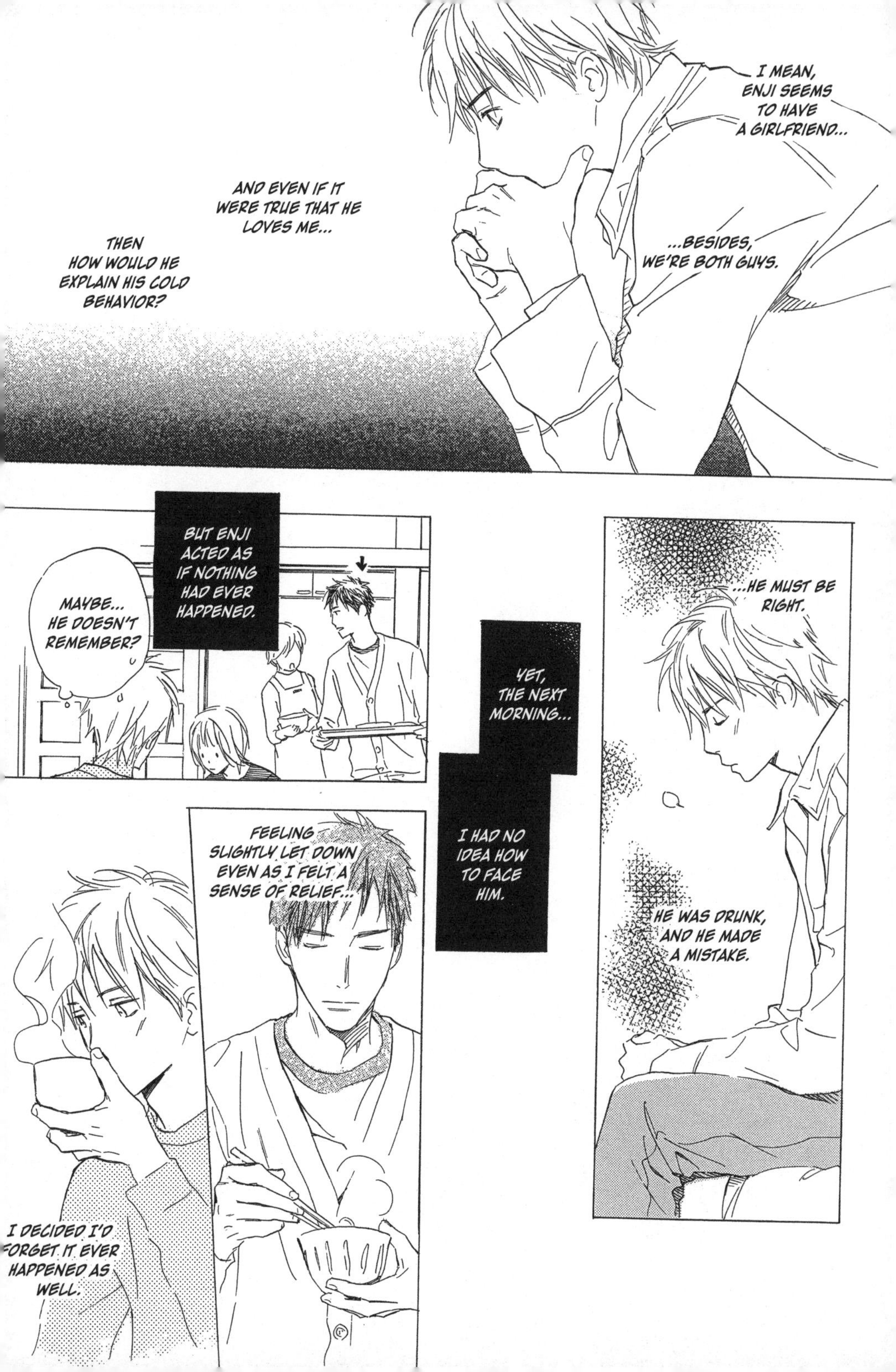
I MEAN, ENJI SEEMS TO HAVE A GIRLFRIEND...
...BESIDES, WE'RE BOTH GUYS.
AND EVEN IF IT WERE TRUE THAT HE LOVES ME...
THEN HOW WOULD HE EXPLAIN HIS COLD BEHAVIOR?
...HE MUST BE RIGHT.
HE WAS DRUNK, AND HE MADE A MISTAKE.
YET, THE NEXT MORNING...
I HAD NO IDEA HOW TO FACE HIM.
BUT ENJI ACTED AS IF NOTHING HAD EVER HAPPENED.
MAYBE... HE DOESN'T REMEMBER?
FEELING SLIGHTLY LET DOWN EVEN AS I FELT A SENSE OF RELIEF...
I DECIDED I'D FORGET IT EVER HAPPENED AS WELL.

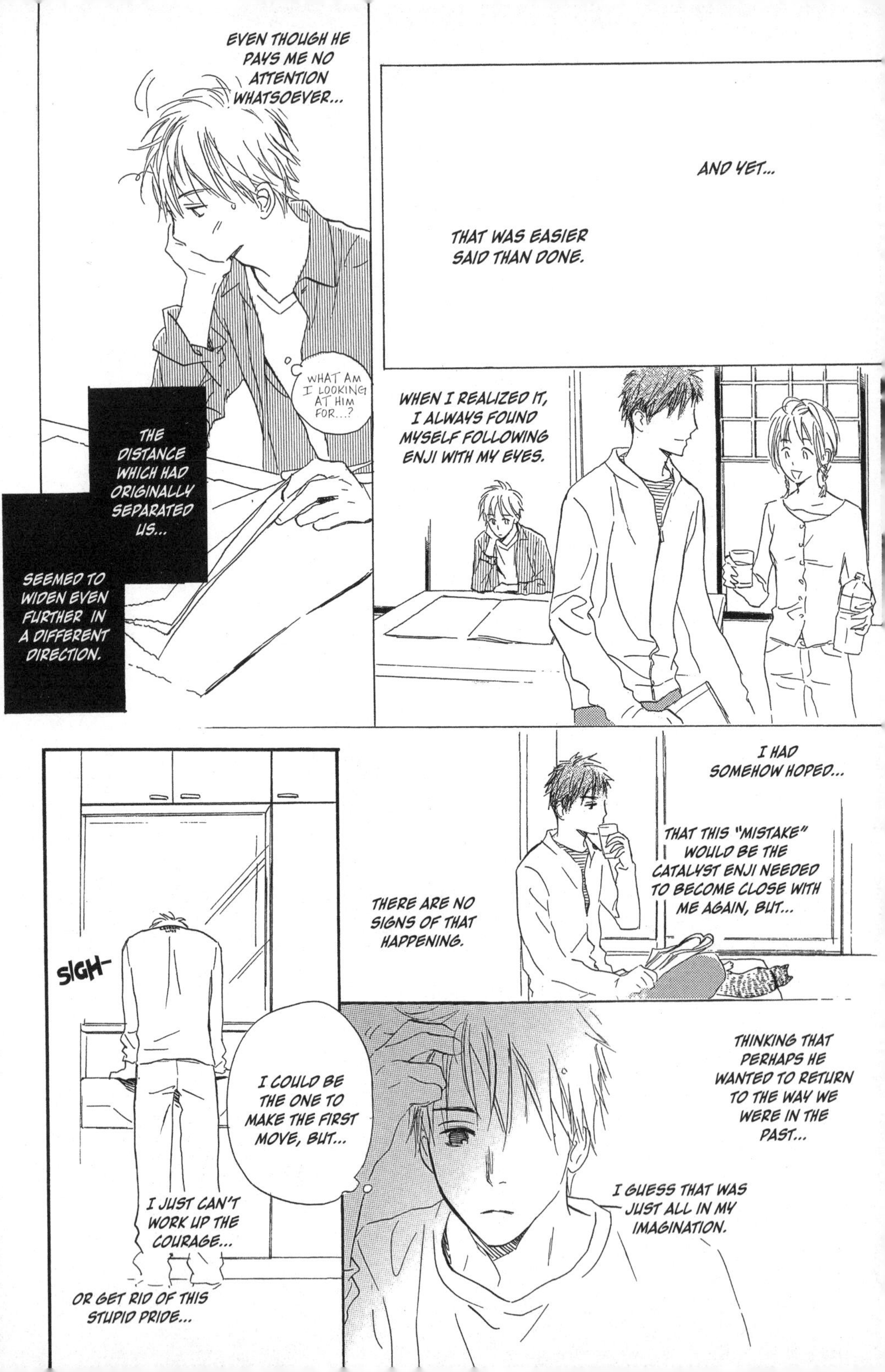
AND YET...
THAT WAS EASIER SAID THAN DONE.
WHEN I REALIZED IT, I ALWAYS FOUND MYSELF FOLLOWING ENJI WITH MY EYES.
EVEN THOUGH HE PAYS ME NO ATTENTION WHATSOEVER...
WHAT AM I LOOKING AT HIM FOR...?
THE DISTANCE WHICH HAD ORIGINALLY SEPARATED US...
SEEMED TO WIDEN EVEN FURTHER IN A DIFFERENT DIRECTION.
I HAD SOMEHOW HOPED...
THAT THIS "MISTAKE" WOULD BE THE CATALYST ENJI NEEDED TO BECOME CLOSE WITH ME AGAIN, BUT...
THERE ARE NO SIGNS OF THAT HAPPENING.
THINKING THAT PERHAPS HE WANTED TO RETURN TO THE WAY WE WERE IN THE PAST...
I GUESS THAT WAS JUST ALL IN MY IMAGINATION.
SIGH-
I COULD BE THE ONE TO MAKE THE FIRST MOVE, BUT...
I JUST CAN'T WORK UP THE COURAGE...
OR GET RID OF THIS STUPID PRIDE...

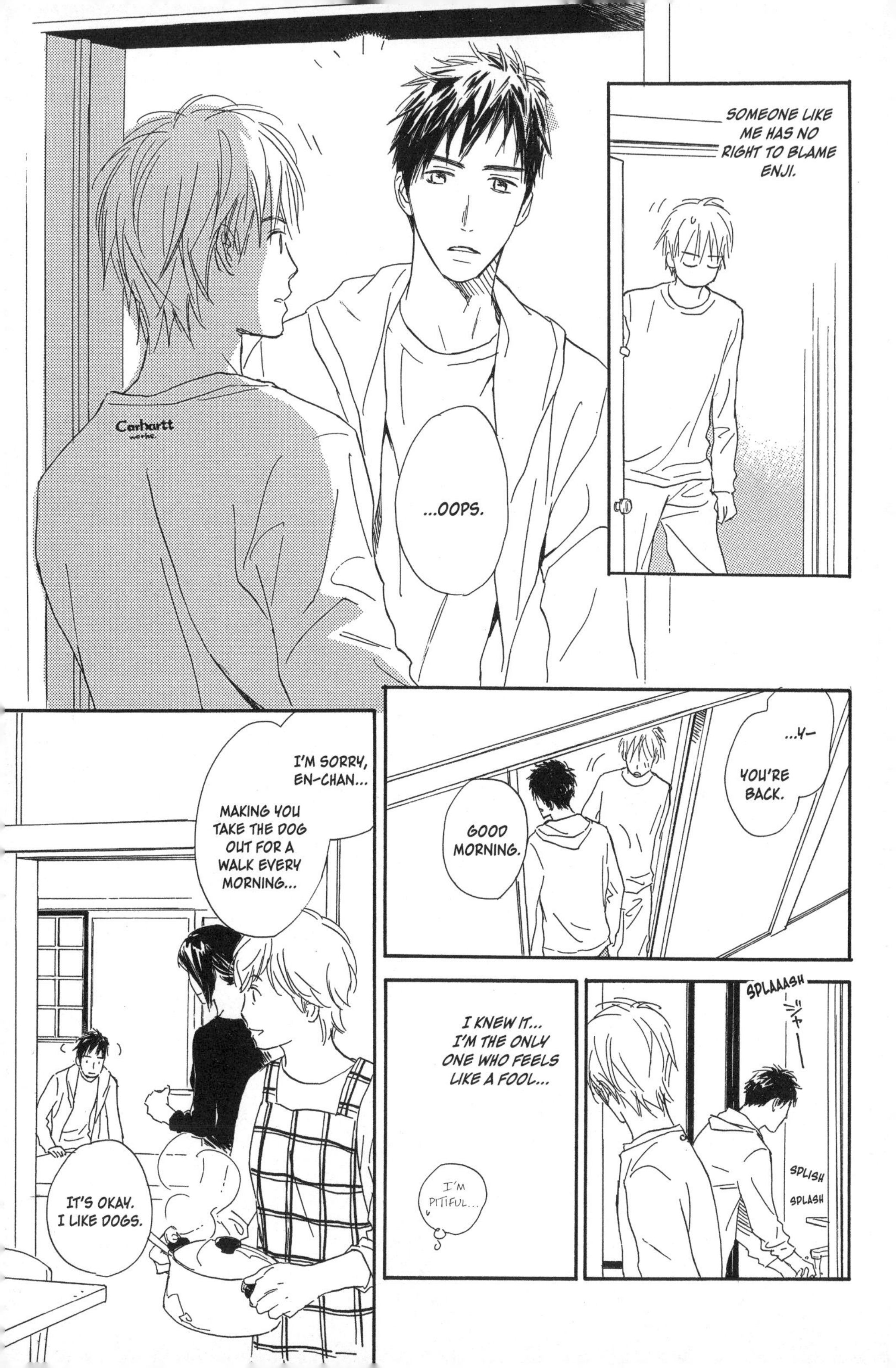
SOMEONE LIKE ME HAS NO RIGHT TO BLAME ENJI.
Carhartt
...OOPS.
...Y-
YOU'RE BACK.
GOOD MORNING.
SPLAAASH
ジャー
SPLISH
SPLASH
I KNEW IT... I'M THE ONLY ONE WHO FEELS LIKE A FOOL...
I'M PITIFUL...
I'M SORRY, EN-CHAN...
MAKING YOU TAKE THE DOG OUT FOR A WALK EVERY MORNING...
IT'S OKAY. I LIKE DOGS.

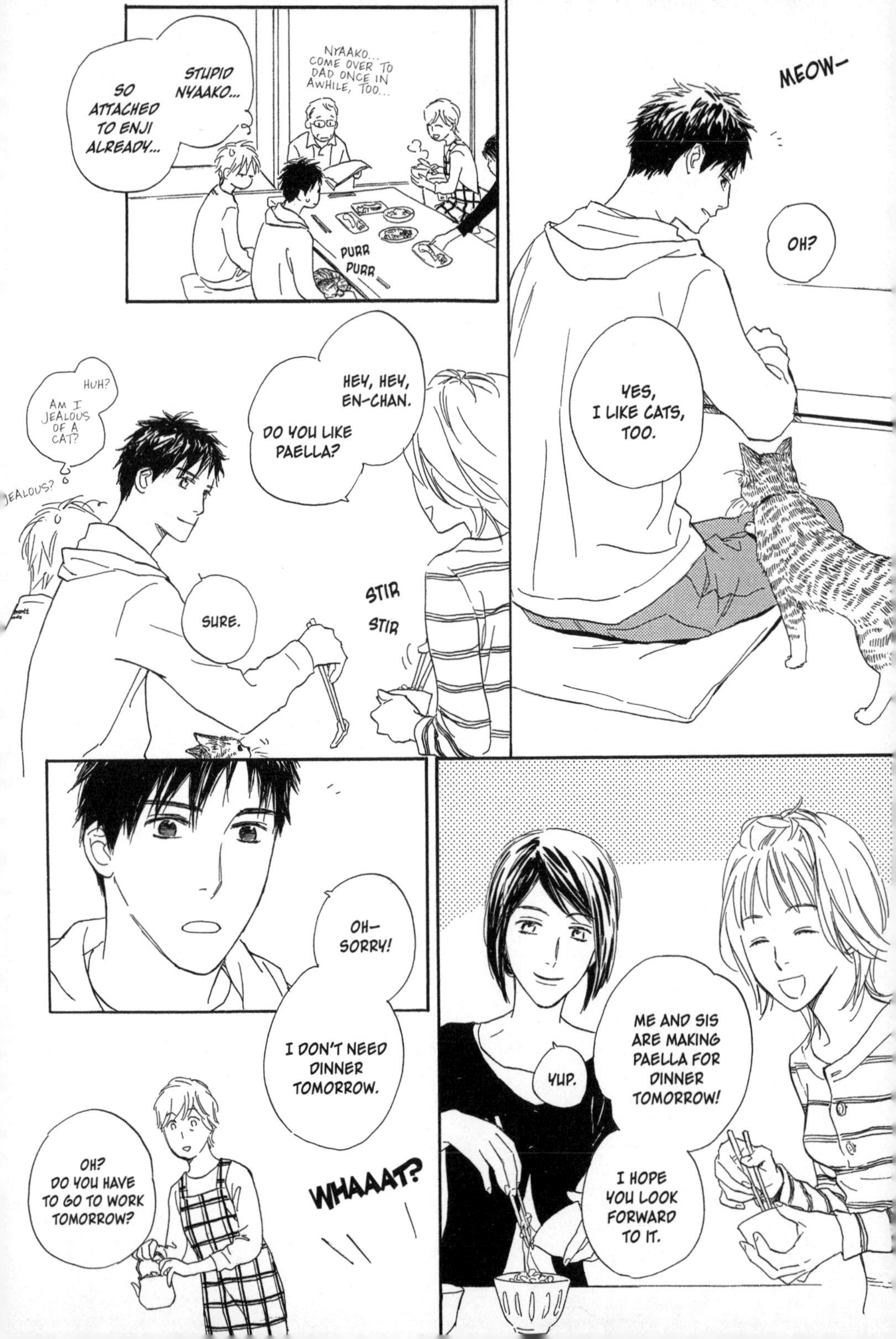
MEOW–
OH?
YES, I LIKE CATS, TOO.
NYAAKO... COME OVER TO DAD ONCE IN AWHILE, TOO...
STUPID NYAAKO...
SO ATTACHED TO ENJI ALREADY...
PURR PURR
HEY, HEY, EN-CHAN.
DO YOU LIKE PAELLA?
STIR STIR
SURE.
HUH?
AM I JEALOUS OF A CAT?
JEALOUS?
ME AND SIS ARE MAKING PAELLA FOR DINNER TOMORROW!
YUP.
I HOPE YOU LOOK FORWARD TO IT.
OH– SORRY!
I DON'T NEED DINNER TOMORROW.
WHAAAT?
OH? DO YOU HAVE TO GO TO WORK TOMORROW?

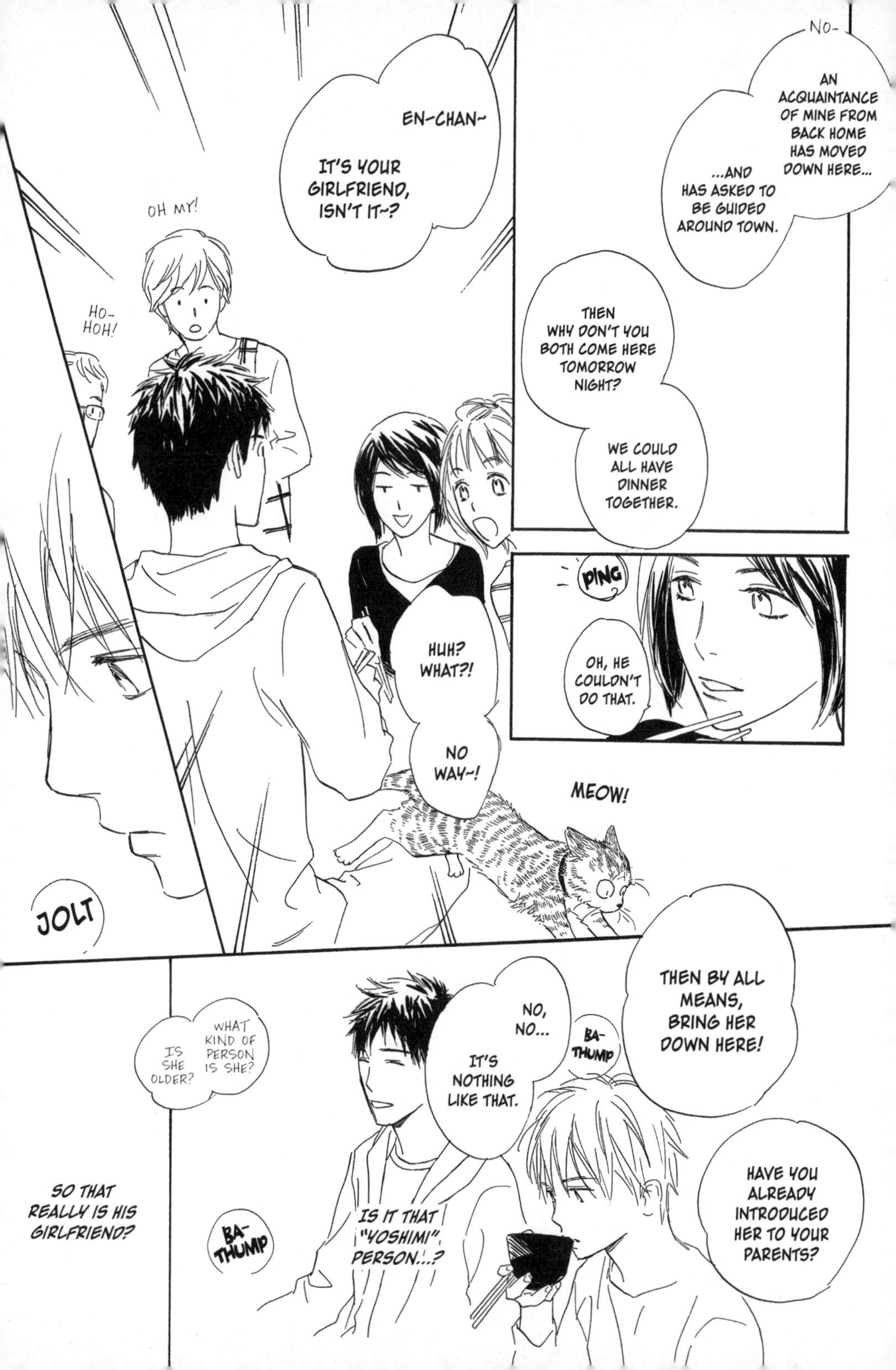
NO-
AN ACQUAINTANCE OF MINE FROM BACK HOME HAS MOVED DOWN HERE...
...AND HAS ASKED TO BE GUIDED AROUND TOWN.
THEN WHY DON'T YOU BOTH COME HERE TOMORROW NIGHT?
WE COULD ALL HAVE DINNER TOGETHER.
PING
OH, HE COULDN'T DO THAT.
EN-CHAN~
IT'S YOUR GIRLFRIEND, ISN'T IT~?
OH MY!
HO-HOH!
HUH? WHAT?!
NO WAY~!
MEOW!
JOLT
THEN BY ALL MEANS, BRING HER DOWN HERE!
HAVE YOU ALREADY INTRODUCED HER TO YOUR PARENTS?
BA-THUMP
NO, NO...
IT'S NOTHING LIKE THAT.
IS IT THAT "YOSHIMI" PERSON...?
BA-THUMP
WHAT KIND OF PERSON IS SHE?
IS SHE OLDER?
SO THAT REALLY IS HIS GIRLFRIEND?

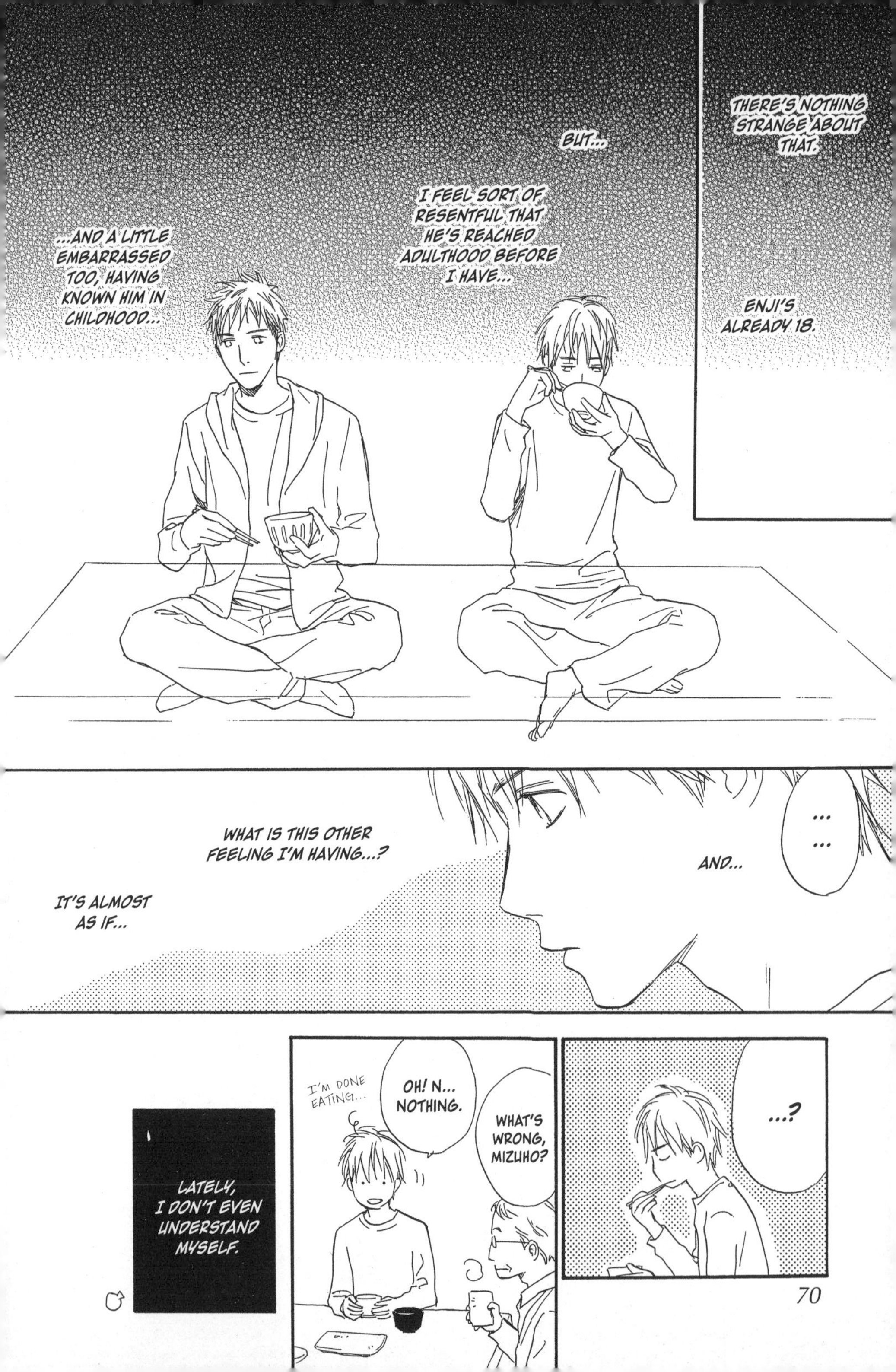
THERE'S NOTHING STRANGE ABOUT THAT.
ENJI'S ALREADY 18.
BUT...
I FEEL SORT OF RESENTFUL THAT HE'S REACHED ADULTHOOD BEFORE I HAVE...
...AND A LITTLE EMBARRASSED TOO, HAVING KNOWN HIM IN CHILDHOOD...
... ...
AND...
WHAT IS THIS OTHER FEELING I'M HAVING...?
IT'S ALMOST AS IF...
...?
WHAT'S WRONG, MIZUHO?
OH! N... NOTHING.
I'M DONE EATING...
LATELY, I DON'T EVEN UNDERSTAND MYSELF.

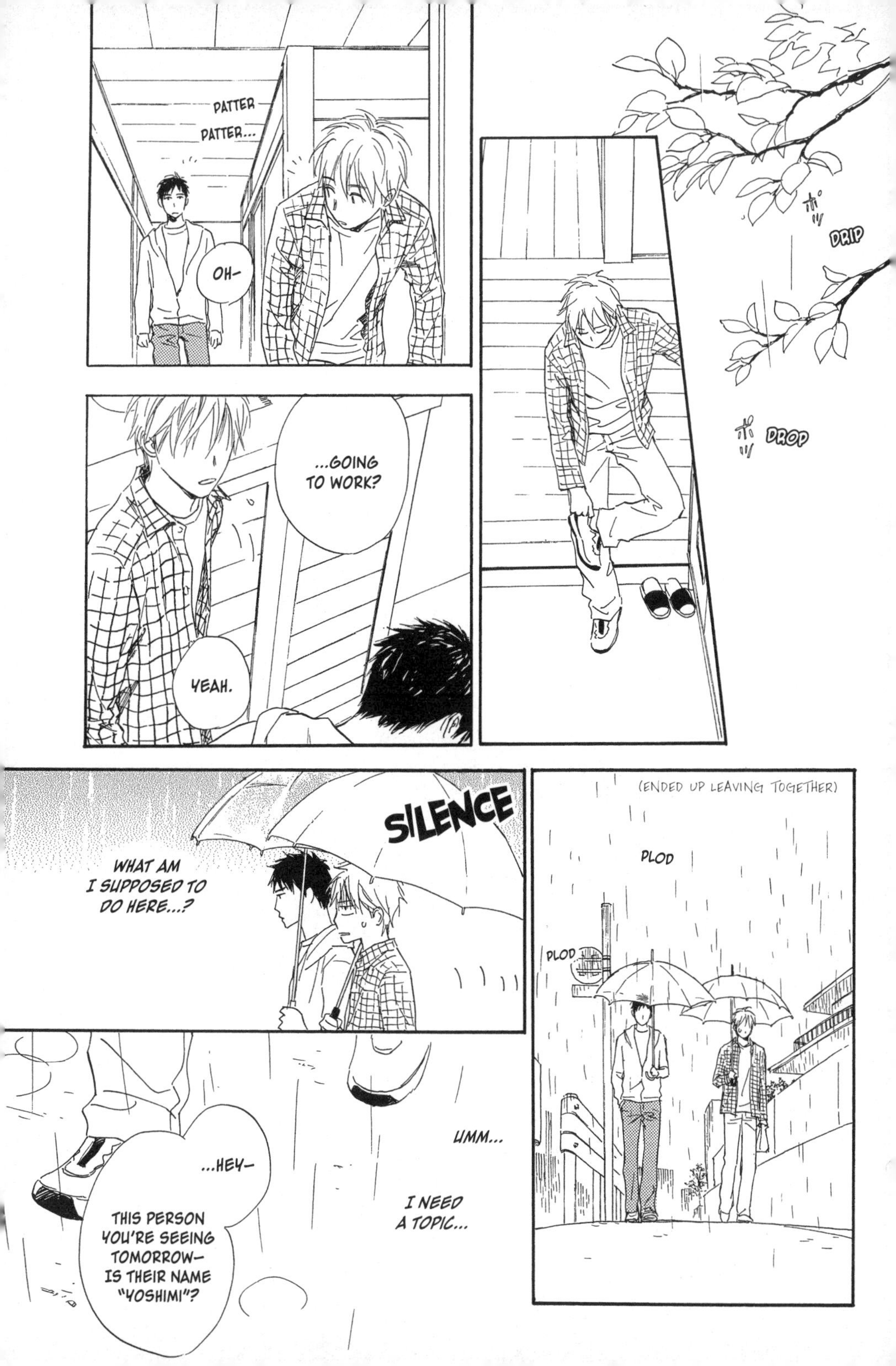
DRIP
DROP
PATTER
PATTER...
OH-
...GOING TO WORK?
YEAH.
(ENDED UP LEAVING TOGETHER)
PLOD
PLOD
SILENCE
WHAT AM I SUPPOSED TO DO HERE...?
UMM...
I NEED A TOPIC...
...HEY-
THIS PERSON YOU'RE SEEING TOMORROW- IS THEIR NAME "YOSHIMI"?

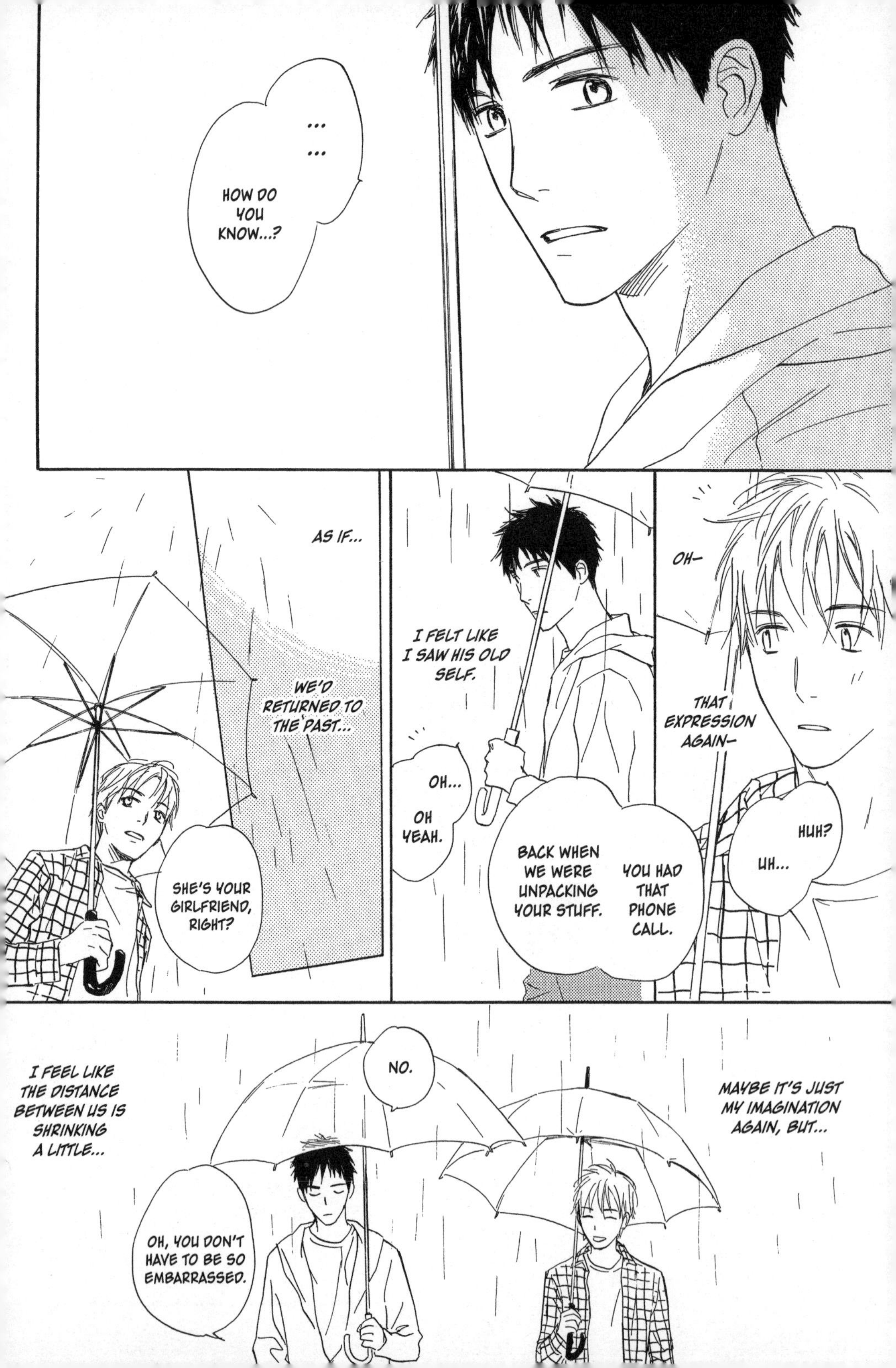

...
...
HOW DO YOU KNOW...?
OH—
THAT EXPRESSION AGAIN—
HUH?
UH...
I FELT LIKE I SAW HIS OLD SELF.
YOU HAD THAT PHONE CALL.
BACK WHEN WE WERE UNPACKING YOUR STUFF.
OH...
OH YEAH.
AS IF...
WE'D RETURNED TO THE PAST...
SHE'S YOUR GIRLFRIEND, RIGHT?
MAYBE IT'S JUST MY IMAGINATION AGAIN, BUT...
NO.
I FEEL LIKE THE DISTANCE BETWEEN US IS SHRINKING A LITTLE...
OH, YOU DON'T HAVE TO BE SO EMBARRASSED.

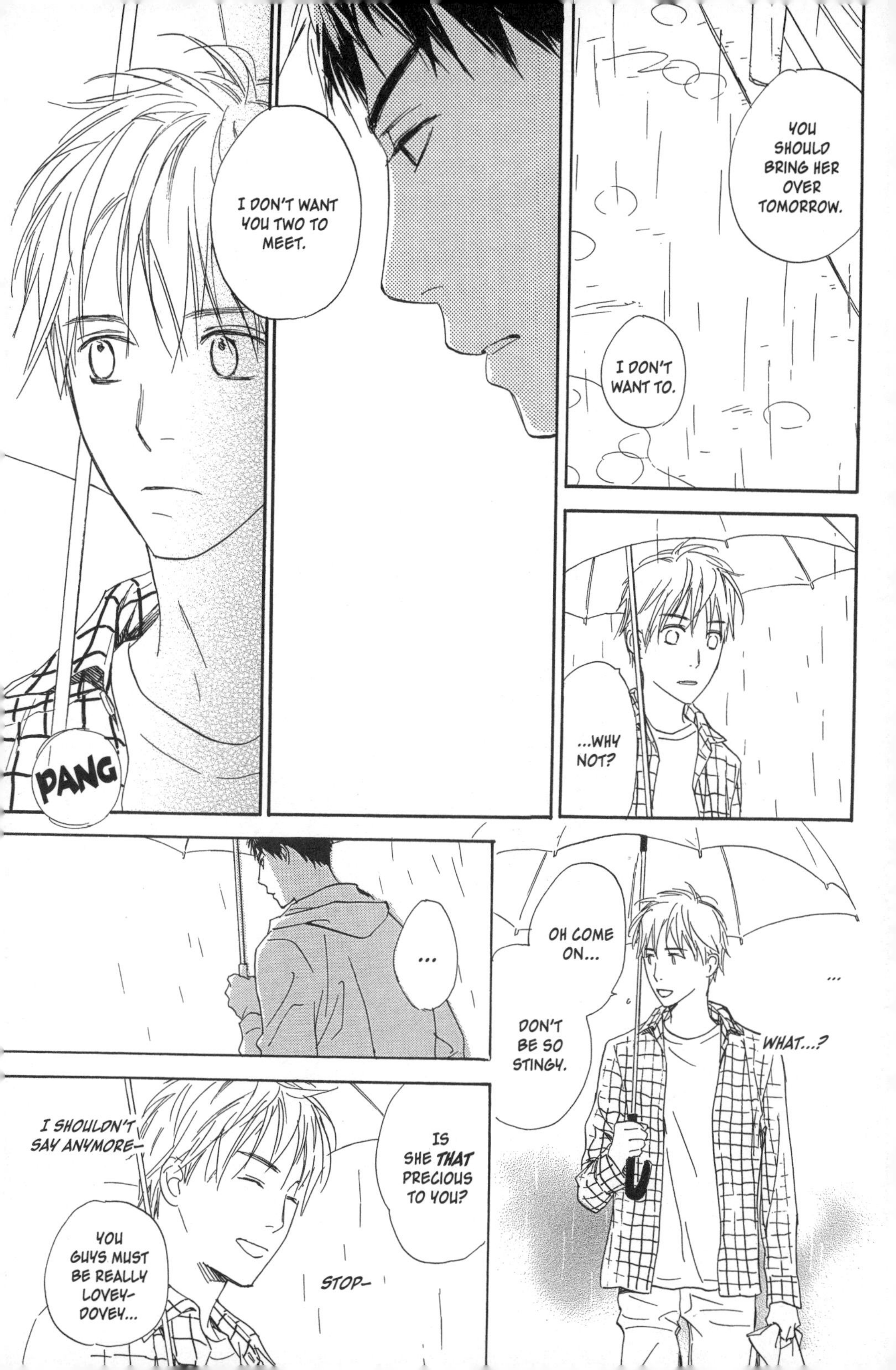
YOU SHOULD BRING HER OVER TOMORROW.
I DON'T WANT TO.
...WHY NOT?
I DON'T WANT YOU TWO TO MEET.
PANG
OH COME ON...
DON'T BE SO STINGY.
...
WHAT...?
...
IS SHE *THAT* PRECIOUS TO YOU?
I SHOULDN'T SAY ANYMORE—
YOU GUYS MUST BE REALLY LOVEY-DOVEY...
STOP—

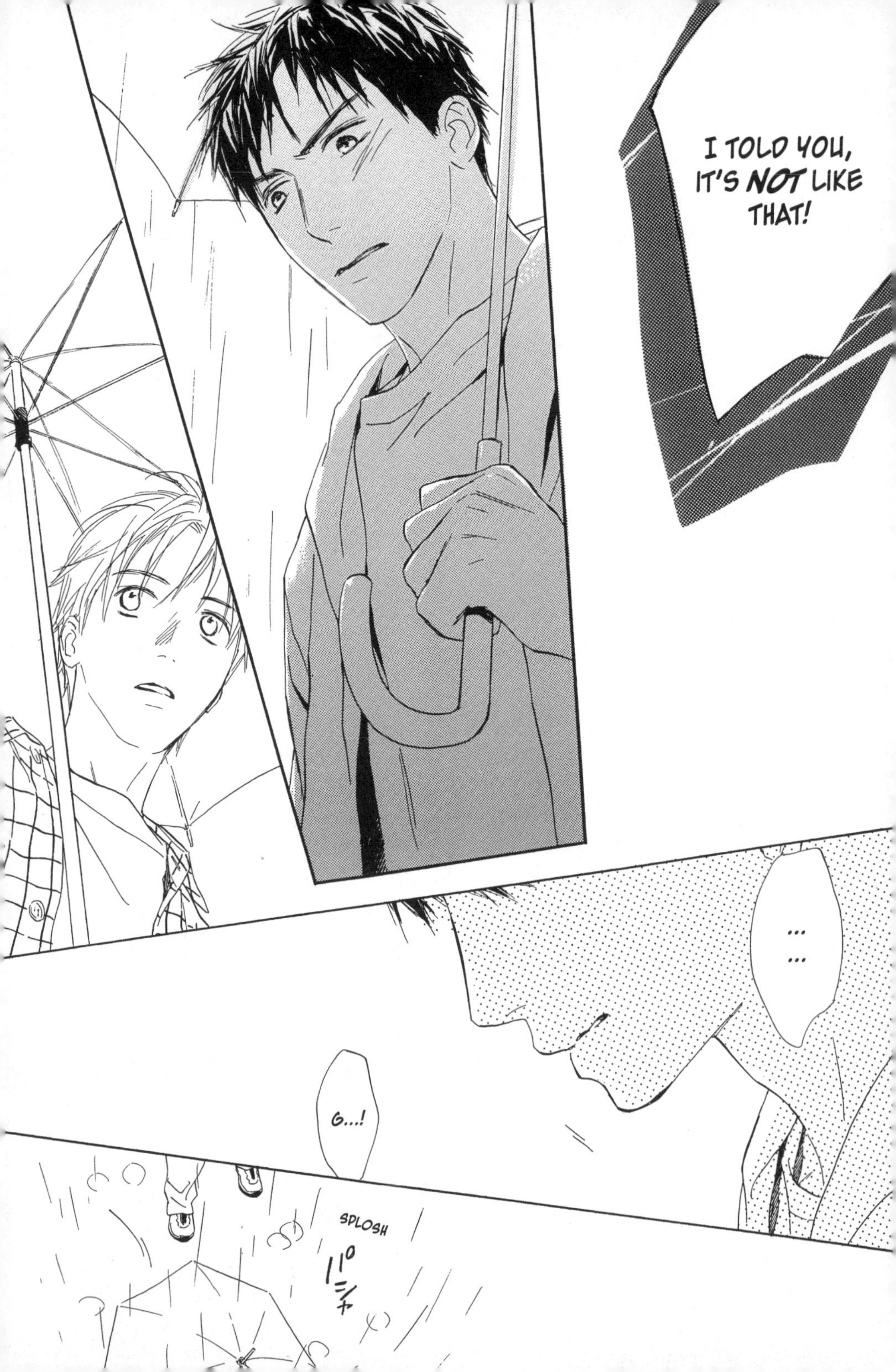
I TOLD YOU, IT'S **NOT** LIKE THAT!
...
...
G...!
SPLOSH
パシャ

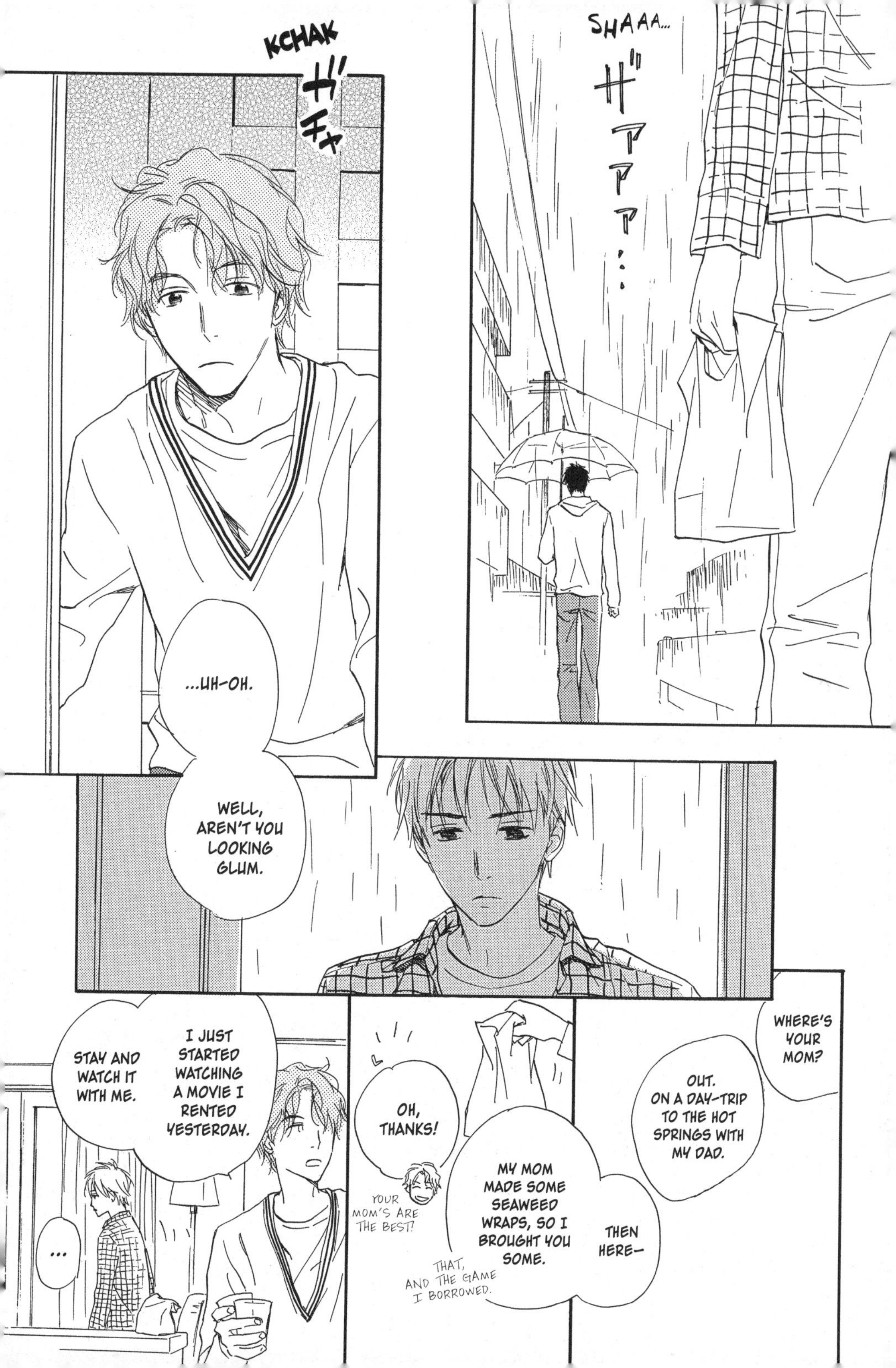
SHAAA...
ザアア...
KCHAK
ガチャ
...UH-OH.
WELL, AREN'T YOU LOOKING GLUM.
WHERE'S YOUR MOM?
OUT. ON A DAY-TRIP TO THE HOT SPRINGS WITH MY DAD.
THEN HERE—
MY MOM MADE SOME SEAWEED WRAPS, SO I BROUGHT YOU SOME.
THAT, AND THE GAME I BORROWED.
OH, THANKS!
YOUR MOM'S ARE THE BEST!
I JUST STARTED WATCHING A MOVIE I RENTED YESTERDAY.
STAY AND WATCH IT WITH ME.
...

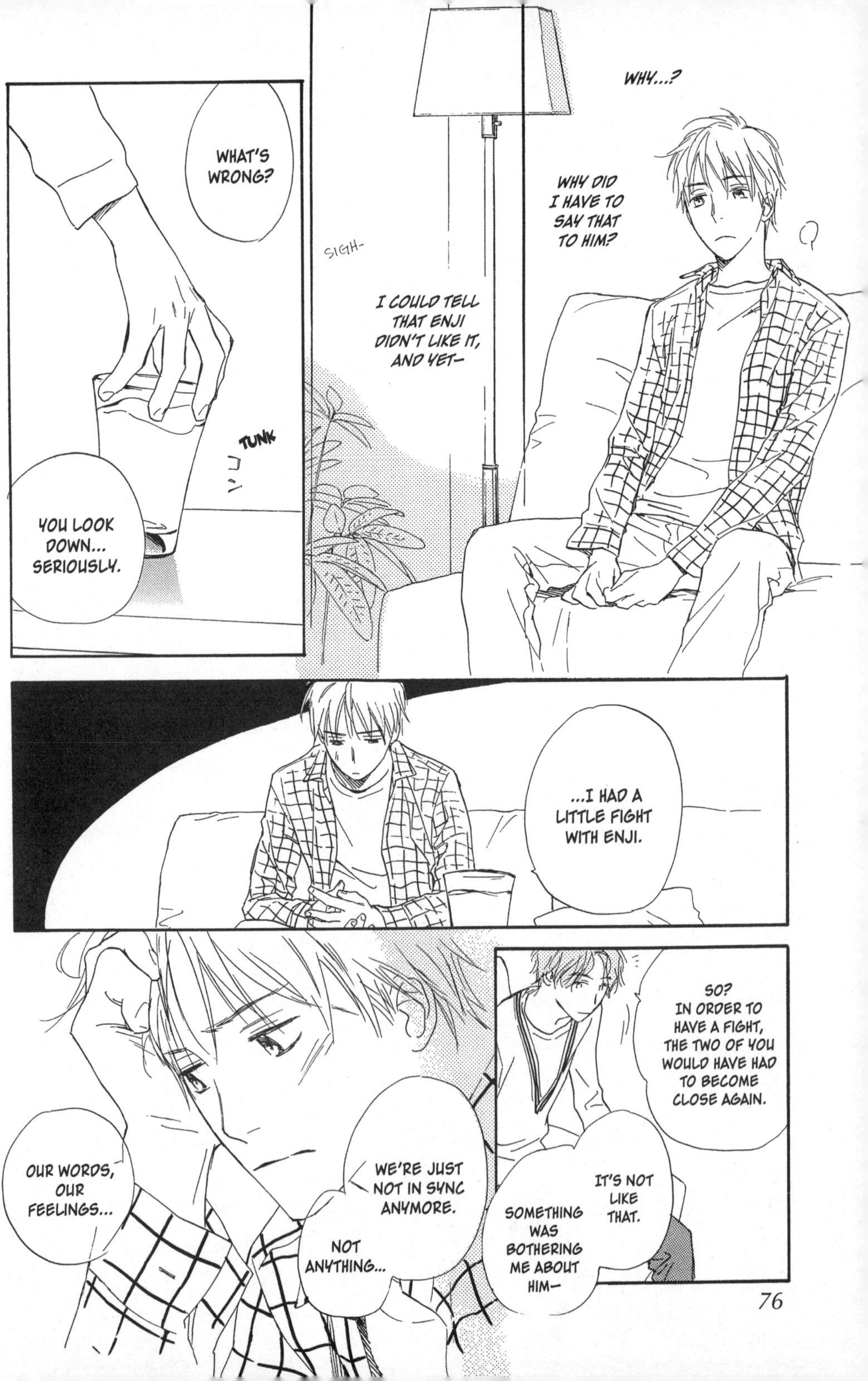
WHY...?
WHY DID I HAVE TO SAY THAT TO HIM?
SIGH-
I COULD TELL THAT ENJI DIDN'T LIKE IT, AND YET-
WHAT'S WRONG?
TUNK
YOU LOOK DOWN... SERIOUSLY.
...I HAD A LITTLE FIGHT WITH ENJI.
SO? IN ORDER TO HAVE A FIGHT, THE TWO OF YOU WOULD HAVE HAD TO BECOME CLOSE AGAIN.
IT'S NOT LIKE THAT.
SOMETHING WAS BOTHERING ME ABOUT HIM-
WE'RE JUST NOT IN SYNC ANYMORE.
NOT ANYTHING...
OUR WORDS, OUR FEELINGS...

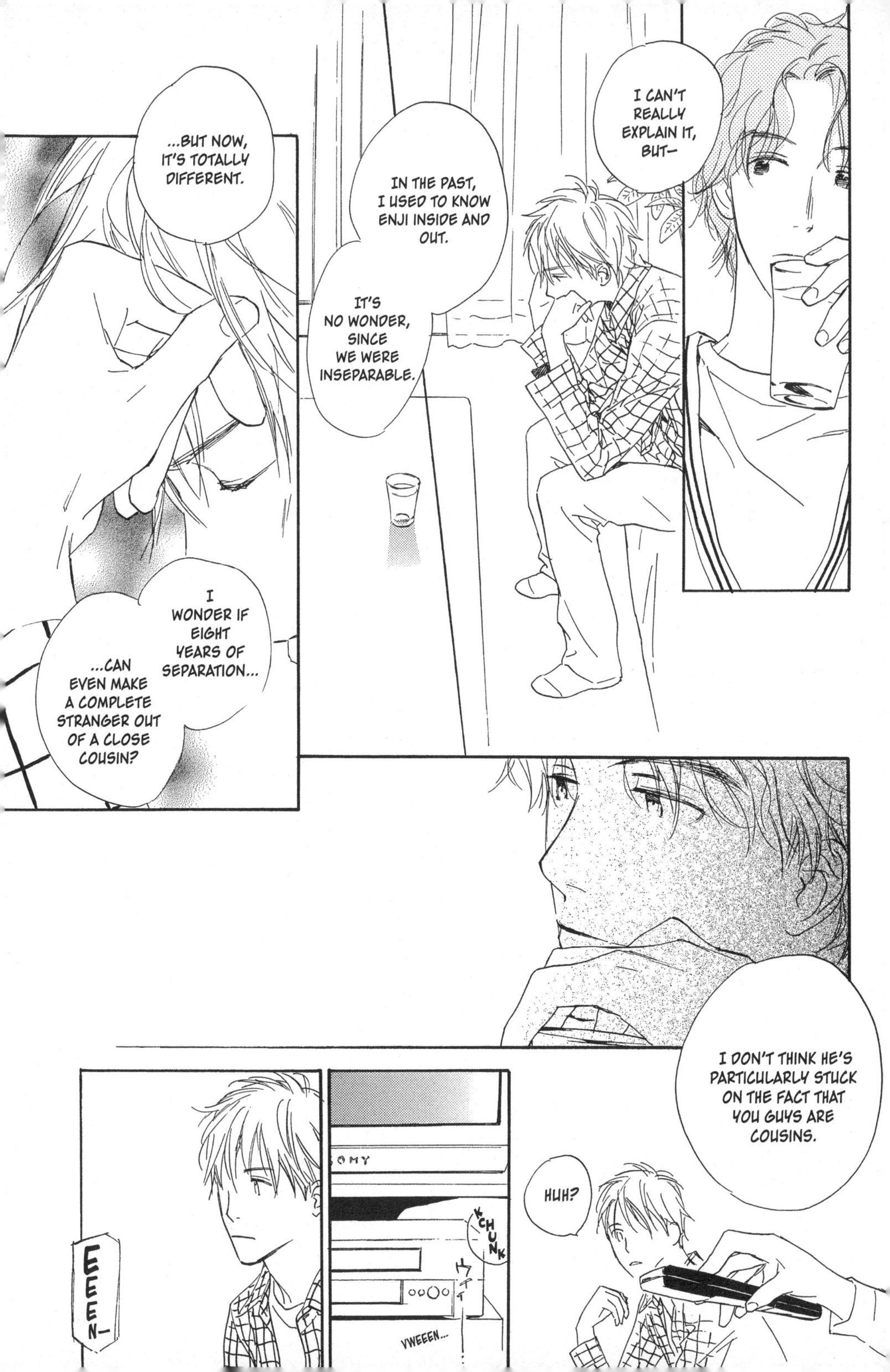
I CAN'T REALLY EXPLAIN IT, BUT—
IN THE PAST, I USED TO KNOW ENJI INSIDE AND OUT.
IT'S NO WONDER, SINCE WE WERE INSEPARABLE.
...BUT NOW, IT'S TOTALLY DIFFERENT.
I WONDER IF EIGHT YEARS OF SEPARATION...
...CAN EVEN MAKE A COMPLETE STRANGER OUT OF A CLOSE COUSIN?
I DON'T THINK HE'S PARTICULARLY STUCK ON THE FACT THAT YOU GUYS ARE COUSINS.
HUH?
KCHUNK
VWEEEN...
EEEEN—

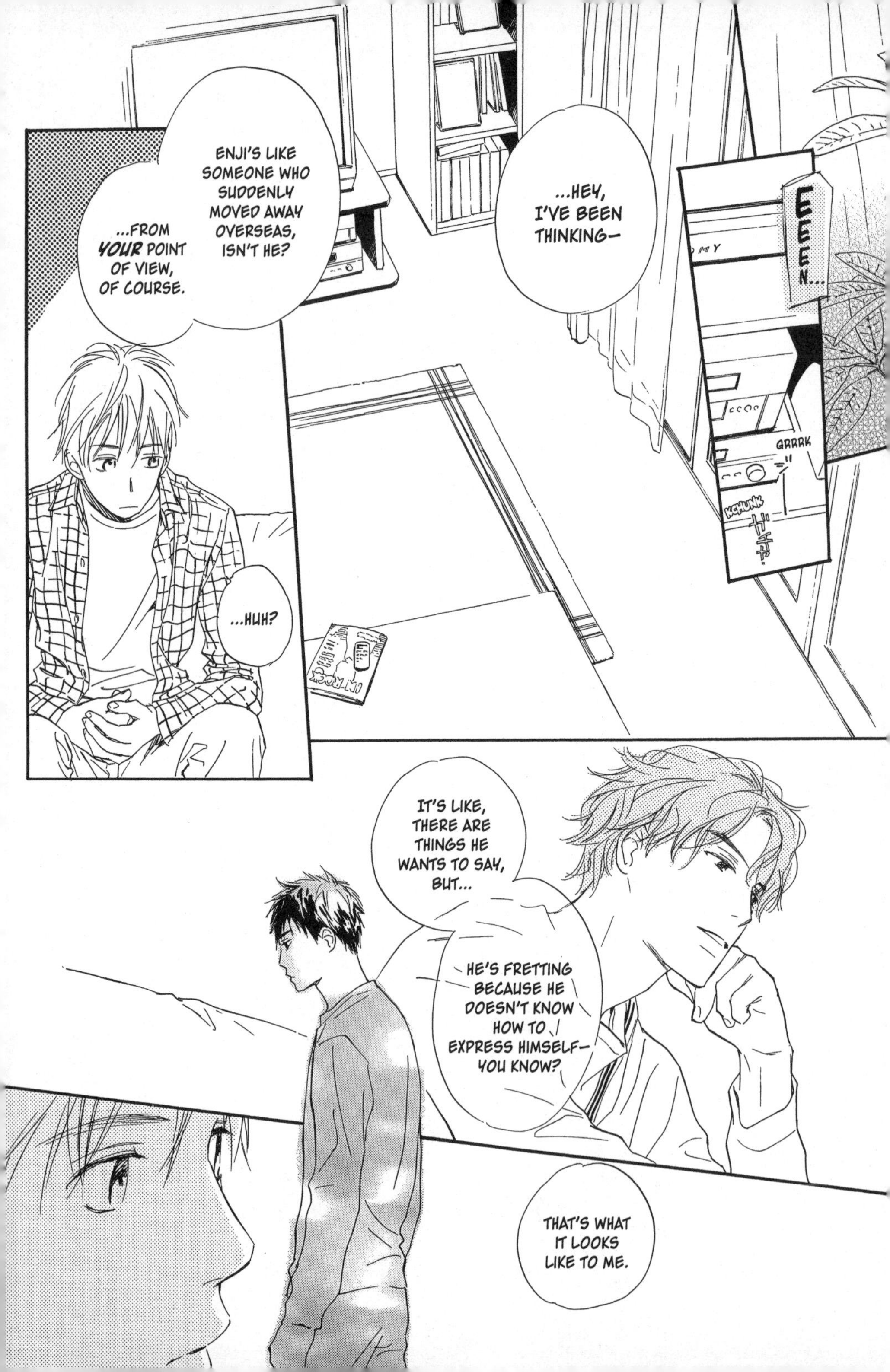
...HEY, I'VE BEEN THINKING—
EEEN...
GRRRK
KCHUNK
ENJI'S LIKE SOMEONE WHO SUDDENLY MOVED AWAY OVERSEAS, ISN'T HE?
...FROM YOUR POINT OF VIEW, OF COURSE.
...HUH?
IT'S LIKE, THERE ARE THINGS HE WANTS TO SAY, BUT...
HE'S FRETTING BECAUSE HE DOESN'T KNOW HOW TO EXPRESS HIMSELF— YOU KNOW?
THAT'S WHAT IT LOOKS LIKE TO ME.

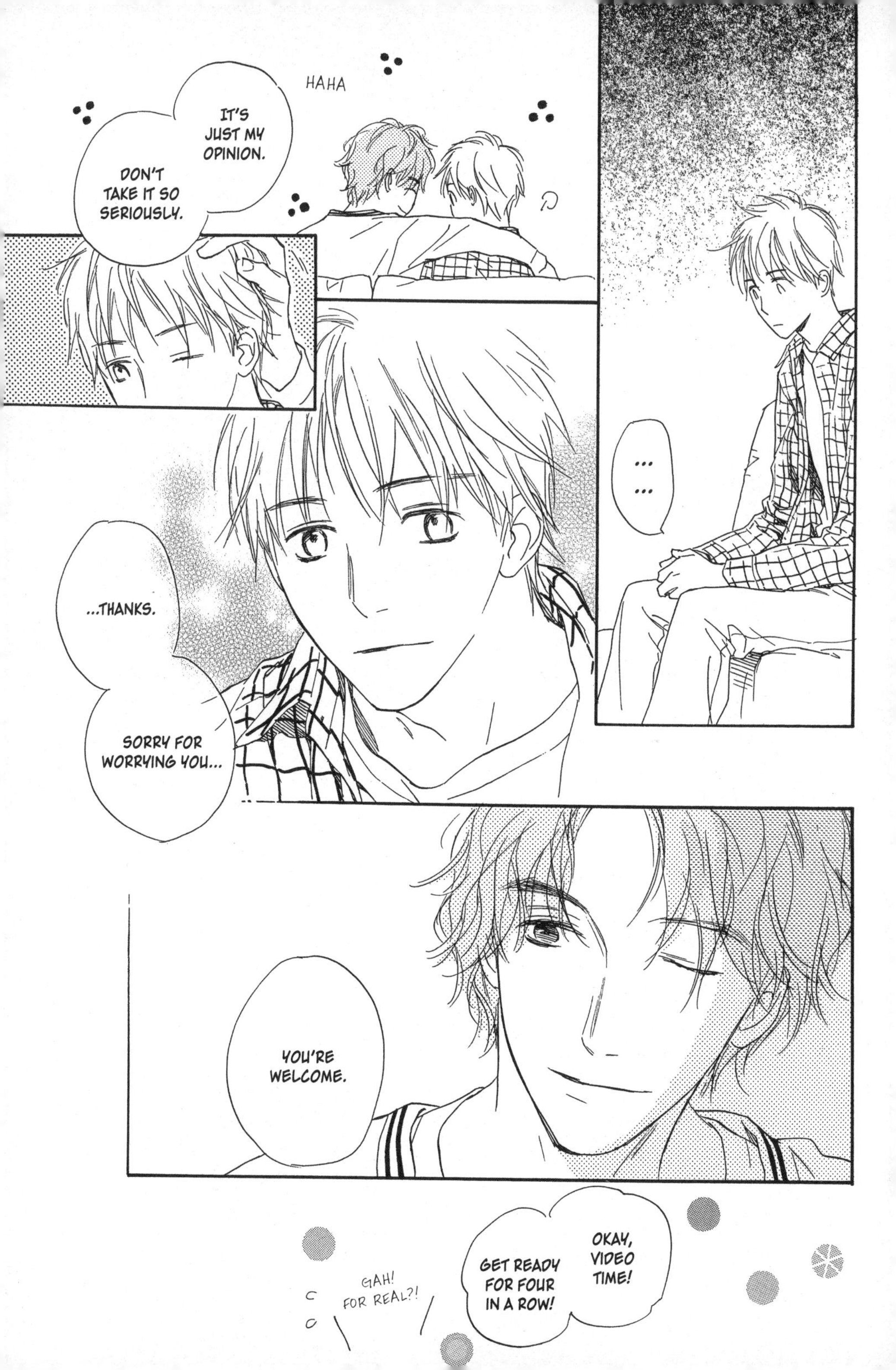

... ...
HAHA
IT'S JUST MY OPINION. DON'T TAKE IT SO SERIOUSLY.
...THANKS.
SORRY FOR WORRYING YOU...
YOU'RE WELCOME.
OKAY, VIDEO TIME! GET READY FOR FOUR IN A ROW!
GAH! FOR REAL?!

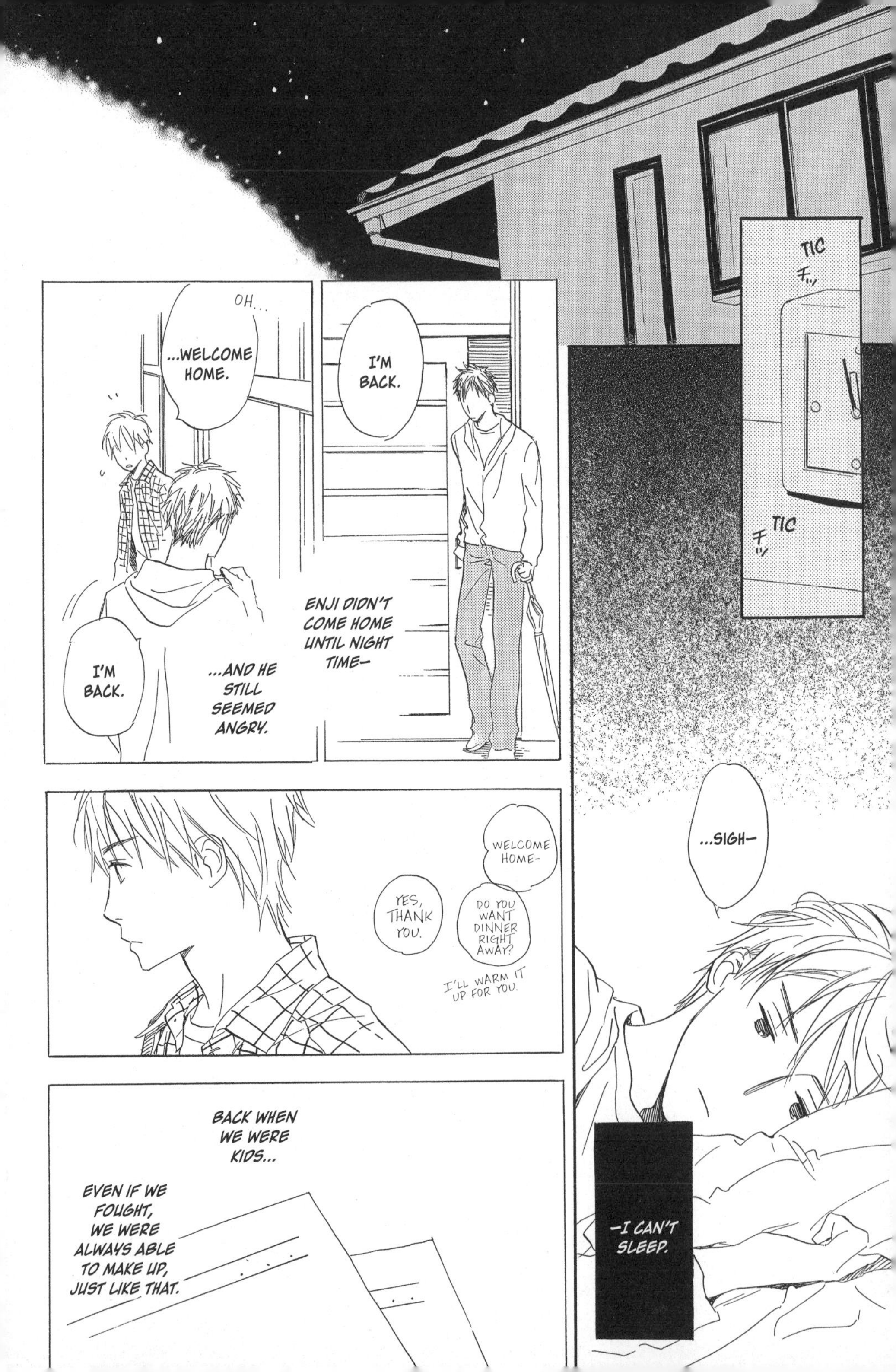
TIC
TIC
...SIGH—
—I CAN'T SLEEP.
I'M BACK.
ENJI DIDN'T COME HOME UNTIL NIGHT TIME—
OH...
...WELCOME HOME.
I'M BACK.
...AND HE STILL SEEMED ANGRY.
WELCOME HOME-
DO YOU WANT DINNER RIGHT AWAY?
I'LL WARM IT UP FOR YOU.
YES, THANK YOU.
BACK WHEN WE WERE KIDS...
EVEN IF WE FOUGHT, WE WERE ALWAYS ABLE TO MAKE UP, JUST LIKE THAT.

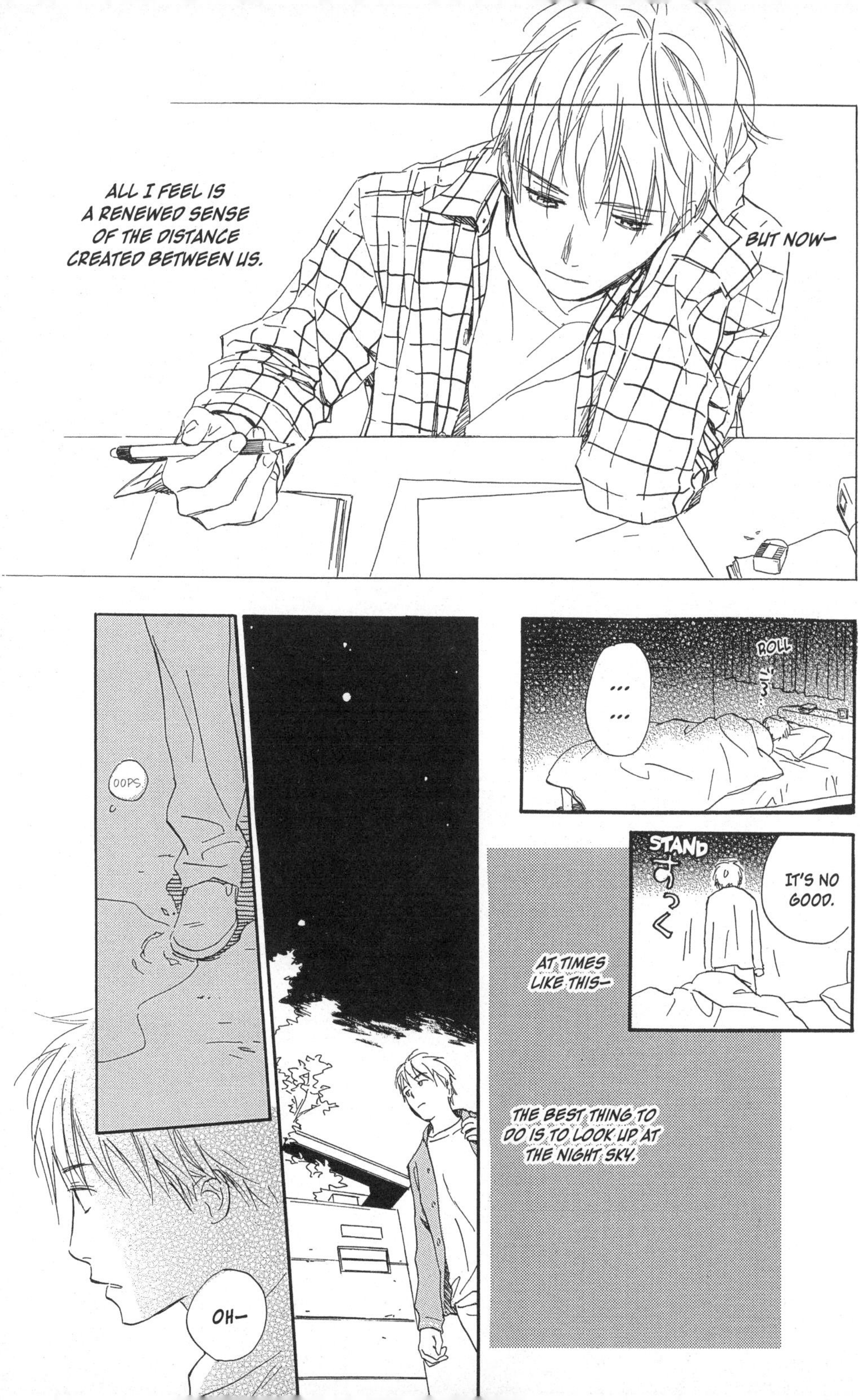
BUT NOW—
ALL I FEEL IS A RENEWED SENSE OF THE DISTANCE CREATED BETWEEN US.
ROLL
…
…
STAND
IT'S NO GOOD.
AT TIMES LIKE THIS—
THE BEST THING TO DO IS TO LOOK UP AT THE NIGHT SKY.
OOPS.
OH—

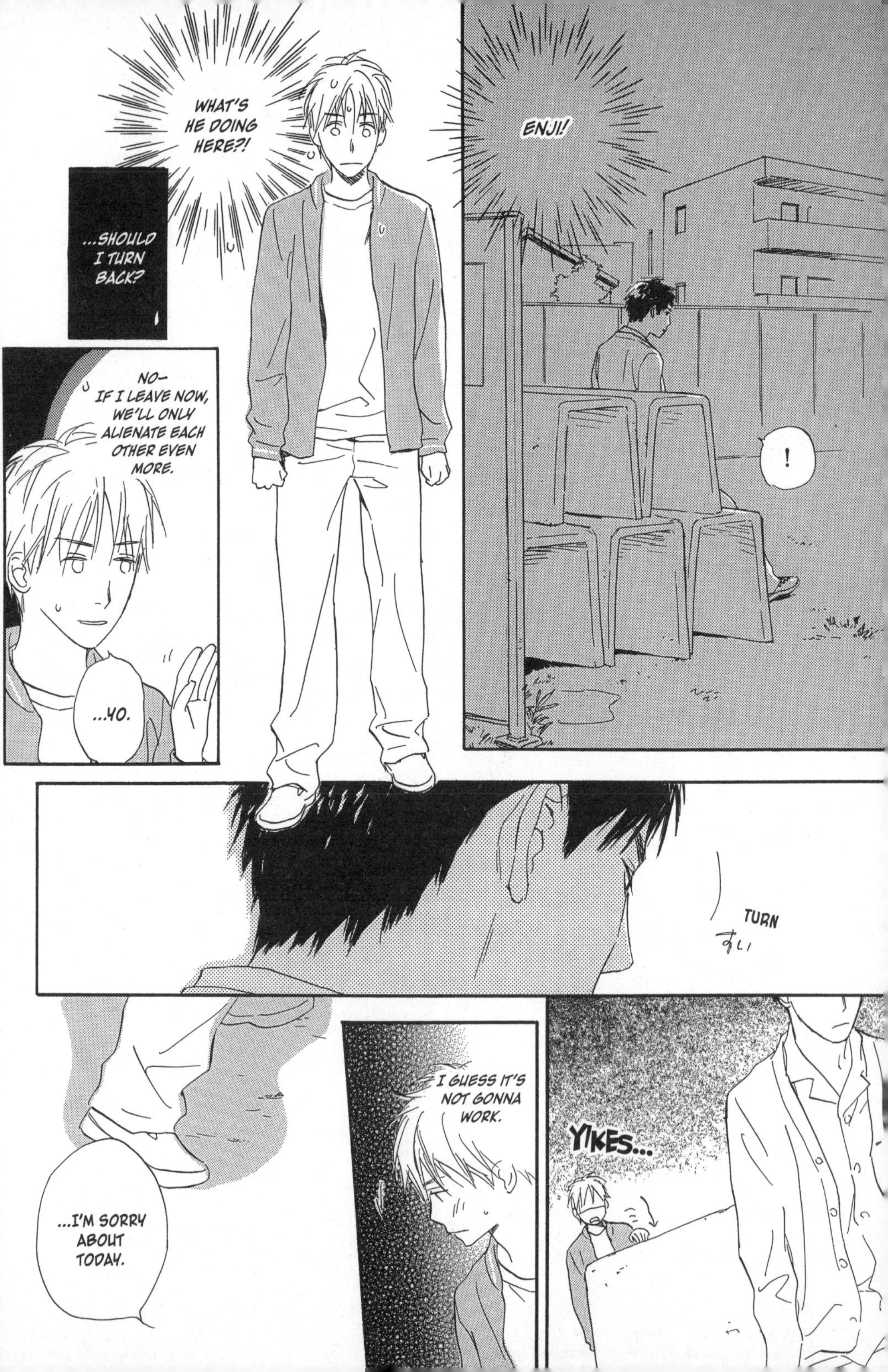
ENJI!
!
WHAT'S HE DOING HERE?!
...SHOULD I TURN BACK?
NO— IF I LEAVE NOW, WE'LL ONLY ALIENATE EACH OTHER EVEN MORE.
...YO.
TURN
すい
YIKES...
I GUESS IT'S NOT GONNA WORK.
...I'M SORRY ABOUT TODAY.

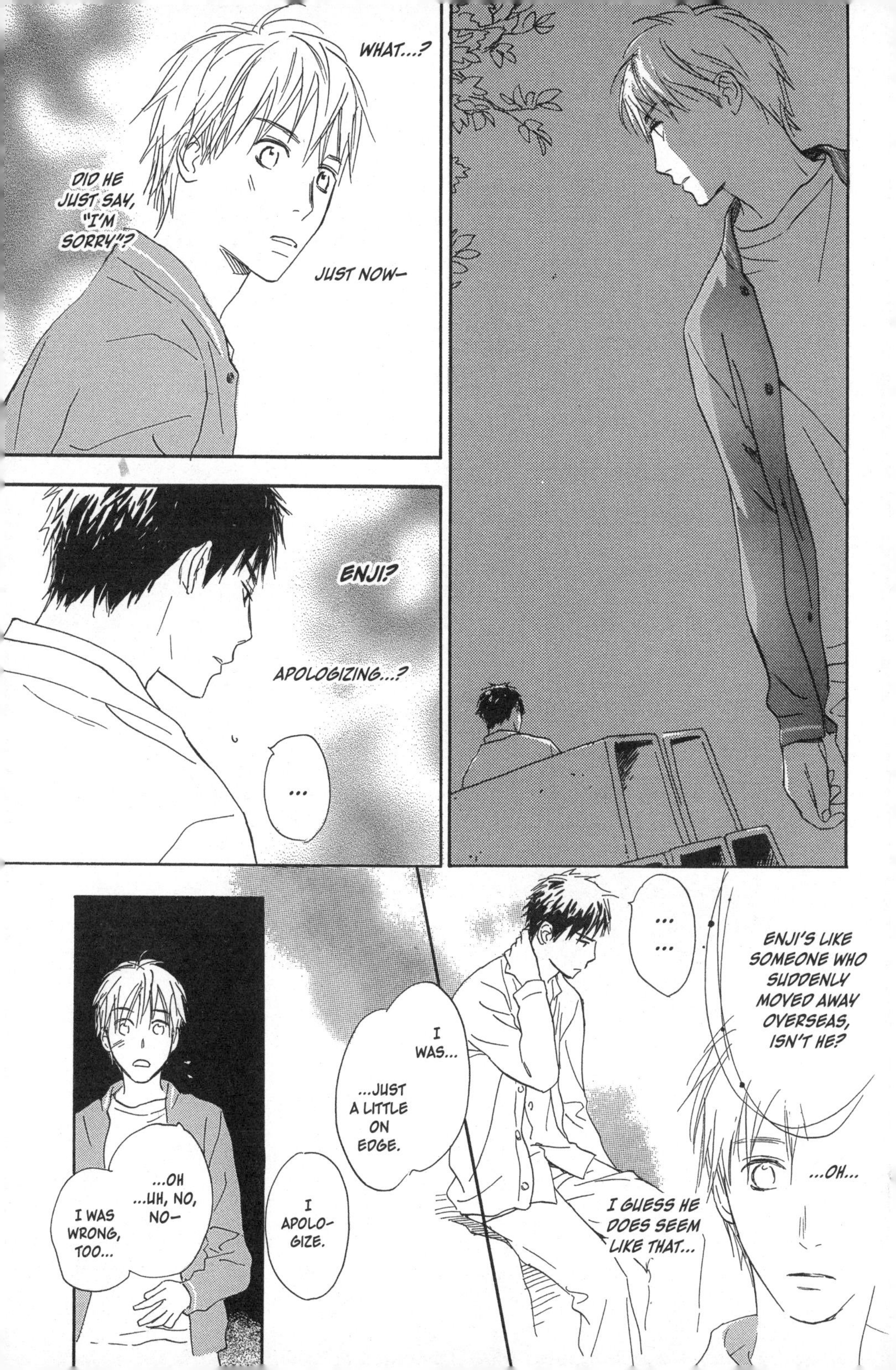
WHAT...?
DID HE JUST SAY, "I'M SORRY"?
JUST NOW—
ENJI?
APOLOGIZING...?
...
ENJI'S LIKE SOMEONE WHO SUDDENLY MOVED AWAY OVERSEAS, ISN'T HE?
...OH...
I GUESS HE DOES SEEM LIKE THAT...
... ...
I WAS...
...JUST A LITTLE ON EDGE.
I APOLOGIZE.
...OH ...UH, NO, NO—
I WAS WRONG, TOO...

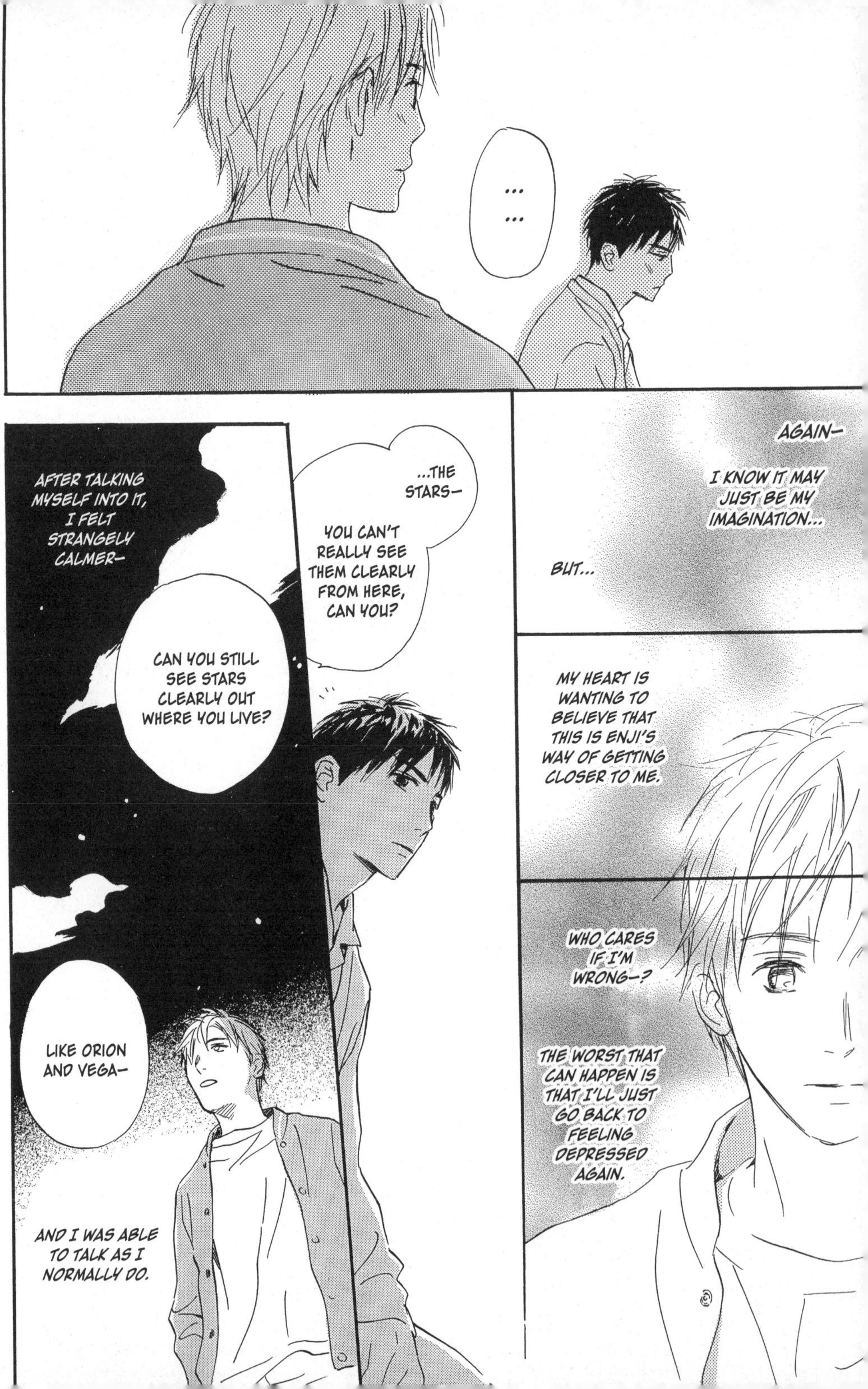
……
AGAIN—
I KNOW IT MAY JUST BE MY IMAGINATION...
BUT...
MY HEART IS WANTING TO BELIEVE THAT THIS IS ENJI'S WAY OF GETTING CLOSER TO ME.
WHO CARES IF I'M WRONG—?
THE WORST THAT CAN HAPPEN IS THAT I'LL JUST GO BACK TO FEELING DEPRESSED AGAIN.
...THE STARS—
YOU CAN'T REALLY SEE THEM CLEARLY FROM HERE, CAN YOU?
AFTER TALKING MYSELF INTO IT, I FELT STRANGELY CALMER—
CAN YOU STILL SEE STARS CLEARLY OUT WHERE YOU LIVE?
LIKE ORION AND VEGA—
AND I WAS ABLE TO TALK AS I NORMALLY DO.

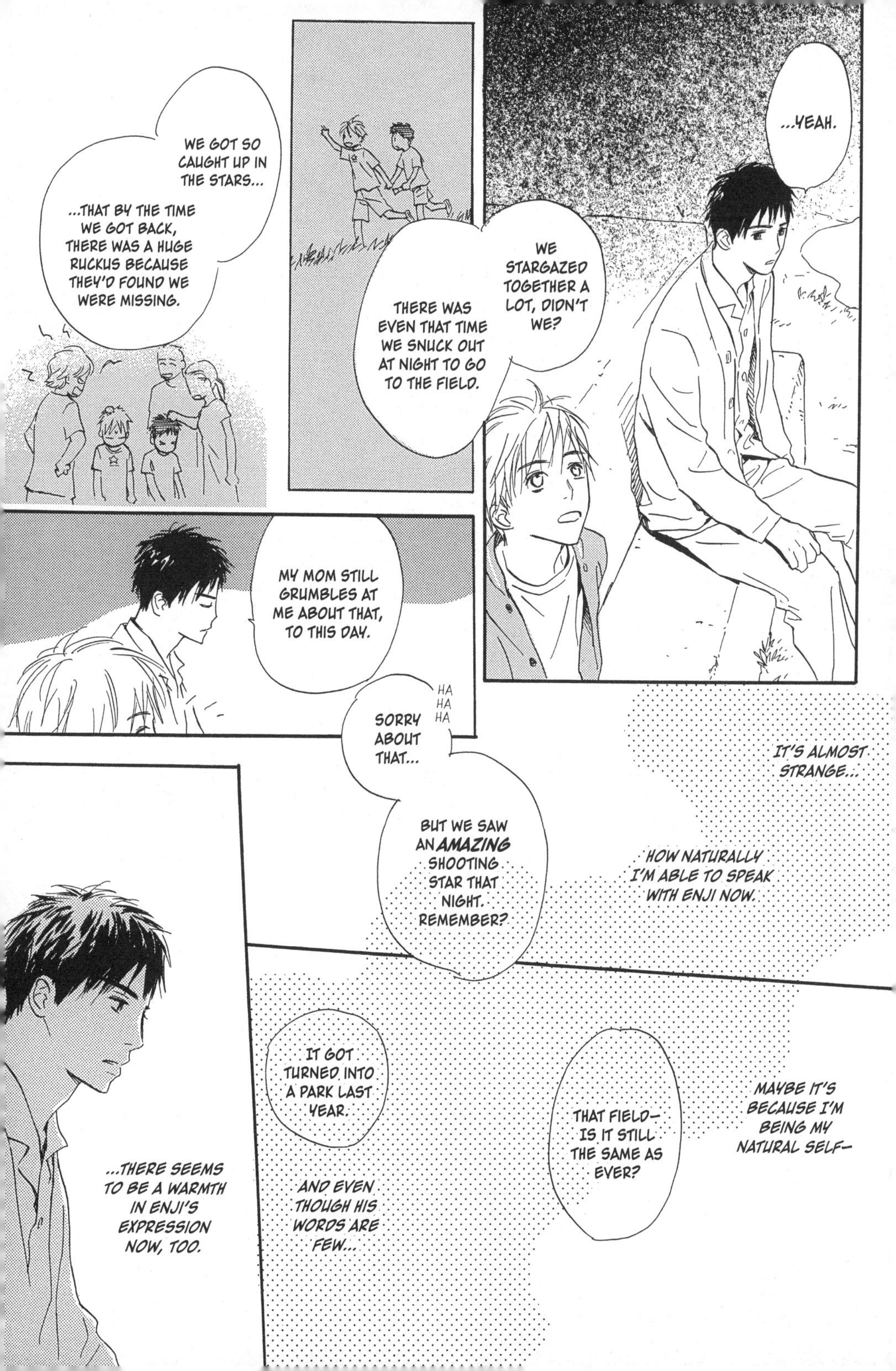
...YEAH.
WE STARGAZED TOGETHER A LOT, DIDN'T WE?
THERE WAS EVEN THAT TIME WE SNUCK OUT AT NIGHT TO GO TO THE FIELD.
WE GOT SO CAUGHT UP IN THE STARS...
...THAT BY THE TIME WE GOT BACK, THERE WAS A HUGE RUCKUS BECAUSE THEY'D FOUND WE WERE MISSING.
MY MOM STILL GRUMBLES AT ME ABOUT THAT, TO THIS DAY.
HA HA HA
SORRY ABOUT THAT...
BUT WE SAW AN ***AMAZING*** SHOOTING STAR THAT NIGHT. REMEMBER?
IT'S ALMOST STRANGE...
HOW NATURALLY I'M ABLE TO SPEAK WITH ENJI NOW.
MAYBE IT'S BECAUSE I'M BEING MY NATURAL SELF—
THAT FIELD— IS IT STILL THE SAME AS EVER?
IT GOT TURNED INTO A PARK LAST YEAR.
AND EVEN THOUGH HIS WORDS ARE FEW...
...THERE SEEMS TO BE A WARMTH IN ENJI'S EXPRESSION NOW, TOO.

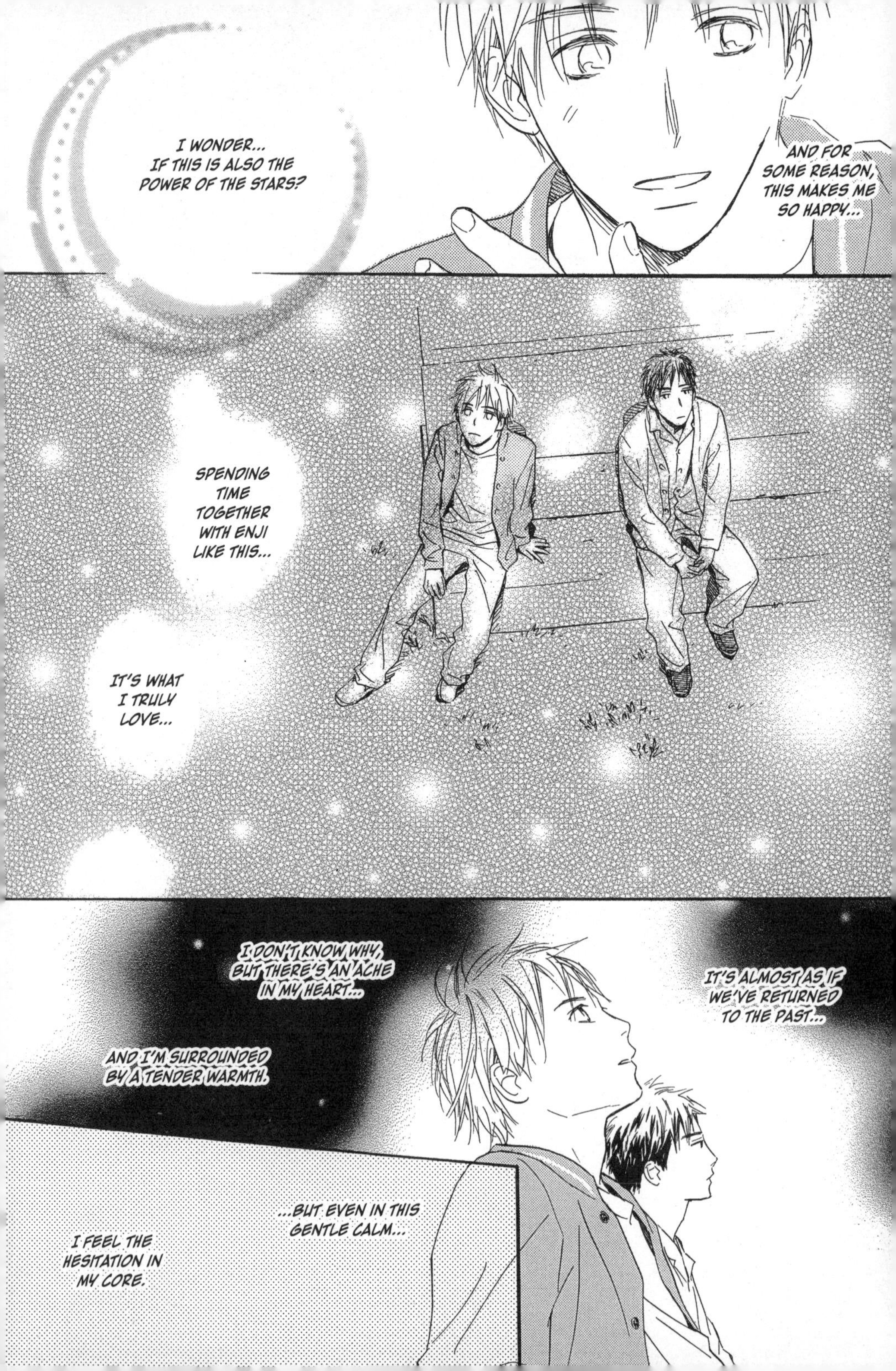
AND FOR SOME REASON, THIS MAKES ME SO HAPPY...
I WONDER... IF THIS IS ALSO THE POWER OF THE STARS?
SPENDING TIME TOGETHER WITH ENJI LIKE THIS...
IT'S WHAT I TRULY LOVE...
IT'S ALMOST AS IF WE'VE RETURNED TO THE PAST...
I DON'T KNOW WHY, BUT THERE'S AN ACHE IN MY HEART...
AND I'M SURROUNDED BY A TENDER WARMTH.
...BUT EVEN IN THIS GENTLE CALM...
I FEEL THE HESITATION IN MY CORE.

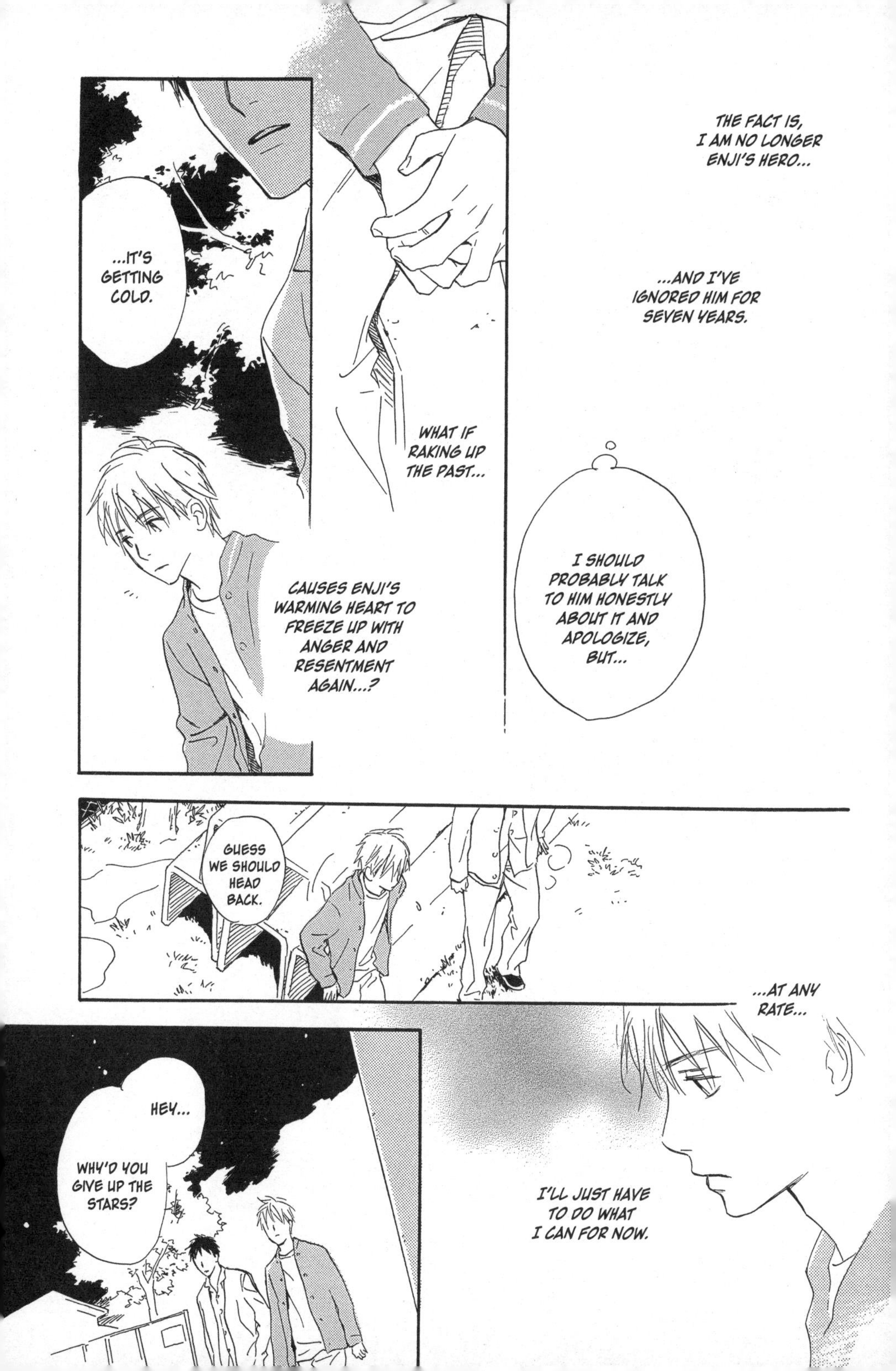

THE FACT IS, I AM NO LONGER ENJI'S HERO...
...AND I'VE IGNORED HIM FOR SEVEN YEARS.
I SHOULD PROBABLY TALK TO HIM HONESTLY ABOUT IT AND APOLOGIZE, BUT...
WHAT IF RAKING UP THE PAST...
CAUSES ENJI'S WARMING HEART TO FREEZE UP WITH ANGER AND RESENTMENT AGAIN...?
...IT'S GETTING COLD.
GUESS WE SHOULD HEAD BACK.
...AT ANY RATE...
I'LL JUST HAVE TO DO WHAT I CAN FOR NOW.
HEY...
WHY'D YOU GIVE UP THE STARS?

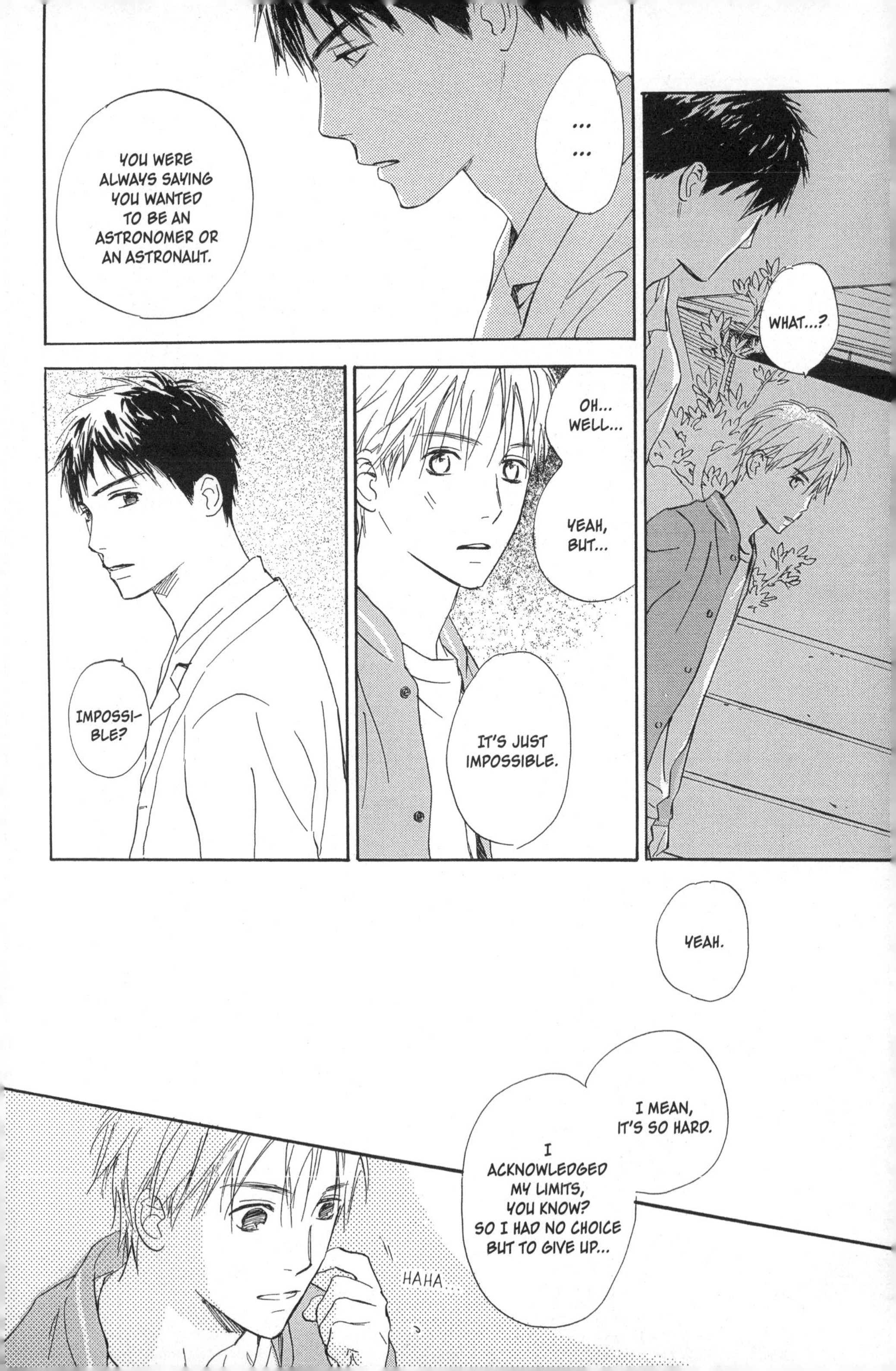

...
...
YOU WERE ALWAYS SAYING YOU WANTED TO BE AN ASTRONOMER OR AN ASTRONAUT.
WHAT...?
OH... WELL...
YEAH, BUT...
IT'S JUST IMPOSSIBLE.
IMPOSSI-BLE?
YEAH.
I MEAN, IT'S SO HARD.
I ACKNOWLEDGED MY LIMITS, YOU KNOW? SO I HAD NO CHOICE BUT TO GIVE UP...
HAHA

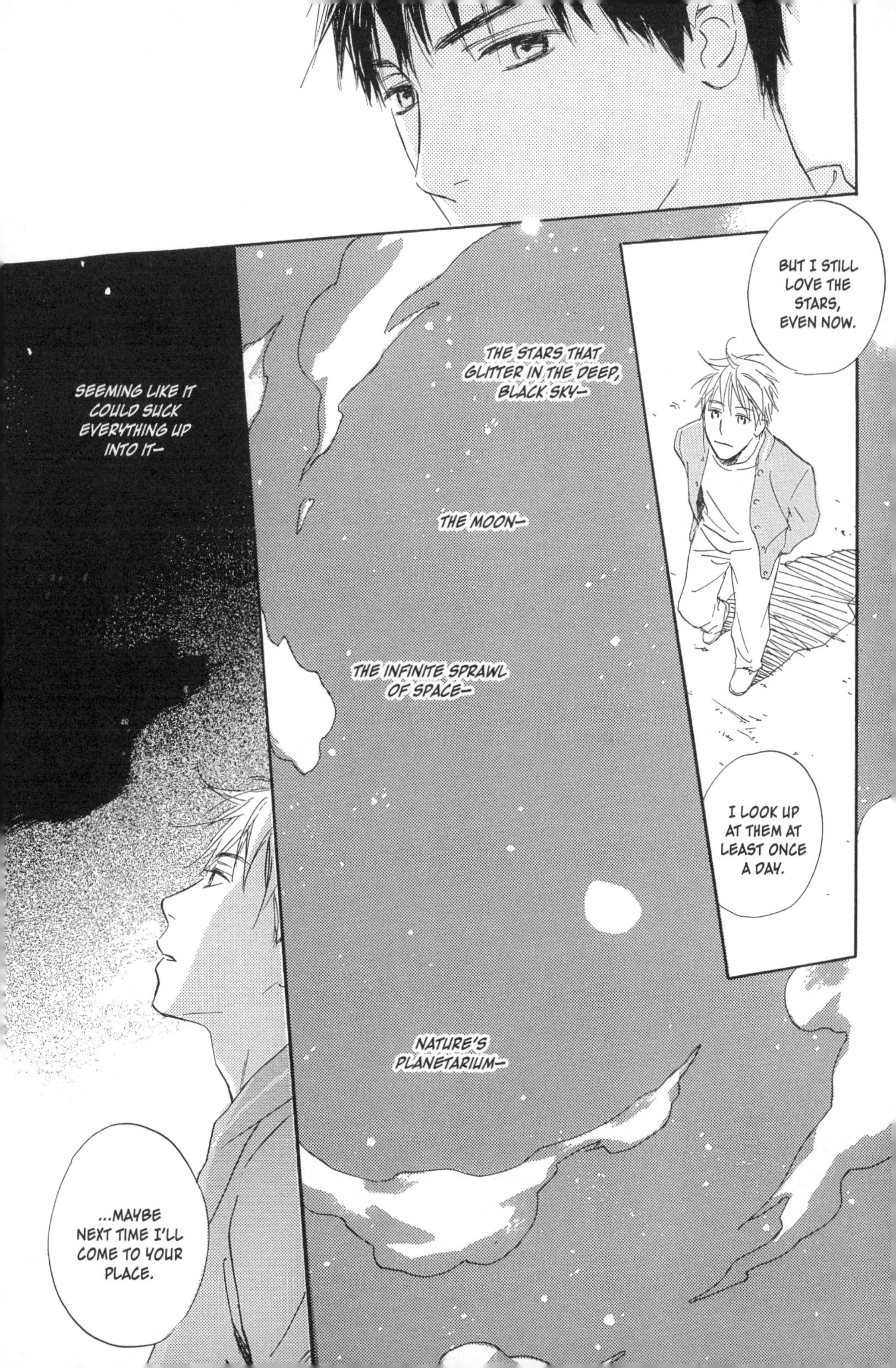
BUT I STILL LOVE THE STARS, EVEN NOW.
I LOOK UP AT THEM AT LEAST ONCE A DAY.
THE STARS THAT GLITTER IN THE DEEP, BLACK SKY—
THE MOON—
THE INFINITE SPRAWL OF SPACE—
NATURE'S PLANETARIUM—
SEEMING LIKE IT COULD SUCK EVERYTHING UP INTO IT—
...MAYBE NEXT TIME I'LL COME TO YOUR PLACE.

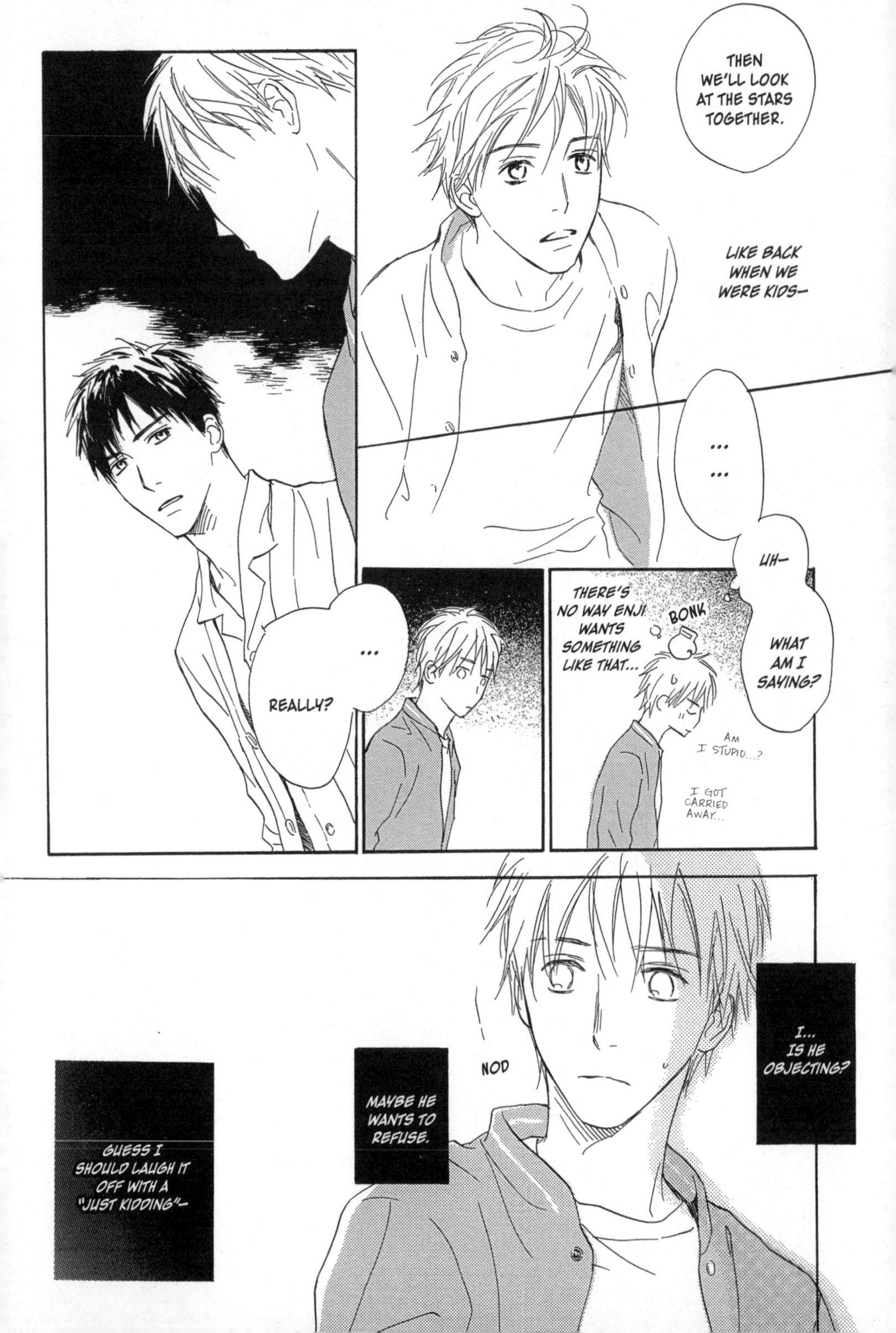
THEN WE'LL LOOK AT THE STARS TOGETHER.
LIKE BACK WHEN WE WERE KIDS—
... ...
UH—
WHAT AM I SAYING?
THERE'S NO WAY ENJI WANTS SOMETHING LIKE THAT...
BONK
AM I STUPID...?
I GOT CARRIED AWAY...
...
REALLY?
I... IS HE OBJECTING?
NOD
MAYBE HE WANTS TO REFUSE.
GUESS I SHOULD LAUGH IT OFF WITH A "JUST KIDDING"—

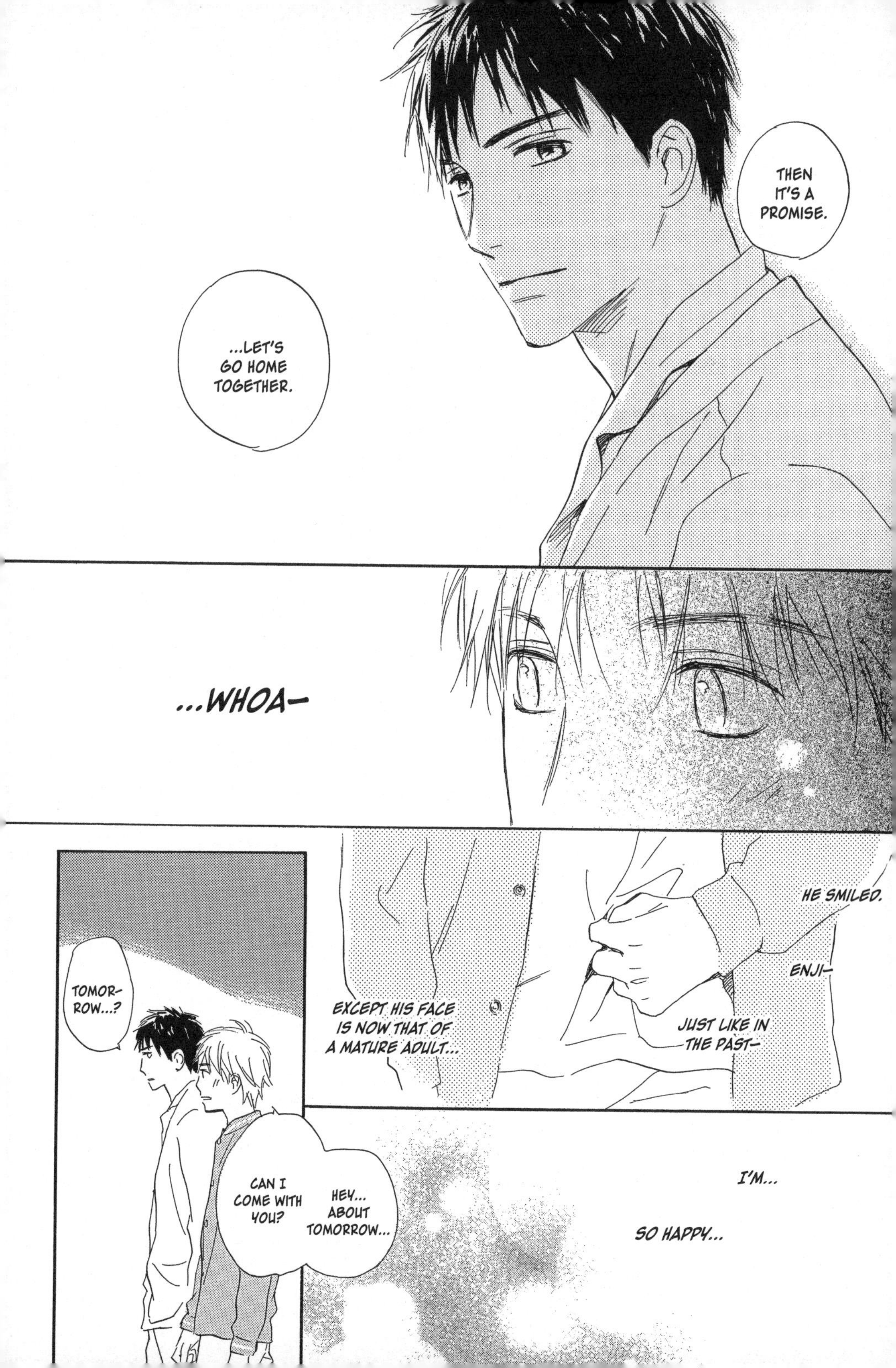

THEN IT'S A PROMISE.
...LET'S GO HOME TOGETHER.
...WHOA—
HE SMILED.
ENJI—
JUST LIKE IN THE PAST—
EXCEPT HIS FACE IS NOW THAT OF A MATURE ADULT...
I'M...
SO HAPPY...
HEY... ABOUT TOMORROW...
CAN I COME WITH YOU?
TOMOR-ROW...?

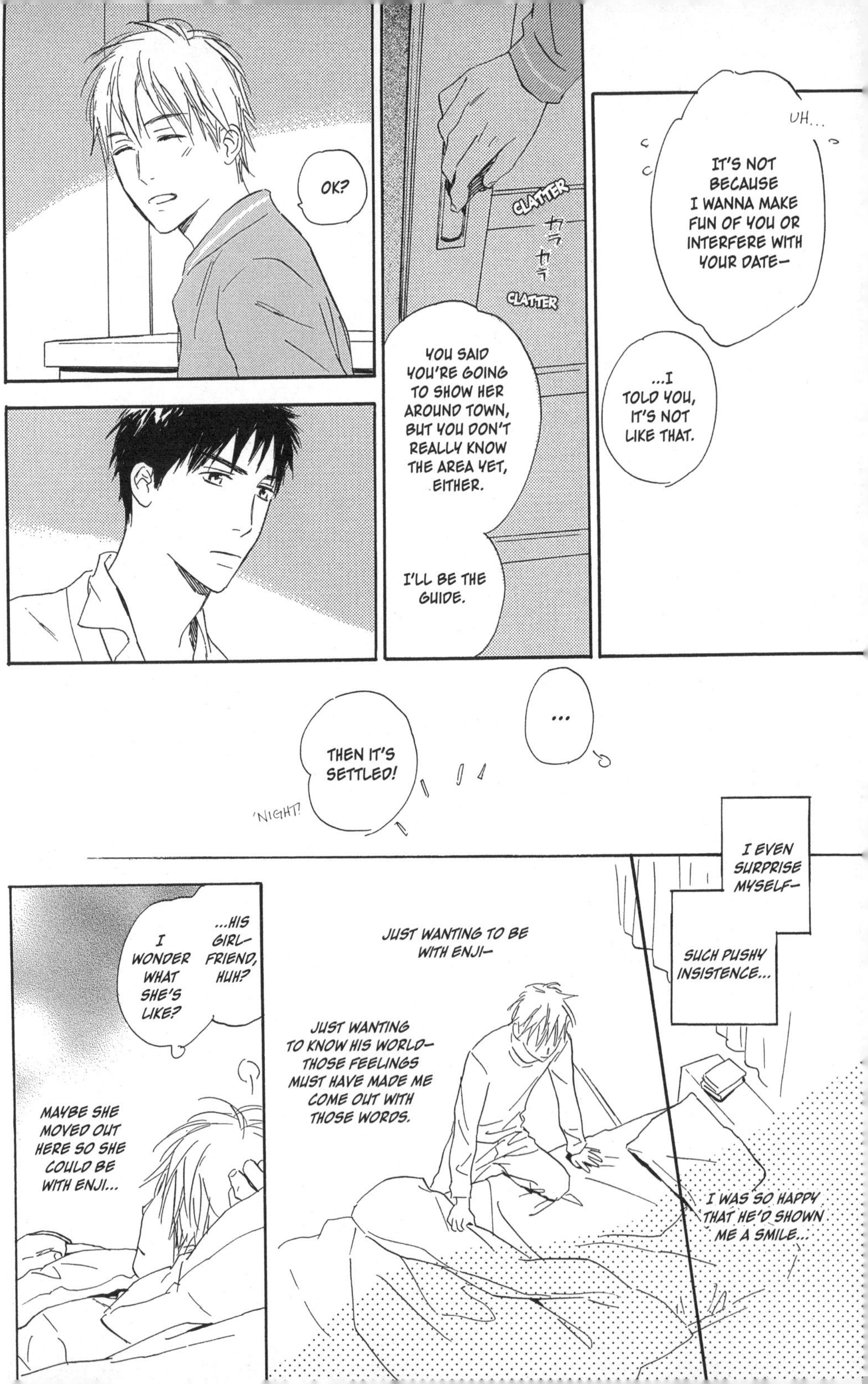
UH...
IT'S NOT BECAUSE I WANNA MAKE FUN OF YOU OR INTERFERE WITH YOUR DATE—
...I TOLD YOU, IT'S NOT LIKE THAT.
CLATTER
カラ
カラ
CLATTER
YOU SAID YOU'RE GOING TO SHOW HER AROUND TOWN, BUT YOU DON'T REALLY KNOW THE AREA YET, EITHER.
I'LL BE THE GUIDE.
OK?
...
THEN IT'S SETTLED!
'NIGHT!
I EVEN SURPRISE MYSELF—
SUCH PUSHY INSISTENCE...
JUST WANTING TO BE WITH ENJI—
JUST WANTING TO KNOW HIS WORLD— THOSE FEELINGS MUST HAVE MADE ME COME OUT WITH THOSE WORDS.
I WAS SO HAPPY THAT HE'D SHOWN ME A SMILE...
...HIS GIRLFRIEND, HUH?
I WONDER WHAT SHE'S LIKE?
MAYBE SHE MOVED OUT HERE SO SHE COULD BE WITH ENJI...

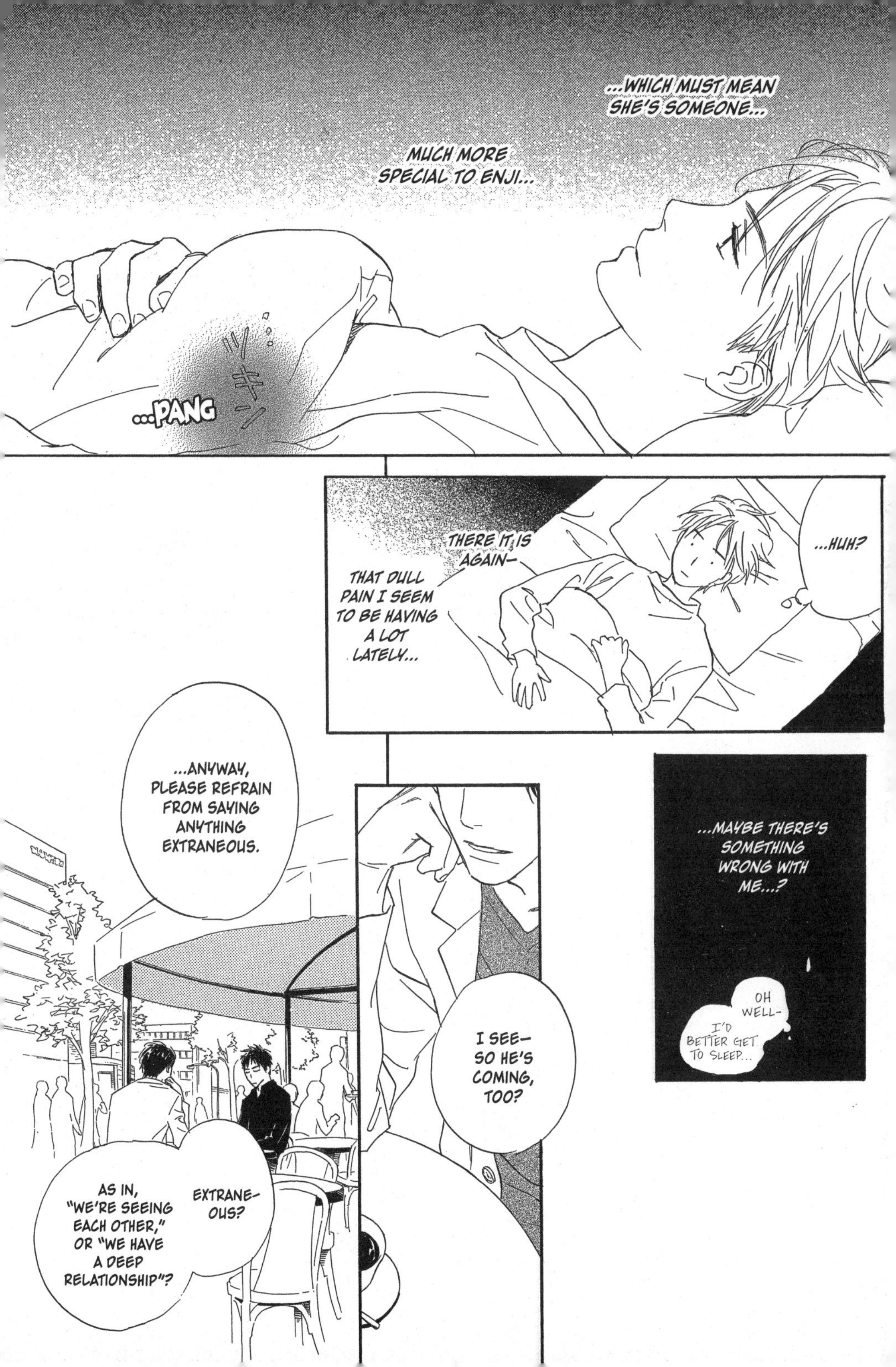

...WHICH MUST MEAN SHE'S SOMEONE...
MUCH MORE SPECIAL TO ENJI...
...PANG
...HUH?
THERE IT IS AGAIN—
THAT DULL PAIN I SEEM TO BE HAVING A LOT LATELY...
...MAYBE THERE'S SOMETHING WRONG WITH ME...?
OH WELL—
I'D BETTER GET TO SLEEP...
I SEE— SO HE'S COMING, TOO?
...ANYWAY, PLEASE REFRAIN FROM SAYING ANYTHING EXTRANEOUS.
EXTRANE-OUS?
AS IN, "WE'RE SEEING EACH OTHER," OR "WE HAVE A DEEP RELATIONSHIP"?

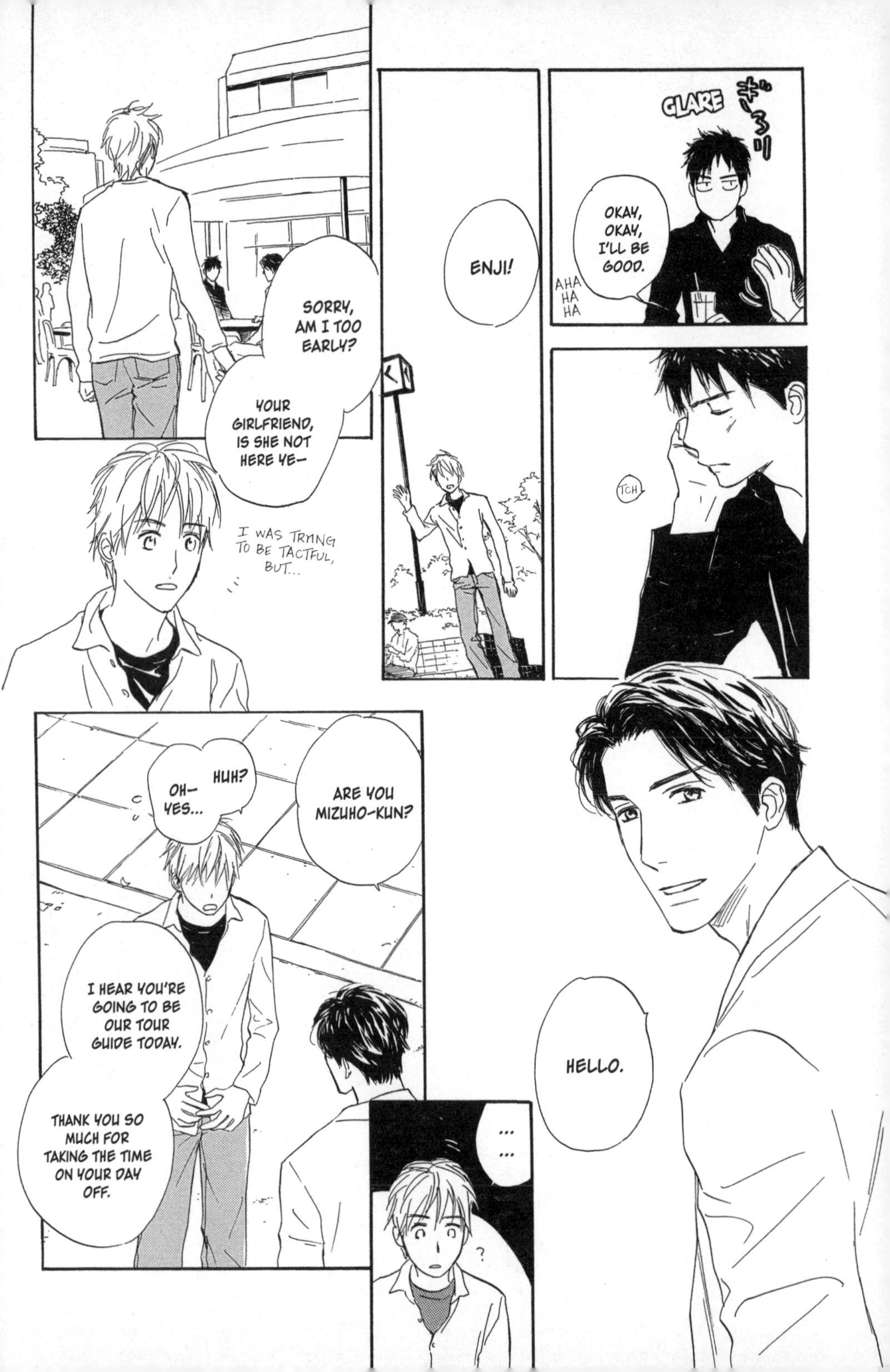
GLARE
ぎろり
OKAY, OKAY, I'LL BE GOOD.
AHA HA HA
TCH
ENJI!
SORRY, AM I TOO EARLY?
YOUR GIRLFRIEND, IS SHE NOT HERE YE—
I WAS TRYING TO BE TACTFUL, BUT...
HELLO.
ARE YOU MIZUHO-KUN?
HUH?
OH— YES...
I HEAR YOU'RE GOING TO BE OUR TOUR GUIDE TODAY.
THANK YOU SO MUCH FOR TAKING THE TIME ON YOUR DAY OFF.
...
...
?

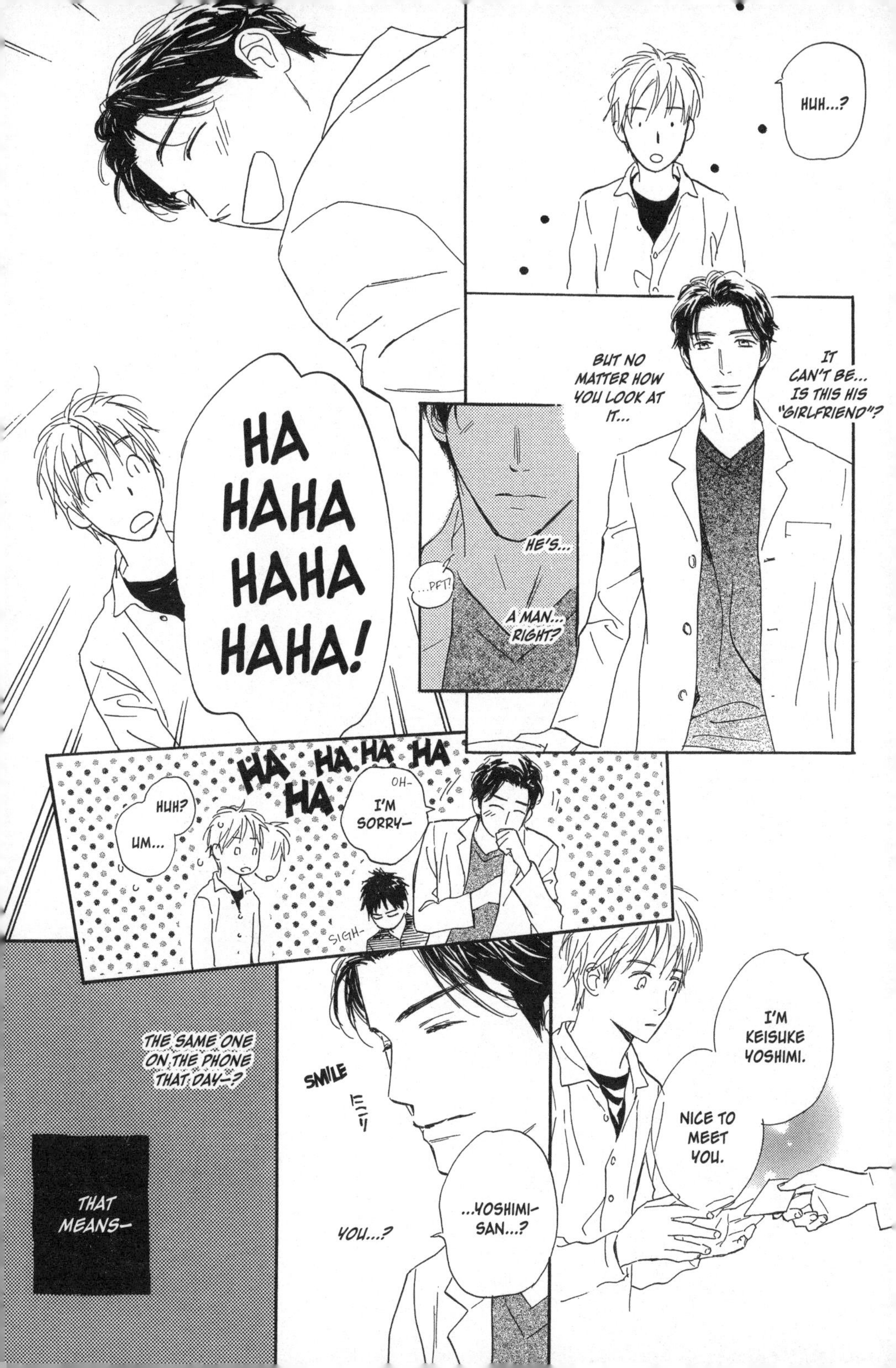
HUH...?
IT CAN'T BE... IS THIS HIS "GIRLFRIEND"?
BUT NO MATTER HOW YOU LOOK AT IT...
HE'S...
A MAN... RIGHT?
...PFT!
HA HAHA HAHA HAHA!
HA HA HA HA HA
OH-
I'M SORRY-
HUH?
UM...
SIGH-
I'M KEISUKE YOSHIMI.
NICE TO MEET YOU.
SMILE
...YOSHIMI-SAN...?
YOU...?
THE SAME ONE ON THE PHONE THAT DAY-?
THAT MEANS-

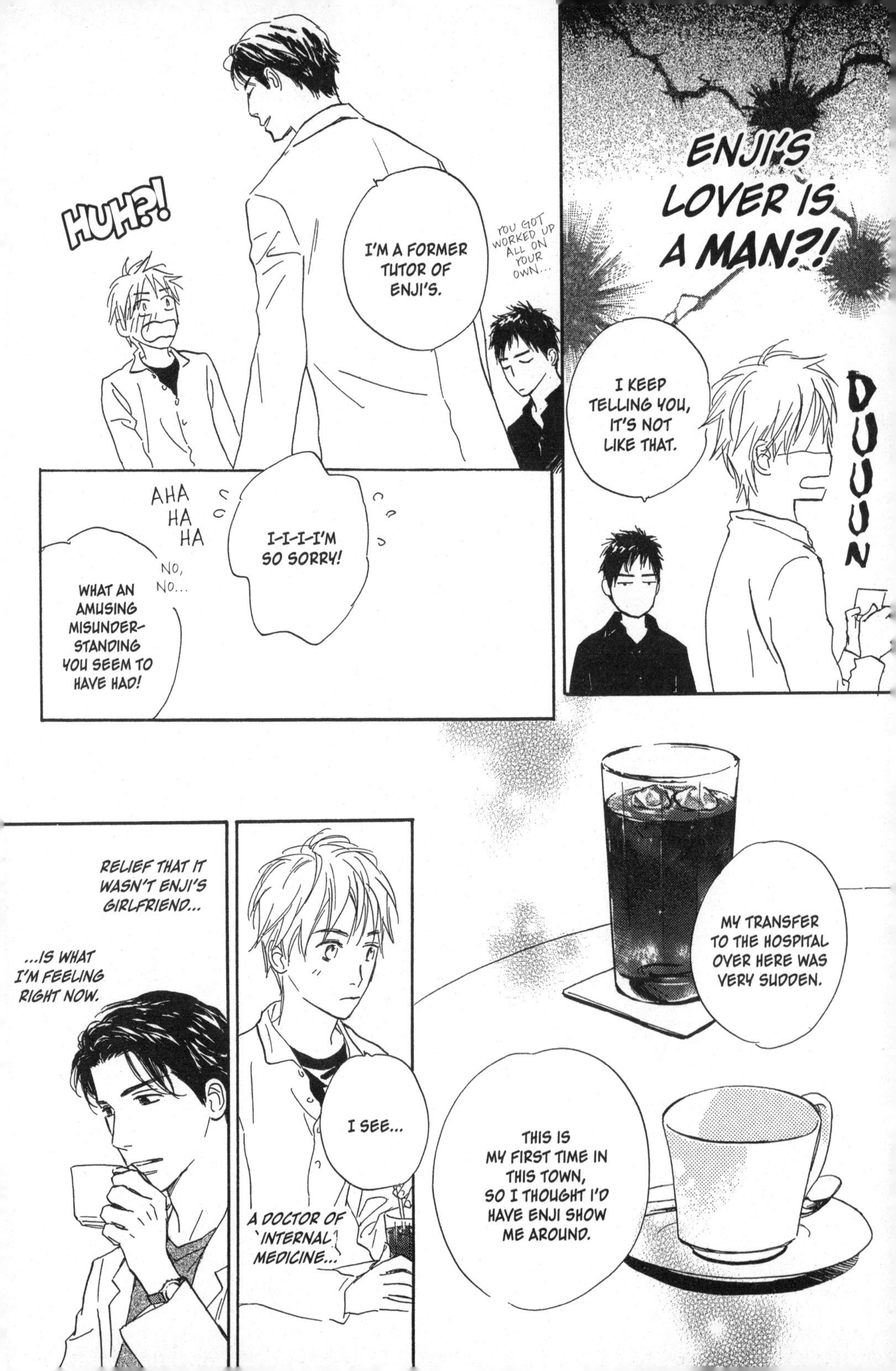
ENJI'S LOVER IS A MAN?!
DUUUN
I KEEP TELLING YOU, IT'S NOT LIKE THAT.
HUH?!
I'M A FORMER TUTOR OF ENJI'S.
YOU GOT WORKED UP ALL ON YOUR OWN...
I-I-I-I'M SO SORRY!
AHA HA HA
NO, NO...
WHAT AN AMUSING MISUNDERSTANDING YOU SEEM TO HAVE HAD!
MY TRANSFER TO THE HOSPITAL OVER HERE WAS VERY SUDDEN.
THIS IS MY FIRST TIME IN THIS TOWN, SO I THOUGHT I'D HAVE ENJI SHOW ME AROUND.
I SEE...
A DOCTOR OF `INTERNAL' MEDICINE...
RELIEF THAT IT WASN'T ENJI'S GIRLFRIEND...
...IS WHAT I'M FEELING RIGHT NOW.

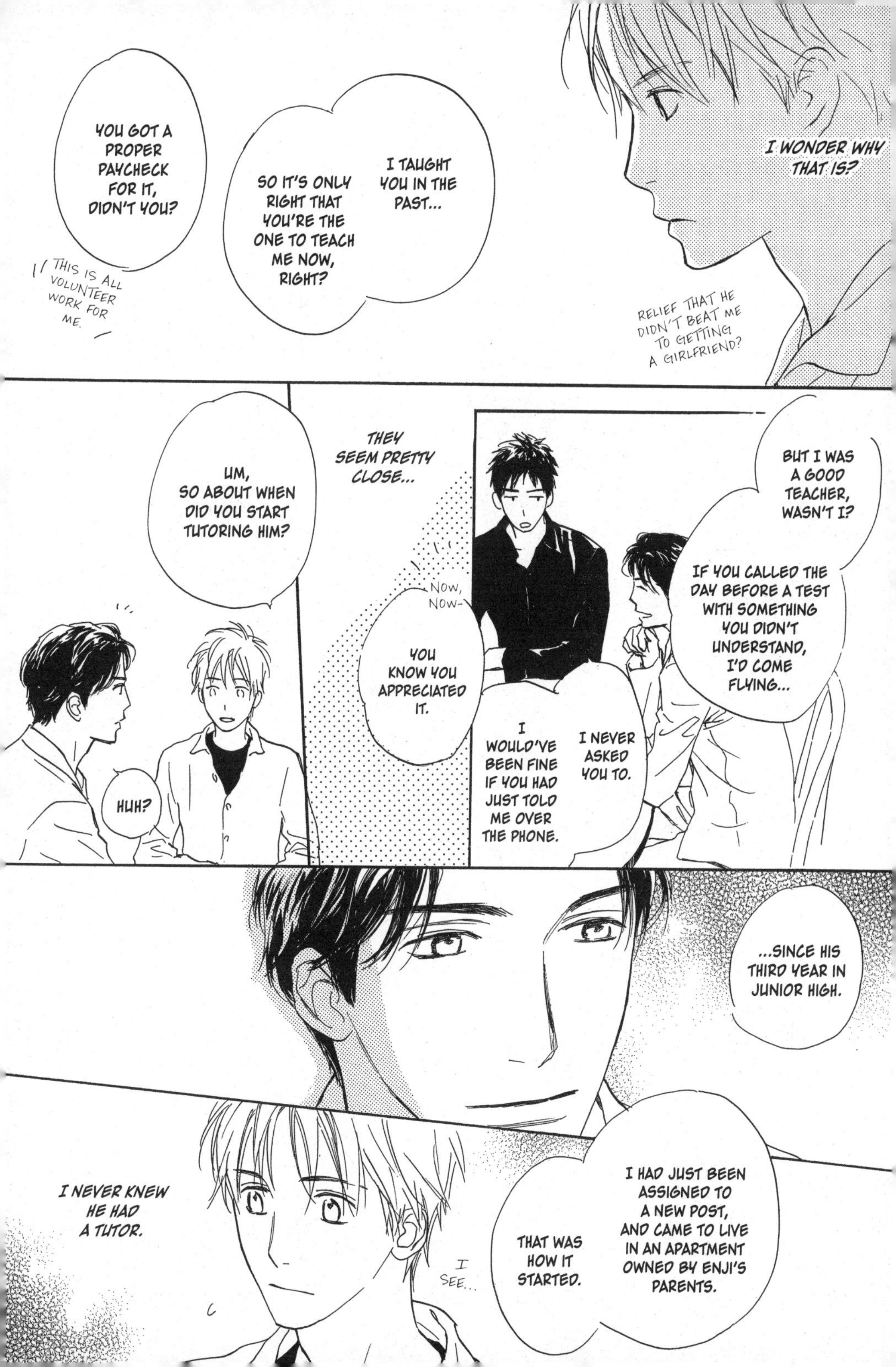
I WONDER WHY THAT IS?
RELIEF THAT HE DIDN'T BEAT ME TO GETTING A GIRLFRIEND?
I TAUGHT YOU IN THE PAST...
SO IT'S ONLY RIGHT THAT YOU'RE THE ONE TO TEACH ME NOW, RIGHT?
YOU GOT A PROPER PAYCHECK FOR IT, DIDN'T YOU?
THIS IS ALL VOLUNTEER WORK FOR ME.
BUT I WAS A GOOD TEACHER, WASN'T I?
IF YOU CALLED THE DAY BEFORE A TEST WITH SOMETHING YOU DIDN'T UNDERSTAND, I'D COME FLYING...
I NEVER ASKED YOU TO.
I WOULD'VE BEEN FINE IF YOU HAD JUST TOLD ME OVER THE PHONE.
THEY SEEM PRETTY CLOSE...
NOW, NOW-
YOU KNOW YOU APPRECIATED IT.
UM, SO ABOUT WHEN DID YOU START TUTORING HIM?
HUH?
...SINCE HIS THIRD YEAR IN JUNIOR HIGH.
I HAD JUST BEEN ASSIGNED TO A NEW POST, AND CAME TO LIVE IN AN APARTMENT OWNED BY ENJI'S PARENTS.
THAT WAS HOW IT STARTED.
I SEE...
I NEVER KNEW HE HAD A TUTOR.

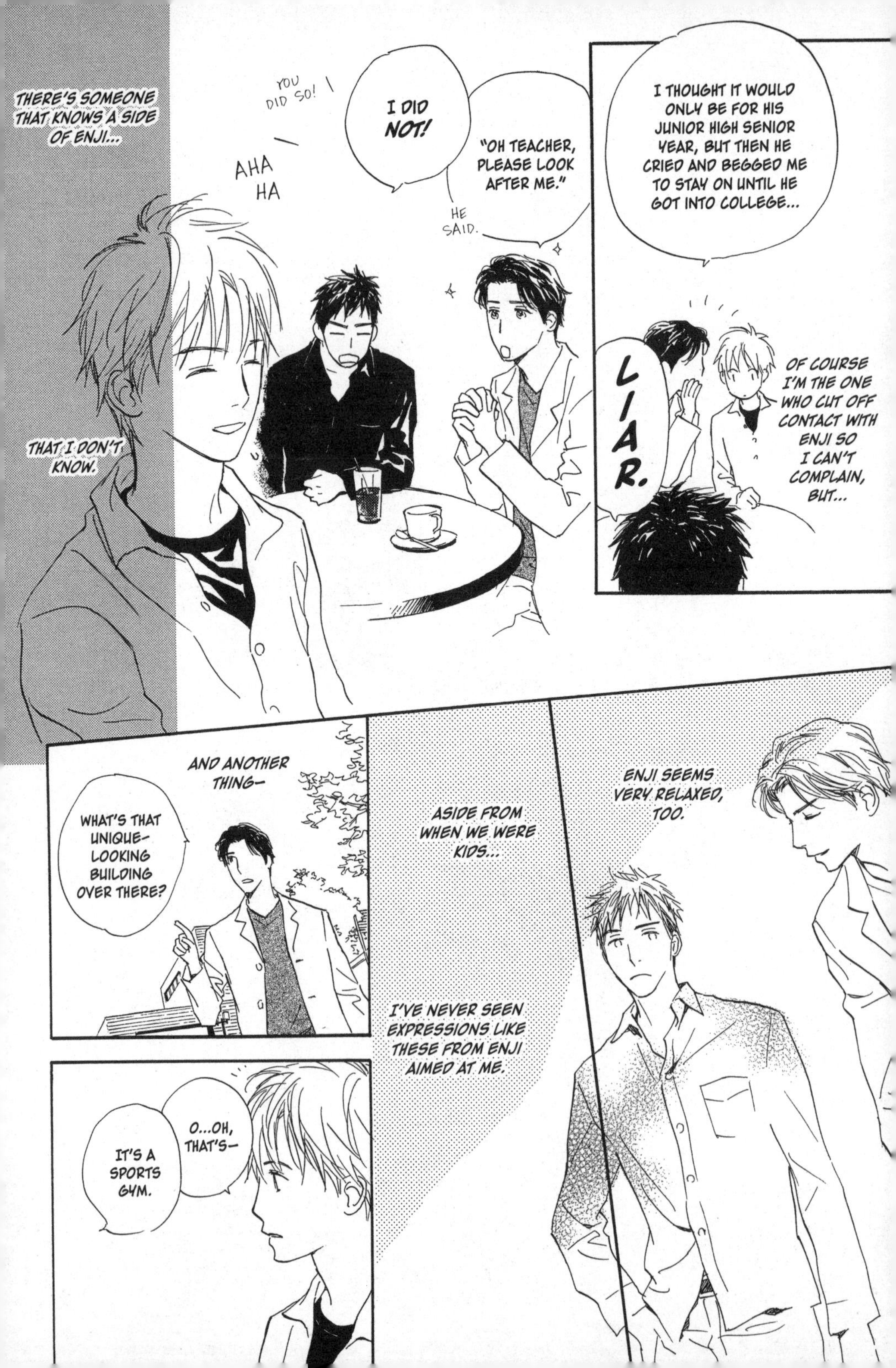
I THOUGHT IT WOULD ONLY BE FOR HIS JUNIOR HIGH SENIOR YEAR, BUT THEN HE CRIED AND BEGGED ME TO STAY ON UNTIL HE GOT INTO COLLEGE...
OF COURSE I'M THE ONE WHO CUT OFF CONTACT WITH ENJI SO I CAN'T COMPLAIN, BUT...
LIAR.
"OH TEACHER, PLEASE LOOK AFTER ME."
HE SAID.
I DID NOT!
YOU DID SO!
AHA HA
THERE'S SOMEONE THAT KNOWS A SIDE OF ENJI...
THAT I DON'T KNOW.
ENJI SEEMS VERY RELAXED, TOO.
ASIDE FROM WHEN WE WERE KIDS...
I'VE NEVER SEEN EXPRESSIONS LIKE THESE FROM ENJI AIMED AT ME.
AND ANOTHER THING—
WHAT'S THAT UNIQUE-LOOKING BUILDING OVER THERE?
O...OH, THAT'S—
IT'S A SPORTS GYM.

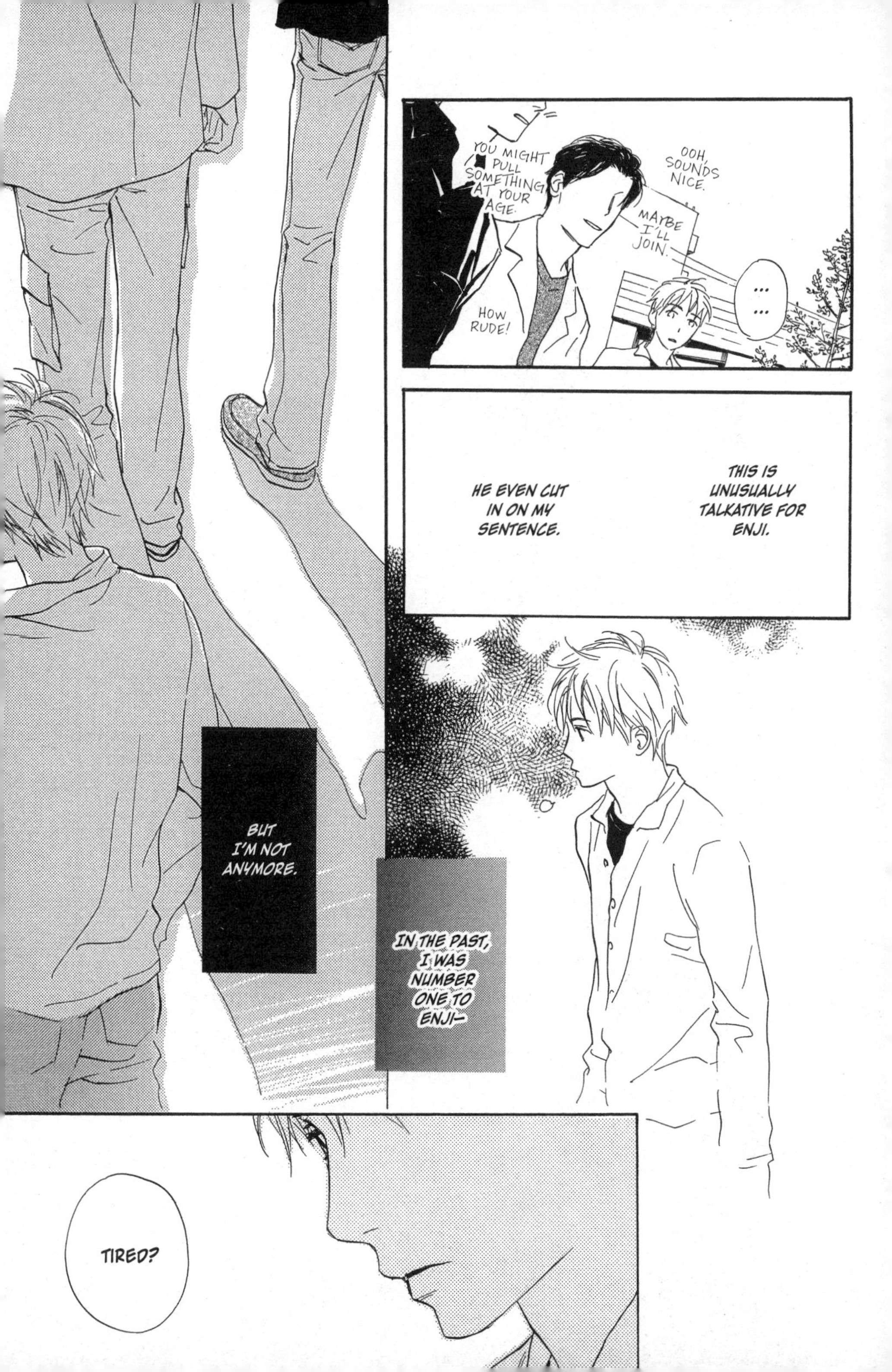

OOH, SOUNDS NICE.
MAYBE I'LL JOIN.
YOU MIGHT PULL SOMETHING AT YOUR AGE.
... ...
HOW RUDE!
THIS IS UNUSUALLY TALKATIVE FOR ENJI.
HE EVEN CUT IN ON MY SENTENCE.
IN THE PAST, I WAS NUMBER ONE TO ENJI—
BUT I'M NOT ANYMORE.
TIRED?

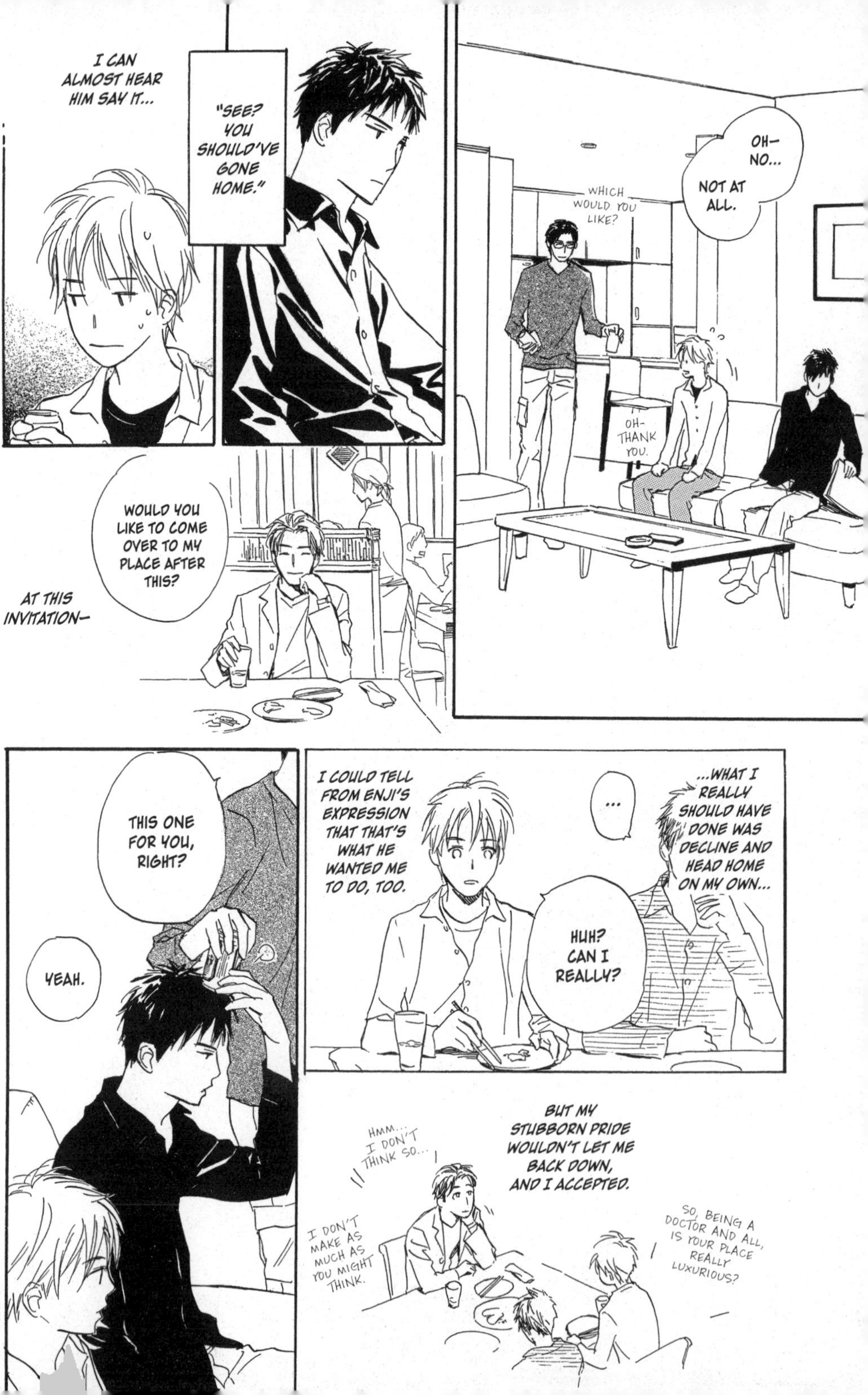
OH— NO... NOT AT ALL.
WHICH WOULD YOU LIKE?
OH— THANK YOU.
"SEE? YOU SHOULD'VE GONE HOME."
I CAN ALMOST HEAR HIM SAY IT...
WOULD YOU LIKE TO COME OVER TO MY PLACE AFTER THIS?
AT THIS INVITATION—
...WHAT I REALLY SHOULD HAVE DONE WAS DECLINE AND HEAD HOME ON MY OWN...
...
HUH? CAN I REALLY?
I COULD TELL FROM ENJI'S EXPRESSION THAT THAT'S WHAT HE WANTED ME TO DO, TOO.
SO, BEING A DOCTOR AND ALL, IS YOUR PLACE REALLY LUXURIOUS?
BUT MY STUBBORN PRIDE WOULDN'T LET ME BACK DOWN, AND I ACCEPTED.
HMM... I DON'T THINK SO...
I DON'T MAKE AS MUCH AS YOU MIGHT THINK.
THIS ONE FOR YOU, RIGHT?
YEAH.

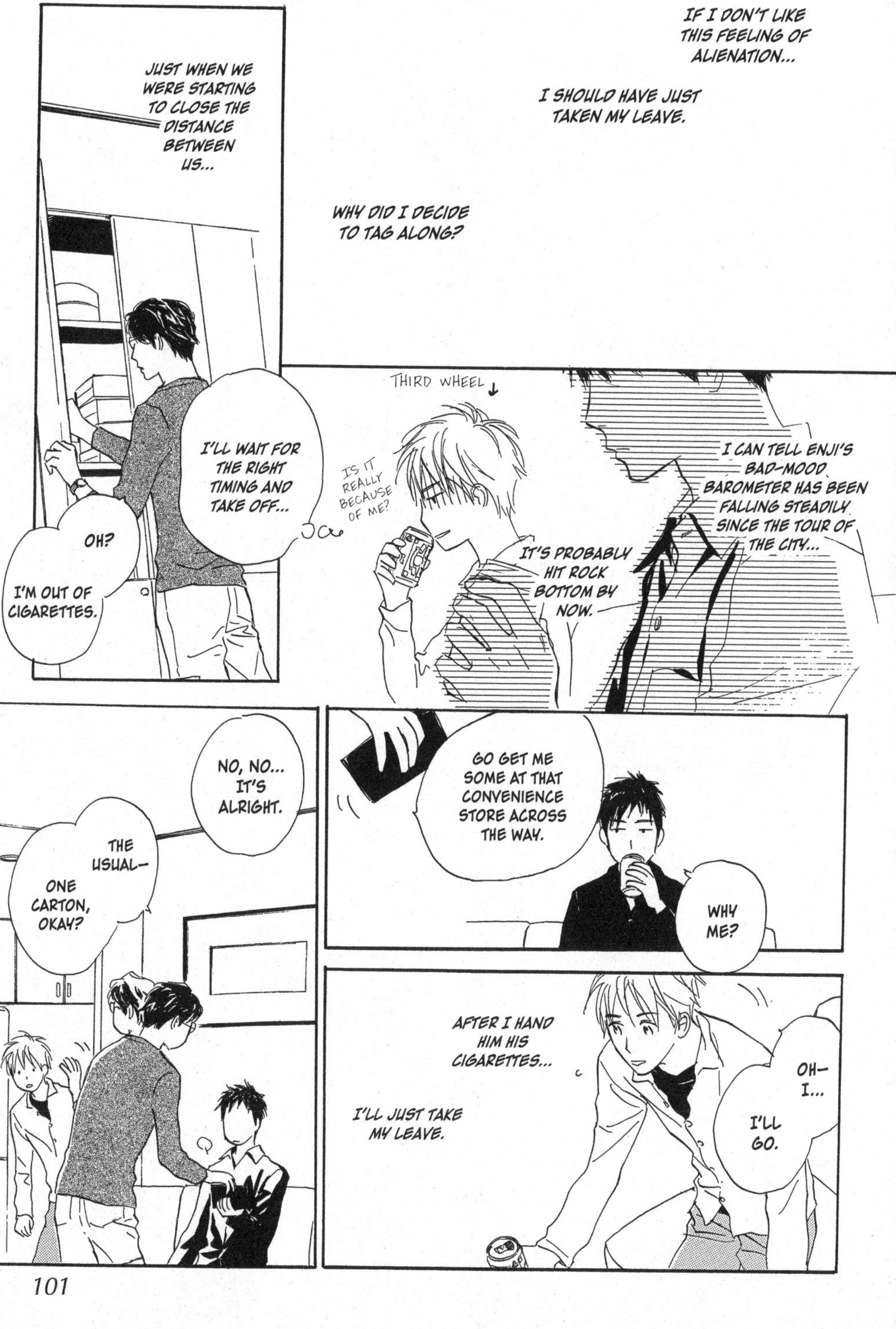
IF I DON'T LIKE THIS FEELING OF ALIENATION...
I SHOULD HAVE JUST TAKEN MY LEAVE.
WHY DID I DECIDE TO TAG ALONG?
I CAN TELL ENJI'S BAD-MOOD BAROMETER HAS BEEN FALLING STEADILY SINCE THE TOUR OF THE CITY...
IT'S PROBABLY HIT ROCK BOTTOM BY NOW.
THIRD WHEEL
IS IT REALLY BECAUSE OF ME?
JUST WHEN WE WERE STARTING TO CLOSE THE DISTANCE BETWEEN US...
I'LL WAIT FOR THE RIGHT TIMING AND TAKE OFF...
OH?
I'M OUT OF CIGARETTES.
GO GET ME SOME AT THAT CONVENIENCE STORE ACROSS THE WAY.
WHY ME?
OH— I... I'LL GO.
AFTER I HAND HIM HIS CIGARETTES...
I'LL JUST TAKE MY LEAVE.
NO, NO... IT'S ALRIGHT.
THE USUAL— ONE CARTON, OKAY?

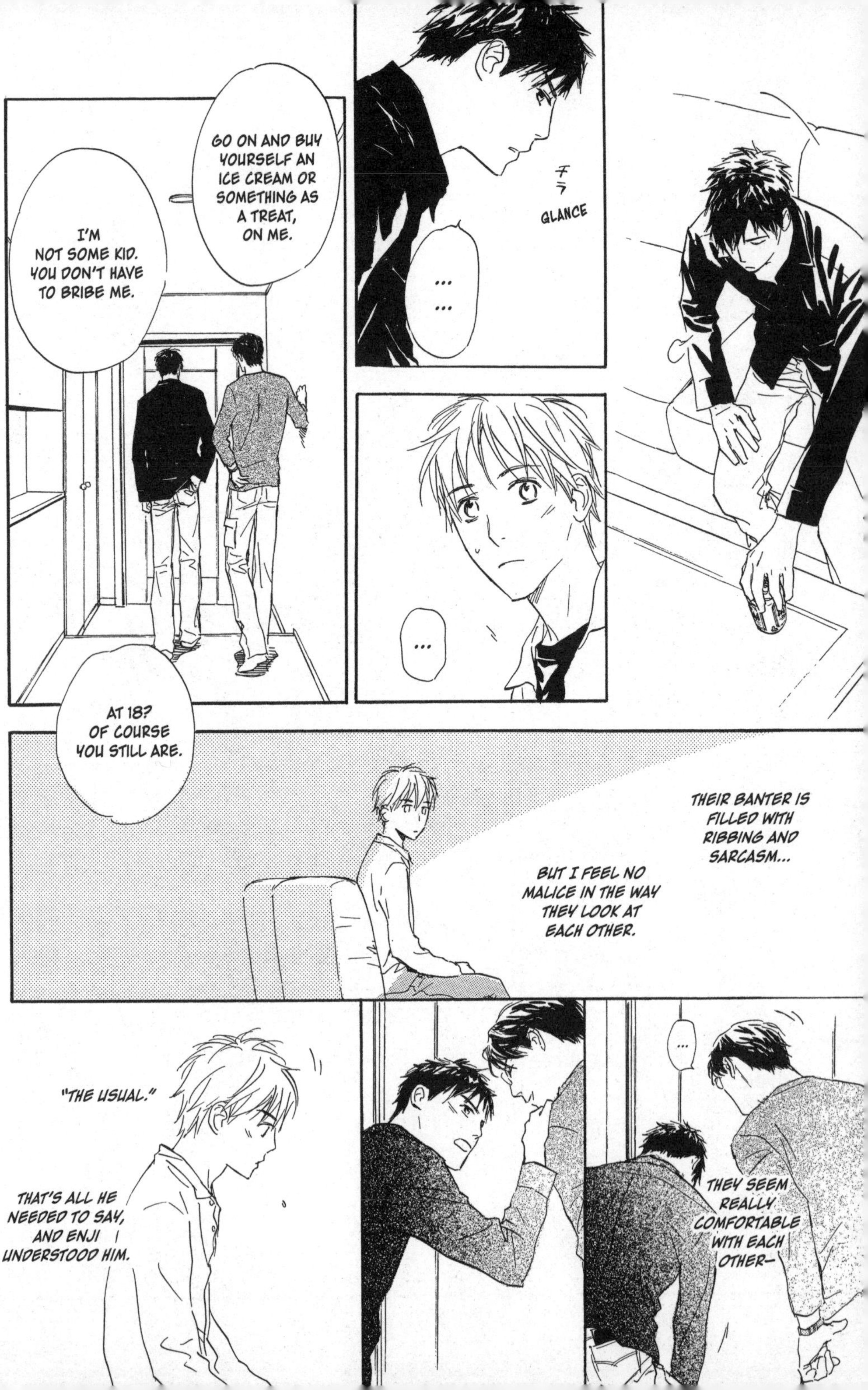

チラ
GLANCE
......
...
GO ON AND BUY YOURSELF AN ICE CREAM OR SOMETHING AS A TREAT, ON ME.
I'M NOT SOME KID. YOU DON'T HAVE TO BRIBE ME.
AT 18? OF COURSE YOU STILL ARE.
THEIR BANTER IS FILLED WITH RIBBING AND SARCASM...
BUT I FEEL NO MALICE IN THE WAY THEY LOOK AT EACH OTHER.
...
THEY SEEM REALLY COMFORTABLE WITH EACH OTHER—
"THE USUAL."
THAT'S ALL HE NEEDED TO SAY, AND ENJI UNDERSTOOD HIM.

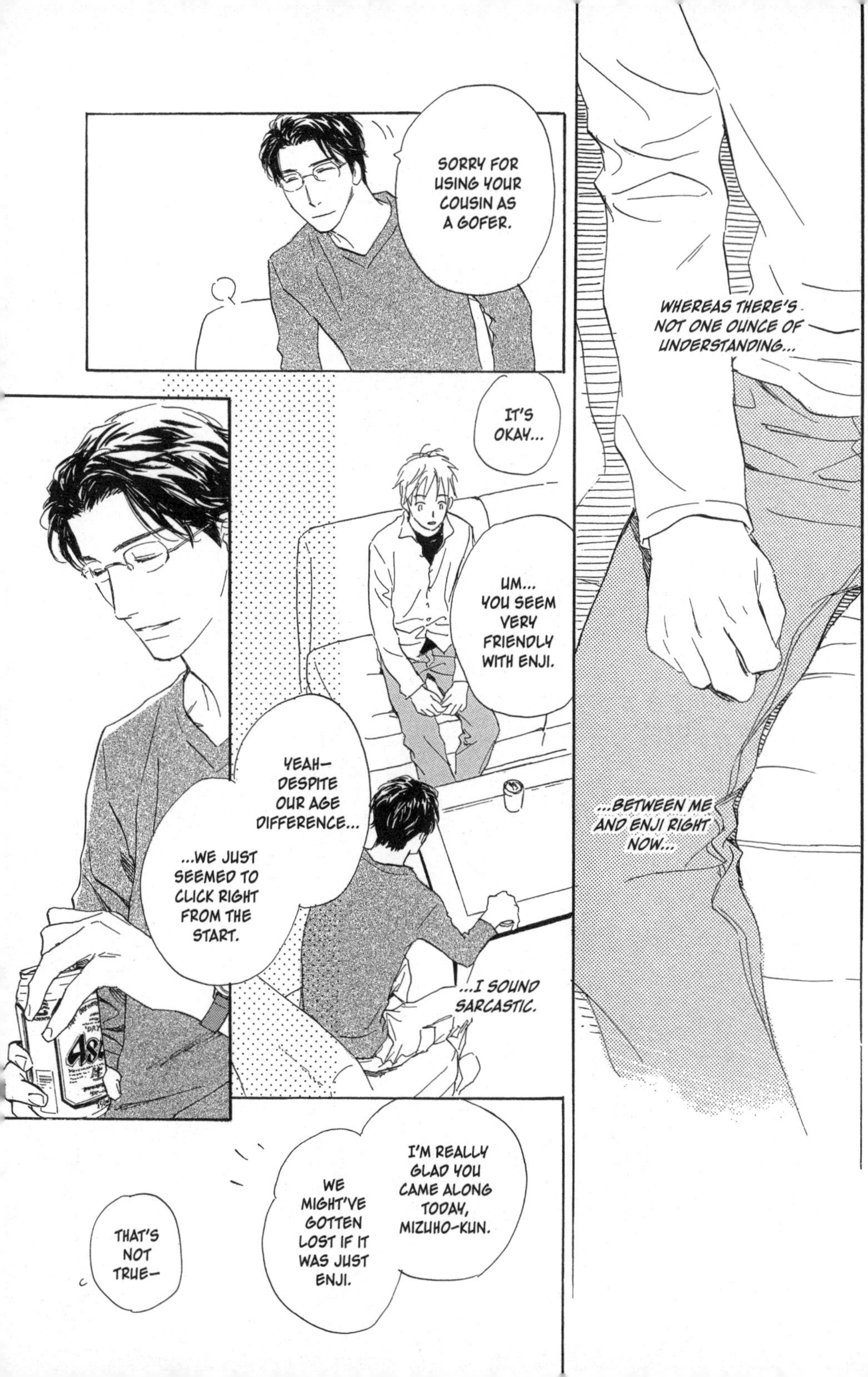
SORRY FOR USING YOUR COUSIN AS A GOFER.
IT'S OKAY...
UM... YOU SEEM VERY FRIENDLY WITH ENJI.
YEAH— DESPITE OUR AGE DIFFERENCE...
...WE JUST SEEMED TO CLICK RIGHT FROM THE START.
...I SOUND SARCASTIC.
WHEREAS THERE'S NOT ONE OUNCE OF UNDERSTANDING...
...BETWEEN ME AND ENJI RIGHT NOW...
I'M REALLY GLAD YOU CAME ALONG TODAY, MIZUHO-KUN.
WE MIGHT'VE GOTTEN LOST IF IT WAS JUST ENJI.
THAT'S NOT TRUE—

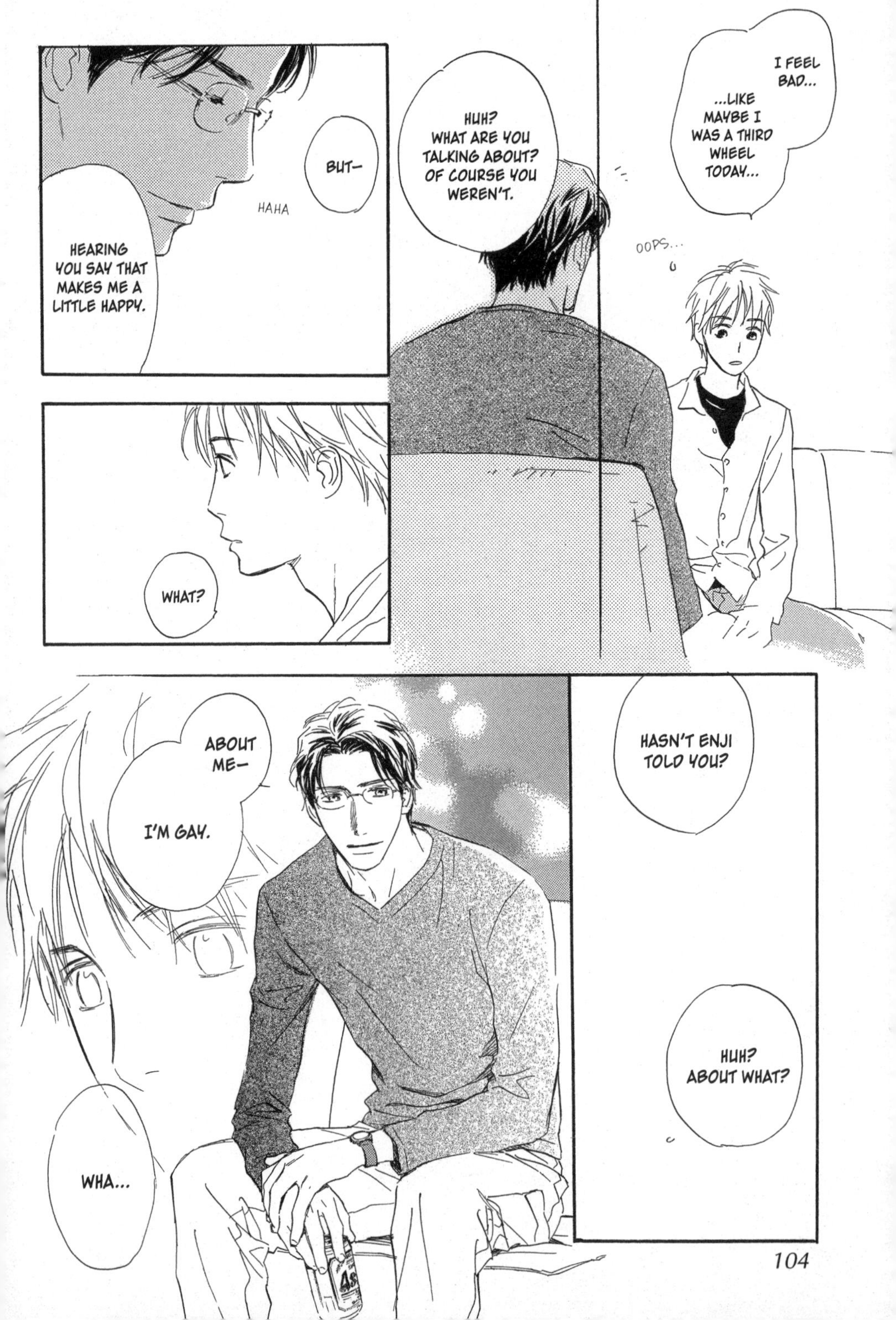

I FEEL BAD...
...LIKE MAYBE I WAS A THIRD WHEEL TODAY...
OOPS...
HUH? WHAT ARE YOU TALKING ABOUT? OF COURSE YOU WEREN'T.
BUT–
HAHA
HEARING YOU SAY THAT MAKES ME A LITTLE HAPPY.
WHAT?
HASN'T ENJI TOLD YOU?
HUH? ABOUT WHAT?
ABOUT ME–
I'M GAY.
WHA...

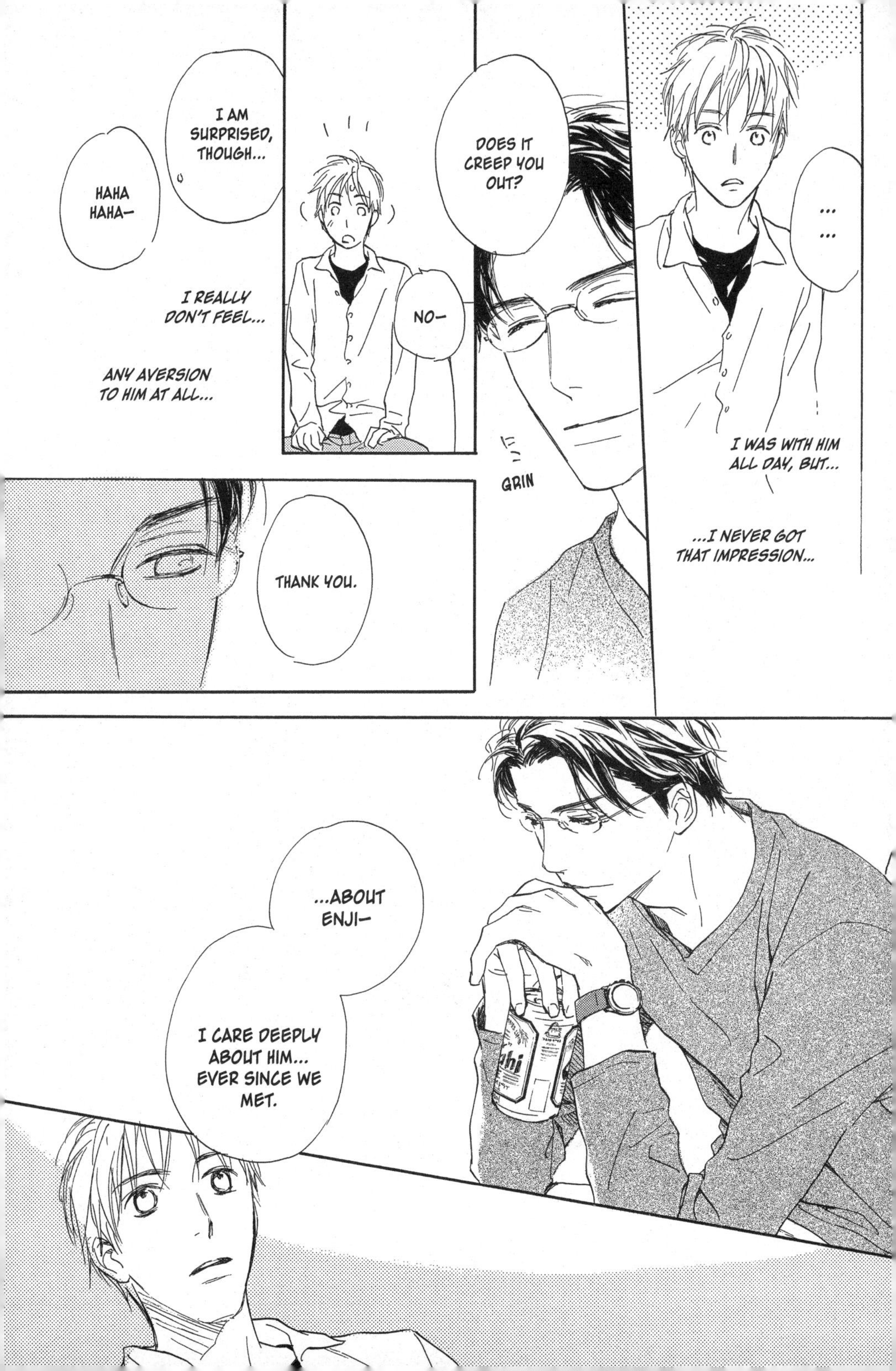
...
...
I WAS WITH HIM ALL DAY, BUT...
...I NEVER GOT THAT IMPRESSION...
DOES IT CREEP YOU OUT?
GRIN
NO—
I AM SURPRISED, THOUGH...
HAHA HAHA—
I REALLY DON'T FEEL...
ANY AVERSION TO HIM AT ALL...
THANK YOU.
...ABOUT ENJI—
I CARE DEEPLY ABOUT HIM... EVER SINCE WE MET.

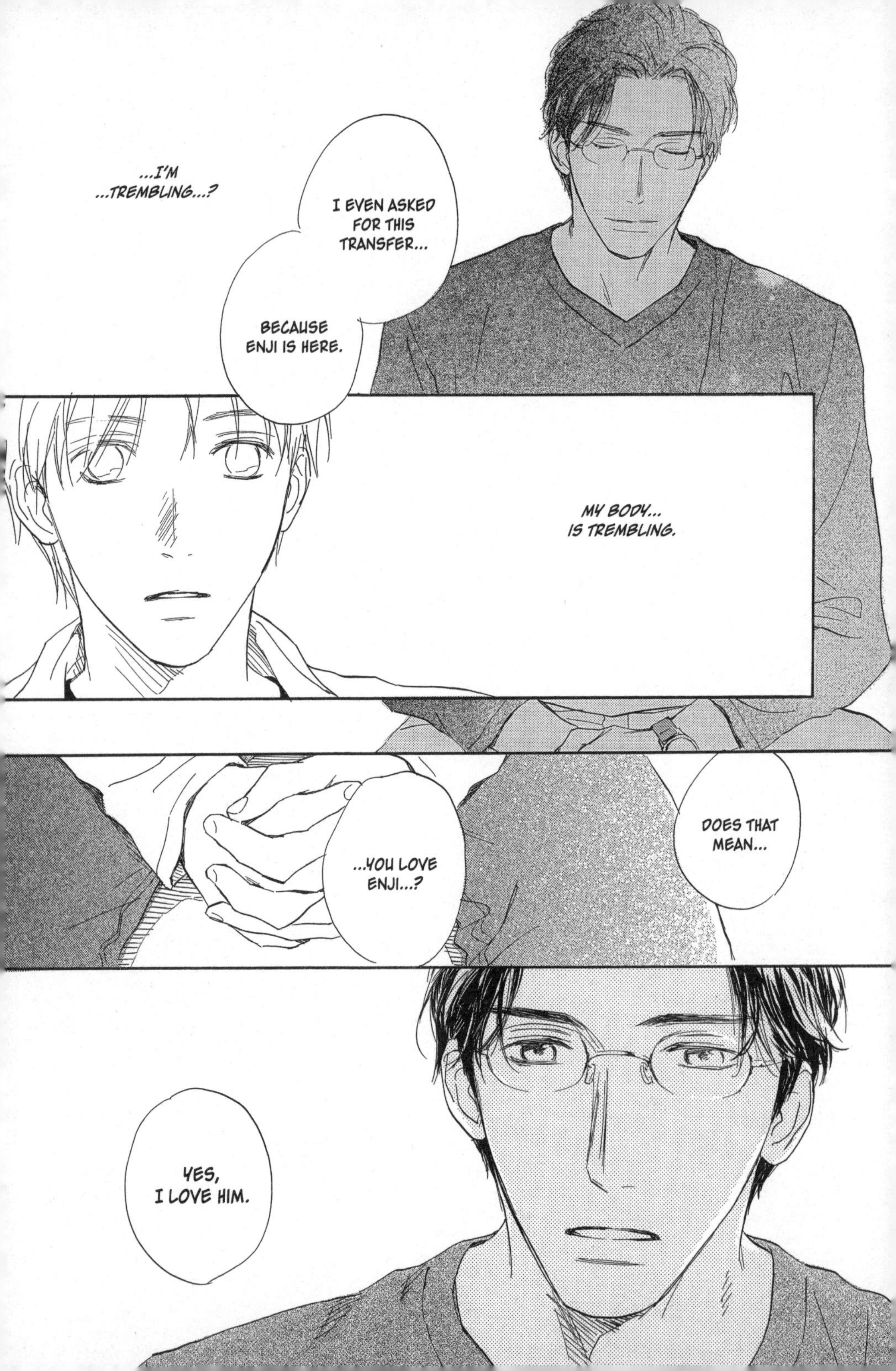
I EVEN ASKED FOR THIS TRANSFER...
BECAUSE ENJI IS HERE.
...I'M ...TREMBLING...?
MY BODY... IS TREMBLING.
DOES THAT MEAN...
...YOU LOVE ENJI...?
YES, I LOVE HIM.

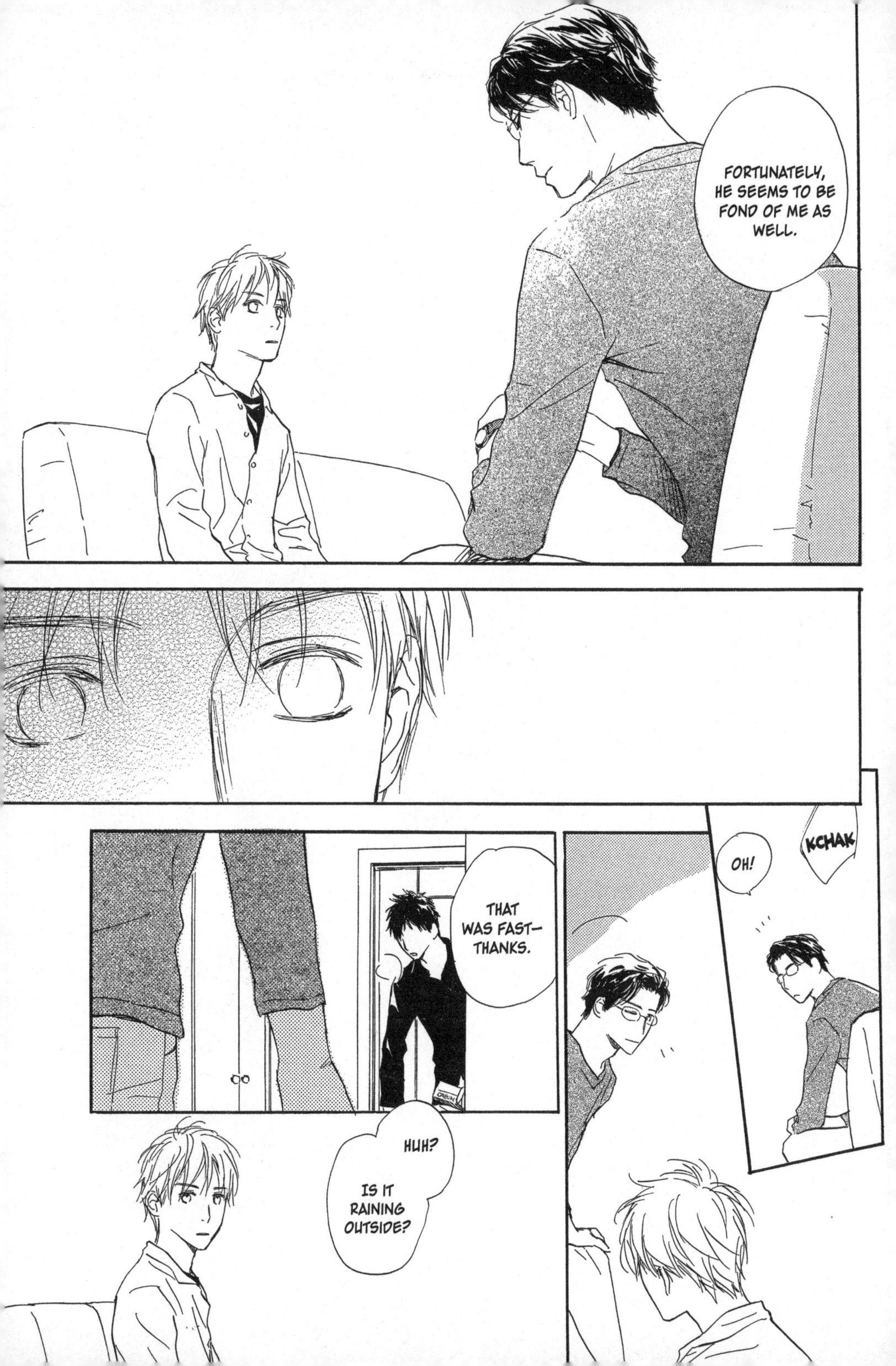
FORTUNATELY, HE SEEMS TO BE FOND OF ME AS WELL.
KCHAK
OH!
THAT WAS FAST— THANKS.
HUH?
IS IT RAINING OUTSIDE?

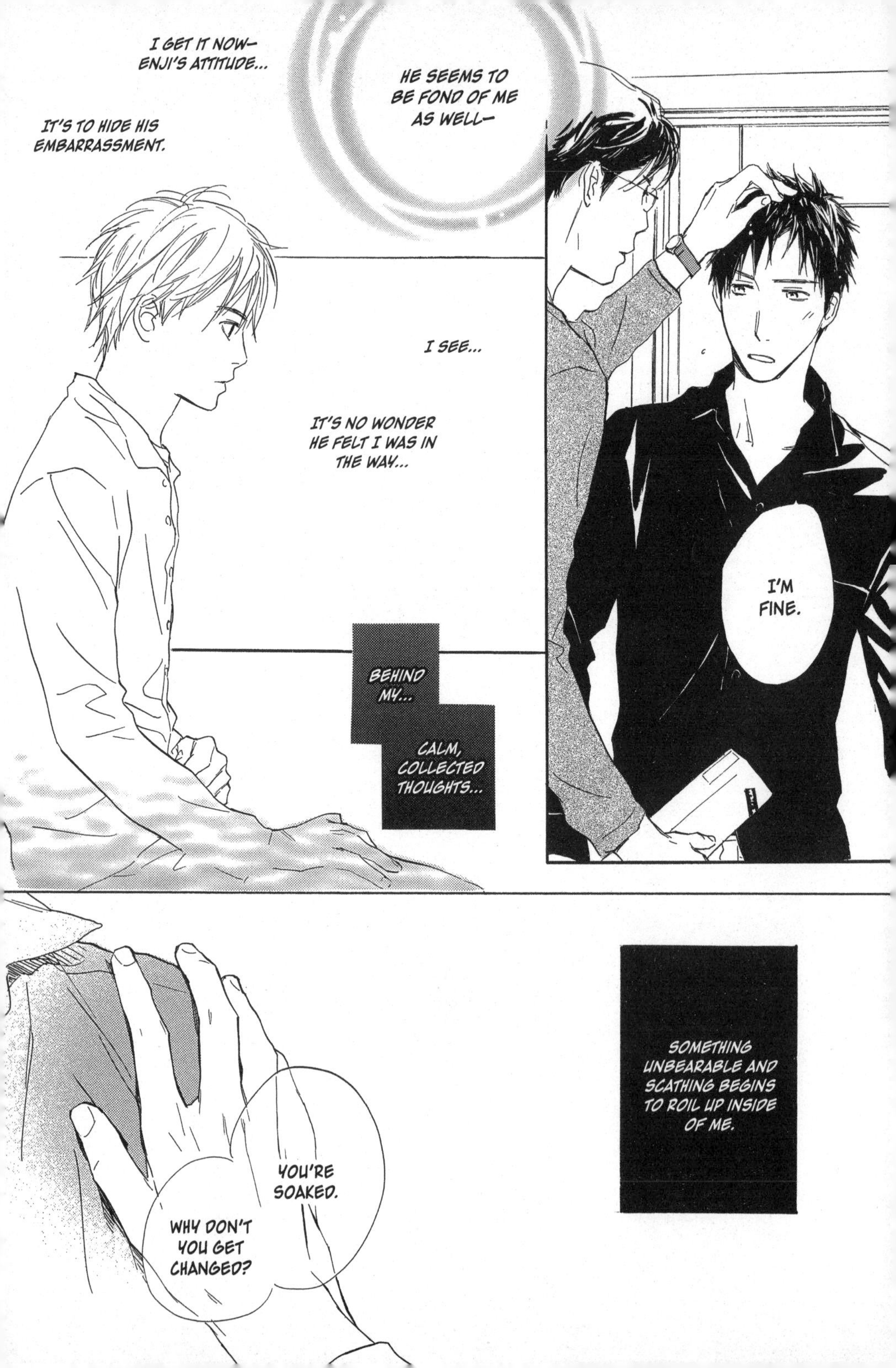
I'M FINE.
HE SEEMS TO BE FOND OF ME AS WELL—
I GET IT NOW— ENJI'S ATTITUDE...
IT'S TO HIDE HIS EMBARRASSMENT.
I SEE...
IT'S NO WONDER HE FELT I WAS IN THE WAY...
BEHIND MY...
CALM, COLLECTED THOUGHTS...
SOMETHING UNBEARABLE AND SCATHING BEGINS TO ROIL UP INSIDE OF ME.
YOU'RE SOAKED.
WHY DON'T YOU GET CHANGED?

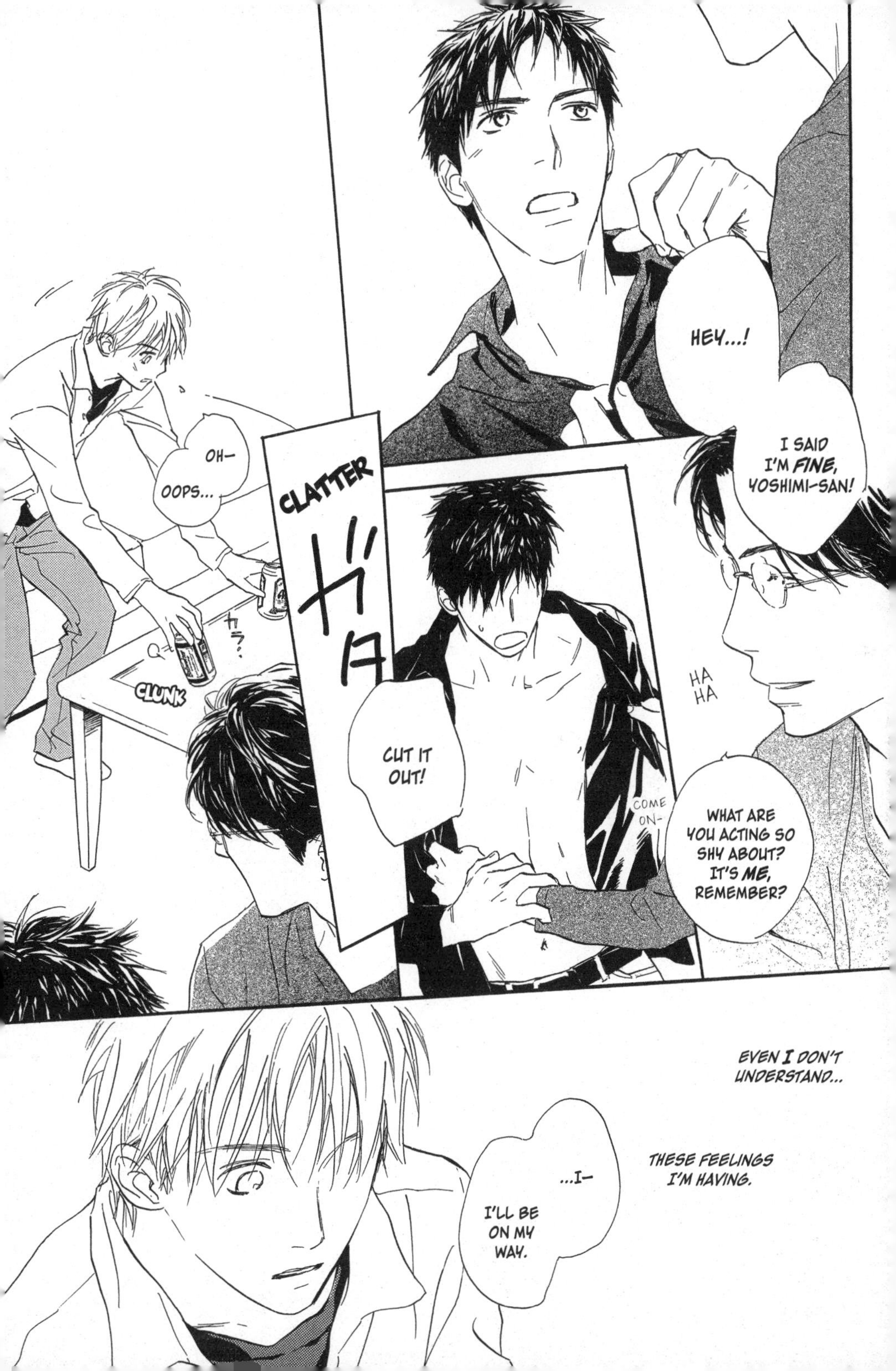
HEY...!
I SAID I'M ***FINE***, YOSHIMI-SAN!
HA HA
WHAT ARE YOU ACTING SO SHY ABOUT? IT'S ***ME***, REMEMBER?
COME ON—
CUT IT OUT!
CLATTER
ガタ
OH— OOPS...
カラ…
CLUNK
EVEN ***I*** DON'T UNDERSTAND...
THESE FEELINGS I'M HAVING.
...I—
I'LL BE ON MY WAY.

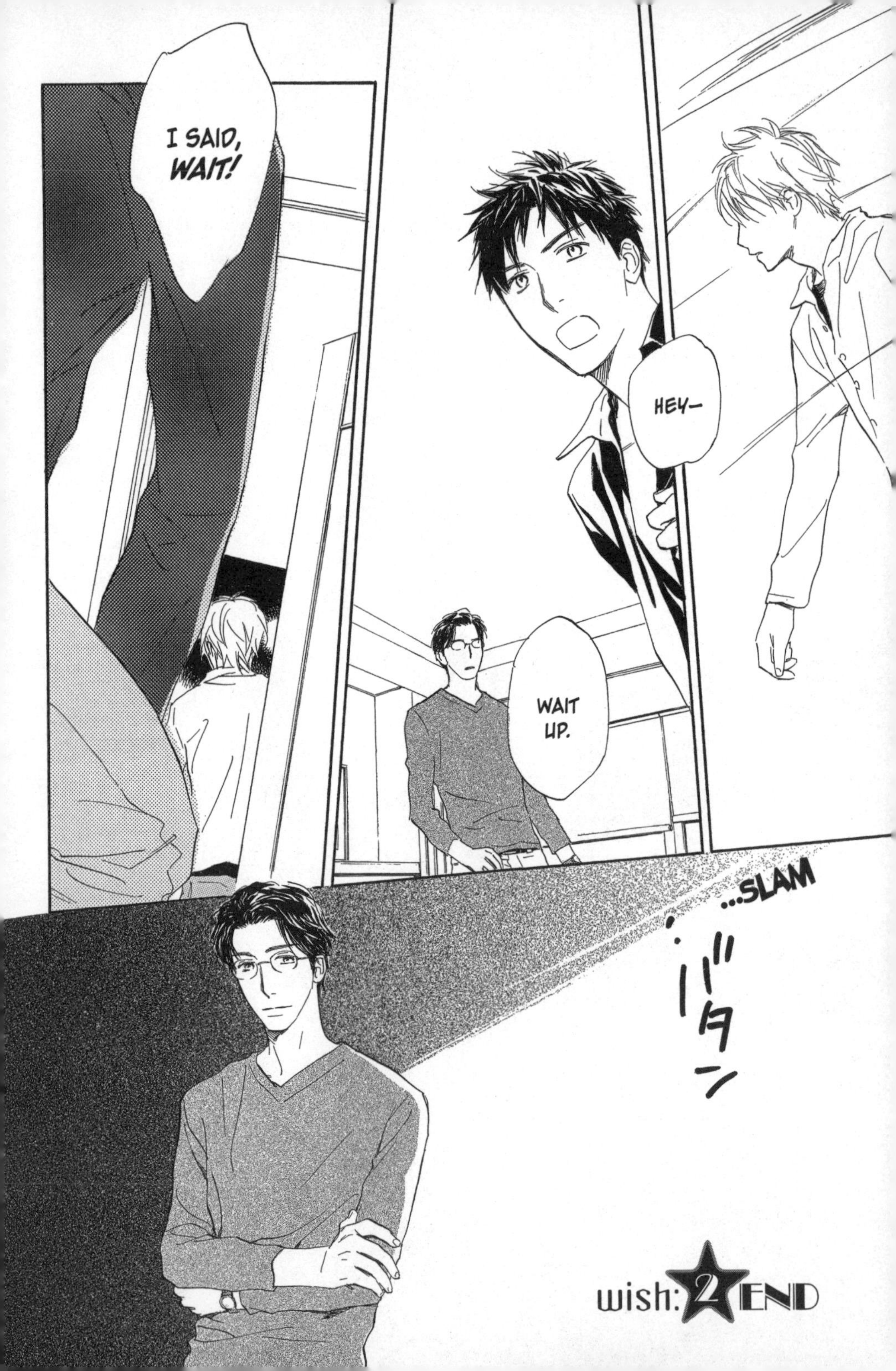
HEY—
WAIT UP.
I SAID, WAIT!
...SLAM
バタン
wish: 2 END

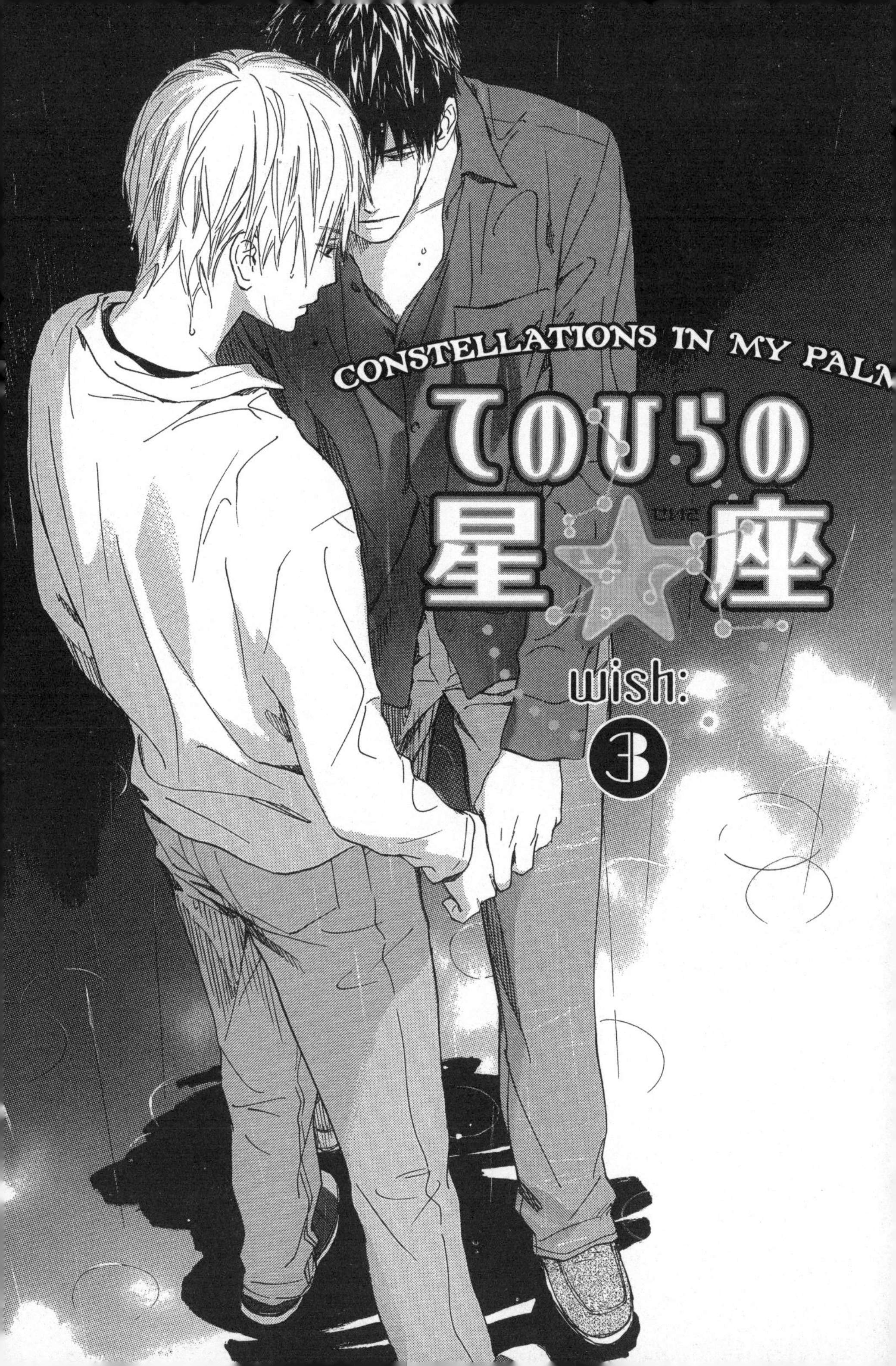
CONSTELLATIONS IN MY PALM
てのひらの
星座
wish:
3

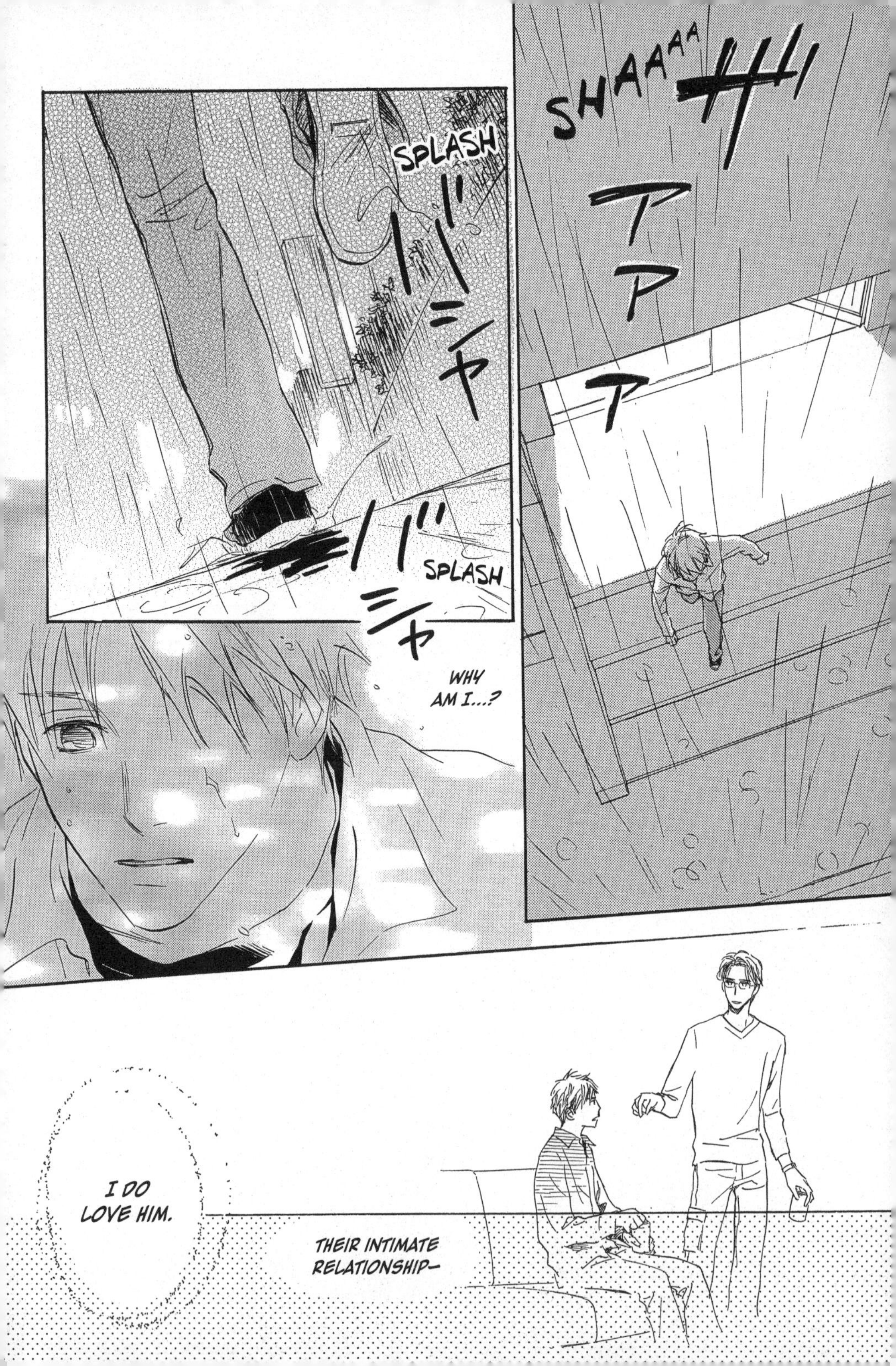
SHAAAA
ザアアア
SPLASH
バシャ
バシャ
SPLASH
WHY AM I...?
THEIR INTIMATE RELATIONSHIP—
I DO LOVE HIM.

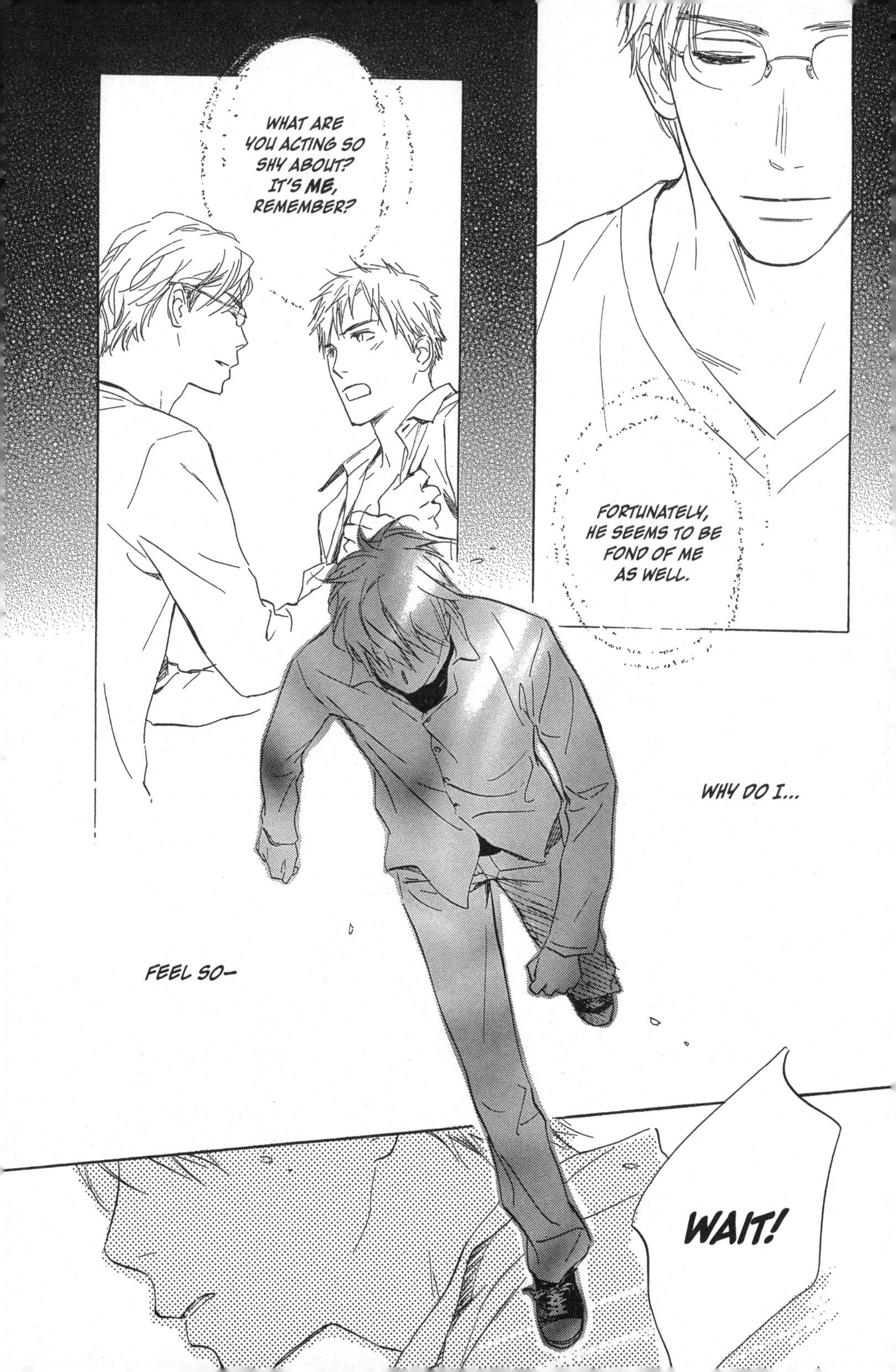
FORTUNATELY, HE SEEMS TO BE FOND OF ME AS WELL.
WHAT ARE YOU ACTING SO SHY ABOUT? IT'S ME, REMEMBER?
WHY DO I...
FEEL SO-
WAIT!

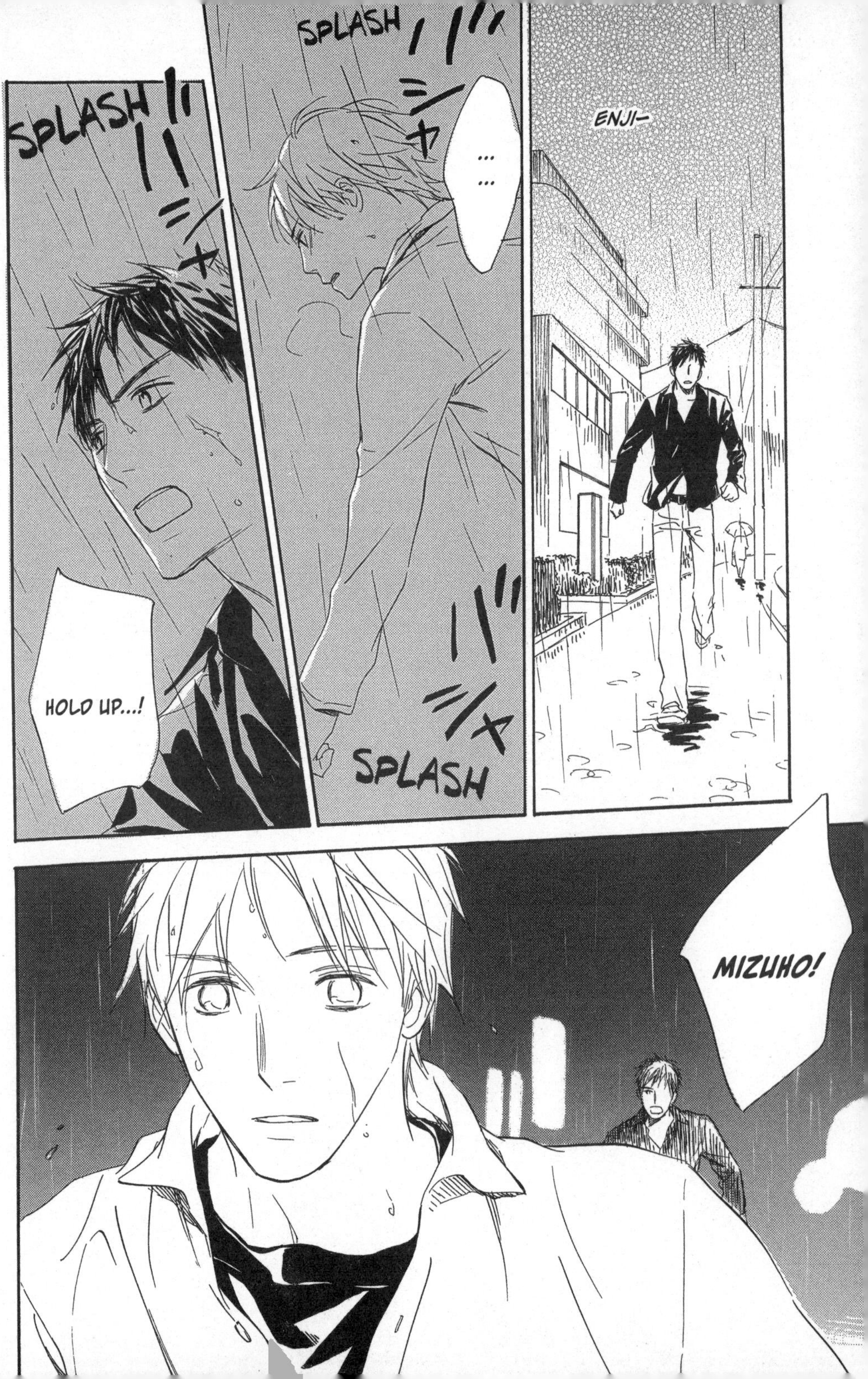
ENJI—
SPLASH
...
...
SPLASH
SPLASH
HOLD UP...!
MIZUHO!

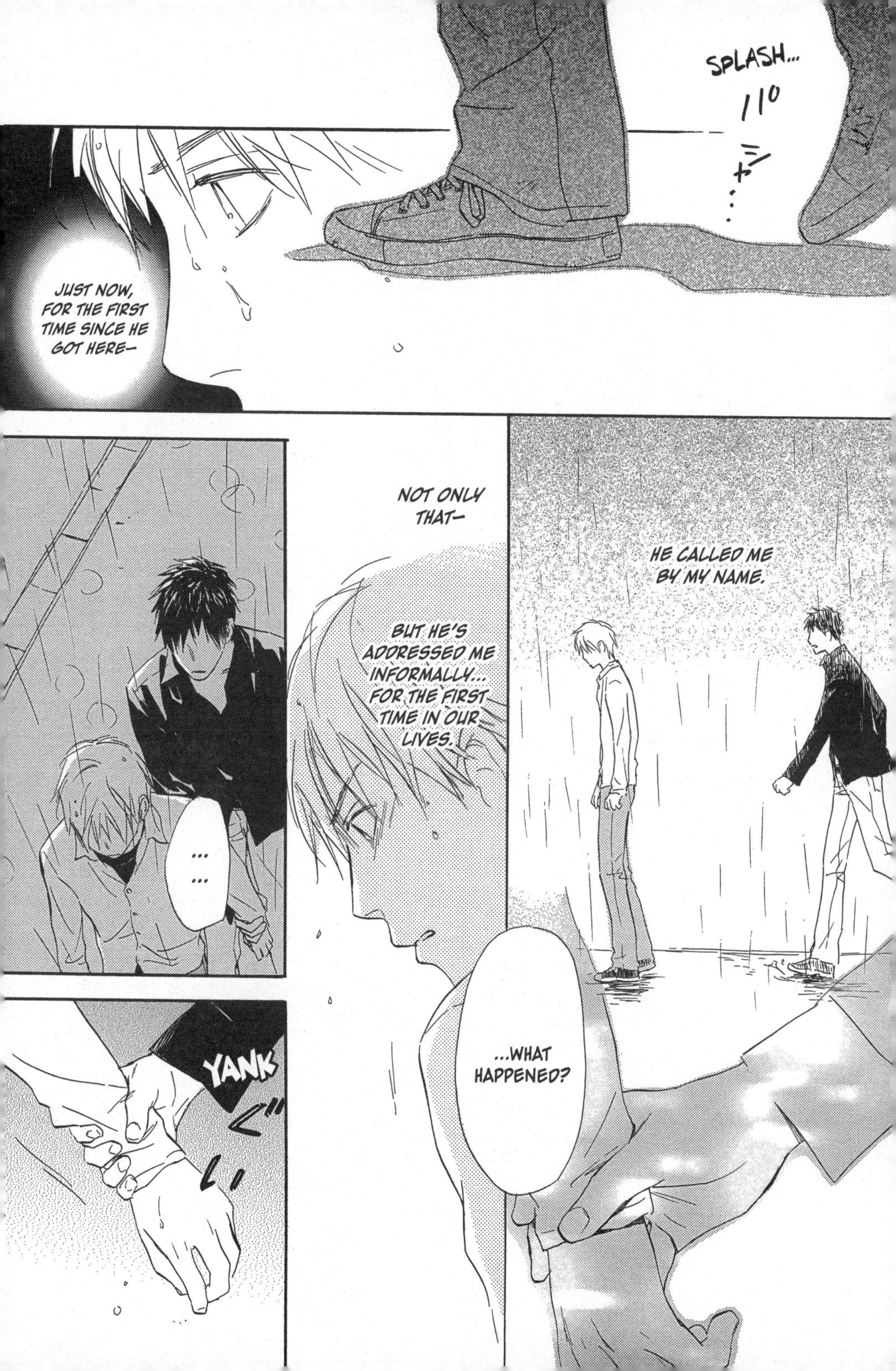
SPLASH...
JUST NOW, FOR THE FIRST TIME SINCE HE GOT HERE—
HE CALLED ME BY MY NAME.
...WHAT HAPPENED?
NOT ONLY THAT—
BUT HE'S ADDRESSED ME INFORMALLY... FOR THE FIRST TIME IN OUR LIVES.
... ...
YANK

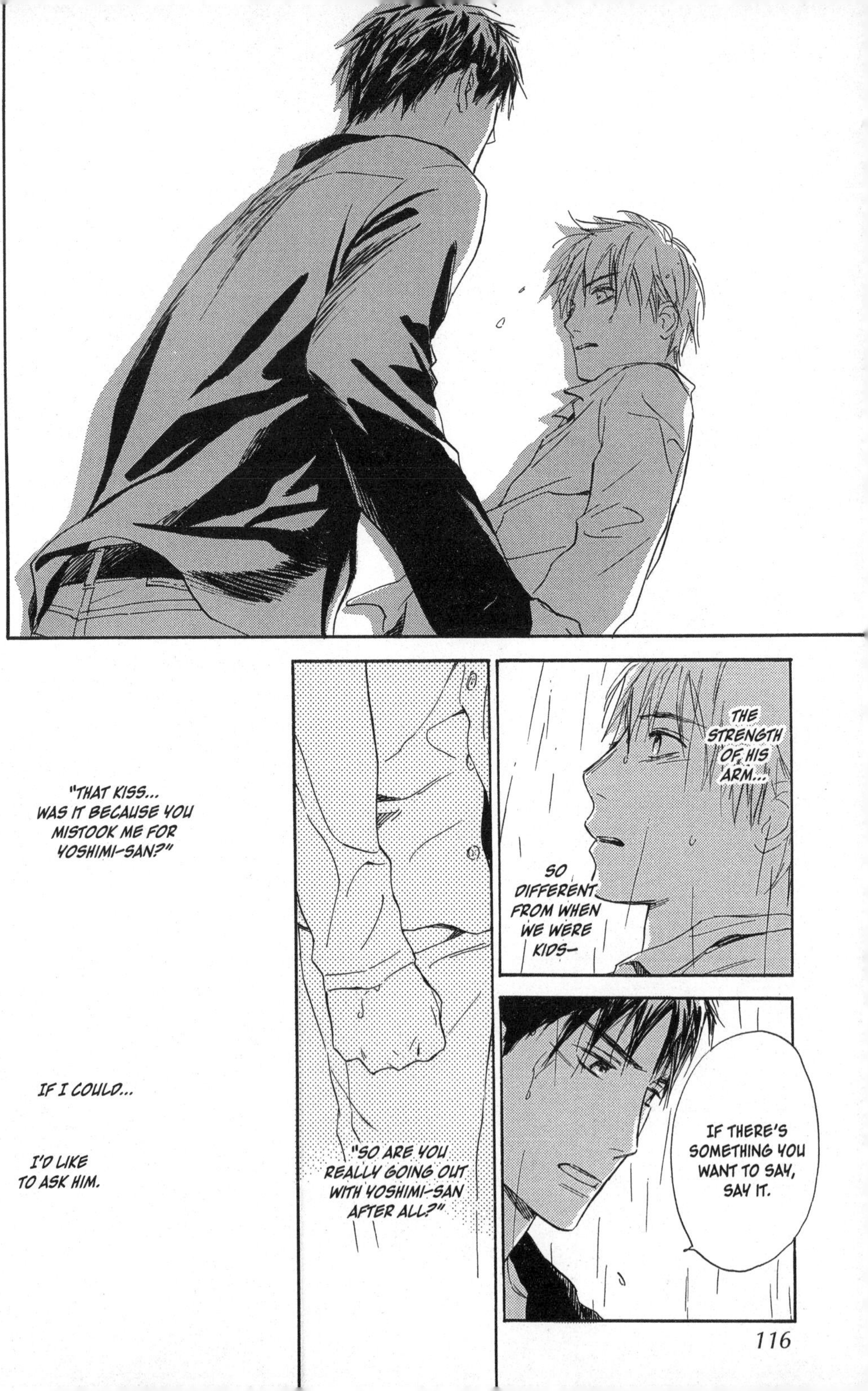
THE STRENGTH OF HIS ARM...
SO DIFFERENT FROM WHEN WE WERE KIDS—
IF THERE'S SOMETHING YOU WANT TO SAY, SAY IT.
"SO ARE YOU REALLY GOING OUT WITH YOSHIMI-SAN AFTER ALL?"
"THAT KISS... WAS IT BECAUSE YOU MISTOOK ME FOR YOSHIMI-SAN?"
IF I COULD...
I'D LIKE TO ASK HIM.

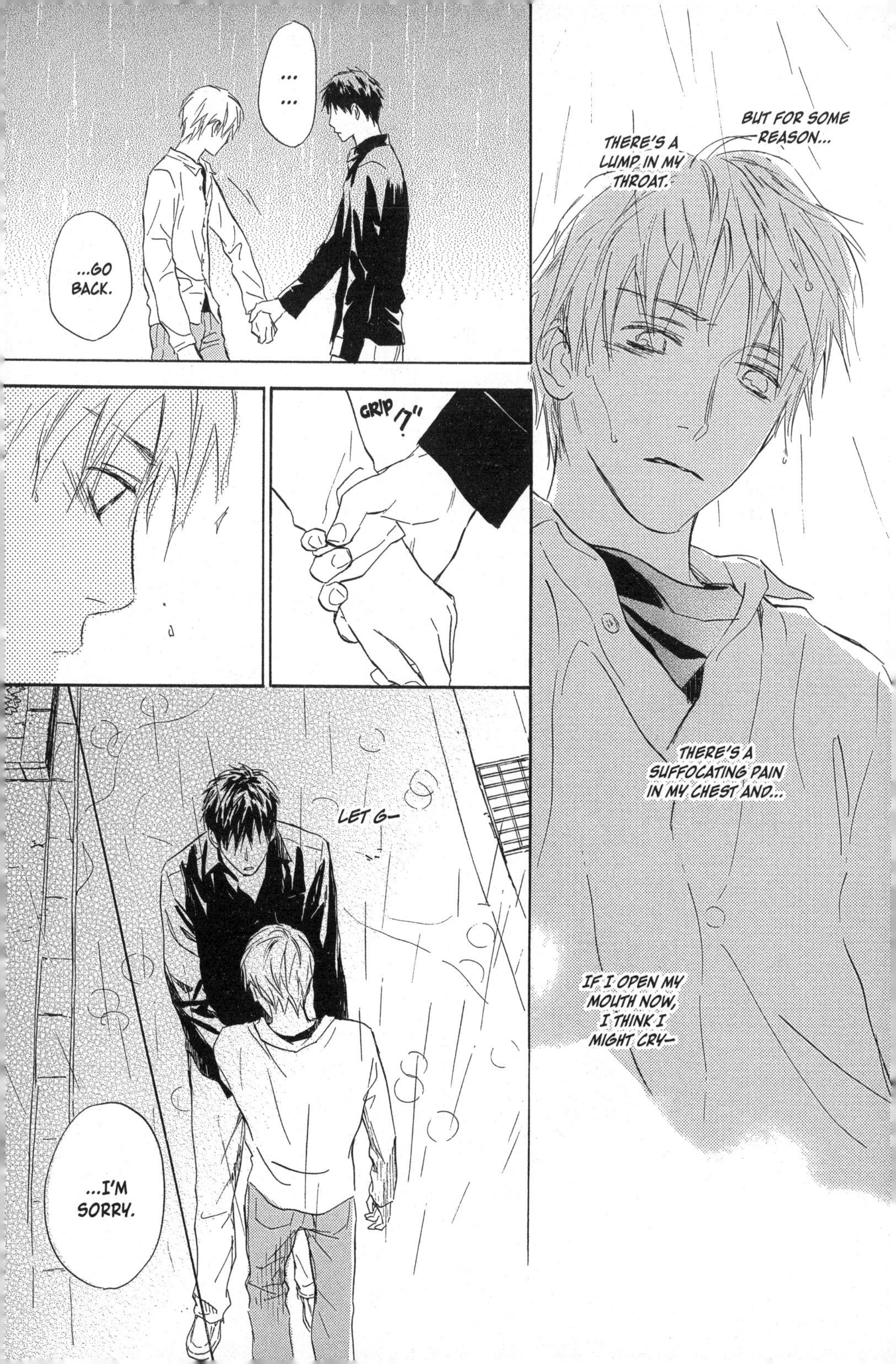

BUT FOR SOME REASON...
THERE'S A LUMP IN MY THROAT.
THERE'S A SUFFOCATING PAIN IN MY CHEST AND...
IF I OPEN MY MOUTH NOW, I THINK I MIGHT CRY—
......
...GO BACK.
GRIP
LET G—
...I'M SORRY.

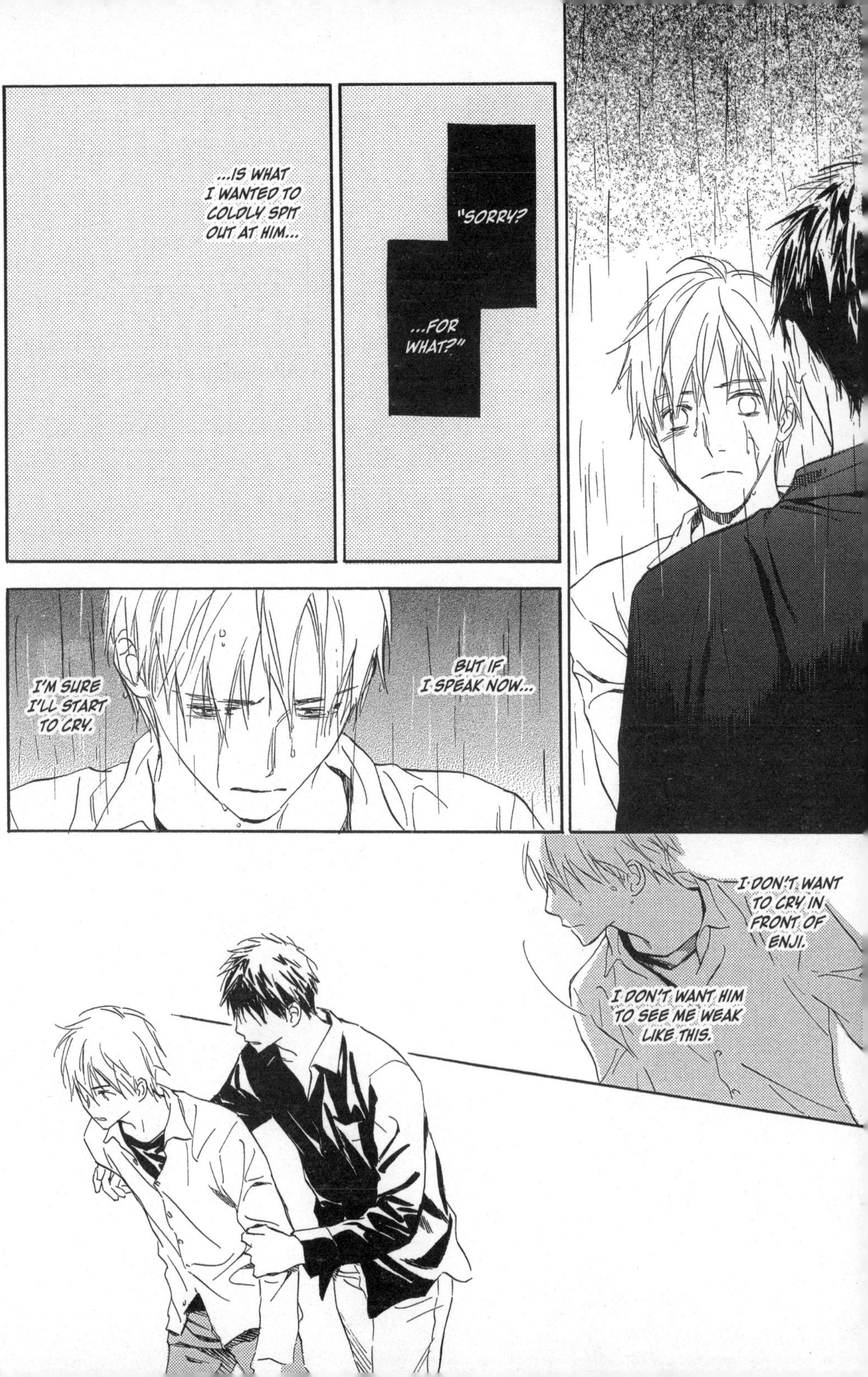
"SORRY?
...FOR WHAT?"
...IS WHAT I WANTED TO COLDLY SPIT OUT AT HIM...
BUT IF I SPEAK NOW...
I'M SURE I'LL START TO CRY.
I DON'T WANT TO CRY IN FRONT OF ENJI.
I DON'T WANT HIM TO SEE ME WEAK LIKE THIS.

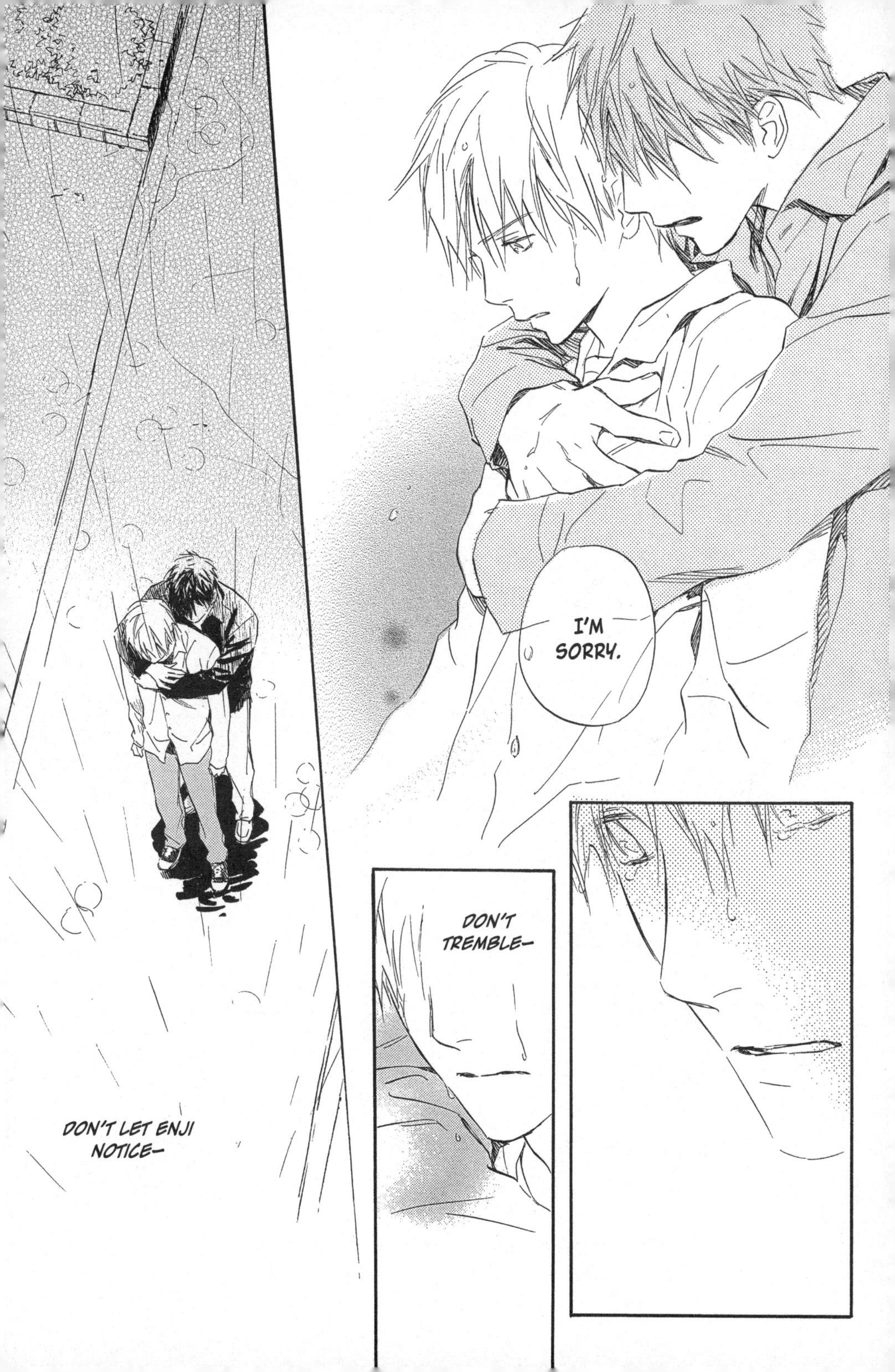
I'M SORRY.
DON'T TREMBLE—
DON'T LET ENJI NOTICE—

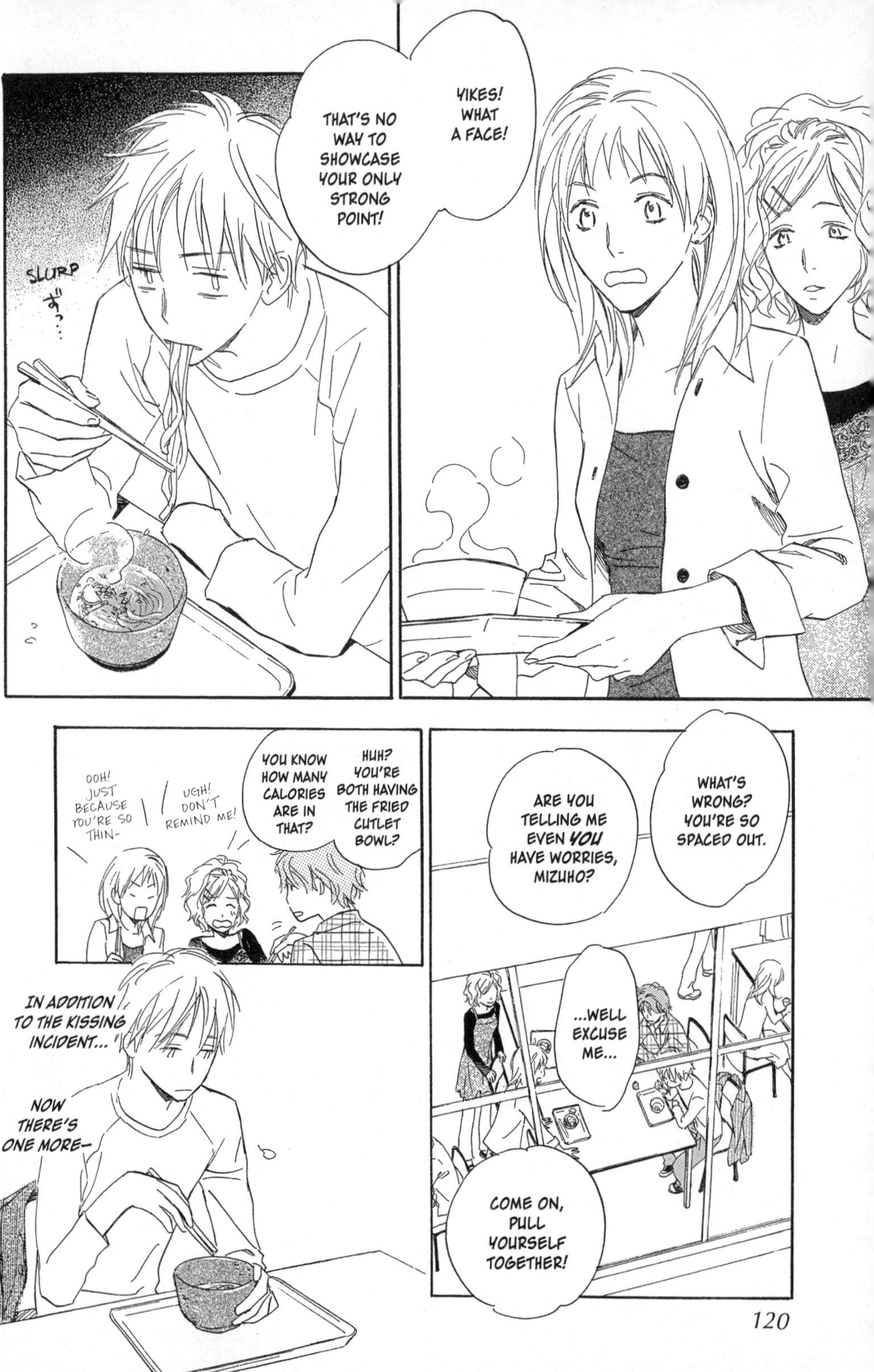
YIKES! WHAT A FACE!
THAT'S NO WAY TO SHOWCASE YOUR ONLY STRONG POINT!
SLURP
ずっ…
WHAT'S WRONG? YOU'RE SO SPACED OUT.
ARE YOU TELLING ME EVEN *YOU* HAVE WORRIES, MIZUHO?
...WELL EXCUSE ME...
COME ON, PULL YOURSELF TOGETHER!
HUH? YOU'RE BOTH HAVING THE FRIED CUTLET BOWL?
YOU KNOW HOW MANY CALORIES ARE IN THAT?
UGH! DON'T REMIND ME!
OOH! JUST BECAUSE YOU'RE SO THIN-
IN ADDITION TO THE KISSING INCIDENT...
NOW THERE'S ONE MORE—

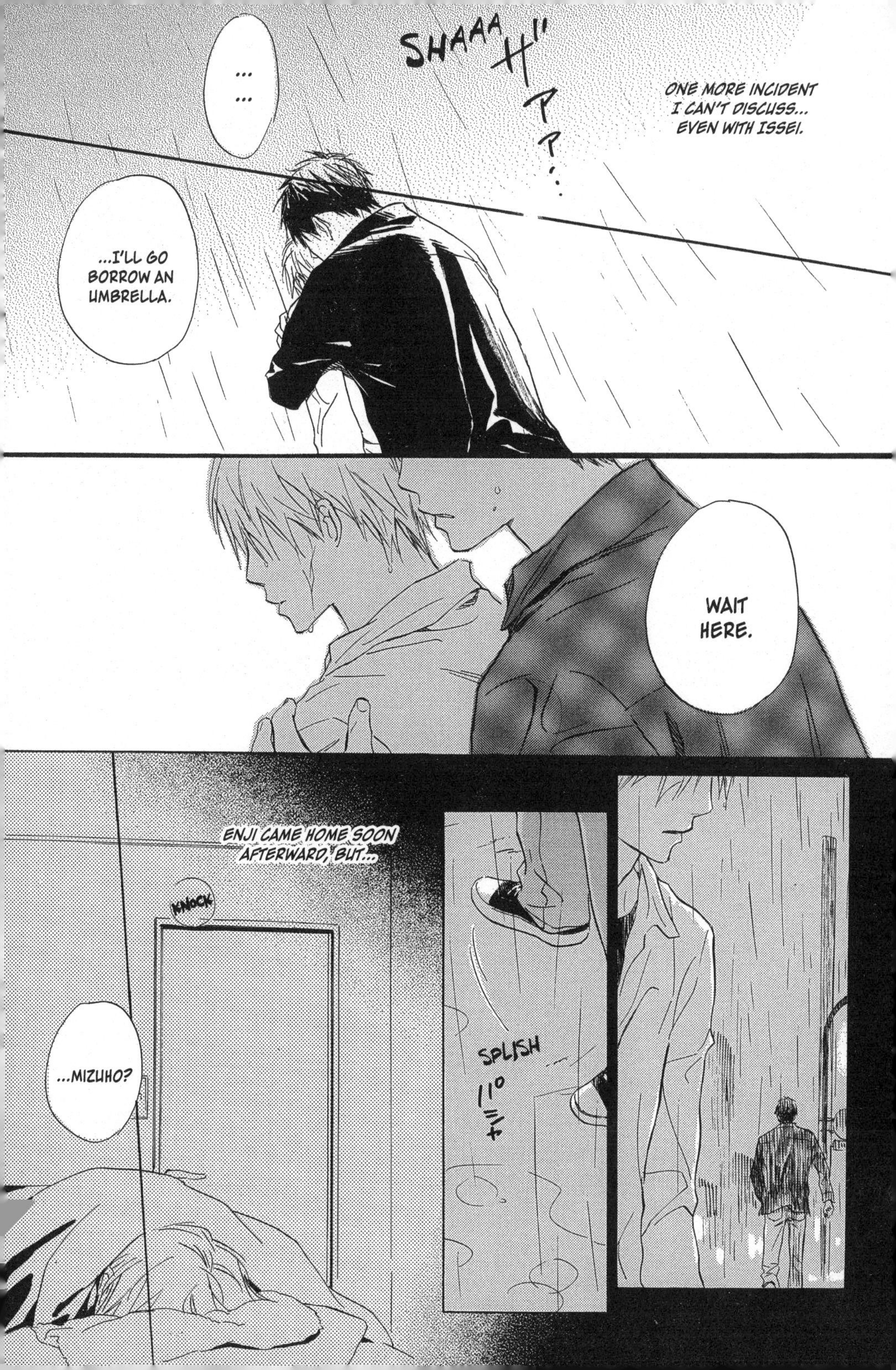
ONE MORE INCIDENT I CAN'T DISCUSS... EVEN WITH ISSEI.
SHAAA
...
...
...I'LL GO BORROW AN UMBRELLA.
WAIT HERE.
SPLISH
ENJI CAME HOME SOON AFTERWARD, BUT...
KNOCK
...MIZUHO?

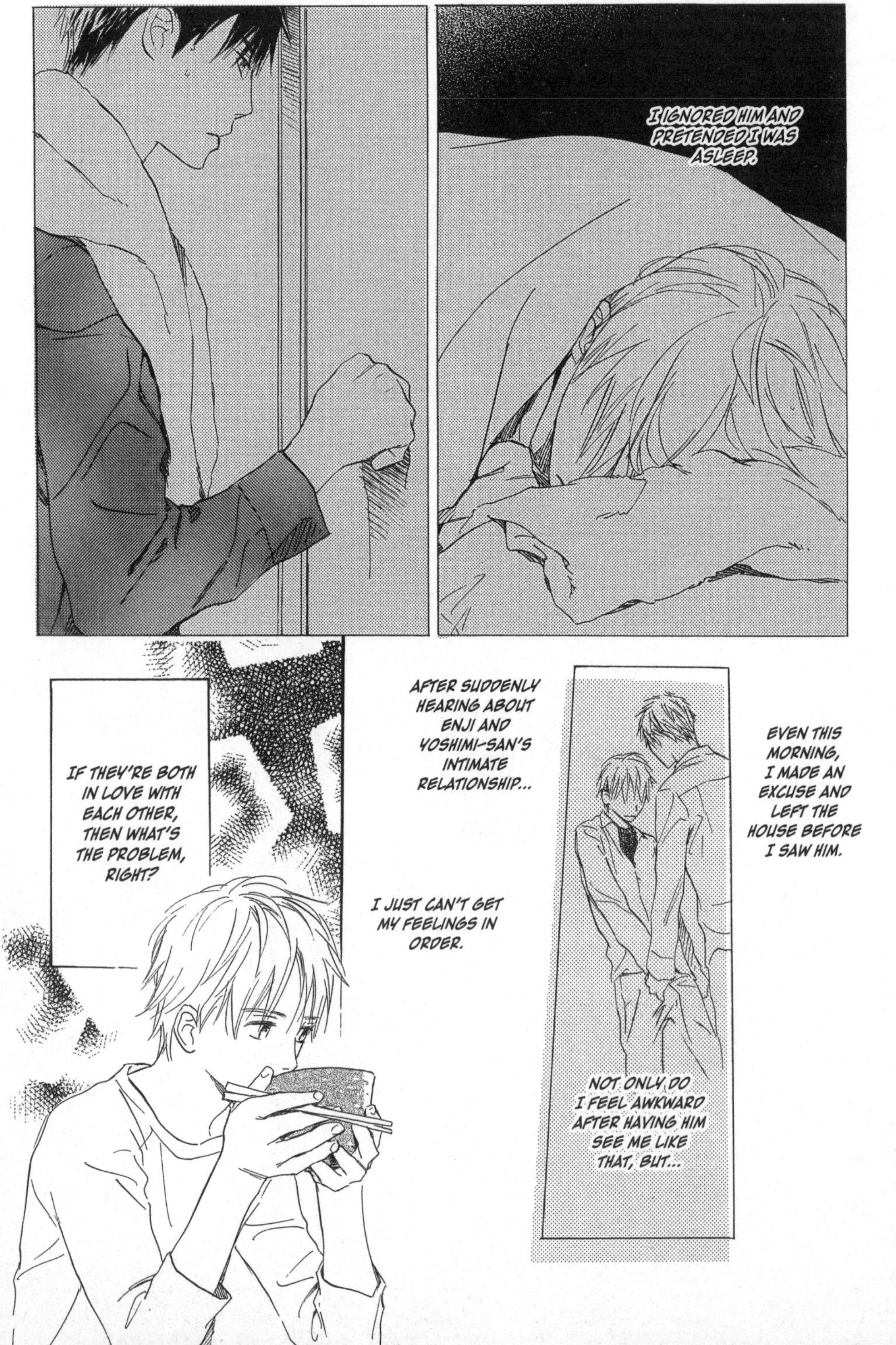
I IGNORED HIM AND PRETENDED I WAS ASLEEP.
EVEN THIS MORNING, I MADE AN EXCUSE AND LEFT THE HOUSE BEFORE I SAW HIM.
NOT ONLY DO I FEEL AWKWARD AFTER HAVING HIM SEE ME LIKE THAT, BUT...
AFTER SUDDENLY HEARING ABOUT ENJI AND YOSHIMI-SAN'S INTIMATE RELATIONSHIP...
I JUST CAN'T GET MY FEELINGS IN ORDER.
IF THEY'RE BOTH IN LOVE WITH EACH OTHER, THEN WHAT'S THE PROBLEM, RIGHT?

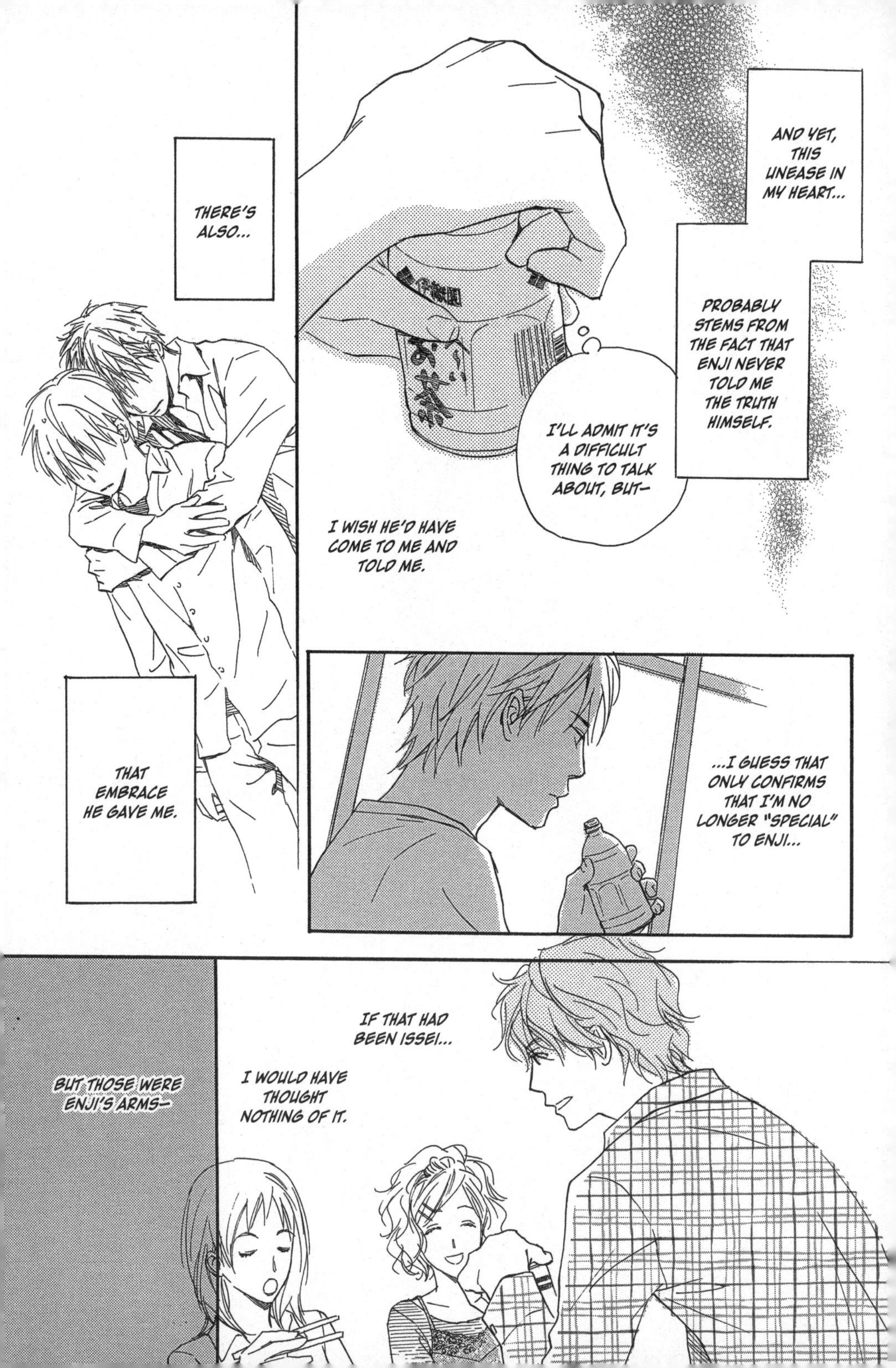
AND YET, THIS UNEASE IN MY HEART...
PROBABLY STEMS FROM THE FACT THAT ENJI NEVER TOLD ME THE TRUTH HIMSELF.
I'LL ADMIT IT'S A DIFFICULT THING TO TALK ABOUT, BUT—
I WISH HE'D HAVE COME TO ME AND TOLD ME.
...I GUESS THAT ONLY CONFIRMS THAT I'M NO LONGER "SPECIAL" TO ENJI...
THERE'S ALSO...
THAT EMBRACE HE GAVE ME.
IF THAT HAD BEEN ISSEI...
I WOULD HAVE THOUGHT NOTHING OF IT.
BUT THOSE WERE ENJI'S ARMS—

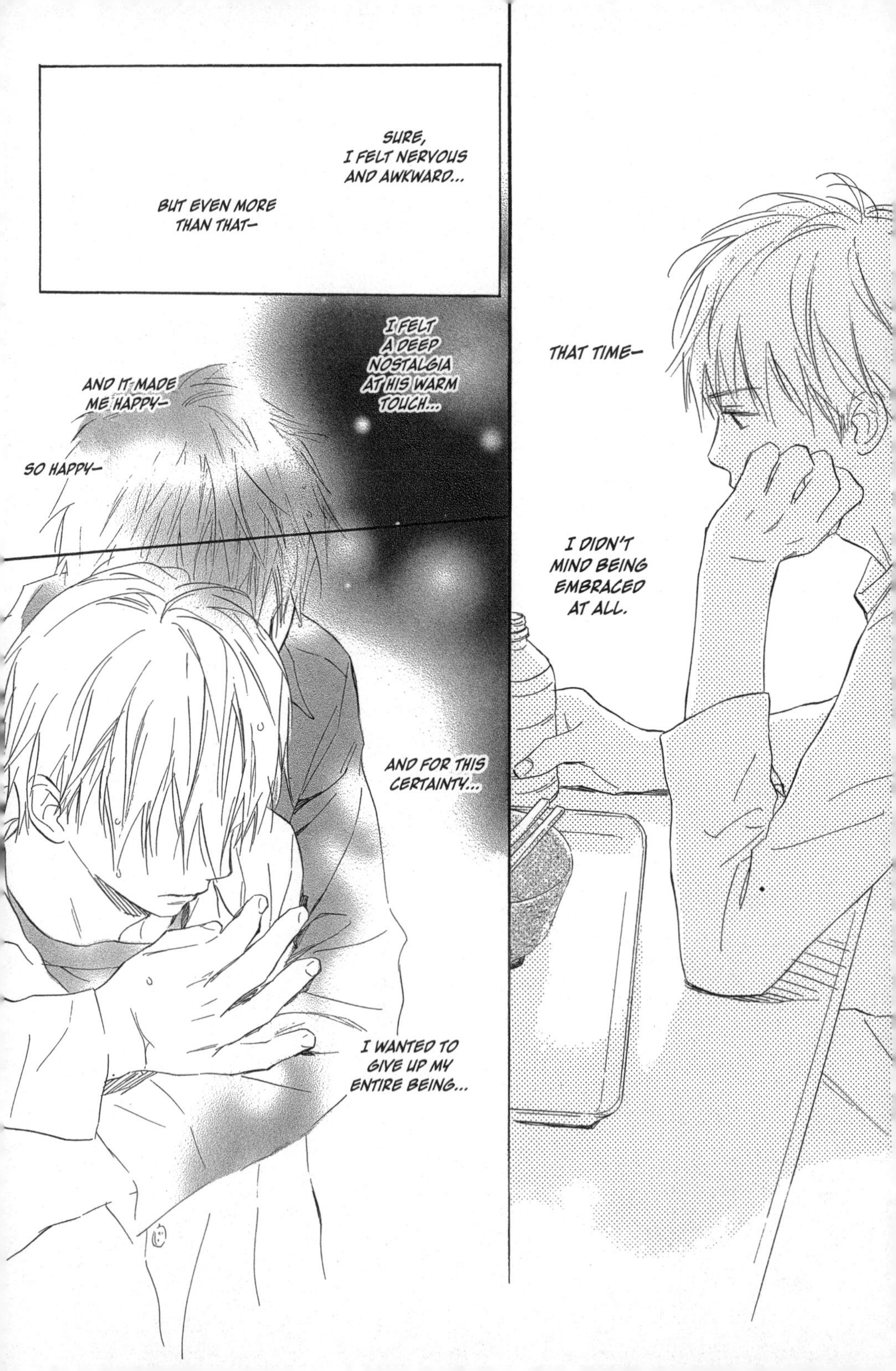
THAT TIME—
I DIDN'T MIND BEING EMBRACED AT ALL.
SURE, I FELT NERVOUS AND AWKWARD...
BUT EVEN MORE THAN THAT—
I FELT A DEEP NOSTALGIA AT HIS WARM TOUCH...
AND IT MADE ME HAPPY—
SO HAPPY—
AND FOR THIS CERTAINTY...
I WANTED TO GIVE UP MY ENTIRE BEING...

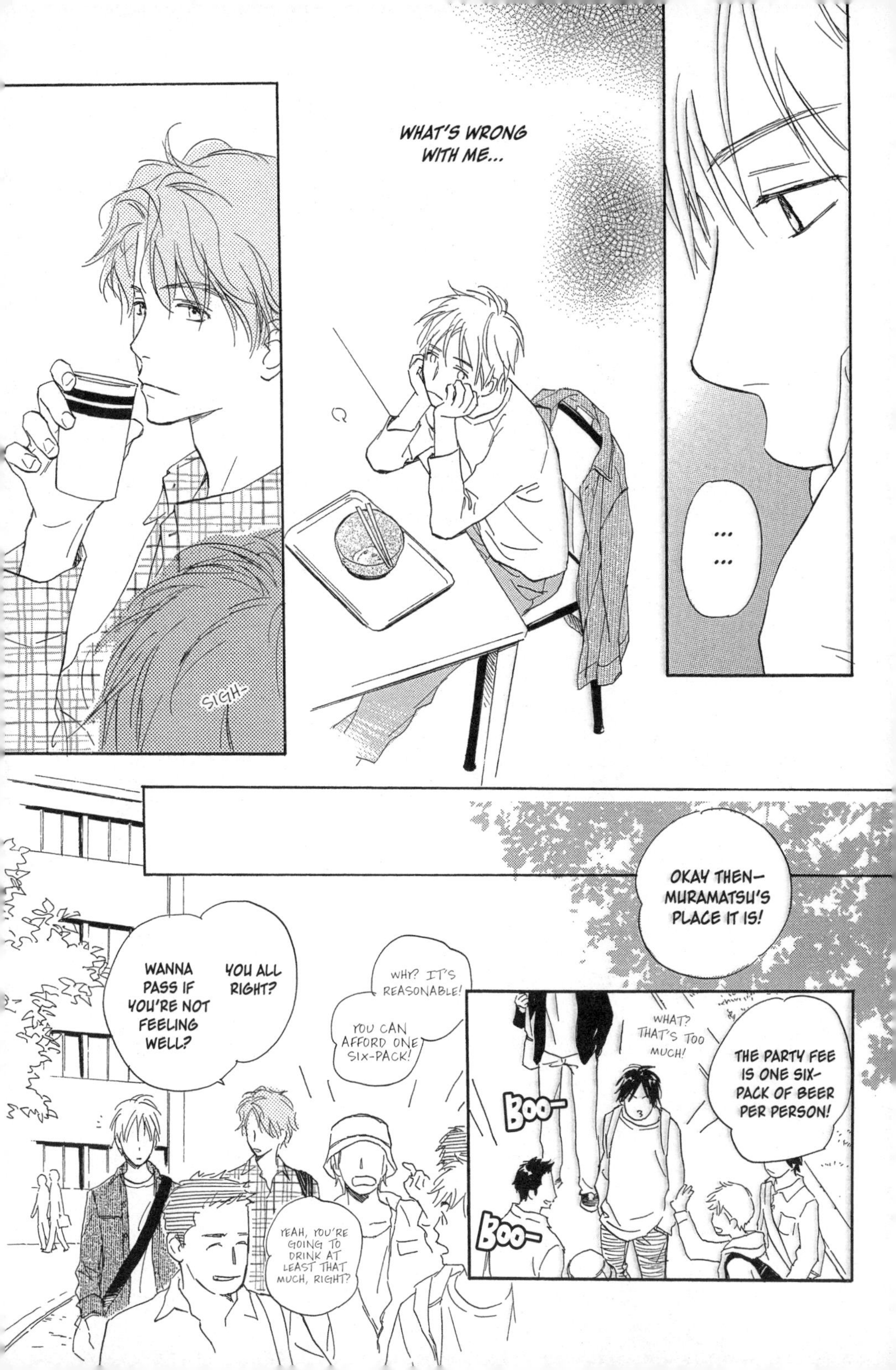
... ...
WHAT'S WRONG WITH ME...
SIGH-
OKAY THEN— MURAMATSU'S PLACE IT IS!
THE PARTY FEE IS ONE SIX-PACK OF BEER PER PERSON!
WHAT? THAT'S TOO MUCH!
BOO-
BOO-
WHY? IT'S REASONABLE!
YOU CAN AFFORD ONE SIX-PACK!
YEAH, YOU'RE GOING TO DRINK AT LEAST THAT MUCH, RIGHT?
YOU ALL RIGHT? WANNA PASS IF YOU'RE NOT FEELING WELL?

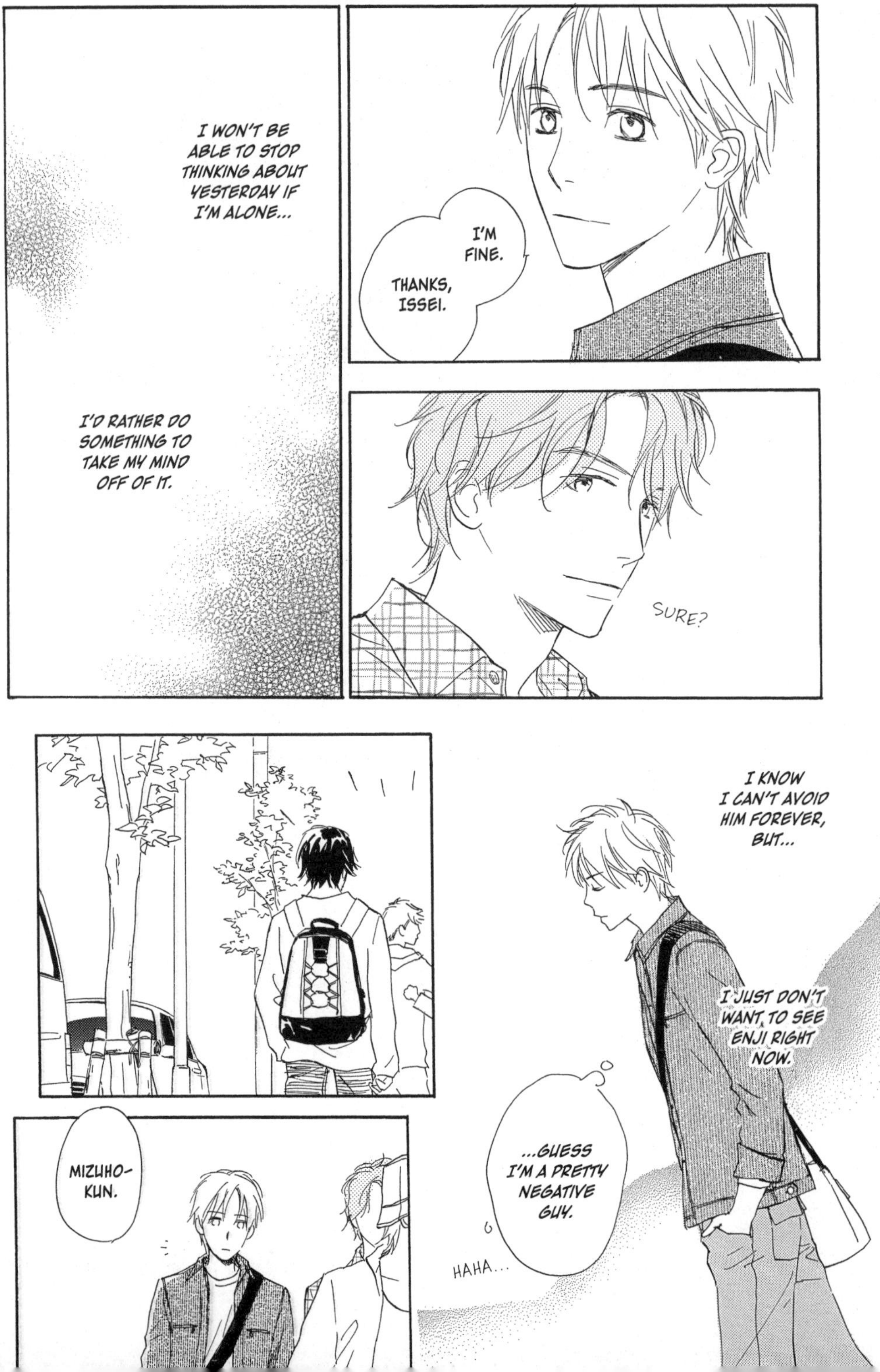
I'M FINE.
THANKS, ISSEI.
SURE?
I WON'T BE ABLE TO STOP THINKING ABOUT YESTERDAY IF I'M ALONE...
I'D RATHER DO SOMETHING TO TAKE MY MIND OFF OF IT.
I KNOW I CAN'T AVOID HIM FOREVER, BUT...
I JUST DON'T WANT TO SEE ENJI RIGHT NOW.
...GUESS I'M A PRETTY NEGATIVE GUY.
HAHA...
MIZUHO-KUN.

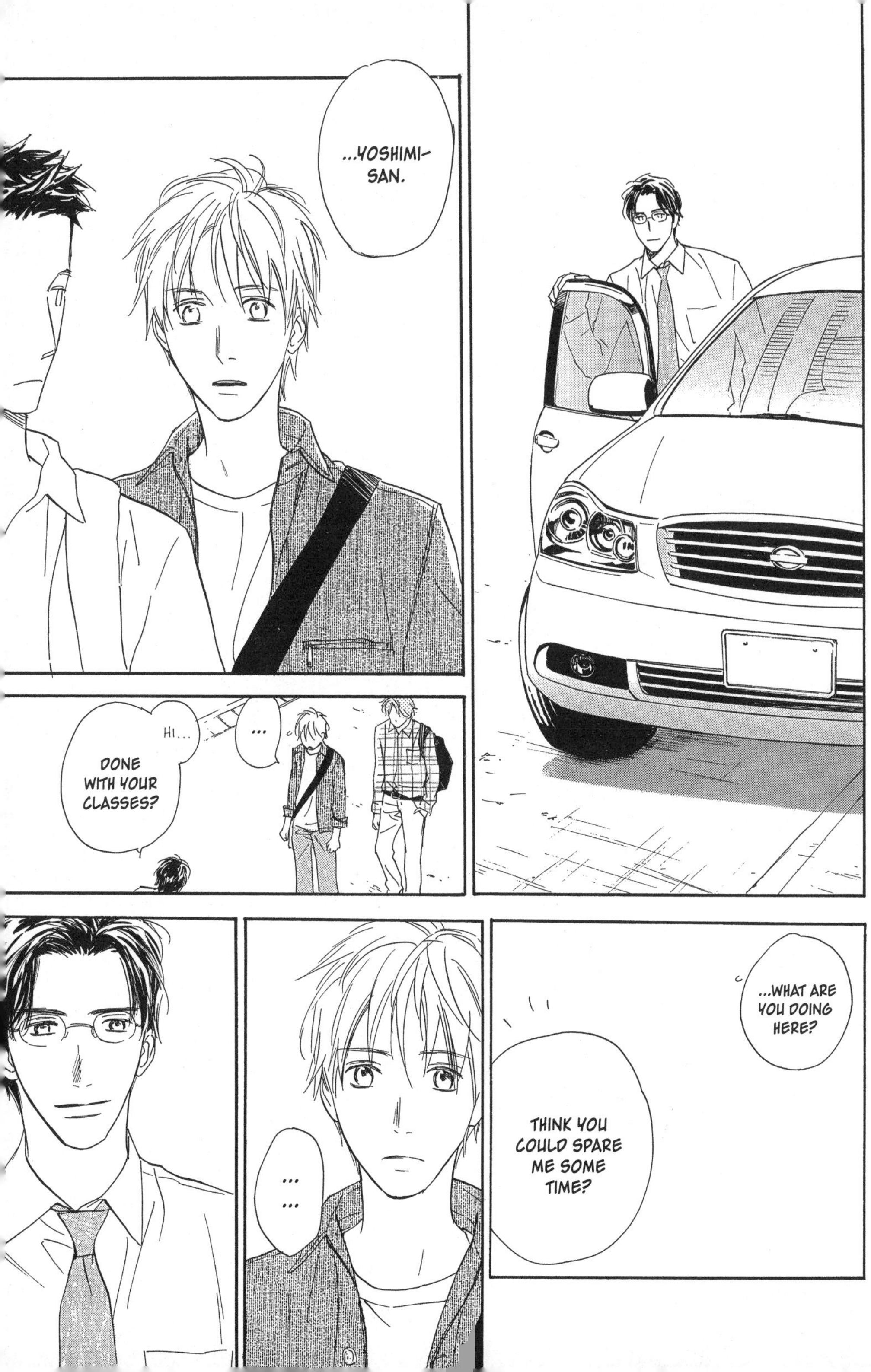
...YOSHIMI-SAN.
...
HI...
DONE WITH YOUR CLASSES?
...WHAT ARE YOU DOING HERE?
THINK YOU COULD SPARE ME SOME TIME?
... ...

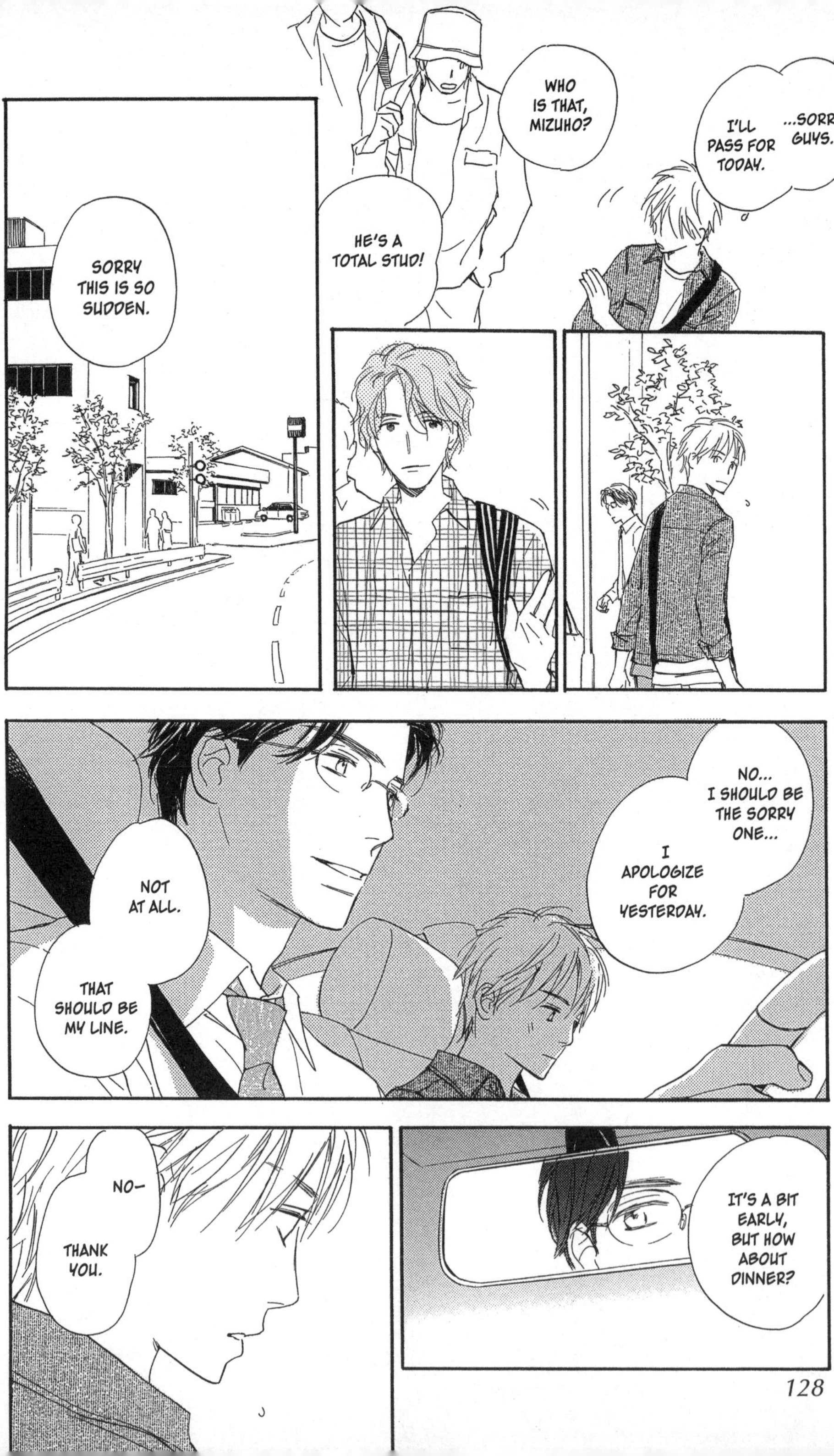
...SORRY, GUYS.
I'LL PASS FOR TODAY.
WHO IS THAT, MIZUHO?
HE'S A TOTAL STUD!
SORRY THIS IS SO SUDDEN.
NO... I SHOULD BE THE SORRY ONE...
I APOLOGIZE FOR YESTERDAY.
NOT AT ALL.
THAT SHOULD BE MY LINE.
IT'S A BIT EARLY, BUT HOW ABOUT DINNER?
NO—
THANK YOU.

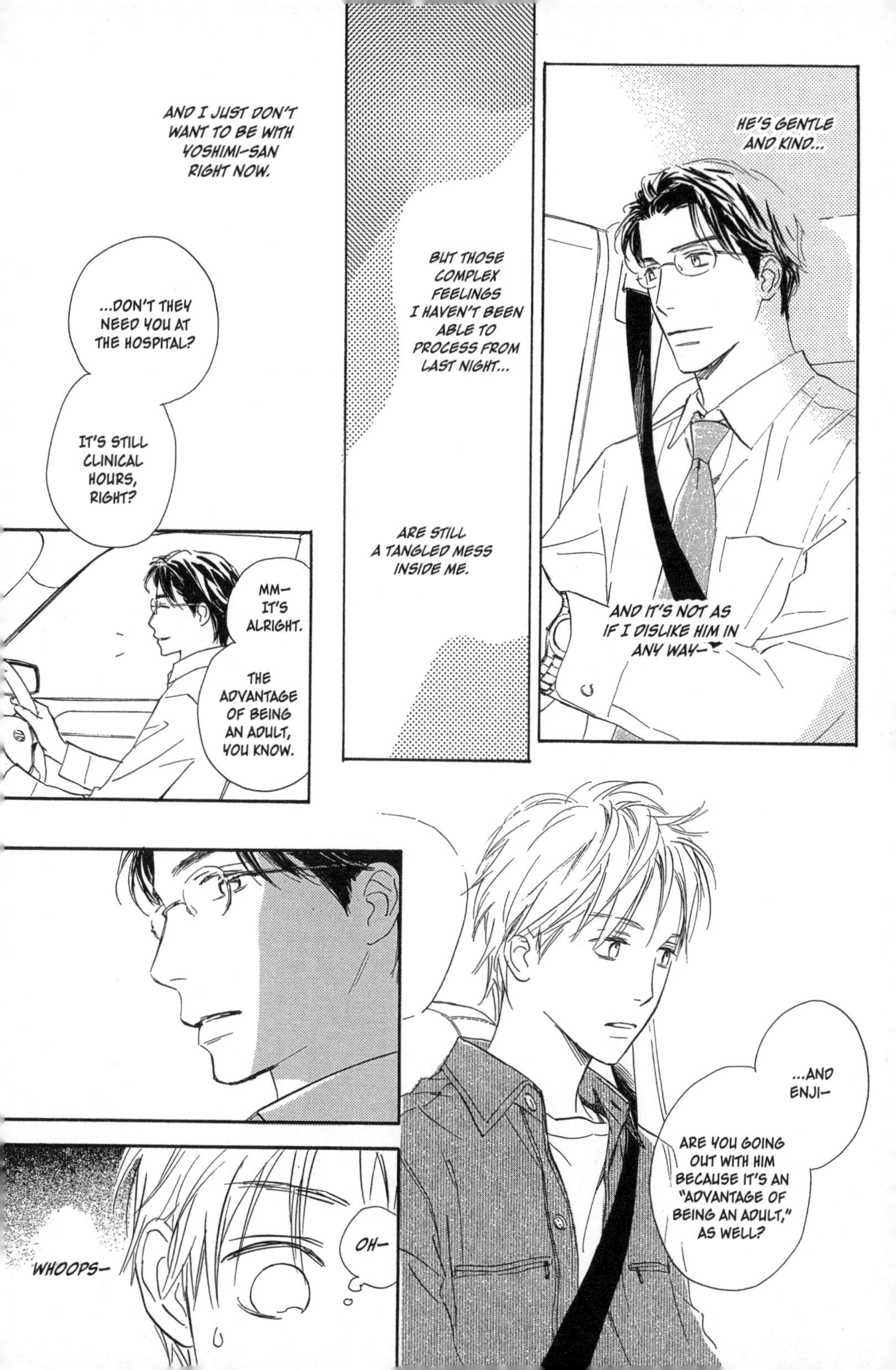
HE'S GENTLE AND KIND...
AND IT'S NOT AS IF I DISLIKE HIM IN ANY WAY—
BUT THOSE COMPLEX FEELINGS I HAVEN'T BEEN ABLE TO PROCESS FROM LAST NIGHT...
ARE STILL A TANGLED MESS INSIDE ME.
AND I JUST DON'T WANT TO BE WITH YOSHIMI-SAN RIGHT NOW.
...DON'T THEY NEED YOU AT THE HOSPITAL?
IT'S STILL CLINICAL HOURS, RIGHT?
MM— IT'S ALRIGHT.
THE ADVANTAGE OF BEING AN ADULT, YOU KNOW.
...AND ENJI—
ARE YOU GOING OUT WITH HIM BECAUSE IT'S AN "ADVANTAGE OF BEING AN ADULT," AS WELL?
OH—
WHOOPS—

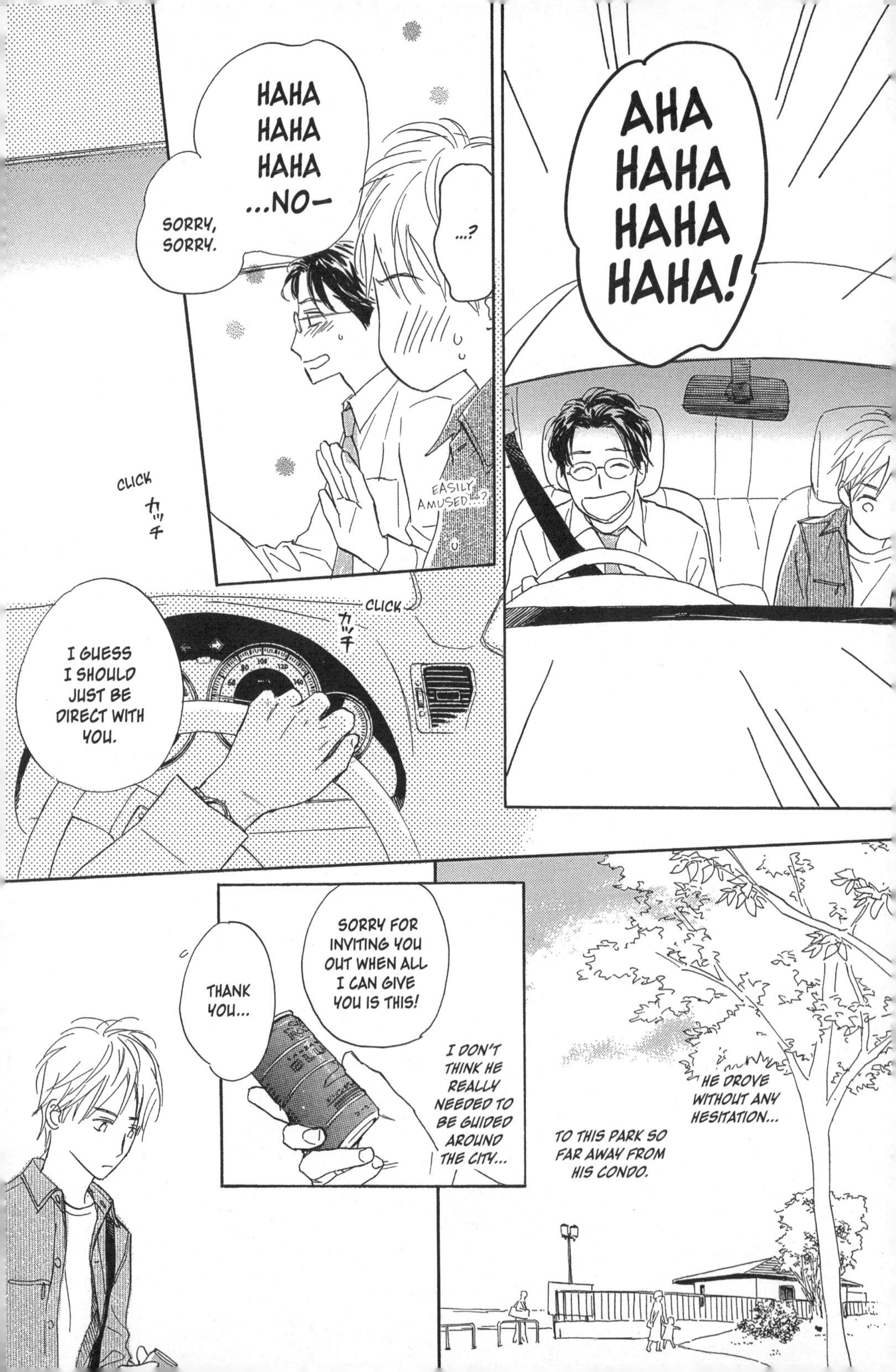
AHA HAHA HAHA HAHA!
HAHA HAHA HAHA ...NO—
...?
SORRY, SORRY.
EASILY AMUSED...?
CLICK
カッチ
CLICK
カッチ
I GUESS I SHOULD JUST BE DIRECT WITH YOU.
HE DROVE WITHOUT ANY HESITATION...
TO THIS PARK SO FAR AWAY FROM HIS CONDO.
SORRY FOR INVITING YOU OUT WHEN ALL I CAN GIVE YOU IS THIS!
I DON'T THINK HE REALLY NEEDED TO BE GUIDED AROUND THE CITY...
THANK YOU...

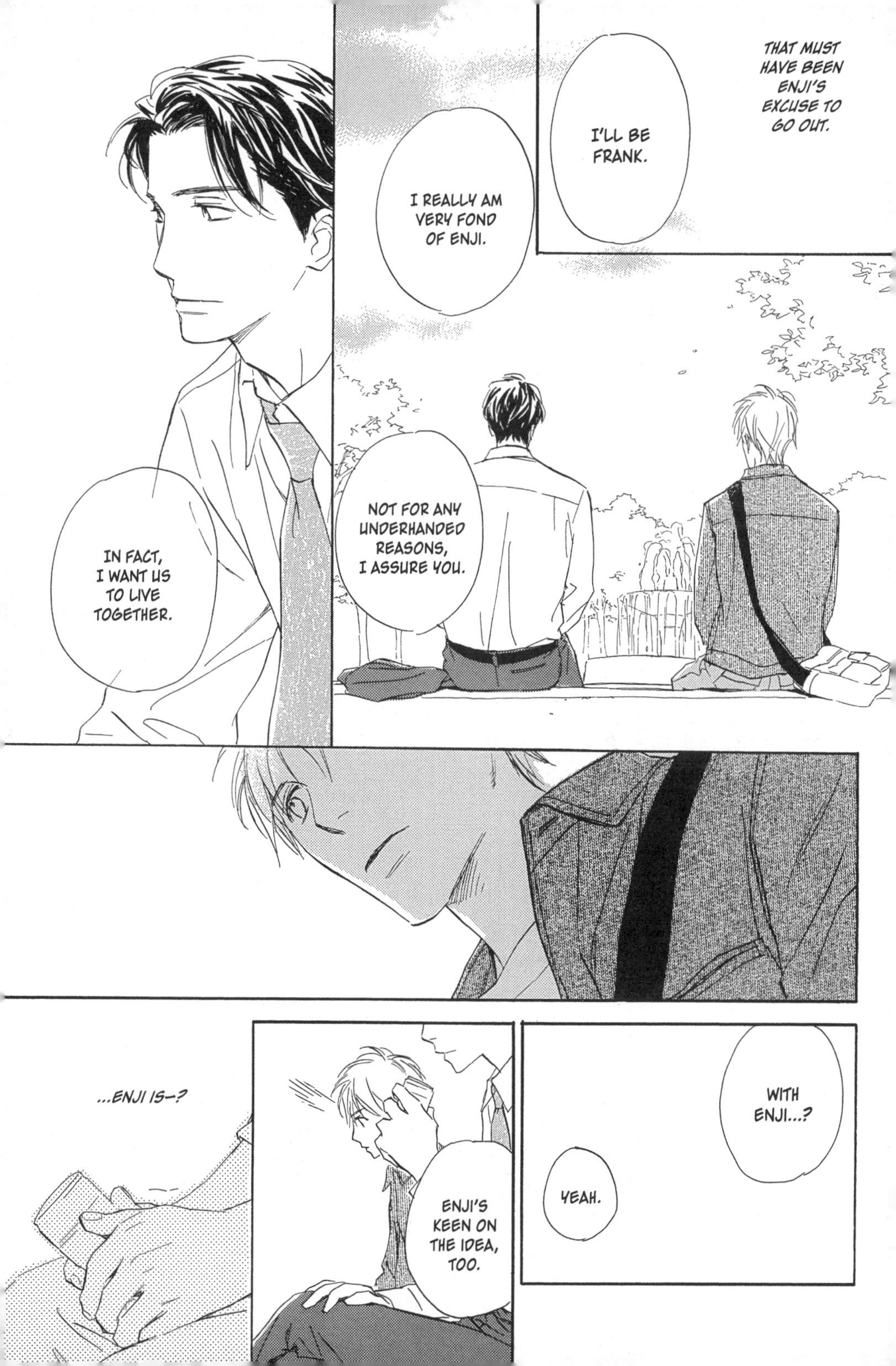
THAT MUST HAVE BEEN ENJI'S EXCUSE TO GO OUT.
I'LL BE FRANK.
I REALLY AM VERY FOND OF ENJI.
NOT FOR ANY UNDERHANDED REASONS, I ASSURE YOU.
IN FACT, I WANT US TO LIVE TOGETHER.
WITH ENJI...?
YEAH.
ENJI'S KEEN ON THE IDEA, TOO.
...ENJI IS—?

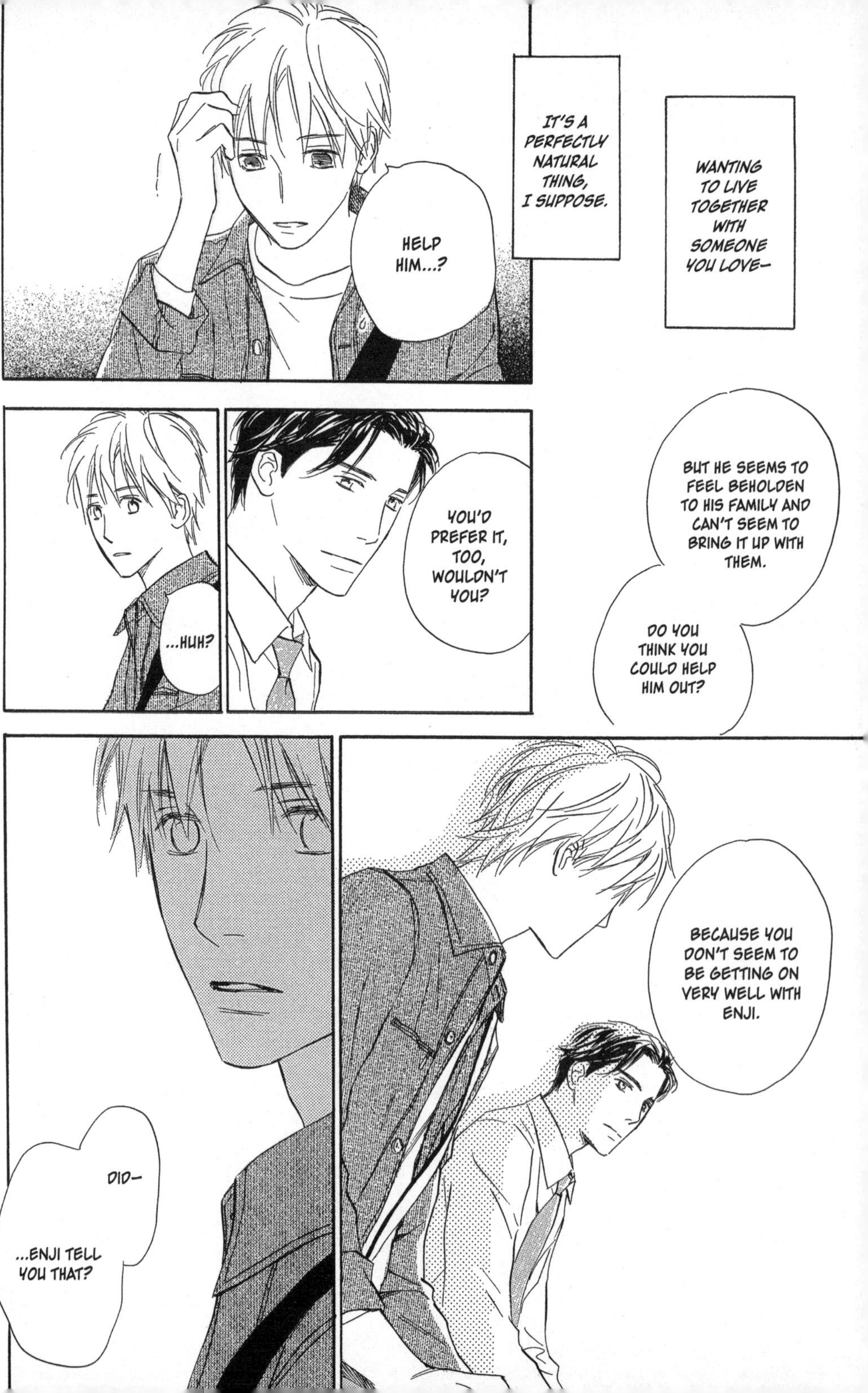
WANTING TO LIVE TOGETHER WITH SOMEONE YOU LOVE—
IT'S A PERFECTLY NATURAL THING, I SUPPOSE.
HELP HIM...?
BUT HE SEEMS TO FEEL BEHOLDEN TO HIS FAMILY AND CAN'T SEEM TO BRING IT UP WITH THEM.
DO YOU THINK YOU COULD HELP HIM OUT?
YOU'D PREFER IT, TOO, WOULDN'T YOU?
...HUH?
BECAUSE YOU DON'T SEEM TO BE GETTING ON VERY WELL WITH ENJI.
DID—
...ENJI TELL YOU THAT?

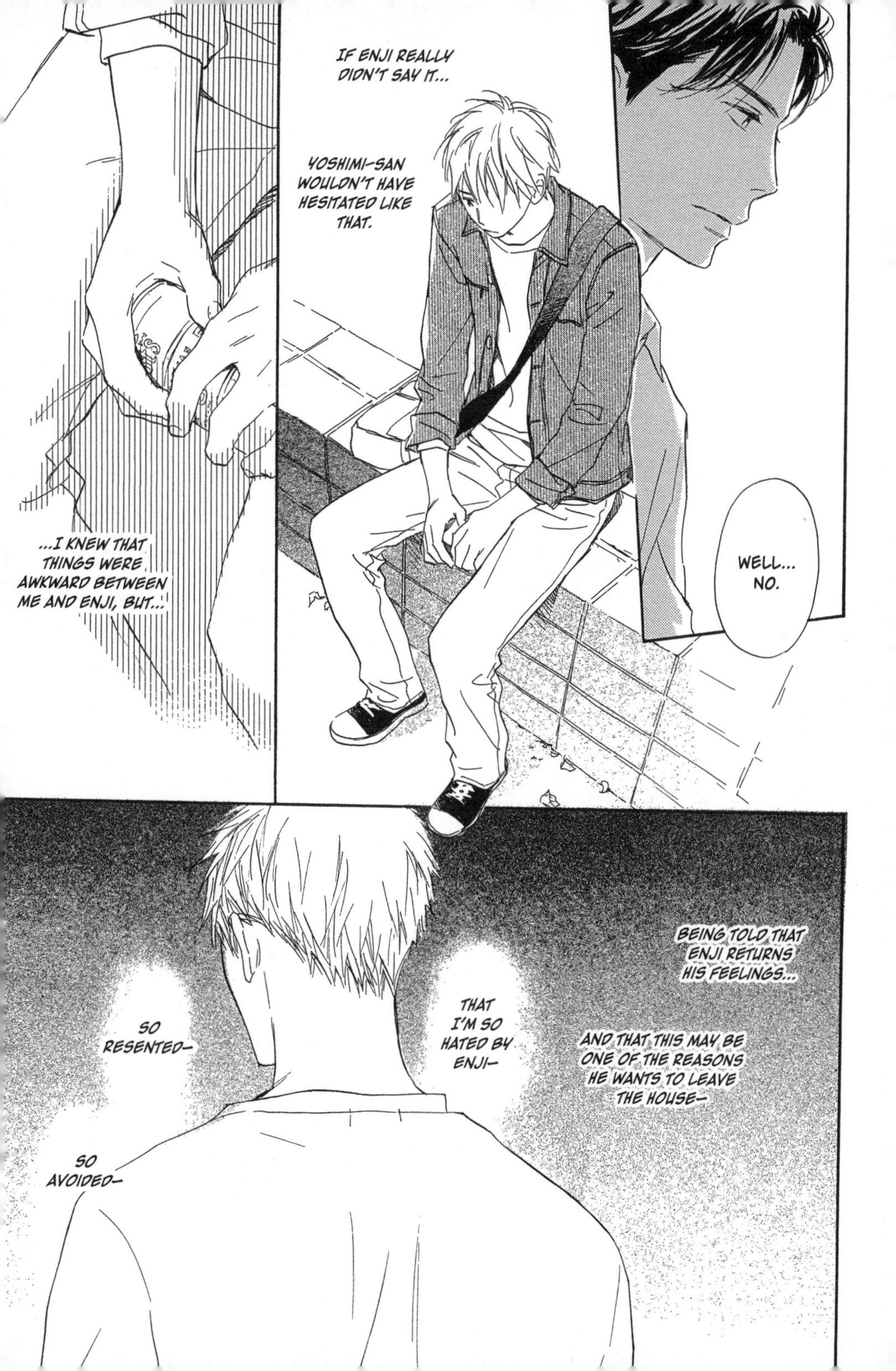
WELL... NO.
IF ENJI REALLY DIDN'T SAY IT...
YOSHIMI-SAN WOULDN'T HAVE HESITATED LIKE THAT.
...I KNEW THAT THINGS WERE AWKWARD BETWEEN ME AND ENJI, BUT...
BEING TOLD THAT ENJI RETURNS HIS FEELINGS...
AND THAT THIS MAY BE ONE OF THE REASONS HE WANTS TO LEAVE THE HOUSE—
THAT I'M SO HATED BY ENJI—
SO RESENTED—
SO AVOIDED—

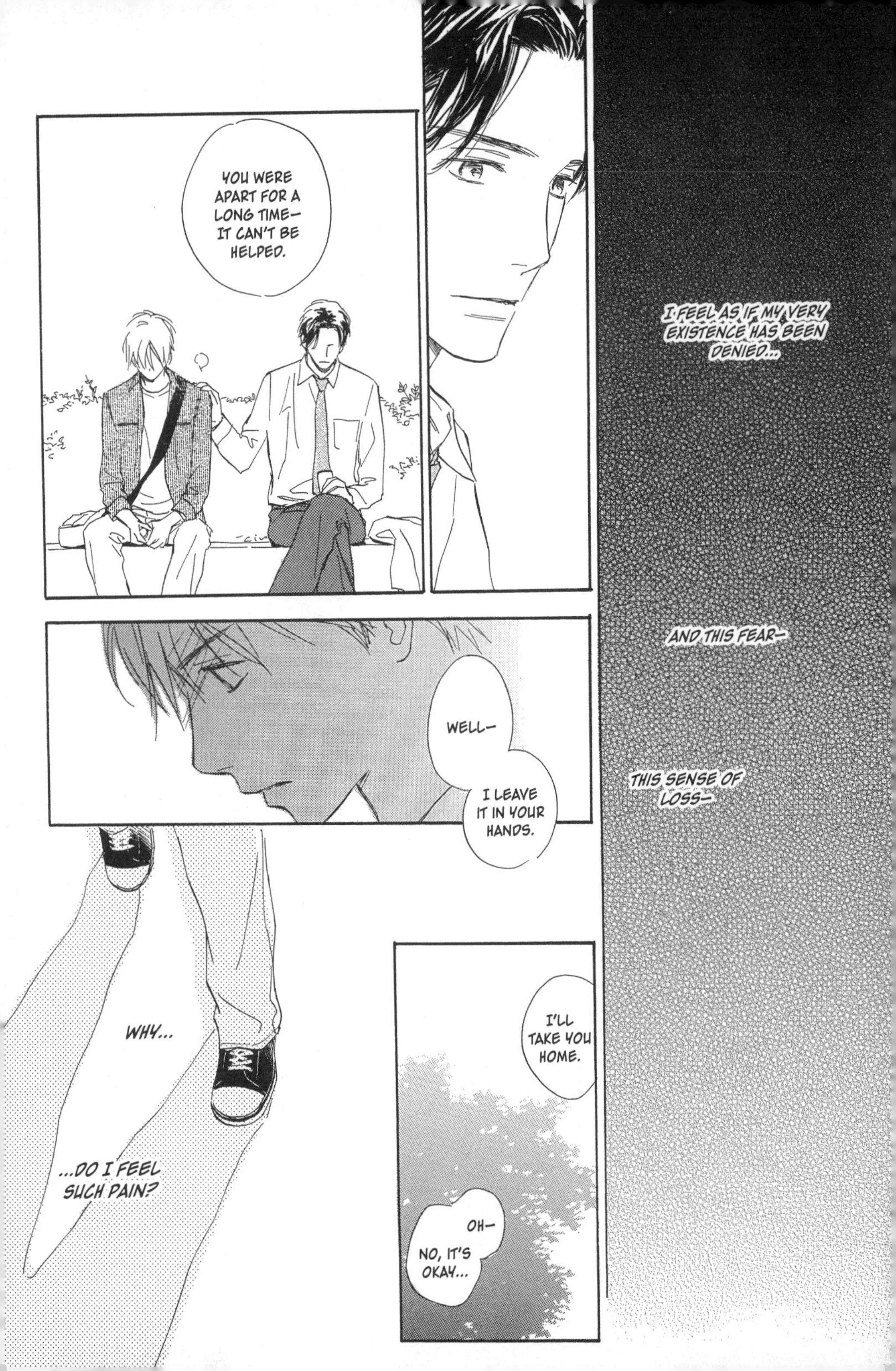
I FEEL AS IF MY VERY EXISTENCE HAS BEEN DENIED...
AND THIS FEAR—
THIS SENSE OF LOSS—
YOU WERE APART FOR A LONG TIME— IT CAN'T BE HELPED.
WELL—
I LEAVE IT IN YOUR HANDS.
I'LL TAKE YOU HOME.
OH—
NO, IT'S OKAY...
WHY...
...DO I FEEL SUCH PAIN?

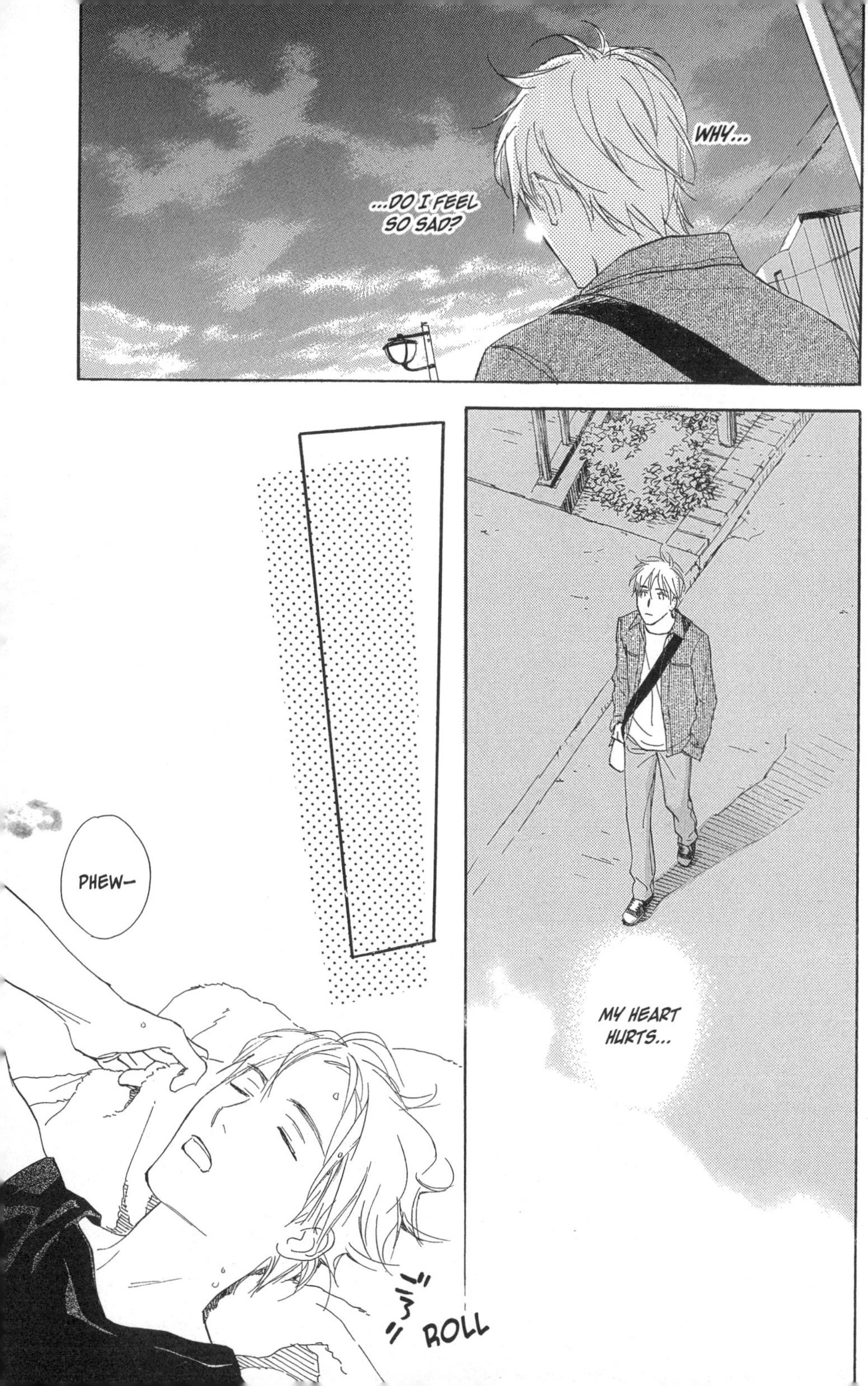
WHY...
...DO I FEEL SO SAD?
MY HEART HURTS...
PHEW–
ROLL

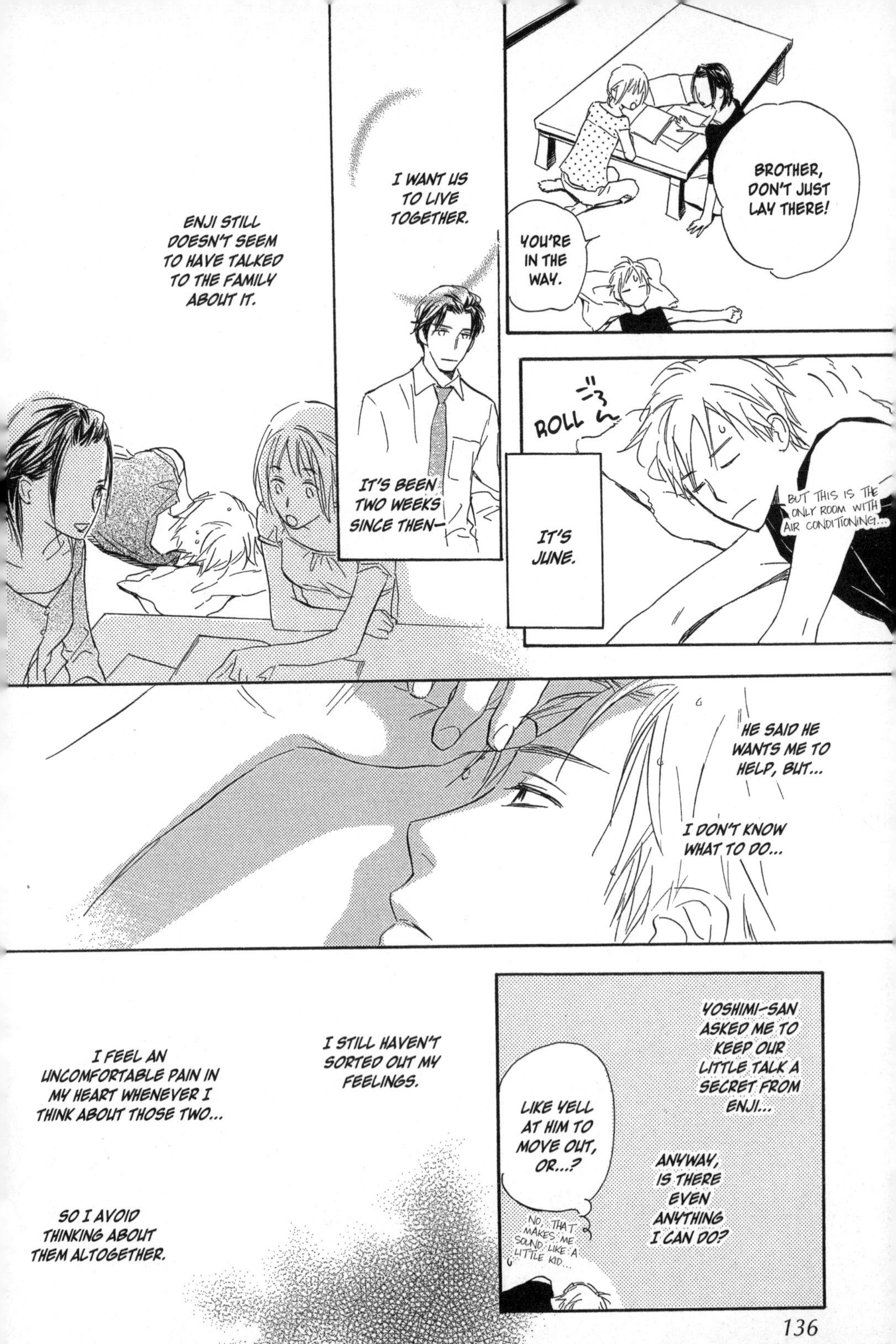
BROTHER, DON'T JUST LAY THERE!
YOU'RE IN THE WAY.
ROLL
BUT THIS IS THE ONLY ROOM WITH AIR CONDITIONING...
IT'S JUNE.
I WANT US TO LIVE TOGETHER.
IT'S BEEN TWO WEEKS SINCE THEN–
ENJI STILL DOESN'T SEEM TO HAVE TALKED TO THE FAMILY ABOUT IT.
HE SAID HE WANTS ME TO HELP, BUT...
I DON'T KNOW WHAT TO DO...
YOSHIMI-SAN ASKED ME TO KEEP OUR LITTLE TALK A SECRET FROM ENJI...
ANYWAY, IS THERE EVEN ANYTHING I CAN DO?
LIKE YELL AT HIM TO MOVE OUT, OR...?
NO, THAT MAKES ME SOUND LIKE A LITTLE KID...
I STILL HAVEN'T SORTED OUT MY FEELINGS.
I FEEL AN UNCOMFORTABLE PAIN IN MY HEART WHENEVER I THINK ABOUT THOSE TWO...
SO I AVOID THINKING ABOUT THEM ALTOGETHER.

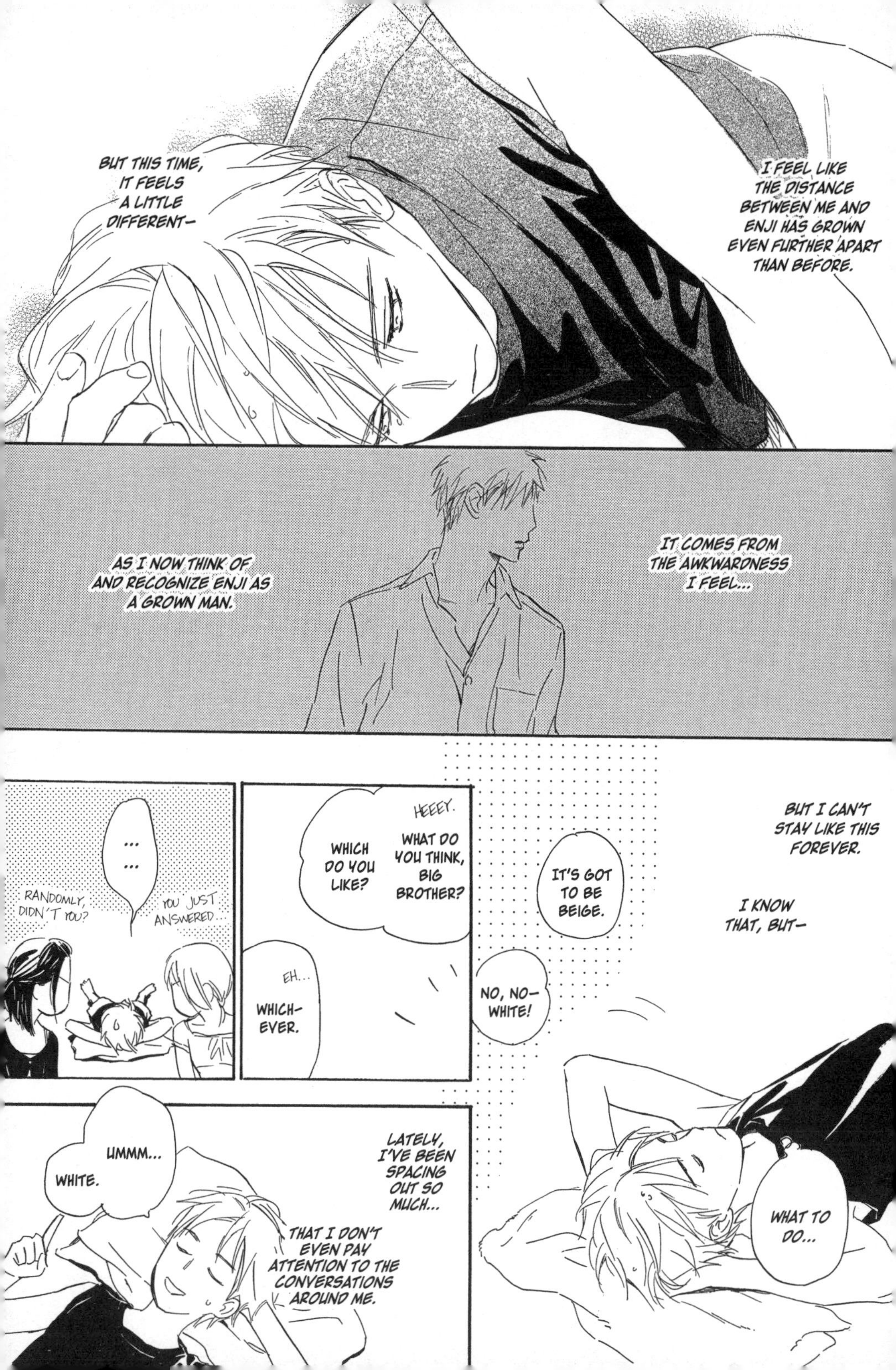
I FEEL LIKE THE DISTANCE BETWEEN ME AND ENJI HAS GROWN EVEN FURTHER APART THAN BEFORE.
BUT THIS TIME, IT FEELS A LITTLE DIFFERENT—
IT COMES FROM THE AWKWARDNESS I FEEL...
AS I NOW THINK OF AND RECOGNIZE ENJI AS A GROWN MAN.
BUT I CAN'T STAY LIKE THIS FOREVER.
I KNOW THAT, BUT—
WHAT TO DO...
HEEEY.
WHAT DO YOU THINK, BIG BROTHER?
WHICH DO YOU LIKE?
IT'S GOT TO BE BEIGE.
NO, NO— WHITE!
EH... WHICH-EVER.
... ...
YOU JUST ANSWERED...
RANDOMLY, DIDN'T YOU?
LATELY, I'VE BEEN SPACING OUT SO MUCH...
THAT I DON'T EVEN PAY ATTENTION TO THE CONVERSATIONS AROUND ME.
UMMM... WHITE.

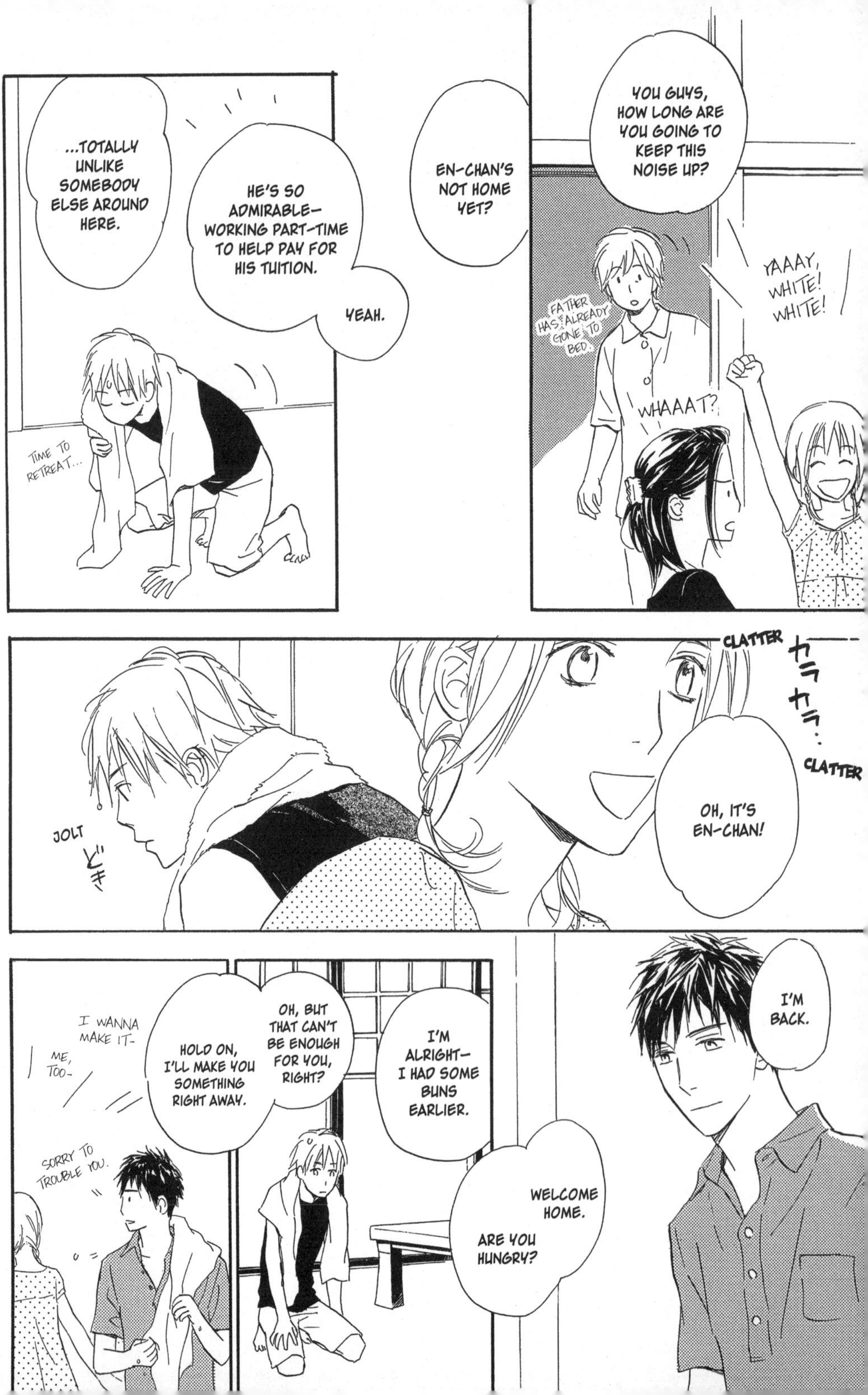
YOU GUYS, HOW LONG ARE YOU GOING TO KEEP THIS NOISE UP?
EN-CHAN'S NOT HOME YET?
FATHER HAS ALREADY GONE TO BED.
YAAAY, WHITE! WHITE!
WHAAAT?
HE'S SO ADMIRABLE—WORKING PART-TIME TO HELP PAY FOR HIS TUITION.
YEAH.
...TOTALLY UNLIKE SOMEBODY ELSE AROUND HERE.
TIME TO RETREAT...
CLATTER
カラ カラ..
CLATTER
OH, IT'S EN-CHAN!
JOLT
ドキ
I'M BACK.
WELCOME HOME.
ARE YOU HUNGRY?
I'M ALRIGHT—I HAD SOME BUNS EARLIER.
OH, BUT THAT CAN'T BE ENOUGH FOR YOU, RIGHT?
HOLD ON, I'LL MAKE YOU SOMETHING RIGHT AWAY.
I WANNA MAKE IT-
ME, TOO-
SORRY TO TROUBLE YOU.

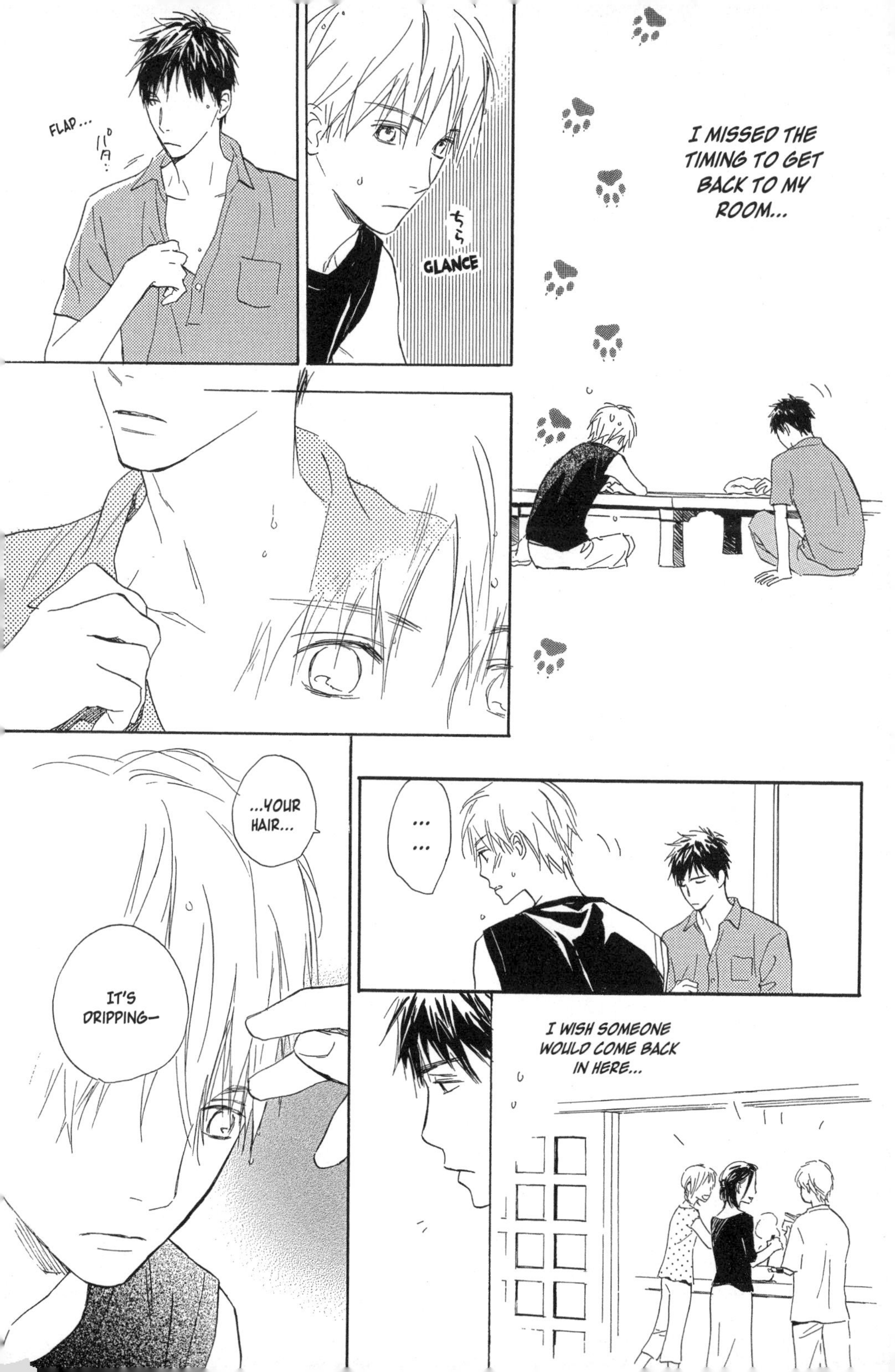
I MISSED THE TIMING TO GET BACK TO MY ROOM...
ちら
GLANCE
FLAP...
パタ
......
I WISH SOMEONE WOULD COME BACK IN HERE...
...YOUR HAIR...
IT'S DRIPPING—

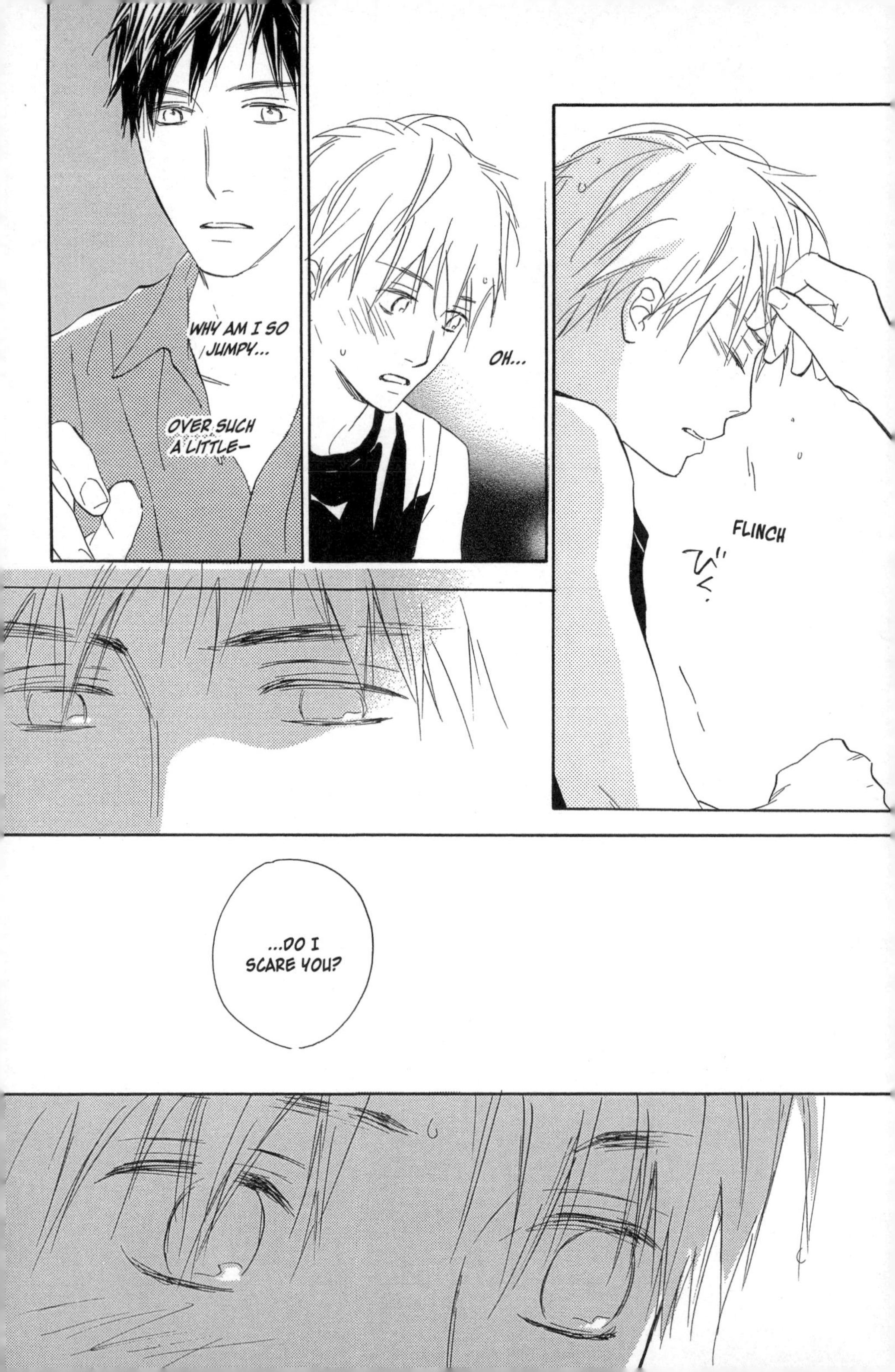
FLINCH
びく
OH...
WHY AM I SO JUMPY...
OVER SUCH A LITTLE—
...DO I SCARE YOU?

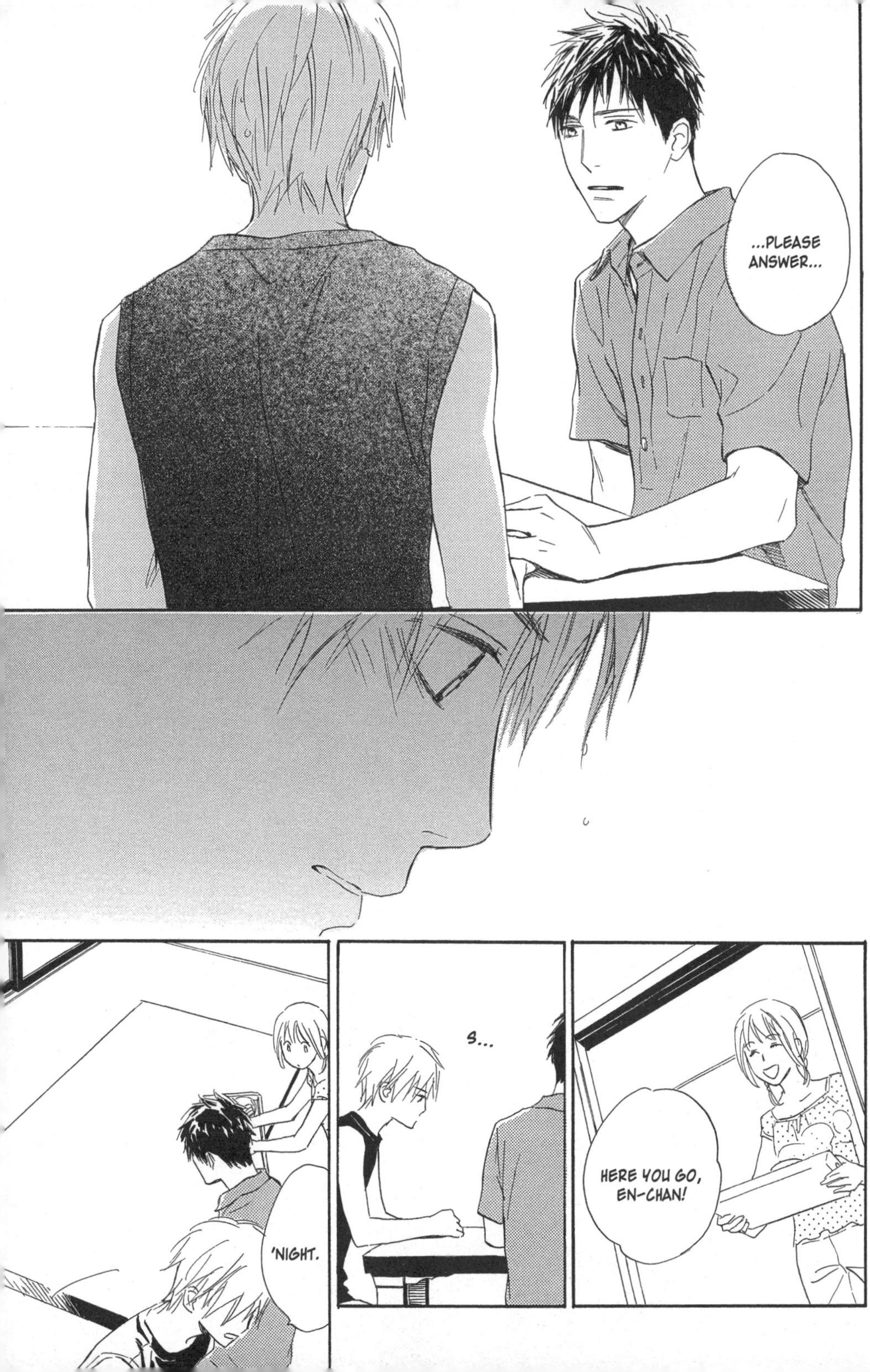
...PLEASE ANSWER...
HERE YOU GO, EN-CHAN!
S...
'NIGHT.

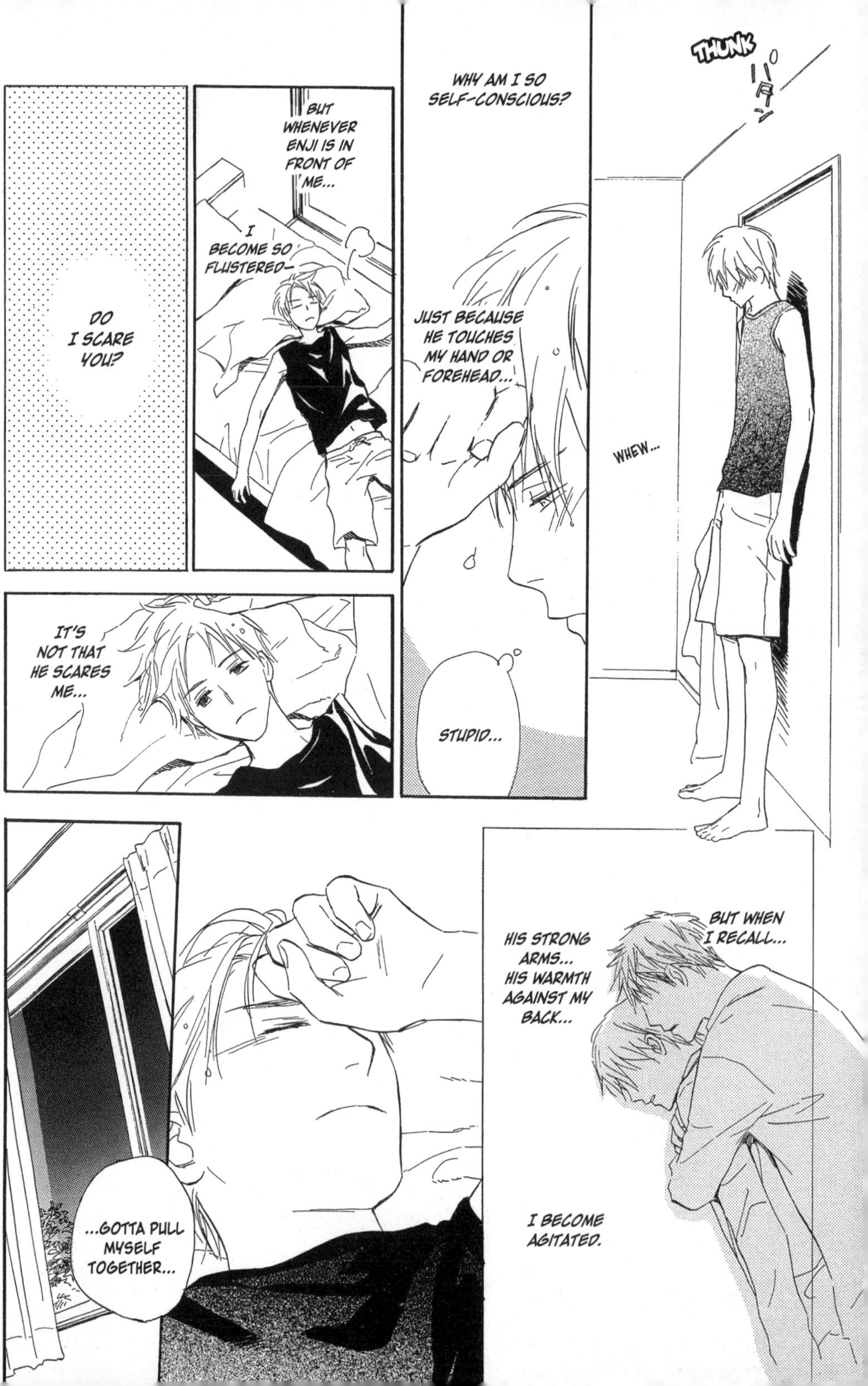
THUNK
WHEW...
WHY AM I SO SELF-CONSCIOUS?
JUST BECAUSE HE TOUCHES MY HAND OR FOREHEAD...
STUPID...
BUT WHENEVER ENJI IS IN FRONT OF ME...
I BECOME SO FLUSTERED—
DO I SCARE YOU?
IT'S NOT THAT HE SCARES ME...
BUT WHEN I RECALL...
HIS STRONG ARMS... HIS WARMTH AGAINST MY BACK...
I BECOME AGITATED.
...GOTTA PULL MYSELF TOGETHER...

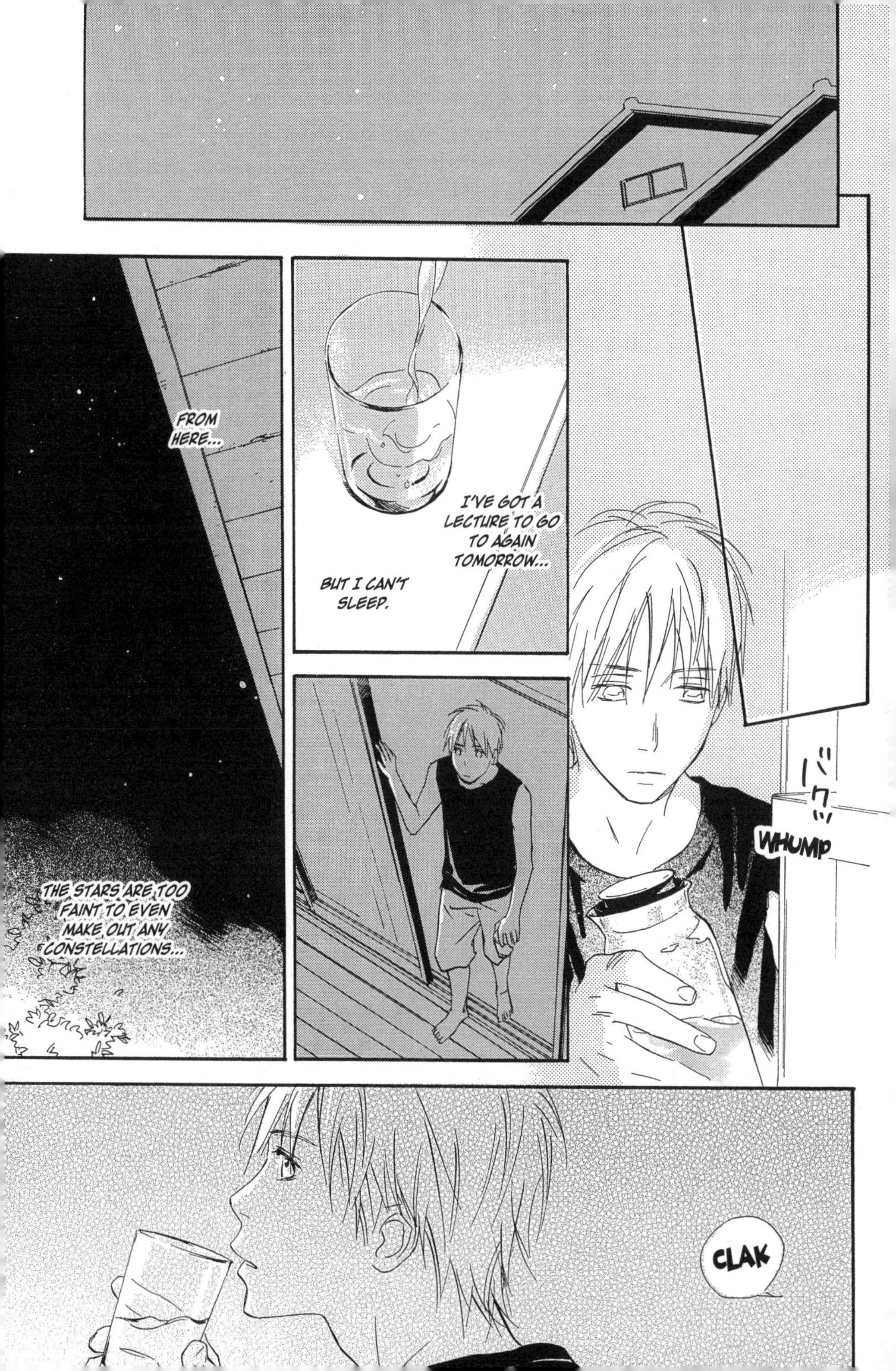

バクッ
WHUMP
I'VE GOT A LECTURE TO GO TO AGAIN TOMORROW...
BUT I CAN'T SLEEP.
FROM HERE...
THE STARS ARE TOO FAINT TO EVEN MAKE OUT ANY CONSTELLATIONS...
CLAK

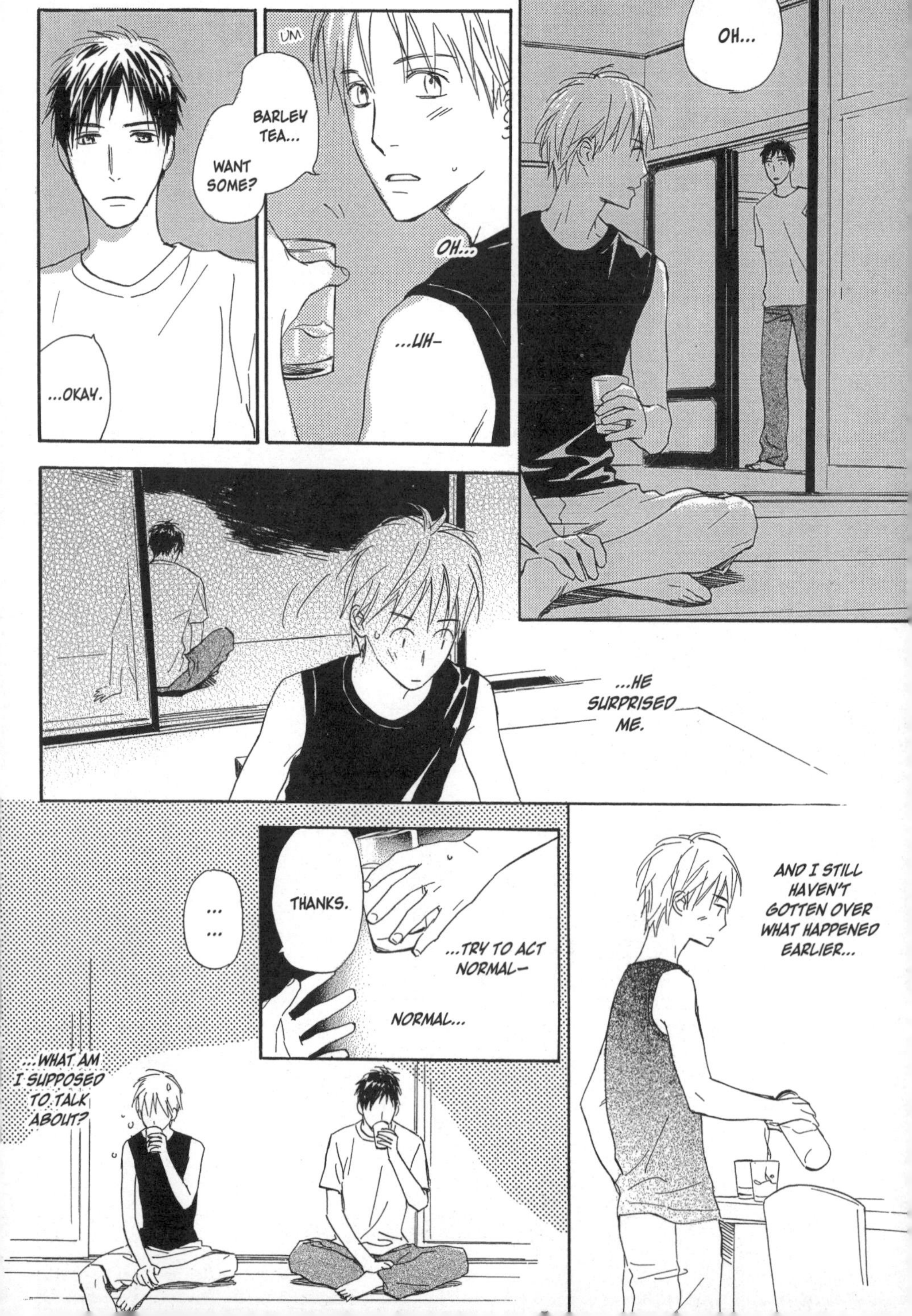
OH...
UM
BARLEY TEA... WANT SOME?
OH...
...UH-
...OKAY.
...HE SURPRISED ME.
AND I STILL HAVEN'T GOTTEN OVER WHAT HAPPENED EARLIER...
... ...
THANKS.
...TRY TO ACT NORMAL—
NORMAL...
...WHAT AM I SUPPOSED TO TALK ABOUT?

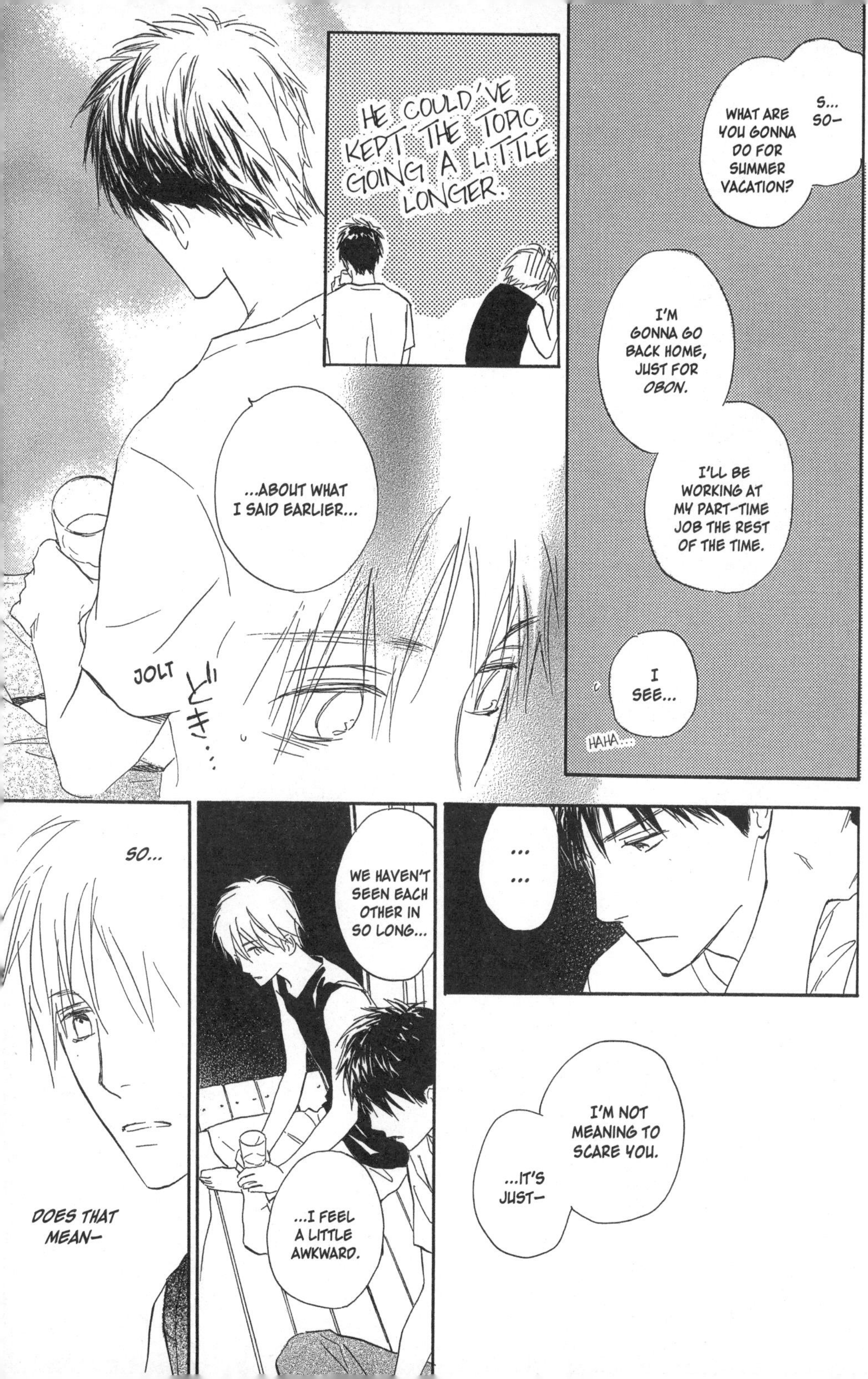
S... SO-
WHAT ARE YOU GONNA DO FOR SUMMER VACATION?
I'M GONNA GO BACK HOME, JUST FOR *OBON.*
I'LL BE WORKING AT MY PART-TIME JOB THE REST OF THE TIME.
I SEE...
HAHA...
HE COULD'VE KEPT THE TOPIC GOING A LITTLE LONGER.
...ABOUT WHAT I SAID EARLIER...
JOLT
どき…
...
...
I'M NOT MEANING TO SCARE YOU.
...IT'S JUST-
WE HAVEN'T SEEN EACH OTHER IN SO LONG...
...I FEEL A LITTLE AWKWARD.
SO...
DOES THAT MEAN-

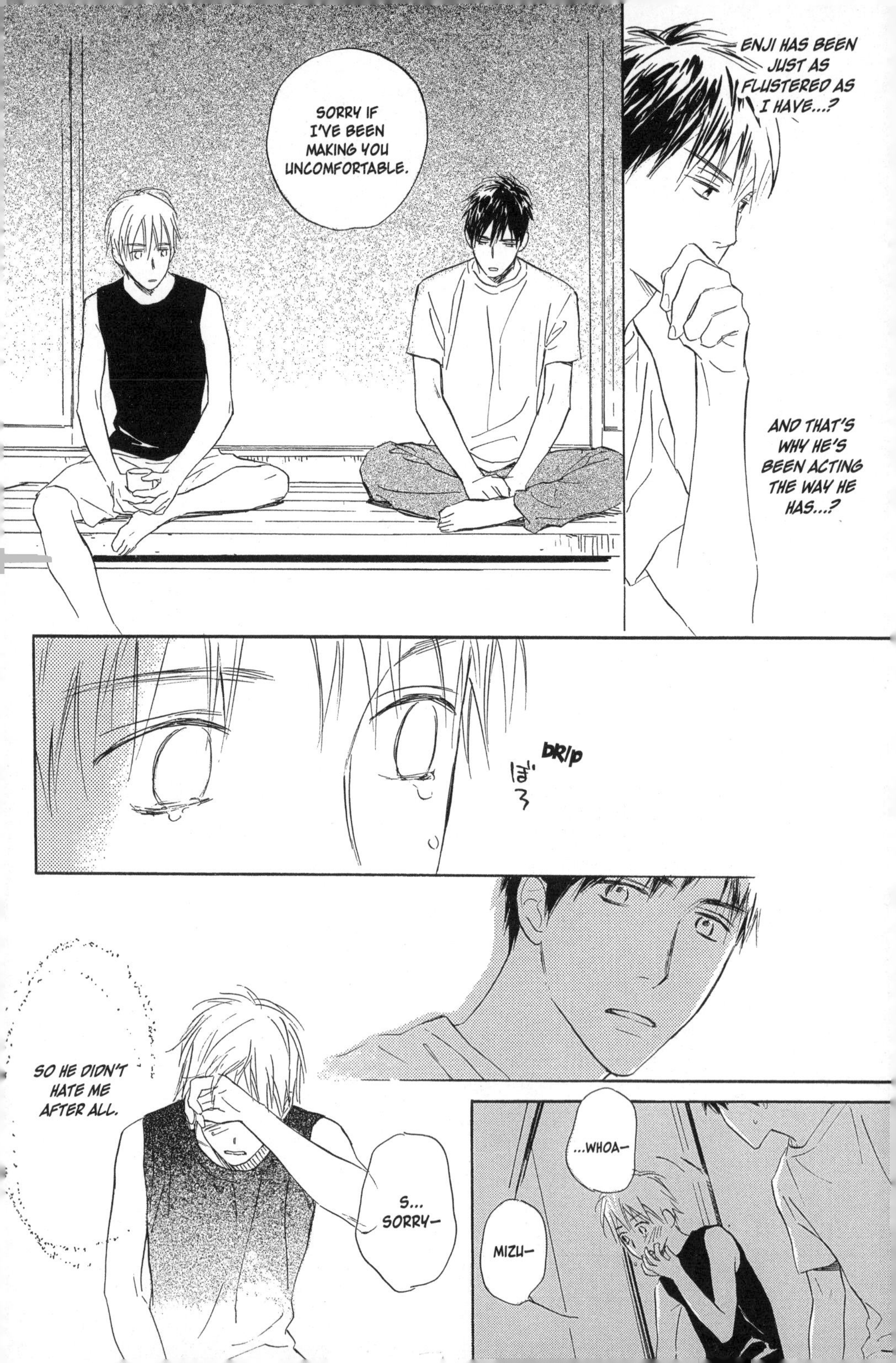

ENJI HAS BEEN JUST AS FLUSTERED AS I HAVE...?
AND THAT'S WHY HE'S BEEN ACTING THE WAY HE HAS...?
SORRY IF I'VE BEEN MAKING YOU UNCOMFORTABLE.
DRIP
ぽろ
...WHOA-
MIZU-
SO HE DIDN'T HATE ME AFTER ALL.
S... SORRY-

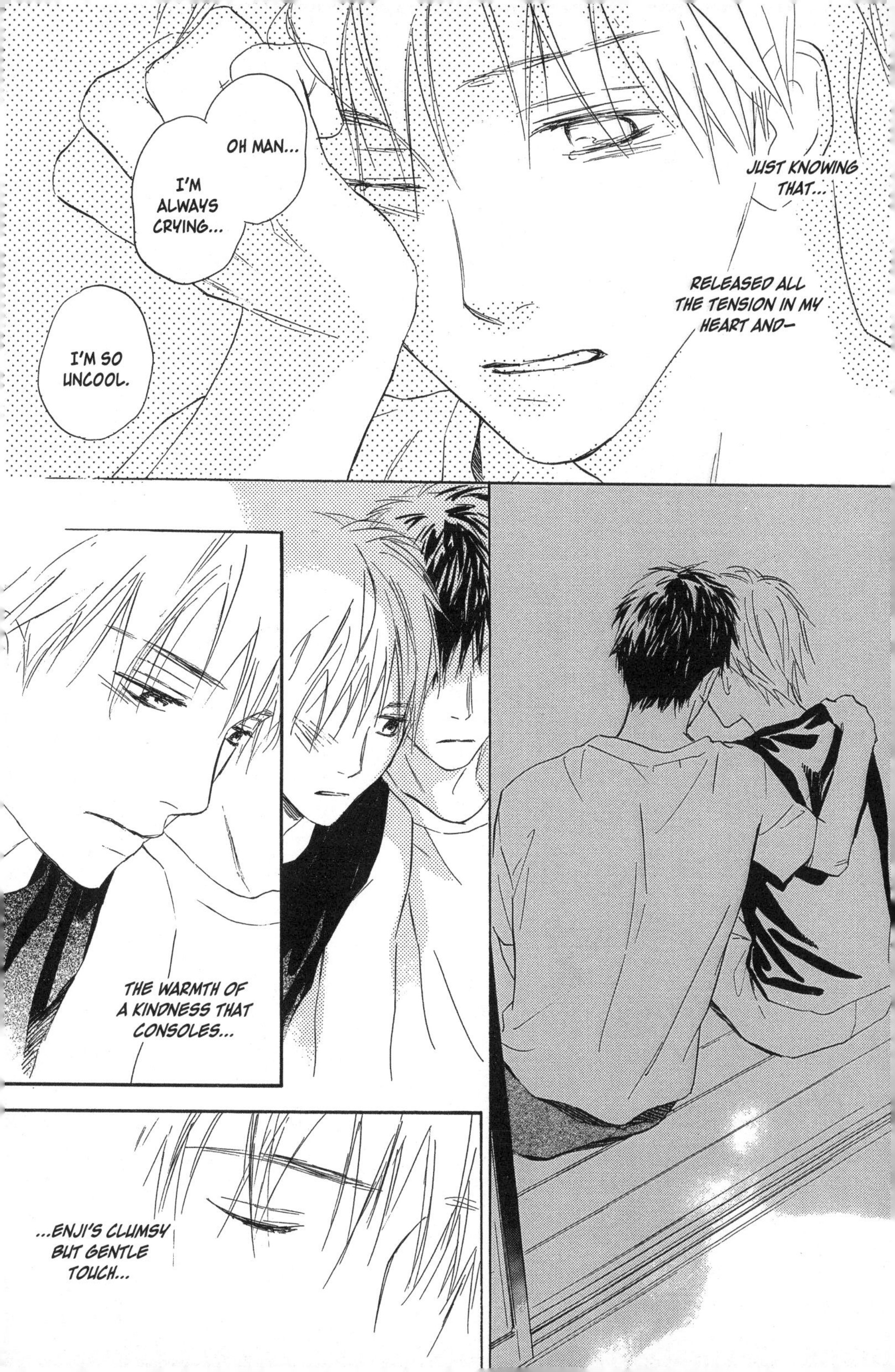
JUST KNOWING THAT...
RELEASED ALL THE TENSION IN MY HEART AND—
OH MAN...
I'M ALWAYS CRYING...
I'M SO UNCOOL.
THE WARMTH OF A KINDNESS THAT CONSOLES...
...ENJI'S CLUMSY BUT GENTLE TOUCH...

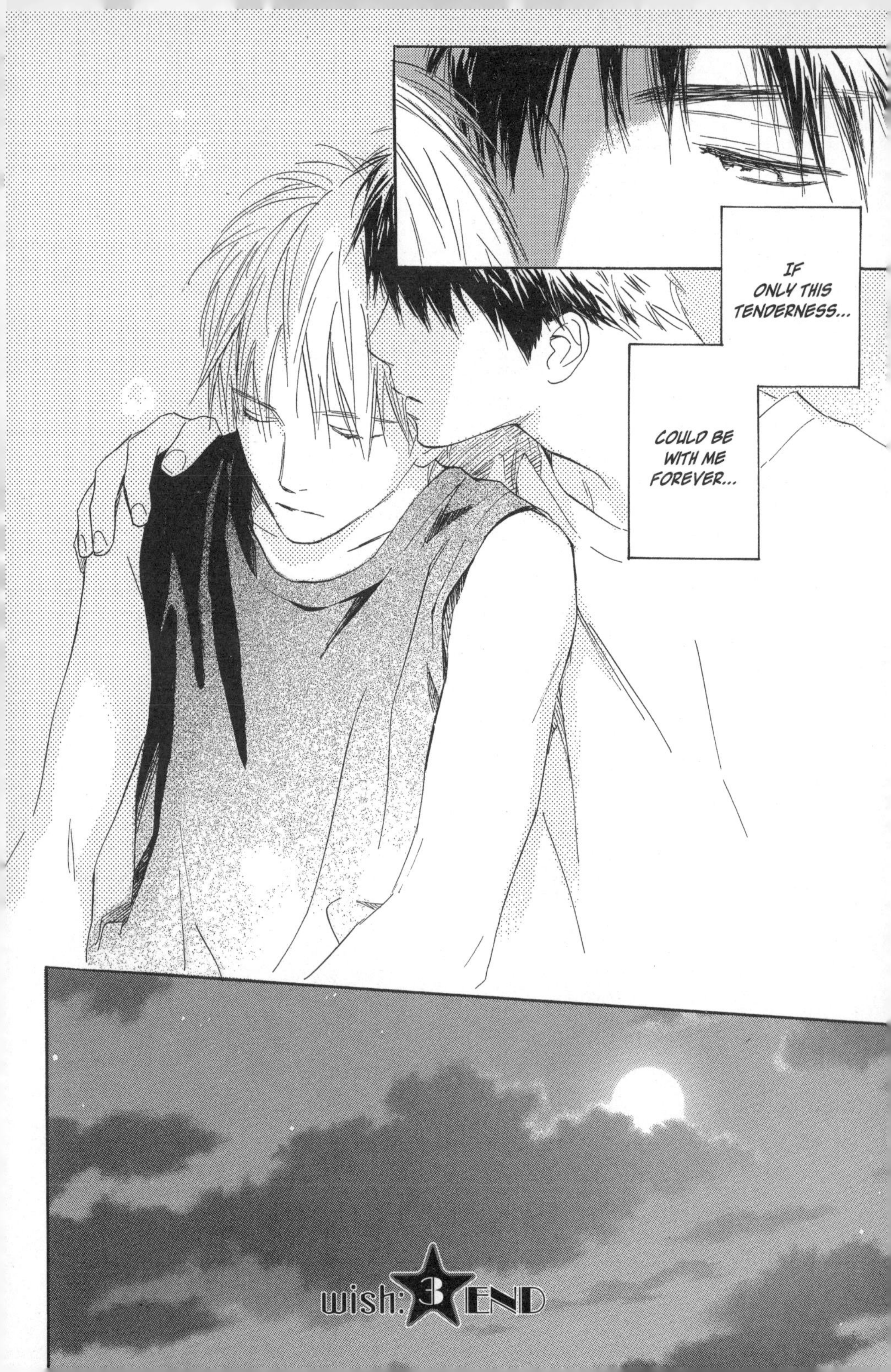
IF ONLY THIS TENDERNESS...
COULD BE WITH ME FOREVER...
wish: 3 END

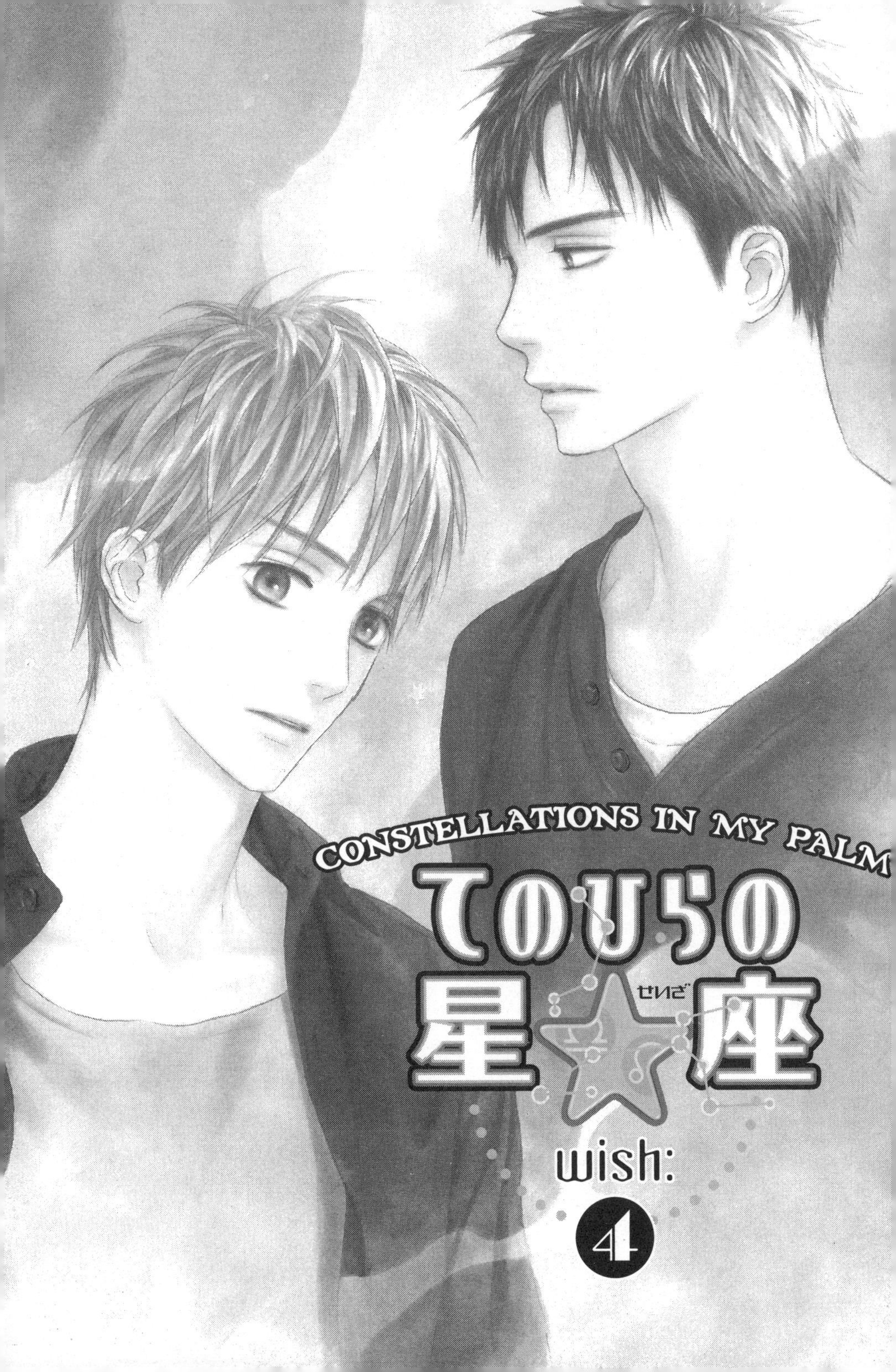
CONSTELLATIONS IN MY PALM
てのひらの
星☆座
せいざ
wish:
4

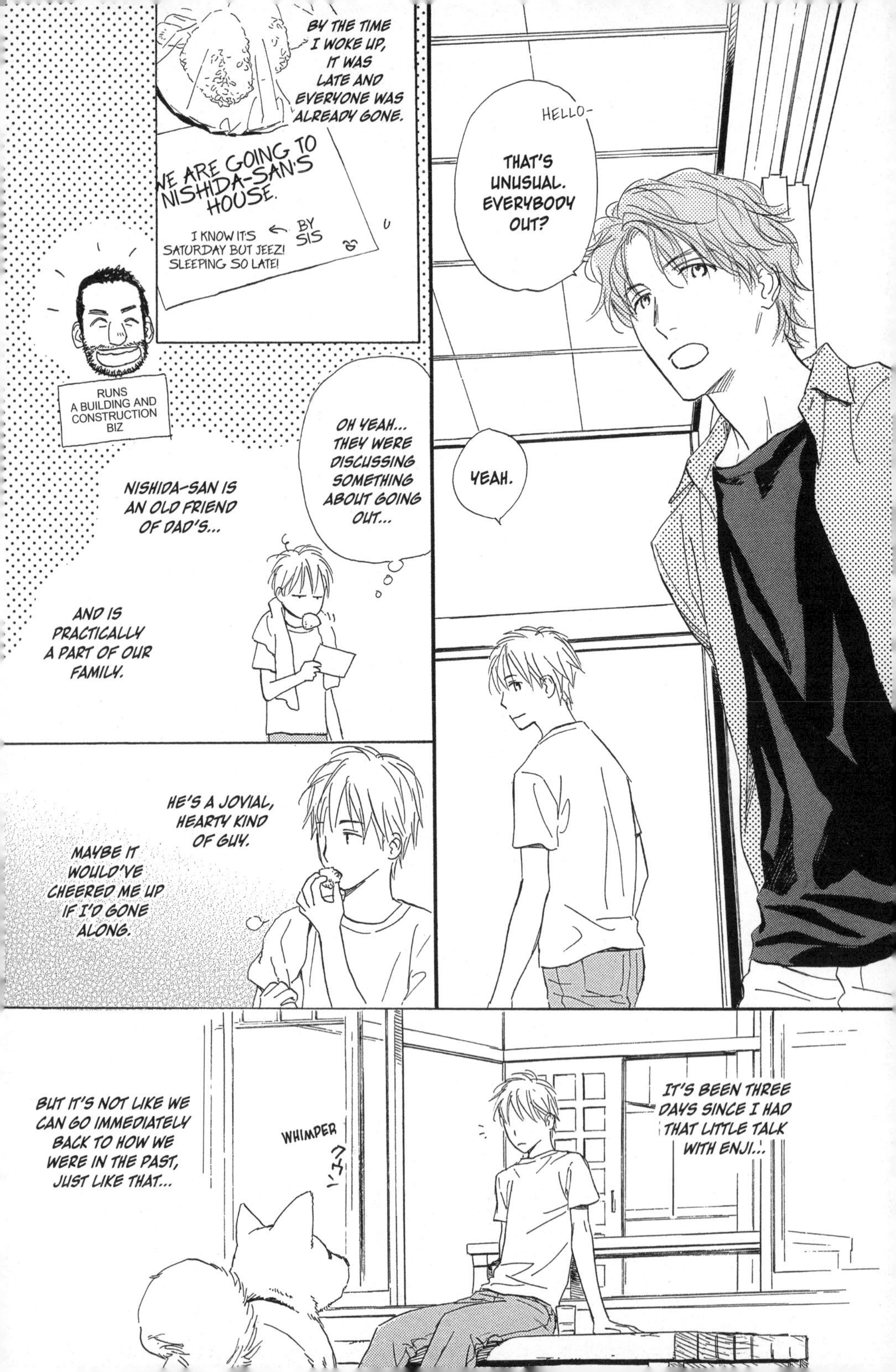
HELLO-
THAT'S UNUSUAL. EVERYBODY OUT?
YEAH.
BY THE TIME I WOKE UP, IT WAS LATE AND EVERYONE WAS ALREADY GONE.
WE ARE GOING TO NISHIDA-SAN'S HOUSE.
BY SIS
I KNOW IT'S SATURDAY BUT JEEZ! SLEEPING SO LATE!
RUNS A BUILDING AND CONSTRUCTION BIZ
OH YEAH... THEY WERE DISCUSSING SOMETHING ABOUT GOING OUT...
NISHIDA-SAN IS AN OLD FRIEND OF DAD'S...
AND IS PRACTICALLY A PART OF OUR FAMILY.
HE'S A JOVIAL, HEARTY KIND OF GUY.
MAYBE IT WOULD'VE CHEERED ME UP IF I'D GONE ALONG.
IT'S BEEN THREE DAYS SINCE I HAD THAT LITTLE TALK WITH ENJI...
WHIMPER
BUT IT'S NOT LIKE WE CAN GO IMMEDIATELY BACK TO HOW WE WERE IN THE PAST, JUST LIKE THAT...

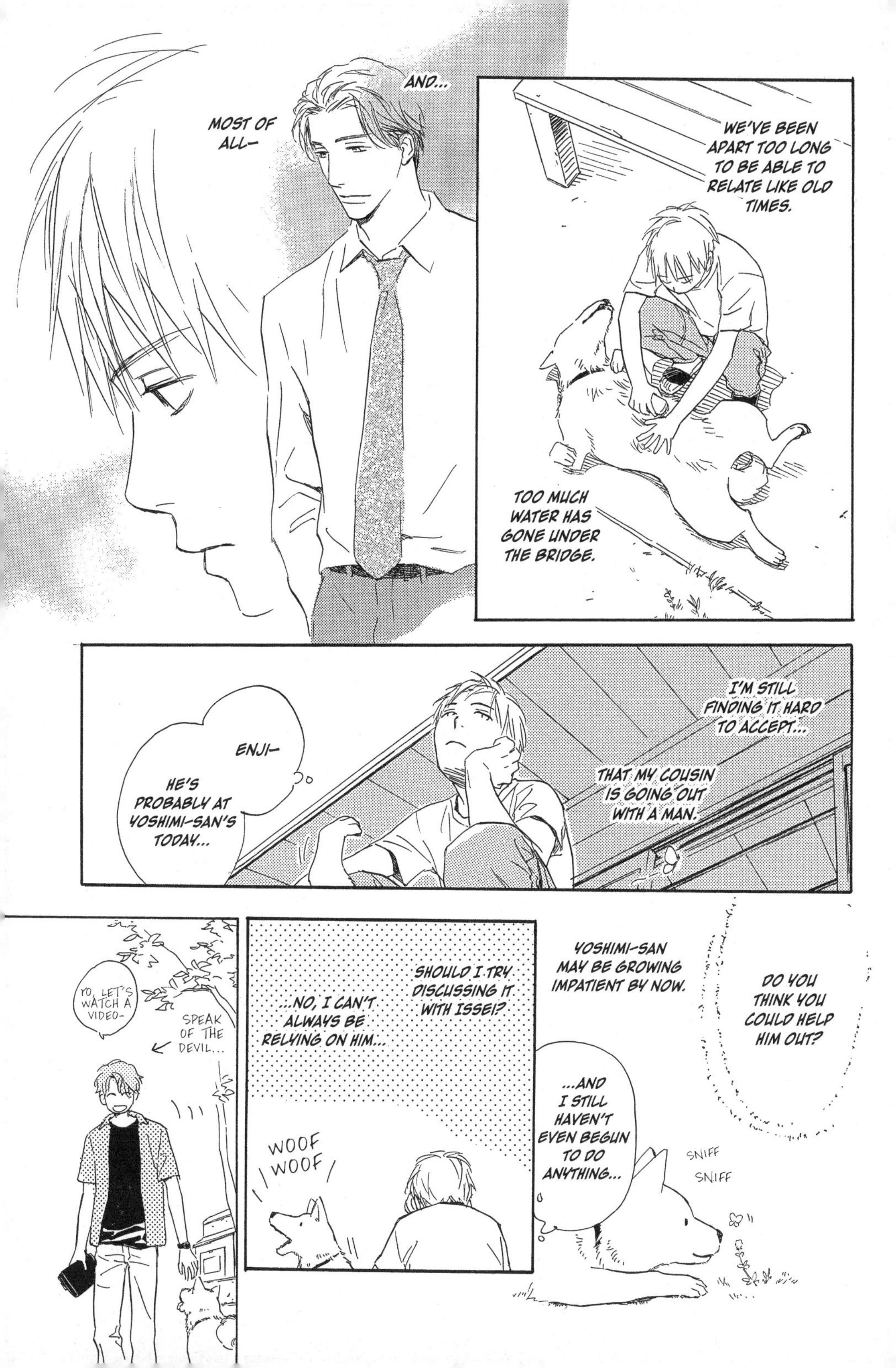
WE'VE BEEN APART TOO LONG TO BE ABLE TO RELATE LIKE OLD TIMES.
TOO MUCH WATER HAS GONE UNDER THE BRIDGE.
AND...
MOST OF ALL-
I'M STILL FINDING IT HARD TO ACCEPT...
THAT MY COUSIN IS GOING OUT WITH A MAN.
ENJI-
HE'S PROBABLY AT YOSHIMI-SAN'S TODAY...
DO YOU THINK YOU COULD HELP HIM OUT?
YOSHIMI-SAN MAY BE GROWING IMPATIENT BY NOW.
...AND I STILL HAVEN'T EVEN BEGUN TO DO ANYTHING...
SNIFF
SNIFF
SHOULD I TRY DISCUSSING IT WITH ISSEI?
...NO, I CAN'T ALWAYS BE RELYING ON HIM...
WOOF WOOF
YO, LET'S WATCH A VIDEO-
SPEAK OF THE DEVIL...

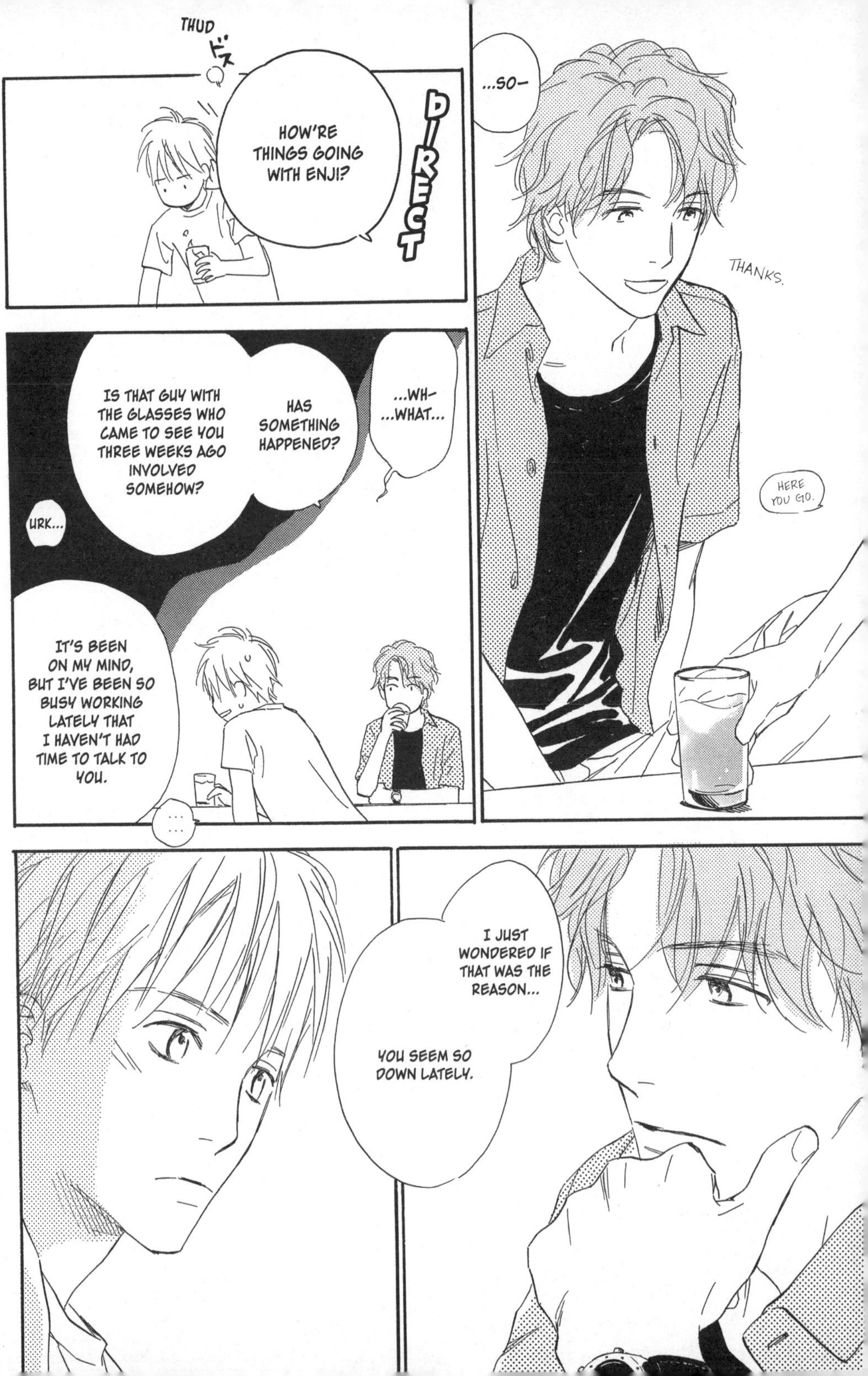

...SO–
THANKS.
HERE YOU GO.
THUD
ドス
HOW'RE THINGS GOING WITH ENJI?
DIRECT
...WH- ...WHAT...
HAS SOMETHING HAPPENED?
IS THAT GUY WITH THE GLASSES WHO CAME TO SEE YOU THREE WEEKS AGO INVOLVED SOMEHOW?
URK...
IT'S BEEN ON MY MIND, BUT I'VE BEEN SO BUSY WORKING LATELY THAT I HAVEN'T HAD TIME TO TALK TO YOU.
... ...
I JUST WONDERED IF THAT WAS THE REASON...
YOU SEEM SO DOWN LATELY.

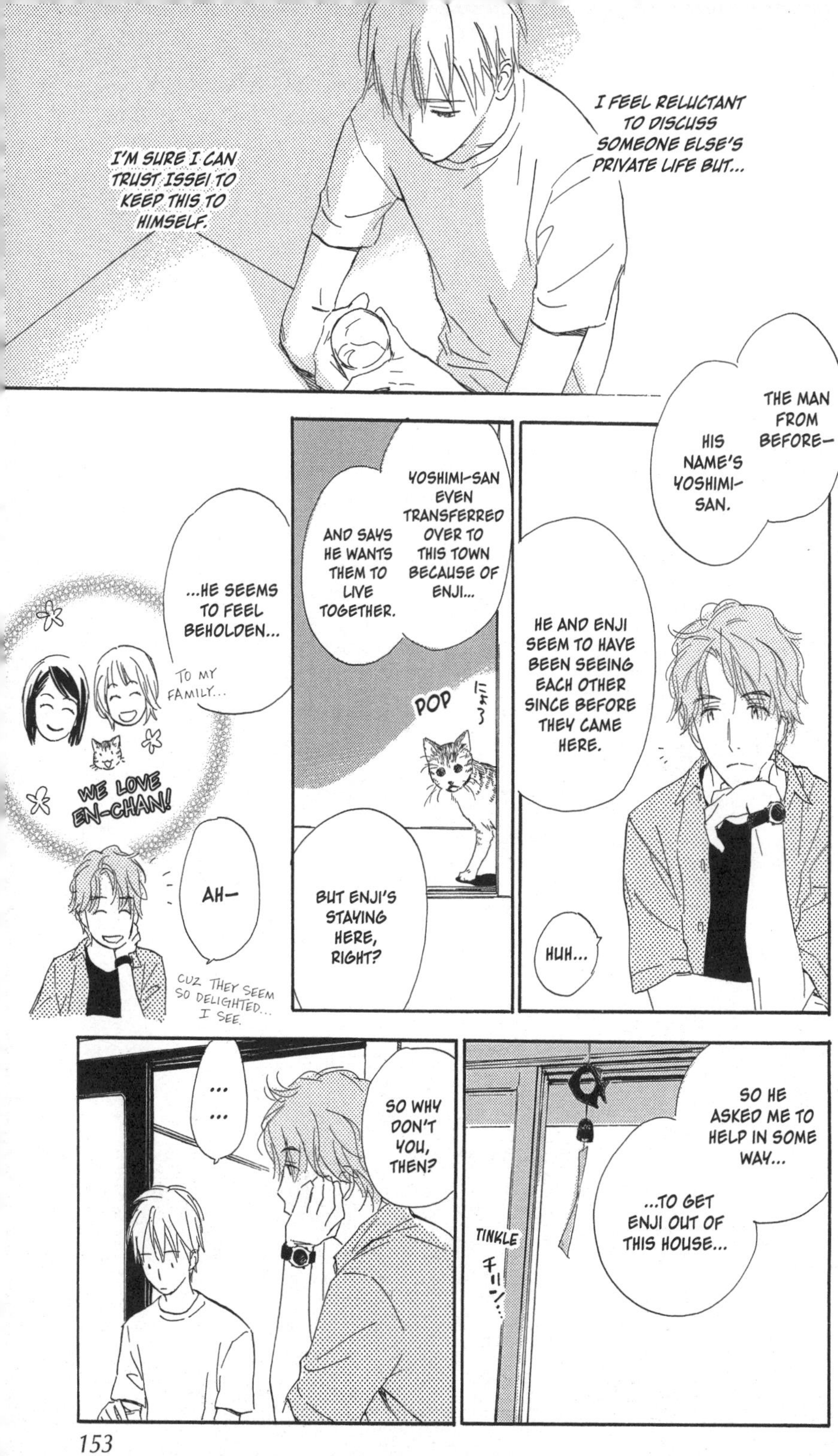
I FEEL RELUCTANT TO DISCUSS SOMEONE ELSE'S PRIVATE LIFE BUT...
I'M SURE I CAN TRUST ISSEI TO KEEP THIS TO HIMSELF.
THE MAN FROM BEFORE—
HIS NAME'S YOSHIMI-SAN.
HE AND ENJI SEEM TO HAVE BEEN SEEING EACH OTHER SINCE BEFORE THEY CAME HERE.
HUH...
YOSHIMI-SAN EVEN TRANSFERRED OVER TO THIS TOWN BECAUSE OF ENJI...
AND SAYS HE WANTS THEM TO LIVE TOGETHER.
POP
BUT ENJI'S STAYING HERE, RIGHT?
...HE SEEMS TO FEEL BEHOLDEN...
TO MY FAMILY...
WE LOVE EN-CHAN!
AH—
CUZ THEY SEEM SO DELIGHTED... I SEE.
SO HE ASKED ME TO HELP IN SOME WAY...
...TO GET ENJI OUT OF THIS HOUSE...
TINKLE
SO WHY DON'T YOU, THEN?
......

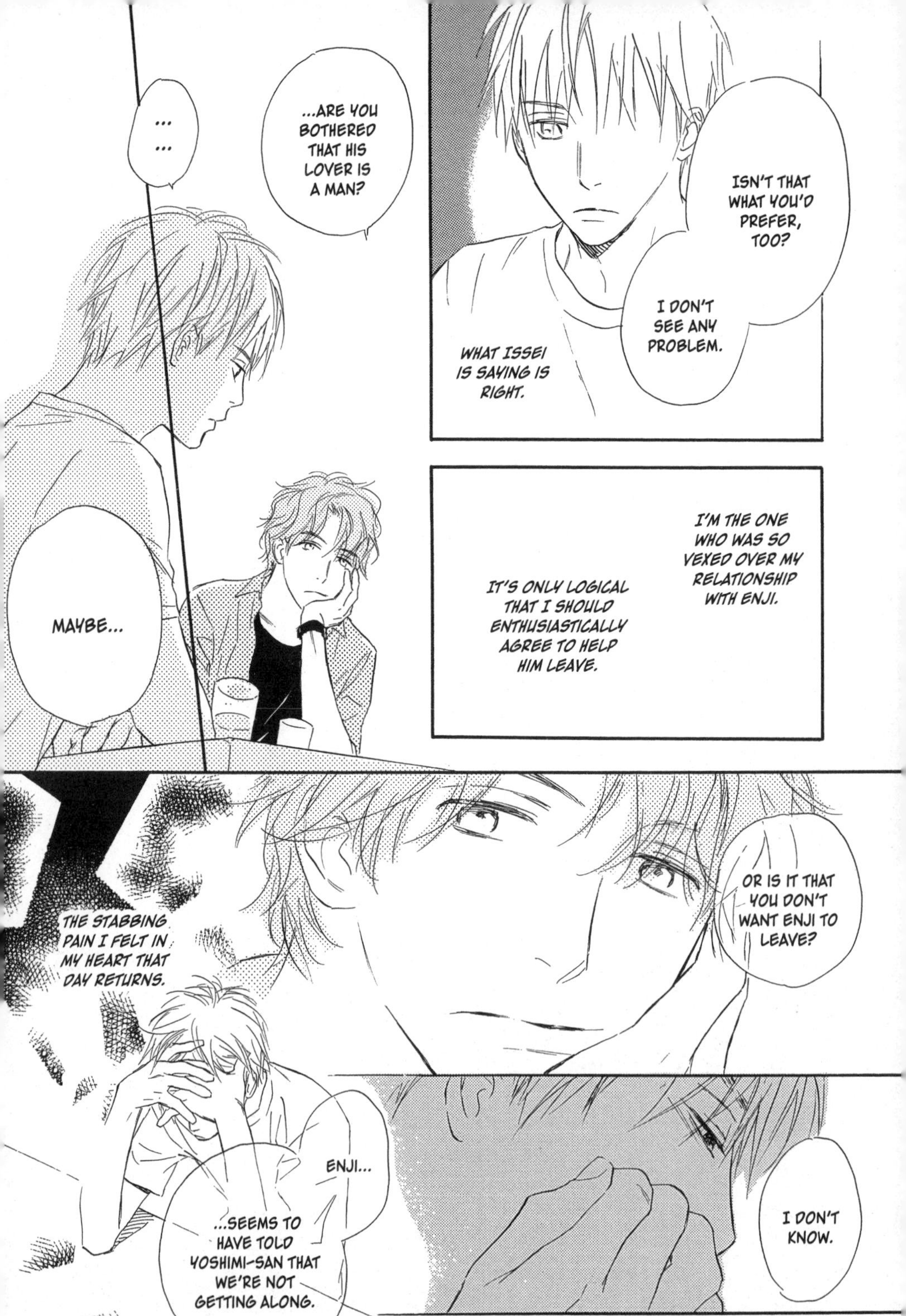
ISN'T THAT WHAT YOU'D PREFER, TOO?
I DON'T SEE ANY PROBLEM.
WHAT ISSEI IS SAYING IS RIGHT.
I'M THE ONE WHO WAS SO VEXED OVER MY RELATIONSHIP WITH ENJI.
IT'S ONLY LOGICAL THAT I SHOULD ENTHUSIASTICALLY AGREE TO HELP HIM LEAVE.
...ARE YOU BOTHERED THAT HIS LOVER IS A MAN?
... ...
MAYBE...
OR IS IT THAT YOU DON'T WANT ENJI TO LEAVE?
THE STABBING PAIN I FELT IN MY HEART THAT DAY RETURNS.
I DON'T KNOW.
ENJI...
...SEEMS TO HAVE TOLD YOSHIMI-SAN THAT WE'RE NOT GETTING ALONG.

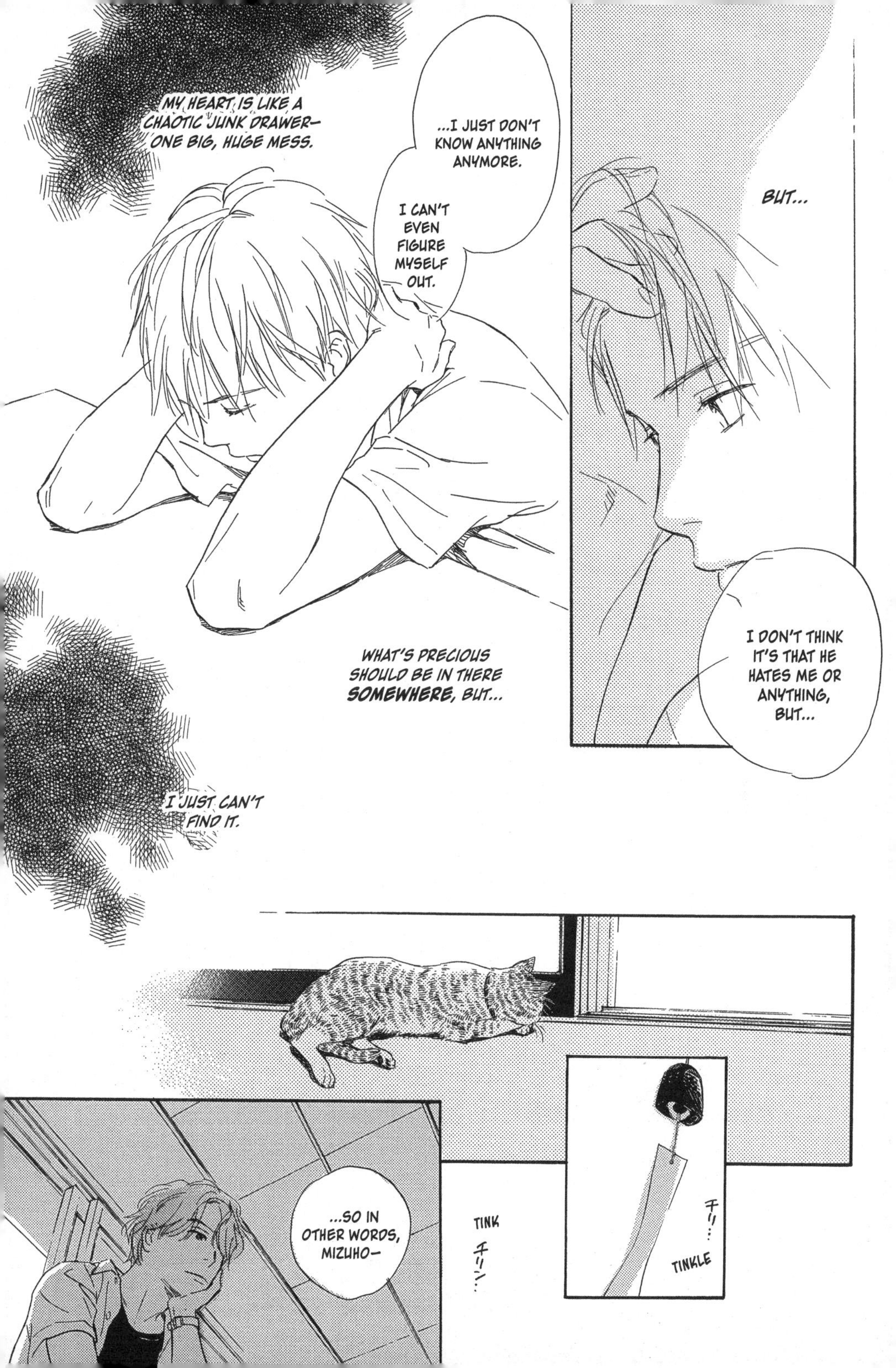
BUT...
I DON'T THINK IT'S THAT HE HATES ME OR ANYTHING, BUT...
MY HEART IS LIKE A CHAOTIC JUNK DRAWER— ONE BIG, HUGE MESS.
...I JUST DON'T KNOW ANYTHING ANYMORE.
I CAN'T EVEN FIGURE MYSELF OUT.
WHAT'S PRECIOUS SHOULD BE IN THERE SOMEWHERE, BUT...
I JUST CAN'T FIND IT.
チリ…
TINKLE
TINK
チリーン…
...SO IN OTHER WORDS, MIZUHO—

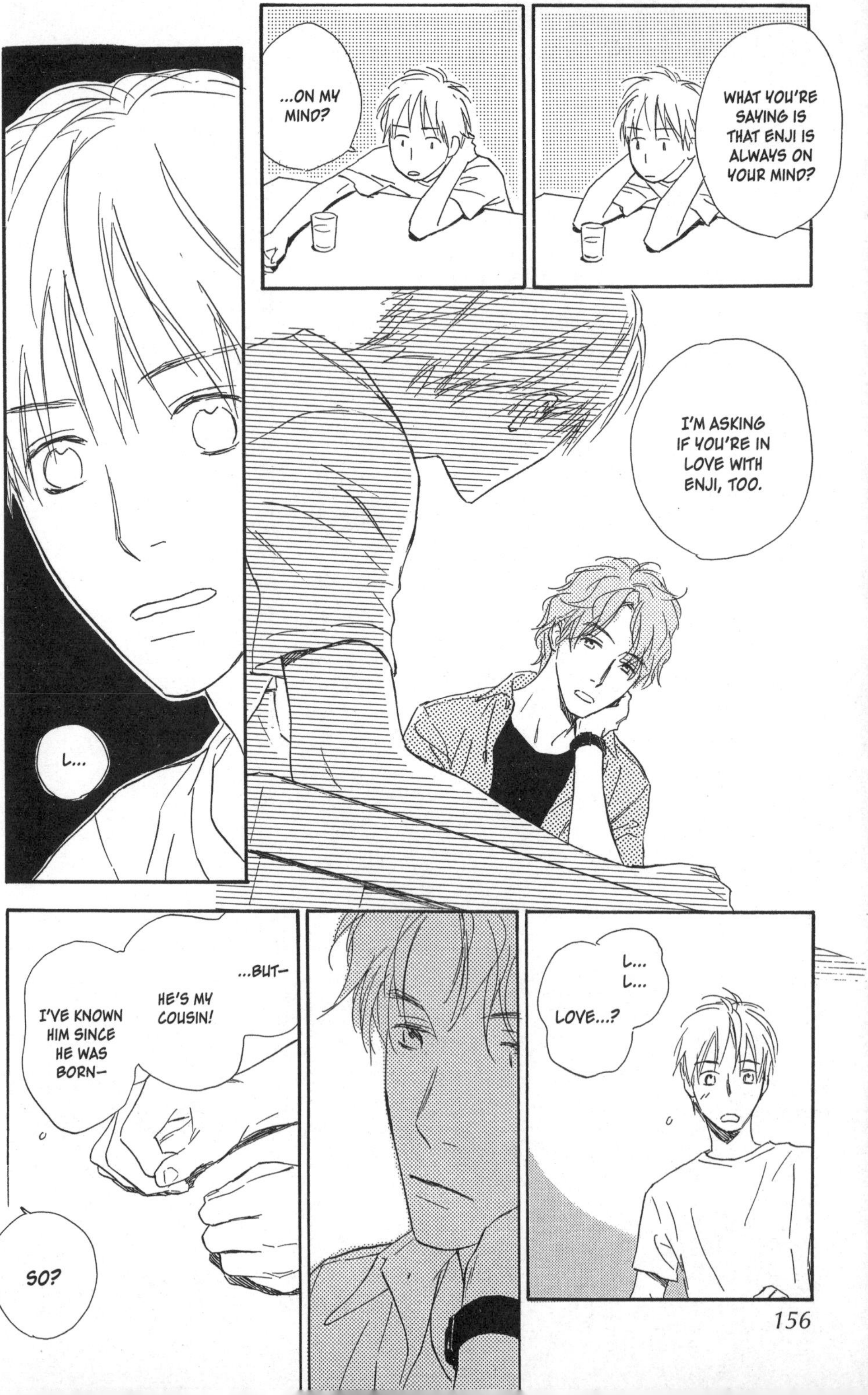
WHAT YOU'RE SAYING IS THAT ENJI IS ALWAYS ON YOUR MIND?
...ON MY MIND?
I'M ASKING IF YOU'RE IN LOVE WITH ENJI, TOO.
I...
I... I...
LOVE...?
...BUT—
HE'S MY COUSIN!
I'VE KNOWN HIM SINCE HE WAS BORN—
SO?

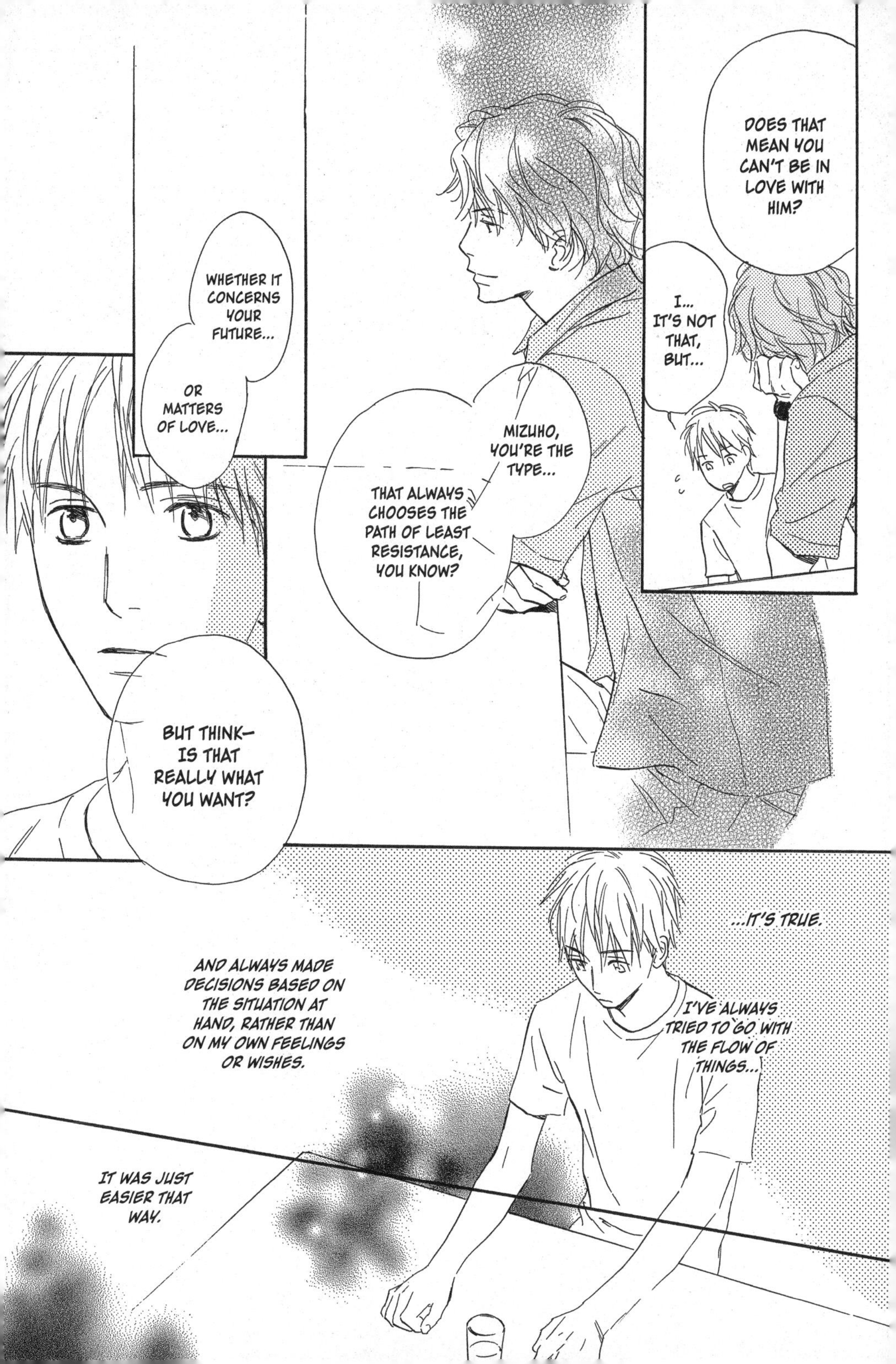
DOES THAT MEAN YOU CAN'T BE IN LOVE WITH HIM?
I... IT'S NOT THAT, BUT...
MIZUHO, YOU'RE THE TYPE...
THAT ALWAYS CHOOSES THE PATH OF LEAST RESISTANCE, YOU KNOW?
WHETHER IT CONCERNS YOUR FUTURE...
OR MATTERS OF LOVE...
BUT THINK— IS THAT REALLY WHAT YOU WANT?
...IT'S TRUE.
I'VE ALWAYS TRIED TO GO WITH THE FLOW OF THINGS...
AND ALWAYS MADE DECISIONS BASED ON THE SITUATION AT HAND, RATHER THAN ON MY OWN FEELINGS OR WISHES.
IT WAS JUST EASIER THAT WAY.

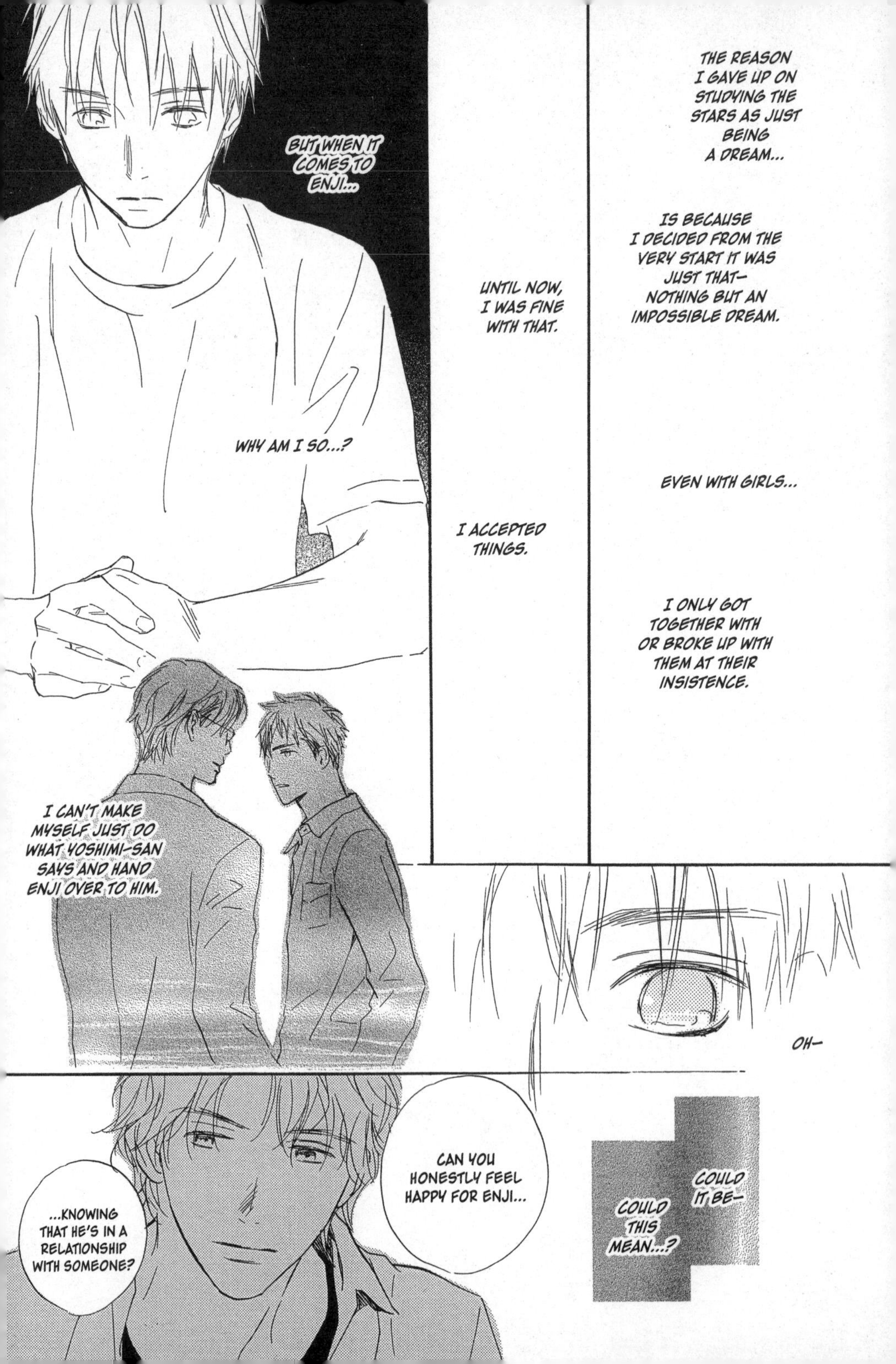
THE REASON I GAVE UP ON STUDYING THE STARS AS JUST BEING A DREAM...
IS BECAUSE I DECIDED FROM THE VERY START IT WAS JUST THAT— NOTHING BUT AN IMPOSSIBLE DREAM.
EVEN WITH GIRLS...
I ONLY GOT TOGETHER WITH OR BROKE UP WITH THEM AT THEIR INSISTENCE.
UNTIL NOW, I WAS FINE WITH THAT.
I ACCEPTED THINGS.
BUT WHEN IT COMES TO ENJI...
WHY AM I SO...?
I CAN'T MAKE MYSELF JUST DO WHAT YOSHIMI-SAN SAYS AND HAND ENJI OVER TO HIM.
OH—
COULD IT BE—
COULD THIS MEAN...?
CAN YOU HONESTLY FEEL HAPPY FOR ENJI...
...KNOWING THAT HE'S IN A RELATIONSHIP WITH SOMEONE?

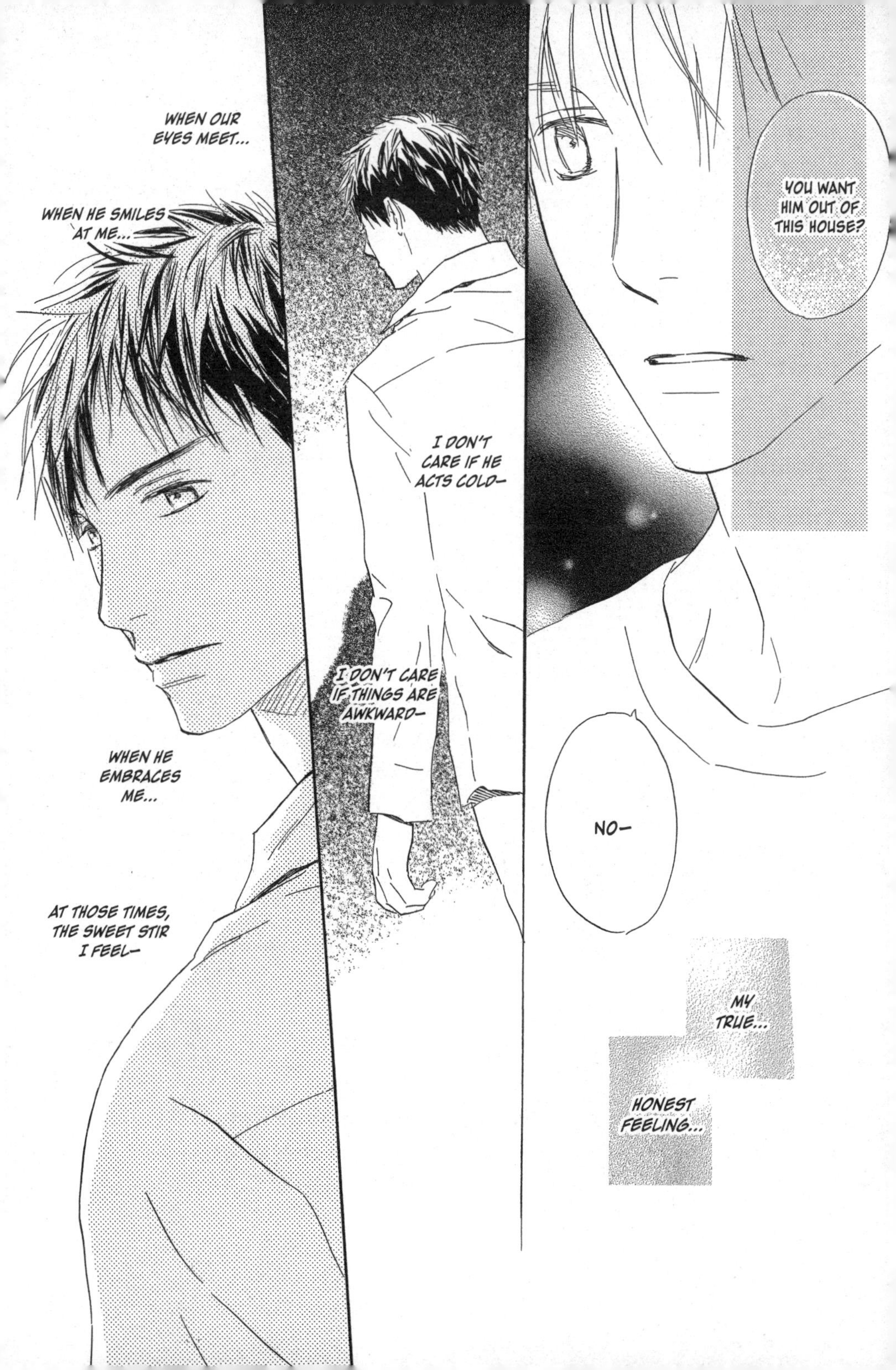
YOU WANT HIM OUT OF THIS HOUSE?
NO—
MY TRUE...
HONEST FEELING...
I DON'T CARE IF HE ACTS COLD—
I DON'T CARE IF THINGS ARE AWKWARD—
WHEN OUR EYES MEET...
WHEN HE SMILES AT ME...
WHEN HE EMBRACES ME...
AT THOSE TIMES, THE SWEET STIR I FEEL—

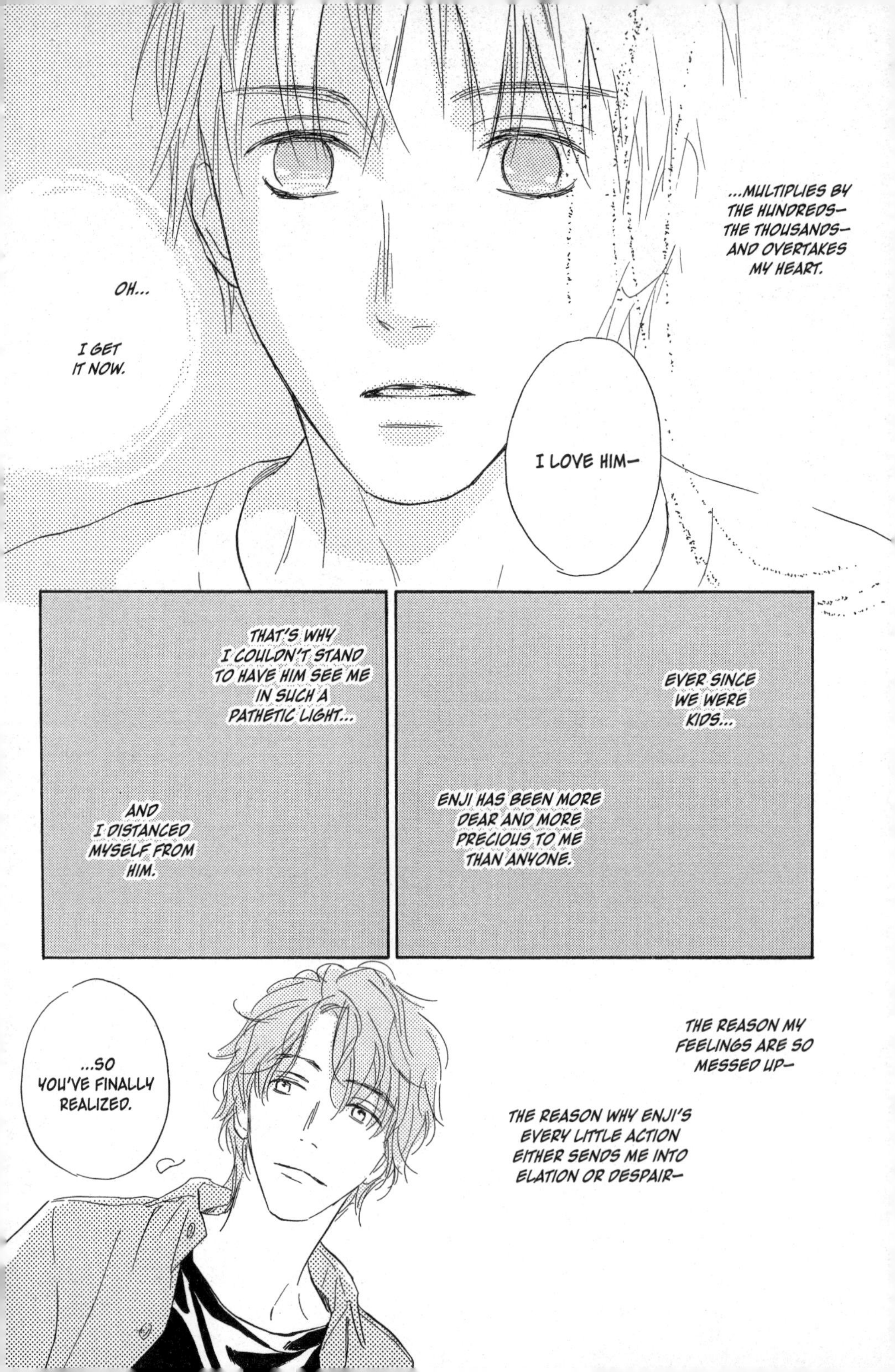
...MULTIPLIES BY THE HUNDREDS— THE THOUSANDS— AND OVERTAKES MY HEART.
OH...
I GET IT NOW.
I LOVE HIM—
EVER SINCE WE WERE KIDS...
ENJI HAS BEEN MORE DEAR AND MORE PRECIOUS TO ME THAN ANYONE.
THAT'S WHY I COULDN'T STAND TO HAVE HIM SEE ME IN SUCH A PATHETIC LIGHT...
AND I DISTANCED MYSELF FROM HIM.
THE REASON MY FEELINGS ARE SO MESSED UP—
THE REASON WHY ENJI'S EVERY LITTLE ACTION EITHER SENDS ME INTO ELATION OR DESPAIR—
...SO YOU'VE FINALLY REALIZED.

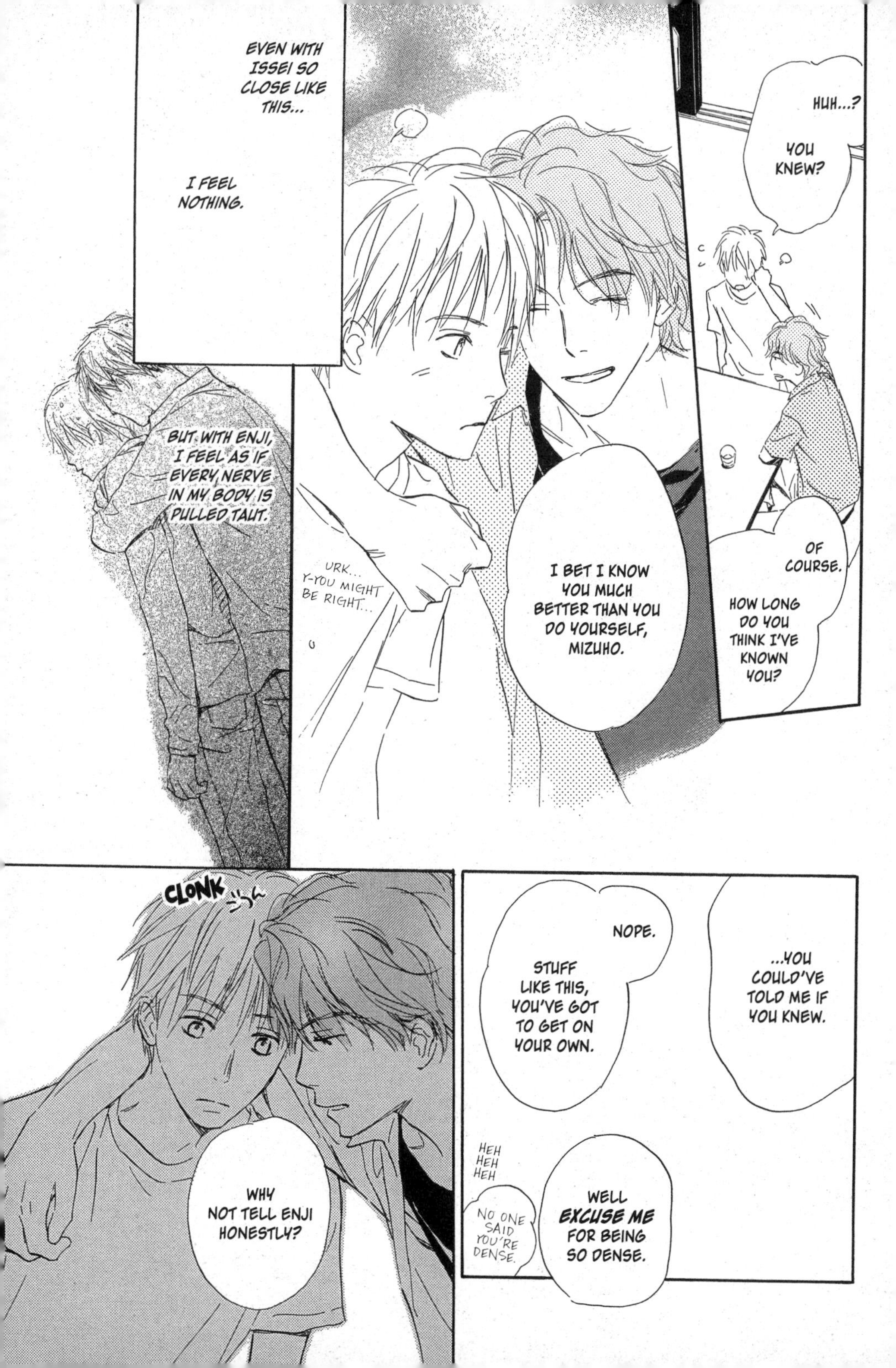
HUH...?
YOU KNEW?
OF COURSE.
HOW LONG DO YOU THINK I'VE KNOWN YOU?
I BET I KNOW YOU MUCH BETTER THAN YOU DO YOURSELF, MIZUHO.
URK... Y-YOU MIGHT BE RIGHT...
EVEN WITH ISSEI SO CLOSE LIKE THIS...
I FEEL NOTHING.
BUT WITH ENJI, I FEEL AS IF EVERY NERVE IN MY BODY IS PULLED TAUT.
...YOU COULD'VE TOLD ME IF YOU KNEW.
NOPE.
STUFF LIKE THIS, YOU'VE GOT TO GET ON YOUR OWN.
WELL EXCUSE ME FOR BEING SO DENSE.
HEH HEH HEH
NO ONE SAID YOU'RE DENSE.
CLONK ごつん
WHY NOT TELL ENJI HONESTLY?

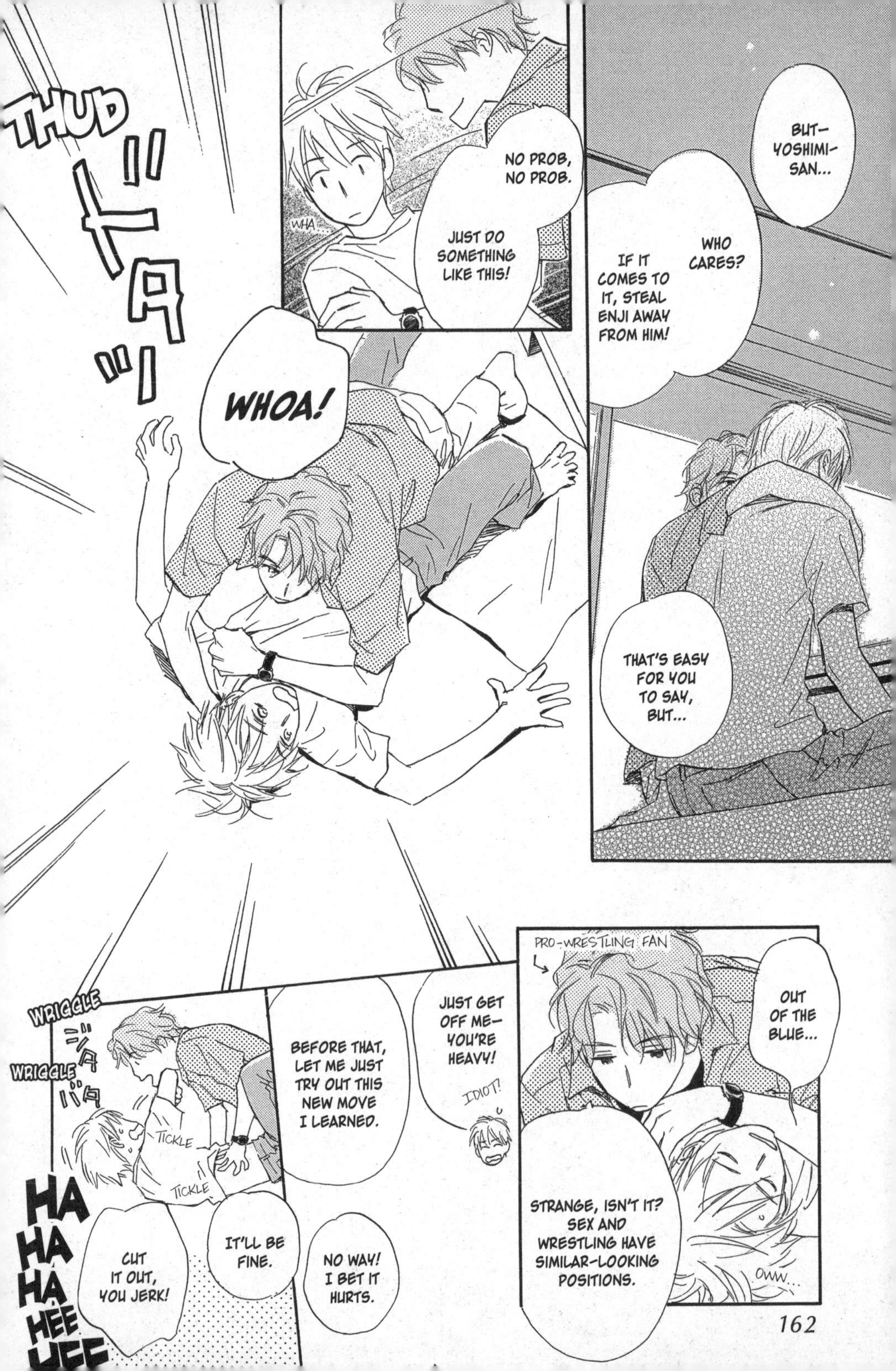
BUT- YOSHIMI-SAN...
WHO CARES?
IF IT COMES TO IT, STEAL ENJI AWAY FROM HIM!
THAT'S EASY FOR YOU TO SAY, BUT...
NO PROB, NO PROB.
JUST DO SOMETHING LIKE THIS!
WHA
THUD
WHOA!
PRO-WRESTLING FAN
OUT OF THE BLUE...
STRANGE, ISN'T IT? SEX AND WRESTLING HAVE SIMILAR-LOOKING POSITIONS.
OWW...
JUST GET OFF ME- YOU'RE HEAVY!
IDIOT!
BEFORE THAT, LET ME JUST TRY OUT THIS NEW MOVE I LEARNED.
NO WAY! I BET IT HURTS.
IT'LL BE FINE.
WRIGGLE
WRIGGLE
TICKLE
TICKLE
CUT IT OUT, YOU JERK!
HA HA HA HEE HEE

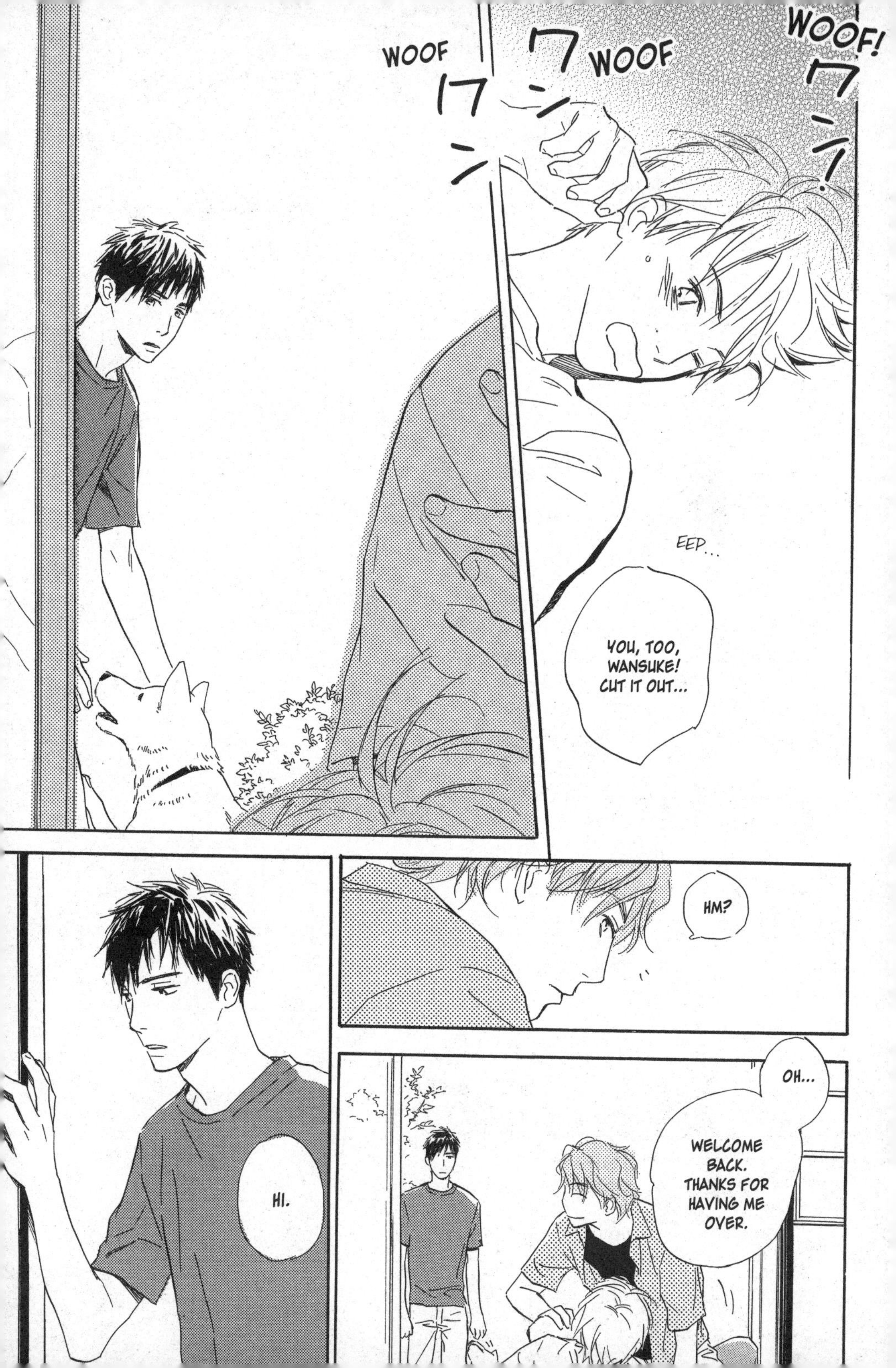
WOOF!
WOOF
WOOF
EEP...
YOU, TOO, WANSUKE! CUT IT OUT...
HM?
OH...
WELCOME BACK. THANKS FOR HAVING ME OVER.
HI.

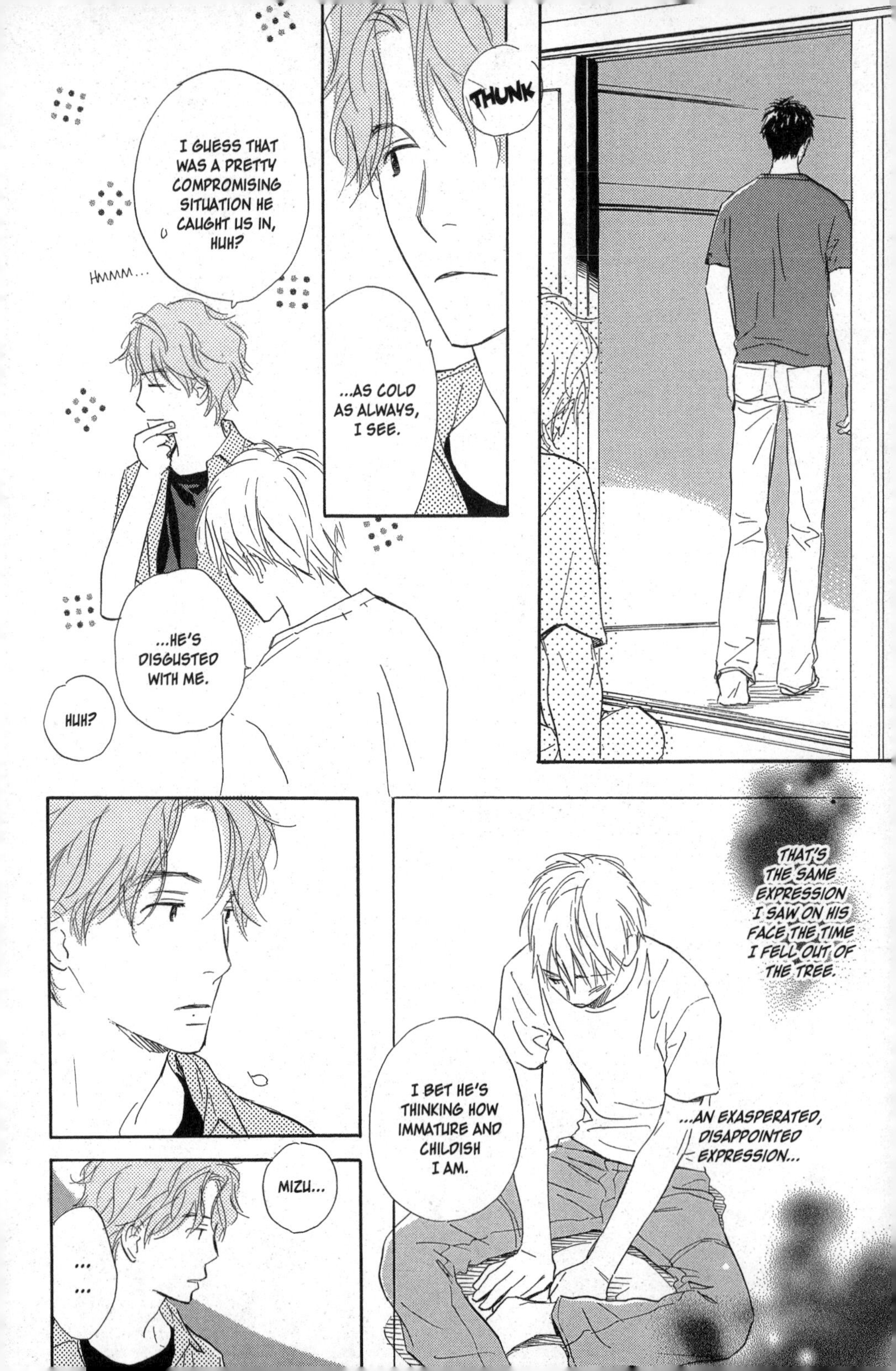
THUNK
...AS COLD AS ALWAYS, I SEE.
I GUESS THAT WAS A PRETTY COMPROMISING SITUATION HE CAUGHT US IN, HUH?
HMMM...
...HE'S DISGUSTED WITH ME.
HUH?
THAT'S THE SAME EXPRESSION I SAW ON HIS FACE THE TIME I FELL OUT OF THE TREE.
...AN EXASPERATED, DISAPPOINTED EXPRESSION...
I BET HE'S THINKING HOW IMMATURE AND CHILDISH I AM.
MIZU...
... ...

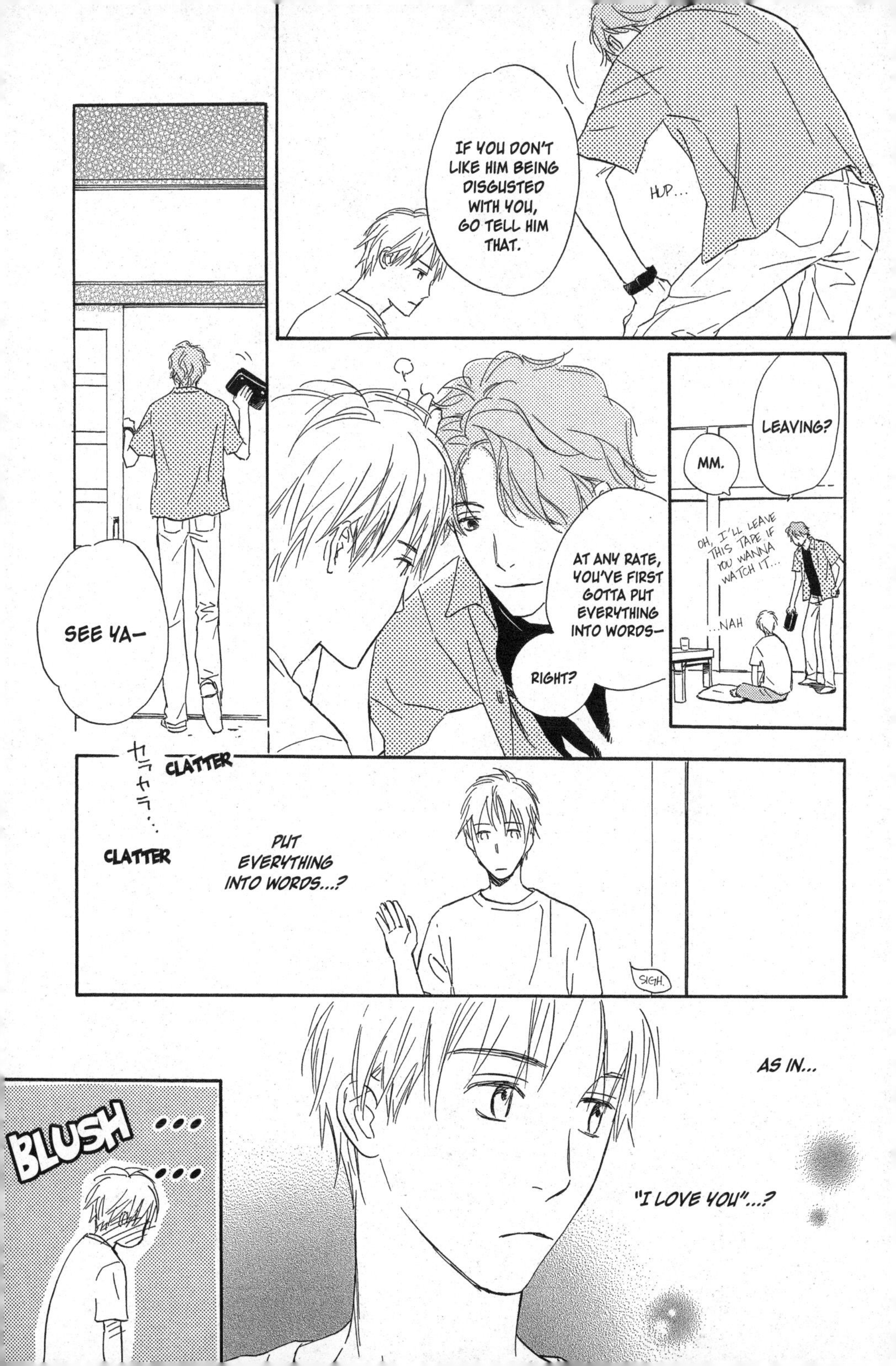

IF YOU DON'T LIKE HIM BEING DISGUSTED WITH YOU, GO TELL HIM THAT.
HUP...
LEAVING?
MM.
OH, I'LL LEAVE THIS TAPE IF YOU WANNA WATCH IT...
...NAH
AT ANY RATE, YOU'VE FIRST GOTTA PUT EVERYTHING INTO WORDS—
RIGHT?
SEE YA—
カラカラ…
CLATTER
CLATTER
SIGH.
PUT EVERYTHING INTO WORDS...?
AS IN...
"I LOVE YOU"...?
BLUSH
...
...

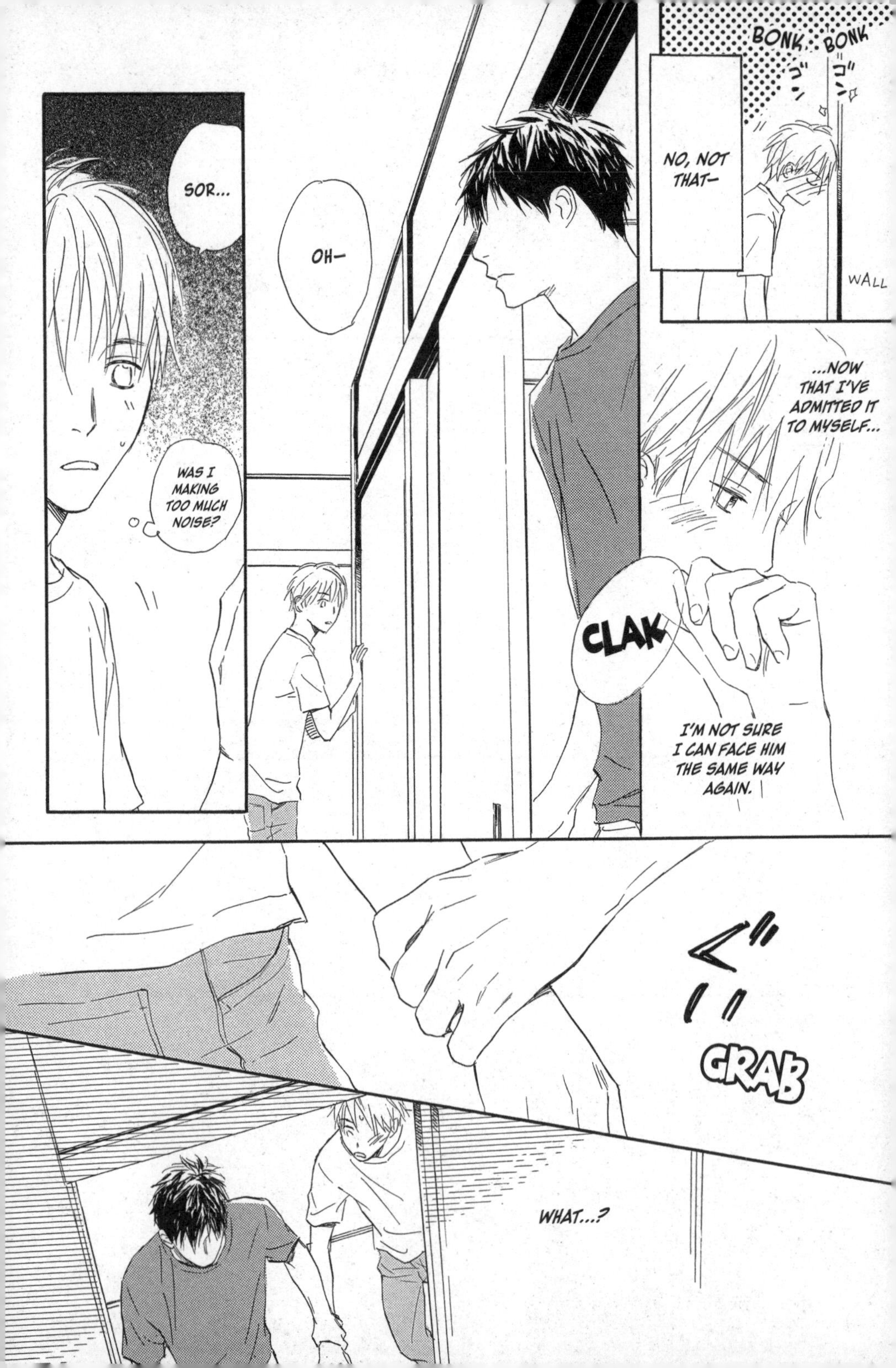
BONK BONK
NO, NOT THAT—
WALL
...NOW THAT I'VE ADMITTED IT TO MYSELF...
CLAK
I'M NOT SURE I CAN FACE HIM THE SAME WAY AGAIN.
OH—
SOR...
WAS I MAKING TOO MUCH NOISE?
GRAB
WHAT...?

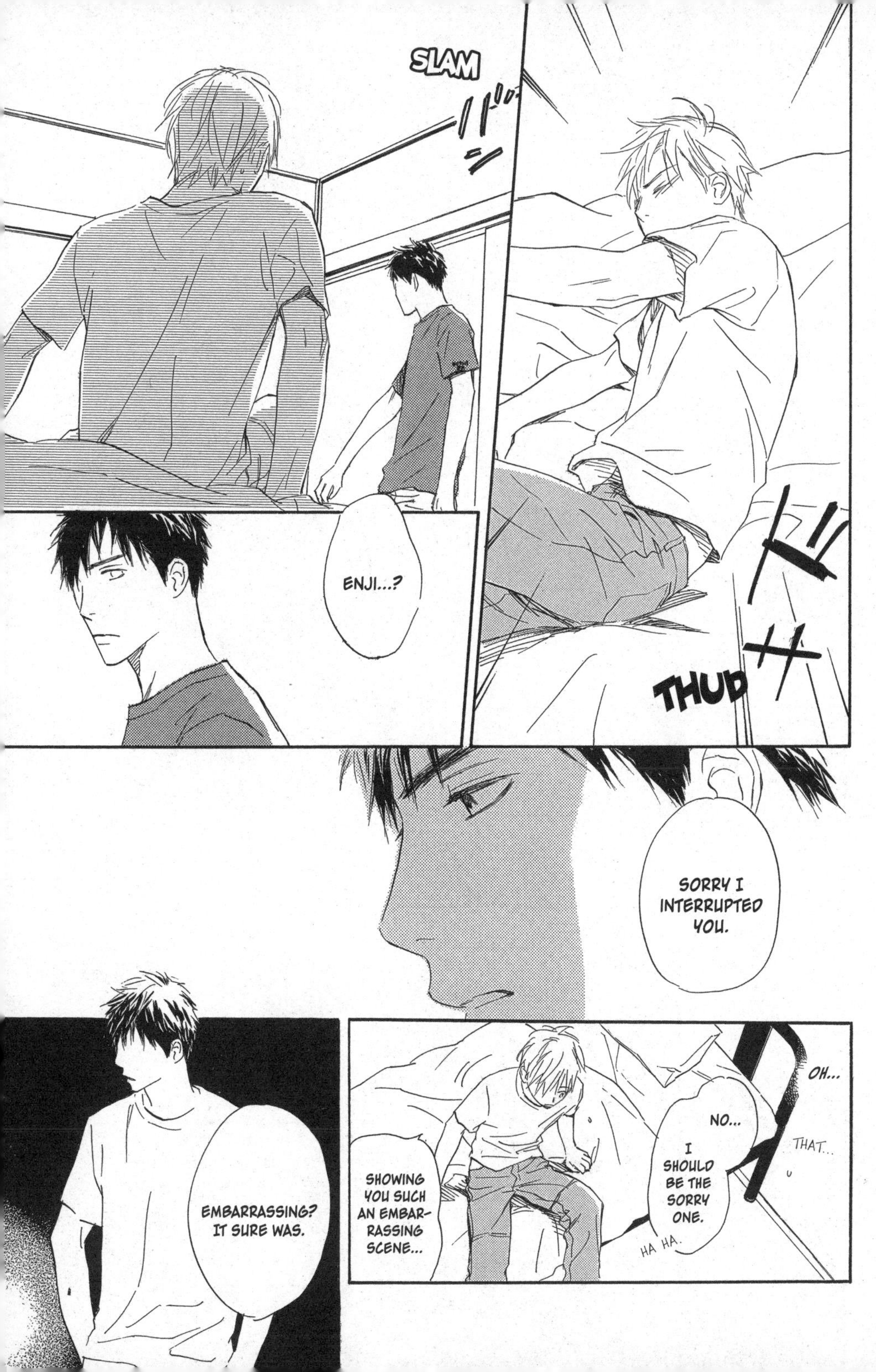
THUD
SLAM
ENJI...?
SORRY I INTERRUPTED YOU.
OH...
NO...
I SHOULD BE THE SORRY ONE.
THAT...
HA HA.
SHOWING YOU SUCH AN EMBAR-RASSING SCENE...
EMBARRASSING? IT SURE WAS.

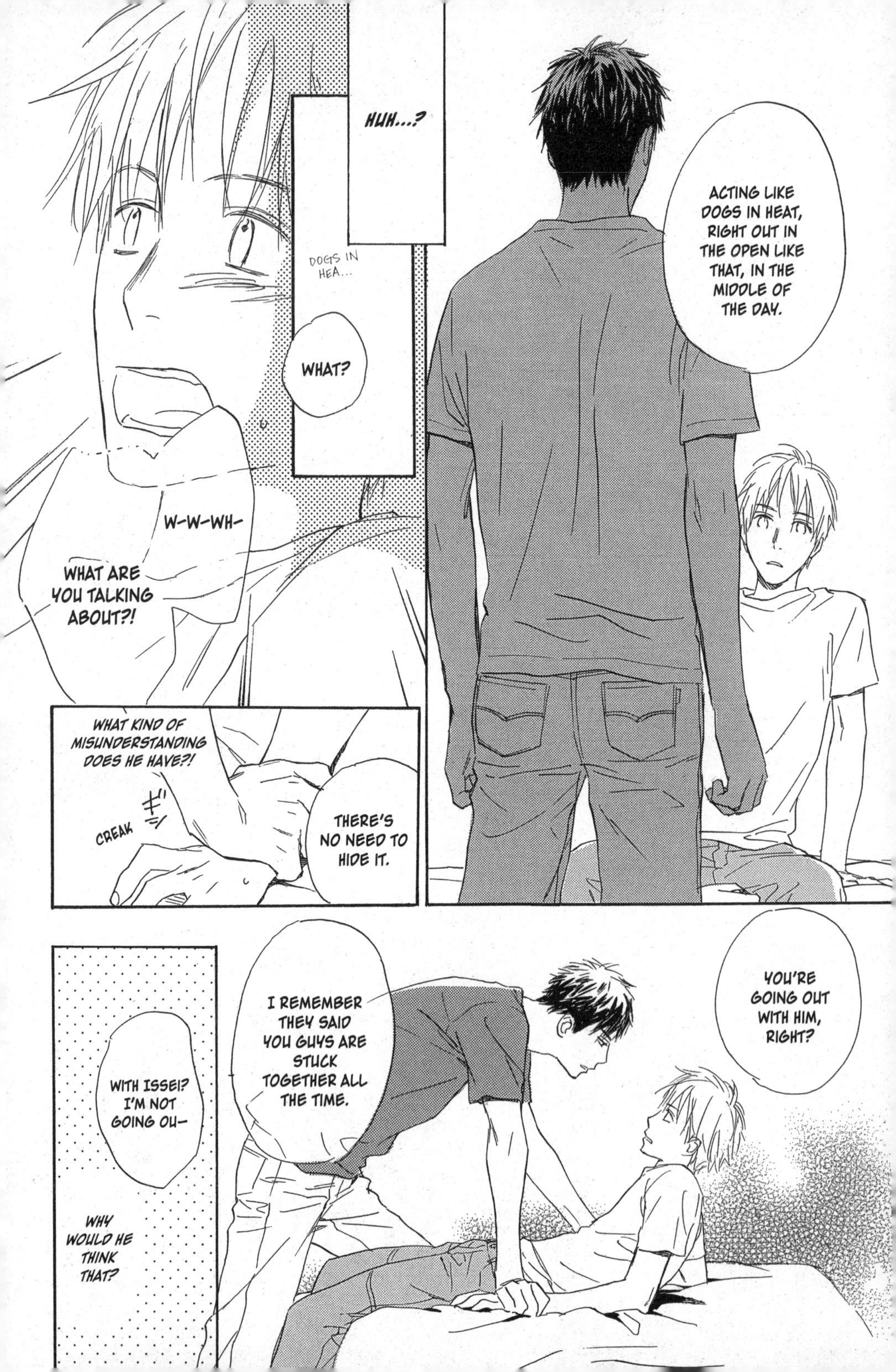
ACTING LIKE DOGS IN HEAT, RIGHT OUT IN THE OPEN LIKE THAT, IN THE MIDDLE OF THE DAY.
HUH...?
DOGS IN HEA...
WHAT?
W-W-WH-
WHAT ARE YOU TALKING ABOUT?!
WHAT KIND OF MISUNDERSTANDING DOES HE HAVE?!
THERE'S NO NEED TO HIDE IT.
CREAK
YOU'RE GOING OUT WITH HIM, RIGHT?
I REMEMBER THEY SAID YOU GUYS ARE STUCK TOGETHER ALL THE TIME.
WITH ISSEI? I'M NOT GOING OU-
WHY WOULD HE THINK THAT?

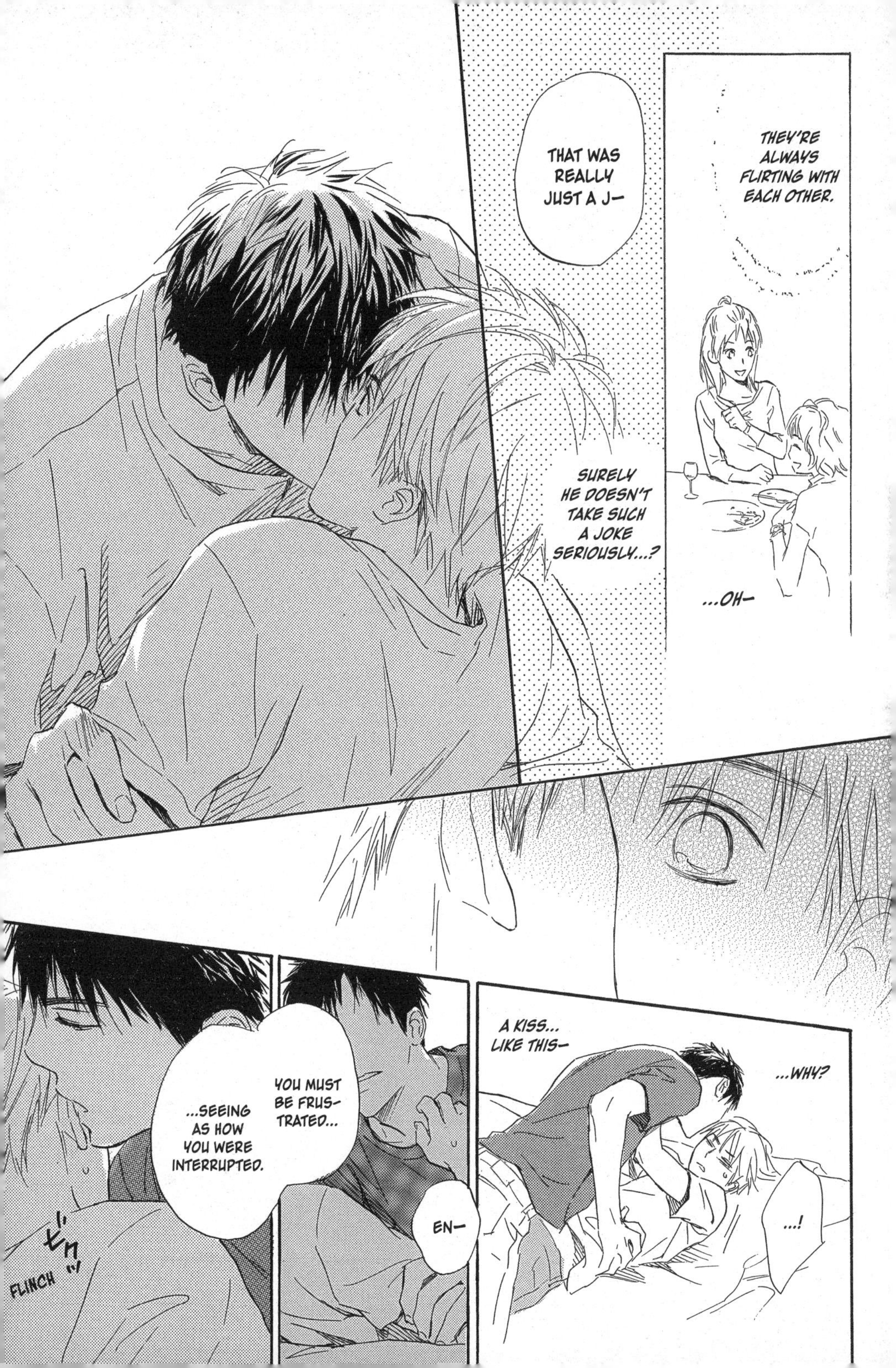

THEY'RE ALWAYS FLIRTING WITH EACH OTHER.
...OH—
THAT WAS REALLY JUST A J—
SURELY HE DOESN'T TAKE SUCH A JOKE SERIOUSLY...?
A KISS... LIKE THIS—
...WHY?
...!
YOU MUST BE FRUS-TRATED...
...SEEING AS HOW YOU WERE INTERRUPTED.
EN—
ビクッ
FLINCH

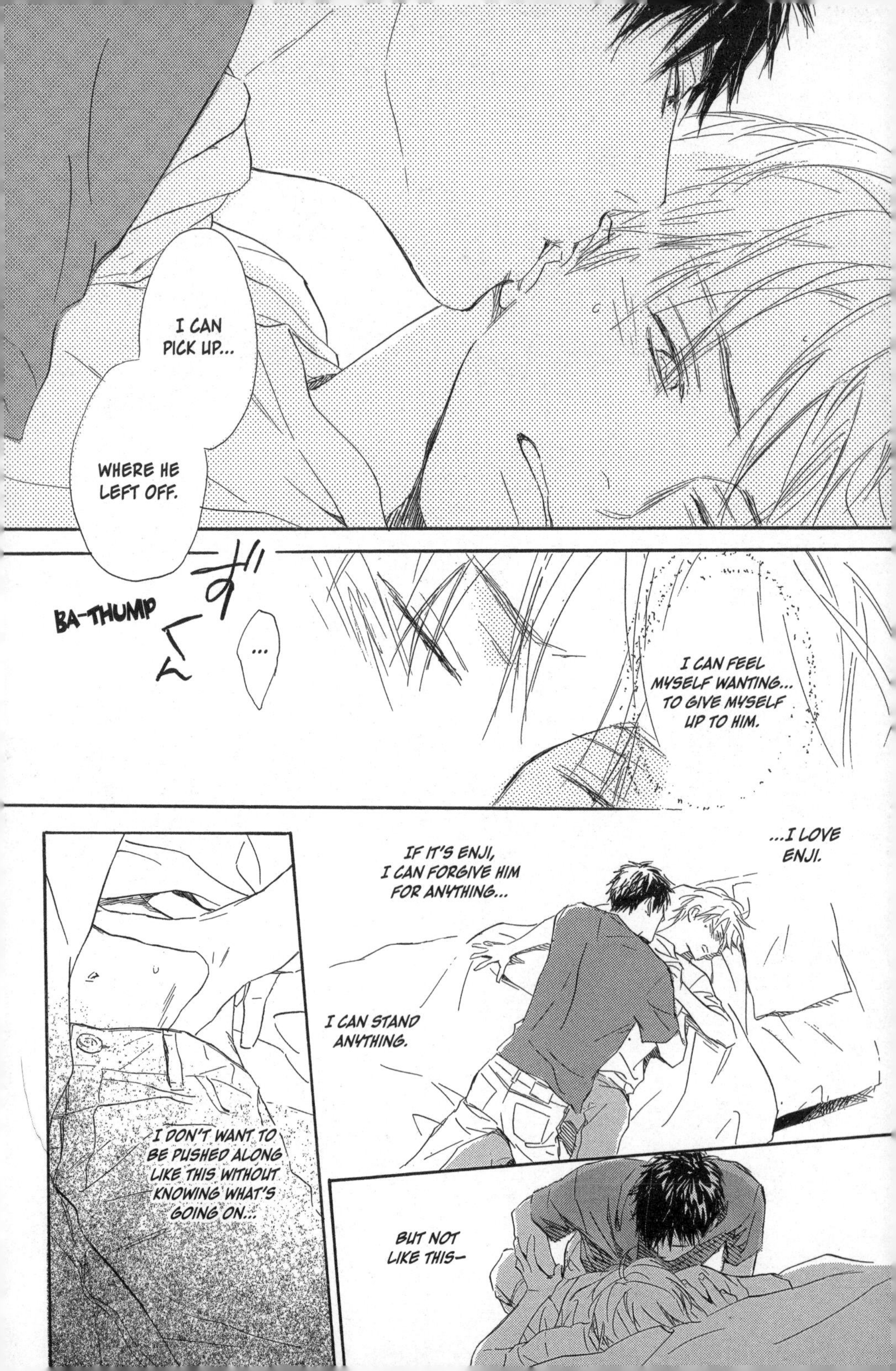
I CAN PICK UP...
WHERE HE LEFT OFF.
I CAN FEEL MYSELF WANTING... TO GIVE MYSELF UP TO HIM.
...
BA-THUMP
ずくん
...I LOVE ENJI.
IF IT'S ENJI, I CAN FORGIVE HIM FOR ANYTHING...
I CAN STAND ANYTHING.
BUT NOT LIKE THIS—
I DON'T WANT TO BE PUSHED ALONG LIKE THIS WITHOUT KNOWING WHAT'S GOING ON...

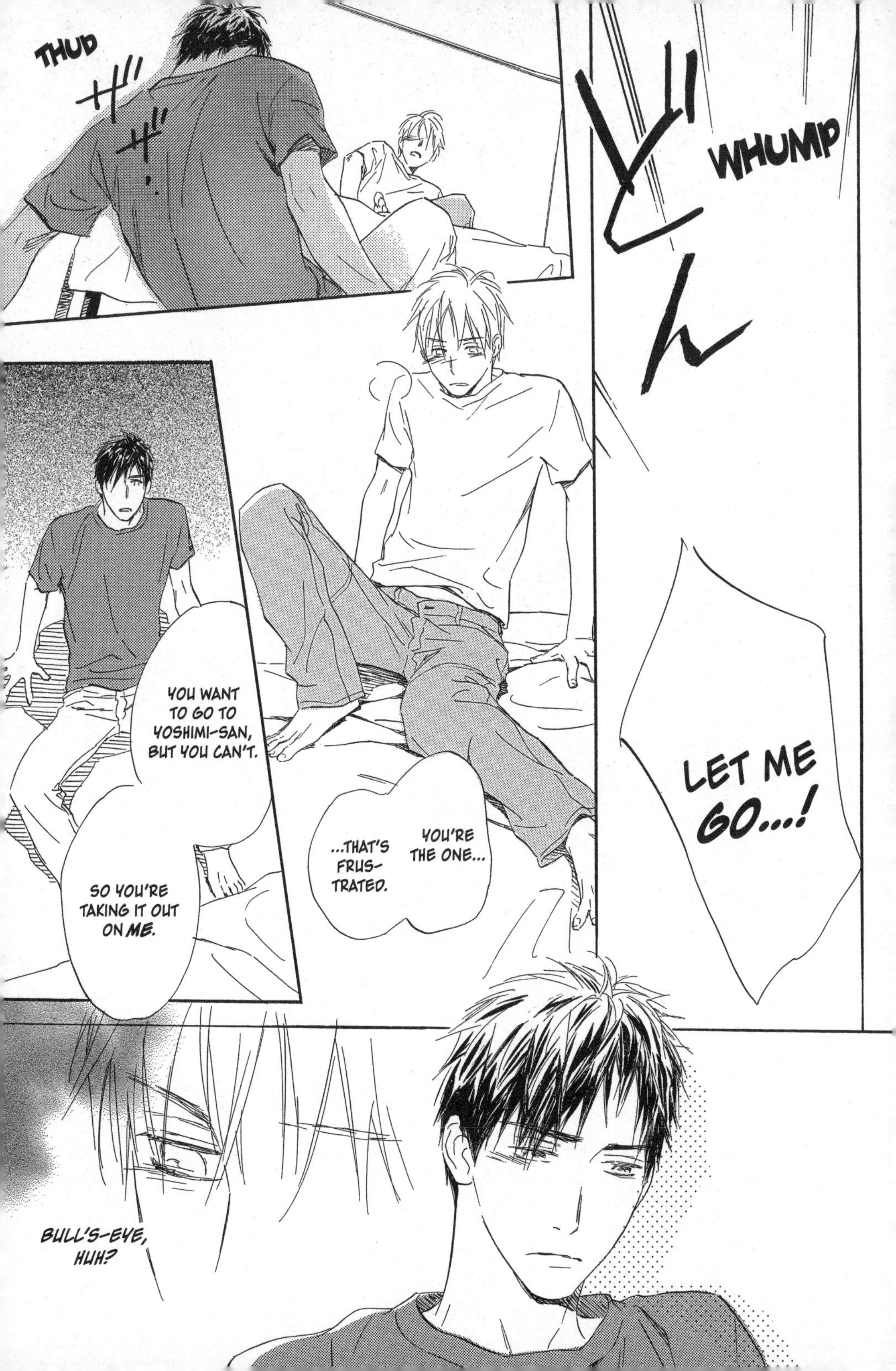
どん
WHUMP
LET ME GO...!
THUD
ザザ
YOU'RE THE ONE...
...THAT'S FRUS-TRATED.
YOU WANT TO GO TO YOSHIMI-SAN, BUT YOU CAN'T.
SO YOU'RE TAKING IT OUT ON *ME*.
BULL'S-EYE, HUH?

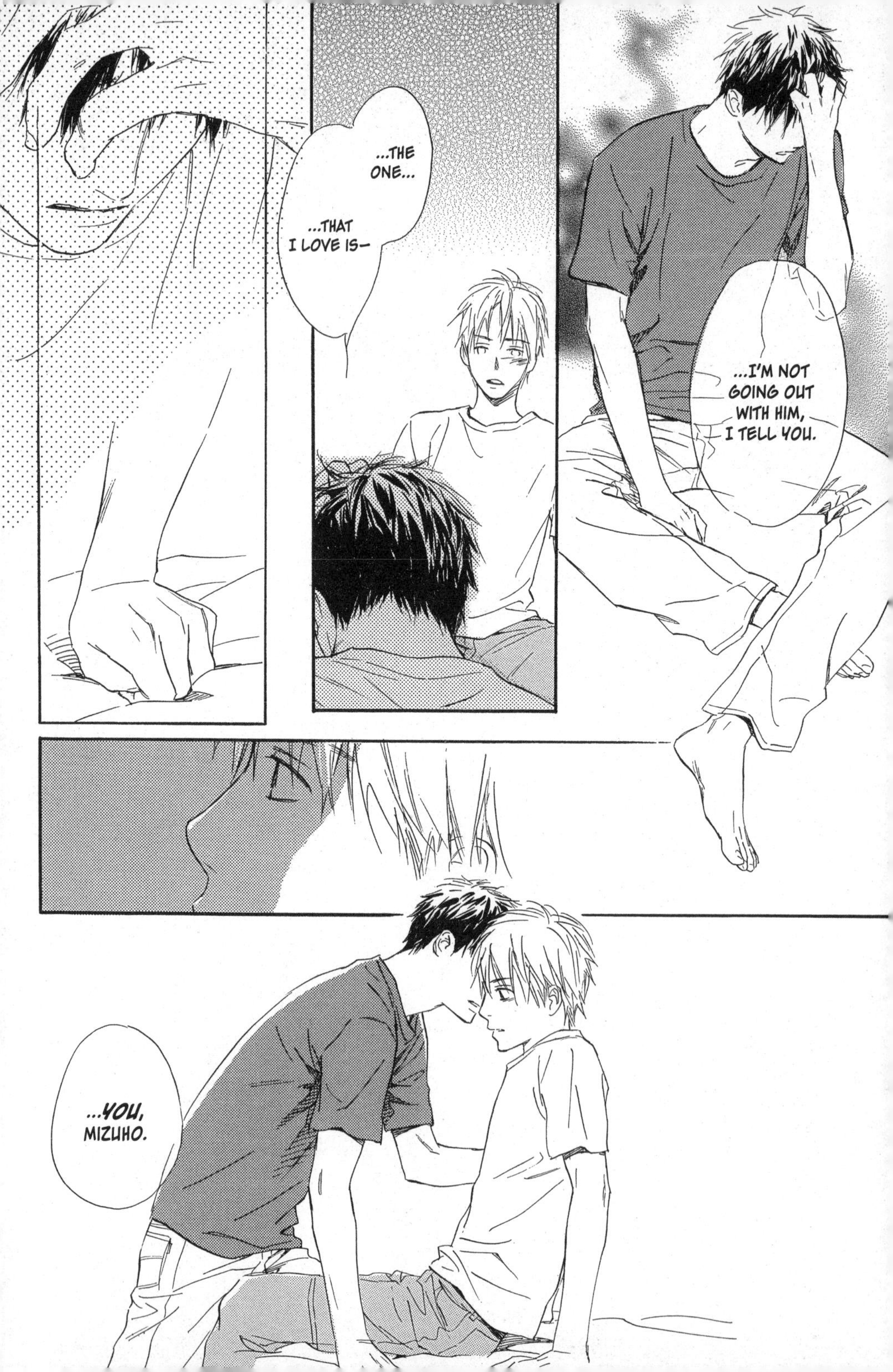
...I'M NOT GOING OUT WITH HIM, I TELL YOU.
...THE ONE...
...THAT I LOVE IS—
...YOU, MIZUHO.

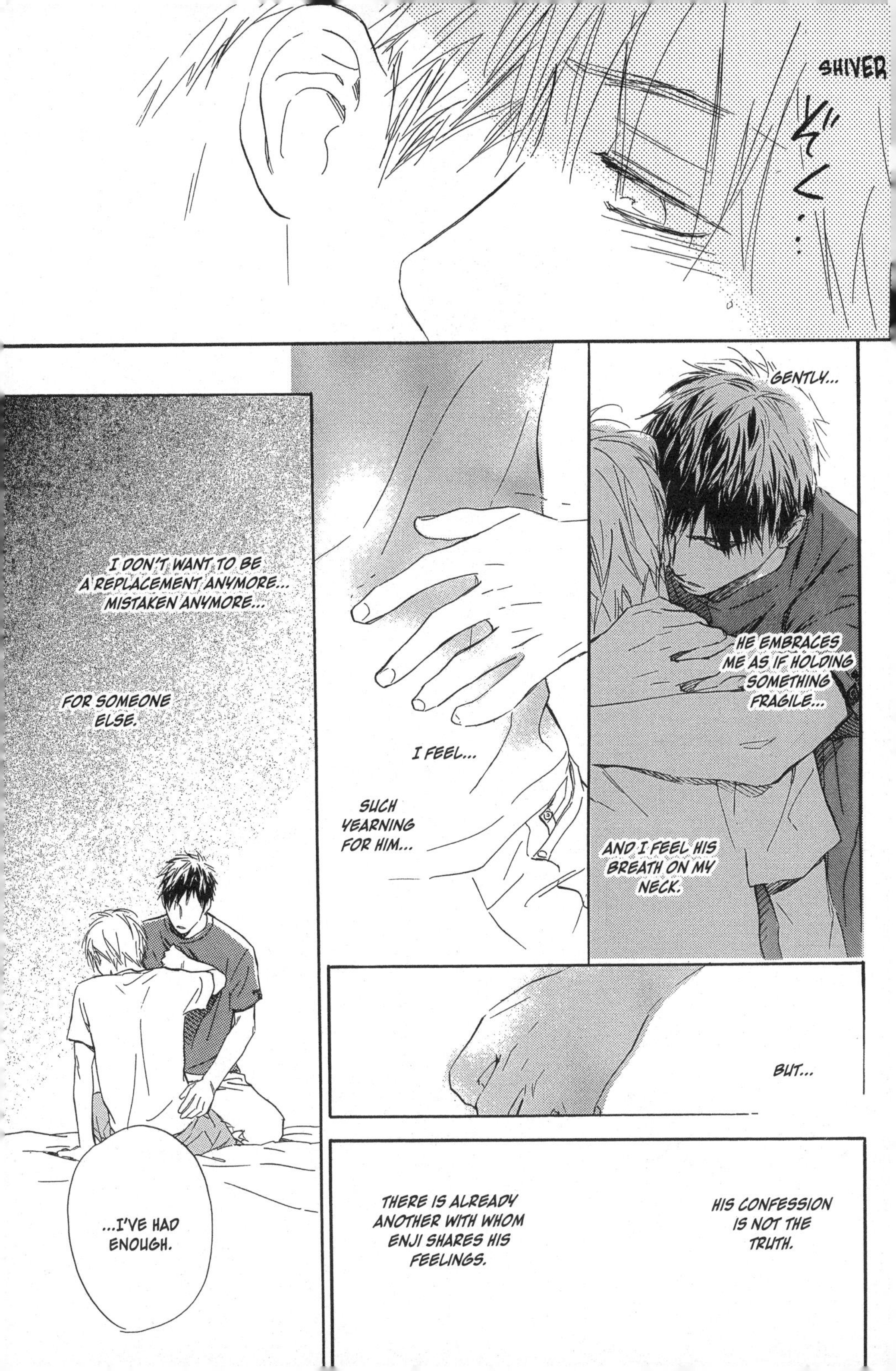
SHIVER
GENTLY...
HE EMBRACES ME AS IF HOLDING SOMETHING FRAGILE...
AND I FEEL HIS BREATH ON MY NECK.
I FEEL...
SUCH YEARNING FOR HIM...
BUT...
HIS CONFESSION IS NOT THE TRUTH.
THERE IS ALREADY ANOTHER WITH WHOM ENJI SHARES HIS FEELINGS.
I DON'T WANT TO BE A REPLACEMENT ANYMORE... MISTAKEN ANYMORE...
FOR SOMEONE ELSE.
...I'VE HAD ENOUGH.

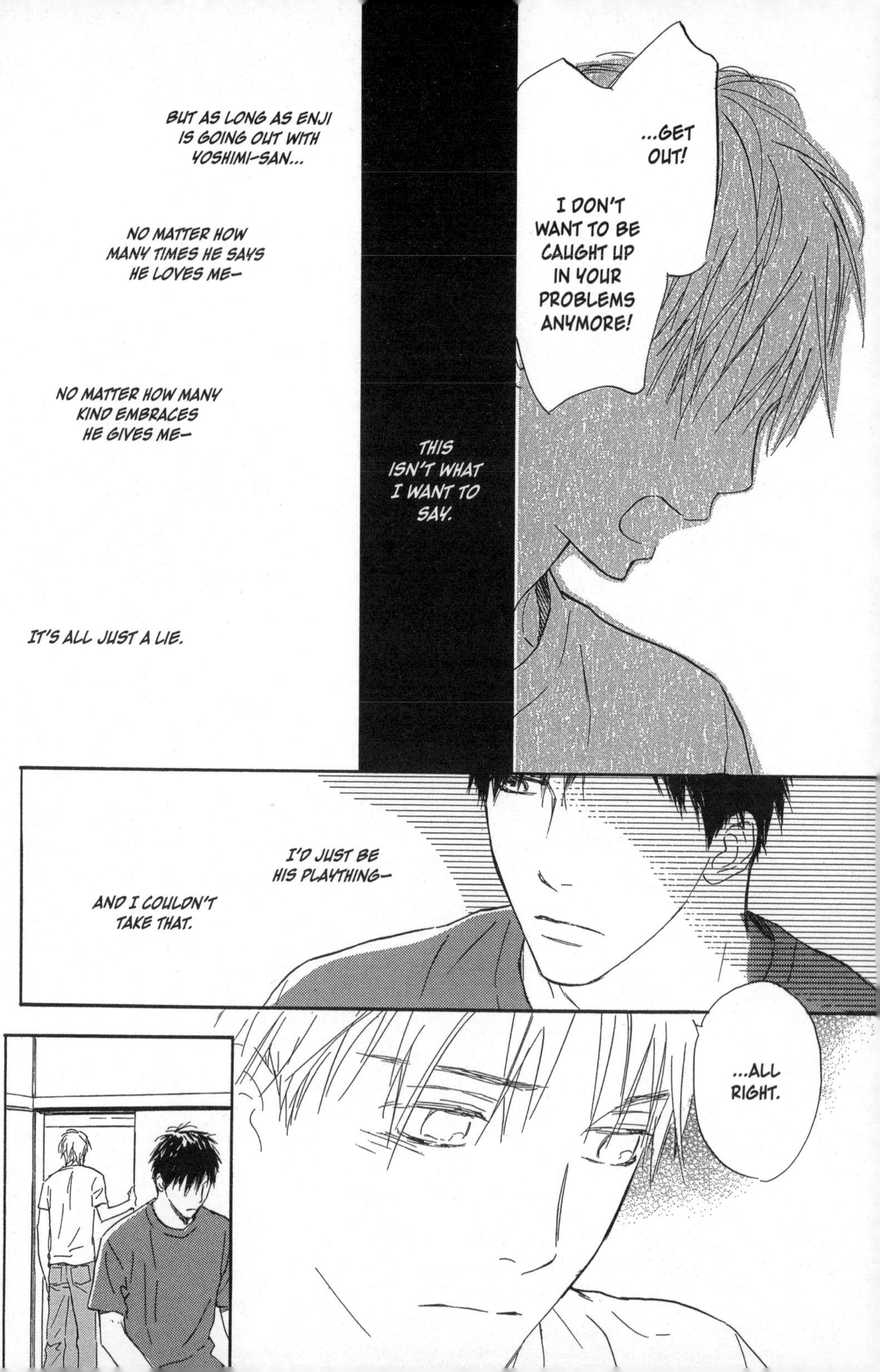
...GET OUT!
I DON'T WANT TO BE CAUGHT UP IN YOUR PROBLEMS ANYMORE!
THIS ISN'T WHAT I WANT TO SAY.
BUT AS LONG AS ENJI IS GOING OUT WITH YOSHIMI-SAN...
NO MATTER HOW MANY TIMES HE SAYS HE LOVES ME—
NO MATTER HOW MANY KIND EMBRACES HE GIVES ME—
IT'S ALL JUST A LIE.
I'D JUST BE HIS PLAYTHING—
AND I COULDN'T TAKE THAT.
...ALL RIGHT.

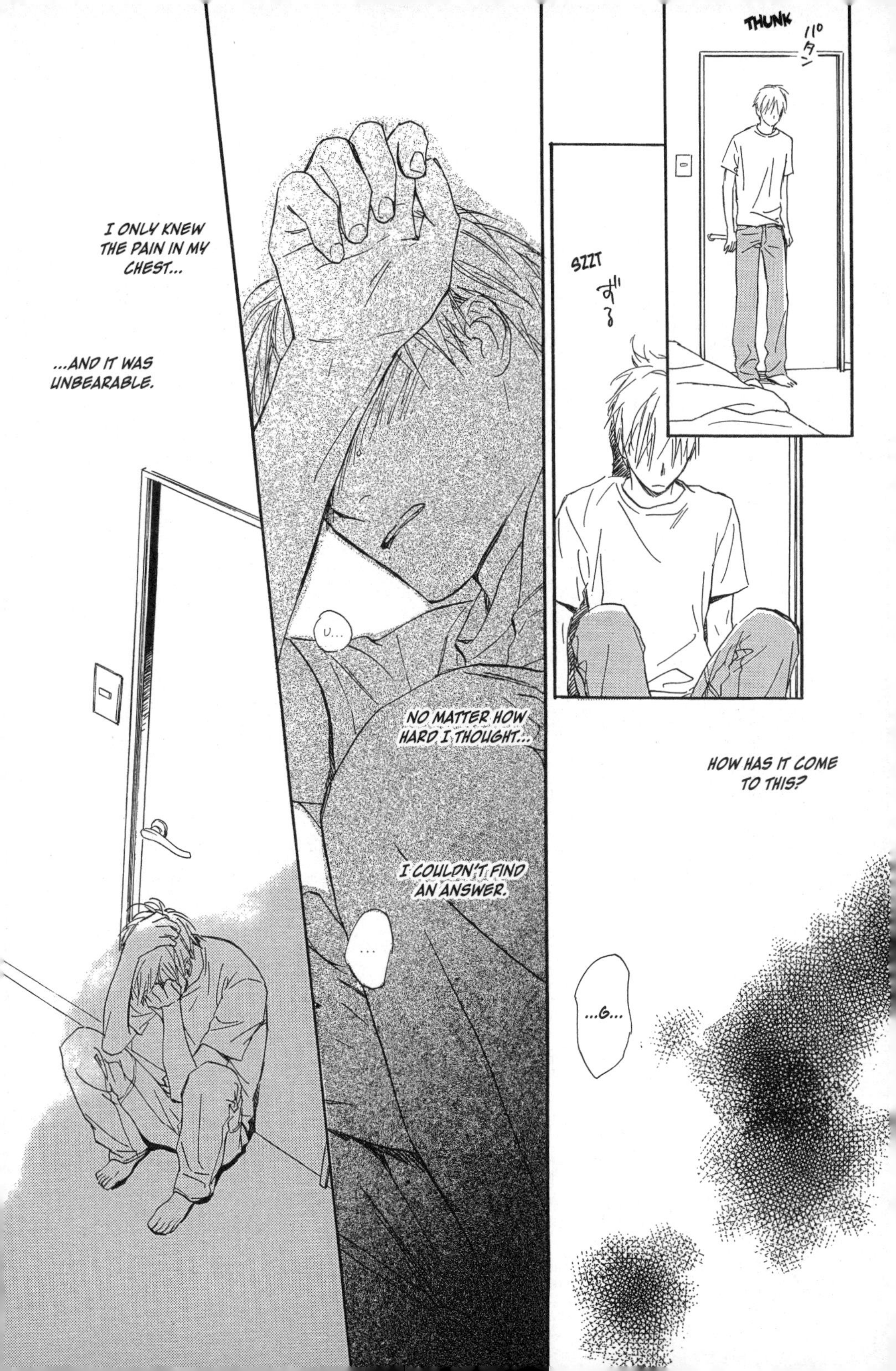
THUNK
SZZT
ずる
HOW HAS IT COME TO THIS?
...G...
U...
NO MATTER HOW HARD I THOUGHT...
I COULDN'T FIND AN ANSWER.
...
I ONLY KNEW THE PAIN IN MY CHEST...
...AND IT WAS UNBEARABLE.

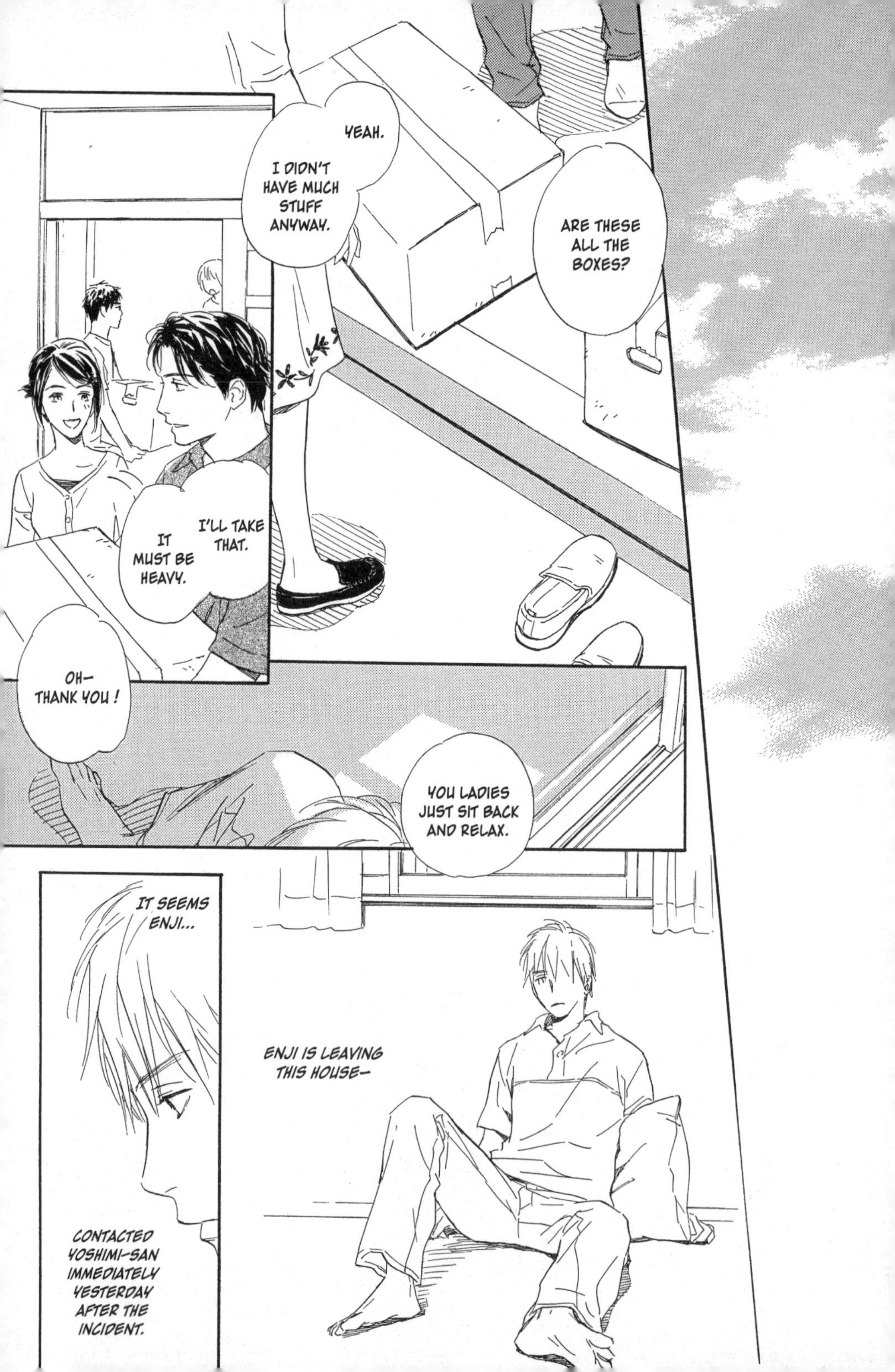
ARE THESE ALL THE BOXES?
YEAH.
I DIDN'T HAVE MUCH STUFF ANYWAY.
I'LL TAKE THAT.
IT MUST BE HEAVY.
OH— THANK YOU!
YOU LADIES JUST SIT BACK AND RELAX.
ENJI IS LEAVING THIS HOUSE—
IT SEEMS ENJI...
CONTACTED YOSHIMI-SAN IMMEDIATELY YESTERDAY AFTER THE INCIDENT.

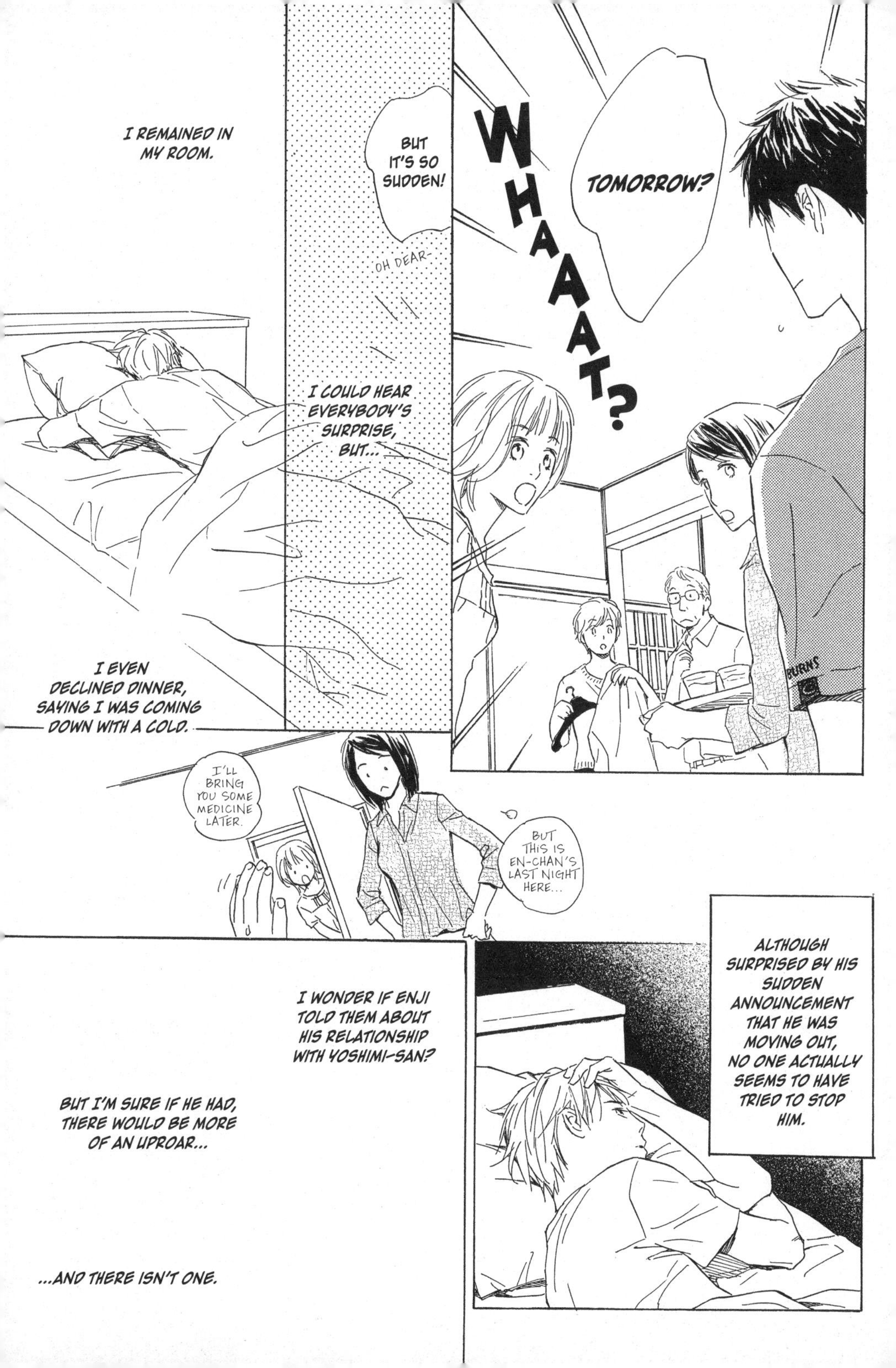
TOMORROW?
WHAAAAT?
BUT IT'S SO SUDDEN!
OH DEAR-
I COULD HEAR EVERYBODY'S SURPRISE, BUT...
I REMAINED IN MY ROOM.
I EVEN DECLINED DINNER, SAYING I WAS COMING DOWN WITH A COLD.
I'LL BRING YOU SOME MEDICINE LATER.
BUT THIS IS EN-CHAN'S LAST NIGHT HERE...
ALTHOUGH SURPRISED BY HIS SUDDEN ANNOUNCEMENT THAT HE WAS MOVING OUT, NO ONE ACTUALLY SEEMS TO HAVE TRIED TO STOP HIM.
I WONDER IF ENJI TOLD THEM ABOUT HIS RELATIONSHIP WITH YOSHIMI-SAN?
BUT I'M SURE IF HE HAD, THERE WOULD BE MORE OF AN UPROAR...
...AND THERE ISN'T ONE.

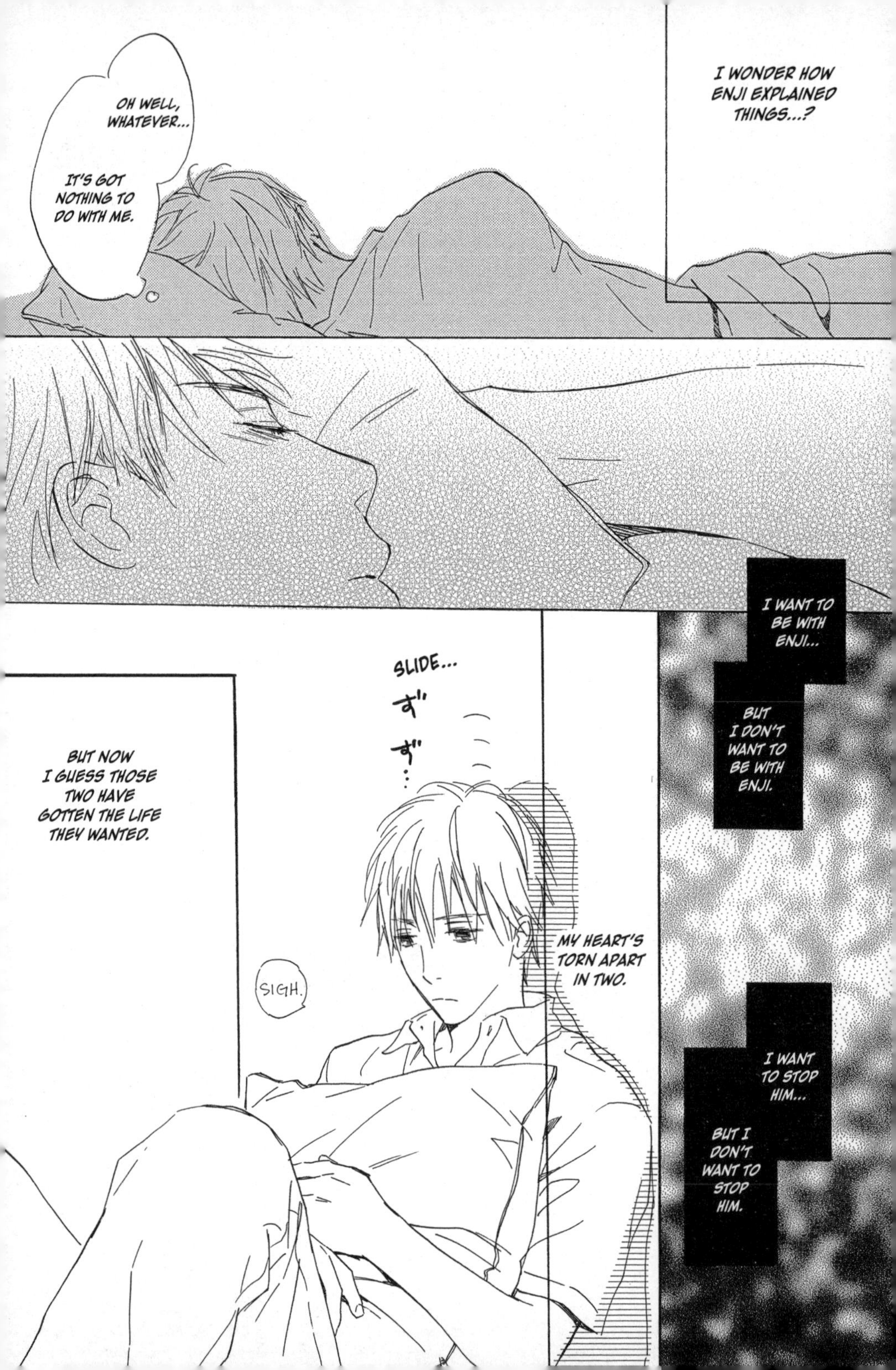
I WONDER HOW ENJI EXPLAINED THINGS...?
OH WELL, WHATEVER...
IT'S GOT NOTHING TO DO WITH ME.
I WANT TO BE WITH ENJI...
BUT I DON'T WANT TO BE WITH ENJI.
I WANT TO STOP HIM...
BUT I DON'T WANT TO STOP HIM.
SLIDE...
ずず...
MY HEART'S TORN APART IN TWO.
SIGH.
BUT NOW I GUESS THOSE TWO HAVE GOTTEN THE LIFE THEY WANTED.

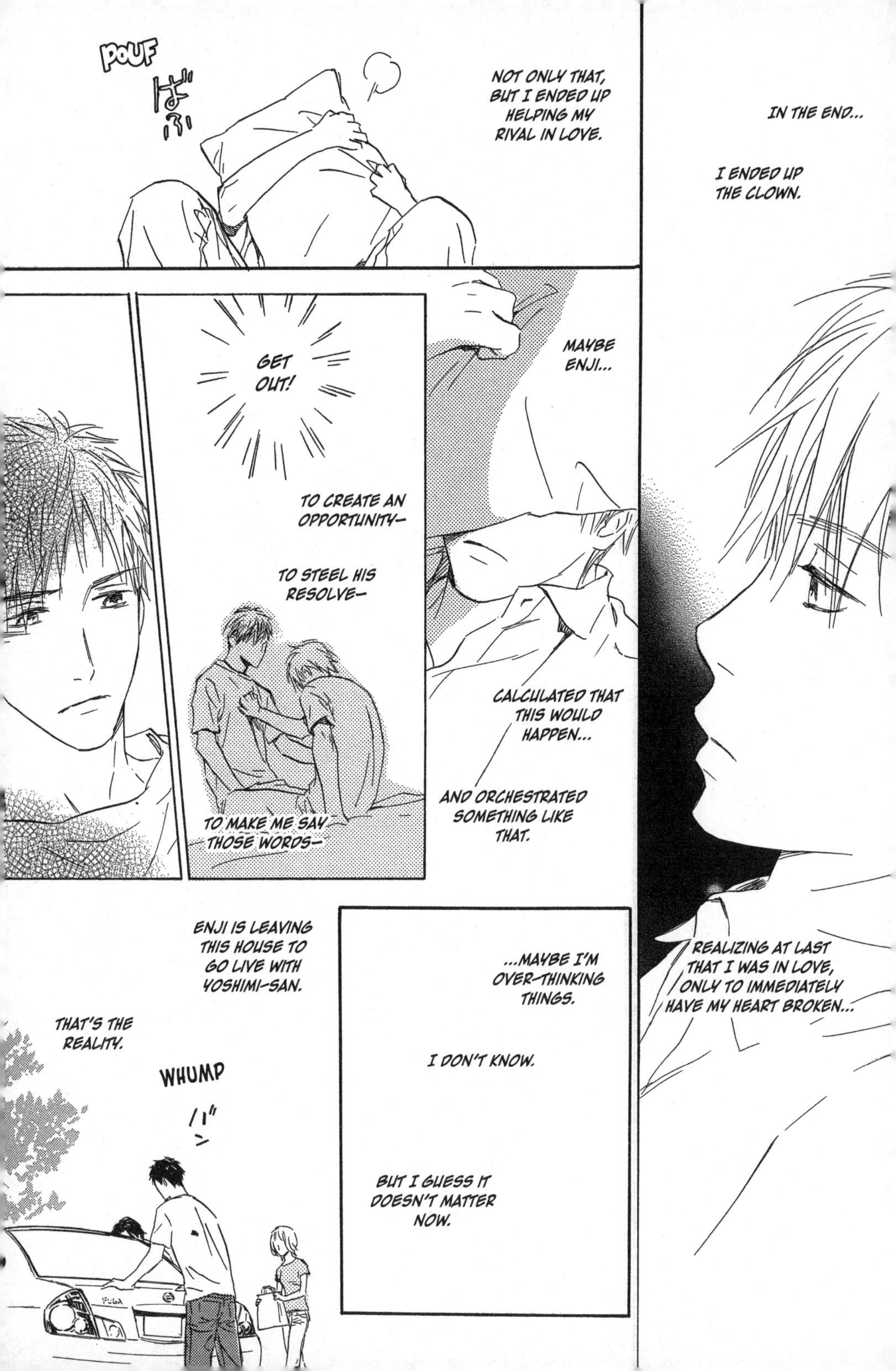

IN THE END...
I ENDED UP THE CLOWN.
REALIZING AT LAST THAT I WAS IN LOVE, ONLY TO IMMEDIATELY HAVE MY HEART BROKEN...
NOT ONLY THAT, BUT I ENDED UP HELPING MY RIVAL IN LOVE.
POUF
ぼふ
MAYBE ENJI...
CALCULATED THAT THIS WOULD HAPPEN...
AND ORCHESTRATED SOMETHING LIKE THAT.
GET OUT!
TO CREATE AN OPPORTUNITY—
TO STEEL HIS RESOLVE—
TO MAKE ME SAY THOSE WORDS—
...MAYBE I'M OVER-THINKING THINGS.
I DON'T KNOW.
BUT I GUESS IT DOESN'T MATTER NOW.
ENJI IS LEAVING THIS HOUSE TO GO LIVE WITH YOSHIMI-SAN.
THAT'S THE REALITY.
WHUMP
バン

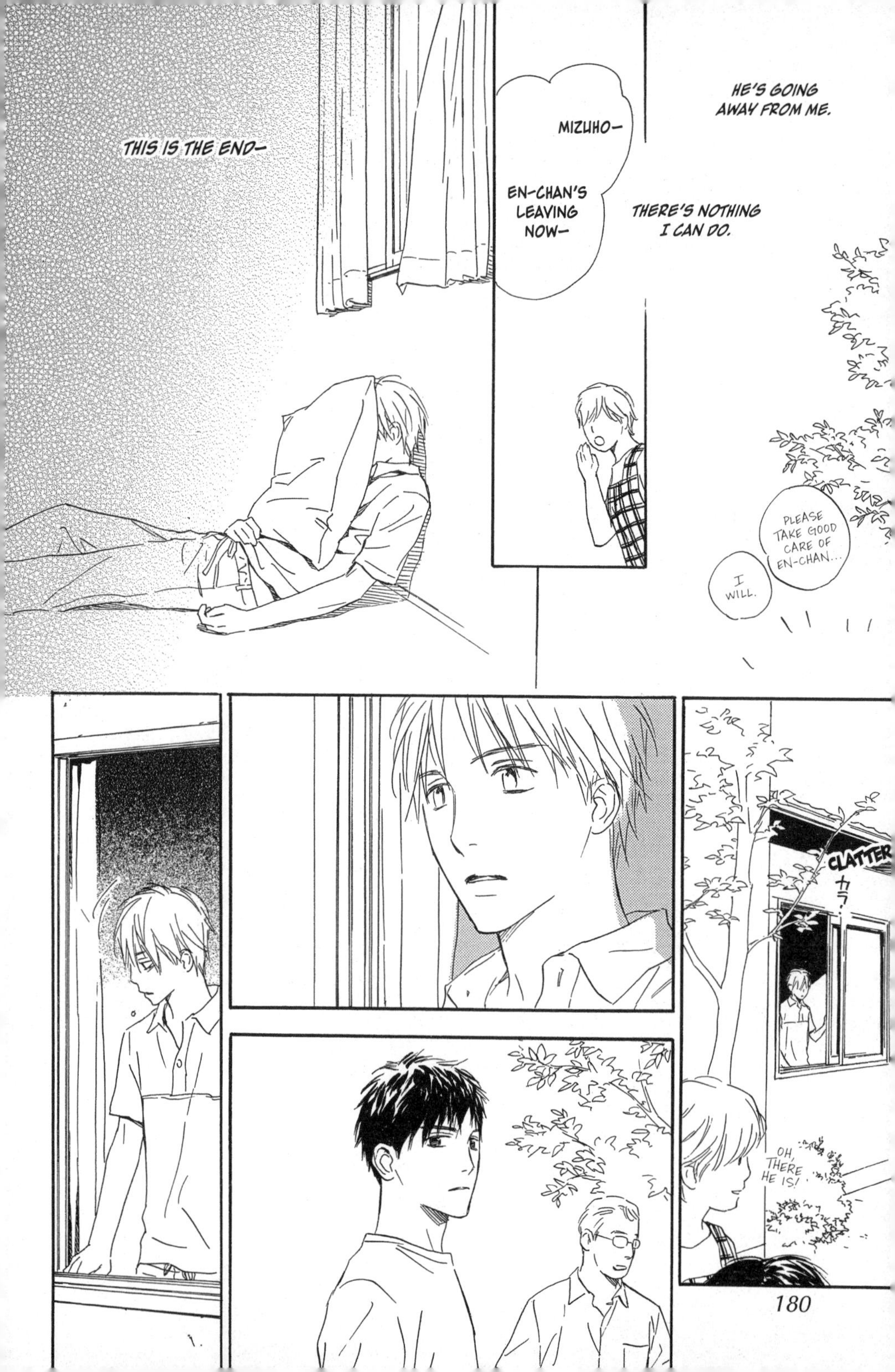
HE'S GOING AWAY FROM ME.
THERE'S NOTHING I CAN DO.
PLEASE TAKE GOOD CARE OF EN-CHAN...
I WILL.
MIZUHO—
EN-CHAN'S LEAVING NOW—
THIS IS THE END—
CLATTER
カラ
OH, THERE HE IS!

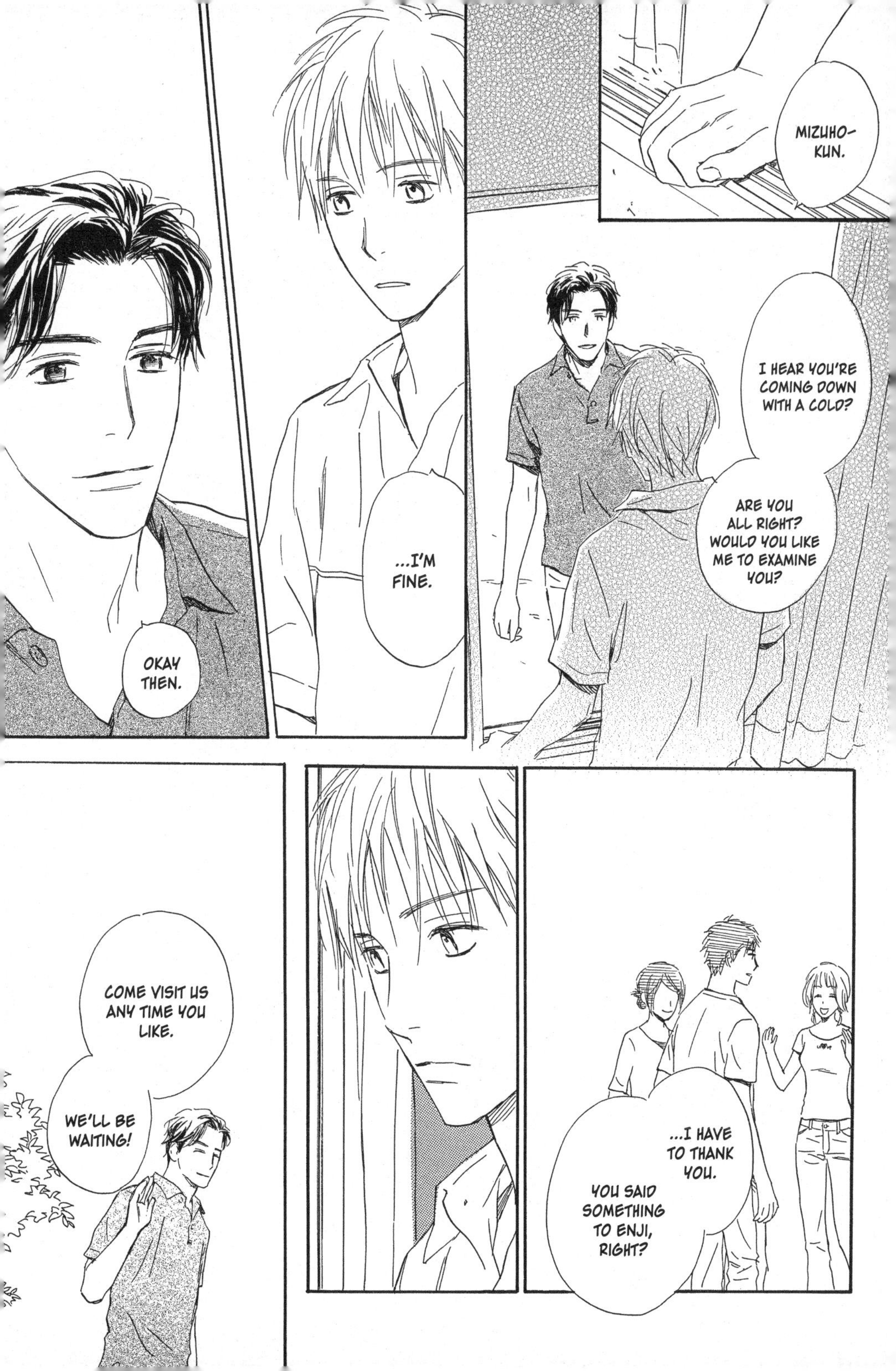
MIZUHO-KUN.
I HEAR YOU'RE COMING DOWN WITH A COLD?
ARE YOU ALL RIGHT? WOULD YOU LIKE ME TO EXAMINE YOU?
...I'M FINE.
OKAY THEN.
...I HAVE TO THANK YOU.
YOU SAID SOMETHING TO ENJI, RIGHT?
COME VISIT US ANY TIME YOU LIKE.
WE'LL BE WAITING!

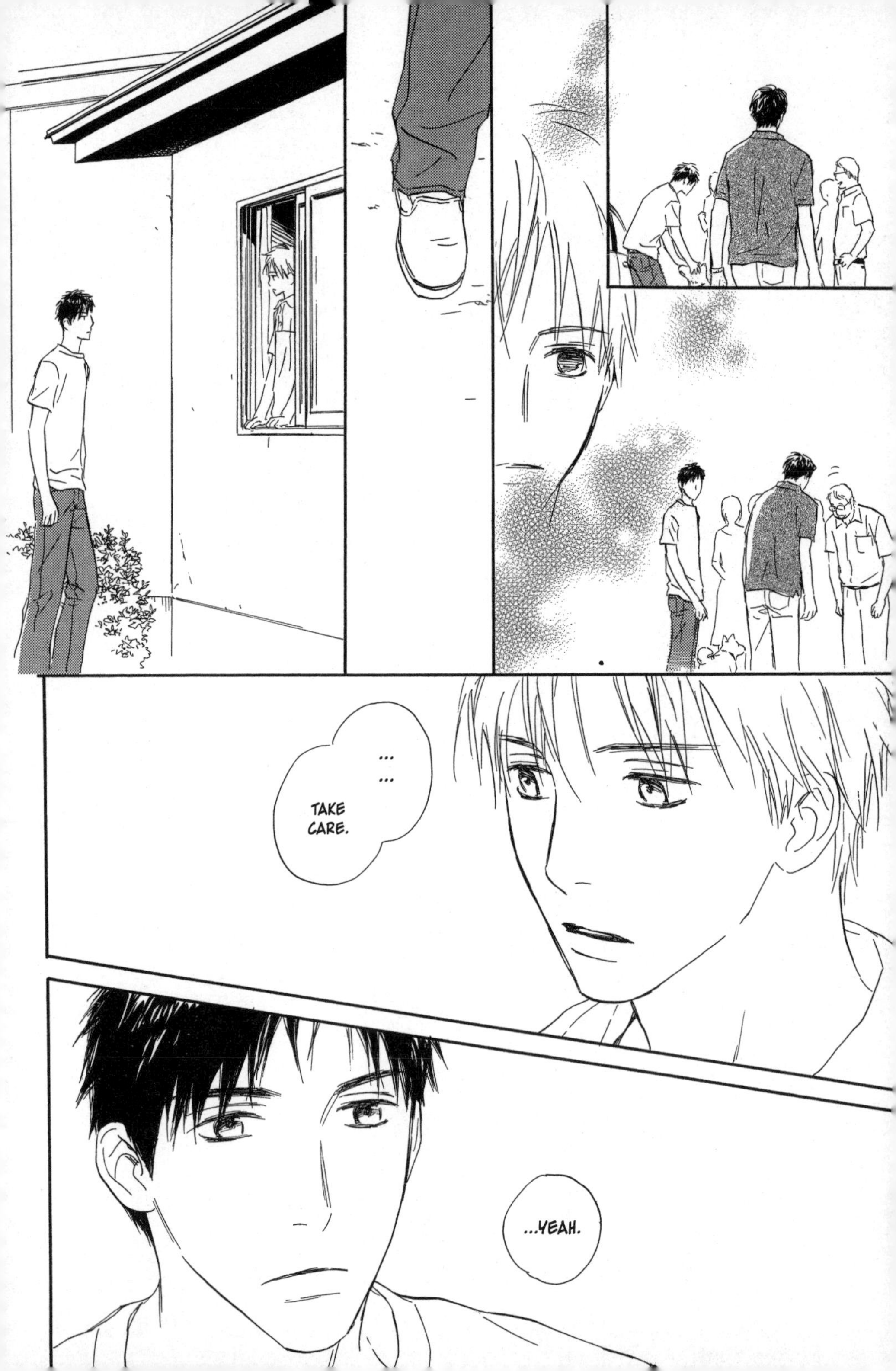
...
...
TAKE CARE.
...YEAH.

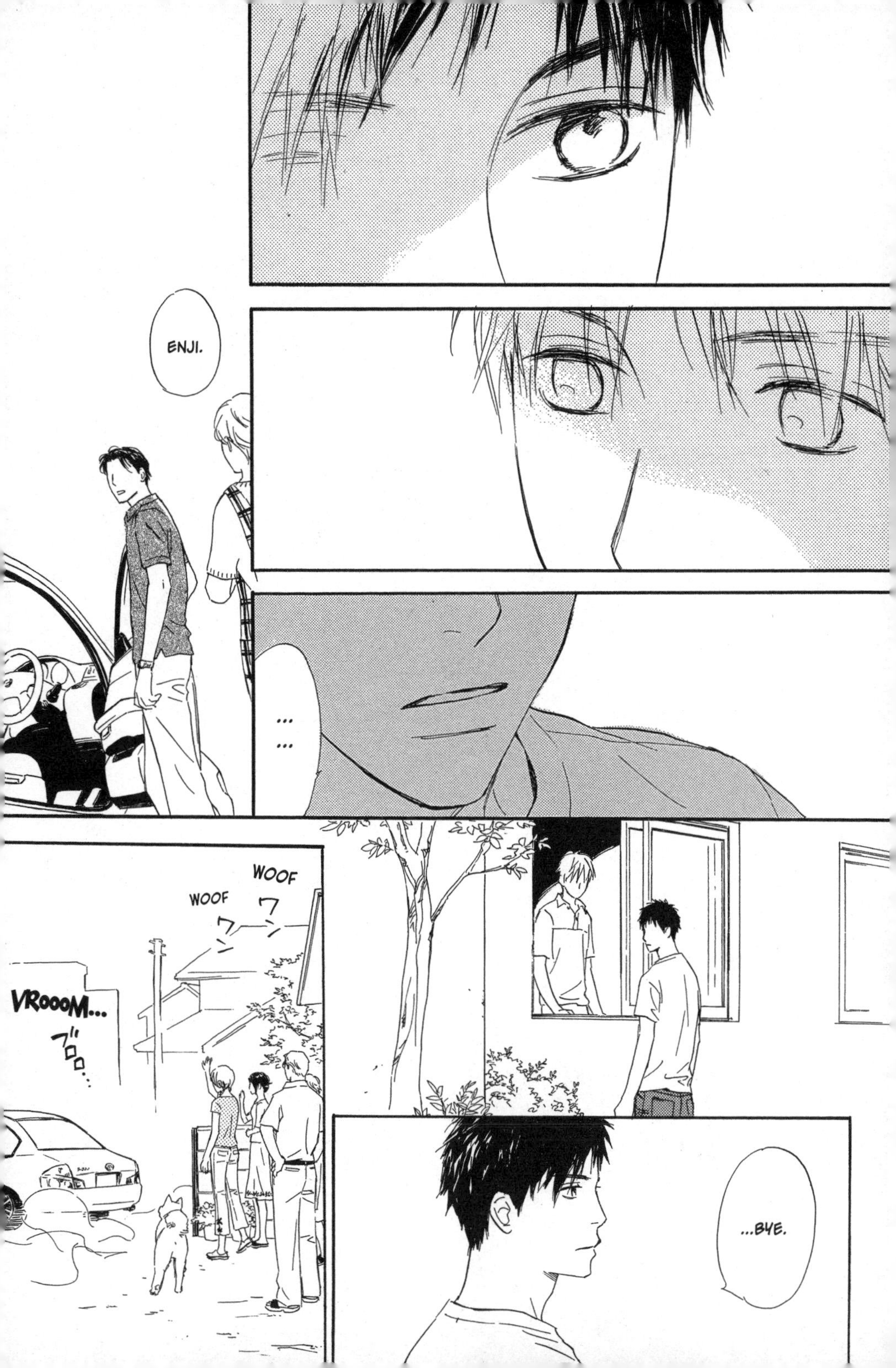
......
ENJI.
...BYE.
WOOF
ワン
WOOF
ワーン
VROOOM...
ブロロ...

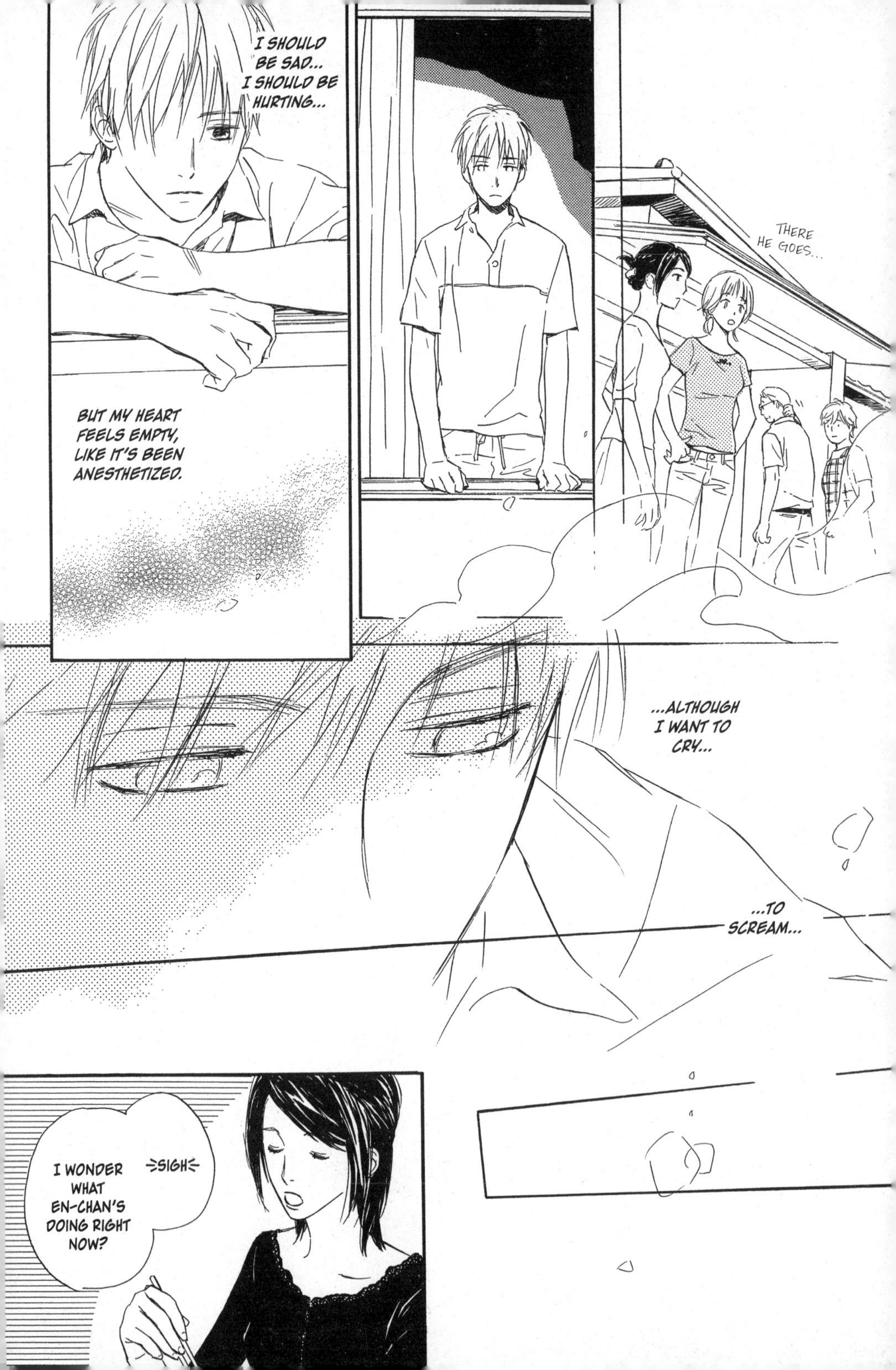
THERE HE GOES...
I SHOULD BE SAD... I SHOULD BE HURTING...
BUT MY HEART FEELS EMPTY, LIKE IT'S BEEN ANESTHETIZED.
...ALTHOUGH I WANT TO CRY...
...TO SCREAM...
SIGH
I WONDER WHAT EN-CHAN'S DOING RIGHT NOW?

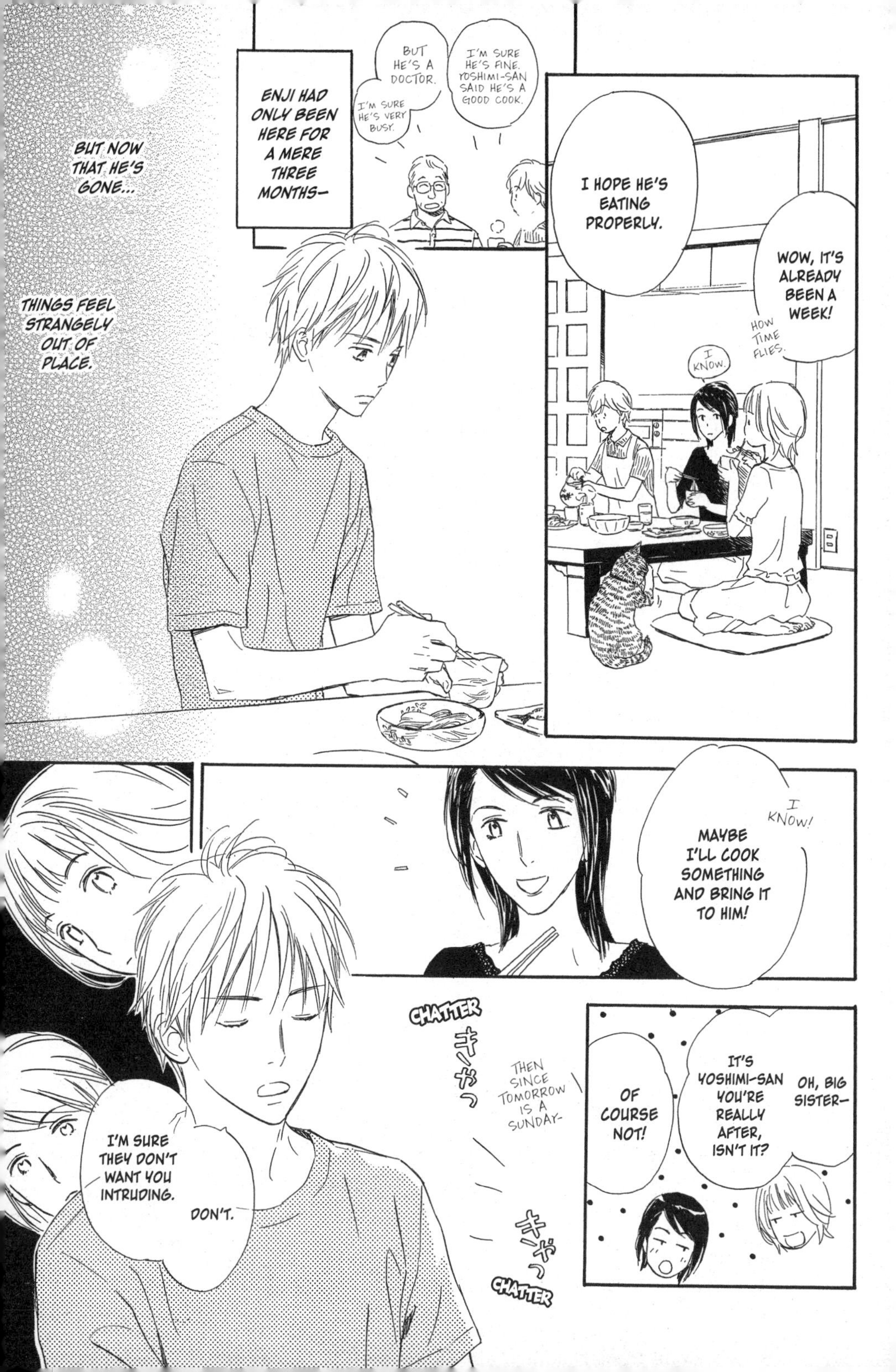

WOW, IT'S ALREADY BEEN A WEEK!
HOW TIME FLIES.
I KNOW.
I HOPE HE'S EATING PROPERLY.
ENJI HAD ONLY BEEN HERE FOR A MERE THREE MONTHS—
I'M SURE HE'S FINE. YOSHIMI-SAN SAID HE'S A GOOD COOK.
BUT HE'S A DOCTOR.
I'M SURE HE'S VERY BUSY.
BUT NOW THAT HE'S GONE...
THINGS FEEL STRANGELY OUT OF PLACE.
I KNOW!
MAYBE I'LL COOK SOMETHING AND BRING IT TO HIM!
OH, BIG SISTER—
IT'S YOSHIMI-SAN YOU'RE REALLY AFTER, ISN'T IT?
OF COURSE NOT!
THEN SINCE TOMORROW IS A SUNDAY-
CHATTER
CHATTER
DON'T.
I'M SURE THEY DON'T WANT YOU INTRUDING.

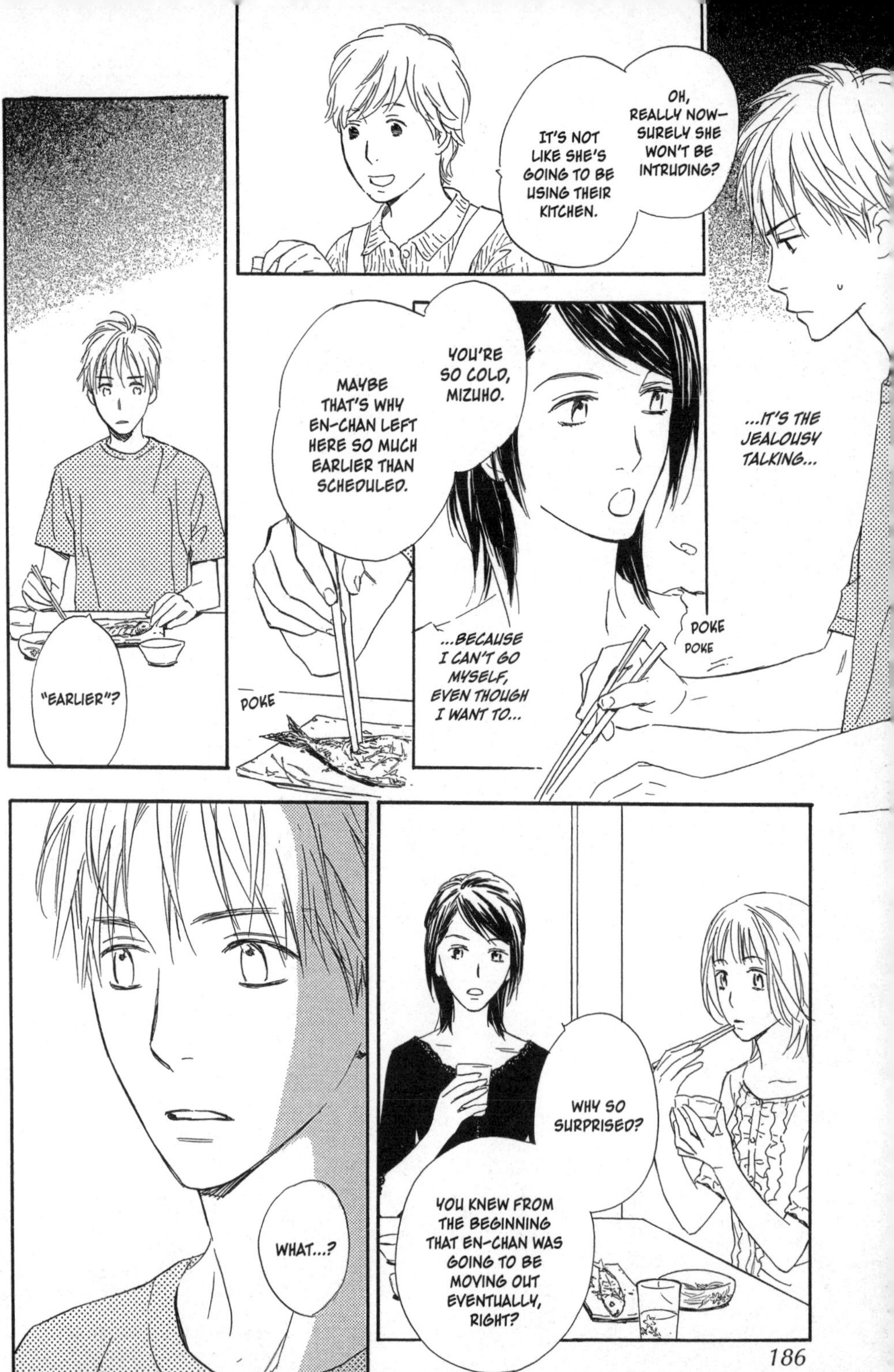

OH, REALLY NOW— SURELY SHE WON'T BE INTRUDING?
IT'S NOT LIKE SHE'S GOING TO BE USING THEIR KITCHEN.
...IT'S THE JEALOUSY TALKING...
YOU'RE SO COLD, MIZUHO.
MAYBE THAT'S WHY EN-CHAN LEFT HERE SO MUCH EARLIER THAN SCHEDULED.
POKE
POKE
...BECAUSE I CAN'T GO MYSELF, EVEN THOUGH I WANT TO...
POKE
"EARLIER"?
WHY SO SURPRISED?
YOU KNEW FROM THE BEGINNING THAT EN-CHAN WAS GOING TO BE MOVING OUT EVENTUALLY, RIGHT?
WHAT...?

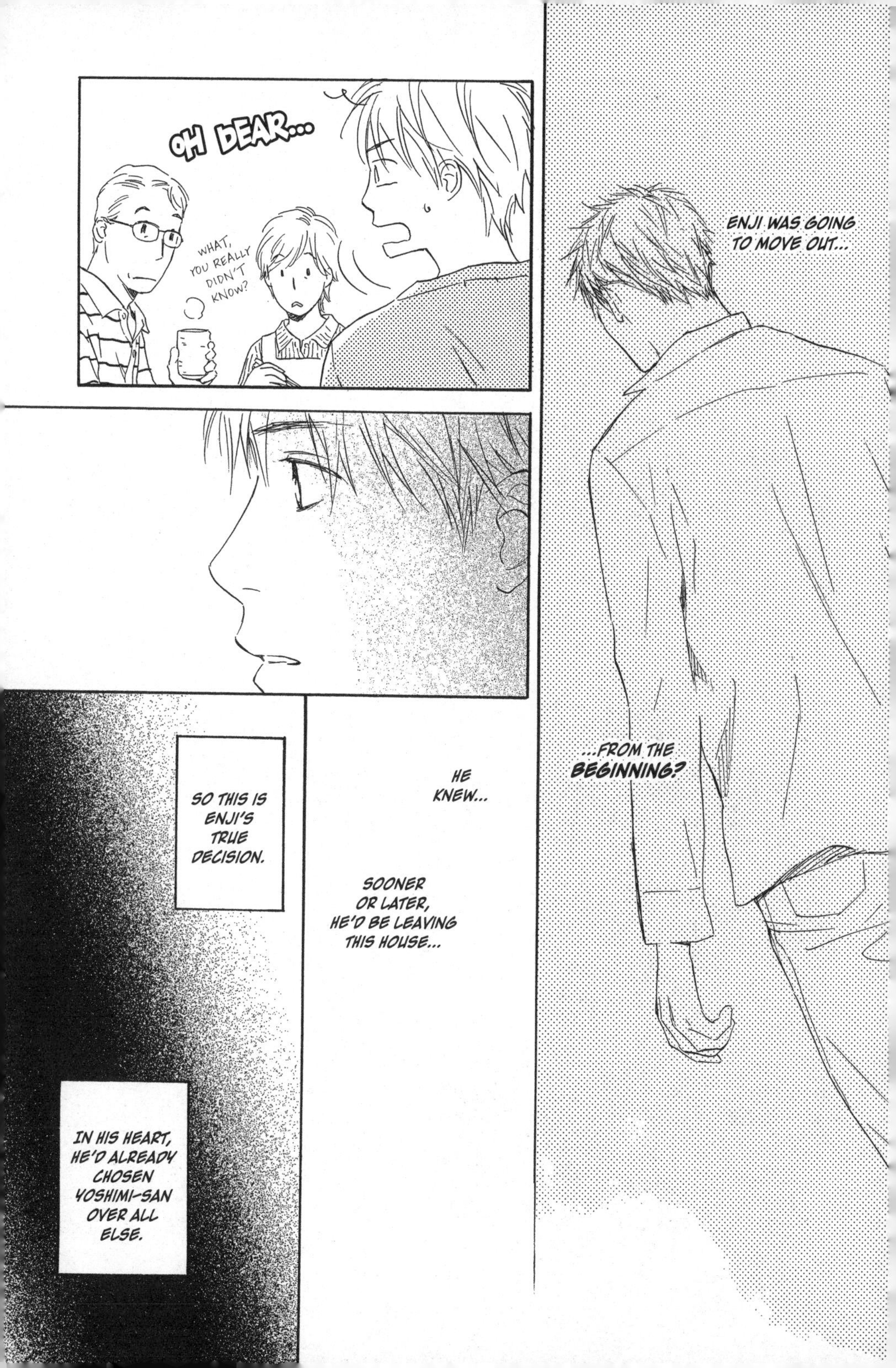
ENJI WAS GOING TO MOVE OUT...
...FROM THE BEGINNING?
OH DEAR...
WHAT, YOU REALLY DIDN'T KNOW?
HE KNEW...
SOONER OR LATER, HE'D BE LEAVING THIS HOUSE...
SO THIS IS ENJI'S TRUE DECISION.
IN HIS HEART, HE'D ALREADY CHOSEN YOSHIMI-SAN OVER ALL ELSE.

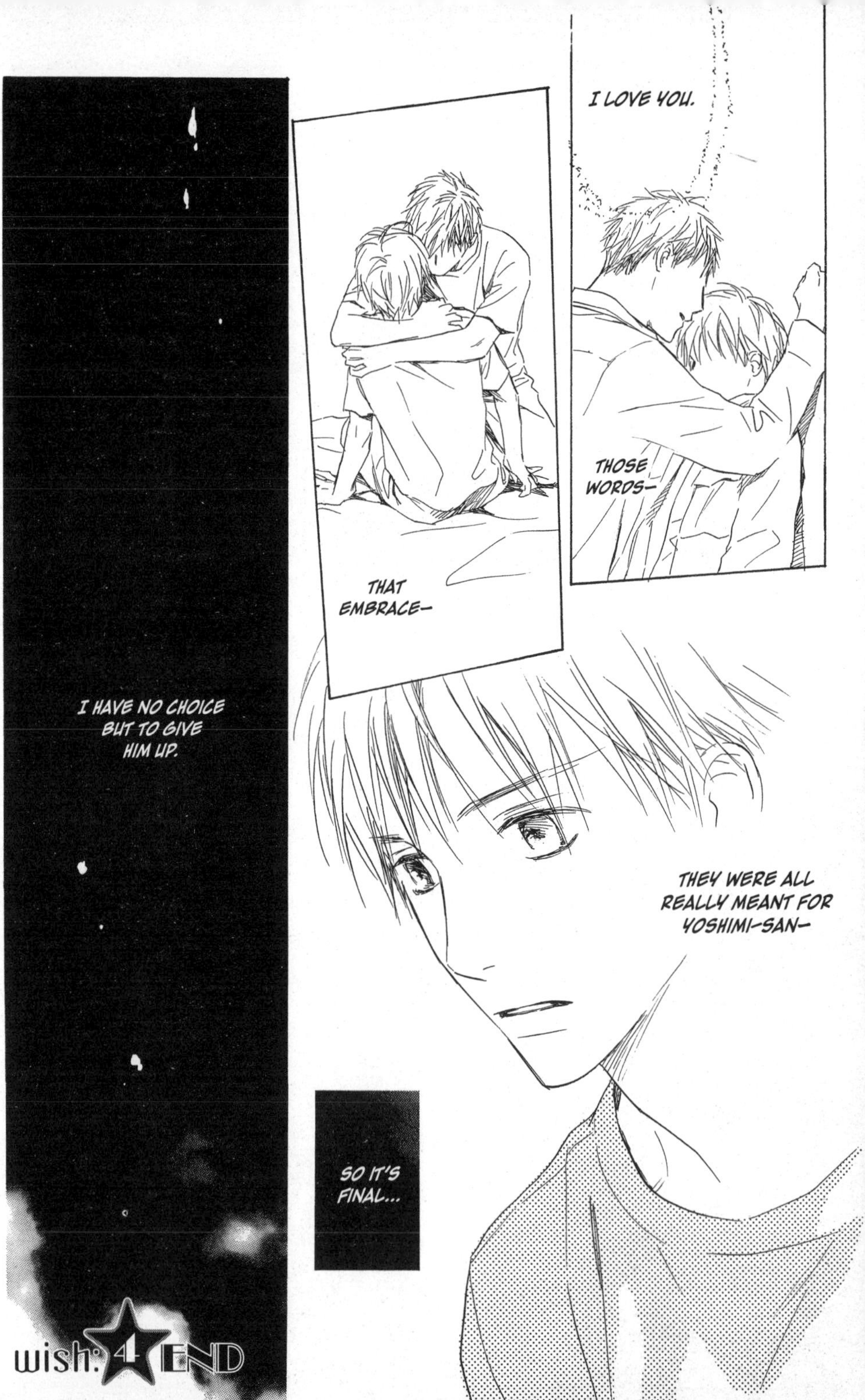
I LOVE YOU.
THOSE WORDS—
THAT EMBRACE—
THEY WERE ALL REALLY MEANT FOR YOSHIMI-SAN—
SO IT'S FINAL...
I HAVE NO CHOICE BUT TO GIVE HIM UP.
wish: 4 END

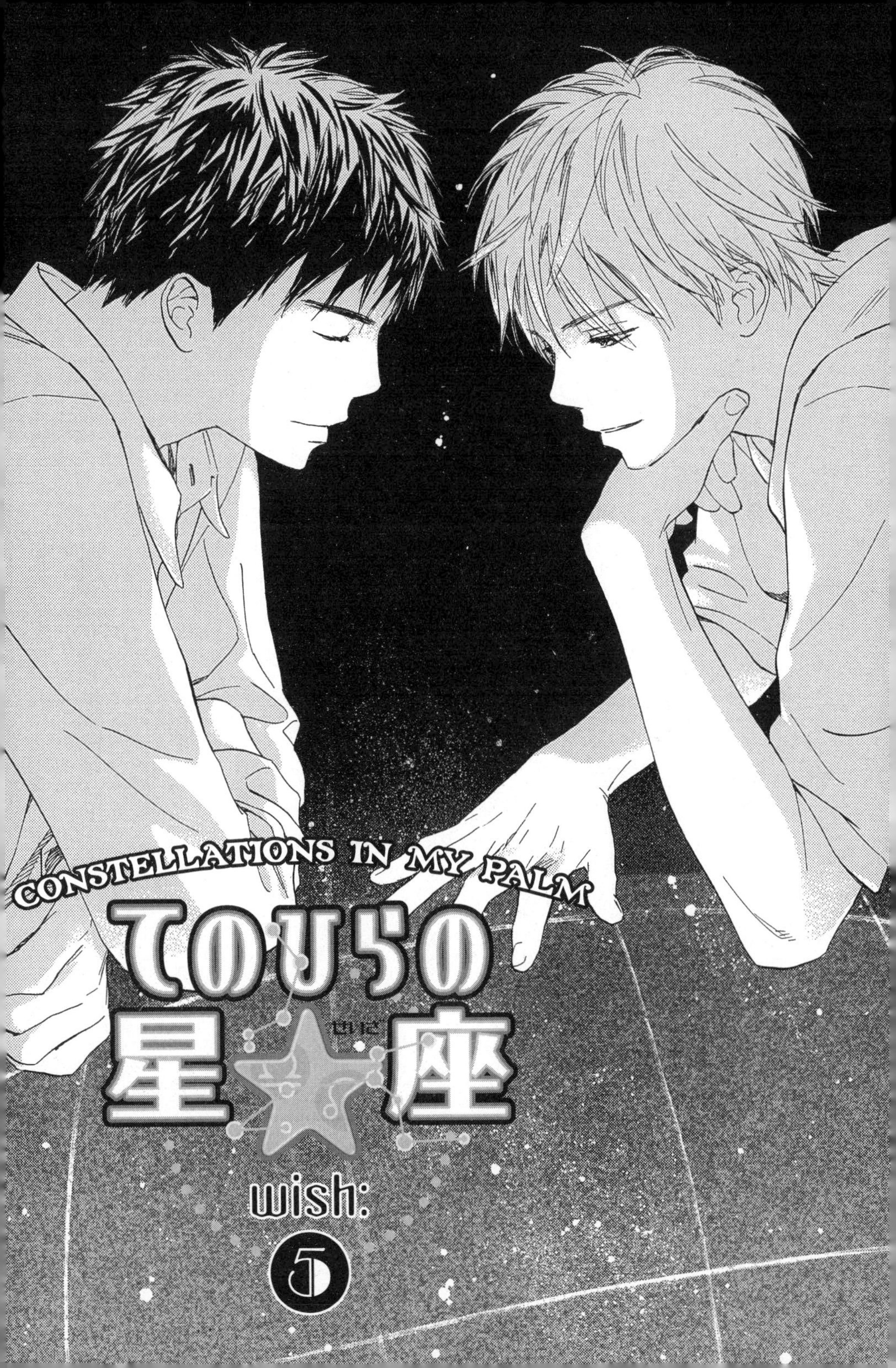
CONSTELLATIONS IN MY PALM
てのひらの星座
せいざ
wish:
5

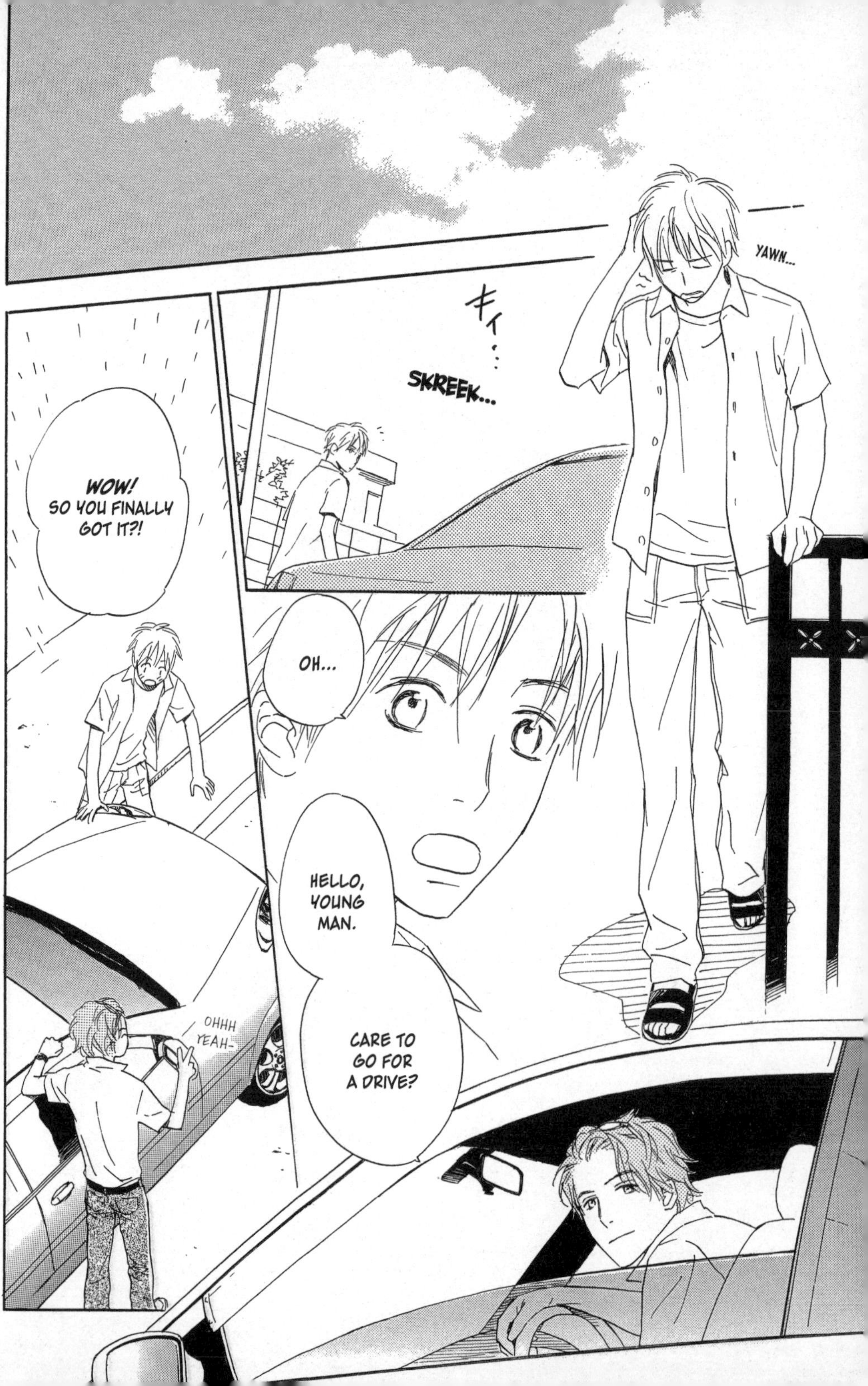
YAWN...
キィ…
SKREEK...
OH...
HELLO, YOUNG MAN.
CARE TO GO FOR A DRIVE?
WOW! SO YOU FINALLY GOT IT?!
OHHH YEAH-

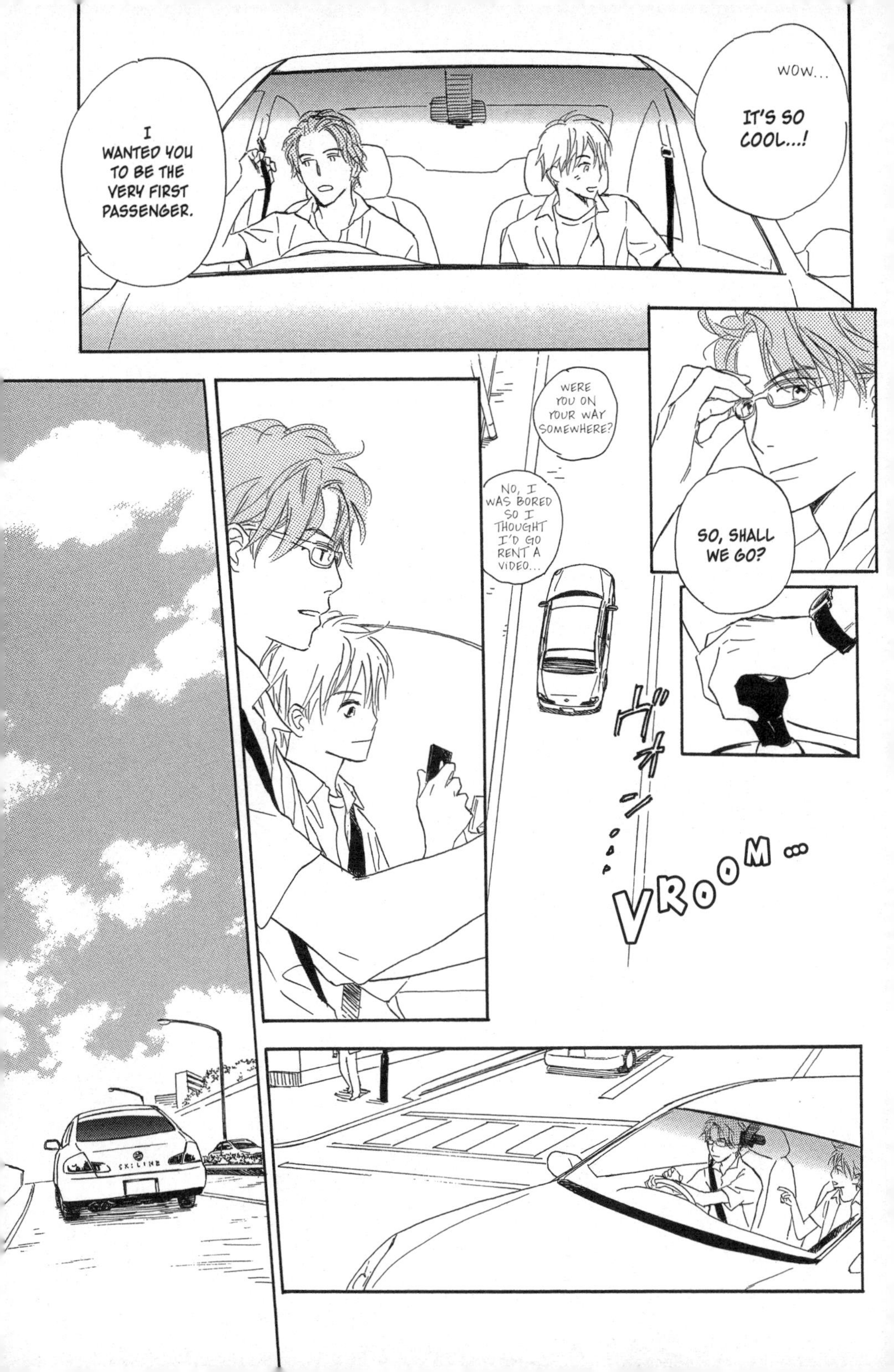
WOW...
IT'S SO COOL...!
I WANTED YOU TO BE THE VERY FIRST PASSENGER.
WERE YOU ON YOUR WAY SOMEWHERE?
NO, I WAS BORED SO I THOUGHT I'D GO RENT A VIDEO...
SO, SHALL WE GO?
ヴォン...
VROOM...
SKYLINE

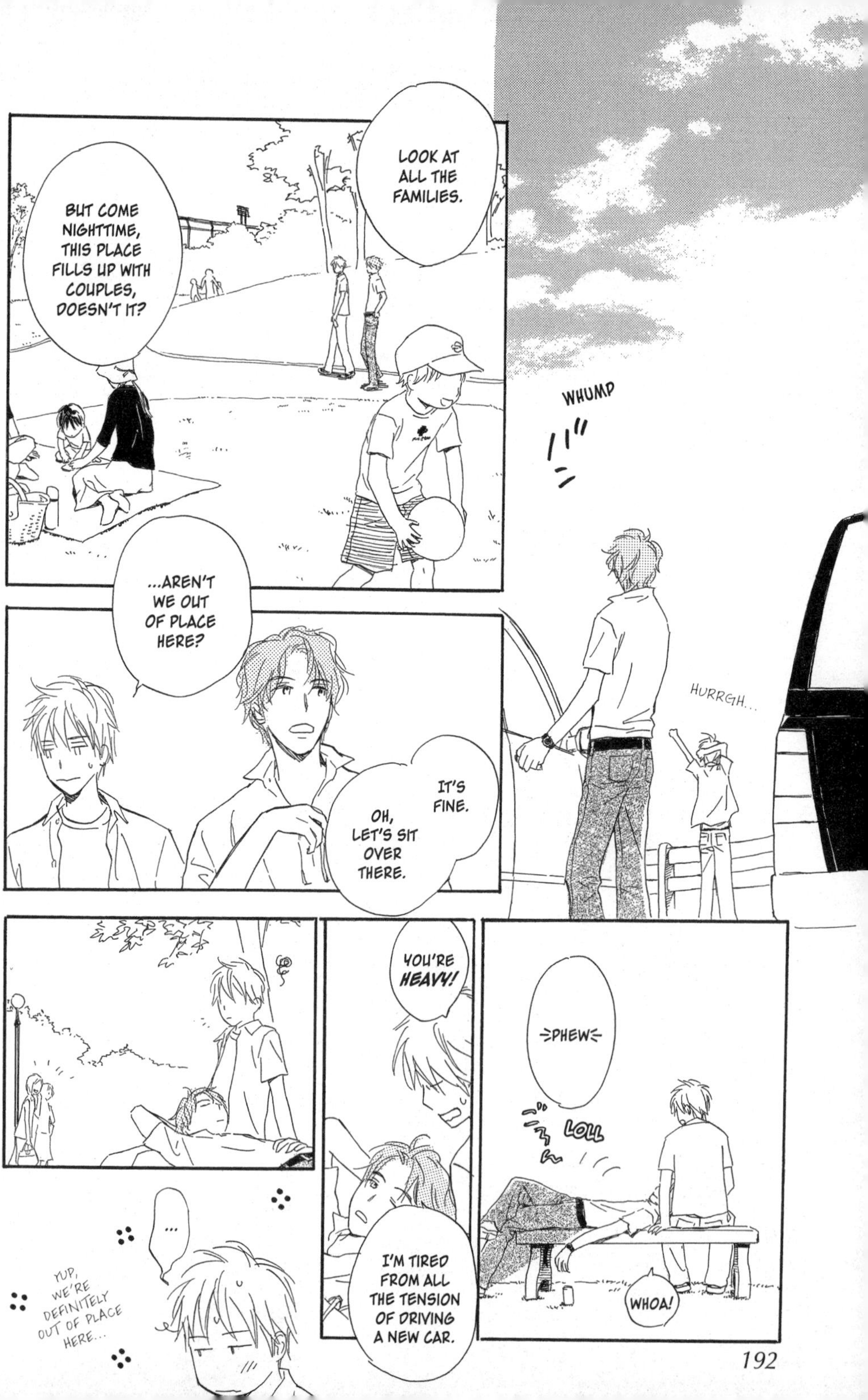
WHUMP
HURRGH...
LOOK AT ALL THE FAMILIES.
BUT COME NIGHTTIME, THIS PLACE FILLS UP WITH COUPLES, DOESN'T IT?
...AREN'T WE OUT OF PLACE HERE?
IT'S FINE.
OH, LET'S SIT OVER THERE.
PHEW
LOLL
WHOA!
YOU'RE HEAVY!
I'M TIRED FROM ALL THE TENSION OF DRIVING A NEW CAR.
...
YUP, WE'RE DEFINITELY OUT OF PLACE HERE...

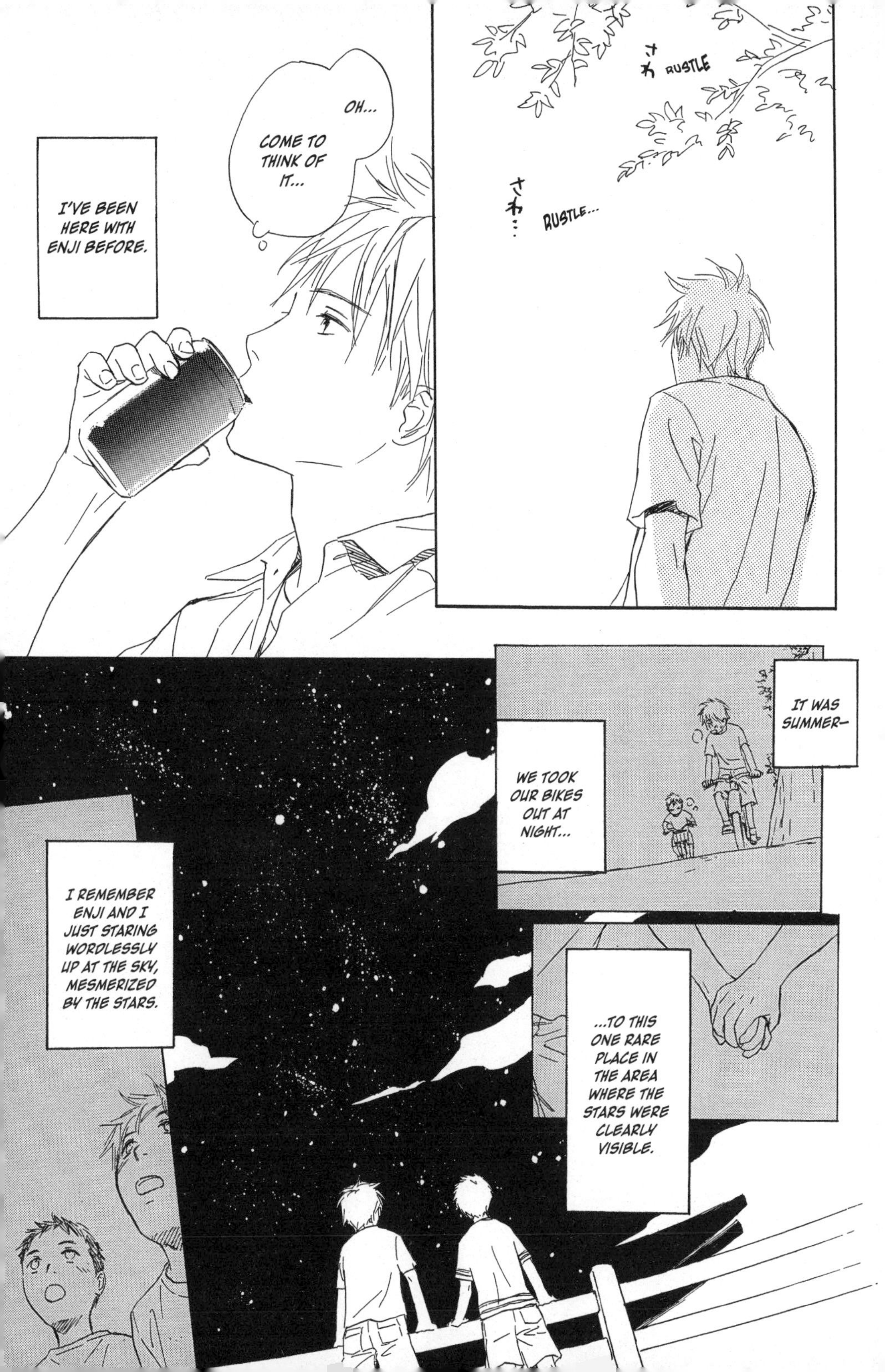
さわ
RUSTLE
さわ…
RUSTLE...
OH...
COME TO THINK OF IT...
I'VE BEEN HERE WITH ENJI BEFORE.
IT WAS SUMMER—
WE TOOK OUR BIKES OUT AT NIGHT...
...TO THIS ONE RARE PLACE IN THE AREA WHERE THE STARS WERE CLEARLY VISIBLE.
I REMEMBER ENJI AND I JUST STARING WORDLESSLY UP AT THE SKY, MESMERIZED BY THE STARS.

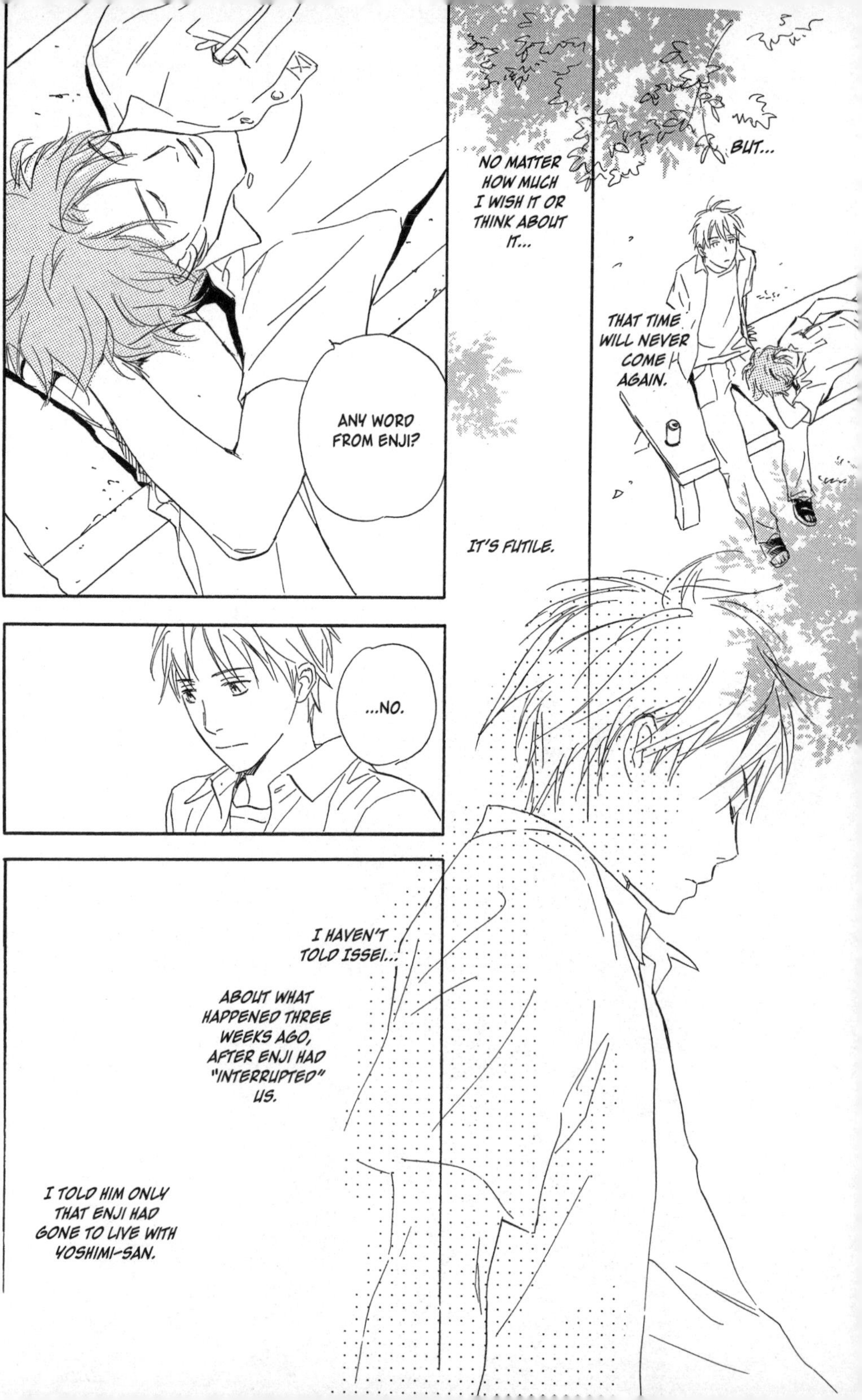
BUT...
THAT TIME WILL NEVER COME AGAIN.
NO MATTER HOW MUCH I WISH IT OR THINK ABOUT IT...
IT'S FUTILE.
ANY WORD FROM ENJI?
...NO.
I HAVEN'T TOLD ISSEI...
ABOUT WHAT HAPPENED THREE WEEKS AGO, AFTER ENJI HAD "INTERRUPTED" US.
I TOLD HIM ONLY THAT ENJI HAD GONE TO LIVE WITH YOSHIMI-SAN.

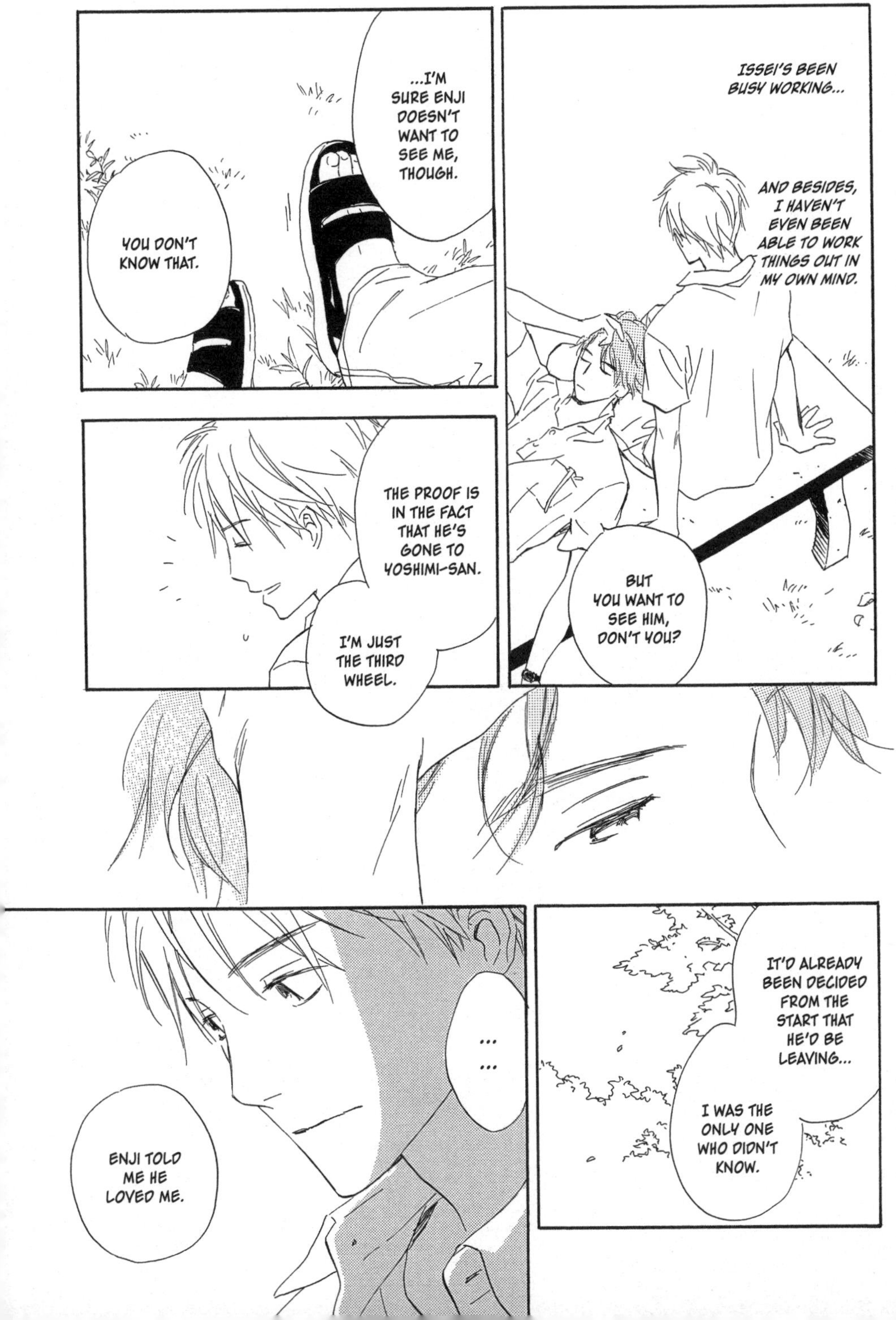
ISSEI'S BEEN BUSY WORKING...
AND BESIDES, I HAVEN'T EVEN BEEN ABLE TO WORK THINGS OUT IN MY OWN MIND.
BUT YOU WANT TO SEE HIM, DON'T YOU?
...I'M SURE ENJI DOESN'T WANT TO SEE ME, THOUGH.
YOU DON'T KNOW THAT.
THE PROOF IS IN THE FACT THAT HE'S GONE TO YOSHIMI-SAN.
I'M JUST THE THIRD WHEEL.
IT'D ALREADY BEEN DECIDED FROM THE START THAT HE'D BE LEAVING...
I WAS THE ONLY ONE WHO DIDN'T KNOW.
... ...
ENJI TOLD ME HE LOVED ME.

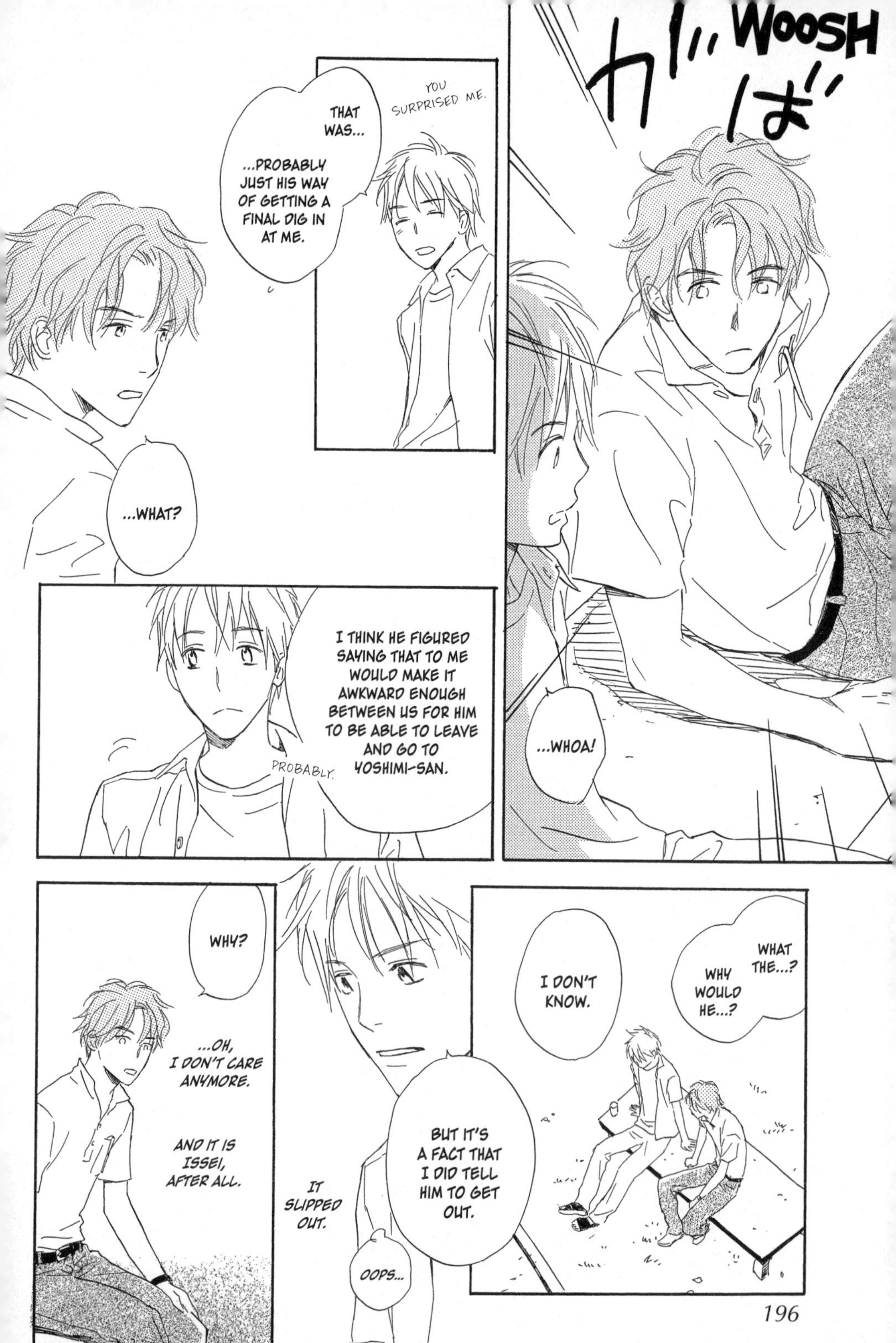
WOOSH
...WHOA!
YOU SURPRISED ME.
THAT WAS...
...PROBABLY JUST HIS WAY OF GETTING A FINAL DIG IN AT ME.
...WHAT?
I THINK HE FIGURED SAYING THAT TO ME WOULD MAKE IT AWKWARD ENOUGH BETWEEN US FOR HIM TO BE ABLE TO LEAVE AND GO TO YOSHIMI-SAN.
PROBABLY.
WHAT THE...? WHY WOULD HE...?
I DON'T KNOW.
BUT IT'S A FACT THAT I DID TELL HIM TO GET OUT.
IT SLIPPED OUT.
OOPS...
WHY?
...OH, I DON'T CARE ANYMORE.
AND IT IS ISSEI, AFTER ALL.

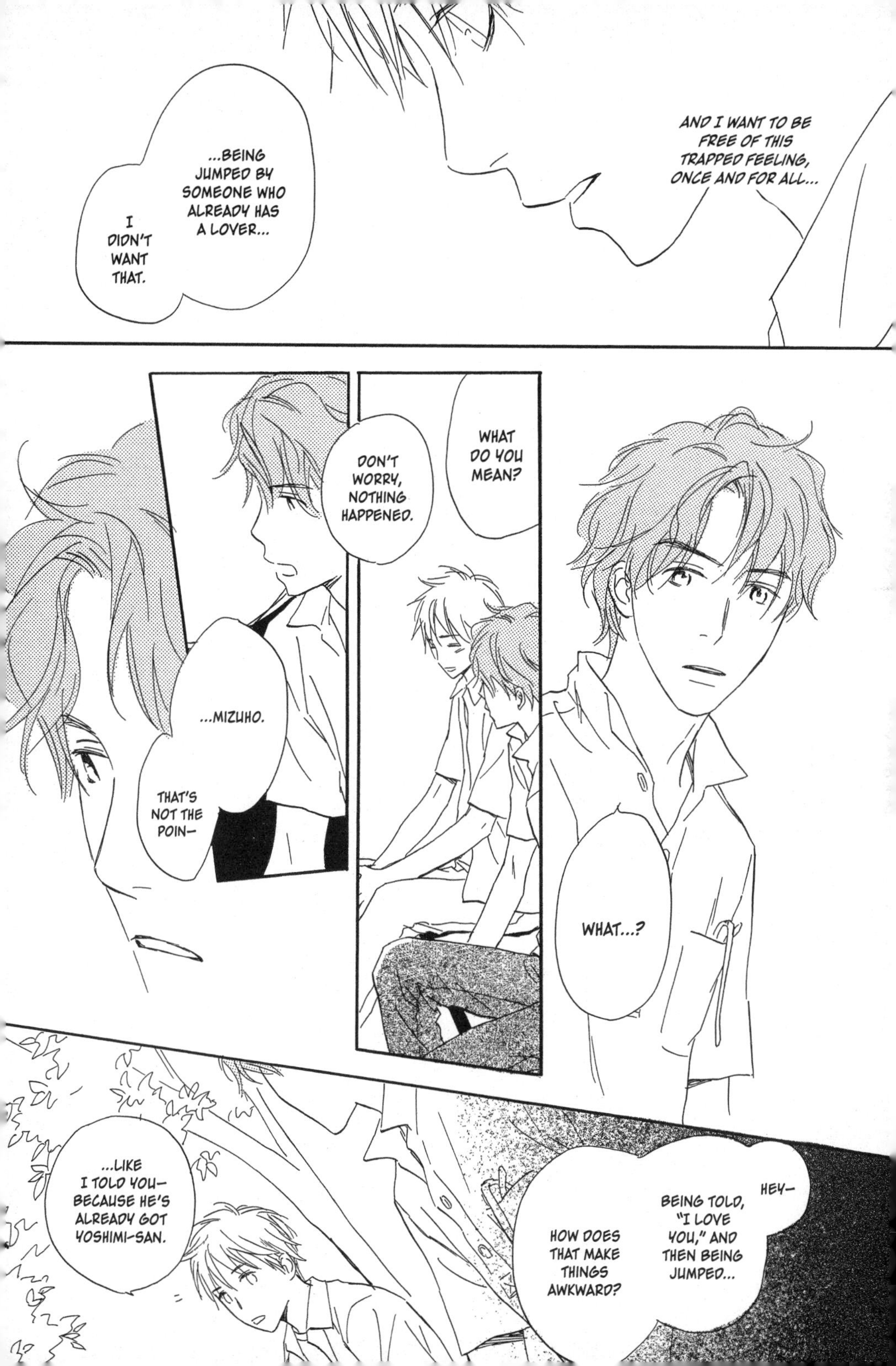
AND I WANT TO BE FREE OF THIS TRAPPED FEELING, ONCE AND FOR ALL...
...BEING JUMPED BY SOMEONE WHO ALREADY HAS A LOVER...
I DIDN'T WANT THAT.
WHAT...?
WHAT DO YOU MEAN?
DON'T WORRY, NOTHING HAPPENED.
...MIZUHO.
THAT'S NOT THE POIN—
HEY—
BEING TOLD, "I LOVE YOU," AND THEN BEING JUMPED...
HOW DOES THAT MAKE THINGS AWKWARD?
...LIKE I TOLD YOU— BECAUSE HE'S ALREADY GOT YOSHIMI-SAN.

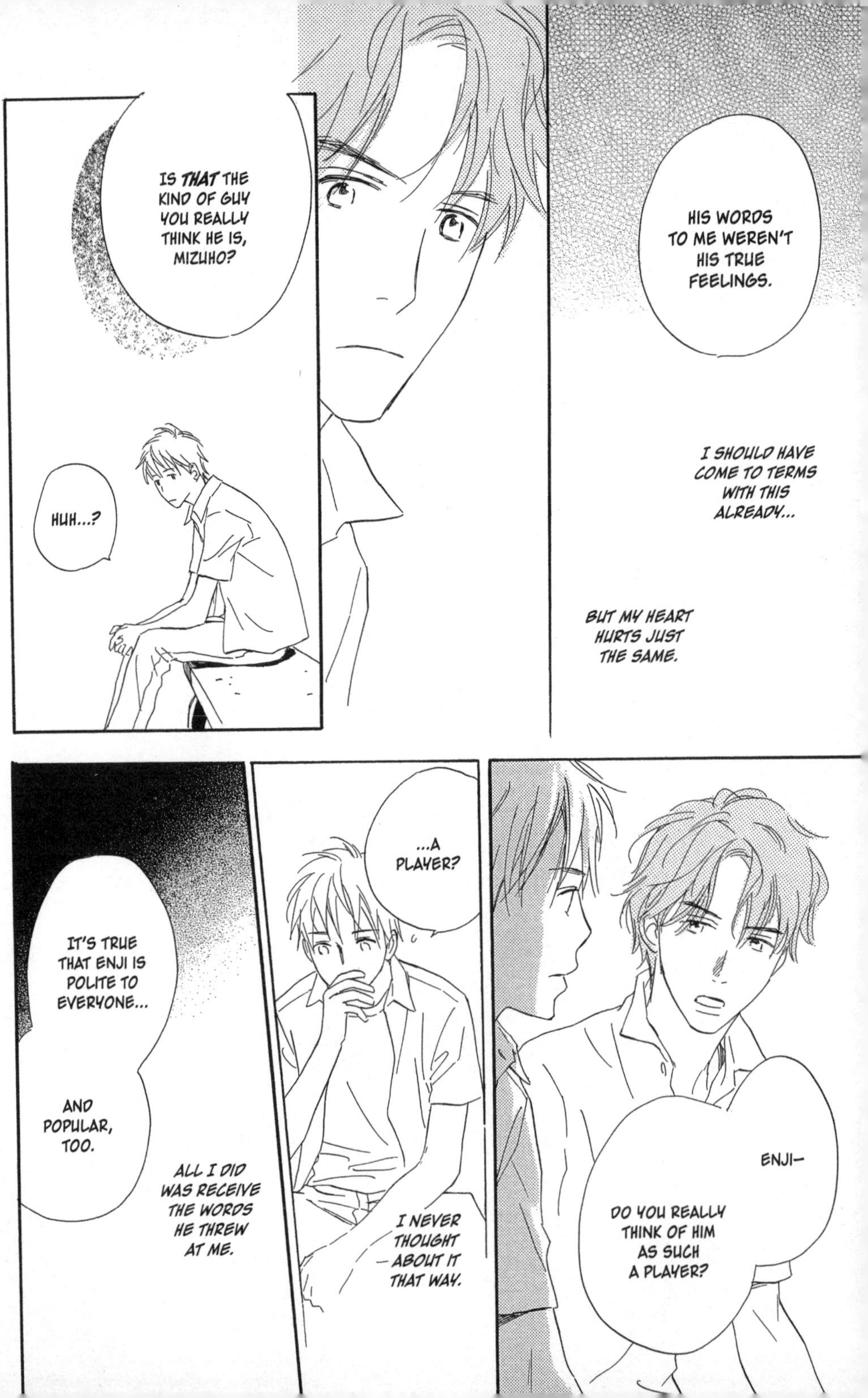
HIS WORDS TO ME WEREN'T HIS TRUE FEELINGS.
I SHOULD HAVE COME TO TERMS WITH THIS ALREADY...
BUT MY HEART HURTS JUST THE SAME.
IS THAT THE KIND OF GUY YOU REALLY THINK HE IS, MIZUHO?
HUH...?
ENJI—
DO YOU REALLY THINK OF HIM AS SUCH A PLAYER?
...A PLAYER?
I NEVER THOUGHT ABOUT IT THAT WAY.
IT'S TRUE THAT ENJI IS POLITE TO EVERYONE...
AND POPULAR, TOO.
ALL I DID WAS RECEIVE THE WORDS HE THREW AT ME.

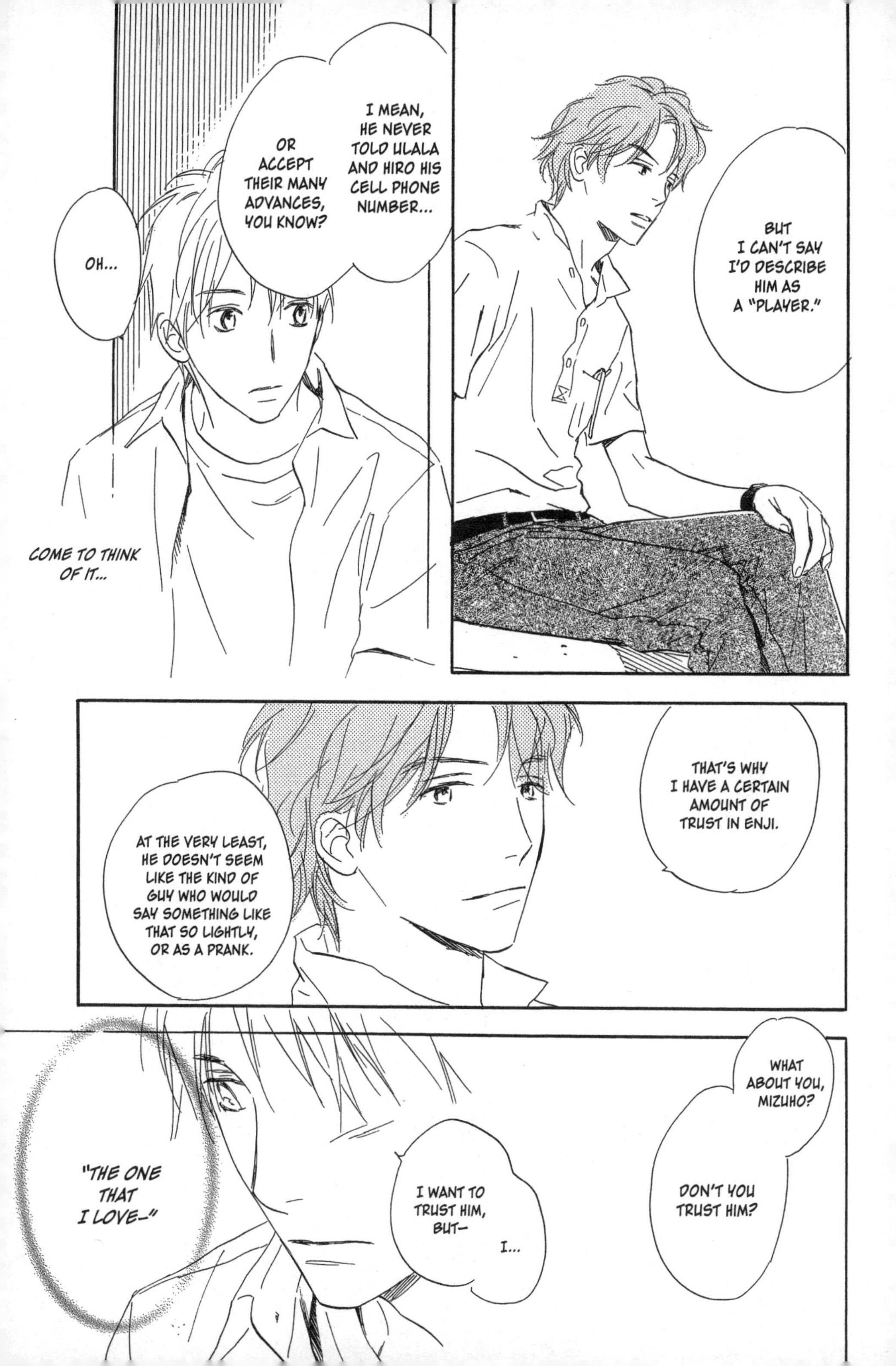
BUT I CAN'T SAY I'D DESCRIBE HIM AS A "PLAYER."
I MEAN, HE NEVER TOLD ULALA AND HIRO HIS CELL PHONE NUMBER...
OR ACCEPT THEIR MANY ADVANCES, YOU KNOW?
OH...
COME TO THINK OF IT...
THAT'S WHY I HAVE A CERTAIN AMOUNT OF TRUST IN ENJI.
AT THE VERY LEAST, HE DOESN'T SEEM LIKE THE KIND OF GUY WHO WOULD SAY SOMETHING LIKE THAT SO LIGHTLY, OR AS A PRANK.
WHAT ABOUT YOU, MIZUHO?
DON'T YOU TRUST HIM?
I WANT TO TRUST HIM, BUT–
I...
"THE ONE THAT I LOVE–"

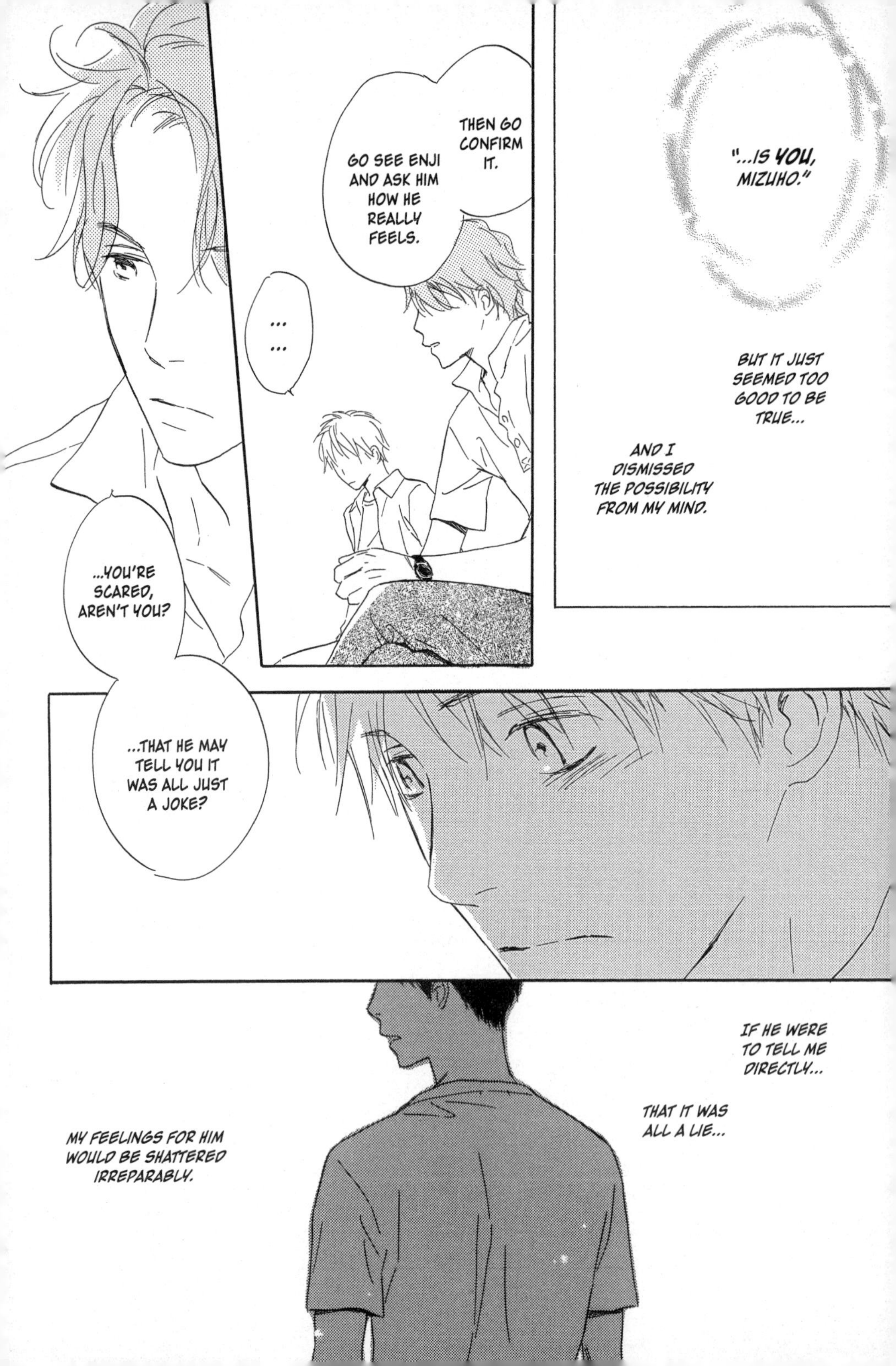
"...IS YOU, MIZUHO."
BUT IT JUST SEEMED TOO GOOD TO BE TRUE...
AND I DISMISSED THE POSSIBILITY FROM MY MIND.
THEN GO CONFIRM IT.
GO SEE ENJI AND ASK HIM HOW HE REALLY FEELS.
......
...YOU'RE SCARED, AREN'T YOU?
...THAT HE MAY TELL YOU IT WAS ALL JUST A JOKE?
IF HE WERE TO TELL ME DIRECTLY...
THAT IT WAS ALL A LIE...
MY FEELINGS FOR HIM WOULD BE SHATTERED IRREPARABLY.

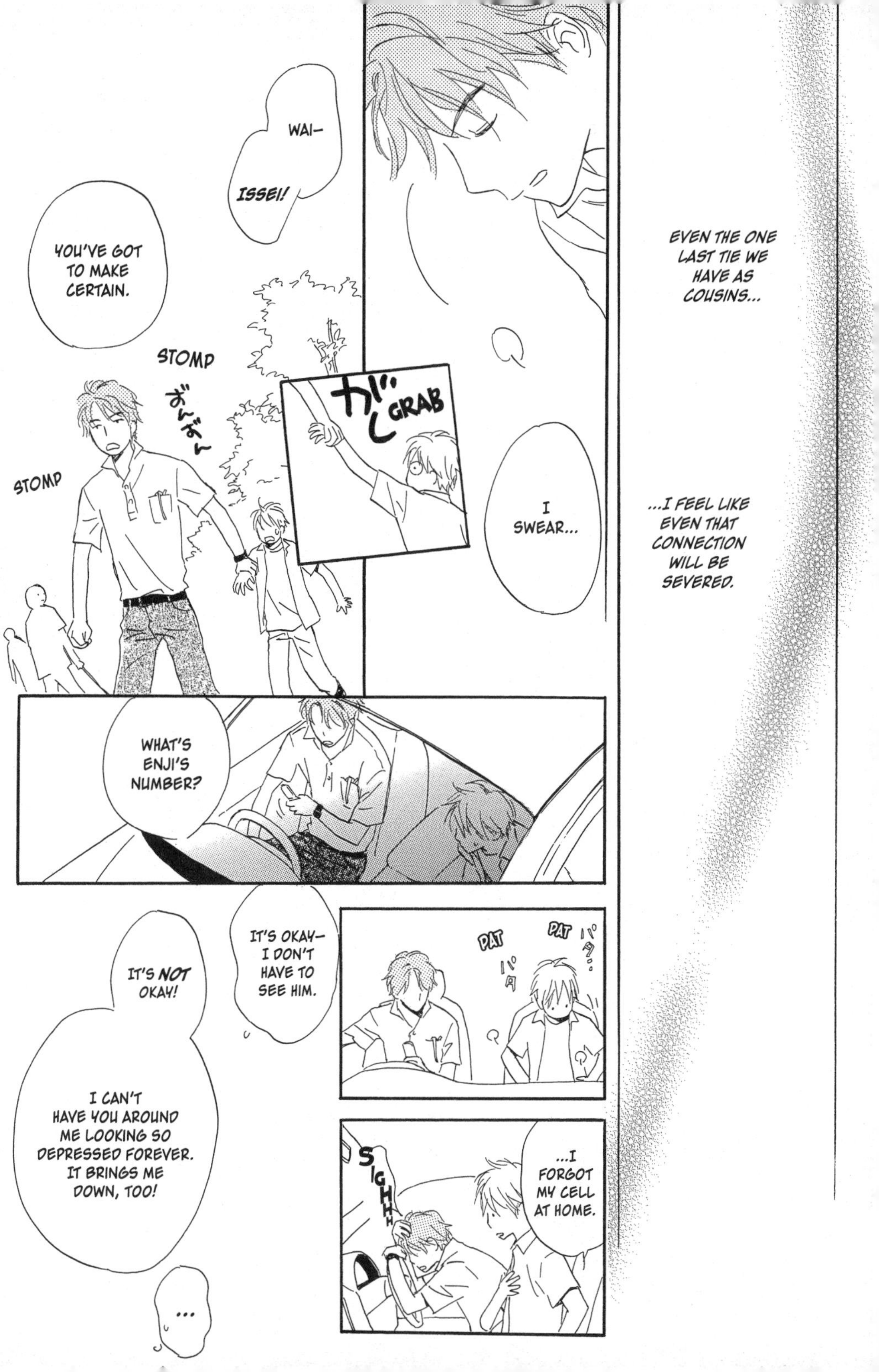

EVEN THE ONE LAST TIE WE HAVE AS COUSINS...
...I FEEL LIKE EVEN THAT CONNECTION WILL BE SEVERED.
I SWEAR...
がし GRAB
WAI—
ISSEI!
YOU'VE GOT TO MAKE CERTAIN.
STOMP
ずんずん
STOMP
WHAT'S ENJI'S NUMBER?
PAT
PAT
パタ
パタ
IT'S OKAY— I DON'T HAVE TO SEE HIM.
IT'S NOT OKAY!
I CAN'T HAVE YOU AROUND ME LOOKING SO DEPRESSED FOREVER. IT BRINGS ME DOWN, TOO!
...I FORGOT MY CELL AT HOME.
SIGHHH
...

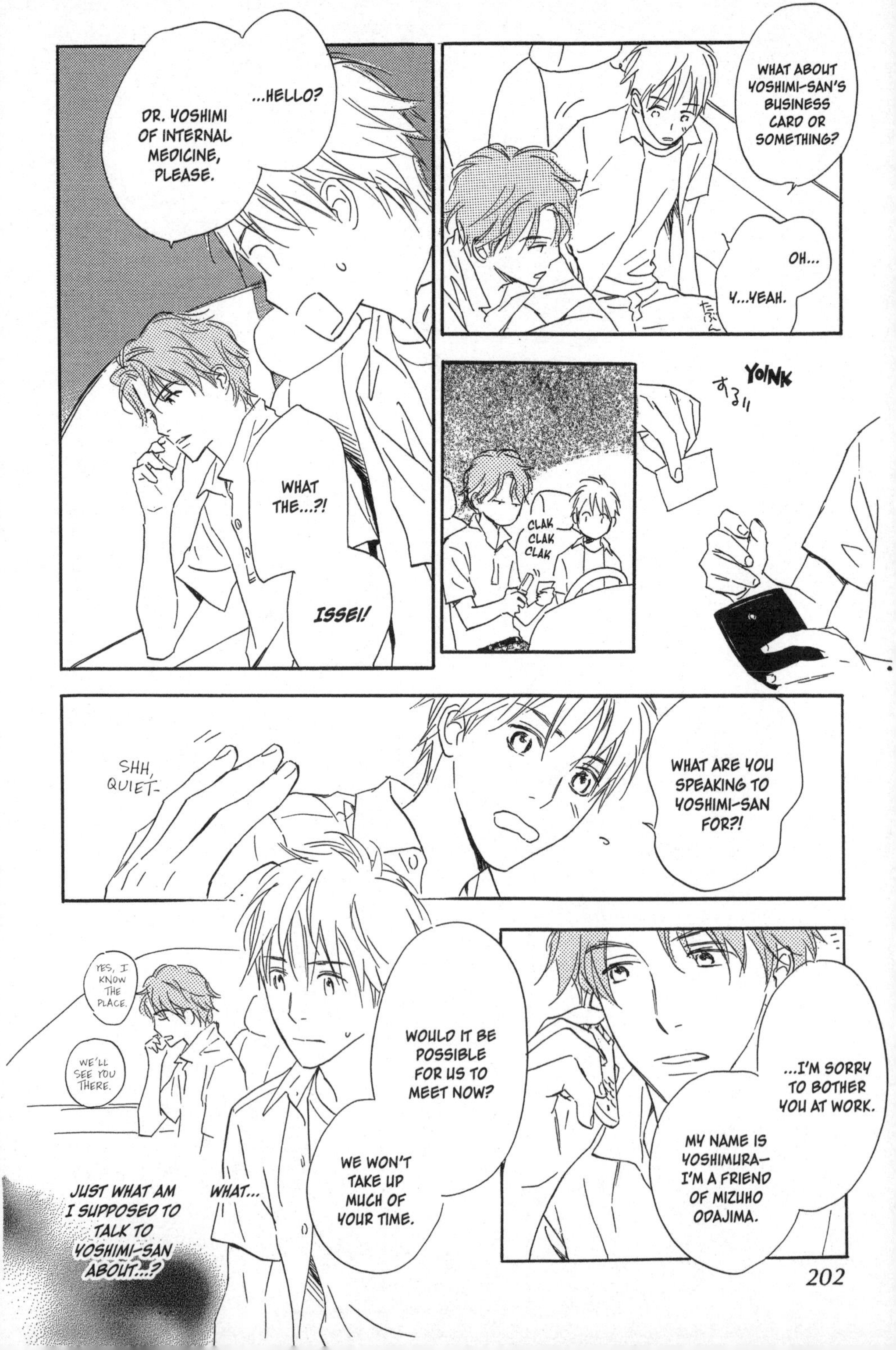
WHAT ABOUT YOSHIMI-SAN'S BUSINESS CARD OR SOMETHING?
OH...
Y...YEAH.
たぶん
YOINK
するり
CLAK CLAK CLAK
...HELLO?
DR. YOSHIMI OF INTERNAL MEDICINE, PLEASE.
WHAT THE...?!
ISSEI!
WHAT ARE YOU SPEAKING TO YOSHIMI-SAN FOR?!
SHH, QUIET-
...I'M SORRY TO BOTHER YOU AT WORK.
MY NAME IS YOSHIMURA— I'M A FRIEND OF MIZUHO ODAJIMA.
WOULD IT BE POSSIBLE FOR US TO MEET NOW?
WE WON'T TAKE UP MUCH OF YOUR TIME.
WHAT...
YES, I KNOW THE PLACE.
WE'LL SEE YOU THERE.
JUST WHAT AM I SUPPOSED TO TALK TO YOSHIMI-SAN ABOUT...?

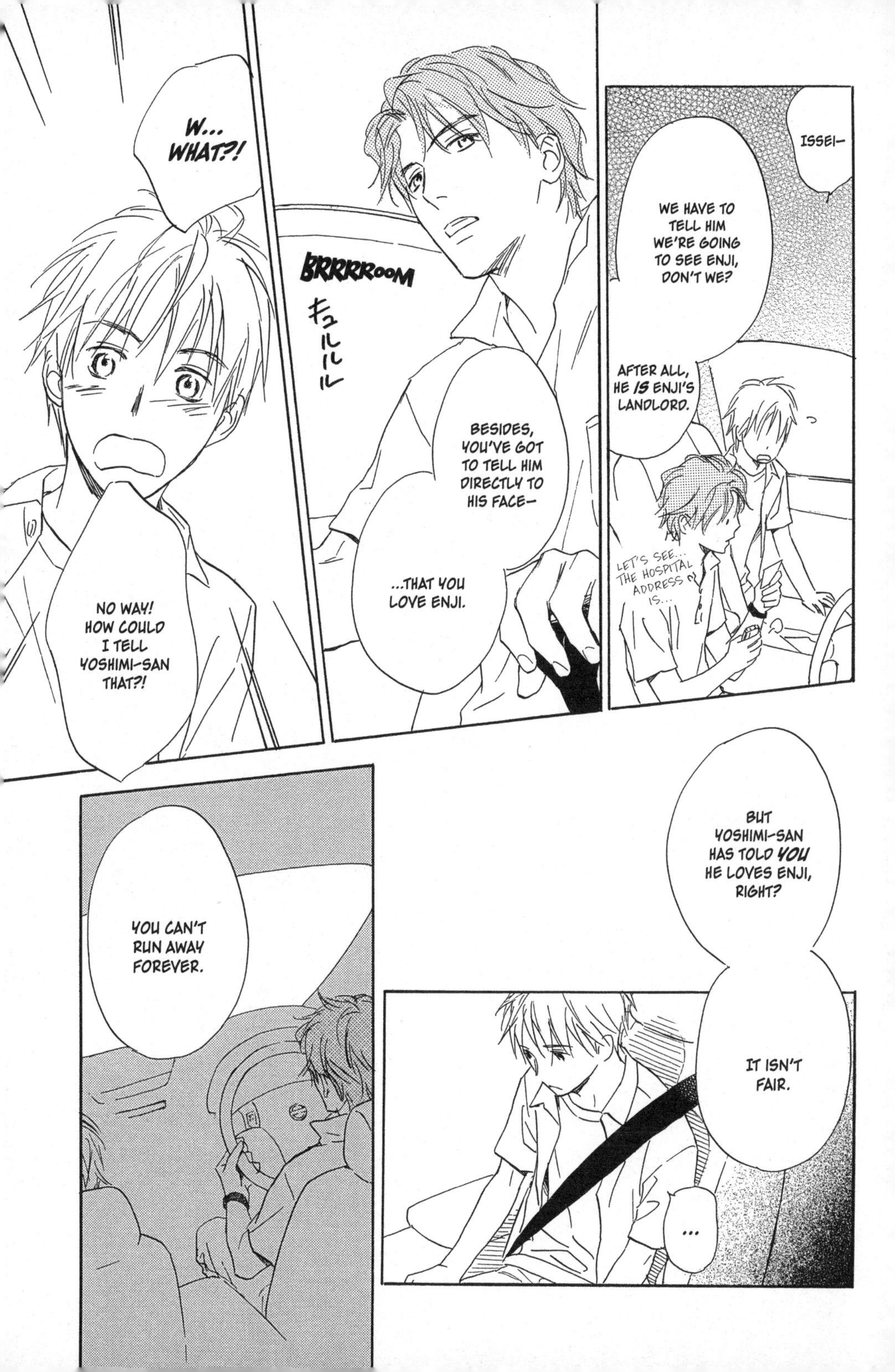
ISSEI—
WE HAVE TO TELL HIM WE'RE GOING TO SEE ENJI, DON'T WE?
AFTER ALL, HE *IS* ENJI'S LANDLORD.
LET'S SEE... THE HOSPITAL ADDRESS IS...
BRRRRoOM
キュルルル
BESIDES, YOU'VE GOT TO TELL HIM DIRECTLY TO HIS FACE—
...THAT YOU LOVE ENJI.
W... WHAT?!
NO WAY! HOW COULD I TELL YOSHIMI-SAN THAT?!
BUT YOSHIMI-SAN HAS TOLD ***YOU*** HE LOVES ENJI, RIGHT?
IT ISN'T FAIR.
...
YOU CAN'T RUN AWAY FOREVER.

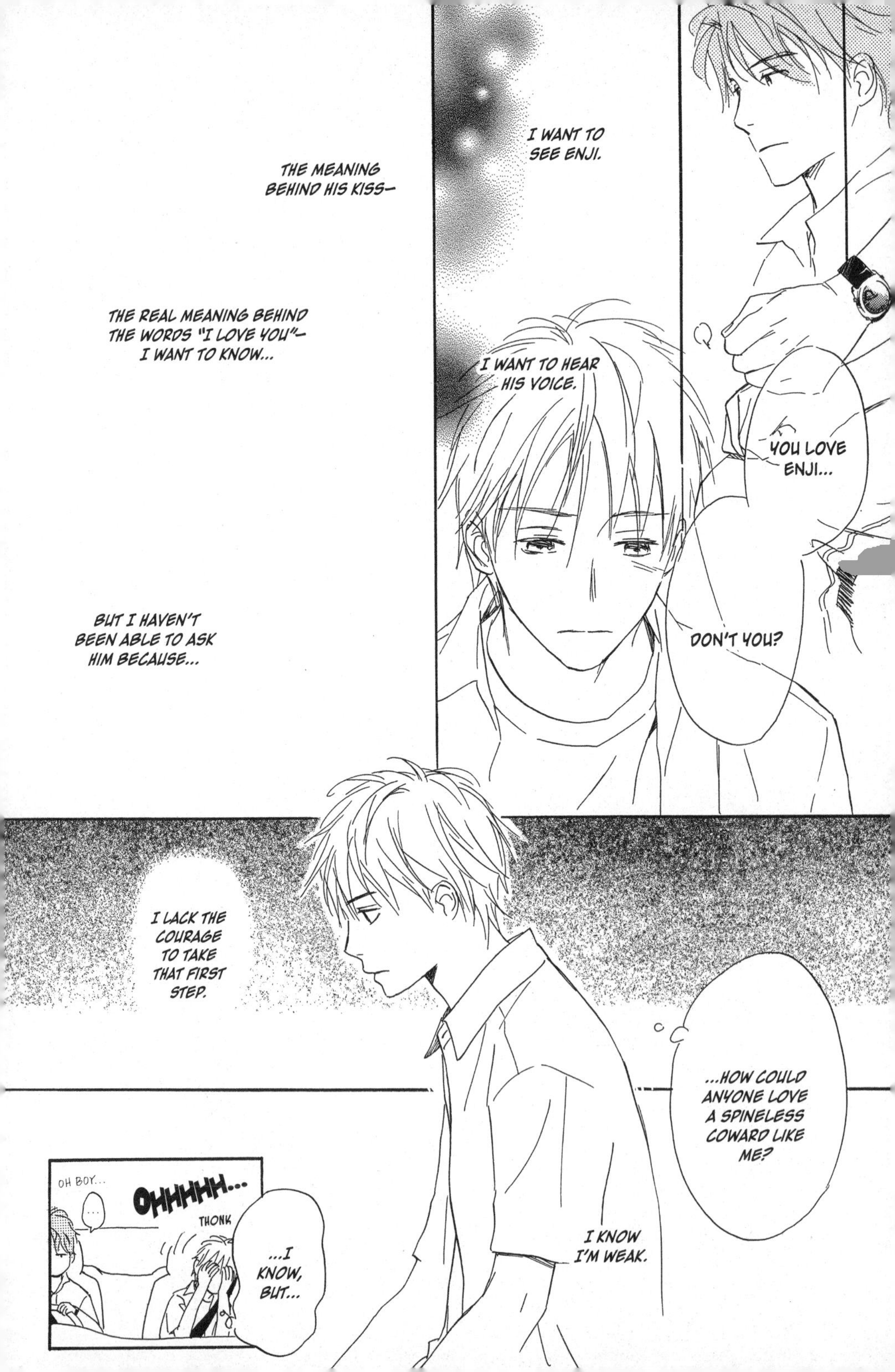
YOU LOVE ENJI...
DON'T YOU?
I WANT TO SEE ENJI.
I WANT TO HEAR HIS VOICE.
THE MEANING BEHIND HIS KISS—
THE REAL MEANING BEHIND THE WORDS "I LOVE YOU"— I WANT TO KNOW...
BUT I HAVEN'T BEEN ABLE TO ASK HIM BECAUSE...
I LACK THE COURAGE TO TAKE THAT FIRST STEP.
...HOW COULD ANYONE LOVE A SPINELESS COWARD LIKE ME?
I KNOW I'M WEAK.
OHHHHH...
...I KNOW, BUT...
THONK
OH BOY...
...

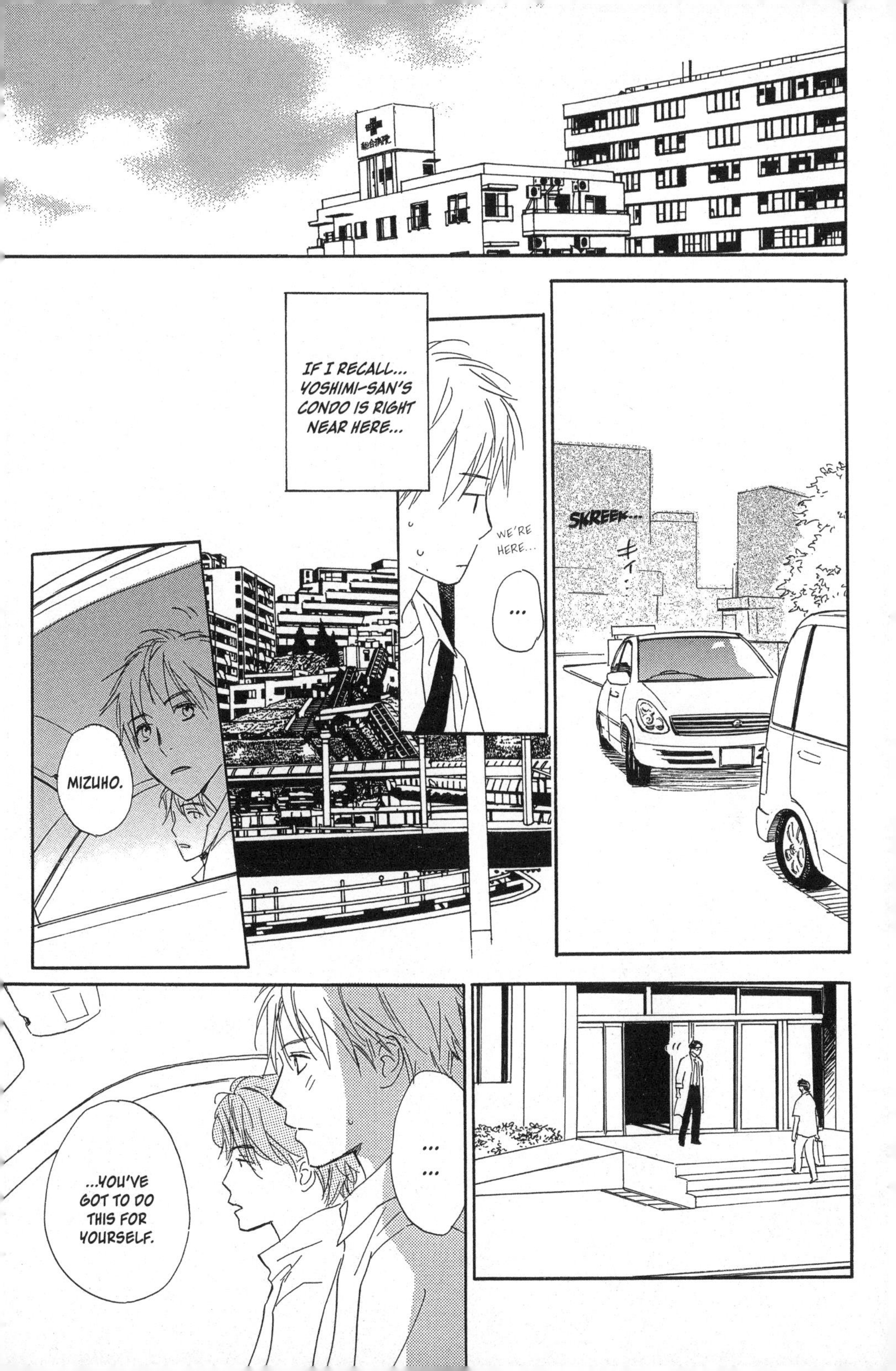
SKREEK...
ギイ…
IF I RECALL... YOSHIMI-SAN'S CONDO IS RIGHT NEAR HERE...
WE'RE HERE...
...
MIZUHO.
...
...
...YOU'VE GOT TO DO THIS FOR YOURSELF.

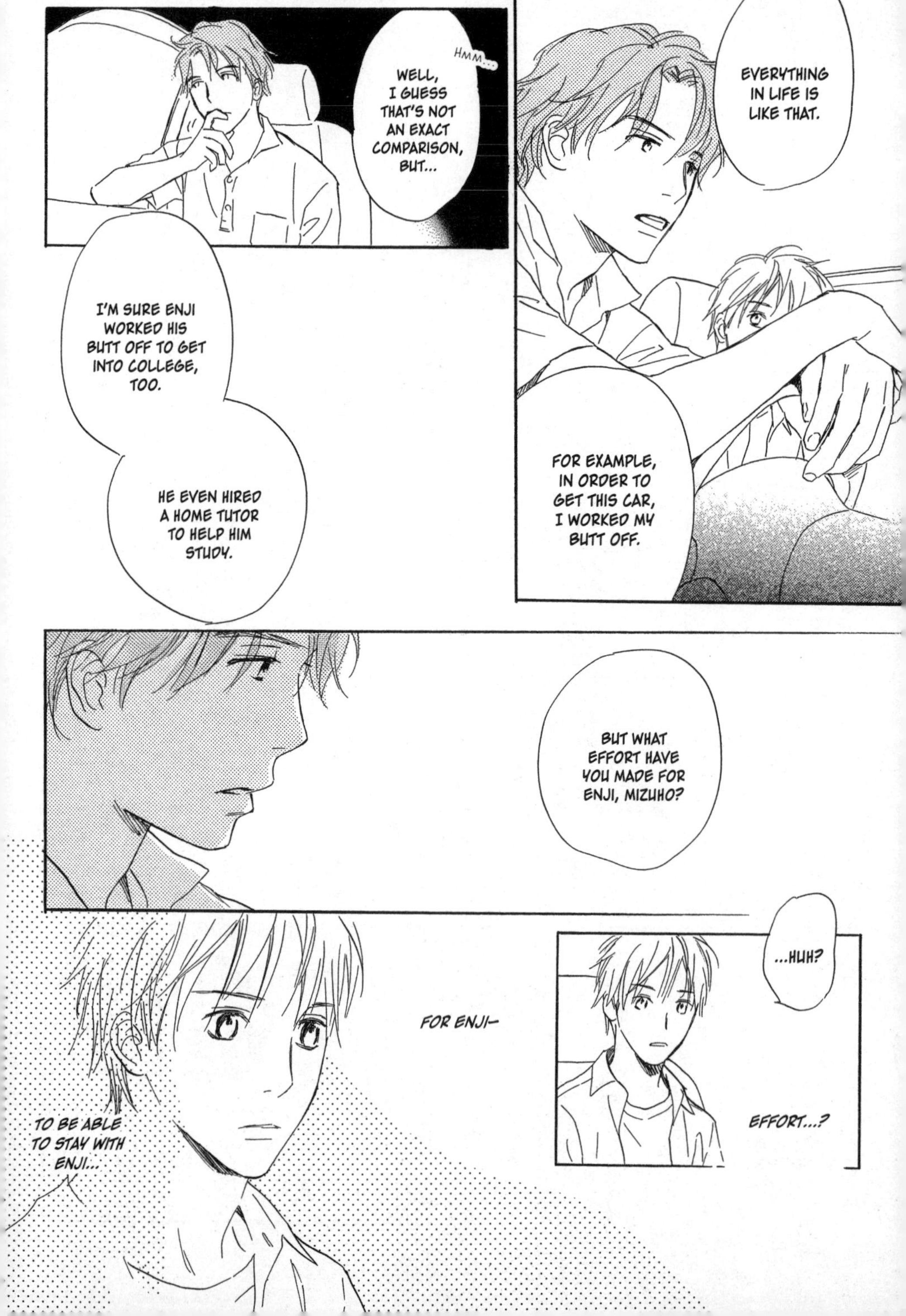
EVERYTHING IN LIFE IS LIKE THAT.
FOR EXAMPLE, IN ORDER TO GET THIS CAR, I WORKED MY BUTT OFF.
HMM...
WELL, I GUESS THAT'S NOT AN EXACT COMPARISON, BUT...
I'M SURE ENJI WORKED HIS BUTT OFF TO GET INTO COLLEGE, TOO.
HE EVEN HIRED A HOME TUTOR TO HELP HIM STUDY.
BUT WHAT EFFORT HAVE YOU MADE FOR ENJI, MIZUHO?
...HUH?
EFFORT...?
FOR ENJI—
TO BE ABLE TO STAY WITH ENJI...

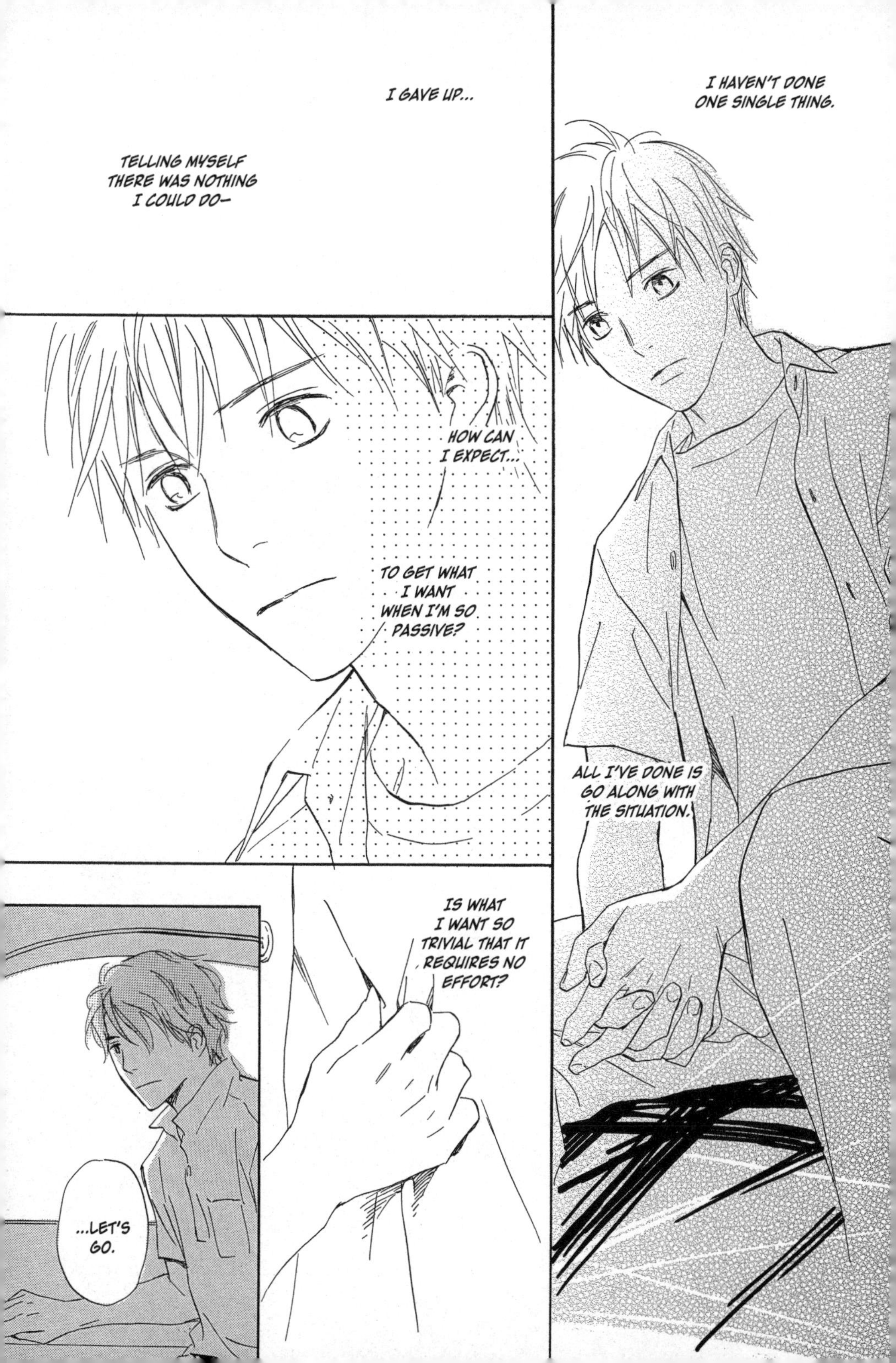
I HAVEN'T DONE ONE SINGLE THING.
ALL I'VE DONE IS GO ALONG WITH THE SITUATION.
I GAVE UP...
TELLING MYSELF THERE WAS NOTHING I COULD DO—
HOW CAN I EXPECT...
TO GET WHAT I WANT WHEN I'M SO PASSIVE?
IS WHAT I WANT SO TRIVIAL THAT IT REQUIRES NO EFFORT?
...LET'S GO.

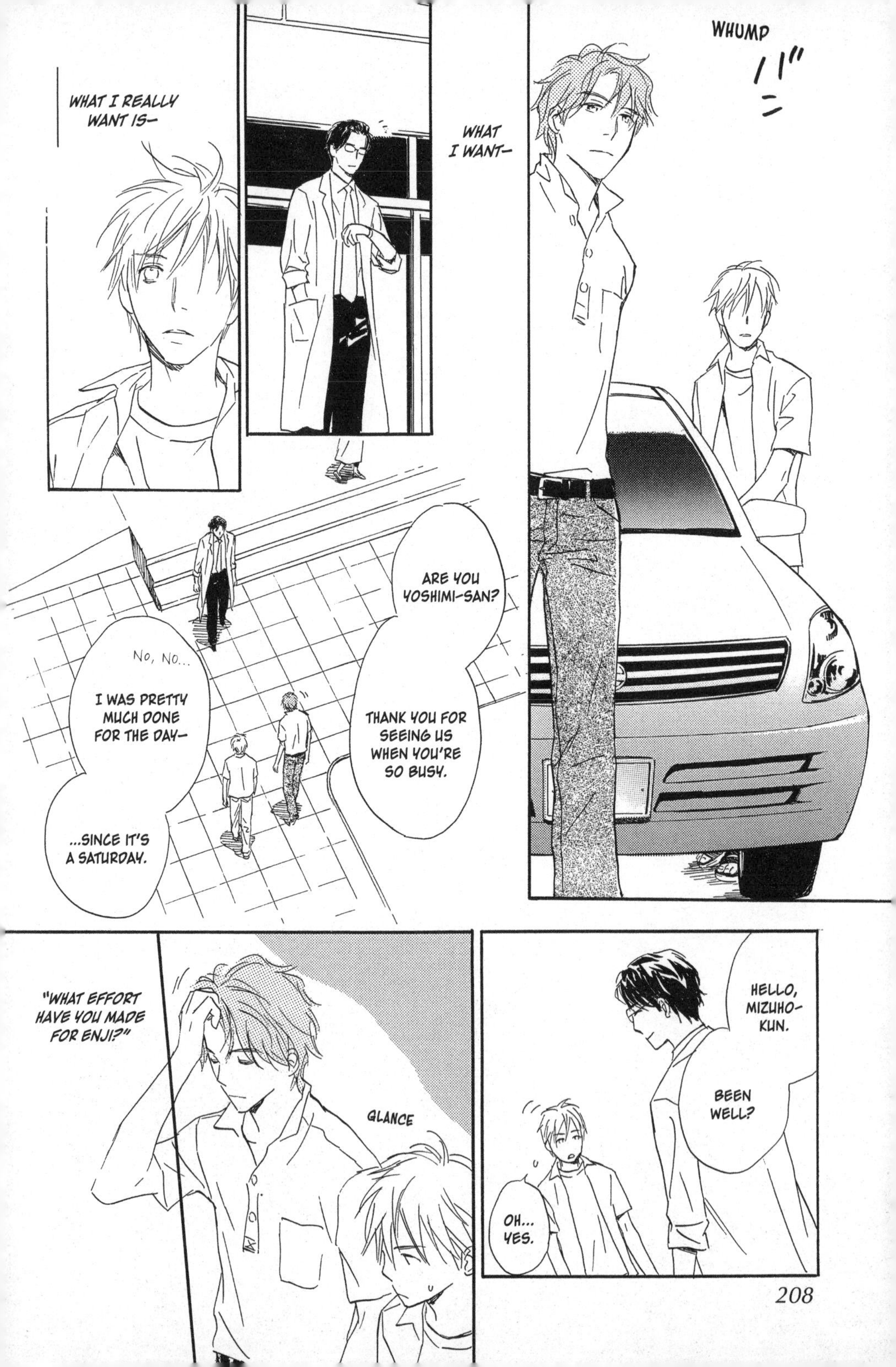
WHUMP
WHAT I WANT—
WHAT I REALLY WANT IS—
ARE YOU YOSHIMI-SAN?
THANK YOU FOR SEEING US WHEN YOU'RE SO BUSY.
No, No...
I WAS PRETTY MUCH DONE FOR THE DAY—
...SINCE IT'S A SATURDAY.
HELLO, MIZUHO-KUN.
BEEN WELL?
OH... YES.
"WHAT EFFORT HAVE YOU MADE FOR ENJI?"
GLANCE

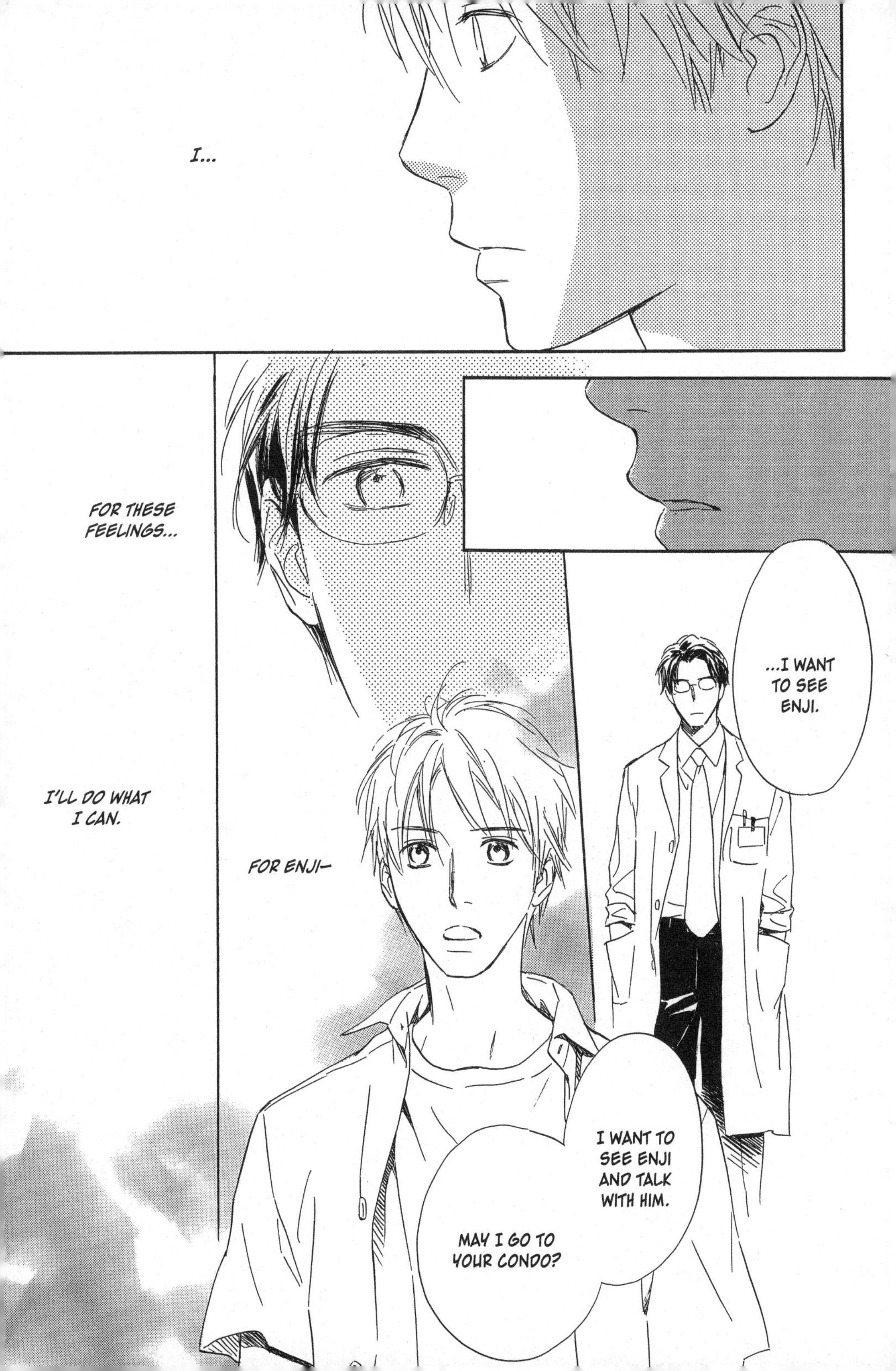
I...
FOR THESE FEELINGS...
I'LL DO WHAT I CAN.
FOR ENJI—
...I WANT TO SEE ENJI.
I WANT TO SEE ENJI AND TALK WITH HIM.
MAY I GO TO YOUR CONDO?

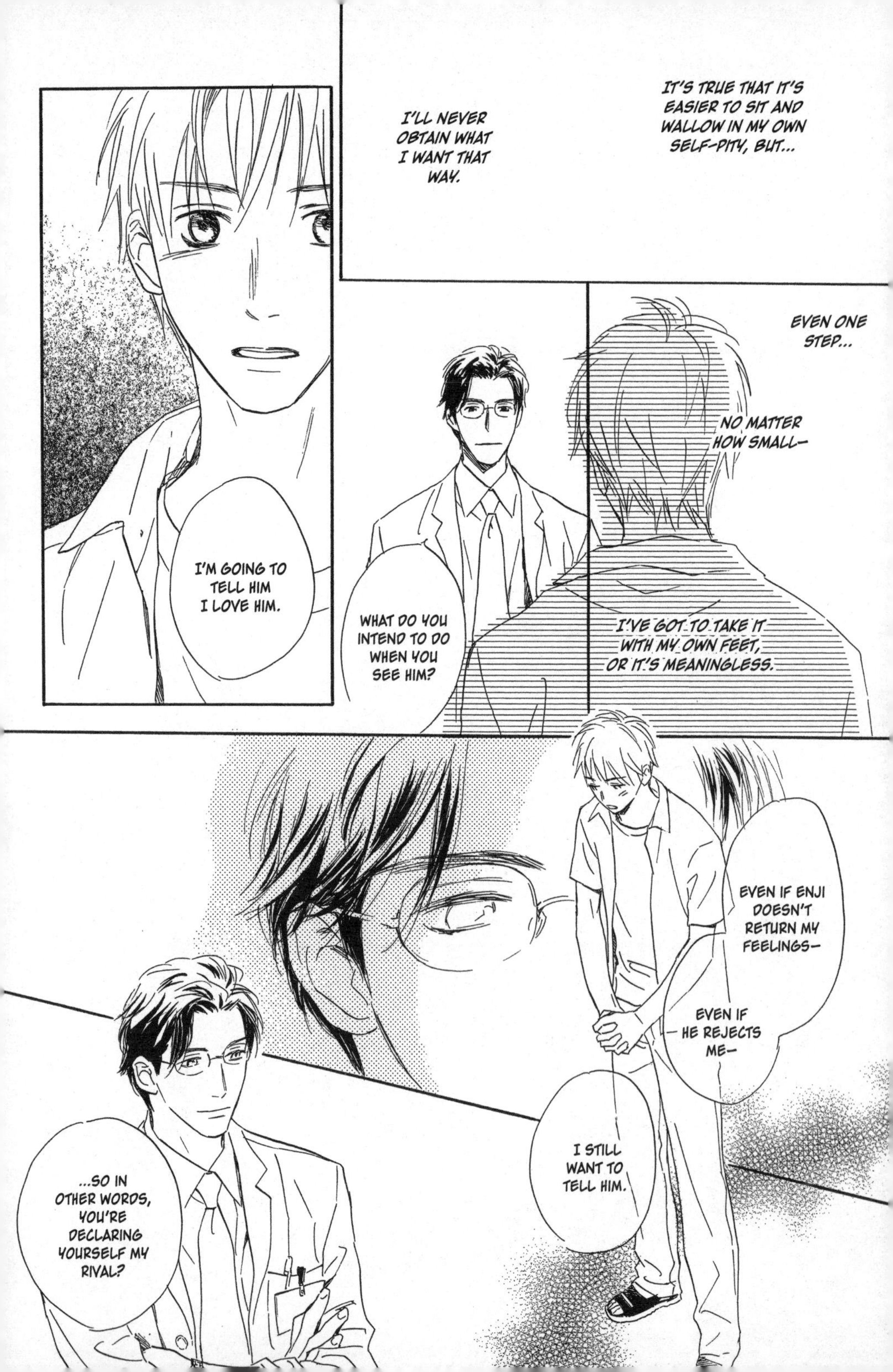
IT'S TRUE THAT IT'S EASIER TO SIT AND WALLOW IN MY OWN SELF-PITY, BUT...
I'LL NEVER OBTAIN WHAT I WANT THAT WAY.
EVEN ONE STEP...
NO MATTER HOW SMALL—
I'VE GOT TO TAKE IT WITH MY OWN FEET, OR IT'S MEANINGLESS.
WHAT DO YOU INTEND TO DO WHEN YOU SEE HIM?
I'M GOING TO TELL HIM I LOVE HIM.
EVEN IF ENJI DOESN'T RETURN MY FEELINGS—
EVEN IF HE REJECTS ME—
I STILL WANT TO TELL HIM.
...SO IN OTHER WORDS, YOU'RE DECLARING YOURSELF MY RIVAL?

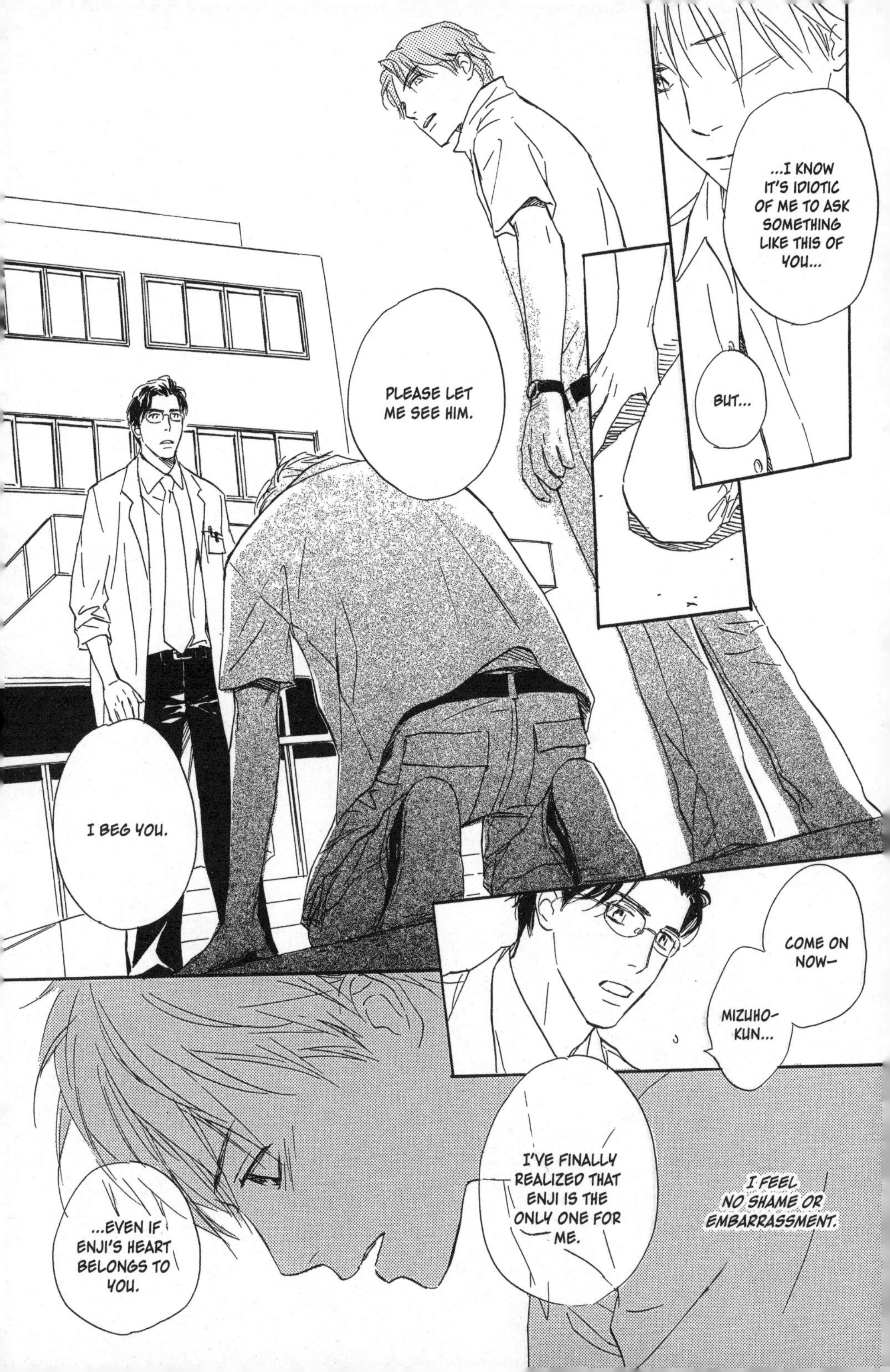
...I KNOW IT'S IDIOTIC OF ME TO ASK SOMETHING LIKE THIS OF YOU...
BUT...
PLEASE LET ME SEE HIM.
I BEG YOU.
COME ON NOW—
MIZUHO-KUN...
I FEEL NO SHAME OR EMBARRASSMENT.
I'VE FINALLY REALIZED THAT ENJI IS THE ONLY ONE FOR ME.
...EVEN IF ENJI'S HEART BELONGS TO YOU.

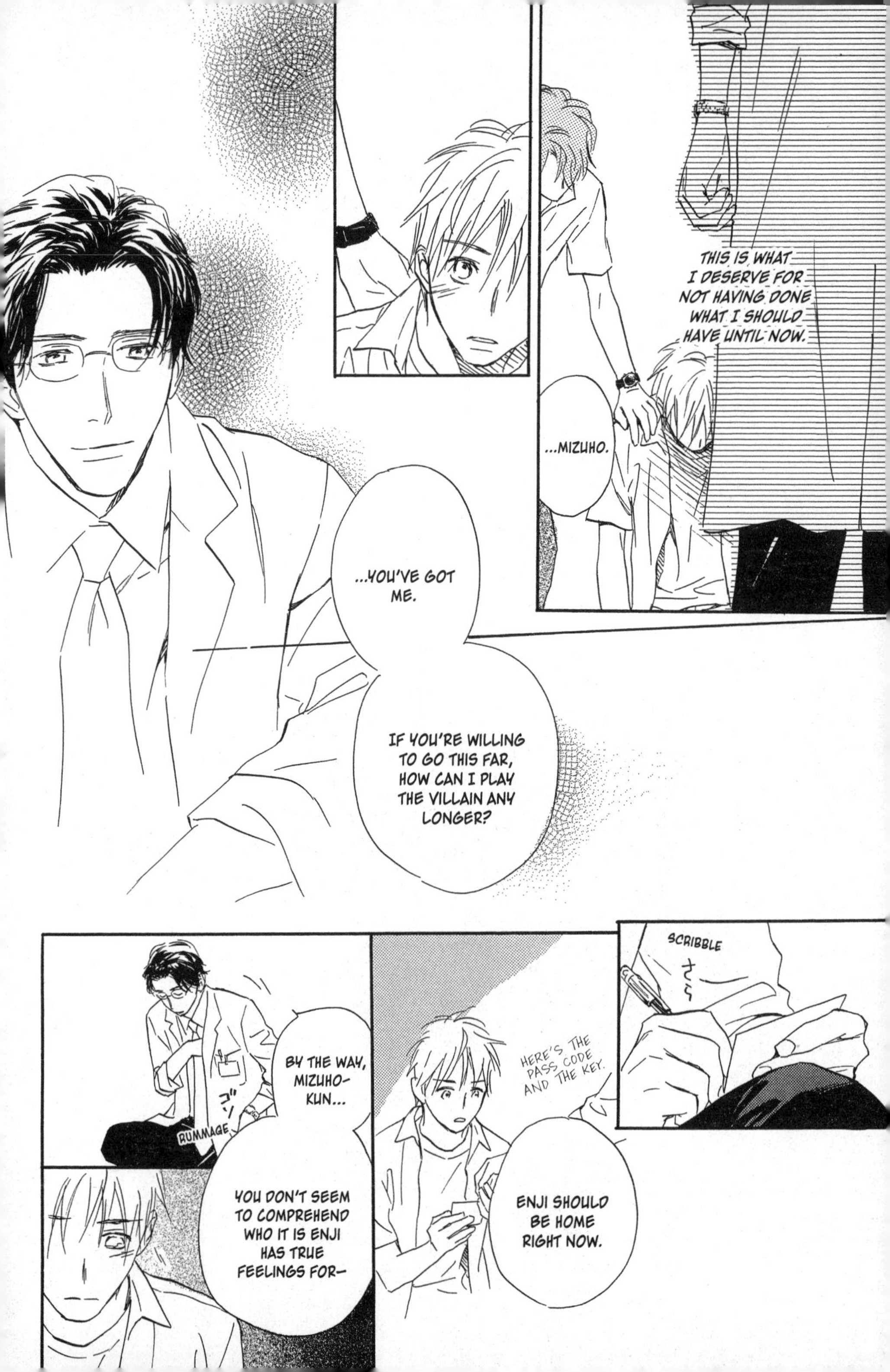
THIS IS WHAT I DESERVE FOR NOT HAVING DONE WHAT I SHOULD HAVE UNTIL NOW.
...MIZUHO.
...YOU'VE GOT ME.
IF YOU'RE WILLING TO GO THIS FAR, HOW CAN I PLAY THE VILLAIN ANY LONGER?
SCRIBBLE
HERE'S THE PASS CODE AND THE KEY.
ENJI SHOULD BE HOME RIGHT NOW.
BY THE WAY, MIZUHO-KUN...
RUMMAGE
YOU DON'T SEEM TO COMPREHEND WHO IT IS ENJI HAS TRUE FEELINGS FOR—

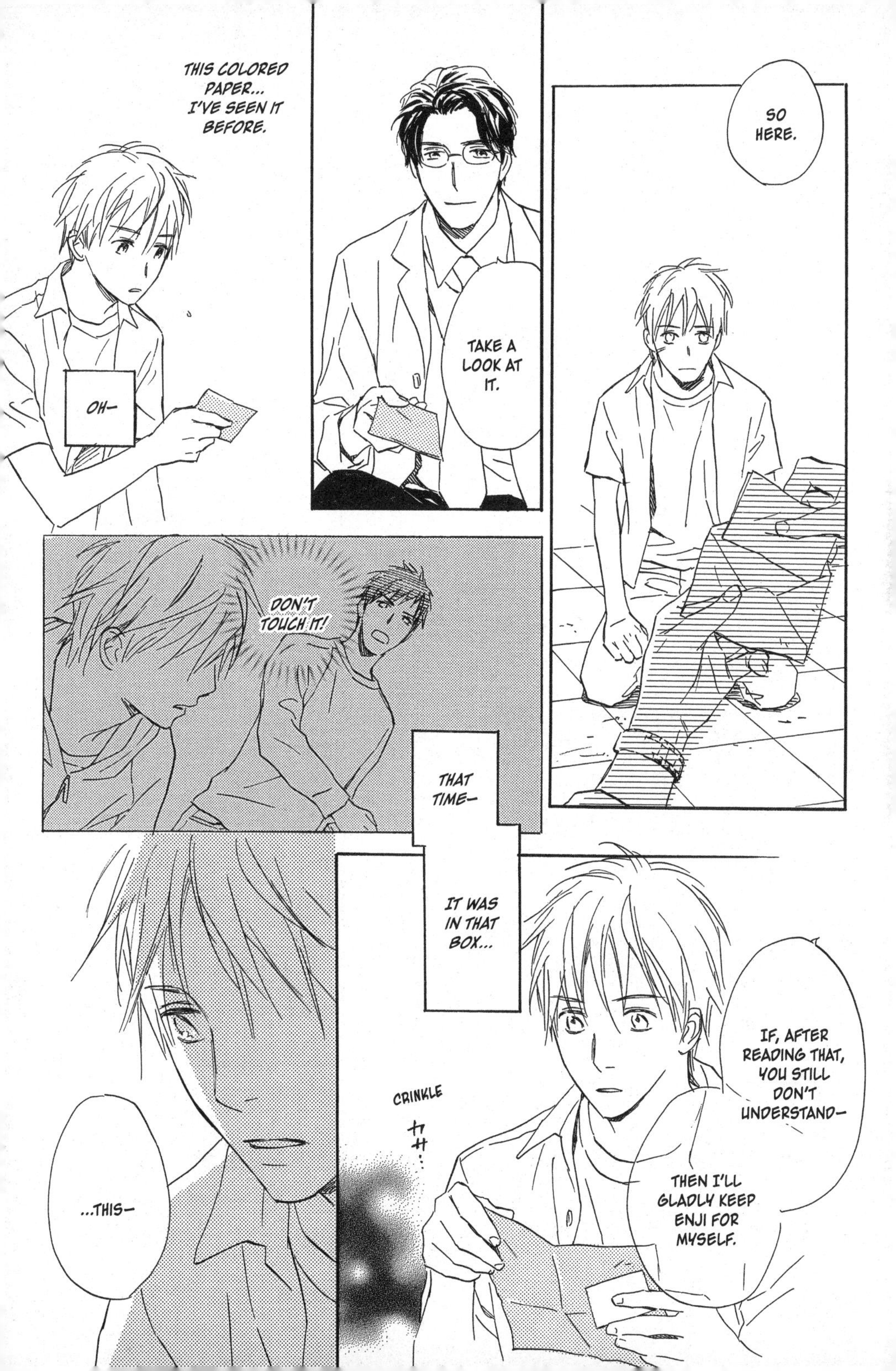
SO HERE.
TAKE A LOOK AT IT.
THIS COLORED PAPER... I'VE SEEN IT BEFORE.
OH—
DON'T TOUCH IT!
THAT TIME—
IT WAS IN THAT BOX...
IF, AFTER READING THAT, YOU STILL DON'T UNDERSTAND—
THEN I'LL GLADLY KEEP ENJI FOR MYSELF.
CRINKLE
...THIS—

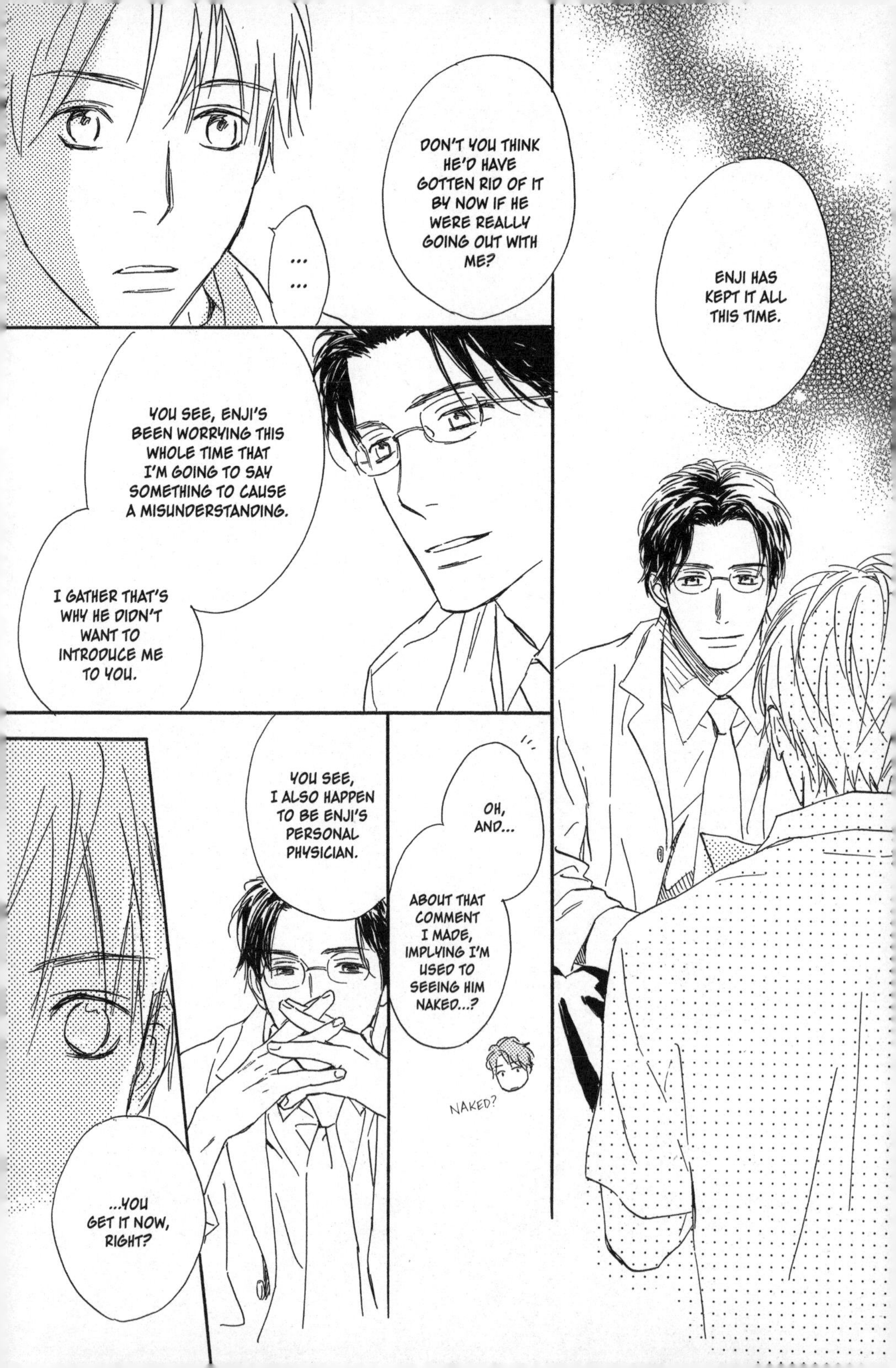
ENJI HAS KEPT IT ALL THIS TIME.
DON'T YOU THINK HE'D HAVE GOTTEN RID OF IT BY NOW IF HE WERE REALLY GOING OUT WITH ME?
... ...
YOU SEE, ENJI'S BEEN WORRYING THIS WHOLE TIME THAT I'M GOING TO SAY SOMETHING TO CAUSE A MISUNDERSTANDING.
I GATHER THAT'S WHY HE DIDN'T WANT TO INTRODUCE ME TO YOU.
OH, AND...
ABOUT THAT COMMENT I MADE, IMPLYING I'M USED TO SEEING HIM NAKED...?
NAKED?
YOU SEE, I ALSO HAPPEN TO BE ENJI'S PERSONAL PHYSICIAN.
...YOU GET IT NOW, RIGHT?

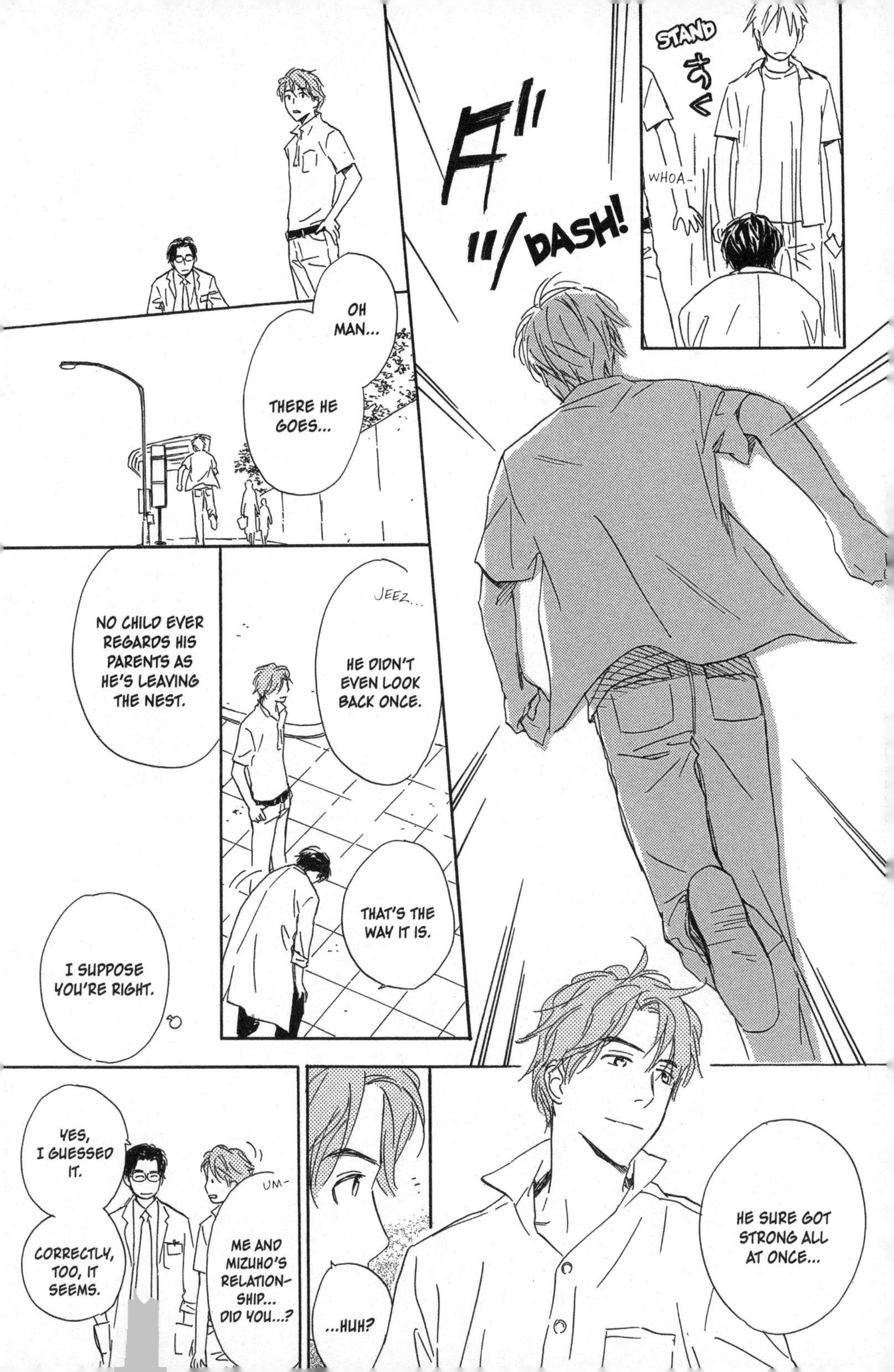
STAND
すっ
WHOA-
DASH!
OH MAN...
THERE HE GOES...
JEEZ...
HE DIDN'T EVEN LOOK BACK ONCE.
THAT'S THE WAY IT IS.
NO CHILD EVER REGARDS HIS PARENTS AS HE'S LEAVING THE NEST.
I SUPPOSE YOU'RE RIGHT.
HE SURE GOT STRONG ALL AT ONCE...
...HUH?
UM-
ME AND MIZUHO'S RELATION-SHIP... DID YOU...?
YES, I GUESSED IT.
CORRECTLY, TOO, IT SEEMS.

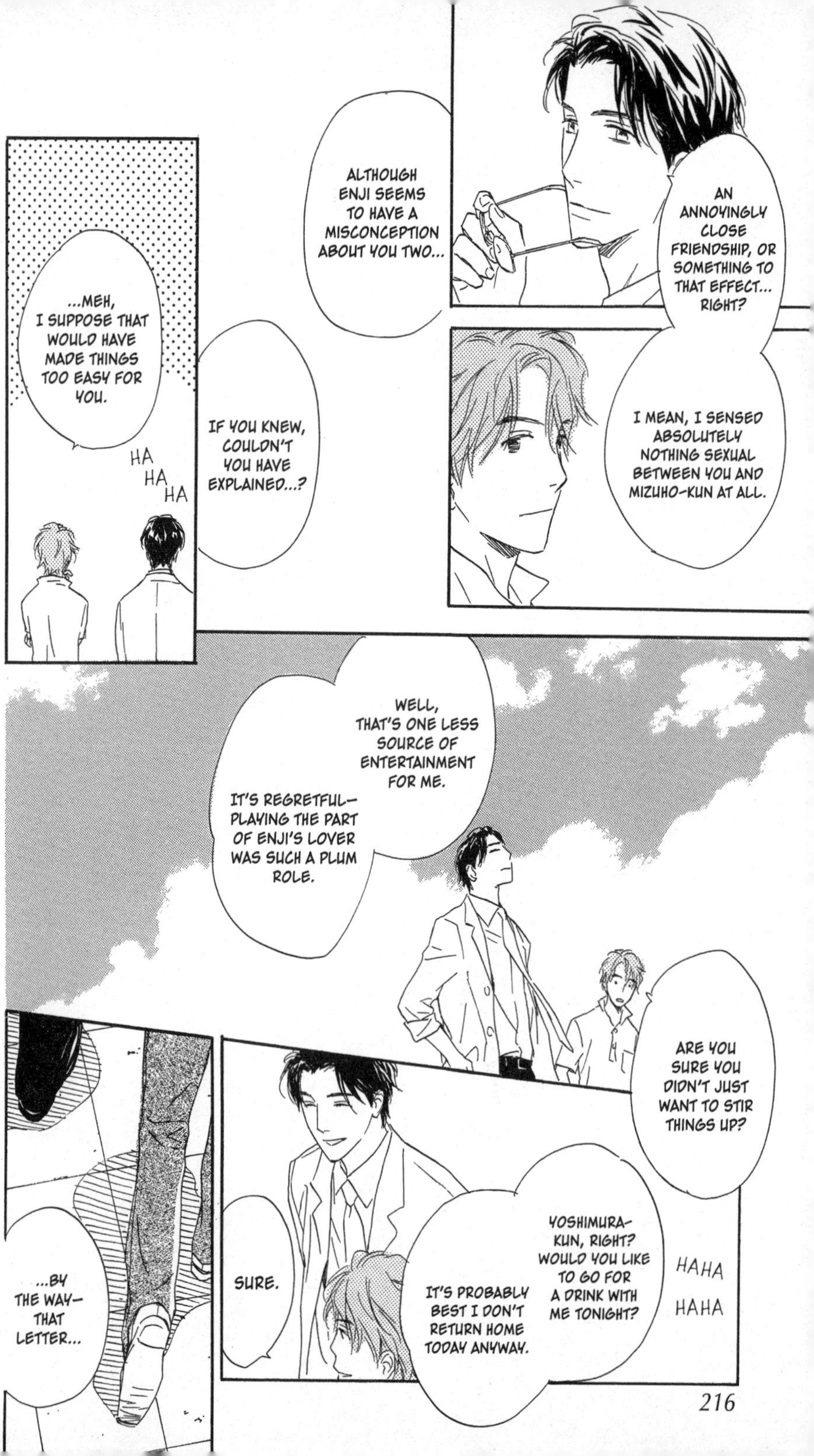
ALTHOUGH ENJI SEEMS TO HAVE A MISCONCEPTION ABOUT YOU TWO...
AN ANNOYINGLY CLOSE FRIENDSHIP, OR SOMETHING TO THAT EFFECT... RIGHT?
I MEAN, I SENSED ABSOLUTELY NOTHING SEXUAL BETWEEN YOU AND MIZUHO-KUN AT ALL.
IF YOU KNEW, COULDN'T YOU HAVE EXPLAINED...?
...MEH, I SUPPOSE THAT WOULD HAVE MADE THINGS TOO EASY FOR YOU.
HA HA HA
WELL, THAT'S ONE LESS SOURCE OF ENTERTAINMENT FOR ME.
IT'S REGRETFUL— PLAYING THE PART OF ENJI'S LOVER WAS SUCH A PLUM ROLE.
ARE YOU SURE YOU DIDN'T JUST WANT TO STIR THINGS UP?
YOSHIMURA-KUN, RIGHT? WOULD YOU LIKE TO GO FOR A DRINK WITH ME TONIGHT?
IT'S PROBABLY BEST I DON'T RETURN HOME TODAY ANYWAY.
HAHA HAHA
SURE.
...BY THE WAY— THAT LETTER...

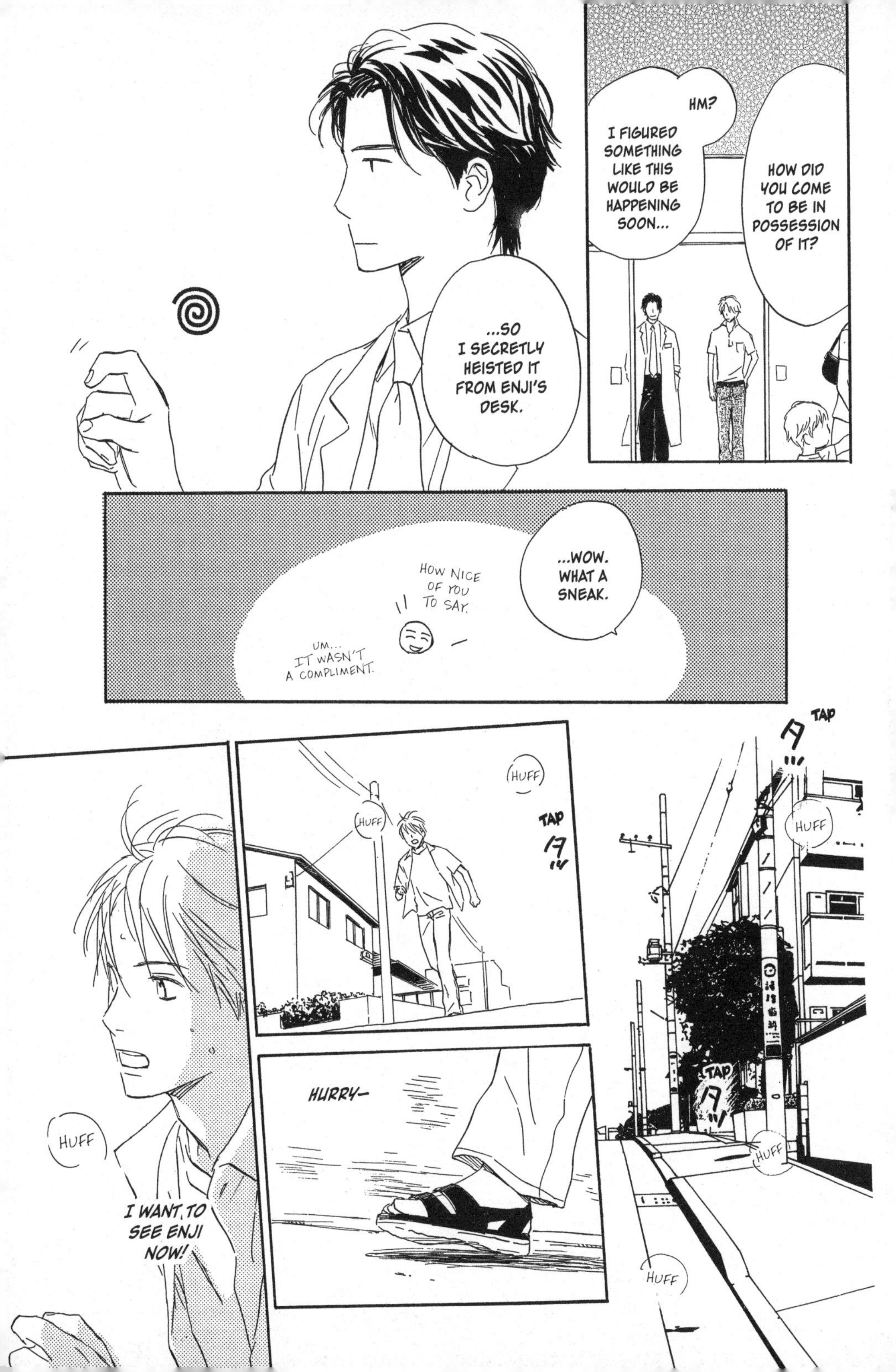
HOW DID YOU COME TO BE IN POSSESSION OF IT?
HM?
I FIGURED SOMETHING LIKE THIS WOULD BE HAPPENING SOON...
...SO I SECRETLY HEISTED IT FROM ENJI'S DESK.
...WOW. WHAT A SNEAK.
HOW NICE OF YOU TO SAY.
UM... IT WASN'T A COMPLIMENT.
TAP
HUFF
TAP
HUFF
HUFF
HUFF
TAP
HUFF
HURRY—
HUFF
I WANT TO SEE ENJI NOW!

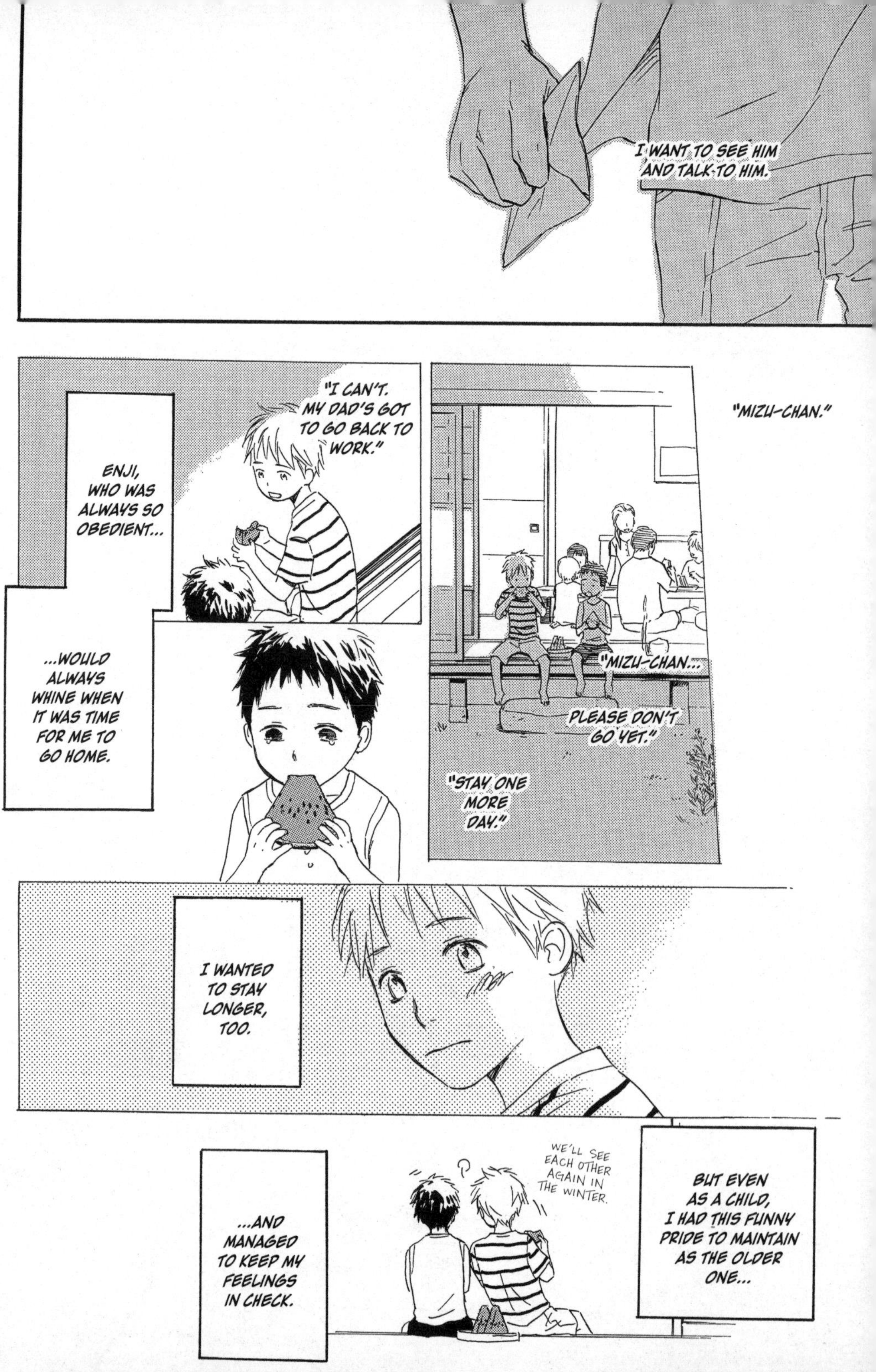
I WANT TO SEE HIM AND TALK TO HIM.
"MIZU-CHAN."
"MIZU-CHAN...
PLEASE DON'T GO YET."
"STAY ONE MORE DAY."
"I CAN'T. MY DAD'S GOT TO GO BACK TO WORK."
ENJI, WHO WAS ALWAYS SO OBEDIENT...
...WOULD ALWAYS WHINE WHEN IT WAS TIME FOR ME TO GO HOME.
I WANTED TO STAY LONGER, TOO.
BUT EVEN AS A CHILD, I HAD THIS FUNNY PRIDE TO MAINTAIN AS THE OLDER ONE...
WE'LL SEE EACH OTHER AGAIN IN THE WINTER.
...AND MANAGED TO KEEP MY FEELINGS IN CHECK.

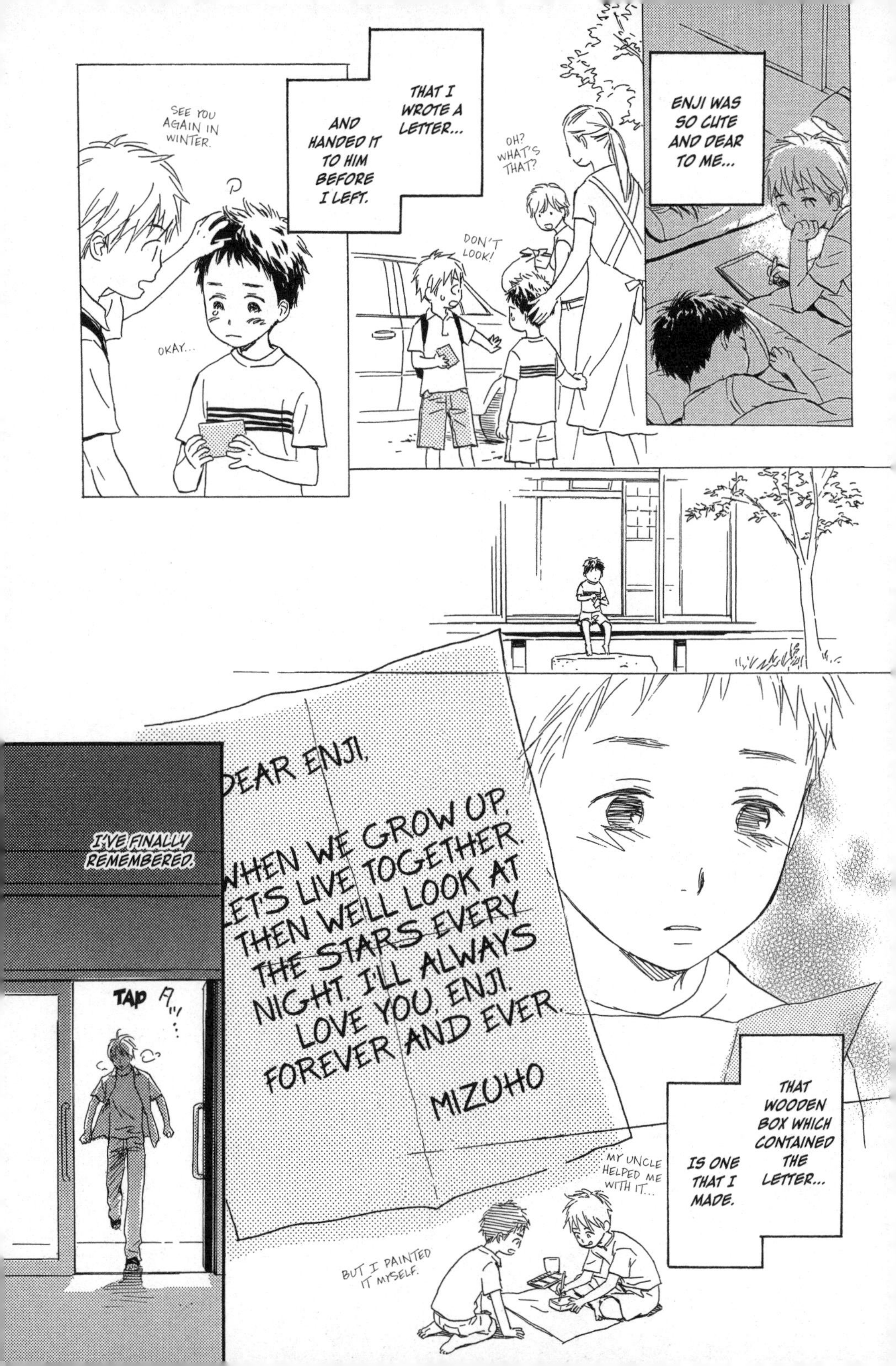
ENJI WAS SO CUTE AND DEAR TO ME...
THAT I WROTE A LETTER...
AND HANDED IT TO HIM BEFORE I LEFT.
OH? WHAT'S THAT?
DON'T LOOK!
SEE YOU AGAIN IN WINTER.
?
OKAY...
DEAR ENJI,
WHEN WE GROW UP, LET'S LIVE TOGETHER. THEN WE'LL LOOK AT THE STARS EVERY NIGHT. I'LL ALWAYS LOVE YOU, ENJI. FOREVER AND EVER.
MIZUHO
THAT WOODEN BOX WHICH CONTAINED THE LETTER...
IS ONE THAT I MADE.
MY UNCLE HELPED ME WITH IT...
BUT I PAINTED IT MYSELF.
I'VE FINALLY REMEMBERED.
TAP

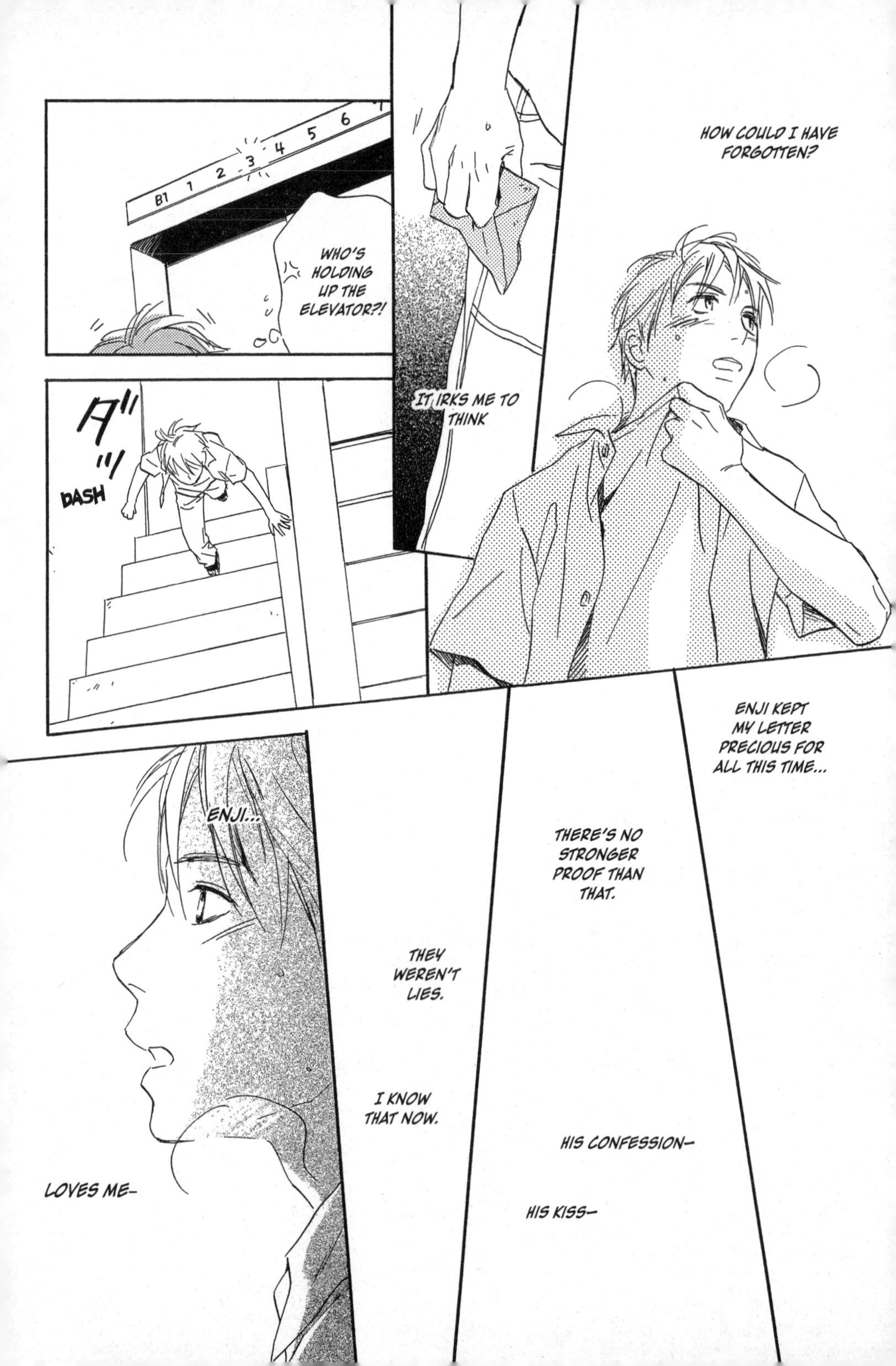
HOW COULD I HAVE FORGOTTEN?
IT IRKS ME TO THINK
B1 1 2 3 4 5 6
WHO'S HOLDING UP THE ELEVATOR?!
DASH
ENJI KEPT MY LETTER PRECIOUS FOR ALL THIS TIME...
THERE'S NO STRONGER PROOF THAN THAT.
HIS CONFESSION—
HIS KISS—
ENJI...
THEY WEREN'T LIES.
I KNOW THAT NOW.
LOVES ME—

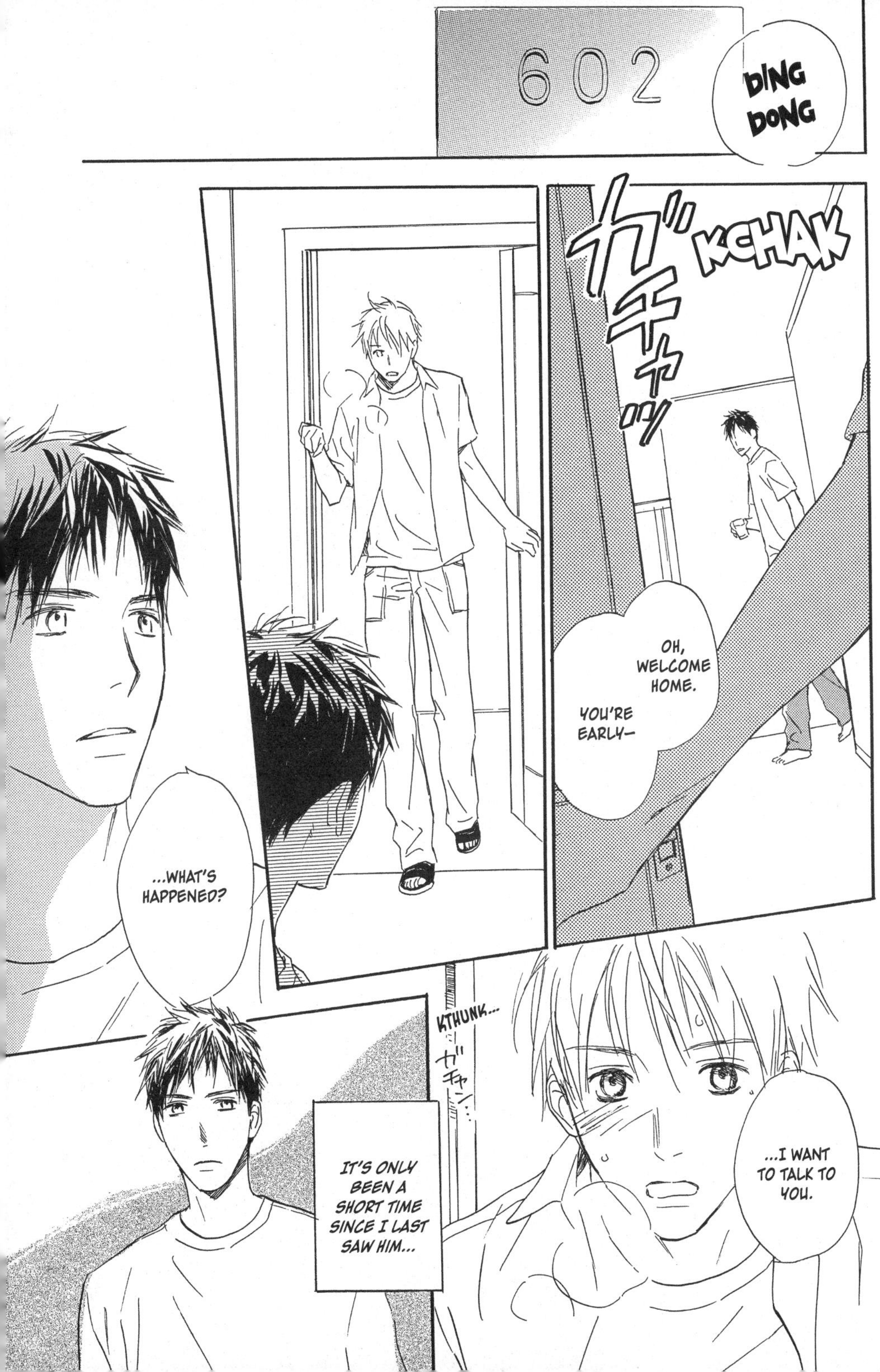
602
DING DONG
ガチャッ
KCHAK
OH, WELCOME HOME.
YOU'RE EARLY—
...WHAT'S HAPPENED?
...I WANT TO TALK TO YOU.
KTHUNK...
ガチャン…
IT'S ONLY BEEN A SHORT TIME SINCE I LAST SAW HIM...

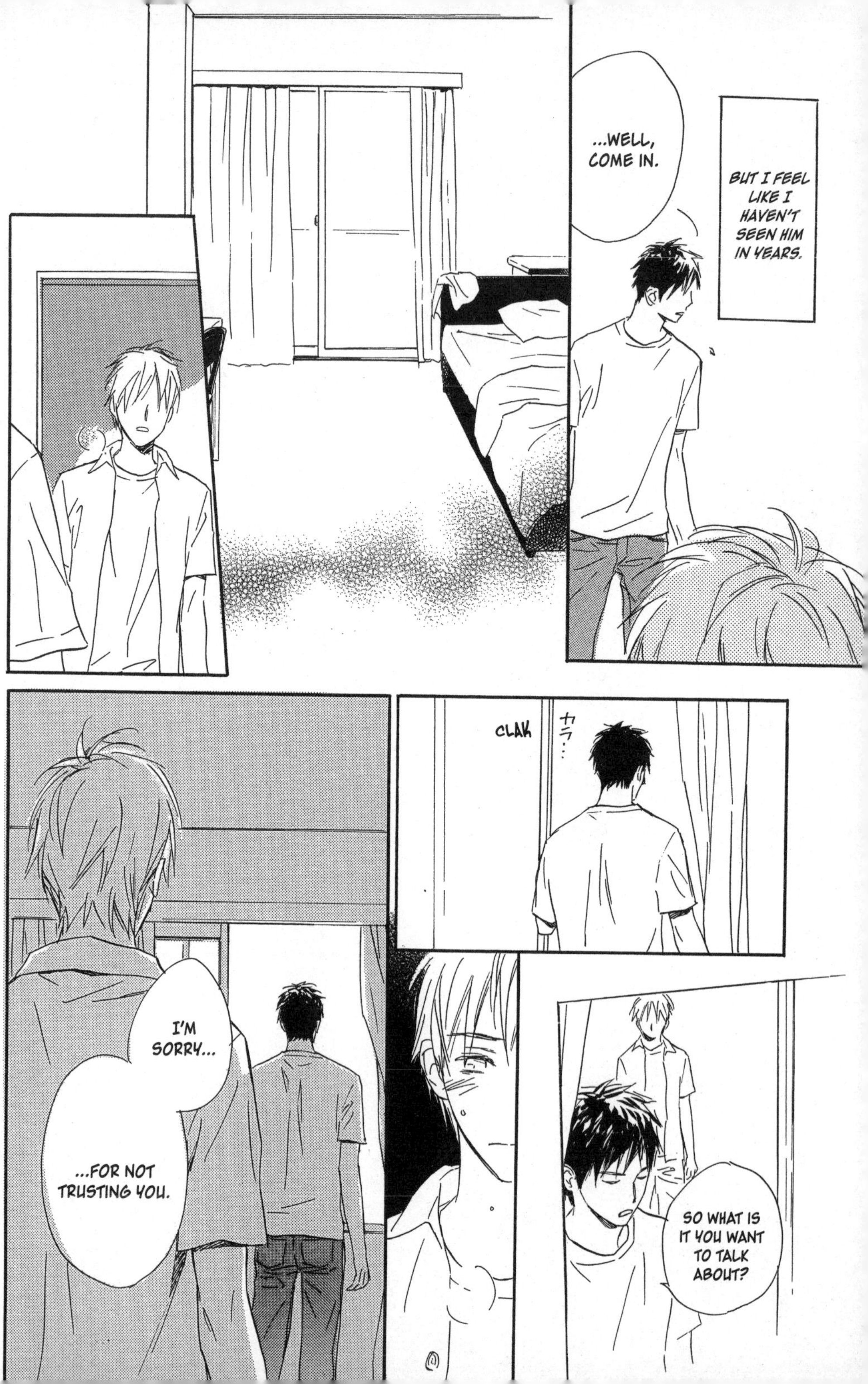
BUT I FEEL LIKE I HAVEN'T SEEN HIM IN YEARS.
...WELL, COME IN.
CLAK
カラ…
SO WHAT IS IT YOU WANT TO TALK ABOUT?
I'M SORRY...
...FOR NOT TRUSTING YOU.

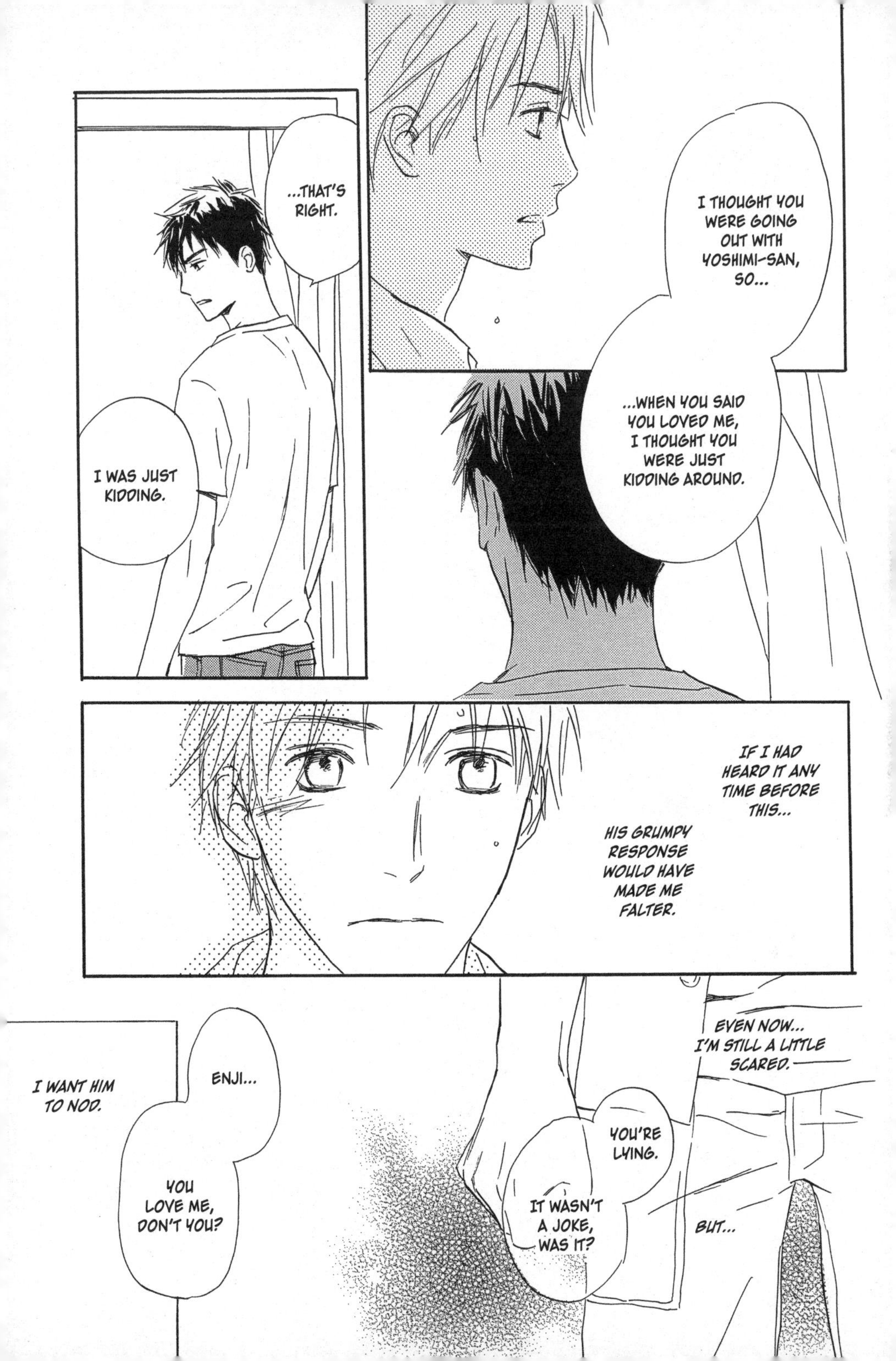
I THOUGHT YOU WERE GOING OUT WITH YOSHIMI-SAN, SO...
...WHEN YOU SAID YOU LOVED ME, I THOUGHT YOU WERE JUST KIDDING AROUND.
...THAT'S RIGHT.
I WAS JUST KIDDING.
IF I HAD HEARD IT ANY TIME BEFORE THIS...
HIS GRUMPY RESPONSE WOULD HAVE MADE ME FALTER.
EVEN NOW... I'M STILL A LITTLE SCARED.
BUT...
YOU'RE LYING.
IT WASN'T A JOKE, WAS IT?
ENJI...
YOU LOVE ME, DON'T YOU?
I WANT HIM TO NOD.

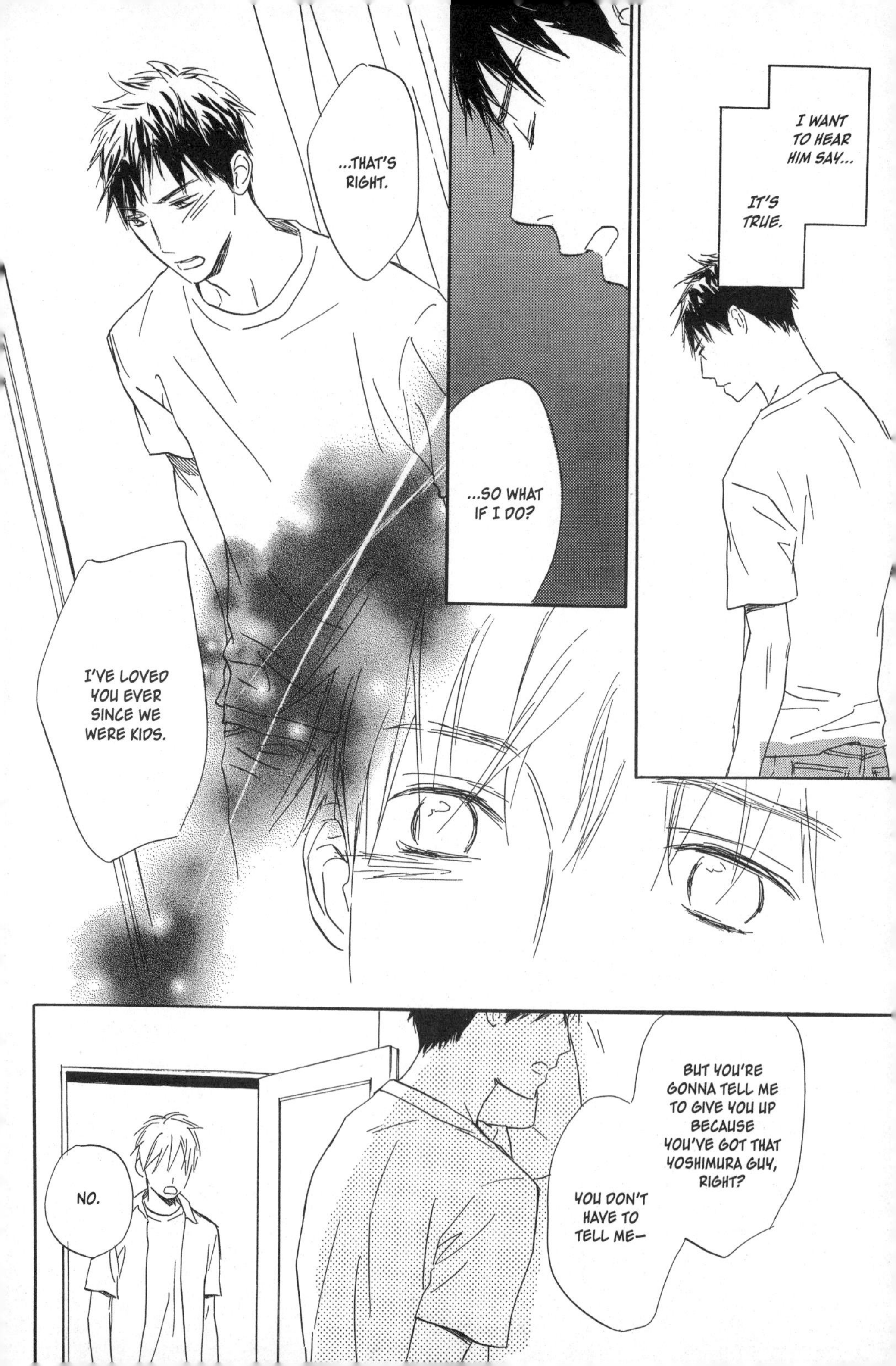
I WANT TO HEAR HIM SAY...
IT'S TRUE.
...SO WHAT IF I DO?
...THAT'S RIGHT.
I'VE LOVED YOU EVER SINCE WE WERE KIDS.
BUT YOU'RE GONNA TELL ME TO GIVE YOU UP BECAUSE YOU'VE GOT THAT YOSHIMURA GUY, RIGHT?
YOU DON'T HAVE TO TELL ME—
NO.

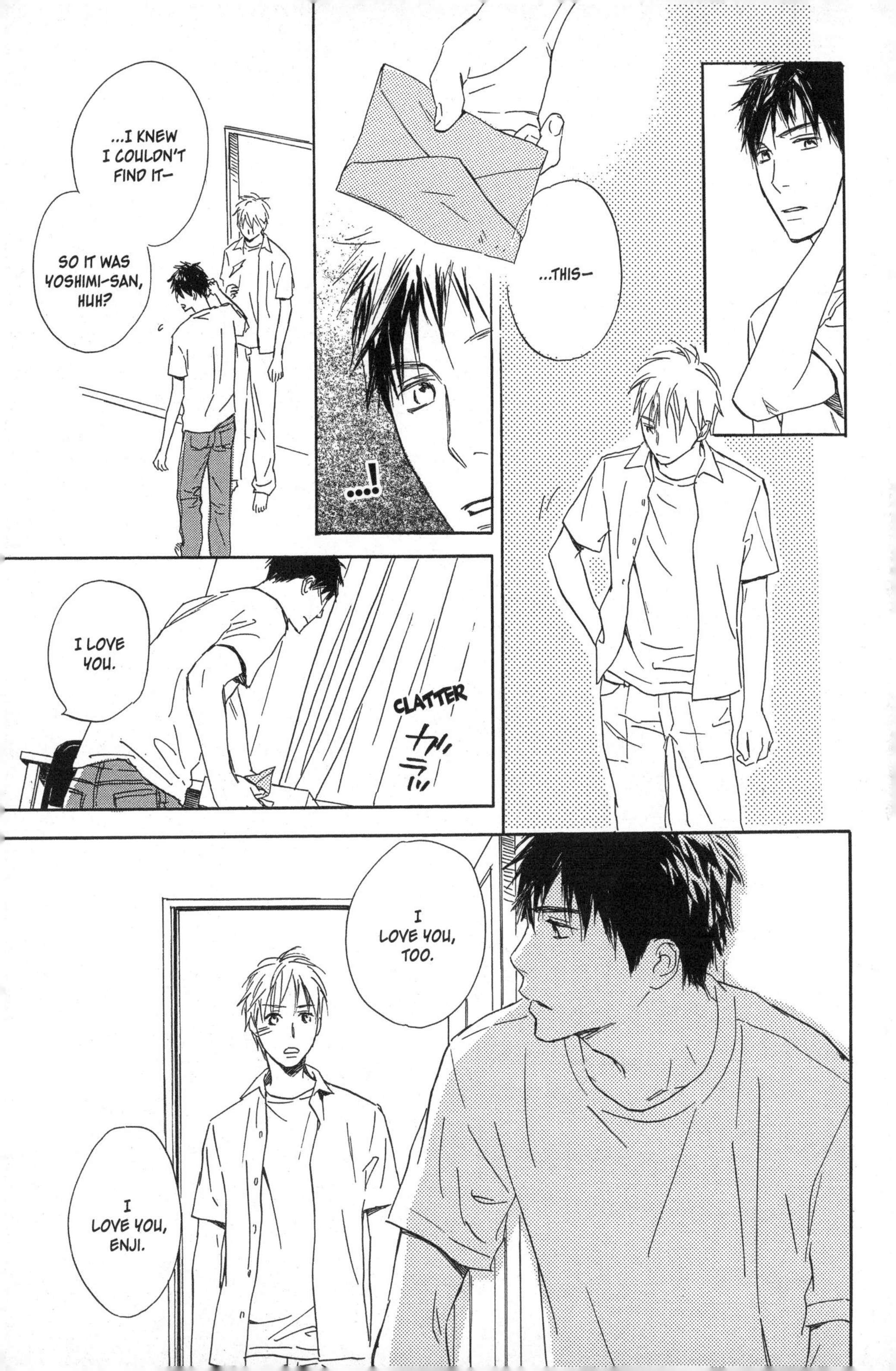
...THIS—
...!
...I KNEW I COULDN'T FIND IT—
SO IT WAS YOSHIMI-SAN, HUH?
I LOVE YOU.
CLATTER
I LOVE YOU, TOO.
I LOVE YOU, ENJI.

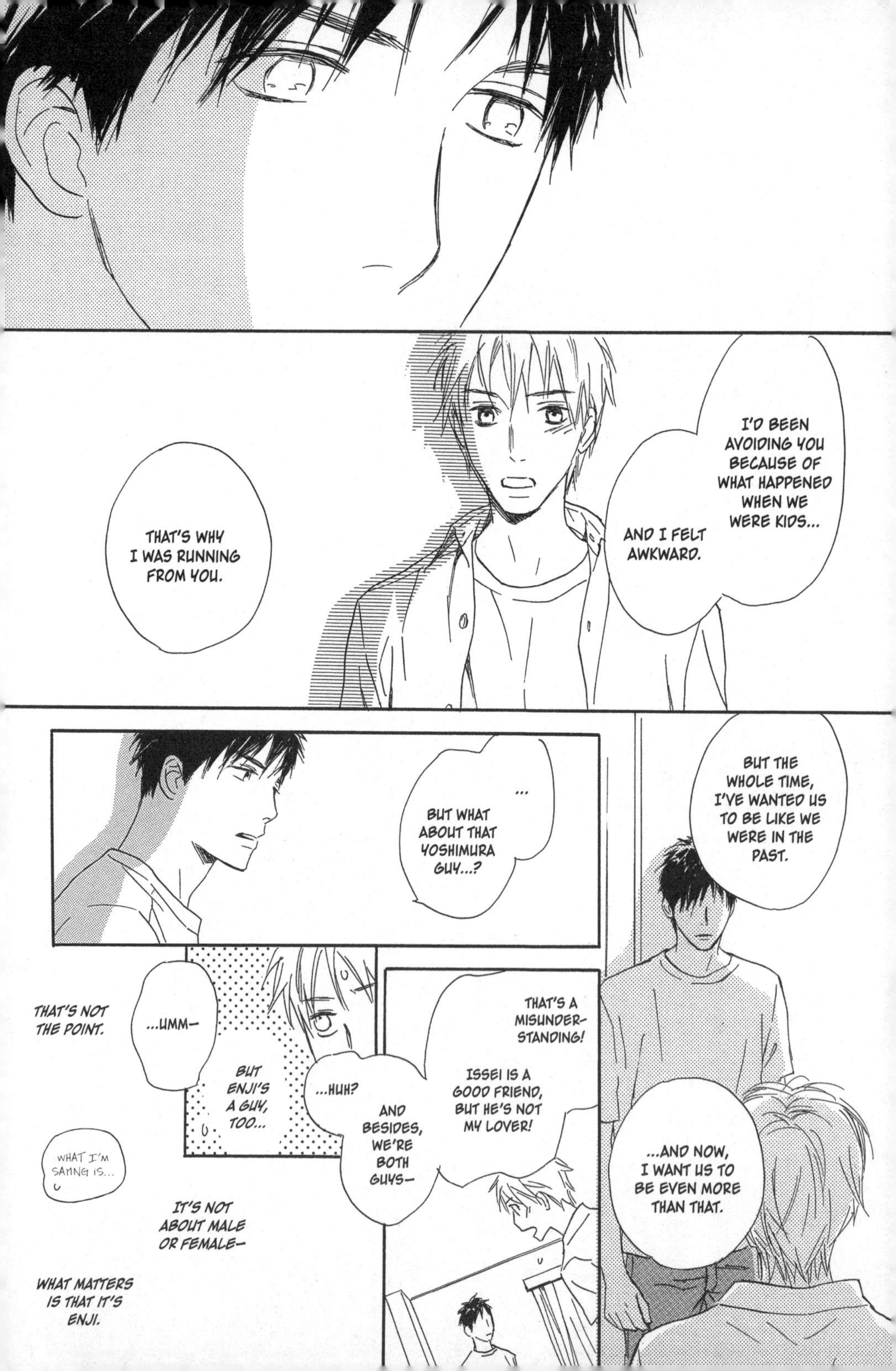
I'D BEEN AVOIDING YOU BECAUSE OF WHAT HAPPENED WHEN WE WERE KIDS...
AND I FELT AWKWARD.
THAT'S WHY I WAS RUNNING FROM YOU.
BUT THE WHOLE TIME, I'VE WANTED US TO BE LIKE WE WERE IN THE PAST.
...AND NOW, I WANT US TO BE EVEN MORE THAN THAT.
...
BUT WHAT ABOUT THAT YOSHIMURA GUY...?
THAT'S A MISUNDER-STANDING!
ISSEI IS A GOOD FRIEND, BUT HE'S NOT MY LOVER!
AND BESIDES, WE'RE BOTH GUYS—
...HUH?
...UMM—
BUT ENJI'S A GUY, TOO...
THAT'S NOT THE POINT.
WHAT I'M SAYING IS...
IT'S NOT ABOUT MALE OR FEMALE—
WHAT MATTERS IS THAT IT'S ENJI.

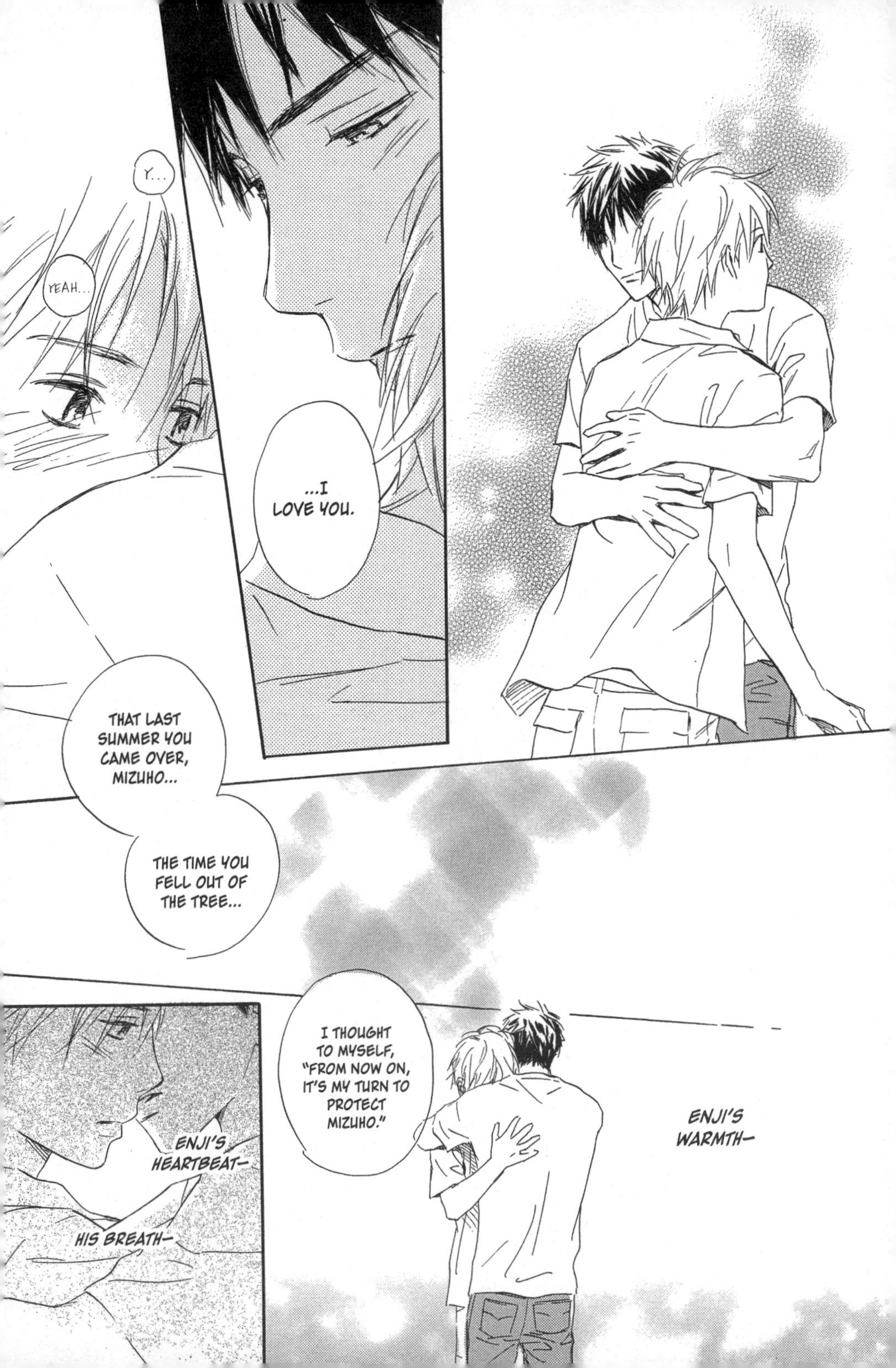
...I LOVE YOU.
Y...
YEAH...
THAT LAST SUMMER YOU CAME OVER, MIZUHO...
THE TIME YOU FELL OUT OF THE TREE...
I THOUGHT TO MYSELF, "FROM NOW ON, IT'S MY TURN TO PROTECT MIZUHO."
ENJI'S WARMTH—
ENJI'S HEARTBEAT—
HIS BREATH—

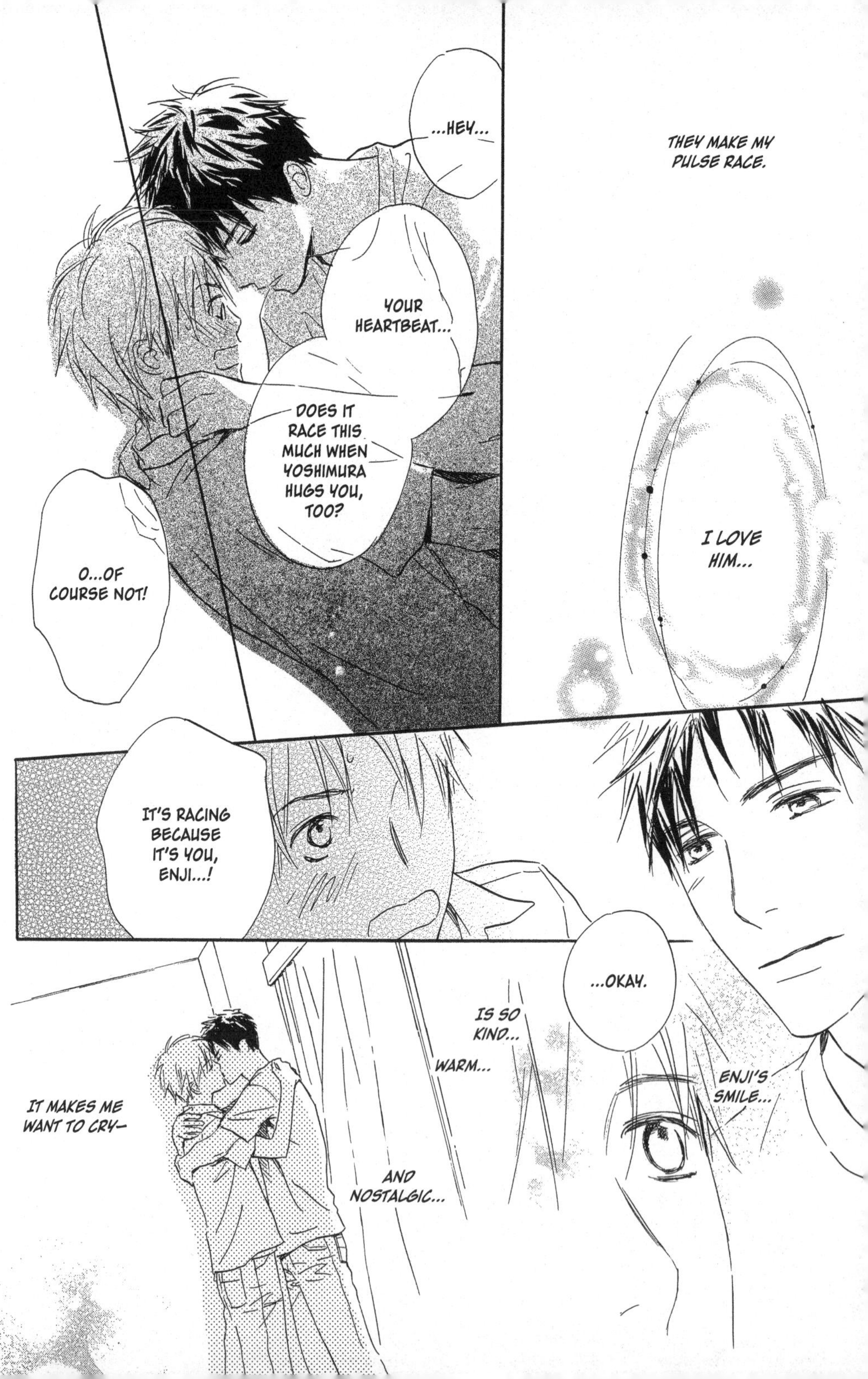

THEY MAKE MY PULSE RACE.
I LOVE HIM...
...HEY...
YOUR HEARTBEAT...
DOES IT RACE THIS MUCH WHEN YOSHIMURA HUGS YOU, TOO?
O...OF COURSE NOT!
IT'S RACING BECAUSE IT'S YOU, ENJI...!
...OKAY.
ENJI'S SMILE...
IS SO KIND...
WARM...
AND NOSTALGIC...
IT MAKES ME WANT TO CRY—

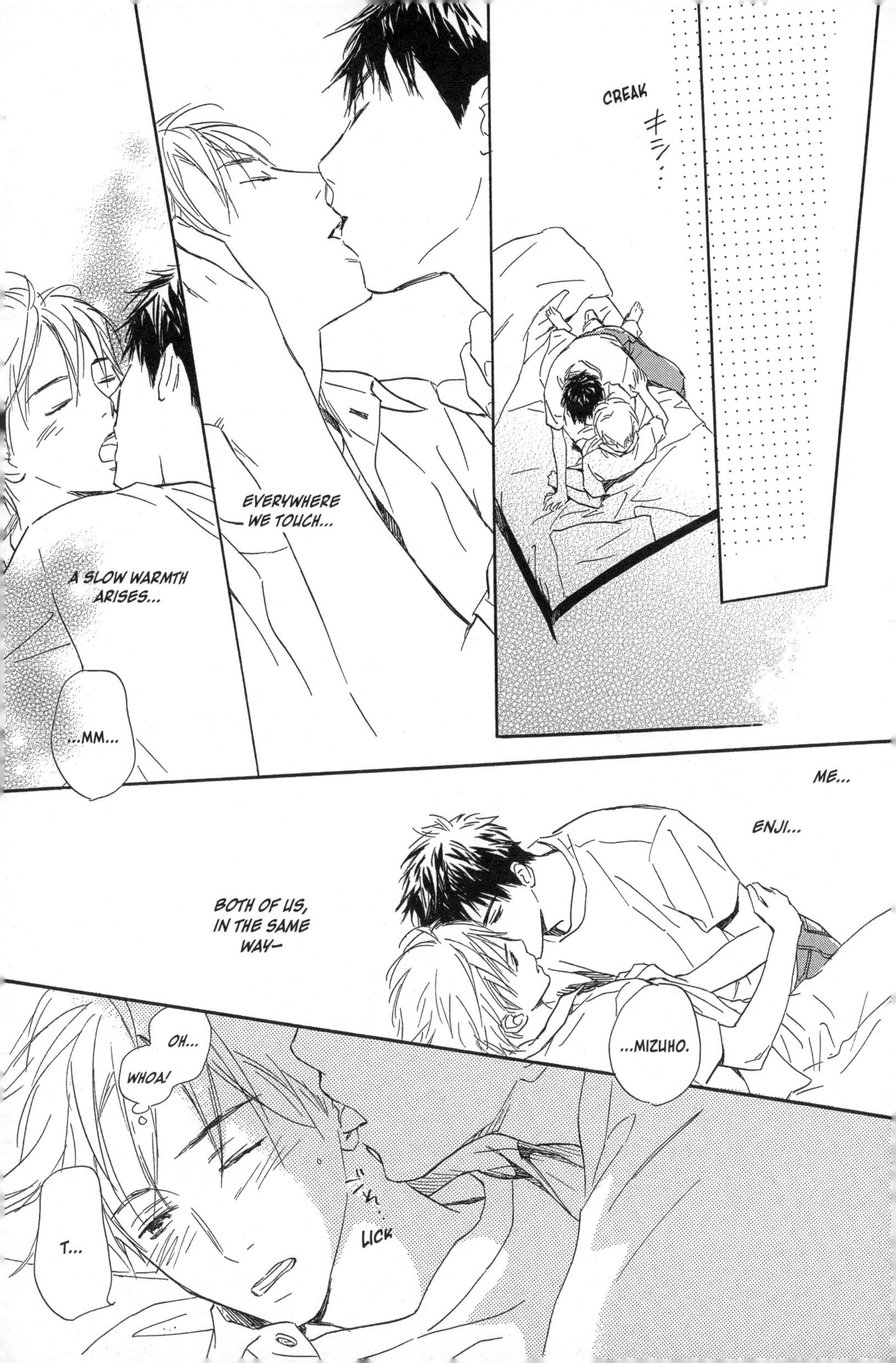

CREAK
キシ…
EVERYWHERE WE TOUCH...
A SLOW WARMTH ARISES...
...MM...
ME...
ENJI...
BOTH OF US, IN THE SAME WAY—
...MIZUHO.
OH...
WHOA!
LICK
T...

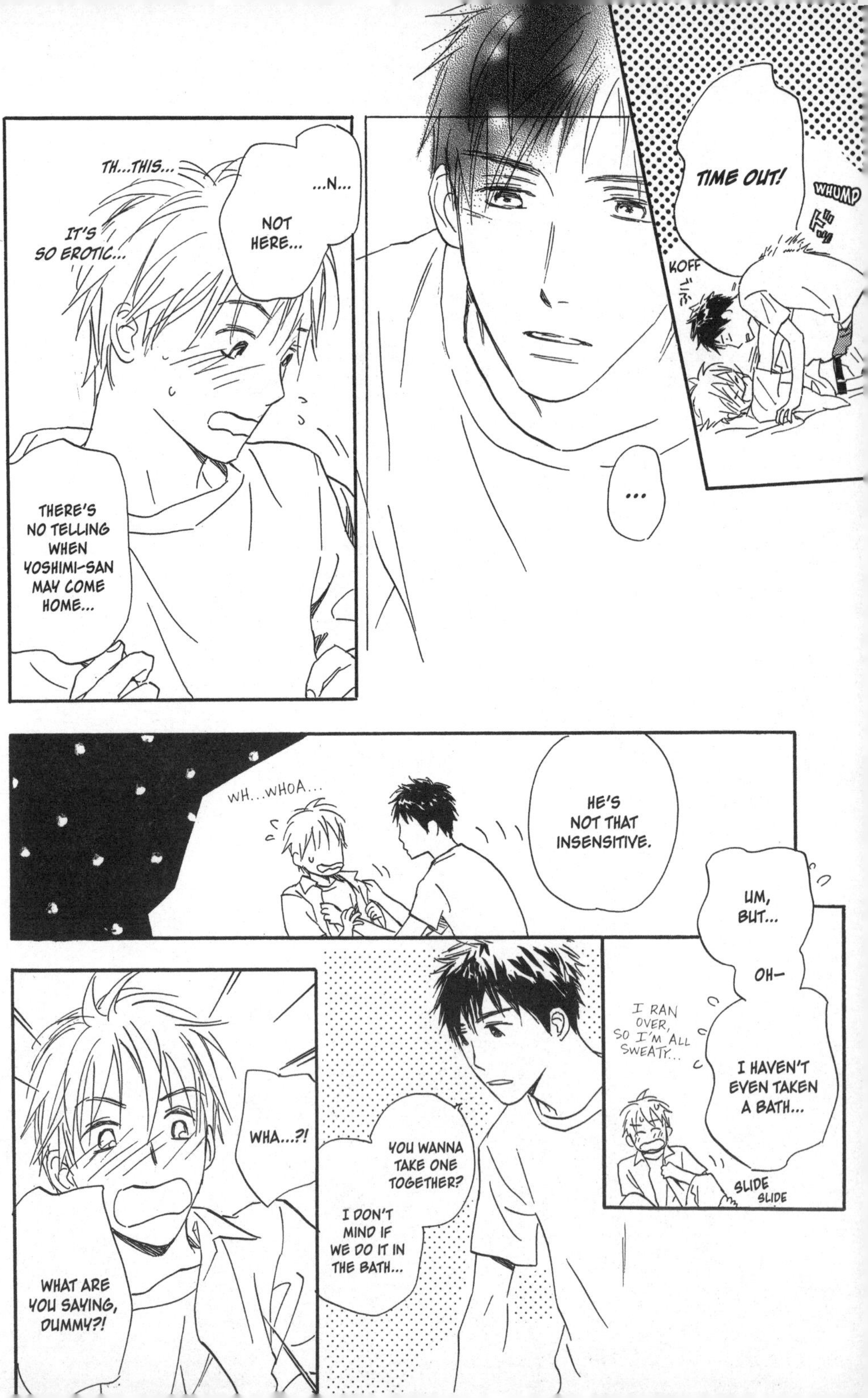
TIME OUT!
WHUMP
KOFF
...
...N...
NOT HERE...
TH...THIS...
IT'S SO EROTIC...
THERE'S NO TELLING WHEN YOSHIMI-SAN MAY COME HOME...
HE'S NOT THAT INSENSITIVE.
WH...WHOA...
UM, BUT...
OH—
I HAVEN'T EVEN TAKEN A BATH...
I RAN OVER, SO I'M ALL SWEATY...
SLIDE
SLIDE
YOU WANNA TAKE ONE TOGETHER?
I DON'T MIND IF WE DO IT IN THE BATH...
WHA...?!
WHAT ARE YOU SAYING, DUMMY?!

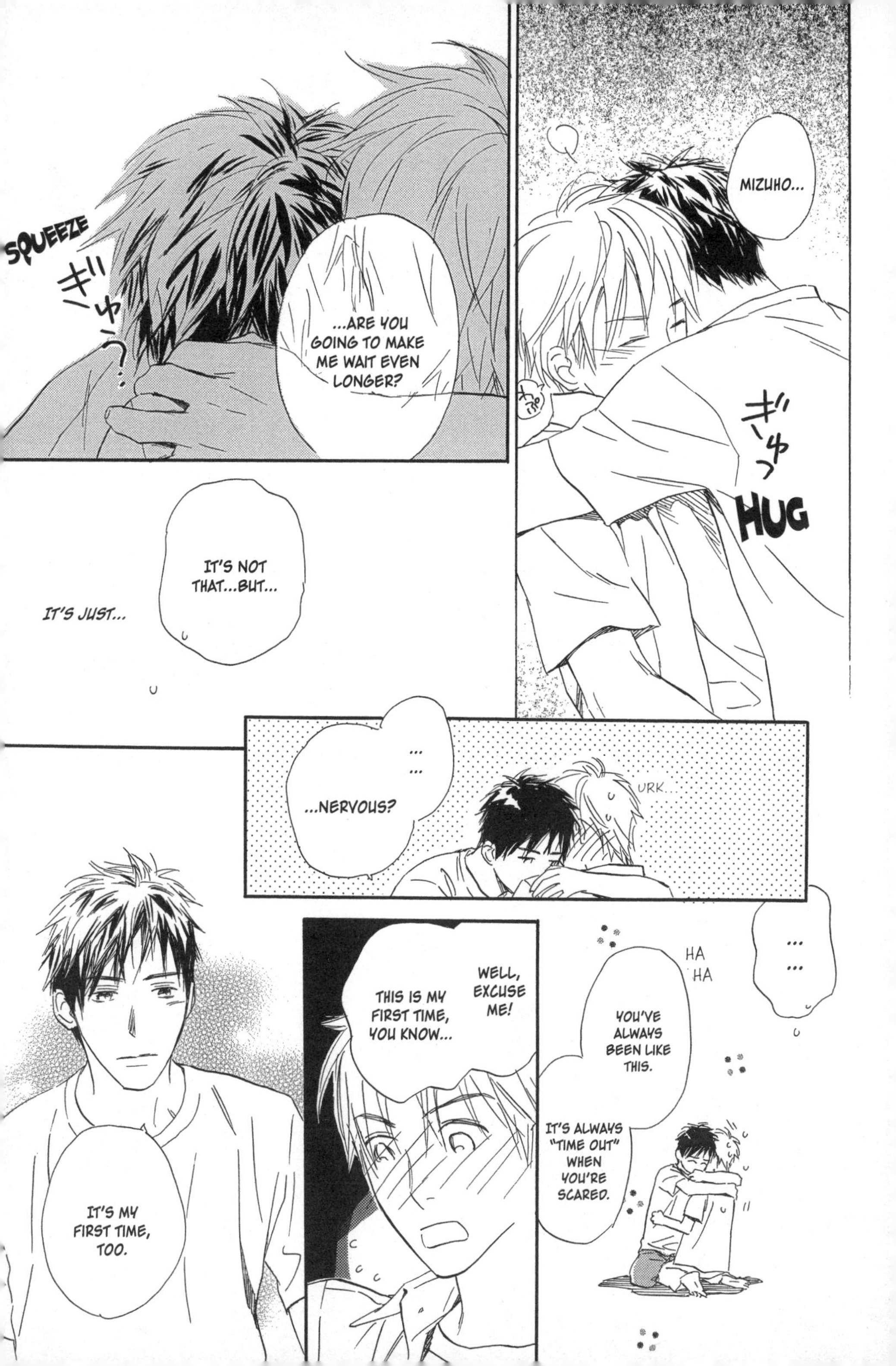
MIZUHO...
ぎゅっ
HUG
...ARE YOU GOING TO MAKE ME WAIT EVEN LONGER?
SQUEEZE
ぎゅっ
IT'S NOT THAT...BUT...
IT'S JUST...
URK...
... ...
...NERVOUS?
... ...
HA HA
YOU'VE ALWAYS BEEN LIKE THIS.
IT'S ALWAYS "TIME OUT" WHEN YOU'RE SCARED.
WELL, EXCUSE ME!
THIS IS MY FIRST TIME, YOU KNOW...
IT'S MY FIRST TIME, TOO.

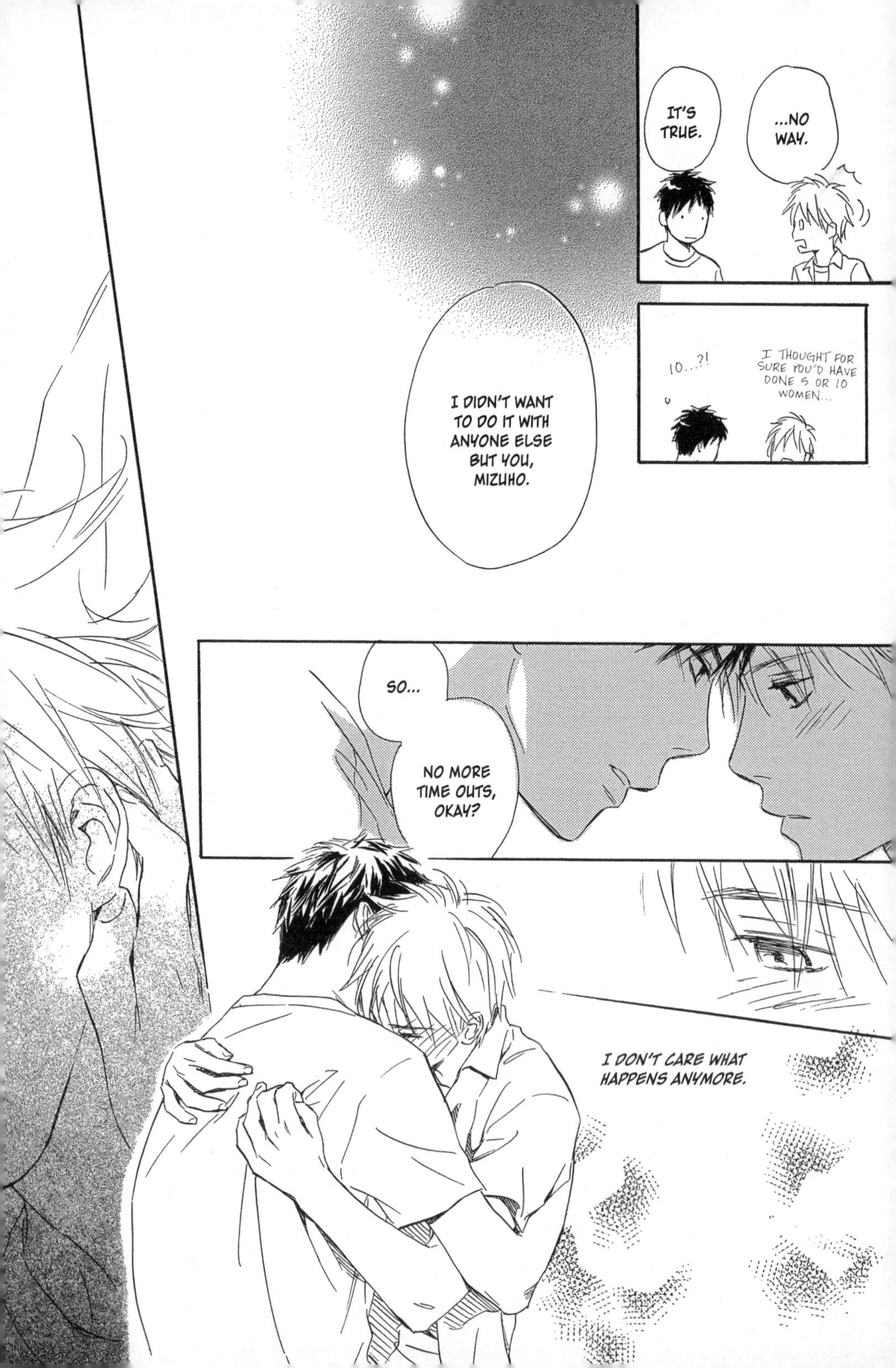
...NO WAY.
IT'S TRUE.
I THOUGHT FOR SURE YOU'D HAVE DONE 5 OR 10 WOMEN...
10...?!
I DIDN'T WANT TO DO IT WITH ANYONE ELSE BUT YOU, MIZUHO.
SO...
NO MORE TIME OUTS, OKAY?
I DON'T CARE WHAT HAPPENS ANYMORE.

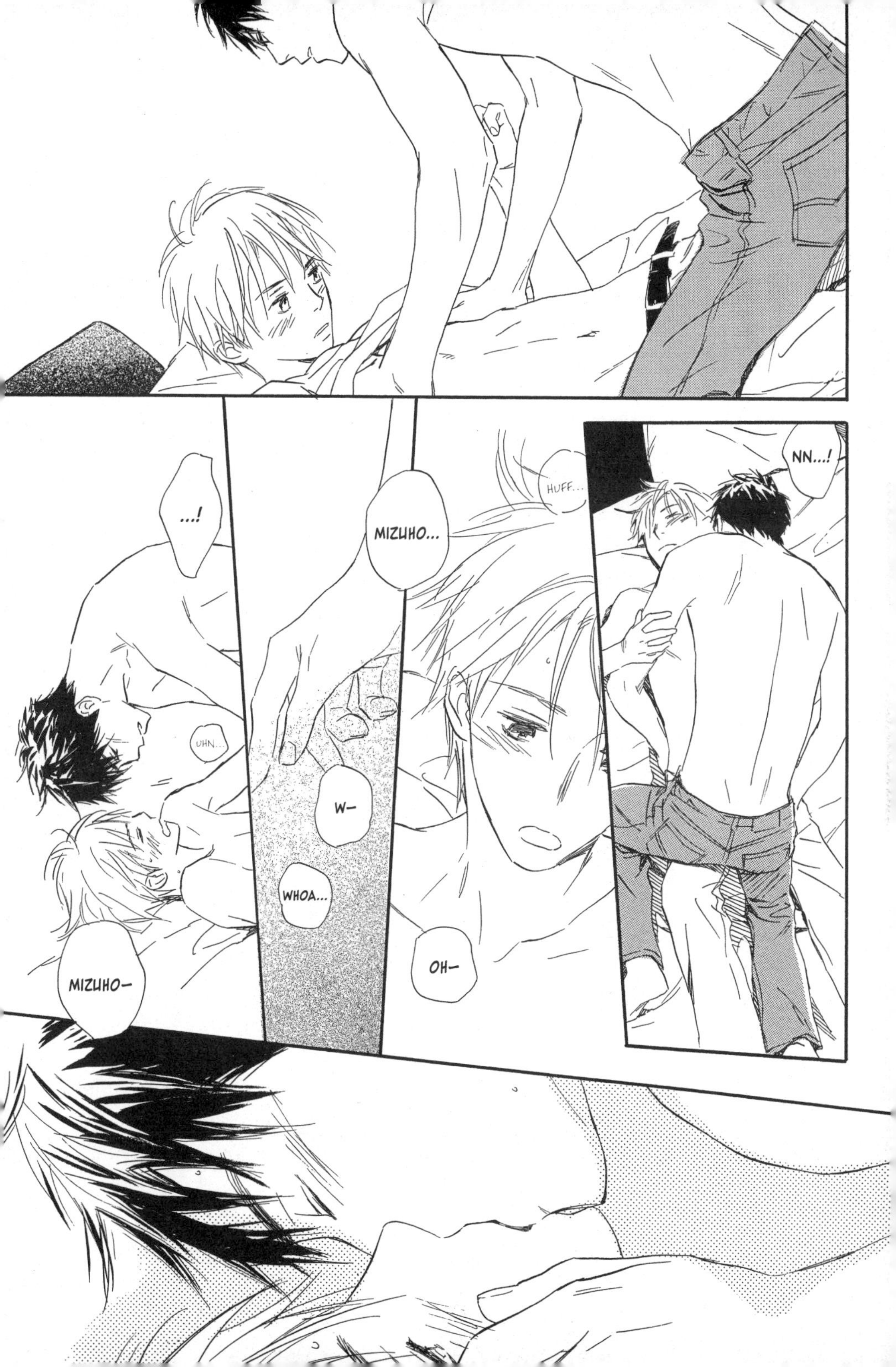
NN...!
HUFF...
OH–
MIZUHO...
W–
WHOA...
...!
UHN...
MIZUHO–

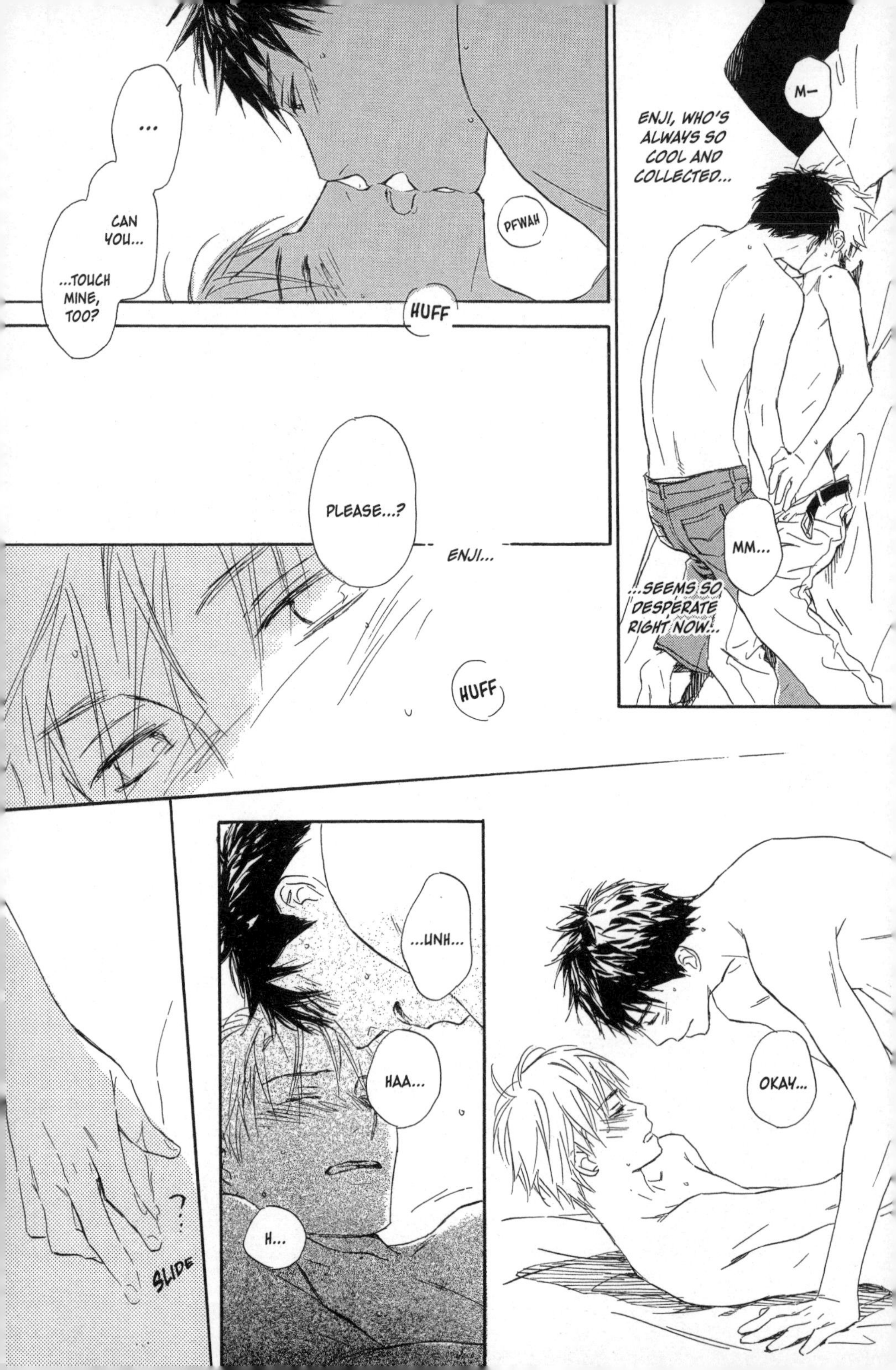
M—
ENJI, WHO'S ALWAYS SO COOL AND COLLECTED...
MM...
...SEEMS SO DESPERATE RIGHT NOW...
PFWAH
...
CAN YOU...
...TOUCH MINE, TOO?
HUFF
PLEASE...?
ENJI...
HUFF
OKAY...
...UNH...
HAA...
H...
?...
SLIDE

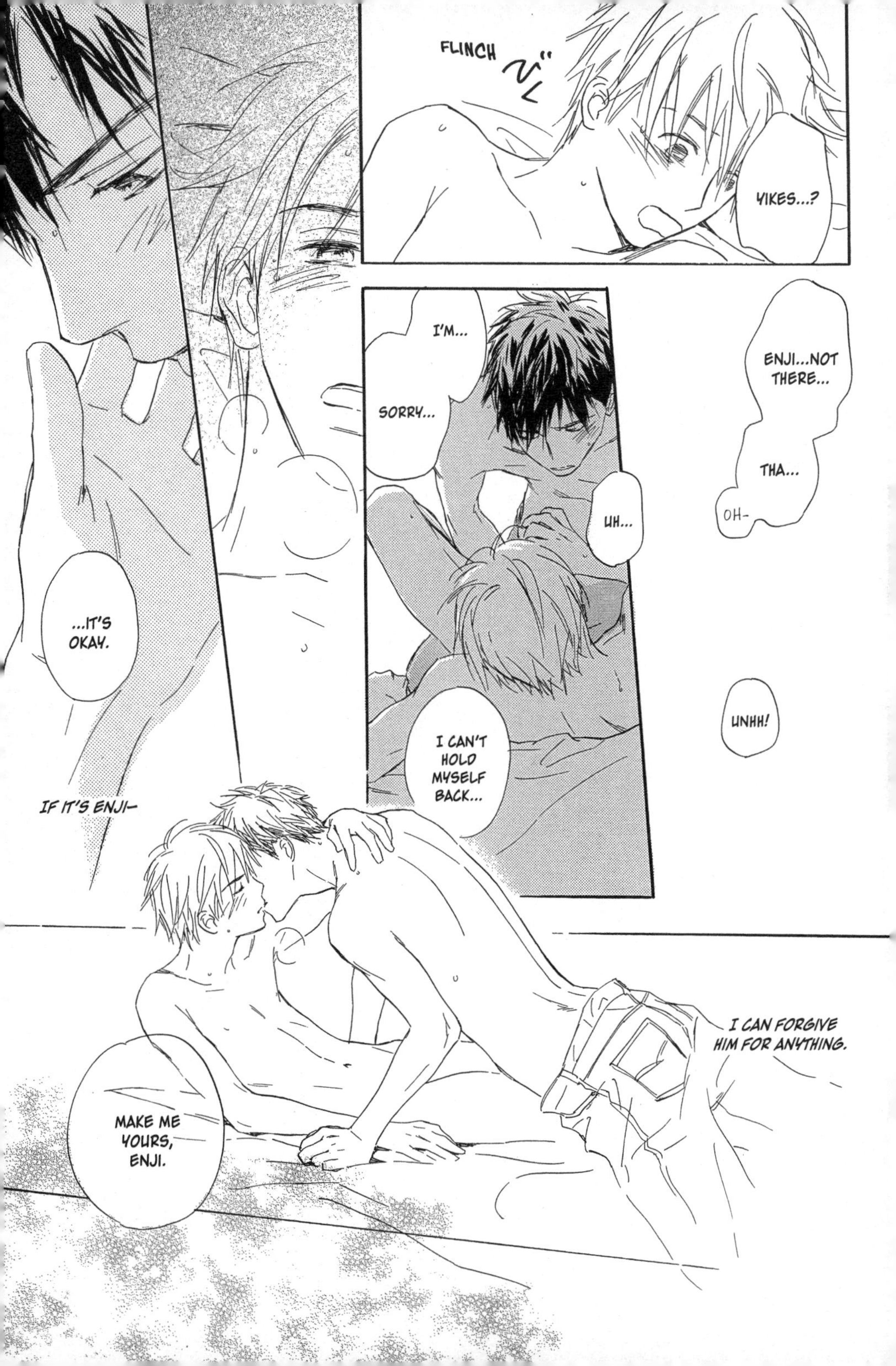
FLINCH
YIKES...?
ENJI...NOT THERE...
THA...
OH-
I'M...
SORRY...
UH...
I CAN'T HOLD MYSELF BACK...
UNHH!
...IT'S OKAY.
IF IT'S ENJI—
I CAN FORGIVE HIM FOR ANYTHING.
MAKE ME YOURS, ENJI.

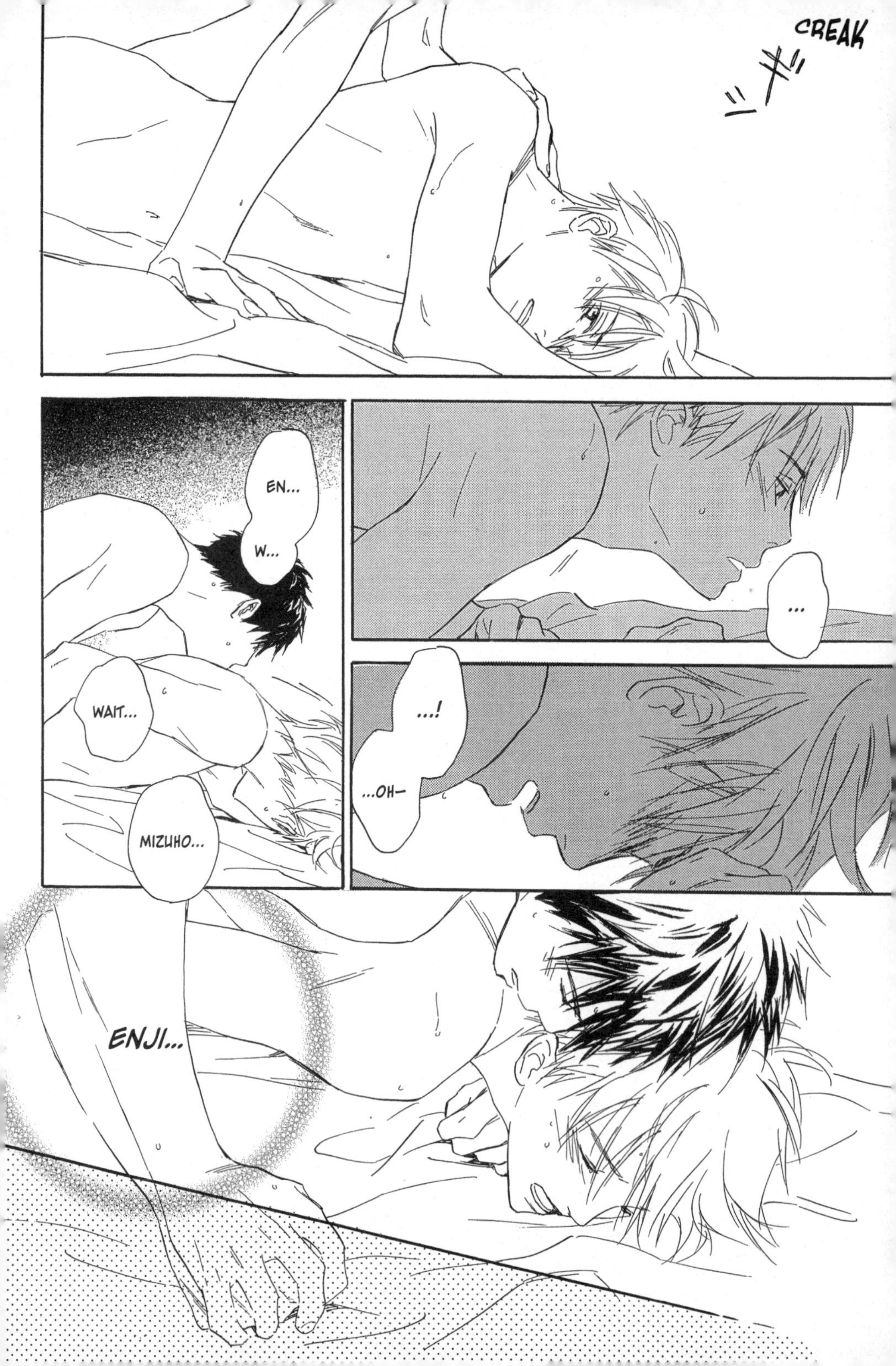
CREAK
...
...!
...OH—
EN...
W...
WAIT...
MIZUHO...
ENJI...

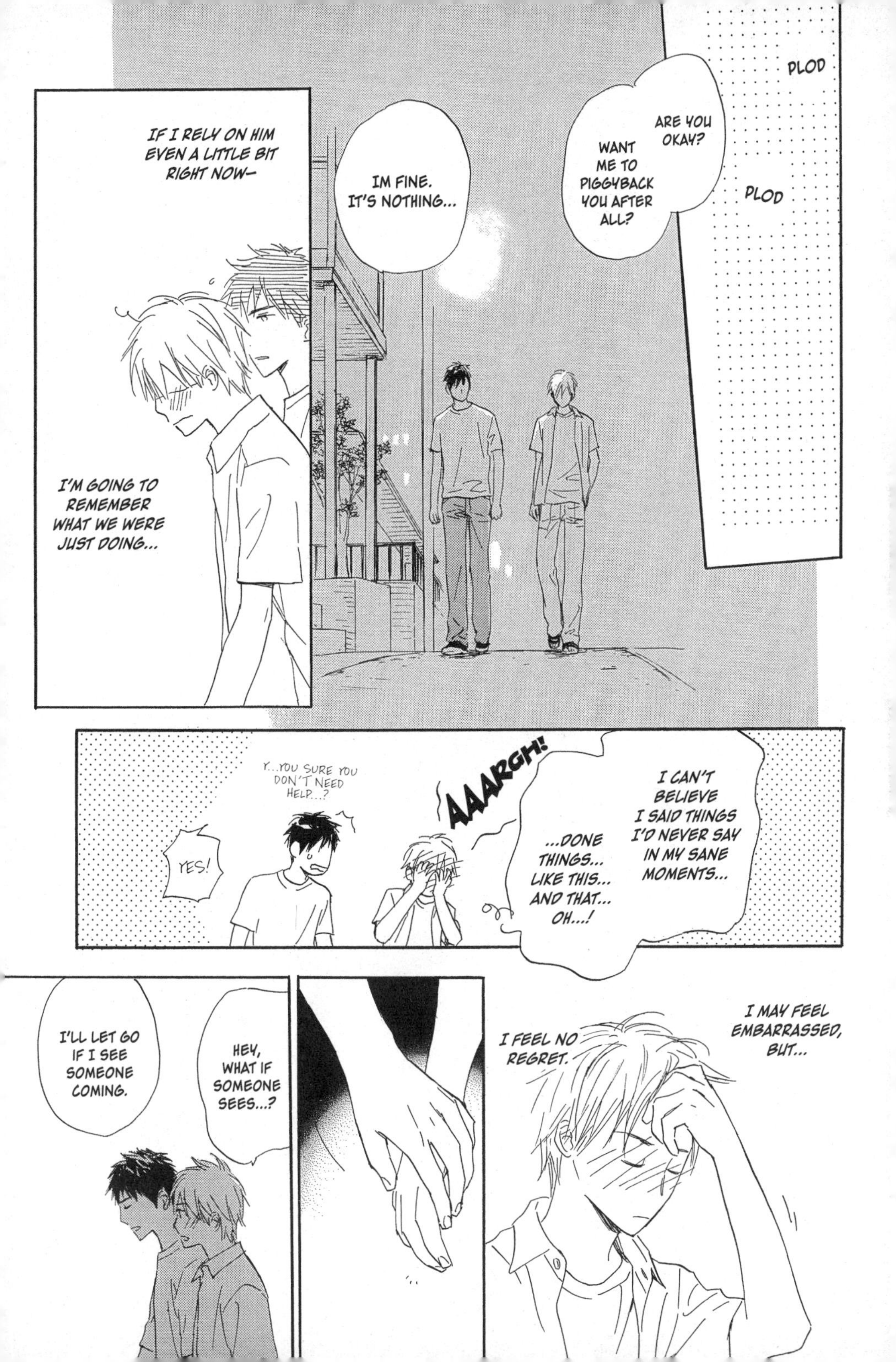
PLOD
PLOD
ARE YOU OKAY?
WANT ME TO PIGGYBACK YOU AFTER ALL?
IM FINE. IT'S NOTHING...
IF I RELY ON HIM EVEN A LITTLE BIT RIGHT NOW—
I'M GOING TO REMEMBER WHAT WE WERE JUST DOING...
I CAN'T BELIEVE I SAID THINGS I'D NEVER SAY IN MY SANE MOMENTS...
...DONE THINGS... LIKE THIS... AND THAT... OH...!
AAARGH!
Y...YOU SURE YOU DON'T NEED HELP...?
YES!
I MAY FEEL EMBARRASSED, BUT...
I FEEL NO REGRET.
HEY, WHAT IF SOMEONE SEES...?
I'LL LET GO IF I SEE SOMEONE COMING.

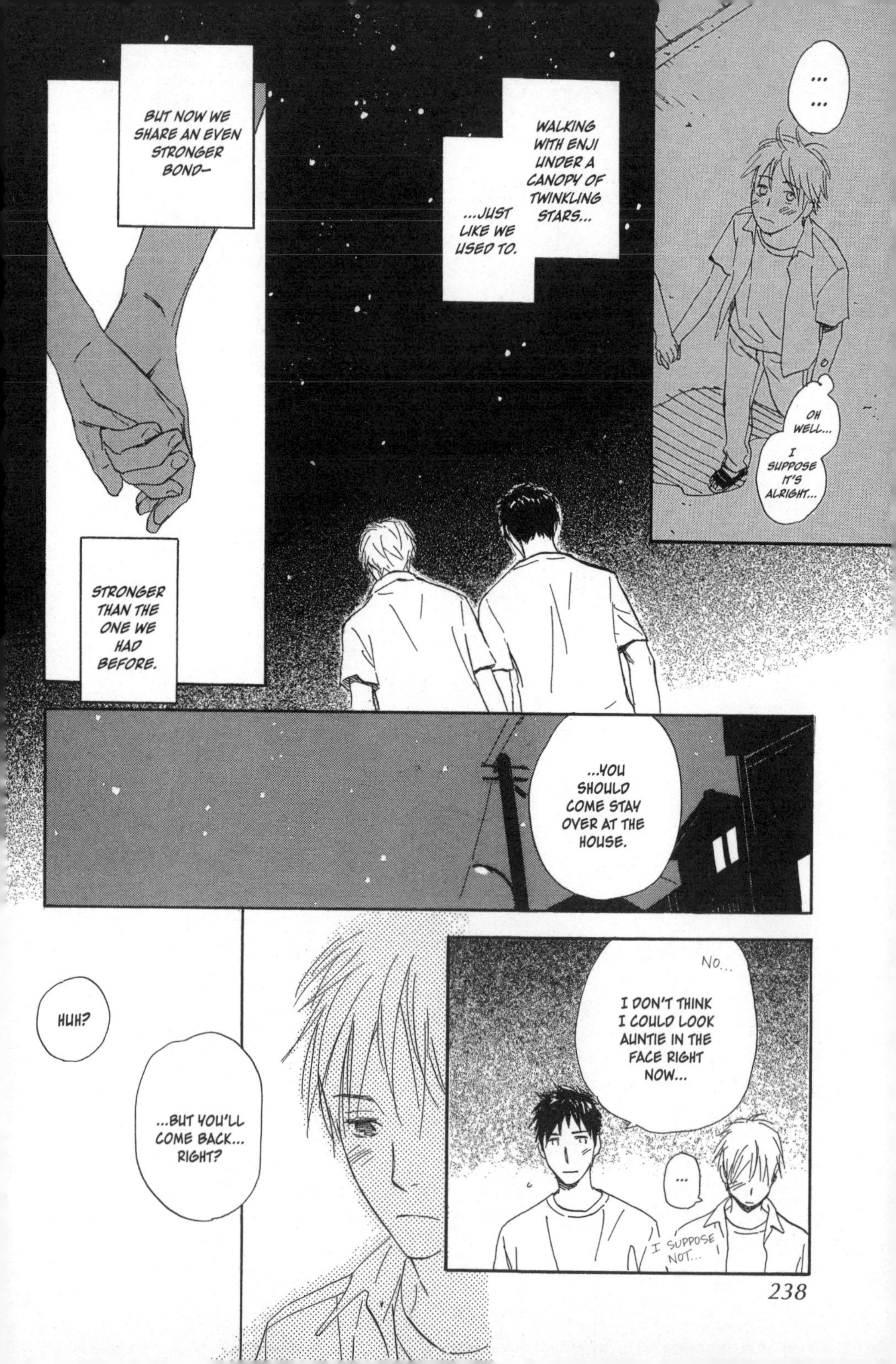
...
...
OH WELL...
I SUPPOSE IT'S ALRIGHT...
WALKING WITH ENJI UNDER A CANOPY OF TWINKLING STARS...
...JUST LIKE WE USED TO.
BUT NOW WE SHARE AN EVEN STRONGER BOND—
STRONGER THAN THE ONE WE HAD BEFORE.
...YOU SHOULD COME STAY OVER AT THE HOUSE.
NO...
I DON'T THINK I COULD LOOK AUNTIE IN THE FACE RIGHT NOW...
...
I SUPPOSE NOT...
HUH?
...BUT YOU'LL COME BACK... RIGHT?

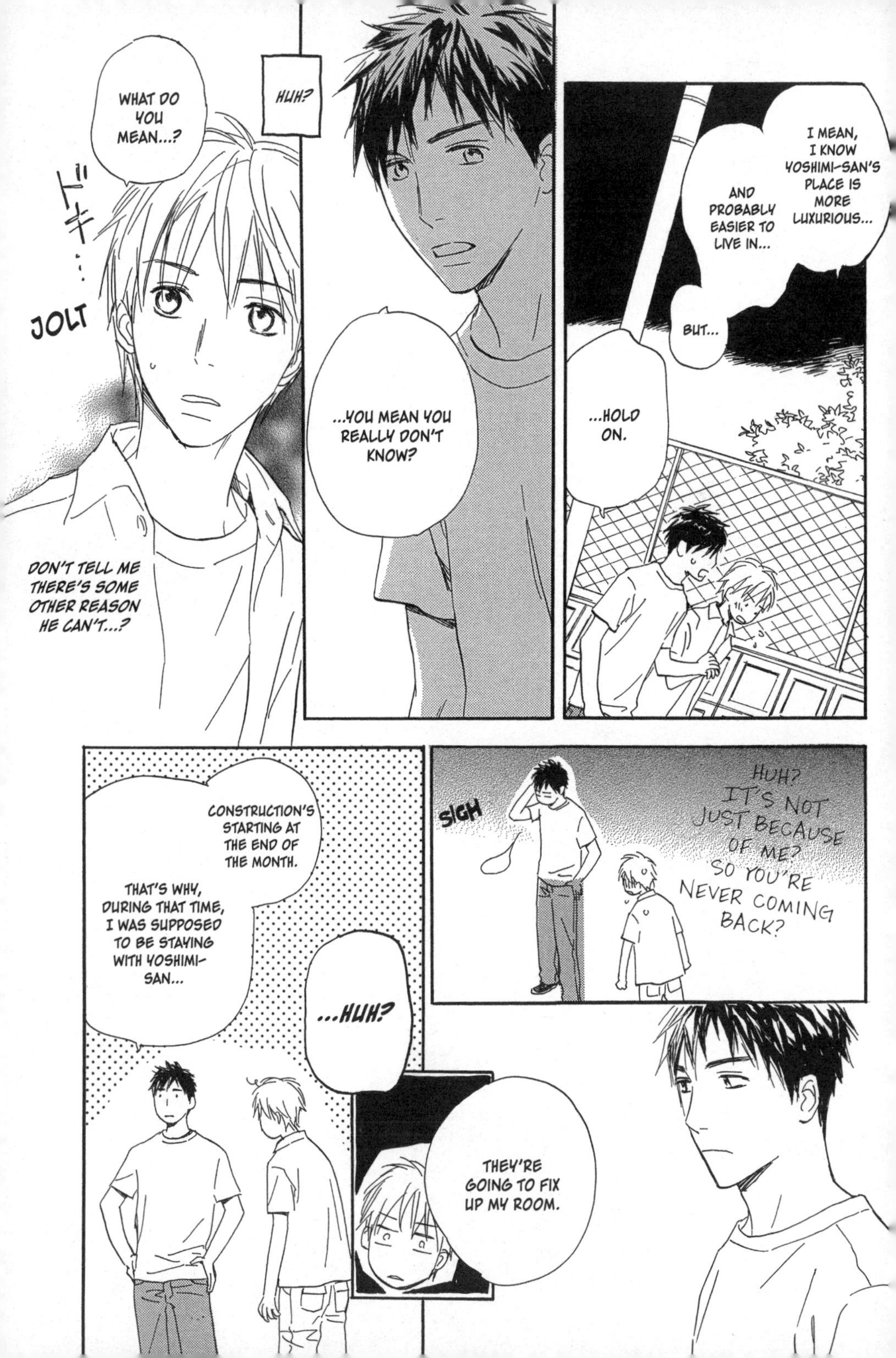
I MEAN, I KNOW YOSHIMI-SAN'S PLACE IS MORE LUXURIOUS...
AND PROBABLY EASIER TO LIVE IN...
BUT...
...HOLD ON.
HUH?
...YOU MEAN YOU REALLY DON'T KNOW?
WHAT DO YOU MEAN...?
ドキ...
JOLT
DON'T TELL ME THERE'S SOME OTHER REASON HE CAN'T...?
SIGH
HUH? IT'S NOT JUST BECAUSE OF ME? SO YOU'RE NEVER COMING BACK?
THEY'RE GOING TO FIX UP MY ROOM.
CONSTRUCTION'S STARTING AT THE END OF THE MONTH.
THAT'S WHY, DURING THAT TIME, I WAS SUPPOSED TO BE STAYING WITH YOSHIMI-SAN...
...HUH?

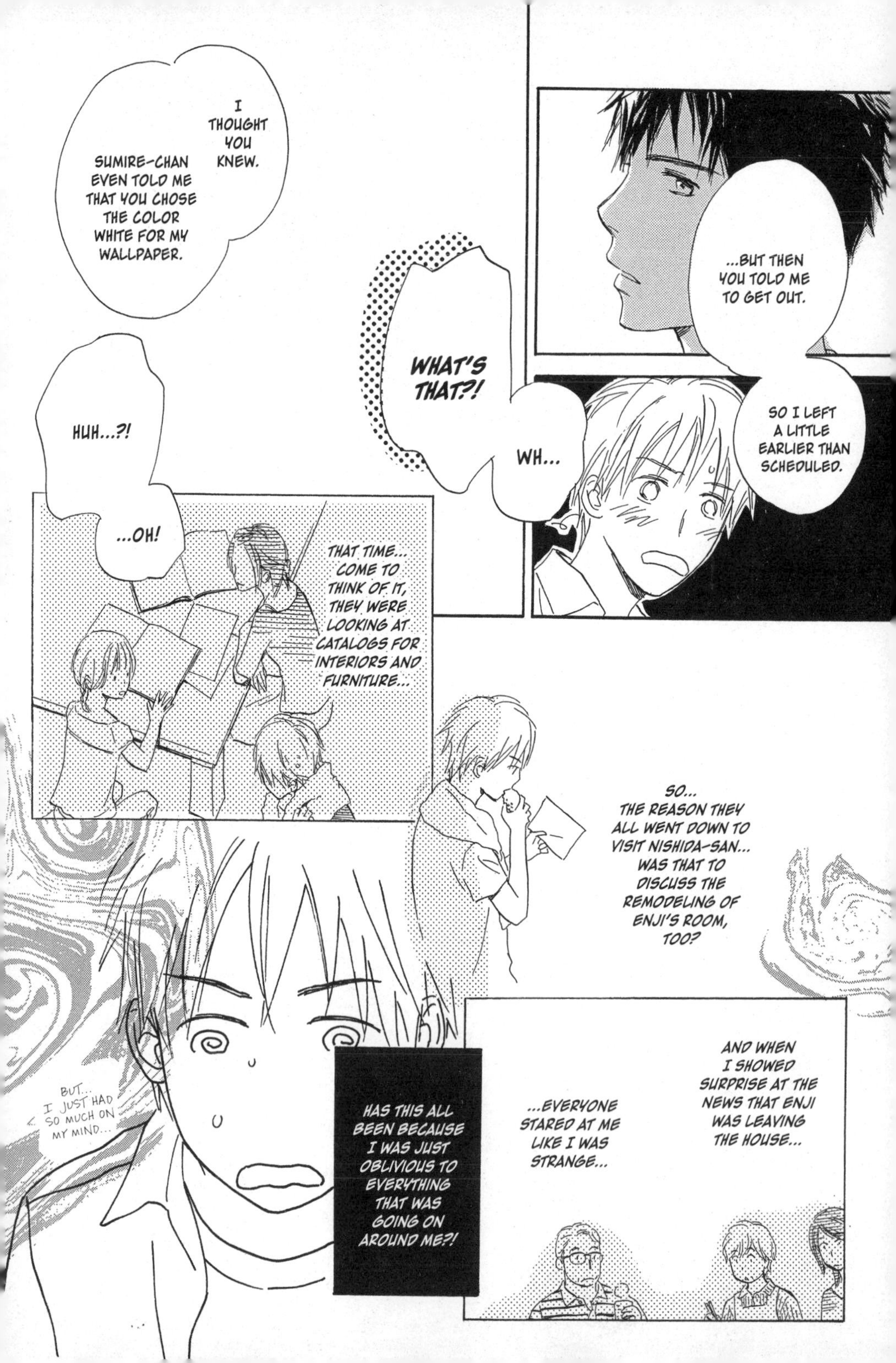
...BUT THEN YOU TOLD ME TO GET OUT.
SO I LEFT A LITTLE EARLIER THAN SCHEDULED.
WH...
WHAT'S THAT?!
I THOUGHT YOU KNEW.
SUMIRE-CHAN EVEN TOLD ME THAT YOU CHOSE THE COLOR WHITE FOR MY WALLPAPER.
HUH...?!
...OH!
THAT TIME... COME TO THINK OF IT, THEY WERE LOOKING AT CATALOGS FOR INTERIORS AND FURNITURE...
SO... THE REASON THEY ALL WENT DOWN TO VISIT NISHIDA-SAN... WAS THAT TO DISCUSS THE REMODELING OF ENJI'S ROOM, TOO?
AND WHEN I SHOWED SURPRISE AT THE NEWS THAT ENJI WAS LEAVING THE HOUSE...
...EVERYONE STARED AT ME LIKE I WAS STRANGE...
HAS THIS ALL BEEN BECAUSE I WAS JUST OBLIVIOUS TO EVERYTHING THAT WAS GOING ON AROUND ME?!
BUT... I JUST HAD SO MUCH ON MY MIND...

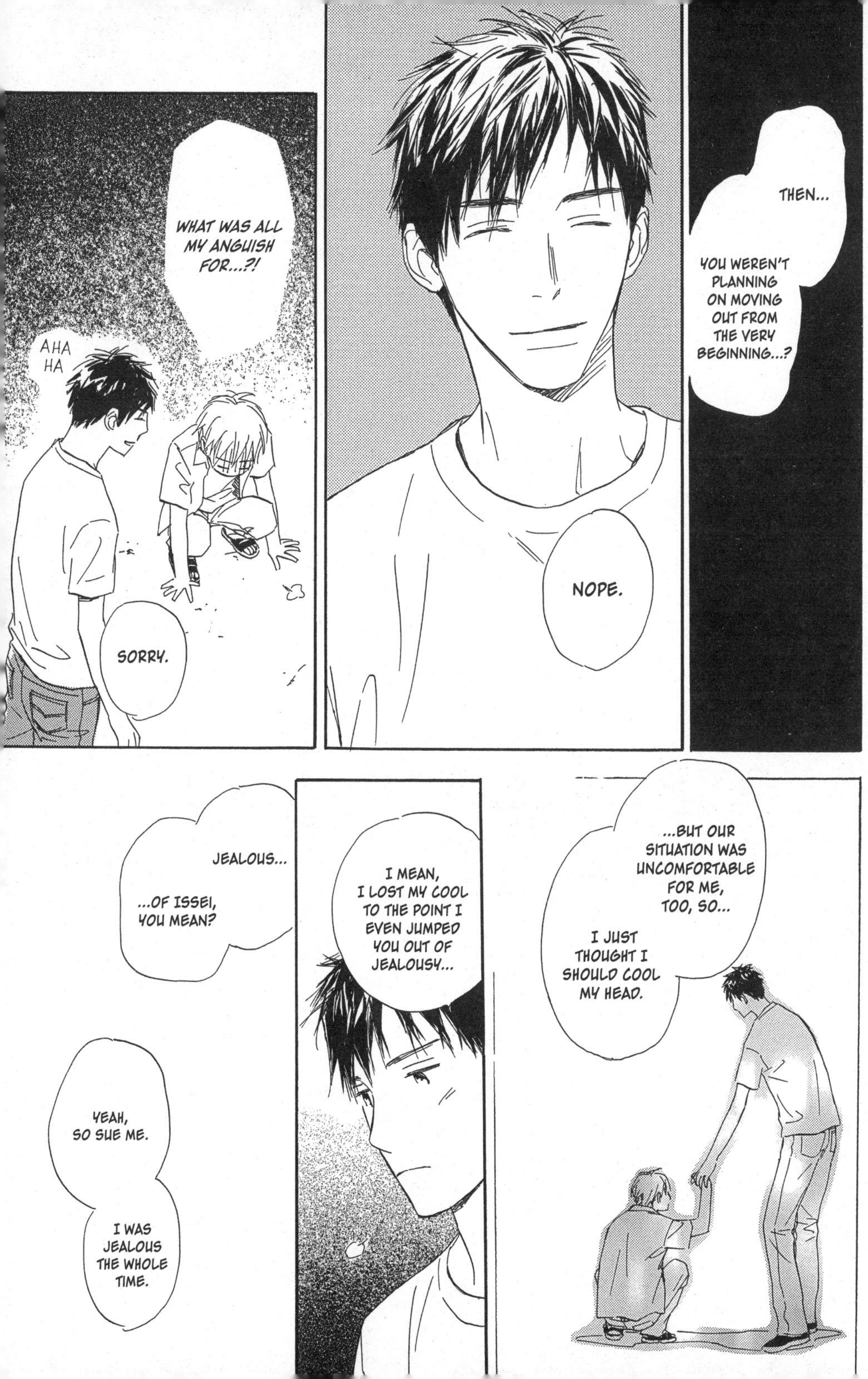
THEN...
YOU WEREN'T PLANNING ON MOVING OUT FROM THE VERY BEGINNING...?
NOPE.
WHAT WAS ALL MY ANGUISH FOR...?!
AHA HA
SORRY.
...BUT OUR SITUATION WAS UNCOMFORTABLE FOR ME, TOO, SO...
I JUST THOUGHT I SHOULD COOL MY HEAD.
I MEAN, I LOST MY COOL TO THE POINT I EVEN JUMPED YOU OUT OF JEALOUSY...
JEALOUS...
...OF ISSEI, YOU MEAN?
YEAH, SO SUE ME.
I WAS JEALOUS THE WHOLE TIME.

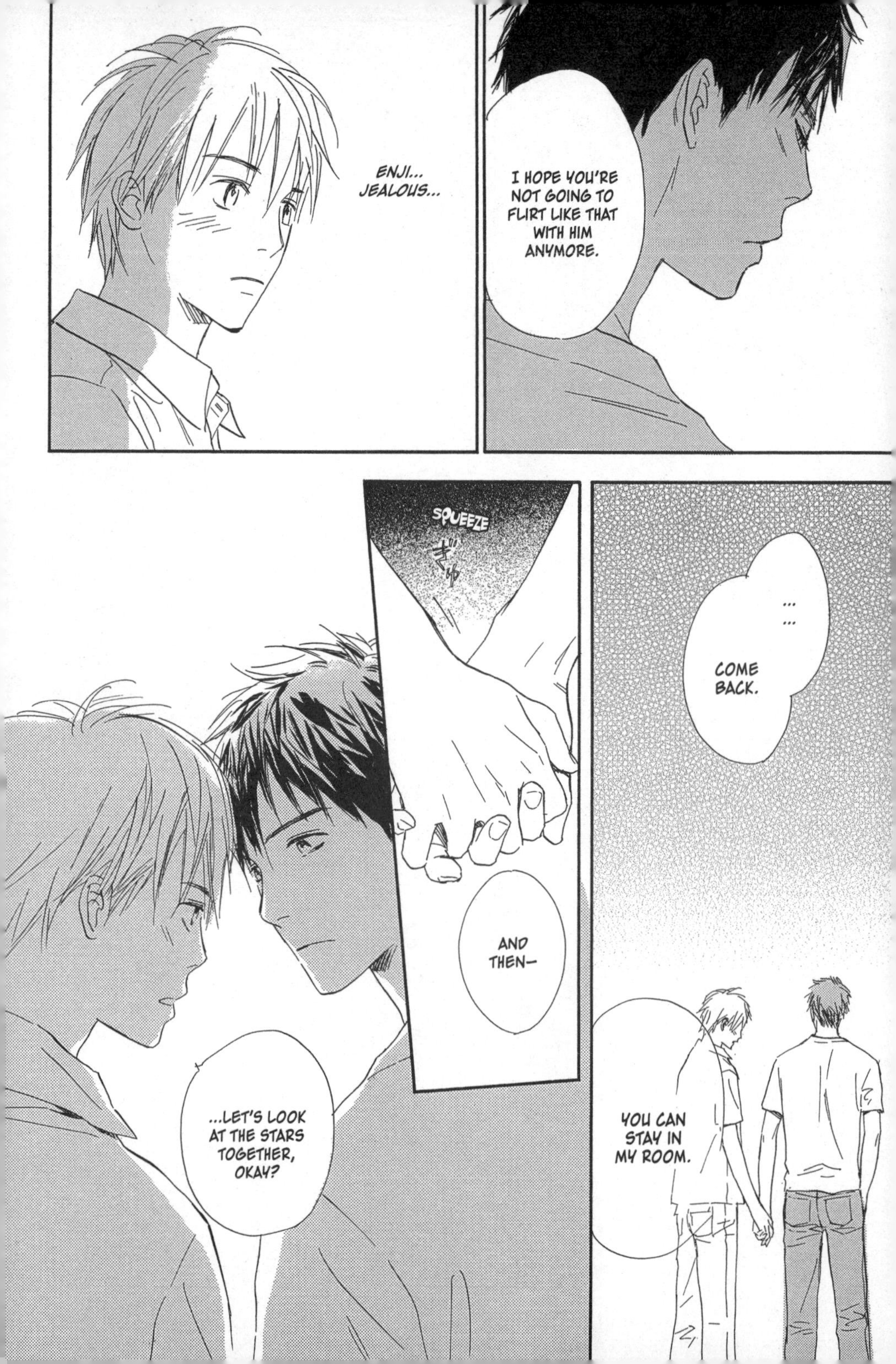
I HOPE YOU'RE NOT GOING TO FLIRT LIKE THAT WITH HIM ANYMORE.
ENJI... JEALOUS...
... ...
COME BACK.
YOU CAN STAY IN MY ROOM.
SQUEEZE
ぎゅ
AND THEN—
...LET'S LOOK AT THE STARS TOGETHER, OKAY?

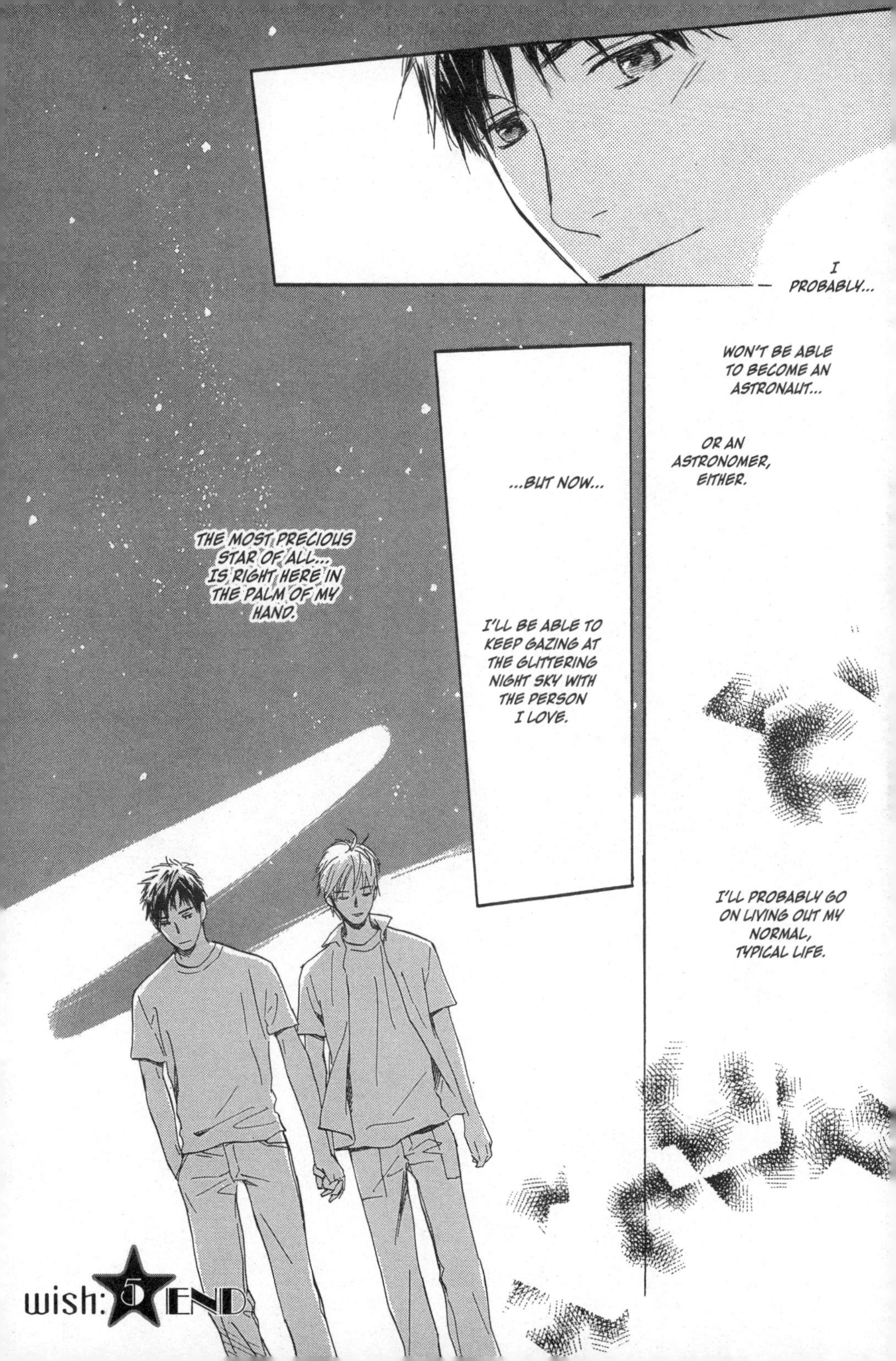

I PROBABLY...
WON'T BE ABLE TO BECOME AN ASTRONAUT...
OR AN ASTRONOMER, EITHER.
I'LL PROBABLY GO ON LIVING OUT MY NORMAL, TYPICAL LIFE.
...BUT NOW...
I'LL BE ABLE TO KEEP GAZING AT THE GLITTERING NIGHT SKY WITH THE PERSON I LOVE.
THE MOST PRECIOUS STAR OF ALL... IS RIGHT HERE IN THE PALM OF MY HAND.
wish: 5 END

# CONSTELLATIONS IN MY PALM

## てのひらの星☆座

### Afterword

HELLO. THIS IS CHISAKO SAKURAGI,
THE WRITER OF THIS STORY.
THANK YOU VERY MUCH FOR TAKING THIS BOOK IN
HAND.

EVER SINCE I WAS A CHILD, I HAVE ALWAYS
LOVED MANGA AND DREAMT OF ONE DAY
BECOMING A MANGA ARTIST MYSELF. AS HOPELESS
AS THIS DREAM WAS FOR ME, WITH THIS PROJECT
I FEEL AS IF MY WISH HAS BEEN PARTIALLY
FULFILLED, AND FOR THIS I AM VERY HAPPY.

BECAUSE I WROTE THIS STORY WHOLLY ACCORDING
TO MY OWN TASTES, I AM SURE IT MUST HAVE
BEEN VERY TRYING AT TIMES FOR HONAMI-SAN
AND EDITOR MITSUHIRO-SAN...BUT I AM IN AWE
AT HONAMI-SAN, WHO MANAGED TO MAKE SUCH
A BEAUTIFUL MANGA OUT OF IT!
HONAMI-SAN, THANK YOU SO VERY MUCH.
I WAS ALWAYS EXCITED TO SEE HONAMI-SAN'S
RENDITIONS OF MIZUHO AND ENJI, A THOUSAND
TIMES MORE FULL OF LIFE THAN IN MY WRITING.
I WENT SERIOUSLY HEAD OVER HEELS FOR YOSHIMI
(LAUGH).

I AM TRULY GRATEFUL TO HAVE BEEN SO BLESSED.
THANK YOU VERY MUCH!

CHISAKO SAKURAGI

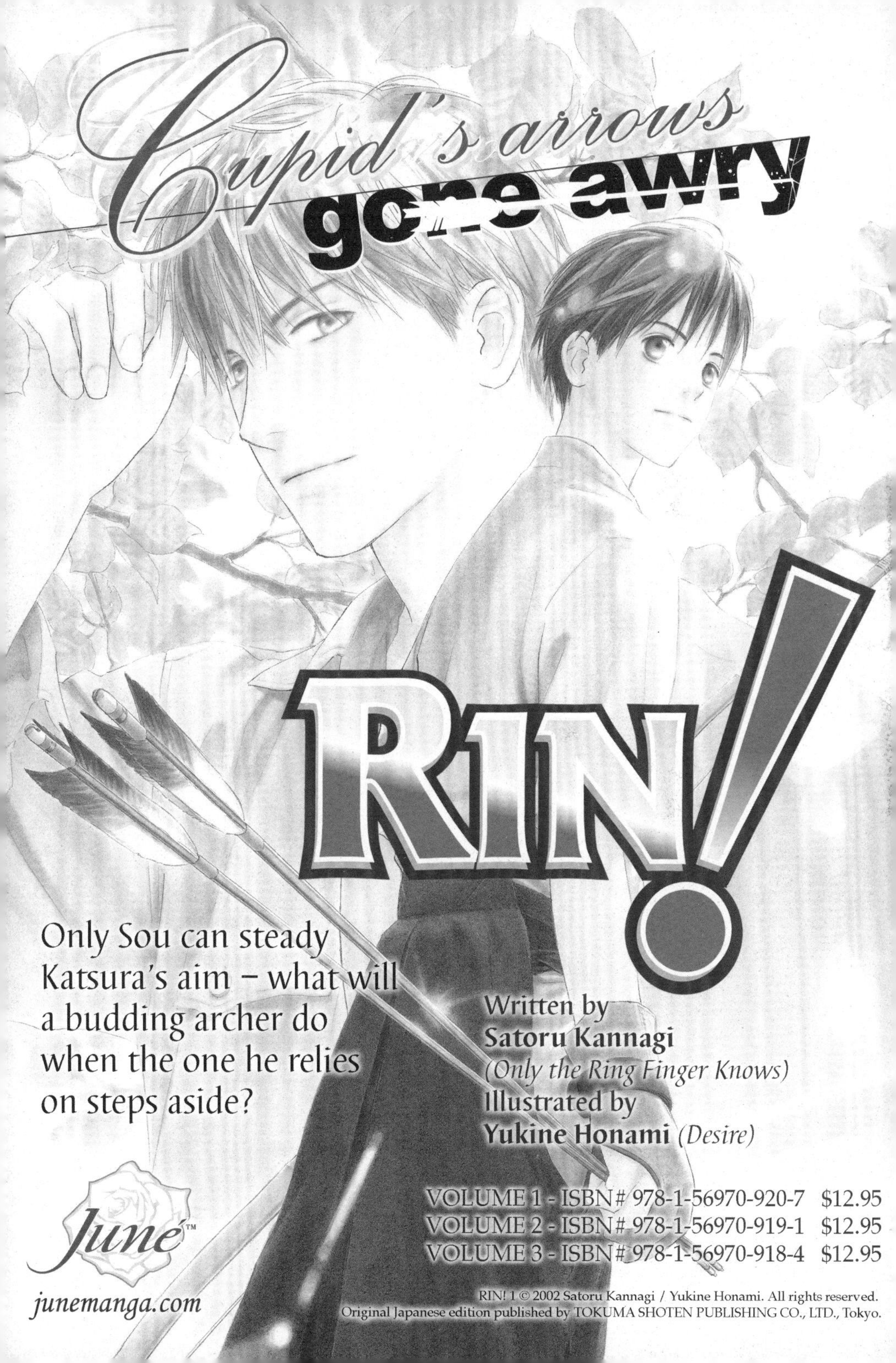
Cupid's arrows gone awry
RIN!
Only Sou can steady Katsura's aim – what will a budding archer do when the one he relies on steps aside?
Written by
Satoru Kannagi
(Only the Ring Finger Knows)
Illustrated by
Yukine Honami (Desire)
VOLUME 1 - ISBN# 978-1-56970-920-7 $12.95
VOLUME 2 - ISBN# 978-1-56970-919-1 $12.95
VOLUME 3 - ISBN# 978-1-56970-918-4 $12.95
June™
junemanga.com
RIN! 1 © 2002 Satoru Kannagi / Yukine Honami. All rights reserved.
Original Japanese edition published by TOKUMA SHOTEN PUBLISHING CO., LTD., Tokyo.

# THE Moon AND Sandals 月とサンダル Vol. 1

## SEE ME AFTER CLASS!

ISBN# 978-1-56970-802-9  SRP $12.95

**June** by DMP

As a newly appointed high school teacher, Ida has yet to gain confidence in his abilities. His insecurity grows worse when he feels someone staring intensely at him during class. The piercing eyes belong to a tall, intimidating student – Koichi Kobayashi. What exactly should Ida do about it? Is it discontent that fuels Kobayashi's sultry gaze… or could it be something else?

*Written and Illustrated by:*
**Fumi Yoshinaga**

junemanga.com

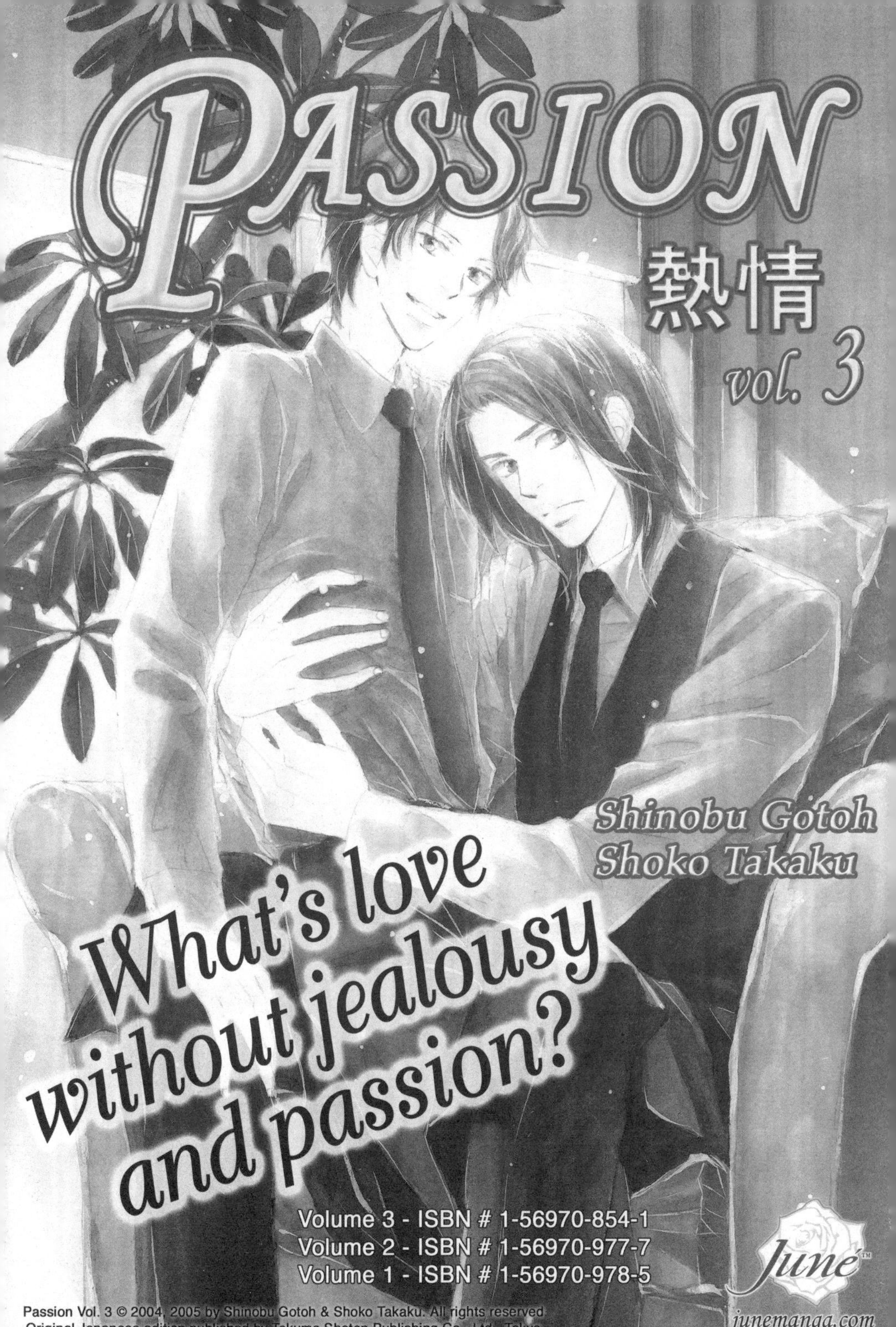

PASSION
熱情
vol. 3
Shinobu Gotoh
Shoko Takaku
What's love without jealousy and passion?
Volume 3 - ISBN # 1-56970-854-1
Volume 2 - ISBN # 1-56970-977-7
Volume 1 - ISBN # 1-56970-978-5
June™
junemanga.com

# He has no luck.
# He has no name.

## Sometimes letting go of the past... requires finding love in the present.

# SEVEN

### BY MOMOKO TENZEN

**June**™

junemanga.com

ISBN# 978-1-56970-849-1  $12.95

SEVEN © Momoko Tenzen 2004.
Originally published in Japan in 2004 by TAIYOH TOSHO Co., Ltd.

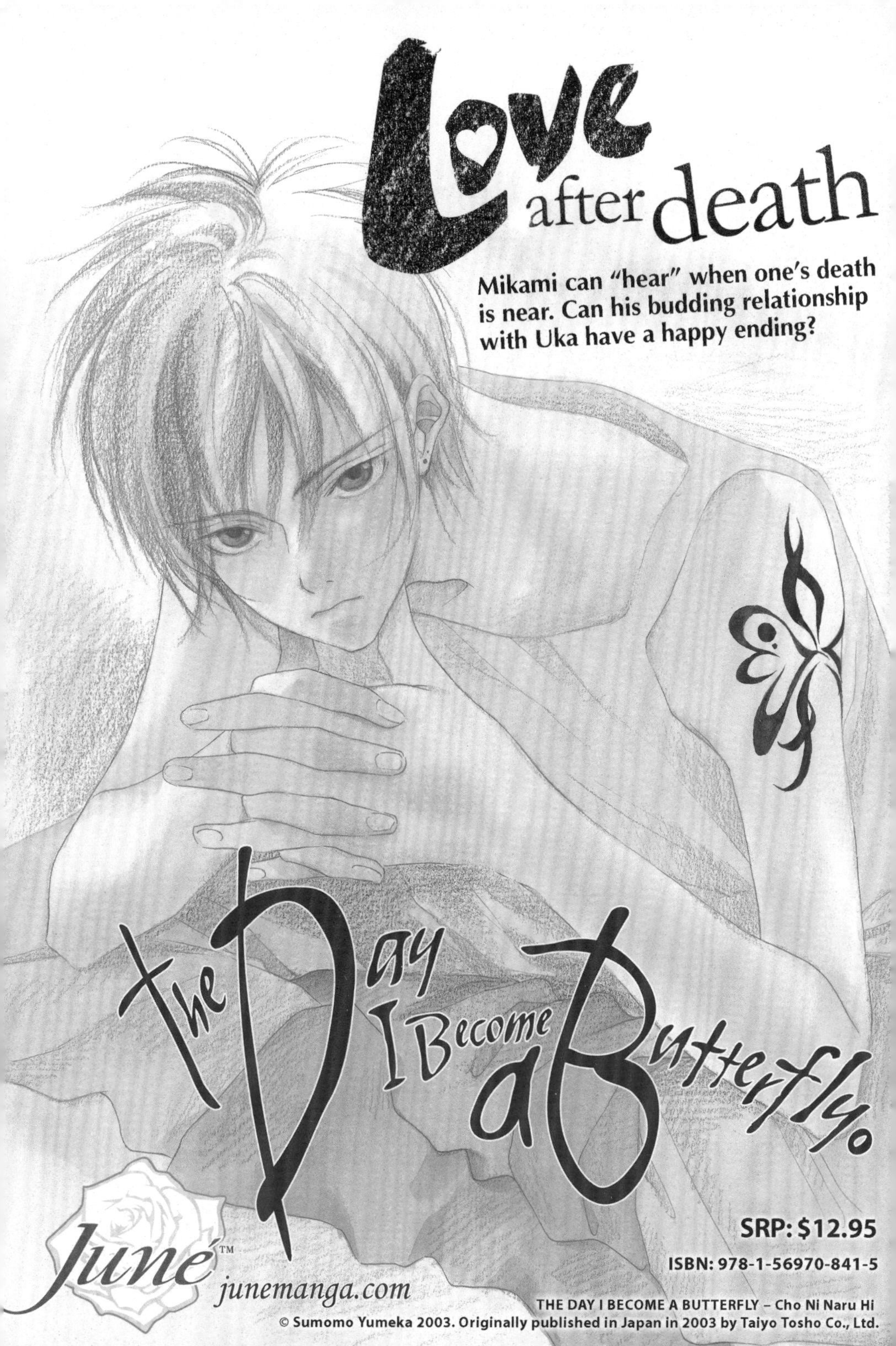
Love after death
Mikami can "hear" when one's death is near. Can his budding relationship with Uka have a happy ending?
The Day I Become a Butterfly
June™
junemanga.com
SRP: $12.95

ISBN: 978-1-56970-841-5

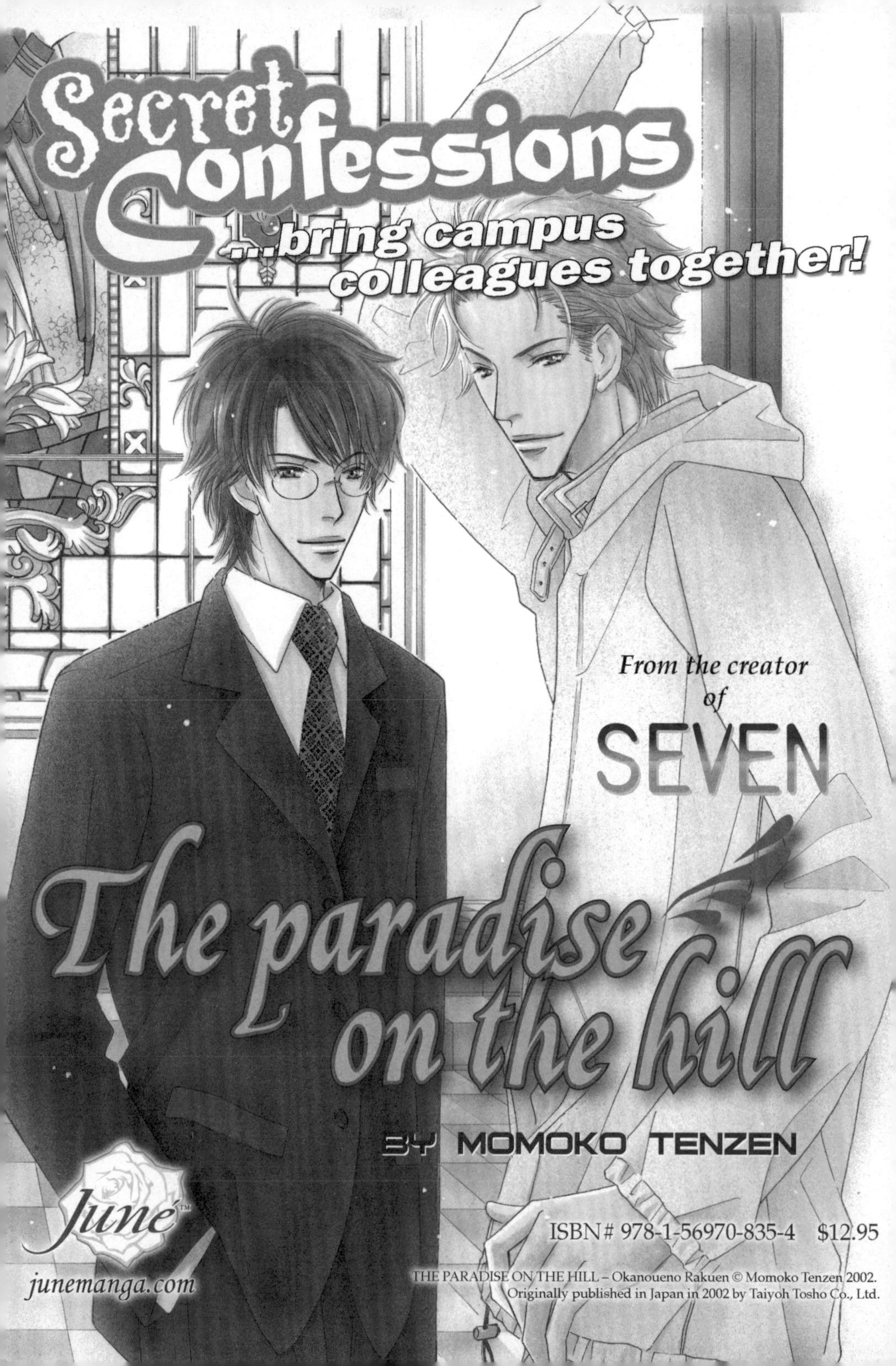
Secret Confessions
...bring campus colleagues together!
From the creator of
SEVEN
The paradise on the hill
BY MOMOKO TENZEN
June™
junemanga.com
ISBN# 978-1-56970-835-4 $12.95
THE PARADISE ON THE HILL – Okanoueno Rakuen © Momoko Tenzen 2002.
Originally published in Japan in 2002 by Taiyoh Tosho Co., Ltd.

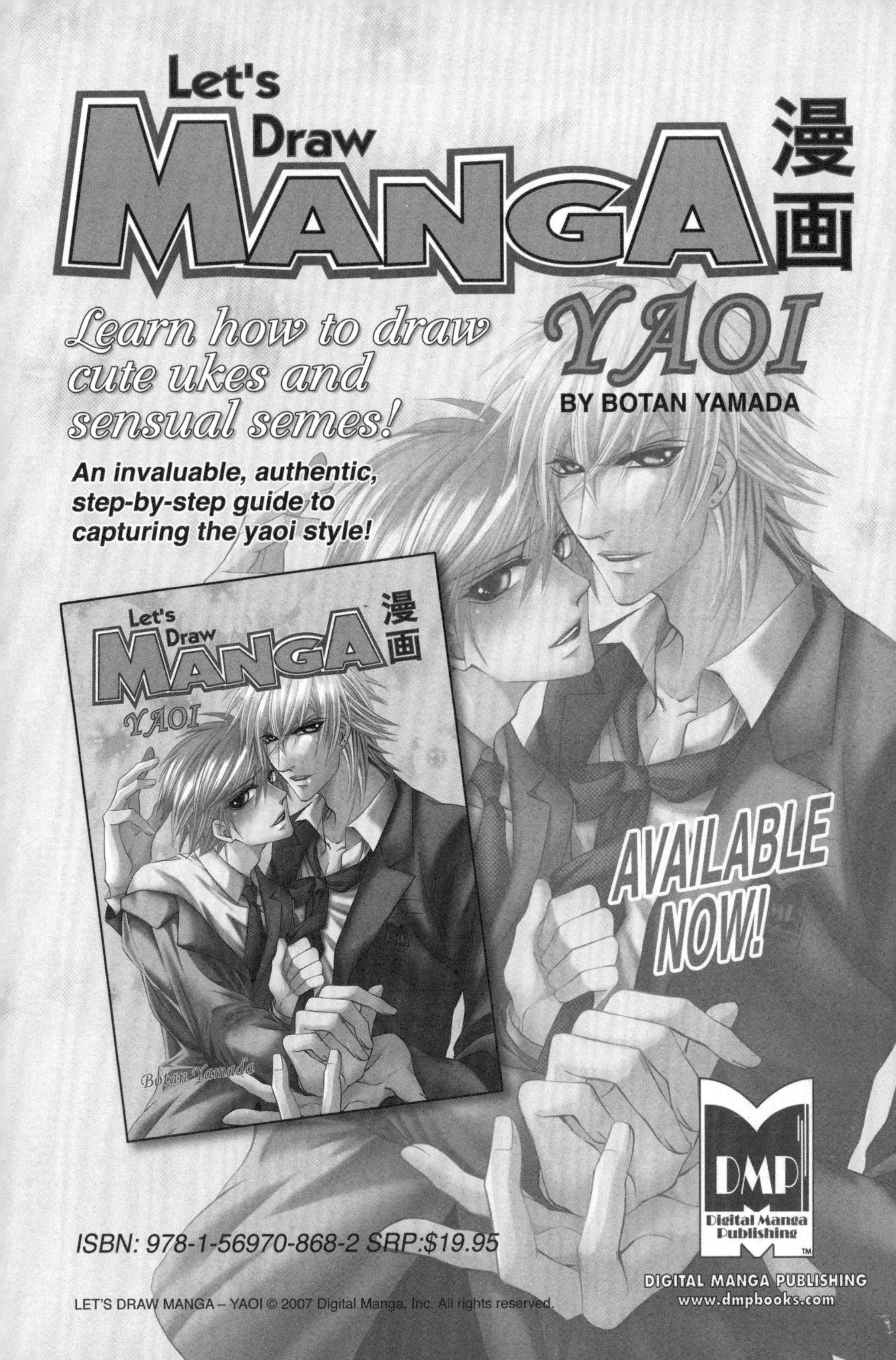
Let's Draw MANGA 漫画
YAOI
BY BOTAN YAMADA
Learn how to draw cute ukes and sensual semes!
An invaluable, authentic, step-by-step guide to capturing the yaoi style!
Let's Draw MANGA 漫画
YAOI
Botan Yamada
AVAILABLE NOW!
DMP
Digital Manga Publishing
ISBN: 978-1-56970-868-2 SRP:$19.95
DIGITAL MANGA PUBLISHING
www.dmpbooks.com
LET'S DRAW MANGA – YAOI © 2007 Digital Manga, Inc. All rights reserved.

# This is the back of the book!
## Start from the other side.

**NATIVE MANGA** readers read manga from *right to left*.

If you run into our **Native Manga** logo on any of our books... you'll know that this manga is published in it's true original native Japanese right to left reading format, as it was intended. Turn to the other side of the book and start reading from right to left, top to bottom.

Follow the diagram to see how its done. **Surf's Up!**

NATIVE MANGA

READ RIGHT TO LEFT